Industrial Organization, Economics and the Law

Industrial Organization, Economics and the Law

Collected Papers of
Franklin M. Fisher

Edited by John Monz

HARVESTER
WHEATSHEAF

New York   London   Toronto   Sydney   Tokyo   Singapore

First published 1990 by
Harvester Wheatsheaf
66 Wood Lane End, Hemel Hempstead
Hertfordshire HP2 4RG
A division of
Simon & Schuster International Group

Typeset in 10/12 pt Times by
Best-Set, Hong Kong

Printed and bound in Great Britain by
BPCC Wheatons Ltd, Exeter.

British Library Cataloguing in Publication Data

Fisher, Franklin M. (Franklin Marvin)
 Industrial organisation, economics and the law.
 1. Industries. Economic aspects
 I. Title II. Monz, John
 338

 ISBN 0-7450-0747-3

1 2 3 4 5 94 93 92 91 90

Contents

Part 2   Regulation of television   233

Part 3   Quantitative methods and the law   323

Acknowledgments

I am indebted to John Monz for very substantial editorial assistance and to Robert Bolick for good advice. I am (as always) grateful to Theresa Benevento for secretarial and organizational assistance.

My family has lived with these papers and the underlying projects for thirty years. I am an inveterate talker, and they have usually been very kind in providing ideas and allowing me to bore them. I trust the reader will be equally kind, if perhaps less bored.

Anyone who is old enough to publish a collection like this is old enough to have grandchildren. This volume was in press when my first grandchild was born. It is dedicated to Elizabeth Rebecca and the others yet to come.

Franklin M. Fisher
Cambridge, Massachusetts

Introduction

Although the earliest paper in this volume was written more than thirty years ago, most of them are of more recent vintage. This reflects a corresponding evolution of my own interests. While industrial organization, and, particularly, antitrust policy, has been an interest of mine throughout my professional life, these subjects have come to be my principal focus in the last ten to twenty years.

That shift in focus is strongly related to my work as a consultant and expert witness. Many (not all) of my publications in these areas grew directly from such work. I have found involvement with the application of economic analysis to real disputes and real problems of microeconomic policy to be a rich source of ideas and, if one is willing to put in the time and labor, of facts as well.

Such work is also a source of lessons about the uses and misuses, the achievements and failings of economic analysis. Those lessons lead to themes that run through a number of the papers in this volume, particularly in the early sections.

I have already hinted at one of the lessons. Economists are fond of ideas. They are less fond of the work and complications required to ensure that those ideas are applicable. When a story makes analytical sense, when it constitutes an interesting analytic tale of what *might* happen, there is a tendency to suppose that one has discovered what must in fact have happened in a real situation.

This is not always – perhaps not even often – true. Real situations involving real companies and industries can be complex, and a more than superficial understanding of the facts involved will often be needed to analyze what those facts mean.

There is another side to this, however. Economic analysis can greatly illuminate the facts. But just as such illumination requires a willingness to work at examining the facts, it also requires more than a superficial understanding of the tools and propositions of economic analysis, their limitations and their uses.

To put it another way, all science consists of simplification. An analytic model of a set of facts must be less complex than the facts themselves or it is merely a description without analysis. Economics provides such simplifications, but one must be careful both to understand the concepts being used and not to do violence to important features in a rush to simplify.

The first chapter in this volume, 'Diagnosing monopoly', deals with the importance of understanding the analytic tools used in the analysis of monopoly versus competition. Monopoly theory is typically taught using a simple one-period equilibrium model. The assumption is made that there are no close substitutes for the good in question, that the monopolist is the only seller, and that there are high barriers to entry. The harmful consequences of monopoly are then adduced.

But the application of that analysis to antitrust policy and, especially, to actual cases, necessarily involves a departure from such assumptions. Real products have substitutes. Real defendants in Sherman Act, Section 2 cases usually have competitors (some of whom may be plaintiffs or have themselves urged prosecution). Real industries can usually be entered, and not everything that keeps real potential entrants out is truly a barrier to entry in a technical sense. Perhaps most important of all, real firms do not operate in a one-period world, and the world is not always in equilibrium.

All of these areas require careful thought by the analyst, and a misunderstanding of them can lead to major litigation involving vast expenditures of time and money. I have elsewhere written in detail about the oustanding example of this – the *IBM* antitrust cases. 'Diagnosing monopoly', written before my testimony in *United States* v. *IBM* as an invited lecture at the University of Illinois, was intended as my first general discussion of the principles and difficulties involved in such matters – principles and difficulties that extend beyond the *IBM* cases.[1] Many of the issues discussed in Chapter 1 occur again in the other chapters.

The first such issue is that of market definition. The question of 'what is *the* relevant market' is one which only occurs in antitrust settings; it is either assumed away or plays no interesting role elsewhere in economics. Nevertheless, it has often taken on a disproportionate importance in antitrust, great cases appearing to turn on whether certain products are 'in' or 'out' of the market.

The view that I took in Chapter 1 (and expanded in *Folded, Spindled and Mutilated*) is that such concentration on dichotomous classification unnecessarily makes classification itself an end rather than an appropriate beginning of analysis. In analyzing the possibility of monopoly power, one should concentrate on the constraints that operate on an alleged monopolist. Those constraints, which can come either from demand or supply substitutability, themselves describe what one wants to know. Attempting to summarize them by 'in' or 'out' statements merely suppresses information. When one has said, for example, that flexible wrapping papers compete with cellophane at high but not at low prices (and quantified the prices in question), one has described the way in which flexible wrapping papers do and do not constrain the pricing behavior of the manufacturer of cellophane. That information is not conveniently summarized either by saying (as the Supreme Court did in *Cellophane*) that flexible wrapping papers and cellophane are in the same market or by saying (as various economist commentators have) that they are not.[2]

The view that market definition should serve as a way of summarizing constraints was not shared by the antitrust authorities in the 1970s. Indeed, market definition analyses tended to become exercises in word use. By the early 1980s, however, some progress had been made. The Department of Justice's 'Merger Guidelines' defined a market in terms of the minimal collection of firms that could, if they colluded, profitably raise prices for a year by 5 per cent.[3] That is a way of ensuring that the relevant market includes the relevant players, those that constrain the pricing of the firm or firms being investigated.

Concentration on market definition is an example of the need for simplification; in this case, it leads to great oversimplification at the expense of analysis. Further, while such concentration occurs more because courts and lawyers seek a 'bright line' than because economists do, the desire to define a clear relevant market occurs in part because of the wish to use market share as a quantification of market power – a wish not restricted to participants in the judicial process. Indeed, the desire to simplify a complex problem by quantification is a natural one for economists. Unfortunately, industrial organization is too complex a subject and industrial organization theory not sufficiently powerful to permit it to be done.

In the case of the use of market shares, this problem is not restricted to the analysis of monopoly power. I discuss in 'Horizontal mergers: Triage and treatment' (Chapter 2) the shaky use of the Hirschman-Herfindahl index of concentration as a way of judging the likelihood of oligopolistic coordination after mergers. That paper considers the use of the 'Merger guidelines' and concludes that the 'Guidelines' are sensible rough standards for deciding whether to investigate further, but that the antitrust authorities sometimes have a natural but deplorable tendency to behave as if the 'Guidelines' themselves were substitutes for detailed analysis.

One example of such a detailed analysis is given in 'Pan American to United: The *Pacific Division Transfer* case' (Chapter 3), a case in which the Antitrust Division and I were on the same side. Such cases are hard ones, and the policy questions difficult. It is natural to wish to avoid such complexities by finding simple rules to apply. Nevertheless, while such rules can serve as 'triage', separating out those cases which are likely to repay the expenditure of time and resources on investigation, they cannot, in the present state of our knowledge, provide a substitute for that investigation.

Returning to monopoly power, the desire to find a simple diagnostic test does not stop with the use of market share. It is also embodied in the use of data on profit rates. Here, indeed, such use is far from restricted to antitrust cases; a large literature has grown up using profit rates as the dependent variable in regressions intended to test elements of the structure–conduct–performance paradigm. Unfortunately, not only is the theory that leads to that paradigm too weak to allow proper specification of the variables and functional forms involved, and not only is the direction of causation from size and concentration to profits open to question, but also the use of accounting profit rates as the touchstone variable is simply wrong.[4]

As my article with John McGowan, 'On the misuse of accounting rates of return to infer monopoly profits' (Chapter 4), pointed out, profit rates are only interesting because they provide the signals for expansion and contraction. A positive present value at a suitably risk-adjusted cost of capital is a signal that profits are positive and that more resources can efficiently be allocated to the business. To the extent this can be expressed in terms of rates of return at all, it means an *economic* or *internal* rate of return in excess of the risk-adjusted cost of capital. Accounting rates of return simply do not correspond to this save in quite special circumstances.

Indeed, the notion that profit rates can be used as an indicator of monopoly or of market power is not well taken in any case. To assert that there are no economic profits in competition (that is, no accounting profits above the rate of return just necessary to keep capital in the business) is to make a statement that is true only in long-run equilibrium. To concentrate on equilibrium in this way is to lose sight of the important role that profits and losses play in the dynamics of competition. It is to substitute for an appreciation of the workings of the Invisible Hand a shallow understanding of what happens when the Invisible Hand has stopped doing anything.

Such fascination with equilibrium is, I believe, a central failing of modern economic theory. Our equilibrium theory is so powerful and so esthetically appealing that we have lost sight of the fact that we typically have no satisfactorily rigorous theory of how, or even *if* equilibrium is attained. I have written extensively elsewhere on disequilibrium and stability theory in the high-theory context of general equilibrium,[5] but the unfortunate, if understandable, mindset that stops at equilibrium pervades all of economics. Industrial organization is no exception.

Returning to the use of profit rates as an index of monopoly power, my article with McGowan showed (partly by theorem and partly by example) that the accounting rate of return is not very informative about the economic (internal) rate of return – the only rate of return of any interest. We had worried about whether our article was publishable, because some of the basic points had been made before,[6] but we need not have been concerned at the amount of new ground we were seen to be breaking. The paper caused a storm of protest – some of which is discussed in the 'Reply' republished here (as Chapter 5) both for completeness and amusement value – and became first quite controversial and then very influential. Not a month goes by in which I do not receive from either editors or authors, papers on this subject.

My own work includes a sequel to the Fisher–McGowan paper. 'On the misuse of the profits–sales ratio to infer monopoly power' (Chapter 6) shows that the same capital-theoretic problems that haunt the use of accounting rates of return on capital also affect the popular use of the profits–sales ratio as the Lerner measure of monopoly power (price less marginal cost all divided by price). The problem arises because of an inadequate understanding of how the standard one-period model of the firm must be applied in a multi-period context.

Properly understood, then, theory does not provide a sound basis for a simple quantitative measure of market power based either on structure (market share) or performance (profits). Further, analysis of conduct must also be undertaken with care. This is exemplified in the two papers on predation – one, 'On predation and victimless crime' (Chapter 7), still on monopoly, and the other, '*Matsushita*: Myth v. analysis in the economics of predation' (Chapter 8), on oligopoly as well. In both cases, care must be taken to distinguish supposedly anti-competitive conduct from that which one would see under competition and to ask whether the alleged anticompetitive program makes any sense.

It must not be thought, however, that I invariably take the view that conduct that appears anticompetitive turns out on closer examination to be just the opposite. In 'Can exclusive franchises be bad?' (Chapter 9) I show that there exist circumstances in which the currently popular view that the suppression of 'intra-brand' competition cannot benefit a manufacturer unless it benefits consumers turns out to be mistaken.

Much of the work discussed so far focuses on the too casual use of theory without real understanding. That problem is not restricted to antitrust policy. My paper with Peter Temin, 'Returns to scale in research and development: What does the Schumpeterian hypothesis imply?' (Chapter 10), discusses another area in which empirical tests were done in the literature without the realization that the predictions of the theory being tested were not what they seemed.

Obviously, I do not believe that the analysis of market power, of the presence or absence of competition, can be simply done. Rather each case must be investigated in detail with the guidance of properly understood microtheory. Unfortunately, that theory is not so rich as to permit the avoidance of such investigations.

A natural question, then, is whether modern industrial organization theory is proceeding in a way that seems likely to help. At least in the oligopoly context, I do not believe it is, and these views are set forth in 'Games economists play: A non-cooperative view' (Chapter 12). I there draw a distinction between what I call 'exemplifying theory' and 'generalizing theory'. Exemplifying theory, as its name implies, is theory by example. It proceeds by using stripped-down models to show that certain things can happen. Generalizing theory, on the other hand, consists of propositions about what *must* happen, if only by showing how outcomes depend on particular factors whose influences need to be quantified. (Demand theory is an example here.)

As explained in the paper, I believe that the central unsolved question of oligopoly theory is that of the influence of the real world context on the likelihood of the joint-maximization solution – what is sometimes called 'tacit collusion' or 'conscious parallelism'. One need only consider the state of merger analysis already discussed to see the importance of the question. A generalizing theory of the likelihood of the joint-maximization outcome would be invaluable for public policy. It would also greatly illuminate the use of cross-industry regressions to study the structure–conduct–performance paradigm. Without such a theory, such regression studies are necessarily in a very sorry state – even apart from their hopeless use of profit rates as dependent variables.

But modern oligopoly theory is not even attempting such an accomplishment. Instead, oligopoly theory (and much other modern industrial organization theory) takes the form of exemplifying theory. It has become a series of formalized anecdotes told in a game-theoretic language. Further, as I argue in the paper, the fashionable and powerful influence of game theory has not been without its cost. It has led to an unwarranted concentration on single-shot games of little interest in the analysis of real situations in which firms face each other repeatedly.

Moreover, with its concentration on equilibrium, game theory is an inconvenient (although not an impossible) language in which to study the influence of real-world contexts on oligopolistic coordination – the real central problem for oligopoly theory.

While only recently published, 'Games economists play' has achieved some notoriety since I gave it as an invited lecture at the Australasian meetings of the Econometric Society in 1987. As expected, not everyone agrees with it, but I note that replies from game theorists tend largely to consist of citing the many accomplishments of game theory as exemplifying theory – and such replies are not replies at all.[7]

This is not to say that I frown on the use of exemplifying theory. (How could I? It is also known as 'MIT-style theory'.) Exemplifying theory is a powerful tool. It is particularly useful for calling attention to possibilities and (perhaps especially) for providing counter-examples to supposedly general propositions. Not only do I view favorably every paper cited in Chapter 12, but also many of my own papers are of this type. The papers already discussed on exclusive franchises and the Schumpeterian hypothesis are examples of this; so, to an extent, are the papers on accounting rates of return.

The remaining two chapters in the first part of the book are two very small contributions to oligopoly theory that I made a long time ago. (Neither of them, I hasten to say, bear much on the central question mentioned above.) Both concern the Cournot model – now once again in vogue because of game theory. The first, 'New developments on the oligopoly front: Cournot and the Bain–Sylos analysis' (Chapter 13), was a comment on Franco Modigliani's famous paper of 1958.[8] It showed that, despite the fact that the new theories of oligopoly with entry had potential entrants making the Cournot-like assumption of no output change by incumbents, the theories were not identical with a Cournot model expanded to include entry.

The second of these chapters, 'The stability of the Cournot oligopoly solution: The effects of speeds of adjustment and increasing marginal costs' (Chapter 14) was also a comment – but one considerably (if not necessarily happily) longer than the paper that inspired it.[9] It was one of a series of papers concerning the extension of the Cournot model beyond its equilibrium to dynamics. Despite my continuing belief in the unrealism of the Cournot model (even in its modern Nash equilibrium form), and despite the fact that the paper itself was soon generalized and somewhat superseded,[10] I have included it here for two reasons. First, it represents my first attempt to break away from the view that equilibrium analysis is all that is involved in economics – a view which, as mentioned above, I find generally pernicious in all areas, including industrial organization.

Second, in terms of stability theory itself, I was surprised on rereading the paper to see that it contains an extremely early suggestion (p. 218) 'that it may be important to worry . . . about the adjustment process at the individual level, rather than simply assuming that some market variable (aggregate or average) adjusts in some specified (but sometimes mysterious) way'. That proposition has proved true in the analysis of the stability of general equilibrium.[11] It reflects the need in industrial organization and other aspects of microeconomics to understand how agents behave when equilibrium assumptions are not satisfied.

The second part of this book is related both to the first and to the third. It contains my published work on the regulation of television – a subject in which I became involved in 1963 and to which I periodically return.

One of the Chapters in this part, 'The financial interest and syndication rules in network television: Regulatory fantasy and reality' (Chapter 18), might just as well have been included in the first part. It concerns the strange and politicized history of regulation of the three major US television networks and the associated antitrust cases brought against them in the 1970s. Both regulation and antitrust action were marked by poor economic analysis and a misunderstanding of how one distinguishes the abuse of market power from the natural results of competition.

The other three chapters – two of them econometric studies and one some reflections on policy issues – have to do with the vexed history of the regulation of cable television. This was a subject that occupied the Federal Communications Commission at frequent intervals for twenty years. Chapter 16, 'Community antenna television systems and local television station audience' (with Victor E. Ferrall, Jr and in association with David Belsley and Bridger M. Mitchell), reports on an empirical study done for the National Association of Broadcasters in one of the earliest of the cable proceedings. It showed the effect of cable systems on local stations and may have (fortunately or unfortunately) contributed to the Commission's decision to regulate cable, a decision that continued in one form or another through the 1970s. (A contribution to a much later proceeding, set forth in Chapter 17, was my paper with John J. McGowan and David S. Evans, 'The audience–revenue relationship for local television stations'.) Chapter 15, 'Community antenna television systems and the regulation of television broadcasting' shows why the area may properly be one for the exercise of regulatory judgment (or, at least, may have been so in the 1960s). It suggests, however, that such judgment may have been misplaced, moving in the direction of shoring up an existing set of local monopolies used for public ends by restricting efficient forms of competition.

The final part of this book contains two types of chapters – some dealing with mathematical and statistical methods applied to certain legal problems and some dealing explicitly with the use of statistical methods in litigation. There is no firm line between the two.

The earliest of these chapters, 'The mathematical analysis of Supreme Court decisions: The use and abuse of quantitative methods' (Chapter 19), deals with an early attempt to apply quantitative analysis to a new area – the prediction of decisions by the US Supreme Court.[12] Unfortunately, the author of that innovative attempt had no understanding of how quantitative methods work. While the concept of quantitatively relating Court decisions to case facts was a promising insight, the result was a piece that could not have been accepted in an economics journal, and, I trust, could not now be accepted in journals of political science. Nevertheless, his paper purported to produce a perfect predictor of decisions in a complex series of cases, causing great consternation among some members of the Harvard Government Department with whom I was friendly and who urged me to explain why this impossible thing was in fact not true. I did so, but what happened afterwards is worth telling.

The original author, Fred Kort, had adopted a method of calculating coefficients which began with initial estimates (the derivation of which need not concern us) and used square roots, sums of squares, weights of 10 and $\frac{1}{10}$ and an additive constant of 5 to generate final estimates. He explained this transformation as involving 'necessary technical modifications' to avoid negative values. I pointed out that such a criterion did not determine the formula to be used, stating (p. 337) that 'one could, instead, . . . , multiply [each initial value] . . . by 23.99π, add 482, and subtract the sum of the other [initial values]'. I soon learned about the uses of such heavy-handed irony in a context where mathematics is unfamiliar. Kort wrote a reply in which he observed that he had tried my suggestion and it did indeed avoid negative values, but he was unable to understand what the result meant. The *American Political Science Review*, perhaps understandably sick of the whole business, did not let me see his Reply before publication and refused to publish a rejoinder. I kept up with the later literature for a little while, but soon discovered that these pieces were cited together as 'Kort's work has been criticized by a mathematician, and he has replied'. I stopped reading after a few of these, and can only hope that the authors, including Kort who had the vision to see that such things were possible, have mastered the techniques they are using.

Other (less amusing) stories of the misuse of quantitative methods can be found in some of the other pieces. Chapter 20 'On the feasibility of identifying the crime function in a simultaneous model of crime rates and sanction levels' (with Daniel Nagin) tackles the literature on punishment as a deterrent to crime and casts doubt on the ability of most of the studies to measure the deterrent effect. It dates from my participation in a National Academy of Sciences panel on the subject. (For a description of how I was induced to participate, see the end of Chapter 24.)

'Statisticians, econometricians and adversary proceedings' (Chapter 24) discusses for the professionals named in the title some of the issues involved in participation in litigation. It also details some war stories of good and bad use of statistical methods. Its companion piece, 'Multiple regression in legal proceedings' (Chapter 23), serves as an expository article for attorneys. Despite the fact that there is nothing of a general nature therein that cannot be found well exposited in many other places, the fact that it was published in a law review has caused it to be cited a number of times in judicial opinions (usually accurately).

The fact that I used the example of statistical tests of discrimination in Chapter 23 caused me to become involved in a few such cases. 'Employment discrimination and statistical science: Comment' (Chapter 25) was an outgrowth of that experience. One point of that chapter is that the use of quantitative methods ought not to blind one to the ethical and policy implications of what one is saying. That is also the main point of Chapter 21, 'Empirically-based sentencing guidelines and ethical considerations' (with Joseph B. Kadane), written for another National Science Foundation panel. If one of the points of some of my papers is that badly understood science can be positively harmful, another is that even well-understood science must be judiciously used.

Finally, Chapter 22, 'Janis Joplin's yearbook and the theory of damages' (with R. Craig Romaine) discusses the complex problem of how damages should be awarded to 'make the plaintiff whole'. The issues here involve the treatment of pre-judgment interest and the use of hindsight. As with many of the chapters in this volume, this one was stimulated by experience in an actual case.

I add an editorial note. Nobody's work is free of mistakes. Alas, mine is no exception, and I can, of course, only report on what has been done with the ones of which I am aware. Where only a typographical error is involved, it has been corrected without comment. In one case (the chapters with Peter Temin on the Schumpeterian hypotheses), the correction given in a later paper is self-explanatory. In two other cases, Chapters 19 and 25, the present version corrects an error in the original, with the correction indicated. In neither case did the errors matter to the principal points being made.[13]

In a number of cases, my chapters were comments on or published together with work by others, naturally not reprinted here. I believe that the reader will find the reprinted papers sufficiently self-contained so that this will present no more than a minor inconvenience, if any.

Notes

1. See F.M. Fisher, J.J. McGowan and J.E. Greenwood, *Folded, Spindled and Mutilated: Economic Analysis and US v. IBM* (Cambridge, Massachusetts: MIT Press, 1983). The late John McGowan remarked to me on reading 'Diagnosing monopoly', that while the case is never mentioned, anyone who knew about it could see that *United States v. IBM* was firmly held in mind at every page.
2. *United States v. E.I. du Pont de Nemours and Company*, 351 US 377 (1956). See R.A. Posner, *Antitrust Law: An Economic Perspective* (Chicago and London: University of Chicago Press, 1976), pp. 127–8; G.W. Stocking and W.F. Mueller, 'The Cellophane case and the new competition', *American Economic Review* 45 (1955) pp. 29–63; and C. Kaysen and D.F. Turner, *Antitrust Policy* (Cambridge, Massachusetts: Harvard University Press, 1959), p. 102.
3. US Department of Justice, 'Merger guidelines', *Federal Register*, **49** (1984), 26284.
4. For reviews of the literature, see L.W. Weiss, 'The concentration–profits relationship and antitrust' in H.J. Goldschmid *et al.* (eds) *Industrial Concentration: The New Learning* (Boston: Little, Brown, 1974) and F.M. Scherer, *Industrial Market Structure and Economic Performance* (Chicago: Rand McNally, 1980), pp. 267–95. H. Demsetz challenged the direction of causation. See his 'Industry structure, market rivalry and public policy', *Journal of Law and Economics* 16 (1973) pp. 1–10.
5. See F.M. Fisher, *Disequilibrium Foundations of Equilibrium Economics* (Cambridge: Cambridge University Press, 1983).
6. T.R. Stauffer, 'The measurement of corporate rates of return: a generalized formulation', *Bell Journal of Economics* 2 (1971) pp. 434–69, proved some of the theorems. E. Solomon, 'Alternative rate of return concepts and their implications for utility regulation', *Bell Journal of Economics* 1 (1970) pp. 65–81 presented an expository treatment. Even earlier, G.C. Harcourt, 'The accountant in a golden age', *Oxford Economic Papers* 17 (1965) pp. 66–80 had provided similar results.
7. An excellent example is the paper by Karl Shapiro, 'The theory of business behavior', published by the *RAND Journal* as a companion piece to mine.
8. F. Modigliani, 'New developments on the oligopoly front', *Journal of Political Economy* LXVI (1958) pp. 215–32.
9. R.D. Theocharis, 'On the stability of the Cournot solution of the oligopoly problem', *Review of Economic Studies* XXVII (1959–60) pp. 133–4.
10. F.H. Hahn, 'The stability of the Cournot oligopoly solution', *Review of Economic Studies* XXIX (1961–62) pp. 329–31.
11. See *Disequilibrium Foundations of Equilibrium Economics* (cf. especially pp. 28–9).
12. F. Kort, 'Predicting Supreme Court decisions mathematically: a quantitative analysis of the "Right to Counsel" cases', *American Political Science Review* 51 (1957) pp. 1–12.

13. In the case of Chapter 19, I corrected the error in a later publication. As noted above, the *American Political Science Review* was sick of the whole business, so the correction appeared (along with other material) in an obscure mimeographed journal called *MULL* (*Modern Uses of Logic in Law*). After thirty years, neither I nor any convenient library appear to have a copy, so I have been unable to republish the piece here.

PART 1
Antitrust: Monopoly and oligopoly

1

Diagnosing monopoly (1979)

It is difficult being an expert in a subject everybody understands. It may even be more difficult to be an expert in a subject which everybody thinks they understand. In this regard, I do not envy football coaches, but being an economist has something of the same aspect.

Perhaps because economics deals with matters which touch everyone's life fairly closely, people tend to suppose that economic analysis must be just a matter of common sense requiring no special expertise. The difficulty is compounded by the fact that economists often use words which are in common use and whose everyday meanings are not in fact the same as their technical definitions. (This may be the only really good excuse that one can think of for the tendency of economists to create their own jargon.)

This sort of difficulty is perhaps most familiar to macroeconomists. The problem of explaining why a balanced budget does not mean the same thing for the economy as a whole as it does for an individual household is perhaps the best-known example. Yet the difficulty exists at the level of microeconomics as well. In particular, it is true of the problem which is the subject of this paper – the problem of deciding when a particular firm is or is not a monopoly. That problem, as indeed the word 'monopoly' itself, is surrounded by a miasma of not always consistent connotations. The man in the street, the legal profession, and the economist (not to mention competitors of the alleged monopolist) all have something different in mind when they talk of 'monopoly'.

The David Kinley Lecture, presented at the University of Illinois, Urbana-Champaign, October 20, 1978.

Those different definitions need not always conflict, but they certainly tend to confuse. Moreover, the problem of deciding whether a real-life firm has monopoly power is further exacerbated by the fact that some economists take a very simplistic view of what it is that economic analysis has to say about the matter.

The world would be much simpler if one could determine that someone had a monopoly by observing that he owned Park Place and Boardwalk and was building hotels apace. (In that case, one might add, the monopolist could be sent directly to jail.) Similarly, the world would be a simpler place if one could decide that some firm has a monopoly by observing that it has 100 per cent of whatever it is that the firm is selling. After all, competition must mean that everybody who wants to can get in and survive, and monopoly, as everybody knows, means that one firm has it all. Unfortunately, that too is too easy.

In order to understand why such simplistic notions are wrong and to lay some foundation for examining the issues which arise, I shall begin with a brief review of the economic theory of competition and monopoly. Have done so, I shall then go on to consider the various issues which tend to arise in real-life cases. Generally, these can be grouped under the following headings:

- market definition
- the role of market share
- profits and their meaning
- barriers to entry and
- conduct and predation.

In almost every one of these issues we shall see that there is a certain amount of confusion in part engendered by the vocabulary and in part, perhaps, engendered by badly understood analytics. A little economics is a dangerous thing. What is true about a lot of economics, I am not prepared to say.

The pure theory of competition and monopoly

The static case

Imagine a market where there are many firms each selling the same homogeneous product for which there are no close substitutes, with each firm sufficiently small that it correctly believes that it cannot have an appreciable effect on the price. Suppose further that the consumers of the product are informed about prices and product quality, so that they know what is going on. Further, suppose that the owners of the factors of production (the workers, the suppliers of capital equipment, and so forth) all understand perfectly well the contribution that they make to the production processes of the firms and can change firms with no difficulty.

In such an ideal world, any given firm will have no choice as to the price it charges its customers or pays its suppliers and workers. Seeking to maximize profit, it will produce at a point where marginal cost equals price – that is, at a point at which the price consumers are just willing to pay for another unit of the product exactly covers the cost of making it. Further, each supplier of a factor of production will be paid their marginal contribution to revenues, so that the firm, at the margin anyway, acts as a conduit passing what consumers are just willing to pay for another unit of the product back to the factors of production which just require that payment to produce it.

Will such a firm make profit? Well, that depends on what you mean by 'profit'. The firm will certainly receive sufficient money to keep it in the business. Economists like to count that sort of thing as a cost rather than a profit. It represents, in effect, the return to the firm for its own services as a factor of production – the factor which puts all the other factors together and takes risks, so to speak.

Will profits be earned beyond this? Not in the long run. If firms are earning profits in the short run, then other firms, perceiving the opportunity to do likewise, will enter the business. That entry will expand supply of the product and bid down the price. It will also expand demand for the factors of production and bid up their prices. The end of the process will be a situation in which no profits (beyond the ones conventionally included in costs) are being earned.

What happens to inefficient firms in this situation? They cannot survive. Firms who do not adopt the most efficient means of production and are more costly than necessary, will find that they lose money. They are undercut by others whose costs are low enough to provide lower prices and they must either become more efficient or go out of business.

This suggests, and indeed it is true, that there is something good about competition. Not only is it true that firms must use the most efficient means of production, but also the marginal conditions already referred to ensure that consumers get what they are just willing to pay for, where the cost is computed using the most efficient means of production possible. Where such a situation prevails in all markets, it can be shown that it is not possible to rearrange things to make some consumer better off without making other consumers worse off.

Now let me complicate this simplified picture somewhat by introducing product differentiation. Suppose that there are different varieties of the same product, all close substitutes. Now firms must not only choose how much to produce and how to produce it, but also what variety of the product to produce. Nevertheless, despite this complication, in broad outline the result will be roughly the same. Firms will produce any variety for which there is a demand creating a profitable opportunity. The end result of the process will be that consumers (who this time care not only about price but also about the type of product) receive a menu of product varieties each produced in the most efficient manner, each with the marginal cost of production just equal to its price, and each varying from the other in the sense that the cost of converting production from one variety to another just reflects at the margin what consumers would be willing to pay to make that change. (What has been left out of this picture, of course, is the process of invention of new product varieties and the question of how consumers come to learn about them. I shall take up those matters later.)

Let us contrast this happy state with that of monopoly. Suppose that we have a single firm producing the original homogeneous product for which there are no close substitutes. Such a firm would be foolish not to notice that the price it can charge depends on the amount that it wants to sell. The firm will not produce where marginal cost equals price; rather it will produce where marginal cost equals marginal revenue. This is because it will find it profitable to increase output up to the point where the cost of the last unit just equals the return from selling that unit, but unlike the case of the competitive firm, that return must take into account not only the price at which the unit is sold but also the fact that the price on all previous units will have to be lowered in order to sell all the units including the last one.

Another way of saying this is that although there are consumers who would be willing to pay the direct cost of producing another unit, they do not get the opportunity to do so, because the monopolist perceives costs as including not only the direct costs of manufacture but also the reduction in revenue on all previous units consequent on having to move the price down. Output ends up less and price ends up greater than in competitive equilibrium.

Does the monopolist earn a profit? In general yes. (I ignore the possibility that monopoly profits might be non-positive.) Unlike the competitive case, however, the profits can persist because entry by other firms does not take place. Without something blocking entry, no firm can be a monopolist.

Can a monopolist be inefficient? The answer is yes. If a monopolist is inefficient, less profit is made, but unlike the competitive case, making less profit need not mean making losses. It has been said 'the best of all monopoly profits is the quiet life' [Hicks, 1935, p. 8]. And a monopolist may in fact choose to take out the profits, as it were, in not aggressively pursuing efficiency. Moreover, as the discussion of the marginal conditions indicate, the situation is not efficient in a larger sense. Even if the monopolist is using the most efficient methods of production, it would remain true that consumers willing to pay the costs of producing an extra unit will not be able to do so.

This simplistic contrasting of competition and monopoly forms a background for the rest of this paper. It should be remembered in proceeding that it is simplistic and that my purpose is to concentrate on the diagnosis of monopoly. There are, in fact, a number of intermediate market structures, such as oligopoly, which present their own problems. My remarks should not be taken as applying to them. This is perhaps particularly so when introducing the first complication of the simple model, the consideration of innovation and change.

Innovation and change

So far, this discussion has been almost exclusively static, essentially comparing points of equilibrium. But competition (or the lack of it) is a dynamic process and takes place in time. Since we typically only obtain snapshots of a moving process rather than observing it only after equilibrium has been reached, it is important to consider the way in which things change over time. This is particularly true in industries characterized by large amounts of innovation.

What does competition in such an innovative industry look like? For simplicity, I concentrate on innovation which takes the form of the introduction of new goods, although much the same story could be told of other types of innovation and, in particular, of the discovery of more efficient methods of production.

Start from a position of long-run equilibrium in a competitive industry. Revenues balance costs; no profits are being earned. Now someone – the innovator – discovers a better product and brings it to market. If the product is truly better (indeed, this is a definition of what 'better' means), consumers will prefer it to the existing products. They will be willing to pay more for it. This means that, during the initial period as the only one producing this product, the innovator will be able to charge a high price for it and will earn profits.

Just as in the static model, however, the presence of such profits will lure others into the business. If there are no barriers to imitation, other firms, through reverse engineering, for example, will learn how to make the new product and begin bringing it out. This will bid down the price, since some price advantage will generally be necessary to lure customers from the original to the copy. Moreover, the imitators will generally have lower research and development (R & D) costs than did the initial innovator and they will be able to afford to get into the imitation business in the first place at a price lower than that which would have brought a reasonable return for heavier R & D expenses. At the same time, the general progress of technology or simply the experience of those who have gone before may enable imitators to make slight improvements on the product and other innovators will make further improvements, bringing in newer and better products. This too will cause customers to leave the original innovator.

Faced with the erosion of business and profits caused by the entry of imitators and rival innovators, the original innovator will not be able to maintain the price which brought the profits of the initial period. In order to stay in business, the price must be lowered on what is now the old innovation and, to make still further profits, still better products must be brought out.

In some respects, the story just told is not very different from the static competitive case. Once again, the lure of profit induces entry and that entry bids the price down and the profits away. Once again, firms are forced to seek the most efficient means of production or, in this case, the best product, or leave the business. Yet the innovative competition story clearly highlights somewhat different points than does the static one and they are worth taking a minute to point out.

The first of these is the necessary role of profits and what they represent. Profits in the initial period of the competitive process just discussed are the reward to the innovator. They are what caused investment in innovative activities to be made and they represent a return on those activities. The US Constitution recognizes the importance of such returns in encouraging innovation in the form of the patent system.

Related to this is the fact that one cannot look at profits during the initial period and attribute them only to the manufacturing process (this is in addition to all the problems associated with using accounting data for profits which I shall discuss later). The profits being earned represent not merely the return on capital invested in manufacturing but also on the investment made in research and development.

Third, and perhaps most important of all, it is a mistake to look at an industry in the midst of such a process and conclude anything at all about it without considering where the process came from and where it is going. A single frame will give a misleading impression of the movie. Looking at the industry during the period just after the innovation is made, one sees the world beating a path to the door of the mousetrap inventor. One sees the mousetrap inventor making profits. One sees the mousetrap inventor alone in the field. One ought not, however, to conclude therefore that a monopoly of mousetraps exists. Indeed, what really matters, in some sense, is whether there is a monopoly of technical progress in the industry. Similarly, when prices come down after the imitators enter, it would be wrong to conclude that the monopolist is engaging in 'predatory pricing' in order to maintain market share. Rather, what one is seeing is competition seriously at work.

What would a monopolist look like in such an industry? In effect, a monopolist would be someone, as in the static case, insulated from entry, from the pressures of imitators and other innovators. New products might very well be brought out because that would be a profitable thing to do, but the crucial fact would be that it is not necessary. As in the static case, the crucial difference between monopoly and competition is the compulsion which market forces place on the competitor and the lack of it on the monopolist.

Monopoly and monopoly power

Since the case of a monopolist with 100 per cent of an economically relevant market (see what follows) is very rare, the analysis of monopoly in the economics of antitrust policy tends to go in terms of 'monopoly power'. This is entirely proper. Such power is in fact the lack of compulsion we have spoken of. The courts have defined monopoly power as 'the power to set prices and exclude competitors', and from the point of view of economic analysis, that is an excellent definition if it is properly understood. Clearly, a monopolist has the ability to earn profits while excluding competitors. This generally means setting high prices while excluding competitors. Whether one ought to infer monopoly power from the ability to *cut* prices and thus exclude competitors is another matter to which I shall return.

The question of identifying a firm with such monopoly power when observed in the field, however, is not a simple one. I turn now to a deeper discussion of some of the problems which beset the enthusiastic monopoly-watcher.

Market definition

The conventional first step in analyzing whether a given firm does or does not have monopoly power is to define the relevant market in which the alleged power is exercised. Unfortunately, this is not as simple as it sounds and tends to lead to confusion, if not abuse.

In my discussion of competition, and especially monopoly, I simply started off by assuming that there was a single homogeneous product with no close substitutes. Now it is all very well, if that happens to be the case in real life, but one frequently encounters the problem that products are differentiated. Typically, in such cases, we are talking not about a single product, but about a group of products. Market definition might be described as the problem of deciding where the relevant group begins and ends. This turns out not to be an easy task and I shall point out in a moment that it may be an unnecessary one, yet common sense (and Supreme Court decisions) suggest it has to be undertaken. After all, one might say, in order to decide whether a firm has monopolized, it is necessary to decide *what* it may have monopolized. In order to decide whether a firm can exclude competitors, it is necessary to decide from what they can be excluded.

The position which I shall take here is that, properly done, trying to answer such questions does indeed yield information about monopoly power. The catch lies in the words 'properly done'.

Let us begin by recalling what the purpose is of market definition. It is the beginning of an analysis of monopoly power. Monopoly power, however, is the ability to act in an unconstrained way. Hence, market definition, if it is to be an aid to analysis, has to place in the relevant market those products and services and firms whose presence and actions can serve as a constraint on the policies of the alleged monopolist. Recall that market definition will be used essentially for two things (both of which I shall discuss later): the computation of market share and the analysis of barriers to entry. A market will thus be well defined if and only if the share measurements to which it leads provide some reasonable index of the true power of the alleged firm; the discussion of entry really then supplements the share measure to show the ability of that firm to maintain share when earning supranormal profits.

Thus, the primary question in defining a relevant market ought to be that of the constraints on the alleged monopolist. The principal constraints can be of two types, those relating to demand and those relating to supply. The courts have paid appropriate attention to demand and supply substitutability – appropriate because those are criteria by which to judge the constraints on the alleged monopolist. It should not be forgotten, however, that it is the constraints which are the object of analysis and not the properties of substitutability themselves.

Demand substitutability refers to the ease with which consumers of the alleged monopolist's products can substitute the products of others. If this is relatively easy, then an attempt by the alleged monopolist to raise prices and earn supranormal profits will lead consumers to switch away. Notice, however, that such substitutability is a question which depends on relative prices. Any firm which raises its price far enough will lose customers. The issue is whether over a range of actually encountered prices consumers are in fact able to substitute.

Note further that such substitution is often not as simple as meets the eye. Consider the following example. My wife and older daughter who (like the rest of the Fishers) enjoy skiing, have chosen to use for their bindings (the device which holds the ski boot to the ski and releases in an otherwise dangerous fall) the Spademan binding which has a particular design. It happens that, because of the design of the Spademan, there are relatively few ski boots which are compatible with it. Many otherwise desirable boots cannot be used with the Spademan binding. Would it be correct to assume that Spademan-compatible boots constitute a market because owners of Spademan bindings cannot directly substitute non-Spademan-compatible boots for Spademan-compatible ones?

The answer is that it would not, even restricting our attention to demand substitutability. It is true that once my wife and daughter acquired the Spademan binding, they limited their immediate range of substitution. An attempt by the makers of Spademan-compatible boots to raise prices and earn supranormal profits would not and could not lead my family to try to ski with Spademan bindings and non-Spademan-compatible boots. But that kind of substitution is not the only kind which constrains the behavior in question.

In the first place, a sufficiently high price for Spademan-compatible boots will lead my wife and daughter to discard their Spademan bindings and acquire other bindings. Moreover, such a price need not be terribly high – the price of the boot is often more than 50 per cent of the boot–binding combination. Second, below that is a price at which, when their current bindings wear out, they will replace them with non-Spademan bindings rather than have to pay the high price for Spademan-compatible boots. Third, and more important, new customers, deciding on what binding–boot combinations to buy will rationally look at the high price of Spademan-compatible boots and make the binding–boot choice taking that into account. It is a great mistake to look at substitution as though all that mattered was rolling out one product and rolling in the other once everything else is fixed. Rather, a major kind of substitution occurs at the stage before everything gets fixed. To the extent that new (or replacement) binding customers are important, the makers of Spademan-compatible boots will have to think twice before attempting to take advantage of those who have temporarily acquired Spademan bindings.

The same example may be used to illustrate some other principles. To the extent that certain boots are associated with certain bindings (I am wandering somewhat from what is really true about ski boots), the real competition takes place between binding–boot combinations. It would be wrong to consider the market for boots alone, even if boots are sold without bindings, if there is a substantial business in binding–boot combinations and the price of the boot affects the choice of the combination.

But what if there are some people who simply want a particular boot because they feel committed to the use of a particular binding, for example? One might add, what if there are people who particularly want a chartreuse boot with seven buckles and a monogram? Does that mean that such people constitute a relevant market and that the maker of such a boot (if there is only one) has monopoly power? It would be a mistake to conclude this automatically. Once we leave the theoretical world of perfect competition and examine real-life firms with differentiated products, we find that every such firm tends to have customers who would be willing to pay more for the product than other customers. This is what it means to have a downward-sloping demand curve. Yet it would be foolish to conclude that this means that there are lots of little markets, each one consisting of such customers, with the corresponding firm having monopoly power. There is no relevant sense in which that is true. To content oneself with the question of whether there are any substitutes for a given product which can be used by those who happen to want the particular product, with exactly the specifications and properties that that product has, is to ignore the real forces at work in the market and to beg the question of market definition which arises when products are differentiated.

The second kind of consideration in market definition is that of substitutability in supply. Let us continue with the ski boot example. Suppose that the makers of non-Spademan-compatible boots could very easily produce Spademan-compatible boots if it were profitable to do so. In that case, an attempt by the makers of Spademan-compatible boots to earn supranormal profits would induce other bootmakers to change their production and bid away those profits. In such a case, it is not very sensible (even apart from demand substitutability considerations) to talk of a market for Spademan-compatible boots. To do so and then to look at the market share as indicating anything, is simply to ignore the important constraints on any power of Spademan-compatible-boot manufacturers placed by the presence of the other boot manufacturers. It would obviously be more sensible to count the latter in the same market.

Here again, it is important to realize what kind of substitution is involved. The issue is not whether, once a non-Spademan-compatible boot is produced, the manufacturer can easily convert it into a Spademan-compatible one by retrofitting. If that is possible, of course, it is important. Rather, the issue is whether the production facilities can be adjusted to make Spademan-compatible boots.

Obviously, such substitutability is a matter of degree. Where supply substitutability is somewhat more difficult or slower, we may prefer to draw the boundary of the relevant market and refer to the ability of firms outside it to make the product inside it in terms of ease or difficulty of entry, a matter I shall take up later. Indeed, properly done, it matters not at all where we draw the market boundary from the supply substitutability point of view. If we draw it very narrowly, we shall have to say that entry is extremely easy. If we define the market much more broadly, we shall have to remain aware that not everyone in it puts an equal constraint on the power of the alleged monopolist.

As this last point suggests, I do not believe that the question of what is the relevant market is the fundamentally right question to ask, even though answering it in a sensible way can be an aid to analysis. The fundamental question is that of the constraints on power. Focusing on the question of relevant market can often lead to losing sight of that fact.

Let me elaborate. The inevitable next step which comes after a market has been defined is the computation of market share, about which I shall have more to say in the next section. Ever since Judge Hand's dictum in the *Alcoa* case as to the various market shares which might lead one to infer or not infer a monopoly, plaintiffs have struggled to prove shares to be higher and defendants have struggled to prove them lower than the points he named. Obviously, if a market is defined sufficiently narrowly, one can do it so that the share of the alleged monopolist is high. Similarly, if the market is defined sufficiently broadly, one can get the share of an alleged monopolist to be lower.

Yet all this is in some sense beside the point. Whatever shares may mean, their meaning depends on how the market is defined. In a market defined overly narrowly, a high share does not carry much information. Similarly, in a market defined overly broadly, a low share also does not. In the former case, not all constraints on the alleged monopolist's behavior have been taken into account. In the latter case, not all the things which have been taken into account constrain that behavior equally.

If one always remembers this, there is no positive harm in engaging in the market definition exercise. Indeed, viewed correctly, arguments concerning whether products are in or out of the market which are made in terms of demand and supply substitutability, and hence in terms of constraints, are exactly the arguments which one would have to decide in looking at the constraints directly. The trouble is that it is too easy to forget what the analysis is all about. By focusing on whether products are in or out of the market, one converts a necessarily continuous question into a question of yes or no. The temptation is to regard products which are in as all counting equally and products which are out as not counting at all.

The result of this tendency in antitrust cases is for plaintiffs to argue for narrow market definitions not in terms of constraints and their implications but in other terms altogether. Thus, where concentration should be on the competition faced by the defendant, private plaintiffs who compete with the defendant in some part of the latter's business try to define the market in terms of the competition they themselves face, something which would tell one about the constraints on the plaintiff but not about the constraints on the defendant.

Moreover, as the foregoing discussion should indicate, the term 'market' as used in this kind of analysis is a term of art. It is not the same as the ordinary use of the word. Yet there is a tendency to adopt ordinary usage as though it had technical meaning so that a tendency of business executives to speak of the 'market' for a particular kind of their own product becomes converted into a supposed recognition that such is the relevant market for economic analysis. This is not only bad practice, but it would make economic experts unnecessary and is therefore to be frowned upon.

Such a practice is closely related to another one. When dealing with records or statistics on differentiated products, it is natural to categorize those products and to treat each variety separately. Yet such record-keeping treatment cannot convert the categories involved into economically relevant markets for the analysis of monopoly. Similarly, one cannot look at the definition of words and construct markets. To the extent that market definition really is a matter of definition, it has to be only a way of looking at the problem – a way which cannot affect the answer. To the extent that it reflects a real part of the analysis, one must bear that always in mind.

Let me take an example from a real case about which I know almost nothing (as it happens, this is a merger, rather than a monopoly case, but the principle is the same). It is my understanding that the Federal Trade Commission has challenged Nestlé's acquisition of Stouffer's and has claimed that the relevant market is that for high-priced, non-ethnic, frozen entrées (main courses). Let me just take a moment to be sure that that sinks in. High-priced, non-ethnic, frozen entrées. Not only are all non-frozen foods excluded, but so are any frozen dinners (or combination of frozen entrée and unfrozen vegetables), anything such as meatpie (low-priced), and any Chinese, Mexican or Italian food (ethnic). I have no opinion whatsoever on whether or not the merger involved tends to reduce competition, but it is not necessary to know that in order to see that if adults wish to make the question of whether high-priced, non-ethnic, frozen entrées is a relevant market, the question on which the analysis turns, then somebody's eye is badly off the ball. One suspects that whoever made that up has lost track of what the whole business is supposed to be about. (It is amusing that sometime after the case was brought, Stouffer's ran a series of commercials on television which showed someone tasting a Stouffer's entrée and saying things such as 'It's like lasagna, but it isn't lasagna'. Whatever the motivation behind such commercials, the implication is that certain ethnic entrées compete directly with Stouffer's products.)

Market share

As already observed, the big point in defining a relevant market is to proceed to the computation of market share on the supposition that this tells us something about monopoly. After all, everybody knows that a pure monopolist has 100 per cent of the market. Presumably the higher the share the more likely the inference of monopoly power. Is this correct?

I have already emphasized the importance of getting the market definition part of the analysis right if one is going to try to make inferences from share. The computation of share in a market with differentiated products is an attempt to summarize a complex set of relationships and to read into a single number a number of items of somewhat different weight. If market definition is done properly, that can be an aid to analysis, so long as one remembers that one is summarizing and possibly leaving out important information.

Suppose then that market definition has been properly done (whatever that may mean). What does economic analysis tell us about the relation of share and monopoly power? Well, the one proposition which most people believe is that a small share shows the absence of monopoly power and a large share its presence. (Note that I am careful not to say how small is small, however.) This is not true. The right question is that of what happens to share, or, more generally, to a firm's business when monopoly profits are sought. The fundamental issue is whether competitors are able to grow.

Thus, consider a firm which has a very large share of a particularly defined market. It may very well be that such a firm is merely efficient and has achieved that share by charging low prices. Alternatively, we may be looking at a case of innovative competition in the initial period when the mousetrap has been invented. Should we infer monopoly power from a large share in such cases? The answer is no, not necessarily. The right question to ask is whether that large share would survive an attempt to charge high prices and earn monopoly profits. If the share is maintained solely because of low prices or better products, then we are looking at what competition is supposed to do and not at a monopoly. This is, of course, closely related to the legal position that a monopoly acquired and maintained by 'superior skill, efficiency or foresight' does not violate the antitrust laws. I would prefer to say that a large share acquired and maintained in such ways is not a monopoly at all.

The confusion of monopoly with large share is dangerous in complicated cases. When combined with the related concentration on market definition as the great touchstone question, it leads to analytic confusion.

Profits

If one cannot be sure one is observing a monopoly by observing a large share, are there any other simple features of monopoly that might enable one to conclude that it is present? The one most commonly pointed to is profits. My discussion of share, just given, suggests that the crucial issue regarding that variable is what happens to it if supranormal profits are earned. The discussion of the foregoing competitive case shows that it is the lure of profits which leads to entry which then bids the profits away, a matter I shall take up later. Is it then true that one can look at a firm's profit rate and conclude very simply that there is monopoly power if it is high and an absence of such power if it is low?

The answer is no, and I am sorry to say that there are a number of studies in the literature which attempt to examine the relation between profits and concentration which automatically equate profits with monopoly and tend to make other errors as well. Such issues also creep into antitrust cases in analytically foolish ways.

The analytically correct issue here is the measurement of what is called 'the economic rate of return' and its comparison with some competitive standard. The economic rate of return is a profit rate relating profits to capital (profits on sales are not involved). It is defined as follows.

Consider an investment which costs a certain amount and which over time brings in a stream of net revenues as a result of having been made. (Net revenues are the difference between gross revenues and the costs associated with maintaining the revenue stream.) The economic rate of return on the investment is that interest rate such that, using that rate, the discounted present value of the stream of net revenues is just equal to the capital cost of the investment. It is, in effect, the interest rate such that, if one could get it at a bank, one could deposit the capital value of the investment and just manage to draw out the same stream of net revenues as the investment generates. It is the expectation of a high economic rate of return relative to similar opportunities elsewhere which draws capital into a competitive market.

Obviously, calculating the economic rate of return in any but the simplest situation is not a simple matter. Calculating it for a firm as a whole involves knowing a great deal about the past, present and, indeed, future history of the firm. Yet the important fact for our purposes is that calculations involving so-called 'accounting rates of return' which can be read fairly easily from the firm's books are no substitute whatsoever.

This is true for a number of reasons, some obvious and some more subtle. The accounting rate of return is essentially current profits divided by some measure of the value of current assets. (Sometimes it is taken as current profits divided by the value of stockholders equity. I ignore this version, for simplicity.) The most obvious reason that such measures can be misleading concerns the question of what is included in profits and what in the value of assets for accounting purposes. This involves such questions as the treatment of depreciation for accounting purposes as opposed to true economic depreciation, but it involves other issues as well.

To take one of the easier issues, many firms choose to write off research and development or advertising expenses as part of current costs. This is a conservative method of accounting and may in fact be useful for tax purposes. Yet research and development expenses or even advertising may be analytically equivalent to capital expenses. I do not know what du Pont's accounting practices were, but it ought to be plain that the very large research and development expenses for the intro-duction of nylon, for example, carried on over several years, were analytically equivalent to an investment producing a stream of much later returns. Properly calculated for the purpose of assessing the economic rate of return, such expenses should be capitalized and placed in the asset base rather than subtracted from current revenues. The effect of making such a change on the calculated rate of return is complicated.

There is a much more important problem with the accounting rate of return of which, in some respects, the one just discussed is a subcase. It is easiest to highlight this with a numerical example. Suppose that a typical investment consists of the purchase of a machine costing $100. Suppose further that such an investment brings in nothing the year it is made but, starting one year later, brings in $11 per year in perpetuity. It is not hard to see that the economic rate of return on such an investment has to be 10 per cent. (That is, $110 invested at 10 per cent will bring in $11 per year in perpetuity. Thus, the stream of returns is equivalent to $110 invested *one year after the machine is bought* at 10 per cent. But $110 one year away is the equivalent of $100 now at 10 per cent so the rate of return on the whole thing must be 10 per cent.)

Now, I have chosen 10 per cent to make the numbers easy, but let us suppose that 10 per cent is in fact a high enough return so that the firm wishes to make such investments and to make them at quite a substantial rate. Suppose that it does so as follows. In the first year, it buys one machine. In that year, capital stock is $100 and profits are zero; the firm's accounting rate of return is thus also zero. In the second year, it buys another machine so that it doubles its capital stock. Since there is no depreciation in this example, the value of the capital stock is now $200, but the firm begins to earn the $11 per year brought in by the first machine. Its accounting rate of return is now 5.5 per cent. In the next year, suppose the firm again doubles its capital stock, investing in two more machines and bringing the total value of its capital stock to $400. It now earns $11 from the first two machines for a total of $22 and an accounting rate of return still 5.5 per cent. In fact, if the firm goes on doubling in size every year, its accounting rate of return will always (except for the very first year) be 5.5 per cent, about half of the true economic rate of return.

Evidently, from this example, the relations between the accounting rate of return and the economic rate of return depend a great deal on the rate of growth of the asset base of the firm. At least in this example, the faster the firm grows, the lower the accounting rate of return will be, leading to the anomaly that very high economic rates of return which would induce the firm to grow very fast will produce very low accounting rates of return. Moreover, outside of such a simple example, the problem is not always one way. Depending on the rate at which firms invest, the rate at which investments depreciate and the time pattern of the returns from an investment, it is quite possible to have a low economic rate of return correspond to a very high accounting rate of return. One cannot make inferences about monopoly profits from this sort of thing. The correct analysis is not a simple one.

I regard the problem of calculating the economic rate of return as the most serious one in trying to use the profit rate for a judgment about monopoly power and the use of the accounting rate of return as the worst mistake therein. Nevertheless, even if one somehow succeeded in getting around this sort of timing problem in estimating the economic rate of return, there would still remain problems with using the results to make inferences about monopoly power. As with some of the problems raised previously, the issues here involve what is appropriately called profits.

Recall that, in the competitive model, a certain amount of what accountants and firms consider profits is included in costs for the purposes of economic analysis. Expressed as a rate of return, the amount so included represents the rate of return just necessary to keep the firm in the business; it represents the rate of return that the firm's capital could earn elsewhere. Thus, when one says that long-run profits in a competitive industry are zero, one does not mean that measured profits will be zero, but merely that measured profits will be at that level at which there is no inducement to entry or exit.

Now that is all very well in theory, but in practice, one is going to make a judgment about monopoly power by deciding whether the given level of profits is at a competitive level or whether it is above that level with entry somehow blocked. This would be easier to do if there were a single measure of a competitive rate of return.

There is no such single measure, however, and this is largely due to the fact that risks in different industries vary. When I outlined the competitive model, I took the usual course of ignoring risk altogether. But real-world industries, even real-world competitive industries, experience risk and part of the rate of return necessary to keep capital in the business is a reward for risk-taking. Accordingly, the competitive rate of return in high risk industries is going to be higher than in low risk ones.

Nobody knows exactly how to quantify that effect, yet it is obviously an important issue. Consider, for example, a very high risk industry in which those who gamble and fail leave. The profit rates earned by those who gamble and succeed and thus remain in the industry will be high, yet it would be wrong to conclude that one is looking at a situation of monopoly profit. If one looks only at the rate of return earned on their investment by winners of the Massachusetts State Lottery, for example, one will quickly conclude that it is an extremely good investment (a view which the advertisements put on by the state would like to encourage). Yet this is clearly wrong. What matters is the rate of return for both winners and losers.

Moreover, there is an additional, somewhat related, issue. Suppose that one looks at an industry and manages to calculate the economic rates of return for the firms therein and finds that there is one firm with a very high rate of return and others with rather lower ones. Can one then conclude that the most profitable firm has monopoly power? After all, in competition, are not all firms' profits supposed to be the same and equal to the competitive rate? Even if one cannot tell what that rate is, cannot one conclude something from differential profits?

Unfortunately, the answer is once again in the negative. In the risk-taking case, this is because there may be differential outcomes for winners and the rate of return earned by the luckiest winner may be more than that necessary to remain in the business. Even so, monopoly profits are not earned because what is involved is the *ex ante* expected rate of return involved when the gamble is taken. More generally, what is involved here is what economists call 'unimputed rents'.

The simple model of competition supposes that every firm is just as efficient as every other firm and has access to all the same factors of production. Yet in practice, this may not be the case. One firm may be more efficient than another. To take three examples, it may have more efficient people working for it; it may be more favorably situated geographically; or it may at some time in the past have made a successful innovation which, perhaps just because it was first, cannot be successfully duplicated.

How does one reconcile such cases with the competitive model? One way to do it is to define the apparent excess profits being earned as really being something else. This is the sort of thing that economists are very good at, and so it is in this case. Such apparent profits are called 'rents'. They represent returns which do not affect economic decisions and which can be thought of as belonging to something other than the firm's manufacturing activity. Thus, if the firm's management is particularly skillful, the extra money coming in really represents returns to managerial talent rather than profits to the firm. Similarly, a firm with an advantageous location ought to be thought of as making its extra money as a return on that location – a true 'rent' which the firm pays to itself as a landlord. Finally, the firm with the past successful innovation is earning money as the owner of the rights to that innovation rather than in its current production activity.

Now, in some circumstances, one would not expect to see such rents appearing in the profit statements of firms. If greater efficiency is due to the skills of only a few people, then, in a competitive industry, such people, if they are not paid for their skills, can be bid away by new entrants or other competitors. The end result will be that their wages go up and apparent profits go down. Similarly, in some very long-run sense, a firm with an especially advantageous location could lease that location to another firm at a high price and go into business at a less advantageous location. If it did that, it would record the same amount of incoming money, but what appeared to be profits would be properly recorded as rent coming into the firm in its landholding capacity. Analytically considered, the firm ought to keep its books in that form whether or not it actually engages in such activities. Similarly, the holder of the rights to an innovation ought to value those rights at what they can be sold for and keep books in two capacities, one as a manufacturing firm and one as the holder of such rights.

But, of course, firms do not keep their books in such ways. Moreover, even the case of special managerial skills need not result in rents being fully imputed to the factors of production with which they are properly associated. Particularly in large firms dealing with complicated and delicate technologies, it is perfectly possible for the added efficiency to accrue not to any small group of individuals but to the firm as a whole. If that is true, then while it would be possible for others to bid away any small group of individuals, the managerial efficiencies would still rest in the organization, the whole being greater than the sum of its parts. In that circumstance, there would still be unimputed rents which will show up as profits in the accounting records.

Obviously, I believe that judgments about profits as an index of monopoly power are very difficult, if not impossible to make. This is particularly unfortunate because of the associated difficulty it produces in assessing barriers to entry, a subject to which I now turn.

Barriers to entry

It should be clear from what has been said that a consideration of the role of entry plays a major part in any assessment of monopoly power. Where entry is easy, no monopoly power can persist. Where entry is difficult, provided there are not already many existing competitors, monopoly power can survive. It is entry which is induced by supranormal profits in a competitive industry and entry which bids those profits away. (Actually, this is literally true only if one reads 'entry' to include the expansion of existing competitors.)

Clearly then, correct analysis of entry or barriers to entry lies at the heart of an assessment of monopoly power. This is particularly true, since, as we saw when discussing market definition, the choice of an arbitrary line for the boundary of the market on grounds of supply substitutability will not affect the outcome provided that one is careful about entry from entities left outside the line. Whether considered as a phenomenon of new firms coming into the business or a phenomenon of older firms able to expand (when the line is drawn rather more widely), the analysis of entry conditions is the analysis of a central phenomenon which places or does not place constraints on the behavior of the alleged monopolist.

It is therefore with some regret that I have to say that the analysis of barriers to entry is, in my view, the single most misunderstood topic in the analysis of competition and monopoly. Even the confusion associated with market definition probably takes a second place. In large part, this may be due to an unfortunate terminology, but whatever the cause, it is a matter for considerable concern.

To see what the problem is, it is important to understand the economic relevance of a barrier to entry. A barrier to entry exists when entry would be socially beneficial but is somehow prevented. That is a fairly fancy way of describing a situation in which unnecessarily high profits are being earned and society would be better off if they were competed away, but firms cannot enter to do this. The social benefit–cost calculation is not correctly reflected in the private benefit–cost calculation of the potential entrant.

Now, that definition, which is drawn in terms of the results one wants entry to have, departs rather sharply from what one might think would be meant by a 'barrier to entry' in terms of something which makes entry difficult. Nevertheless, it turns out to be the useful way to look at it. (I have been aided greatly in thinking about this problem by the recently published work of C.C. von Weizsäcker, 1980.)

Consider, for example, an industry, entry into which requires the construction of a large plant, a distribution network and other large investments. Leave aside for the moment the question of whether the scale required for entry is big relative to demand and assume that firms can borrow at rates which correctly reflect perceptions of risk, both matters to which I shall return. The question I want to focus on now is that of whether the mere fact that a large amount of money has to be spent to get into the business and that certain skills and equipment have to be acquired means that there is a barrier to entry.

This is where economic analysis and ordinary language part company. It is not true that the situation I have just described is necessarily one of high barriers to entry. Just to focus attention, let me point out that there are not necessarily high barriers, even if the incumbent firms are currently making very high profits. Why should this be the case?

An economically relevant barrier to entry is one in which unnecessarily high profits are not bid away by entry. That is a situation in which society would be benefited by entry but in which the attractiveness of entry from the point of view of society is not the same as attractiveness from the point of view of the entrant. In the large investment example just described, however, there is no reason to believe that it is necessarily the case that profits, *properly considered*, are excessive. If a large lumpy investment has to be made to get into the industry, then the right consideration for an entrant is what the rate of return will be on all the expenses, including that lumpy investment; but if the incumbent firms had to make similar lumpy investments, then consideration of the rate of return being earned by those firms (even apart from many of the issues raised in the previous section) has to take into account the fact that their current apparently high profits come as the result of having made those investments. What has to be considered is the rate of return being earned by the incumbent on the entire process, including the initial investment. To look only at the short-run profits after that investment has been amortized for tax purposes, for example, is to miss the point.

Let me put it another way. If it is technically necessary to make a lumpy investment to get into the industry, the right question from the point of view of society is whether or not the rate of profit to be earned on the entire activity of entry, production and sale, including that lumpy investment, is higher than the rate of return which can be earned in other industries (adjusting for risk). The fact that a large investment has to be made at the outset makes this a long-run question, but it is the right question nevertheless. In the situation described, there is no reason to suppose that the calculation made by the potential entrant is any different from the calculation which society would wish to be made. There is no reason to believe that there are any social benefits or costs which are not reflected in private incentives. In the situation described, the potential entrant will not enter if the profits foreseen in the long run will not be sufficient to justify the initial lumpy investment. But that is exactly the same calculation which one would make on behalf of society. It would be socially wasteful to encourage such investment if the resulting profits will not be sufficiently high to earn the rate of return which could be earned by investing the resources 'elsewhere.

The same general principle applies to other situations sometimes thought to represent barriers to entry. Take, for example, the situation in which an existing manufacturer has achieved a deserved reputation for reliability and quality of product. Suppose that a new manufacturer, even though able to produce a product which is technically as good, or even better, cannot induce customers to buy this alternative except by offering a price premium. Does that disadvantage signal a barrier to entry?

The answer is no. Customers, when they buy a product in such a circumstance, buy not only the physical characteristics of the product but also take risks as to its quality and its reliability. One way of looking at it is to say that in buying the established products, customers are buying less risk or, if you will, more information. Investment in providing that service has already been made by the incumbent. The new entrant can also provide it by offering a price premium which will induce customers to try the new product and thus gain a reputation. But it is not to society's advantage for customers to be forced to take risks with untried products in such a situation. Just as in the case of the building of a plant, the question is whether the profits to be earned by ultimately attaining a reputation equivalent to that of the incumbent are such as to justify the investment which will have to be made to attain it. If so, then both society and the entrant will be served by entering; if not, then neither will be.

This is an important and easily misunderstood point, so let me distinguish it from some related matters. In the first place, I am talking about deserved reputation – reputation which correctly reflects product quality. It may also be that customers have irrational brand preferences. It is hard to describe exactly what that would mean, but it would certainly be different.

Second, there is no doubt that society would be better off and entry easier, in some sense, if information were perfect and the risks of trying different products either did not exist or could be assessed free of cost. The fact that experience is necessary to reduce risks certainly makes the incumbent better able to earn profits than the potential entrant. Further, competition would be enhanced if the information and risk problem did not exist. Given that it does exist, however, there is no true barrier to entry in the fact that the incumbent, but not the potential entrant, has already invested in overcoming it. Exactly the same thing is true of investment in plants. If it were not necessary to build a plant to get into a business, then more people would be in it. In a world with that kind of technology, competition would be different from what it actually is. However, what makes the difference is not the fact that incumbents have already invested in the plant necessary to overcome the difficulties. That is the cure, not the disease. Given that such an investment has to be made, either to build a plant or to establish a reputation, the question both for society and for potential entrants is whether it is worth making.

Now, the fact that I have been careful to point out that two things which are commonly thought to be barriers to entry are not really that at all does not mean that barriers to entry do not exist. There certainly can be such barriers. Here are some examples.

Incumbent firms may possess all there is to possess of some scarce resource. It may be that they are not even using that resource to capacity but are, as it were, stockpiling it. In such an event, society would be better served if entry could take place and expansion of output occur.

Next, although the need to make a large investment may not in itself be a barrier to entry, it may be that it is associated with something that is a barrier to entry. Suppose that the minimum scale which is necessary for efficient production is large relative to demand. In such a case, an incumbent firm may be able to earn monopoly profits because an entrant will properly make the calculation of what profits will be *after* entry, rather than before, and will perceive that with one more minimum scale firm in the market the addition to supply will be such as to reduce prices to a point where profits cannot be earned. Note that, even here, if costs decrease sharply up to minimum size and the market is not big enough to support one more firm when all firms are of minimum size, then the social benefit–cost calculation is the same as the private benefit–cost calculation and one ought not to talk of barriers to entry. In somewhat less black and white situations, however, what matters in part is what the entrant believes will happen to incumbents' outputs upon entry. There can be cases in which society would be benefited by the expansion of output consequent on entry, but in which entry does not take place because the entrant believes there will not be enough room. (Conduct-related issues are discussed in the next section.)

It may also be the case that credit markets function imperfectly, so that the rate of interest which must be paid by a small firm to make the lumpy investment required for entry is higher than that which would be paid by an incumbent firm to make a similar investment and higher in a way which does not simply reflect the greater risks involved. In the limit, it may be that a potential entrant cannot borrow the money at all.

The question of the existence of such capital barriers to entry is a matter of some dispute. I shall only touch on some of the issues. Aside from the difficulty of assessing whether differential borrowing rates actually reflect differential risks or not (if they do, then society's interests are appropriately reflected in the rates), potential entrants into many industries are not small firms but large firms who operate outside those industries. Since credit rationing, to the extent that it exists, is generally supposed to involve the size of the borrower rather than the size of the borrower in a particular business, the importance of capital barriers in practice has been questioned.

Further, it is important not to make mistakes by looking at the extent to which incumbents can finance expansion with retained earnings while new entrants have to raise new equity or borrow. That is not in itself an issue of the imperfection of capital markets. An incumbent who uses retained earnings to finance expansion is forgoing the opportunity to invest those earnings elsewhere, thus paying what is technically known as the 'opportunity cost' of investing in the business. Retained earnings are not free. It may, of course, very well be that internal financing is cheaper than external financing. But this may simply reflect differential assessments of risk rather than a true capital barrier. It is not an easy thing to decide.

There may also be conduct-related barriers to entry; I take these up in the next section.

In general, in deciding on barriers to entry, it is important to look at the whole picture. In particular, one has to look at the long-run picture. Take the case of innovation. After the mousetrap has been invented (and possibly, but not necessarily, patented), society would be better off in the short run if other firms had instant access to the mousetrap technology and could imitate it and produce it right away. But it is very shortsighted to suppose that the fact that they cannot do so is a barrier to entry or, indeed, is socially detrimental. The profits earned by the mousetrap inventor in the initial period of success represent in part a return on the investment in innovation, an investment which society presumably wishes to encourage. If immediate imitation were to take place, the unnecessary profits on the mousetrap *after the mousetrap has been invented* would indeed be bid away. There would then, however, not be sufficient profits to be earned in the innovation business to induce such innovations in the first place. The right issue is not whether there are barriers to entry into the production of a particular mousetrap, but whether there are barriers to entry into *innovation* in mousetraps. As is always true, the still picture can provide useful publicity but can also give a very misleading idea about the movie.

Conduct and predatory pricing

> Thou hast it now: King, Cawdor, Glamis, all,
> and I fear,
> Thou play'dst most foully for't.
> *Macbeth*, Act III, Scene I

If we think of the conventional structure–conduct–performance paradigm, this discussion has been mostly about structure (an exception being some of the discussion of profits). Unfortunately, it has turned out that many of the structural issues are quite complicated. Is it possible to go about the matter in a different way, by looking at the way an actual monopolist behaves? Are there certain kinds of activity which one can point to as clear evidence of monopolizing behavior?

Put the matter a different way. Aside from the relevance of an examination of conduct to analysis of attempts to monopolize (an offense related to, but different from that of monopolization under the Sherman Act), suppose that we observe a firm with monopoly power; indeed, suppose (what is not the same thing at all, but is a good deal easier to observe) that we observe a firm with a high share of the market. The question naturally arises as to how that share was obtained. The courts have said that it matters whether or not it was obtained by 'superior skill, efficiency and foresight' or 'by conduct honestly industrial, but not economically inevitable'. What kind of conduct ought then to be permitted?

This is a good question for public policy. As I have already indicated, however, I believe that it is awkwardly expressed from the point of view of economic analysis, even though the issues which must be considered in order to answer it are the same no matter how it is posed. A firm which maintains a large share of the market because of behavior forced on it ('economically inevitable') or solely because of being better ('superior skill, efficiency and foresight') is a firm which does not have monopoly power at all. Monopoly power is the power to maintain a high share and earn supranormal profits *without* being better. A firm which has acquired a large share simply by winning the competitive race through competitive means is not a firm which is a monopoly. The view that it can be a monopoly, but one which is nevertheless to be encouraged stems, I think, from the confusion of high market share with monopoly power which I have already discussed.

Still, whichever way one wants to put it, the question of what kind of conduct is to be encouraged and what prohibited in the course of attaining a large share is an important one. Moreover, the fact that the law can be violated by conduct not in itself illegal but which is 'honestly industrial but not economically inevitable' makes the question of prohibited conduct a difficult one to answer. It also leads to arguments from plaintiffs about all sorts of innocent-appearing and quite possibly actually innocent and competitive conduct.

Is there any rule that one can apply in assessing conduct? I think there are two principles which one can state. The first such principle is that conduct, to be suspect, ought at least to be more restrictive than necessary. The example of the United Shoe Machinery Company which required very long leases and enforced penalty clauses differentially depending on whether or not the customer went to a competitive machine comes immediately to mind. So does the example of Alcoa which bought up power sites far in advance of any use of them (although there the question of distinguishing that behavior from the use of superior foresight at least arises). In both cases, one can say that the conduct involved restrictions to competition which basically had no other purpose. The market could have functioned and the firms been profitable with less restrictive action.

The second principle (and the one the overlooking of which leads to confusion) is that conduct should not be condemned if it is precisely the conduct which competition would lead us to expect. One has to be careful to distinguish between cases in which competition is forcing firms to react and cases in which firms are taking unnecessary action to forestall competition. The competitive model itself points to situations in which firms, faced with competition, will be forced to do certain things or lose business. Firms observed to be doing those things in those situations should not be regarded as monopolizing. They are engaging in conduct which competition makes 'economically inevitable'.

This can be made clearer by considering a leading example, the analysis of predatory pricing. The notion of a monopolist setting a predatorily low price in order to stifle competitors is a popular one (although less popular among economists than among others). It is certainly fostered by those firms which have to compete against low prices. What can be said on this issue? (Actually quite a lot can be and has been said on this issue and I can do no more than touch on what seem to me to be the really basic points. Recent papers include Areeda and Turner (1975, 1976), Posner (1976), Scherer (1976) and Williamson (1977). The view taken here is closest to that of Areeda and Turner.)

Most economists would at least agree with the following proposition. At any moment in time, there are costs to producing a product which are sunk and costs which can be avoided if the product is not produced. Planning at any moment, a firm should price so that anticipated revenues at least cover the avoidable costs. Deliberate pricing lower than that should be deemed predatory. A firm engaging in that kind of pricing is deliberately earning losses which it could have avoided.

Note, however, that what matters here is the expected revenue and costs as of the time plans are made. In the event it may turn out that demand was considerably weaker than had been expected and products actually make losses. Indeed, after a product is introduced and fails to sell, the best a firm may be able to do is to lower the price of the product to bring in some return on the *then* still avoidable costs. The fact that, viewed after the event, the firm failed to earn a profit on the original investment in developing and producing the product is beside the point. Failures are not necessarily predatory.

Note also, that in assessing what expected revenues and avoidable costs were, one needs to take everything into account. Consider, for example, a firm which bids on a contract to develop a high technology product for the government in the expectation that the experience so gained will be useful in the profitable production of a similar product later on for the commercial market. Such a firm is not necessarily engaging in predatory conduct if it bids for the government contract at a price that does not return its costs in the original development. The revenues from engaging in the development properly include the profits earned later from gaining experience with the technology.

Of course one has to be careful about this sort of thing. A firm which does engage in predatory pricing is presumably doing so because, after competition is forced out, it will earn monopoly profits. Considered as a long-run proposition, the pricing behavior engaged in in the first place was profitable, including in revenues the monopoly profit later earned as a result. Still, it is possible to make sensible judgments about what later effects should and should not properly be included.

The issue over which there is considerable confusion, however, is that of whether prices which are planned to be remunerative, even considering only direct effects, can also be predatory prices. Imagine a firm charging a relatively high price. Suppose that other firms attempt to enter and produce the same product. Suppose that the first firm, which for some reason is more efficient than the others, drops its price below the costs of the other firms but not below its own costs. Is this 'below-cost pricing' and therefore predatory? Does not it reveal that the initial firm had monopoly power? After all, apparently it had the power 'to set prices and exclude competitors'.

Anybody who is ready to answer 'yes' to those questions should stay after school, because they have missed a good deal of the point of what I have been saying about the analysis of competition and monopoly. Monopoly power is the power to keep prices *high*, earn supranormal profits, and *still* exclude competitors. *Any* firm which is more efficient than its rival always has the power to exclude competitors by setting prices low. That is what competition is supposed to encourage. Further, suppose firms are equally efficient. Then the firm with the largest supply of cash has the power to set prices low and drive out its competitors because it will go out of business last. This is wholly irrelevant. Where competitors are forced out or entry forestalled only by prices being kept low, competition is doing its job. The hallmark of monopoly power is the ability to set *high* prices and earn *high* profits without inducing entry and competitive growth. It is always possible to set *low* prices and earn *low* profits without doing so.

Let me consider two somewhat more specific examples to drive this home. Consider first a firm producing two varieties of the same product. Suppose that it perceives a special demand for one of the varieties and raises the price for it, hoping to earn profits. Suppose it then turns out that others discover a way to make the low-priced variety into the high-priced variety at relatively low cost and that they then begin to purchase the low-priced variety from the original firm, alter it and resell it, undercutting the original firm's price for the high-priced variety. The original firm then finds it cannot maintain the price differential and it readjusts its prices accordingly. The arbitraging firms then find that the profit opportunity disappears and they leave the business. Was the readjustment in prices predatory?

I should hope the answer would clearly be seen to be 'no'. What I have described is exactly what is supposed to happen under competition. A price differential which does not reflect a cost differential is bid away. Had the original firm been able to sustain that differential, there would have been monopoly power. The closing of the differential was in fact 'economically inevitable'.

It is worth commenting further on this example. Note how misleading it is to look at it only as the arbitraging firms are driven out. By concentrating on the lowering of the price differential, one can pretend one is seeing an attempt to drive out competitors; but that would only make sense if, after they are driven out, it is possible to increase the differential again without bringing them back. That requires some other barrier to competition than merely the lowering of the prices.

Further, competition does not take place in real markets in an impersonal way. The original firm in this example is very likely to understand what is happening and to consider in some detail the costs that the arbitraging firms incur in changing one product into the other. It may even know that it will put them out of the arbitrage business by lowering its price. Even so, it is not committing a predatory act. It is forced, in the example, to lower the price differential or lose business in the high-priced good. What we are observing is competition driving that price differential down to the differential cost of the product, nothing else.

To take a second example, consider the process of innovative competition which I have previously described. In the initial phase, the inventor of the better mousetrap is charging a high price and earning apparently supranormal profits which represent the return on the innovation. Then the imitators come in and bid the price down. *What on earth does bidding the price down mean if it does not mean that the original firm has to lower its price or else lose market share?* Is such a lowering of the price predatory? Surely not. Again, had it been possible to keep the price up without losing share, monopoly power would have been present. Competition will force the innovator to lower the price and, if the innovator's costs are lower than those of the imitators, it will force the price down to the point where the imitators cannot make a profit. Moreover, the innovator may lower its price quite knowingly.

To condemn such conduct as predatory is to condemn exactly the kind of conduct that competition is supposed to foster. If 'economically inevitable' means anything at all, it means this sort of thing. If market share gained by 'superior efficiency' is to mean anything at all, it must mean lower prices by the efficient firm. One can certainly expect cries of outrage and even lawsuits from the others involved, but protection of competition does not mean the protection of individual competitors. Where competitors are being kept out by low prices, competition is doing its job.

That is not to say that low prices cannot form part of an anti-competitive plan. There may be cases in which firms lower prices, thus driving out temporarily less efficient competitors, and in which barriers to entry of some other kind then arise which enable the formerly low-priced firm to become high-priced with impunity. Further, at least in theory, if every attempt to enter is met with aggressive behavior and this is combined with economies of scale, then some less efficient potential entrants may get the message that there is no room to make profits and the incumbent firm may be able to make profits itself by raising prices; but fully efficient firms (whose entry would clearly benefit society) cannot be deterred in this way unless prices are cut below the incumbent firm's own cost. Moreover, even firms which would become efficient if they stayed and overcame initial scale or other obstacles can only be so deterred if the capital market fails to provide funds in a way commensurate with the true risk involved – the problematic capital barrier to entry already discussed. (Note that *correct* assessment of the high risk involved in overcoming initial inefficiency does not count here even if it makes borrowing difficult.) Even here it seems to me that public policy would be better served by a program of loan subsidies than by trying to discourage firms from choosing the low but remunerative prices that competition is supposed to bring about.

Note further, that where predatory pricing is an issue, a crucial question is whether prices will later be high. Where entrants are merely kept out by low prices and prices cannot be raised without encouraging entry, then competition is working. Competition is supposed to bid prices down. A firm charging high prices, faced with competition, is supposed to lower such prices. Even a firm with 100 per cent of the market, which is only able to maintain that share by so-called 'limit pricing' in which it must keep the prices below the costs of potential entrants, is not by that fact alone engaging in monopoly.

In short, then, while predatory pricing is a possibility, one has to be careful to distinguish it from the behavior competition is supposed to produce. Certainly, in any actual monopoly antitrust case in which most or all of the behavior challenged consists of low rather than high prices, one should be very suspicious.

Conclusion

The message just given relating to predatory pricing is, of course, the message that has run throughout this chapter. In diagnosing monopoly, one has to be careful to distinguish the symptoms from those of competition. Surprisingly, that is not as easy as might be supposed.

I have said relatively little about performance in this regard. By performance, economists generally mean the extent to which a particular market produces the results that one might expect from a competitive market (low profit margin – appropriately measured; efficient means of production employed; and technical progress). It is not always possible to tell when a market's performance is competitive, although it is usually possible to tell when it is reasonably good. The difficulty with using performance as an index of monopoly power is that, while clearly bad performance would signal the lack of competition, the discretion which monopolists have means that good performance can result even when competition is not structurally present. It is logically true, therefore, that one cannot infer the absence of monopoly power from good performance.

Nevertheless, performance seems to me to be quite a relevant indicator in the following sense. I have tried to show in this chapter how difficult it is to tell monopoly from competition even on grounds of structure and conduct. Doing so is not impossible, but it is easy to become confused and to accept simplistic solutions. Where the performance of a market appears to be good, it seems to me particularly important to be careful about the analysis of structure and conduct. Economists and others ought to approach the public policy problems involved in these areas with a certain humility. Real industries tend to be very complicated. One ought not to tinker with a well-performing industry on the basis of simplistic judgments. The diagnosis of the monopoly disease is sufficiently difficult that one ought not to proceed to surgery without a thorough examination of the patient and a thorough understanding of the medical principles involved.

References

P. Areeda and D.F. Turner, 'Predatory pricing and related practices under Section 2 of the Sherman Act', *Harvard Law Review*, Vol. 88 (February 1975), pp. 697–733.

P. Areeda and D.F. Turner, 'Scherer on predatory pricing: a reply', *Harvard Law Review*, Vol. 89 (March 1976), pp. 891–903.

J.R. Hicks, 'Annual survey of economic theory: the theory of monopoly', *Econometrica*, Vol. 3 (January 1935), pp. 1–20.

R.A. Posner, *Antitrust Law, an Economic Perspective* (Chicago: University of Chicago Press, 1976), pp. 184–96.

F.M. Scherer, 'Predatory pricing and the Sherman Act: a comment', *Harvard Law Review*, Vol. 89 (March 1976), pp. 869–90.

C.C. von Weizsäcker, *Barriers to Entry: A Theoretical Treatment*, (Berlin, Heidelberg, New York: Springer-Verlag, 1980).

Oliver Williamson, 'Predatory pricing: a strategic and welfare analysis', *Yale Law Journal*, Vol. 87 (December 1977), pp. 284–340.

2

Horizontal mergers: Triage and treatment (1987)

Introduction: The 'incipiency' doctrine

For some years now, antitrust policy towards horizontal mergers has been evolving. It is plain to me that some sort of change was badly needed; whether the changes that have taken place or those proposed by the Reagan Administration were the appropriate ones is not quite so clear.

In the years following *Brown Shoe*[1] two views became perniciously intertwined. These were: first, the older view that Section 7 of the Clayton Act was designed to thwart monopoly power 'in its incipiency';[2] second, that the definition of markets or submarkets (whatever 'submarkets' are) is readily accomplished, with the parlance of business executives ('the Chicago drug-store market', 'the high-fashion shoe market') substituting for serious economic analysis. The result was that mergers could be and often were successfully challenged if the merging firms overlapped in their product lines and had even a small fraction of some economic 'market', even if it was obvious that the merger by itself could not materially affect competition. (Perhaps the ultimate case of the incipiency doctrine was *United States* v. *Von's Grocery Co.*, 384 US 270 (1966). In that case a grocery store acquisition in Los Angeles was ruled illegal even though the merged firms had only 7.5 per cent of retail grocery business, there were 150 grocery chains and 3,800 stores in operation, and entry could hardly be said to be difficult.) Since mergers can occur for procompetitive efficiency reasons, an overstringent policy will inflict clear social costs.

The language of Section 7 lends itself to the incipiency doctrine by speaking in terms of mergers the effect of which 'may be substantially to lessen competition or to tend to create a monopoly'. Presumably for this reason, the administration proposes to change the language to 'substantially reduce competition' and thus at least partially negate the incipiency doctrine. But despite the excesses to which the incipiency doctrine has led, there are substantive reasons for not changing the language of Section 7.

The incipiency doctrine may be viewed as filling a void in the legal treatment of oligopoly. In the case of single-firm monopolies, the *Alcoa* case can be read as permitting non-competitive market structures to be attacked even if the firm involved has done nothing wrongful in itself, provided the firm has deliberately acted to achieve the market structure in question.[3] There has never been a parallel structural doctrine in the law for the case of tight oligopoly.[4] Hence, even where the enforcement authorities are sure that the structure of the market is highly conducive to tacit collusion, no antitrust attack on that structure is likely to succeed (or even be attempted). With the exception of acts designed to exclude new entrants, only explicitly or implicitly collusive acts can be successfully attacked, and even a win by the government in a collusion case will leave in place the very structure that makes it likely that similar anticompetitive events will occur again.[5]

Of course, sometimes no structural remedy for tight oligopoly is possible. Just as there are natural monopolies, there are natural oligopolies, and just as the inevitability of a monopoly-like structure is (or ought to be) a defense to a structure case under Section 2 of the Sherman Act, so the inevitability of a tight oligopoly structure ought to be a defense to a structure case under any structurally-oriented anti-oligopoly act. But at present that defense is not an issue, because such an act does not exist.

In the case of monopoly, merger policy plays a natural role as part of a structural policy. If deliberately acquired monopoly power is to be considered a violation of the antitrust laws, then it makes sense to prohibit such deliberate acquisition before it occurs. Banning mergers that 'tend to create a monopoly' is far easier than ordering complex divestiture afterwards. On the other hand, the fact that deliberately acquired monopoly power is a violation does allow later antitrust attack if a particular merger proves part of a pattern that does lead to monopoly.

In the case of oligopoly, however, no such later attack is likely to be possible, and merger policy is the only existing way to prevent a permanent non-competitive structure from arising. Where a merger or a series of mergers will result in a tight oligopoly structure, Section 7 with its present language permits enforcement agencies to prevent it. What is more, the move to a tight oligopoly structure can be halted at a time when the 'inevitability' of that structure can be most easily examined by weighing the pro- and anticompetitive effects of the merger before it occurs. In the absence of any other structurally-oriented oligopoly policy, dealing with tight oligopolies 'in their incipiency' may be the only way of dealing with them at all.

There are problems here, however. Consider the case in which a tight oligopoly structure will be attained through a series of mergers if they are not stopped. In such a situation, dealing with the problem through merger policy encounters possible difficulties. On the one hand, if antitrust attack begins with an early merger in the series (as in *Brown Shoe* and *Von's Grocery*), it may stop an innocent or even procompetitive merger simply because the Court or the Department of Justice envisages it as the forerunner of a line of mergers that may never happen. On the other hand, suppose that antitrust attack waits for later mergers when anticompetitive effect seems certain. Then, at least when a series of mergers occurs in a relatively short time period, one can regard the participants in later mergers as being treated unfairly (unless the first firms to perceive the possibility of later non-competitive profits are regarded as innovators).[6] Further, such a policy can provide an incentive to merge while the merging is good, providing an artificial incentive to get in under the antitrust wire.

While something can be said on both sides of this issue, actual merger policy as applied by the courts has not been particularly ambivalent about it. Instead, merger policy has tended to err in the direction of the first problem – attacking particular mergers because the Kantian categorical imperative shows that many mergers like them would together be anticompetitive. Such a policy carries the incipiency doctrine too far. On the other hand, the attempt of the administration to change the language of Section 7 to require a 'substantial reduction in competition' is likely to lead to the second problem – attacking only later mergers in an otherwise symmetric series.

This latter problem may not seem particularly troublesome. After all, why not deal with the problems created by each merger as they arise? Why prohibit early mergers in a series just because later ones may create a non-competitive structure? Presumably the early mergers are undertaken without (or with relatively little) anticompetitive intent, while the proponents of later mergers must realize what they are doing.

The problem with this argument is that it supposes that we really know how to draw the line, that the place at which the next merger makes the industry non-competitive is easy to spot, perhaps with the aid of some quantitative measure. As I shall repeatedly emphasize, this is simply not the case. Early mergers can contribute to some departure from competition, and a policy of asymmetric treatment can encourage such mergers to occur, rewarding anticompetitive foresight while penalizing late arrivals.

A two-stage procedure

Indeed, the pursuit of any sort of structural policy towards oligopoly – whether through merger policy or otherwise – presupposes that we can recognize anticompetitive structures when we see them. That requirement is especially crucial for the necessarily indirect approach embodied in merger policy. Unfortunately, that requisite is not easy to meet, and there is a temptation to avoid difficult analysis in favor of standards that are apparently precise but in fact very approximate. This problem pervades all aspects of merger policy.

For this reason, when considering merger standards, it is important to bear in mind that policy takes place in stages. In particular, there is a difference between deciding on guidelines for triage – guidelines as to what cases to investigate or oppose – and for treatment, the judicial standard to be used. Arbitrary rules are inevitable and may even be appropriate in the first context. They are a menace in the second. The Department of Justice has not always recognized the difference, particularly when it comes to the use of concentration measures.

I believe merger policy should be explicitly conducted as a two-stage process. In the first stage, fairly simple tests should be used to decide what cases should be further investigated. I would use concentration measures heavily (but not exclusively) here and would consider a variety of reasonable market definitions.

In the second stage, prospective mergers that fail such tests would be investigated in considerably more detail. This investigation will require a more sophisticated approach to market definition and concentration than is needed at the first stage. Such an investigation should begin by examining barriers to entry. If entry is found to be easy, then the merger should be permitted. If not, then the investigation should go on to consider the actual likelihood of tacit collusion (assuming that the merger does not result in a single-firm monopoly). At this stage, such matters as the complexity of the product and the ease with which cheating can be detected should come into play. I would put the burden of proof as to increased concentration and lack of entry barriers on the opponents of the merger, but tentatively would treat both sides equally when considering other factors that make tacit collusion easy or difficult. The proponents of the merger should certainly have the burden of proving that the merger will create efficiencies to offset any increased risk of anticompetitive behavior.

Such a two-stage procedure would be unnecessary, of course, if the tests of the first stage could really pick out anticompetitive mergers from harmless or procompetitive ones. Accordingly, I would have courts put little weight on the fact that a prospective merger has failed the first-stage tests (although the extent of such failure – the level of concentration above the threshold, for example – would continue to be relevant): After all, in such a system, *any* merger that gets as far as trial *must* have failed the first-stage tests.

On the other hand, partly because of the importance of providing a clear guide to firms and partly for reasons given later, I would have the antitrust authorities at least loosely committed not to attack mergers that pass the first-stage tests. Further, I would have courts put more weight on such passage in considering private suits than the small weight to be put on first-stage failure. Because the first-stage tests are mechanistic and rough, however, I would not make them dispositive either way. I shall exemplify and expand on the workings of such a two-stage procedure as I consider various aspects of merger policy.

Market definition

Market definition is an artificial construction created by antitrust litigation. For any other purpose of economic analysis, the binary question of whether particular firms or products are 'in' or 'out' of a given market is a meaningless one. Even in antitrust cases, that question is not a useful one if substantive results turn on the answer. What matters are the constraints that other firms and products put on the power of those whose actions are being examined. The proposition that flexible wrapping papers substitute for cellophane at a high cellophane price but not at lower ones already contains a good deal of information concerning the ability of a sole supplier of cellophane to charge monopoly prices. There is nothing to gain and much to lose by the Procrustean device of summarizing that information either in the statement that flexible wrapping papers and cellophane are 'in' the same market (the Supreme Court's position in the cellophane case) or in the statement that they are 'out' (the position of many commentators).[7]

Such activity, however, has historically been of overwhelming importance in antitrust cases. Instead of market definition being used as a device for summarizing and organizing information, it has often become the principal issue. Worse, the deservedly central but complex issue of constraints on the exercise of market power has often been ignored altogether. To return to merger cases, one need know little about the facts of Nestlé's acquisition of Stouffer's in the mid-1970s to know that analysis in that case was not helped by a debate over whether there is a 'market' consisting of high-priced, frozen, non-ethnic entrées.[8]

If market definition is to be at all useful in antitrust cases, the 'market' must include those firms and services that act to constrain the activities of the firm or firms that are the object of attention. That such constraints may not all be equally powerful merely points to the fact that analysis does not end when the market has been defined and that simple-minded measures of power or concentration, like simple-minded binary treatments of market definition, are unlikely to be adequate substitutes for a full analysis.[9]

The Department of Justice 'Merger Guidelines' (US Department of Justice, 1984) are a major step in the direction of sanity here. In the 1982 version (slightly modified in 1984) the Department of Justice defined a 'market' as the minimum collection of firms that could, if they colluded, profitably raise prices 5 per cent above current levels for a year. Putting the details aside for a moment, this approach is plainly the right one. If prices cannot be so raised, then supply or demand substitutability puts important constraints on the power of those already included. To leave those constraints out of the 'market' would be to have much of the action take place off stage. The implicit focus of the 'Guidelines' on constraints as the principal question to be asked in market definition is absolutely right.

It is less clear that the specific details of the 'Guidelines' approach are correct. Is 5 per cent the correct threshold amount to use for price rises? Is one year the correct amount of time? Should the 5 per cent be applied to current price levels or to something else?

I begin with the third of these questions, since the answer to it has implications for the answers to the first two. As Lawrence White (1987) emphasizes in his paper written for the same symposium as this one, the use of current levels as the base for the test is consistent with the view that merger policy is preventive, designed to keep matters from getting worse. On the other hand, as Richard Schmalensee (1987) states in his symposium constribution, 'it makes sense to define a market as something that could profitably be monopolized, not as something for which price could be profitably increased over current (possibly mono-polistic) levels'.

I agree with Schmalensee here, but more than a semantic point is involved. If one takes the view that merger policy is a substitute for a structural policy towards oligopoly, then there is a strong case for using competitive rather than current price levels. Consider a fairly tight duopoly in which prices have already been raised to the level at which a competitively-produced substitute product (like flexible wrapping papers) can compete. The present 'Guidelines' would let the duopoly merge, since the market would have to include the producers of the substitute. Since tacit collusion may not always be easy to maintain, permitting such a merger may make permanent a situation that otherwise might not last. Further, since the merger of the two duopolists is not 'economically inevitable' or solely the result of 'superior skill, foresight and industry',[10] there is the possible anomaly that the 'Guidelines' used in the administration of the supposedly more stringent Clayton Act would permit a merger leading to a monopoly that might then be successfully challenged under Section 2 of the Sherman Act.

This example suggests that using a competitive price level produces a more stringent standard than using the current level. White argues that this conclusion may not always follow, because fewer firms will be attracted to compete by 5 per cent increases over lower prices than over higher (non-competitive) ones. He gives the example of a cellophane monopolist who wishes to acquire a manufacturer of aluminum foil. In such a circumstance, the use of the competitive price level as the standard might permit the merger, since it would place the two companies in different markets (assuming that aluminum foil does not begin to compete with cellophane until the price of the latter is more than 5 per cent above its competitive level). The use of the current level, on the other hand, would force consideration of the substitution possibilities (assuming that the cellophane company is already exercising its monopoly power and pricing at the point where aluminum foil begins to become a realistic substitute for cellophane).

This argument is an excellent example of the difficulty that can arise when one tries to squeeze a complex set of facts into the binary choice of 'in' or 'out' and then decide what to do solely on the basis of mechanical tests. Obviously, any detailed analysis would uncover and deal with White's problem. One can (and should) ensure that such an analysis will take place by requiring that any serious discrepancy between competitive and current price levels should trigger further (stage two) investigation. There is no need to become a prisoner of one's own 'Guidelines' if one is willing to treat them as merely first-stage thresholds.

Of course, some of this discussion has an apparent precision that is not real. It is not easy to know in practice just what competitive prices would be. Fortunately, this problem is unlikely to matter if the job is done sensibly.[11] The kind of qualitative analysis required to decide whether market participants can raise prices above competitive levels is precisely the kind of analysis required to do a sensible job of market definition by considering the constraints on the behavior of the prospective merged company. It is not particularly different in kind from the qualitative analysis now required by the use of current price levels as the base. Only if detailed quantitative analysis were to be performed would the exact location of competitive price levels matter, and such analysis (typically not practical anyway) does not belong in the first stage of merger analysis. One need not locate competitive price levels with any precision to realize that some apparent substitutes may only reflect existing supracompetitive pricing.

As this discussion suggests, the question of whether 5 per cent is the correct figure for the test may not be very important. The 5 per cent figure does serve to focus attention on the sort of effects that will be considered important, but beyond that it serves only to give a spurious impression of precision to an analysis that is generally imprecise.

Is 5 per cent roughly right? The answer here depends on the costs and benefits involved. By using a high figure, one allows mergers to slip by that may lead to elevated prices and welfare loss. On the other hand, by using a low figure, one runs the risk of prohibiting mergers that are relatively harmless or may promote economic efficiency. Further, society must bear the cost of administrative or judicial proceedings to stop a fairly small harm. Since it is impossible to decide where to draw the line without a detailed analysis of the likely welfare losses and gains in each case, 5 per cent seems to me to be a sensible administrative rule. (One year for the time period seems a little short.) As indicated, however, I would apply it to competitive rather than to current price levels and would investigate further whenever current prices are substantially above competitive ones. This implies a more stringent rule for already non-competitive industries than the Department of Justice now uses. This seems appropriate for the first stage of merger analysis.

The second stage of merger analysis, however, requires a more sophisticated approach. Here I would move away from the simplistic, binary notion that things are either 'in' or 'out' of a 'market' and explicitly consider the fact that different firms and products provide differing degrees of constraints on the success of post-merger anticompetitive arrangements. Serious analysis need not become bogged down in deciding such bogus issues as whether cellophane and other flexible wrapping papers are in or out of the same market; it can come to grips with the real questions such as whether cellophane producers are constrained to price competitively.

Concentration measures

Painful though it may be to economists to admit, the analysis of oligopoly does not yield precise, useful results relating structure to conduct and performance. Economists know in a general way what factors make conscious parallelism more or less likely: number and size distribution of firms, complexity of the product and so on. Unfortunately, such knowledge is nowhere nearly precise enough to substitute for the study of specific situations. In particular, while conscious parallelism clearly seems to be more likely the smaller the number of firms (other things equal), economic analysis has no serious idea as to whether the danger point is reached at four firms rather than five or, indeed, what the function in question looks like. Similarly, while conscious parallelism clearly seems to be more likely the more concentrated is the market (other things equal), no sound reason exists for picking out particular levels of the Herfindahl–Hirschman index (HHI) as danger points. (See p. 202 for a definition of the HHI.)

Indeed, while the HHI seems a reasonable way to measure concentration, neither theory nor reliable econometric evidence shows that the HHI is a sufficient statistic for determining the effects of concentration on non-competitive behavior. Studies attempting to relate profit levels or markups to HHI values are not reliable guides in this regard (see Note 11). Even on their own terms, such studies are not so successful as to warrant basing merger policy on them. It would therefore be a great mistake if the courts (or Congress) were to adopt the practice of judging mergers by looking only or even primarily at pre- and post-merger HHI levels. As with market shares in monopoly cases, the HHI provides only the crudest of indications as to what we want to know. Any serious merger case must ask specifically about the likelihood of tacit collusion, and this question requires considerably more than the computation of the HHI.

Such strictures, however, do not apply to the use of the HHI for first-stage, administrative purposes. With limited resources and finite time, the antitrust authorities must decide somehow what cases to investigate and then pursue. If that decision is not itself to require a full-dress investigation, then some rules must be used that can be applied fairly readily. In that circumstance, the use of the HHI to trigger or turn off investigation appears warranted.

Since I would principally use the HHI in this way, such questions as how to treat foreign competition recede in importance. If quotas exist or are likely, for example, then the availability of foreign capacity does not put the same constraint on post-merger anticompetitive behavior as would the same capacity in independent domestic hands. I would calculate the HHI both including foreign production beyond the quota level and excluding it. If the treatment of foreign production makes a difference, then the issue should be analyzed and investigated further.

There is no point in wasting time arguing which one is the 'right' computation. As in all aspects of market definition, it is a mistake to suppress information. In this case, it is a mistake to suppress the fact that foreign competition may matter in a different way from domestic competition by forcing a decision that foreign competition is either the same as domestic or not present at all. Calculating the HHI ought not to be the point of a merger analysis, but only a signal for further investigation.

Are the HHI levels currently used in the 'Guidelines' the right ones to use as such signals? How can one know? Plainly, a very low post-merger HHI makes it most unlikely that anticompetitive behavior will (or can) result from the merger. Plainly also, a merger that raises the HHI by a very large amount and leaves it very high is one that requires investigation. But what do 'very low' and 'very high' mean? Is the 1800 cut-off the right one? To know this with much certainty would be to know what we emphatically do not know – exactly how the HHI relates to non-competitive behavior. Further, to know the answer with certainty would be to know what cannot be known, for the relation of the likelihood of non-competitive behavior to market structure is too complex to be well-summarized in a single measure.

One can get a little farther, however. The danger of setting the trigger levels of the HHI too high is that anticompetitive mergers will slip through. One of the dangers of setting them too low is that the antitrust authorities will be beset with many cases of HHIs above the threshold with claims of offsetting effects (and may lose such cases if they go to trial). This is particularly likely where the Department of Justice defines the market too narrowly, as it sometimes still does.[12] Analysis of actual experience under the 'Guidelines' might be revealing here. A low trigger level may not necessarily be a bad thing. If the purpose of setting such levels is to trigger investigation, it may well be better to waste resources on an investigation of a merger that is shown to be harmless than to fail to investigate a merger that will turn out to be harmful.

Unfortunately, low trigger levels have other costs. Mergers are sometimes delicate creatures, and antitrust litigation can be extremely expensive. The HHI levels set in the 'Guidelines' can therefore act to deter mergers that involve such levels. Setting the levels low can deter socially useful mergers. This outcome is particularly likely if a two-stage procedure is not followed and the trigger levels are used by the authorities not as signals to investigate but as signals to oppose.[13]

Partly to offset the costs of deterring socially useful mergers by too low a trigger level, I would have the antitrust authorities committed not to oppose mergers that fail the first stage tests save in unusual circumstances. I would also have courts give some weight to such passage in deciding private suits (although I would not make passage of such tests dispositive).

Barriers to entry

After the decision to investigate a proposed merger has been taken on the basis of the HHI, ease of entry is the phenomenon that should be investigated first. That is so, first because of the intrinsic importance of the role of potential entry (or the lack thereof) and second, because a finding that entry is easy should be dispositive. Unfortunately, while the importance of analyzing entry is generally recognized in principle, there is mass confusion over what it involves in practice.

The analytic use of the term 'barriers to entry' comes as part of the proposition: 'Barriers to entry prevent the competitive process from working'. Or similarly: 'Where entry is easy, there can only be a competitive result'. Accordingly, a barrier to entry must be something that interferes with competition. It must be something that allows incumbent firms, if they collude, to charge non-competitive prices and earn supranormal profits.

It follows that not everything that makes entry appear difficult or uninviting is necessarily a barrier to entry. The mere necessity of building a plant when incumbents have already built theirs is not such a barrier (although associated economies of scale with sunk costs can be). Neither is the necessity of advertising or creating a reputation automatically a barrier. To be a barrier, the phenomenon involved must permit incumbents to earn supranormal profits on the whole process of getting into the market and continuing to act, without inducing others to enter and bid those profits away.[14]

Two issues deserve special discussion here, because they involve phenomena that may permit incumbents to earn supranormal profits without their having any special long-run advantage. These are the issues of economies of scale and of the time it takes to enter.

As already indicated, I take the position that economies of scale with sunk costs can be a barrier to entry. If the cost structure requires a new entrant to come in at so large a size that post-entry prices will mean losses, then such a potential entrant will not become an actual one. In such a circumstance, incumbents – provided they can tacitly (or explicitly) collude – can earn supranormal profits. They can do so without inducing entry because it is the expected post-entry profits of the entrant rather than the pre-entry profits of the incumbents that matter in the entry decision.

The case in which entry simply takes a long time presents a different problem. Suppose that incumbents and potential entrants have no differences in this regard. Then it can be said that entry-time is not a barrier and that the profits earned by the incumbents are merely the rewards of foresight. While I would take this view in dealing with a single-firm monopoly case, I do not do so in the case of a prospective merger. Consider, for example, a market that takes a long time to enter and that now contains only two firms of equal size. Those firms may, by their foresight, be entitled to what they can get with the current market structure, but that is no reason to allow them to change that structure and become a (short-run) monopoly. More generally, the foresight that has led firms to enter an industry does not require reward by allowing them to merge and thus increase the likelihood of non-competitive outcomes. If it did, the same argument would permit any merger as a reward to foreseeing the supracompetitive profits to be gained thereby.

The proposition that an entry barrier is only something that permits incumbent firms to earn supranormal profits is not an easy one, and the Antitrust Division does not have a good track record in applying it in practice. A recent example will serve to illustrate the point.[15]

In the recent Northwest–Republic airline merger (in which I was a witness for Northwest), the Department of Justice took quite a narrow view of the market. In addition to the position discussed in Note 12, the Department argued that only another airline also having a hub at Minneapolis would be able to compete effectively for air passenger traffic on routes out of the merged airline's Minneapolis hub. For purposes of the present discussion, I assume that position to be correct.[16]

There were no obvious barriers to another airline constructing such a hub. Landing slots were not a problem, nor were gate facilities. Further, while the fact of the merger of two airlines with hubs at Minneapolis might be taken to imply that economies of scale made hubbing in that city a natural monopoly, the Department of Justice did not contend that this was so, explicitly assuming that economies of scale required no more than the number of flights flown in and out of Minneapolis by Republic (the airline with the smaller of the two pre-merger hubs there).

Why then did the Department of Justice claim that barriers to entry existed and go on to oppose the merger as likely to create a monopoly? Because, said the Antitrust Division, Minneapolis is not an attractive place to have a hub. It is too far north to be an efficient connecting point between major east and west coast cities, and other airlines will not find it attractive to build a hub there in the presence of the large number of flights 'controlled' by the post-merger Northwest.

This position misunderstands the proper analysis of barriers to entry. The issue should have been whether other airlines would find hubbing at Minneapolis attractive *if the post-merger Northwest sought to raise prices and reduce output*. Whether or not other airlines would find Minneapolis attractive with the post-merger Northwest aggressively competing by offering the service previously flown by the two merger partners and doing so at pre-merger prices was irrelevant. Even more obviously irrelevant was the issue of whether Minneapolis is inherently an attractive hub. The geographical position of Minneapolis is not something that gives incumbents an advantage over entrants.[17]

Such a misunderstanding of the analysis of entry barriers is an important failing in the antitrust authorities. Particularly if markets are to be narrowly defined and HHI levels that trigger further investigation set relatively low, the analysis of entry is absolutely crucial. I would put great weight on it in considering a prospective merger.

Having said this, I must go on to caution against attempts to avoid what ought to be a thoughtful and detailed analysis of this important question by the creation of a single summary measure of ease of entry. Just as the state of our knowledge does not permit the HHI to serve as more than a rough signal of the need for further investigation, so also economists know too little to be able to produce a useful quantitative index of ease of entry. While this gap may be filled as the science progresses, and while quantitative or potentially quantitative measures (the degree of how sunk any sunk costs are, for example) can inform and assist the analysis of entry barriers, it is well to avoid the appearance of great precision where little exists in reality. There is a great temptation for the antitrust authorities (and perhaps the courts) to focus on quantitative standards as a substitute for real analysis. Economists ought not to offer such temptation unless the delivery soundly backs up the promise.

Another example drawn from the *Northwest–Republic* case is illustrative here. Correctly observing that airlines are more likely to enter a given city-pair route if they have traffic that feeds into that route (more likely to enter Kansas City–Minneapolis service, for example, if they can collect passengers from other origins at Kansas City), the Department of Justice introduced a measure of likelihood of entry called the 'feed ratio'. That measure was constructed as follows for a given city pair, A and B. Assume for simplicity that a pair of cities served by only one incumbent airline has only one potential entrant. The 'feed ratio' is the ratio of the sum of the potential entrant's total enplanements at A and B to the sum of the incumbent's total enplanements at the two cities. In both cases, enplanements are measured without regard for the destinations of the passengers involved.[18] The Department of Justice argued (at least at first) that the fact that the 'feed ratio' was relatively low for a number of routes involved in the merger showed that entry was difficult.

This argument is nonsense. Consider the Boston–Minneapolis city pair, for example. Passengers wishing to fly between those cities must, by definition, be flying on an incumbent airline. Other passengers enplaning at those cities are certainly going somewhere else. Of what possible relevance to a decision by Delta to enter Boston–Minneapolis service is the fact that my wife, who has no reason to travel to Minneapolis, sometimes flies from Boston to Cincinnati on Delta to visit her parents?

It is thus not surprising that the 'feed ratio' fails to predict actual entry and not surprising that the chief witness for the Department of Justice eventually admitted that it was not an entry predictor.[19] What is disturbing is that the Department made a fair production of putting it forward. I believe this was because of the powerful lure of apparent measurability. That lure should always be resisted lest the measurability prove spurious.

Efficiencies and other matters

Having gone beyond an analysis of entry to an analysis of other factors bearing on effects on competition, I would not merely use those other factors as tiebreakers. Enforcement agencies should first analyze concentration as a threshold matter. They should then analyze entry because it may dispose of the question if the answer comes out a particular way. If concentration is high and entry not easy, analysts ought properly to be quite suspicious. But they must not forget that the theory of oligopoly is not good enough for them to be able to infer anticompetitive results from structure in any precise way. Instead, merger analysts should always bear in mind that the question at issue is the likelihood, or at least the ease, of anticompetitive behavior. The complexity of the product, the extent to which an effective tacit agreement would require implicit collusion on many negotiated transaction prices instead of a single list price, the ease with which cheating on a tacit agreement can be detected, these and similar matters are properly subjects for analysis once it appears that concentration will be high and entry difficult. It tentatively seems appropriate that, once the opponents of a merger have carried the burden of proof as to concentration and entry, the parties should be on an equal footing as to the actual likelihood of tacit collusion, but that is not to say that such matters should only come into play in otherwise doubtful cases.

The burden of proof as to cost savings or other offsetting efficiencies, however, should rest squarely on the proponents of a merger, and here I would require a very high standard. Such claims are easily made and, I think, often too easily believed. Two examples will illustrate this.

When General Motors (GM) and Toyota proposed a joint venture to assemble a small car in California, one would have thought that antitrust considerations would have prevented it. Here two of the largest automobile manufacturers in the world were combining to produce a vehicle. The price of that vehicle was likely to provide an obvious reference point for the setting of other prices. Even though GM and Toyota proposed to set the price in question by reference to a particular average of other car prices, the very use of a particular average seemed likely to facilitate tacit collusion (Salop, 1986a). Yet the Federal Trade Commission approved the joint venture. It did so principally because of the argument that the venture would realize efficiencies, since GM would learn from Toyota the secrets that made Japanese automobile manufacture more efficient than American. Presumably, GM would then be able to use those secrets in other plants.[20]

It is far from clear that the efficiency argument accepted by the Federal Trade Commission was more than superficial. The so-called Japanese secrets may very well not have been secrets at all. The Japanese system of labor relations and inventory management were the likely source of efficiencies. A joint venture was hardly needed to learn about those. Moreover, to the extent that production 'secrets' could be learned, it seemed unlikely that GM would learn very much from an assembly plant when the engines were produced in Japan. Finally, GM already had relations with other Japanese automobile manufacturers.

All in all, the Federal Trade Commission appears to have been too easily swayed by the difficulties of the American automobile industry and the success of the Japanese. One need only contemplate the likely result of a similar application for a joint venture by GM and Ford, for example, to realize the tremendous weight that the efficiency argument was given.

My second example relates again to airlines. Here, the Department of Transportation has approved a whole series of mergers. On the whole, I regard those approvals as warranted. The entire process of airline deregulation rests on the view that city-pair 'markets' (which are usually not really economic markets at all) are contestable. So long as landing slots and other facilities are available (or can be purchased from a large number of airlines), there is a presumption that mergers of domestic airlines cannot result in much market power.

That presumption, however, does not extend to situations where entry is in fact difficult, and it does not automatically extend to acquisitions involving foreign routes. In particular, the Department of Transportation's approval of United Airlines' acquisition of Pan American's Pacific Division is open to very serious question.[21]

Entry into air transportation between the United States and Asia is far from easy, and entry into the vital service between Japan and the United States is especially difficult. Deregulation does not apply to that service; indeed, the Japanese have been historically reluctant to permit expanded service. Further, the use of Tokyo's Narita airport is considerably restricted.

Before the acquisition, service between Japan and the US mainland was quite concentrated (an HHI of 2542 in 1984). The acquisition permitted the number four carrier (United), with about 7 per cent of the market, to combine with the number three carrier (Pan American), which had about 19 per cent. Numbers one and two (Japan Air Lines and Northwest) each had a bit more than than 30 per cent market share. The acquisition (in terms of 1984 figures) caused an increase in the HHI from 2542 to 2812, well beyond the trigger levels set in the 'Guidelines'.[22] Before the acquisition, price competition of various kinds was substantial. United, in particular, had actively sought to increase traffic through its Seattle gateway. On the other hand, it seemed likely that the post-acquisition United would be able to attract traffic without competing on price, first by manipulating its Apollo computer reservation system, and second, because it would be the only airline providing both a really extensive route structure in the United States (acquired during regulation) and a large system of routes connecting at the Tokyo hub – the latter being Pan American's legacy from regulation.

Such integrated service meant a real benefit to passengers. The Department of Transportation very properly regarded this as an efficiency. What is not so clear is whether that efficiency should have justified the acquisition.

Pan American's Pacific Division was profitable; indeed, before the acquisition, it had announced plans for expanded Pacific service for the summer of 1985. Had the acquisition not been approved, Pan American either would have sold its Pacific Division to a different domestic airline not already serving Japan or else would have continued to operate it. In the latter case, Pan American would certainly have continued its program to expand its domestic route structure. Further, Northwest, which had gradually developed its own Tokyo hub, was striving to develop its own domestic route system.[23] Most important of all, United itself could have expanded.[24]

In short, absent the acquisition, three companies might well have been competing to provide integrated service. The acquisition reduced that number to no more than two. In this connection, the Department of Transportation took a very limited view of its responsibilities, refusing, for example, to connect the award of new routes to Japan with the outcome of the case. It appears mostly to have been impressed with the argument that the post-acquisition United would be a stronger competitor than the pre-acquisition Pan American.

As this discussion suggests, I would not approve mergers because of efficiency considerations if the efficiencies involved could be obtained in a less restrictive way. Further, I would hesitate to use such efficiencies as an excuse for permitting a merger if those efficiencies are unlikely to be passed on to customers. In the *Pacific Division Transfer Case*, for example, the benefits of integrated service could have been achieved while maintaining competition. That result would have ensured that the travelling public would benefit from those efficiencies without paying more for them in the form of increased prices. The approval of the acquisition created the efficiencies but also made it very likely that all benefits would be captured by United itself.·

I am, of course, sensible of the argument that transfer payments ought not to matter to economists, so that analysts should only be concerned with the question of whether efficiencies obtained outweigh deadweight loss and not with the question of who captures the savings. In practice, however, I would be very reluctant to approve mergers for efficiency reasons if they seem likely to lead to a restriction of competition. Efficiency arguments are easy to make, but hard to evaluate. The same efficiencies will often be achievable in less restrictive ways; technology has a way of changing. Mergers, on the other hand, have a way of being permanent. Finally, a policy of approving anticompetitive mergers for efficiency reasons is likely to promote a dissipation of resources into rent-seeking.

This view of efficiency arguments, however, supposes that a proper merger analysis has been carried out and the proposed merger found to be anticompetitive. I would certainly accept evidence of efficiencies as showing that the merged enterprise will be a tougher competitor. If merger analysis continues to be dominated by the measurement of concentration, I would put considerable weight on such a showing as offsetting the really crude presumption resulting from market definition and the HHI.

Conclusion

To sum up then, except for their use of current rather than competitive price levels in market definition, I think the Department of Justice 'Guidelines' generally take a sensible approach if properly interpreted and used primarily in the first stage of merger analysis – the decision whether to investigate further. If that is done, then pre-merger screening can serve an important useful purpose, preventing lengthy litigation to force the disgorgement of already digested assets.

On the other hand, the 'Guidelines' are not a substitute for serious analysis, and the Department of Justice staff has tended to focus narrowly on issues of market definition and concentration measures as though such issues were dispositive. That is a mistake. In the present (and likely future) state of our knowledge, serious analysis of market power and oligopoly cannot be subsumed in a few spuriously precise measurements.

I would use the approach of the 'Guidelines' (including an analysis of entry) as a threshold test, committing the enforcement authorities not to oppose mergers that pass that test save in unusual circumstances. Mergers that fail such a test can (and often should) be opposed, but the imprecision of our knowledge means that such failure should not be given much weight in court. The burden of proof as to concentration and entry belongs on the opponents of a merger. Both sides should share that burden as to the other factors (product complexity, ease of detection of cheating and so on) that make tacit collusion more or less likely. The burden of showing that efficiencies will outweigh anticompetitive consequences belongs on the proponents of the merger.

The Reagan Administration has generally been very permissive in its merger policies. To an extent, that permissiveness may be viewed as offsetting at high levels the tendency of the Department of Justice staff to substitute HHI measurement for economics, but only if one thinks of different mergers as substitutes for each other. In fact, mergers have sometimes been wrongly blocked (or at least opposed by the Department of Justice) because of unthinking application of 'Guidelines' standards, and sometimes wrongly approved because of a wish to find efficiency excuses (a wish that may be greatest where competition with foreigners is involved as in GM–Toyota or United–Pan American). The two mistakes do not compensate for each other, and neither approach is a substitute for sound analysis.

One final word. I have deliberately only commented here on mergers that I have studied and have not expressed an opinion about other mergers that I would or would not have permitted. Experience suggests that economists are often too ready to offer opinions about complex situations which they have not studied and which require detailed analysis. A principal point of this chapter is that this proposition applies to mergers.

Acknowledgments

I am indebted to Carl Shapiro, Timothy Taylor and especially Steven Salop for very helpful comments, but retain responsibility for error and for the views expressed.

Notes

1. *Brown Shoe Company* v. *United States*, 370 US 294 (1962). The case involved a merger between Brown Shoe and Kinney Shoe, the third and

eighth largest firms in the industry. In its decision blocking the merger, the Supreme Court took a very narrow view of product markets (or 'submarkets').

2. The 'incipiency' doctrine goes back to Congressional discussion of the original Clayton Act. (See Senate Report No. 698, 63rd Cong., 2nd Sess. (1914), p. 1.) The same language was used when Section 7 was amended in 1950 (Senate Report No. 1775, 81st Cong., 2nd Sess. (1950), pp. 4–5), and by the *Brown Shoe* court (370 US 294 at 317, 346), as well as in later opinions.

3. *United States* v. *Aluminum Company of America, et al.* 148 F. 2d 416 (1945). Judge Learned Hand's opinion held that an alleged monopolist (in this case Alcoa) could be in violation of Section 2 of the Sherman Act (the antimonopoly section) if it had monopoly power and had deliberately achieved that power by means other than 'superior skill, foresight and industry'. Alcoa was held to have violated Section 2 largely by buying up inputs far in advance of any intention to use them. The *Alcoa* standard (which may now be defunct) has not always been wisely applied or well understood. See Fisher *et al.* (1983).

4. This may be the reason that the antitrust authorities have attempted to invent a doctrine of 'shared monopoly'. See *In the Matter of Kellogg Company, et al.* FTC Docket No. 8883 (decided 1981).

5. Consideration of the absence of any serious remedy in the second *American Tobacco* case (*United States* v. *American Tobacco Co.*, 328 US 781 (1946)) or of the history of litigation and investigations in the cement industry will illustrate the problem. I take no position on whether structural remedies would have been effective in these industries.

6. It may be considered an objection to any purely structural policy towards oligopoly that, unlike the case of monopoly, where the pattern of conduct that leads to the non-competitive structure consists of acts all done by a single firm, the acts that lead to a tight oligopoly are the acts of several firms. This means that an *Alcoa*-like standard applied to oligopoly can penalize individual firms because of actions taken by others, even if no one firm's action would be illegal in itself. There is no escape from this problem. Attacking it in terms of merger policy either does not solve it at all or else makes it worse in the sense of penalizing the two merging firms for acts that only *might* later be taken by others.

7. *United States* v. *El du Pont de Nemours and Company*, 353 US 377 (1956). See also Stocking and Mueller (1955), Kaysen and Turner (1959, p. 102), and Posner (1976, pp. 127–8).

8. It may or may not have been a coincidence that, after the acquisition was challenged by the Federal Trade Commission, Stouffer's (which of course favored a wide market definition) began a series of television commercials that featured someone tasting a Stouffer's product and saying something like. 'What is it? It tastes like lasagna, but it isn't lasagna.' The case was eventually settled.

9. For a more detailed discussion of these issues in the context of Sherman Act, Section 2 cases, see Chapter 3 of Fisher *et al.* (1983).

10. *United States* v. *United Shoe Machinery Corporation*, 110 F. Supp. 295 (1953) at 341; *United States* v. *Aluminum Company of America, et al.*, 148 F. 2d 416 (1945) at 430.

11. There is a serious danger that the job would not be done sensibly and that

the antitrust authorities would simply look at profits or profits–sales ratios in a mechanical attempt to compute competitive prices. To do this would be a mistake, both because profits play an important role in competitive industries and are not absent save in long-run equilibrium, and because accounting measures of profits or the profits–sales ratio do not tell one whether firms are exercising market power. See Chapter 7 of Fisher *et al.* (1983) and Chapters 4 and 6 of this book.

12. To take a recent example, in the Northwest–Republic airline merger (*NWA-Republic Acquisition Case*, Department of Transportation Docket 43754 (1986)), the Department of Justice insisted that one-stop or connecting airline service was not in the same market as non-stop service. In so doing, it based its arguments on the undeniable fact that all travelers prefer non-stop service to one-stop or connecting service if the flights leave at the same time and have the same price. Such an argument takes a very limited view of substitution and market definition. In fact, people take one-stop or connecting flights in preference to non-stop flights if they get something thereby. That something can be time-of-day convenience or it can be a lower price. A large box of a particular breakfast cereal typically sells for a higher price than does a small box. That does not put them in different markets, and, in fact, the prices of the different types of flights tend to move together. (I appeared as a witness for Northwest.)

13. Alas, the Antitrust Division has a natural, if distressing tendency to become fascinated with its own 'Guidelines' and to focus on the HHI levels mentioned therein as though failure to pass the tests of the 'Guidelines' were proof that a merger was anticompetitive rather than merely being a signal for further analysis.

14. For an extended discussion of these matters, see von Weizsäcker (1980), Chapter 6 of Fisher *et al.* (1983) and Salop (1986b).

15. For an older example, see Chapter 6 of Fisher *et al.* (1983).

16. That view is not correct. What keeps an airline with a hub at Denver from competing on equal terms with one at Minneapolis for traffic between the two cities? Why cannot an airline with a hub at Dallas, say, and already serving cities between Dallas and Minneapolis simply extend its flights to compete for traffic between Minneapolis and those other cities?

17. I cannot forbear adding that the Department of Justice was factually wrong about the attractiveness of Minneapolis as a hub. In fact, because the earth is a sphere, the usual Mercator projection of North America gives a quite misleading picture. The great circle routes from east to west coast cities pass quite close to Minneapolis, and that, together with prevailing winds and traffic patterns, makes it the second most attractive hub for such flights, a few minutes worse than Chicago. Nevertheless, the Department of Justice's position on this indisputable matter persisted into post-hearing discussions when the higher-ups in the Division made the same argument about Minneapolis's position and were quite surprised to learn that they were wrong. The symbolism is clear. I fear that, at least as regards the analysis of barriers to entry, the Department of Justice believes that the earth is flat.

18. Where there is more than one incumbent–entrant pair, the 'feed ratio' is taken to be the maximum over all such pairs of this ratio of enplanements.

19. *NWA–Republic Acquisition Case*, Department of Transportation Docket 43754 (1986), testimony of Gloria Hurdle, tr. 1429.

20. *General Motors Corp. et al.*, 48 Federal Register 57246 (1983). I was

retained by counsel for Ford, which eventually decided not to bring suit to oppose the joint venture.

21. *Pacific Division Transfer Case*, Department of Transportation Docket 43065 (1985). I was a witness for Northwest Airlines which opposed the acquisition. My views on the matter are set forth at length in Chapter 3.

22. It is worth remarking that the testimony offered by the Department of Justice in opposition to the acquisition was focused very heavily on the HHI and the 'Guidelines'. United and Pan American were ready for this. They had previously prepared a study for use in rebuttal purporting to show the not very surprising fact that city-pair HHIs had little effect on fares. The result was largely to divert argument from the more substantial questions at issue.

23. After the transfer of the Pacific Division, largely because of the need to catch up with the post-acquisition United, Northwest strove to expand quickly by acquiring Republic.

24. United was already creating a rival hub at Seoul. Further, while entry into Japan was difficult, it was not impossible, and the US government could have made expansion by United a primary object of negotiations with Japan. This possibility was very real, because spring 1985 saw an agreement between the two countries to open as many as three new routes. United could have been given those routes.

References

Fisher, Franklin M., John J. McGowan and Joen E. Greenwood, *Folded, Spindled and Mutilated: Economic Analysis and US v. IBM*. Cambridge, Mass.: MIT Press, 1983.

Kaysen, Carl and Donald F. Turner, *Antitrust Policy*. Cambridge, Mass.: Harvard University Press, 1959.

Posner, Richard A., *Antitrust Law: An Economic Perspective*. Chicago and London: University of Chicago Press, 1976.

Salop, Steven C., 'Practices that (credibly) facilitate oligopoly coordination', in Stiglitz, Joseph E. and G. Frank Mathewson, eds., *New Developments in the Analysis of Market Structure*. Cambridge, Mass.: MIT Press, 1986a.

Salop, Steven C., 'Measuring ease of entry', *Antitrust Bulletin*, 1986b, **31**, 551–70.

Stocking, George W. and Willard F. Mueller, 'The Cellophane case and the new competition', *American Economic Review*, 1955, **45**, 29–63.

US Department of Justice, 'Merger Guidelines', *Federal Register*, 1984, **49**, 26284.

von Weizsäcker, Carl Christian, *Barriers to Entry: A Theoretical Treatment*. Berlin, Heidelberg, New York: Springer-Verlag, 1980.

3

Pan American to United: The *Pacific Division Transfer Case* (1987)

Introduction

Since airline deregulation in 1978, there has been a wave of domestic airline mergers. Among others, the combinations of Texas Air–Continental–New York Air–Peoples' Express–Frontier–Eastern, of Delta–Western, of Northwest–Republic and of TWA–Ozark have moved domestic air transportation very much in the direction of an oligopoly dominated by perhaps six large firms. Service on particular city-pair routes has become even more concentrated. Nevertheless, most of the mergers involved have been approved without much difficulty by the Department of Transportation (DOT), which acquired responsibility for such decisions as part of the transition to a deregulated environment.

At least so far as competition on particular city-pair routes is concerned, such approval makes sense if one believes air service on the affected routes to be contestable. Since relatively small sunk costs are involved, a particular city-pair 'market' will be contestable if there is ease of entry. Hence, unless there are entry barriers (a shortage of non-marketable landing slots, for example), airline mergers can be approved without fear that the result will be higher prices and supracompetitive

This chapter is largely based on my testimony on behalf of Northwest Airlines Inc. in the *Pacific Division Transfer Case*, Department of Transportation Docket 43065, 1985. All references are to this case unless otherwise specified. I am indebted to J.W. Campion, George Hall, Kevin Neels, Sheldon L. Pine, Barry S. Spector, Peter Ward, and especially Ronald D. Eastman and William A. Kutzke for assistance and discussion. I thank the editors of the *RAND Journal of Economics* and two referees for helpful criticism of an earlier version, but retain responsibility for any error. The views expressed are my own and not necessarily those of Northwest Airlines.

profits – at least up to the point where concentration in the United States as a whole becomes a cause for concern.

Many city-pair routes in the United States appear to be contestable, and the DOT has tended to take a correspondingly wide view of market definition.[1] Such apparent contestability fails, however, when it comes to international routes, many of which are still regulated, and mergers affecting such routes deserve close scrutiny.

By far the largest recent acquisition involving international routes was United Airlines' purchase of Pan American World Airways' Pacific Division in 1985. In that acquisition United paid Pan American $750 million in exchange for aircraft and other tangible assets and the transfer of Pan American's underlying Pacific route authority. The two airlines applied for approval to the Department of Transportation in April, and after an evidentiary hearing before an Administrative Law Judge (who, however, issued no opinion), Secretary of Transportation Elizabeth Dole approved the transaction at the end of October.

The holding of a hearing reflected the fact that the government took a more serious view of this acquisition than of most purely domestic mergers, which were generally approved without one. Indeed, the transfer of the Pacific Divison was opposed by the Department of Justice, as well as by American, Eastern and Northwest Airlines. I was a witness for Northwest, and this chapter is largely based on my testimony.

The acquisition raised a number of points of concern, some of which may occur in other circumstances. First, the continued regulation of international air service by foreign governments makes entry into the provision of such service difficult, so that mergers or acquisitions involving international routes deserve special scrutiny. Second, entry is also likely to be difficult where there is a shortage of landing slots and no market in such slots enabling potential entrants to acquire them. Third, the history of United's use of its computer reservation system suggests that it may be able to keep prices up while suppressing competition by raising rivals' costs (a phenomenon that would apply to any merger involving United or American Airlines). Fourth, even though the acquisition led to efficiencies, those efficiencies might have been attainable (with some delay) in a way less restrictive of competition. In general, the DOT failed to consider the acquisition as part of a broader view of transportation policy.

Merger analysis: an overview

Before coming to the particulars of the *Pacific Division Transfer Case*, however, it will be useful briefly to set forth my views on the way in which the analysis of any merger ought to proceed and on some of the problems that may arise.[2]

Merger analysis begins (as in the US Department of Justice 'Merger Guidelines' (1984)) with a definition of the market, a definition that should include all the constraints on the merged firms' behavior. Within that market, one goes on to consider concentration measures, on the ground that tacit collusion is more likely, the higher is concentration. If the market in question is concentrated, an analysis of ease of entry is necessary. If entry is easy, then anticompetitive behavior cannot persist. If entry is difficult, then a full investigation is required to assess the ease or difficulty of tacit collusion and the extent to which any efficiencies to be gained by the merger are likely to offset the losses from anticompetitive behavior. Finally, if anticompetitive behavior is likely, but there are offsetting efficiencies, one should inquire as to whether those efficiencies can be obtained in any way that restricts competition less than allowing the merger to go forward.

The application of this procedure is not so simple as it appears, and, indeed, each step presents its own problems. We shall encounter and discuss some of these in later sections as they arise in connection with the *Pacific Division Transfer Case*. One such problem, however, in a way involves the entire procedure and needs to be taken up before proceeding.

The relation between market structure and market conduct and performance is too loosely understood for concentration measures to be more than a very rough guide to the likelihood of tacit collusion. Hence, while it is useful to define a market (or markets) and to compute concentration measures as a way of deciding whether further, detailed investigation is called for, it is a mistake to believe that analysis is complete merely because the Herfindahl–Hirschman index exceeds a particular level.

Unfortunately, merger and acquisition cases are remarkable even among antitrust cases for the extent of their focus on the important, but only preliminary issues of market definition and concentration. The Justice Department, having issued 'Merger Guidelines' (1984) that are broadly sensible as a guide to which cases warrant further analysis, sometimes tends to lapse into believing that its own 'Guidelines' are an adequate judicial or economic standard. This is an understandable tendency in view of the natural desire of attorneys to find a 'bright line', a quantitative standard that can be readily applied. Unfortunately, where, as in the case of the Herfindahl–Hirschman index, the apparent precision of the standard is not real, the desire for such a standard can lead to a focus on the standard to the exclusion of more serious and detailed analysis.

The *Pacific Division Transfer Case* was no exception. Indeed, United and Pan American, correctly foreseeing that the Department of Justice (and possibly others) would rely heavily on presentations involving the Herfindahl–Hirschman indexes, were ready with obviously pre-prepared rebuttal testimony directed solely at the question of whether anything can be concluded from examining raw Herfindahl–Hirschman statistics in international airline 'markets'.[3] As a result, the debate and, especially, Secretary Dole's opinion were misdirected. It gave relatively little attention to the more important competitive issues discussed below.

Nevertheless, market definition and concentration measurement are important threshold issues, and I begin with them.

Market definition

Market definition is only the starting point for antitrust analysis; it defines the universe of discourse within which that analysis will take place. Hence, to be useful, a proposed market definition must include all those firms, products and services that are likely to provide substantial constraints on non-competitive behavior in the proposed market. Such constraints can come either through substitution in demand or through ready substitution in supply (which shades over into ease of entry). In effect, the Department of Justice now takes this view of market definition as a summary of constraints. Its 'Merger Guidelines' (1984) define a 'market' as the minimal collection of firms that could sustain a price rise of stated size for a given period of time.[4]

In previous cases involving post-deregulation airline mergers, the Civil Aeronautics Board (CAB) – the DOT's predecessor in overseeing deregulation – wisely declined to look only at concentration statistics constructed for narrowly defined 'markets' consisting of individual city-pairs. The CAB correctly reasoned that the possibility of entry by other carriers into serving a particular city-pair meant that a wider market definition was called for, even though it was not always clear just what that wider definition should be (Sibley *et al.*, 1982).

The *Pacific Division Transfer Case* presented no such market-definition problems, nor was there much disagreement in this area between proponents and opponents of the acquisition. First, the general conclusions to be drawn from concentration statistics are essentially the same for any reasonable market definition (see Table 3.3). Second, and far more important, air transportation in the Pacific does not take place in a deregulated environment, and (as shown in the section 'Barriers to entry') problems of entry are severe indeed. This

Table 3.1 Number of passengers (thousands) on scheduled service between
the United States and the Far East, 1984.

Between/ and	Total	Honolulu	Guam	Mainland
Total	6,372	2,128	551	3,693
Japan*	4,253	1,516	498	2,239
Hong Kong	557	182	4	371
Korea	526	102	1	423
Taiwan	352	91	15	246
Philippines	330	182	33	115
India	140	–	–	140
Singapore	99	55	–	44
People's Republic of China	70	–	–	70
Thailand	35	–	–	35
Pakistan	9	–	–	9
Malaysia	1	–	–	1

* Including Okinawa (total of 8,000 passengers).

Source: Northwest Airlines (from Immigration and Naturalization Service Form 92).

Table 3.2 Number of passengers (thousands) on scheduled and charter service
between the United States and Japan,* 1984.

Between Japan and	Total	US citizens	Foreign nationals	US carriers	Foreign carriers
Total	4,404	1,357	3,047	2,122	2,282
Per cent		31	69	48	52
Guam	521	43	478	215	306
Per cent		9	91	41	59
Honolulu	1,631	228	1,403	611	1,020
Per cent		14	86	37	63
Mainland	2,252	1,086	1,166	1,296	956
Per cent		48	52	58	42

* Including Okinawa.

Source: Northwest Airlines (from DOT *US International Air Travel Statistics*).

means that contestability is absent and that the market cannot be taken
to include air transportation in other parts of the globe.

As Table 3.1 shows, the largest segment of US–Far East air travel
is between the US mainland and the Far East. The Hawaii–Far East
and Guam–Far East segments predominantly consist of low-fare,
Japan-originating tour-group travel. Table 3.2 shows these segments
(as opposed to Japan–US mainland travel) to comprise primarily
foreign nationals traveling largely by foreign flag carriers. This suggests treating US mainland–Far East travel separately, a suggestion
reinforced by the fact that most of the passengers involved prefer non-

stop routings. Trip routings to Japan via Honolulu, for example, add approximately 1,000 miles and 4 hours to what would otherwise be a 5,200-mile, ten-hour non-stop trip. In what follows I concentrate on US mainland–Far East air travel.[5]

Would a narrower market definition than this be appropriate? So far as the US part of US mainland–Far East air travel is concerned, the answer is negative. Surveys of US-resident air travelers going to the Far East show that only about 32 per cent live in one of the gateway cities (Chicago, Los Angeles, New York, San Francisco and Seattle).[6] Even after adjusting for the fact that travelers residing near but not in a gateway city also use that city's airport as their home airport, it is clear that considerably more than half of all US residents traveling to the Far East do not begin and end their travel at gateways. Such travelers are likely to be indifferent as to which gateway they pass through, and thus to make their choice on the basis of schedule convenience and price.[7] Similarly, many passengers originating in the Orient are unlikely to have strong preferences as to the choice of a US gateway through which to begin or end their visits. These facts suggest that a market definition involving only single US cities would be overly narrow. They also show that Pan American and United competed with each other before the acquisition despite the fact that they served different gateways.[8]

A similar statement does not apply to market definitions that concentrate on particular Asian cities, however. In particular, for reasons of geography, the importance of Japan as a tourist attraction and the overwhelming importance of its economy in that of Asia, the Japanese airports, particularly Tokyo, play a special role in trans-Pacific travel.

Indeed, not only does more than half of trans-Pacific travel originate or terminate in Japan (Table 3.1), but much of the remaining traffic also passes through Tokyo. While it is possible to compete for such traffic by using other hubs (Seoul, for example), the fact that such a large part of the traffic stops, lays over or originates in Tokyo necessarily places the use of such alternatives at a disadvantage. In terms of demand substitutability, the availability of those alternatives places only a weak constraint on the pricing of Japan–US mainland travel.[9]

Market shares and concentration

Whether one defines the market as all US mainland–Far East air travel or restricts attention to Japan, the conclusions to be drawn about concentration are the same. The market was already quite concentrated before the acquisition, and the acquisition increased that concentration significantly.

Table 3.3 1984 market shares (percents) in trans-Pacific air travel*.

Carrier	Share: Mainland–Far East	Share: Mainland–Japan
Northwest	27.5	31.3
JAL	21.9	33.5
Pan American	18.5	19.3
Korean Air	9.3	0.0
United	7.3	7.0
China Airlines	6.8	1.4
Singapore Airlines	2.9	3.1
Thai International Airways	2.2	1.9
CAAC	1.6	—
Philippine Airlines	1.3	1.4
Varig	0.6	1.0
Herfindahl–Hirschman Index	1,782	2,542

* Market shares are for total number of passengers carried. Immigration and Naturalization Service figures on total passengers carried by US flag carriers via each gateway were allocated to Northwest, Pan American and United by using ER586 service segment data.

Source: Immigration and Naturalization Service.

Table 3.3 shows pre-acquisition market shares for both the overly broad US mainland–Far East market and the narrower US mainland–Japan market. In either case the general conclusion is the same. In terms of the Herfindahl–Hirschman index, combining United and Pan American leads to an increase in concentration in the provision of US mainland–Far East service from 1,782 to 2,052. In US mainland–Japan service, the index goes from 2,542 to 2,812. Either case would certainly cause concern in terms of the Justice Department's 'Merger Guidelines' (1984).[10] In either case an already highly concentrated market became significantly more concentrated.

This conclusion is reinforced by the fact that, as discussed in the Appendix, the non-Japanese foreign flag carriers are unlikely to be willing or able to expand their shares of US–Japan air service to take advantage of supracompetitive prices. Since such expansion would be required for those carriers effectively to constrain the larger ones from limiting competition, the Herfindahl–Hirschman index that counts the shares of non-Japanese foreign flag carriers understates the effective degree of concentration and the increase caused by the acquisition.

Barriers to entry

Supply as well as demand considerations point to the relevance of these concentration statistics, for there are serious barriers to entry into the provision of US–Japan air transportation. Unlike domestic air transportation mergers, where ease of entry after deregulation makes for a wider market definition, we are not here dealing with a deregulated environment.

The US–Japan Civil Aviation Agreement, signed in 1952, is a Bermuda-1-type bilateral agreement presenting a formidable barrier to entry into US–Japan service. As over thirty years of experience show, neither US nor Japanese carriers can freely enter. Indeed, in the last several years Japan has favored scrapping the existing route description negotiated in the 1952 agreement in favor of one which, among other changes, would limit or eliminate the existing valuable 'beyond' rights (the right of US carriers to carry traffic beyond Tokyo). The agreement of April 30, 1985, that amended the 1952 agreement to permit a somewhat limited increase in Japan–US service, did not provide a corresponding increase in beyond rights. Indeed, after the acquisition, the Japanese resisted the transfer of Pan American's beyond rights to United. Asking for concessions from the United States, they backed down only under heavy pressure from the US government.

Entry barriers do not only arise from the reluctance of the Japanese to permit entry. There are also severe limitations on the use of Tokyo's Narita airport (and similar problems at Osaka, Japan's secondary international facility). These include operational restrictions, political, legal and environmental factors, and limits on terminal parking stands and gates. As a consequence, airlines serving Narita could together provide only 270 movements per day during the winter of 1985/86. (A take-off and landing constitute two movements.) Operations per hour were also restricted, with only twenty-six movements per hour permitted between 6.00 a.m. and 8.00 p.m., fewer from 8.00 p.m. to 11.00 p.m., and none at all between 11.00 p.m. and 6.00 a.m. There are further constraints on the total number of movements in consecutive three-hour periods. Particularly because flights to or from the United States must use certain time periods to enable passengers to make sensible connections in Asia and the United States, these time-period constraints are far more binding than the overall daily one. As a result, there is no serious prospect for a sizable expansion of operations in the near future.

Is this a cause for concern? In general, whether a shortage of landing slots at a particular airport provides a barrier to entry depends on the ease with which landing slots can be transferred and on the nature of the anticompetitive behavior that is feared. If there is a market in such slots, then the necessity of obtaining slots is no different from the necessity of obtaining other, possibly high-priced inputs. In such a case, if slot ownership is relatively widely dispersed, then, for example, an attempt by a particular airline to raise fares between the airport in question and some particular destination to which it alone flies will induce entry by others, who will either convert their own slots to such service or purchase slots from others to do so. On the other hand, where slots are not freely tradable, or where their ownership is largely concentrated in the hands of the prospective price-raisers, a slot shortage can provide a formidable entry barrier.[11]

In the case of Narita airport, the landing slots at desirable hours for trans-Pacific travel are partly held by the airlines now providing that travel. The remaining slots are largely held by Japan Air Lines (JAL). Slot allocation is not done by the market, but rather by a committee effectively controlled by JAL. Since the anticompetitive behavior that the acquisition may produce is not monopolization by the post-acquisition United, but rather tacit collusion involving JAL, the shortage of landing slots at Narita provides a serious entry barrier.

That barrier is reflected in the price paid by United for the Pacific Division. The principal tangible assets acquired by United from Pan American were aircraft, but these were obsolescent and inefficient. Estimates based on prices for similar equipment show that the costs of the aircraft and other tangibles acquired cannot possibly account for the $750 million price of the transaction.[12]

It follows that a large part of that purchase price was payment for Pan American's route system and rights. Since United already directly served Seoul and Hong Kong, much of the payment for intangibles must have been for the rights to carry passengers to and beyond Japan, which permitted the establishment of a Tokyo hub.

Note, however, that while this fact confirms the view that such rights are scarce, United's willingness to pay for them tells nothing by itself about the likely effects of the merger on competition. Even under competition, such rights could very well carry scarcity rents.[13] While the expectation of later cooperation in reducing output would make those rights more valuable, one cannot conclude from the mere fact that the rights sold for a substantial sum that the value of future monopoly rents was included in their price.

Pre-acquisition price competition

The principal reason for concern over increased concentration where entry is difficult is the fear that such an increase will lead to an avoidance of price competition. Since international air fares are heavily regulated (as domestic fares no longer are), the question naturally arises whether there is any competition to be avoided. Despite the obvious desire of the Japanese government to regulate, the answer in the case of Pacific air travel is affirmative. Before the acquisition, United was especially active in such competition as it attempted to expand by using its Seattle gateway.[14]

The first form that such price competition took involved the combination of a trans-Pacific and an internal US journey. While the fare between Japan and a US gateway city is subject to international tariff-filing requirements, the fare within the United States is not. As a result, a US airline can effectively reduce the price of a Far East–US trip offered to a Japanese (or other Asian) visitor by lowering the price on the segment within the United States. Such price-cutting even applies to some passengers traveling only to US gateways. A passenger traveling from Tokyo to New York, for example, could take advantage of such price cuts by traveling via Seattle instead of directly.

When United first entered the US–Japan market in April 1983, it offered 'Visit USA' (VUSA) fares that were available only to its on-line passengers and enabled them to fly anywhere on its domestic system for a flat fee. In so doing United significantly undercut the VUSA fares already being offered by other airlines. After the CAB (responding to a complaint by JAL) declared VUSA fares to be international fares subject to Japanese tariff-filing requirements, United introduced a different price reduction for its on-line passengers. In November 1983 it began offering fares involving low 'add-ons' for the domestic portion of trans-Pacific travel on United. When, in May 1985, the DOT (again responding to a complaint by JAL) held that these fares also must be filed in international tariffs or be discontinued, United was ready with a third version. It introduced special fares that allowed international passengers to fly up to four domestic segments for a low add-on price ($200 for travel within the western United States). In addition, United apparently had arrangements with certain Asian travel agencies that permitted them not to remit the US domestic part of the special fare.

The second form of price competition involves travel agents. Airlines regularly compete on the commissions paid to travel agents. Since such agents book the lion's share of business, particularly for international travel, such competition is quite important. Here again United is particularly well placed. Its control of the Apollo computer reservation system (discussed below) enables it easily to offer incentives to agents a large share of whose bookings is on United.[15]

Of course, price competition in commissions to travel agents need not always result in lower prices to travelers. Whether it does so depends on the state of competition among travel agents themselves. At least in large cities, however, one would expect increased commissions to be passed on in some form, either as lower prices or as improved service. (This clearly happens in Hong Kong and Taipei, as well as in the so-called ethnic market segment where, for example, American travelers of Chinese origin purchase tickets in Chinese neighborhoods.) Thus, before the acquisition, there was substantial price competition. In particular, United, which had a foothold in serving Japan and was particularly well placed to engage in such competition, was very active in doing so. It fought to fill its flights between Seattle and Japan and to attract traffic from others. It was also investing in a competing hub at Seoul and would have fought to attract traffic there. Whether such price competition would have eventually permitted United to overcome the barriers to entry into Japan is a close question, and I discuss it later. What is certain, however, is that the acquisition removed much of the motive for engaging in price competition. With Pan American's Tokyo and other Pacific service added to its large domestic route system (and with its Apollo computer reservation system), United could expect to attract a large share of the traffic without competing on price.

At the same time, Pan American was taken out of the fight. Its Pacific Division was profitable, and, indeed, shortly before the acquisition, Pan American had announced and published schedules for a major expansion of its Pacific service. The acquisition ended that.

After the acquisition, the principal market participants would be United, JAL and Northwest. United would no longer have the same incentive for price competition as before, while JAL, together with the Japanese government, had historically opposed such competition. Provided Northwest would either go along or else could somehow be hampered, the acquisition seemed likely to reduce price competition, with United and JAL cooperating.[16] Indeed, United forecast that its Los Angeles–Tokyo and San Francisco–Tokyo on-board average fares would increase over Pan American's by 14.9 per cent and 13.3 per cent, respectively.[17]

Efficiencies and competitor opposition: raising rivals' costs

There is more to the matter than this, however. A merger or acquisition can have anticompetitive effects and still promote welfare if it leads to more than offsetting efficiencies whose benefits will be passed on to consumers. Merger proponents, of course, routinely claim that this is so, but deciding such claims is often difficult.

One way of cutting through such difficulty is to consider the attitude of competitors to the transaction in question. In general, competitors are likely to gain from a diminution of price competition, but stand to lose from any efficiency gains resulting from the transaction. Hence, it can be argued that opposition by competitors provides evidence that efficiency gains are likely to outweigh the losses due to the reduction of competition.[18]

This need not be the case. Putting aside the possibility that competitors may not always realize their own best interests, those interests may not always be opposed to those of consumers. First, the merged firm may be able to force out competitors *without* competing on price. This will allow the merged firm to appropriate any efficiency advantages of the merger. Second, the same efficiencies that make competitors fearful may be achievable in less restrictive ways than by permitting the merger. If those less restrictive ways would permit competitors also to attain those efficiencies, then competitor opposition may signal the presence of efficiencies without dictating the conclusion that the merger ought to be permitted. Both these points are relevant to the transfer of the Pacific Division.

There is no reason to suppose that United is directly more cost-efficient than Pan American in flying the Pacific routes, for it uses the same aircraft. Nevertheless, there is no doubt that the post-acquisition United is a stronger competitor than the pre-acquisition Pan American. In particular, United provides single-line service between interior points in the United States and points beyond Tokyo – something Pan American, with a very poor domestic route system, did not do effectively. This is a benefit to the traveling public.[19]

Will the provision of that benefit more than offset the loss of price competition? In this connection it is noteworthy that the acquisition was opposed by Northwest Airlines, the largest US flag carrier in the Pacific, as well as by Eastern and American Airlines, both of which had hoped to acquire Pacific routes. If one looks no further, this suggests that competition by single-line service will be worth more to the traveling public than the price competition that would have continued in the absence of the acquisition.

In fact, that conclusion does not follow. There are reasons for believing that both the public and United's competitors will suffer as a result of the acquisition. As suggested above, the first such reason is the strong possibility that United can damage its competitors without competing on price. It has already demonstrated its ability and willingness to do so in a classic example of raising rivals' costs.[20]

By far the largest part of travel to the Far East is booked through travel agents. Since the middle 1970s, travel agents' bookings have been predominantly made by the use of computer reservation systems. Such systems not only provide up-to-date schedule information, but also inform as to seat availability at different fare levels, communicate with airline computers to book reservations, print tickets and facilitate land arrangements.

With one relatively minor exception, all computer reservation systems are owned by airlines, and the two airlines with the largest domestic route systems, American and United, have by far the largest placements of their systems (named, respectively, 'Sabre' and 'Apollo') with agents.

This is not an accident. In responding to a travel agent's inquiry, not all possible flights and routings can be given equal prominence in the computer display. Generally, there are so many possibilities that they cannot all be displayed at once, and there is a natural tendency for agents to choose from the alternatives on the first screen presented and even from the first line or two on that screen.[21] The order in which flights are displayed is thus a matter of considerable importance to airlines, and there is a great incentive for an airline computer reservation system vendor to favor its own flights. Indeed, the money to be made from so doing is large enough to make it profitable for an airline to offer its computer reservation system to travel agents below cost, or even to pay them for using it.[22]

Both United and American were quick to take advantage of this opportunity. Initially they provided relatively openly biased displays favoring their own flights. After it became plain that this was happening, an investigation by the Department of Justice was begun. That investigation in turn led to proceedings before the CAB, which, in the Fall of 1984, adopted the suggestion of the Justice Department and began regulating the way in which computer reservation system displays are determined. Two private antitrust suits were also filed.

I use the phrase 'began regulating' deliberately, for regulation in this area is likely to be a never-ending task with the vendors always one step ahead of the regulators. An example involves trans-Pacific travel. In 1985 United's Apollo system (unlike other systems) did not list connecting flights where the carrier involved had no authority to carry local traffic. This means that agents using Apollo who booked passengers traveling from the United States to Osaka or Okinawa could not discover that there was an easy on-line connection on Northwest in Tokyo. Instead, they found connections to JAL. Not surprisingly, many of those connections involved United's trans-Pacific flights even though the usual considerations of passenger convenience used in the Apollo algorithm would place the on-line Northwest connection first.[23] There are many other examples of United's pre-acquisition anticompetitive use of Apollo in the Pacific.[24]

Such examples are only the tip of the potential iceberg. They represent abuses already located but not yet cured by regulation. They illustrate the enormous difficulty (indeed the impossibility) of curing the computer reservation system problem through regulation. The algorithms used to determine display order are (necessarily) so complex and the opportunities for misuse of them in subtle ways so varied that the effort to regulate is likely to lead to an endless and continual series of hearings with regulation always struggling to catch up.[25]

Moreover, travel agents in Japan also use a biased computer reservation system, the JAL-controlled JALCOM III. That system, not subject to US regulation, provides a first screen showing only JAL flights. It is conceivable that United could trade JAL special status on Apollo in return for favorable treatment on JALCOM III – an arrangement not available to most of United's American trans-Pacific competitors. (A similar deal was reportedly struck in the Atlantic between American and Lufthansa.) In this way United could extend its biased use of Apollo to involve Japan-originating traffic.

Obviously, diversion of traffic by providing biased or incomplete information is destructive of competition on the merits. Because operating margins are thin on trans-Pacific flights, relatively little traffic needs to be diverted to United for other airlines to find such service unprofitable.[26] The persistence of covert forms of bias after the initial regulations makes this a real possibility.

One need not even take matters so far as this. By diverting traffic by using a biased computer reservation system algorithm, United raises its rivals' costs by forcing them either to fly empty seats or to make extra efforts to fill them. Further, with the imposition of the CAB rules in 1984, United (and American) began charging other airlines high booking fees, an alternative way to raise their costs. By these actions United is able to raise its own price – and to do so without aiding competitors.

In general, courts have tended to give rivals standing to sue to oppose a merger if the transaction seems likely to lead to predatory behavior on the part of the merged firm.[27] That position makes sense only where the feared predation seems likely to materialize, and such cases may be relatively rare.[28] Where competitors' suits are not involved, and enforcement or regulatory authorities are considering whether to permit or to oppose a merger, such arguments ought certainly to be evaluated.

In any event, in the *Pacific Division Transfer Case* the anticipated behavior was not mere speculation. United was already engaging in it, and the acquisition would give it wider scope and incentive to do so. Indeed, without a resolution of the difficult computer reservation system problem, United is likely to be able to use Apollo to raise rivals' costs and to attain a commanding position in trans-Pacific service while pursuing a high-fare policy that does not reflect merely the additional benefits of its on-line service. That was one reason for competitors to oppose the acquisition and a reason for the Department of Transportation to hesitate before approving it.

Efficiencies and competitor opposition: less restrictive alternatives

Even without the possibility of post-merger predatory behavior, the existence of more-than-offsetting efficiencies should not mandate the approval of an otherwise anticompetitive merger. Rather, one must consider the question of whether, absent the merger, such efficiencies can be achieved in a way less restrictive of competition than the merger itself is likely to be. If the merger is not necessary to gain the efficiencies, then permitting it may simply ensure that the efficiency gains are never passed on to consumers or are unnecessarily accompanied by output restriction.

Such considerations ought .to be especially strong where, as in the *Pacific Division Transfer* case, the efficiencies in question do not directly involve cost-savings but rather the provision of an improved product. Where cost-savings are directly involved, it can be argued (not, I think, wholly convincingly) that the merger will achieve resource-use efficiencies, and that the question of whether those efficiencies are passed on to customers is a matter of income distribution. Suppose, on the other hand, that the efficiencies involved do not save resources directly, but rather permit the same (or equivalent) resources to be used to produce a superior product. In such a case it is hard to argue that society should be indifferent as to whether the post-transaction firm extracts much of the consumer surplus from the superior product by charging an offsettingly high price.

In any event, there is no reason to permit an anticompetitive merger for the sake of the efficiencies it brings if those same efficiencies can be obtained without so large a restriction of competition. There is reason for believing that this was the case in the transfer of the Pacific Division.

As a result of half a century of airline regulation, both United and Pan American possessed certain advantages over other airlines when deregulation began. United had the largest route system in the United States, while Pan American, often the favored US flag airline, had a large Pacific system, including beyond-Tokyo rights. Had those advantages both been possessed by a single airline, that airline would doubtless have totally dominated Pacific air travel.

That domination did not occur, and other US airlines – Northwest in particular – could compete because those advantages were not shared. Before the acquisition, United had excellent domestic service but poor service beyond Tokyo. It was striving to develop its Pacific routes. Pan American, on the other hand, had an excellent hub at Tokyo, but very poor domestic feeder service, which expanded from nothing in pre-deregulation days, largely through the acquisition of National Airlines. Competition in the Pacific was provided partly by JAL, the airline of choice for Japanese nationals but one without any internal US routes, by other foreign flag carriers to a limited extent (see the Appendix), and by Northwest. Northwest, in particular, had moved in the post-deregulation period to build its hub at Tokyo and to expand its domestic system, but by 1985 had not come close to having a domestic feeder service that matched United's.

Without the acquisition, Pan American would have had to do something else with its Pacific Division. As already mentioned, that Division was profitable, and Pan American had already announced plans for expansion of service in the Pacific, so one possibility would have been for it to remain as an active competitor, striving for greater efficiency. To succeed in the long run as a major player, it would have had to continue to expand its domestic operations. Alternatively, it could have sold some or all of the Division to another domestic carrier or carriers. Unless that carrier were American Airlines (acquisition of the Pacific Division by whom would present the same computer reservation system problems as acquisition by United), such a sale would have been procompetitive.

Similarly, Northwest would have continued to expand its domestic route system. If both Pan American and Northwest had been successful in their expansion, the result in five to ten years' time might have been that they both would have offered full on-line service from points inside the United States to many points in Asia.

At the same time, United would have had to fight to expand its trans-Pacific service. Given the entry barriers into US–Japan air transportation, however, it is a close question whether such expansion would in fact have taken place, and it may be said that one's view of the case largely depends on how one answers it. On balance, I believe that expansion by United did not require the acquisition and could have been achieved in a less restrictive way. There are three reasons for this.

First, of all US airlines, United was probably the best situated to bypass Japan. Indeed, it had already begun development of an alternative hub at Seoul. By approving the acquisition, the Department of Transportation removed the incentive for that development, which would have provided at least some competition to US–Japan service.

Second, the history of US–Japan negotiations over aviation does reflect progress, although the progress has often been slow. The expansion of Northwest in the Pacific, for example, involved continual pressure by the US government for further rights. Had the US government not approved the acquisition, it could have made further rights for United its first priority in negotiations with Japan. If, indeed, it turned out that Pan American had to retrench, there would have been a strong argument for gradual, piecemeal transfer of unused beyond rights to United. Moreover, a fully procompetitive policy would offer a Japanese carrier the right to carry passengers beyond gateways in exchange for rights beyond Tokyo for United (and other US flag carriers) – an offer that the Japanese government would certainly have to consider.

Third, while beyond rights for United would have to have been the subject of further negotiations, the DOT could itself have assured that United could provide increased trans-Pacific service. In April 1985 (just before the hearing in the case), Japan and the United States signed an agreement providing for up to three additional routes for American carriers offering service to Japan. It was totally in the control of the DOT to assure that United received one (or more) of those routes. This would have ensured that United kept fighting to fill its trans-Pacific planes and would have enhanced the argument that additional beyond rights were required for efficient service.

Thus, had the DOT not approved the acquisition, but instead pursued an aggressive procompetitive policy, the likely long-run result would have involved at least two and probably three American flag carriers providing on-line service on both sides of the Pacific and competing to do so. That competition would have resulted in the benefits of superior on-line service being passed on to the traveling public, rather than being retained by the airlines in the form of higher prices. Certainly, price competition would have continued as United, Pan American and Northwest all fought to gain adequate systems on both sides of the Pacific.

Of course, the provision of on-line service would have been delayed without the acquisition (such delays are a necessary consequence of 'infant industry' arguments such as this one). But, especially with consumers forced to pay high prices for that service, it is at least questionable whether such earlier provision justified the effects on competition.

The acquisition drastically changed the competitive picture. It removed Pan American as an active force and, at one stroke, allowed United to inherit not only its own legacy of regulation, but also that of Pan American. This gave United an immense head start by making it much less likely that Northwest could receive sufficient traffic to grow internally into a second full on-line carrier. As previously noted, it does not take much diversion of traffic on Pacific routes to turn profit into loss.

Similarly, US flag carriers that did not provide US–Asia service before the acquisition are unlikely to impose serious competitive constraints on the post-acquisition United. The April 30, 1985, amendment to the US–Japan bilateral agreement limits the frequency of service and hence the capacity of the carriers newly able to provide trans-Pacific service. Furthermore, the newly certificated US carriers only have rights to Tokyo, not beyond.[29] Had the acquisition not been approved (and the new routes not been awarded to United, as suggested above) the new carriers would have attempted to expand their service, and the United States might well have pressed for beyond rights (perhaps in exchange for parallel concessions to Japanese carriers). Now that United has acquired Pan American's Tokyo hub and beyond rights at a single stroke, however, the pressure of competition from the new carriers who lack such advantages is likely to be relatively low. The Japanese government, having just reluctantly approved the transfer of Pan American's beyond rights to United, is likely strongly to resist granting new ones. This will force the new carriers to grow gradually at best and to sink resources into rent-seeking activity (lobbying the two governments). Further, their expansion is likely to be hampered by United's use of its computer reservation system.

Can competition be preserved in the Pacific or will the acquisition inevitably lead to duopoly cooperation between United and JAL? The most likely source of additional competition remains Northwest, but here the acquisition has set off a predictable (and partly predicted) chain of consequences. As already discussed, United's post-acquisition advantages are too great for Northwest to continue competing through internal growth. Had it attempted to do so, it would have been forced to retrench in the Pacific and to provide very limited service. The alternative (predicted in my testimony) was that Northwest would itself seek a merger partner as a means of quickly acquiring a substantial domestic feed system. At the time, it seemed that the most plausible merger partner was American Airlines with its domestic route system and computer reservation system comparable to United's. In the event, Northwest instead acquired Republic Airlines. A major reason for that merger was Republic's fleet of short-haul aircraft.[30] If Northwest is able to redeploy the acquired aircraft, personnel and other facilities greatly to expand its route structure, there is at least a chance that Northwest can continue to compete effectively in the Pacific.

The decision and the role of the DOT

The DOT has jurisdiction over airline mergers as part of the job of managing the transition to a deregulated environment. That jurisdiction only makes sense if the DOT is willing to consider airline policy as a whole, rather than piecemeal. Thus, even if contestability makes it inappropriate to consider service on a particular domestic city-pair route as a relevant market, it is not irrelevant for the DOT to consider the direction in which the *national* industry structure is evolving.

In evaluating United's acquisition of Pan American's Pacific Division, the fact that Northwest might be forced to merge with another carrier should have been considered by the DOT. The actual Northwest–Republic merger contributed to the movement toward a tighter domestic oligopoly. The fact that approval of that merger required another hearing (in which the merger was opposed by the Department of Justice) at least suggests that its consequences for competition might be a matter of concern.

Unfortunately, when it came to this and the other matters involved in the *Pacific Division Transfer Case*, the DOT explicitly failed to take a broad view of transportation policy. The DOT's fragmented view of its responsibilities was evident not merely in its refusal to take seriously the prospect that the acquisition would lead to further mergers but, more surprisingly, in the way in which it dealt (or, rather, failed to deal) with the other issues raised above. In particular, the DOT gave little attention to the computer reservation system issue and appears never to have seriously considered the question of whether the efficiencies achievable by the acquisition could also be achieved in a way less likely to be destructive of competition.

Given the fact that the computer reservation system problem remains under review (and litigation), one might have expected the DOT to hesitate before expanding its consequences in a major way. This was not the case. Secretary Dole's opinion brushed aside the matter with the comment that it was premature to conclude that the existing computer reservation system rules are inadequate.[31]

The DOT took a similarly narrow view of the larger picture. It accepted Pan American's contention that the airline required a substantial financial commitment to expand. In so doing it passed over Pan American's pre-acquisition announcement of increased service.[32] Even if Pan American's contention had been correct, however, it would not have followed that the acquisition should have been approved. The DOT failed to consider whether the required financial commitment could have been obtained in a way less destructive of competition (sale to an airline not already competing in the Pacific, for example).

The question of United's ability to expand was given a similar treatment. The DOT recognized the entry barriers involved and concluded that United would not be able to overcome them unaided, so that substitution of a strong United for a weak Pan American would increase competition.[33] But, while the DOT recognized the efficiencies that the acquisition would bring, it did not seriously consider the possibility that those efficiencies might be achieved in a less restrictive way and that the DOT itself might aid in bringing about such a result. In particular, it failed to make more than the most cursory connection between the decision on the acquisition and that on the new routes to be awarded under the agreement of April 1985. The DOT stated only that the result of any application by United in the Japan route case 'cannot be predicted here'.[34]

This is an explicit statement of the blinkered view taken by the DOT in discharging its responsibility in overseeing airline mergers. As already remarked, it made sense temporarily to give post-deregulation responsibility for approval of airline mergers to the DOT only because the DOT can take a broad view of transportation policy. Without that it would have been more sensible immediately to entrust such responsibility directly to the courts (or perhaps to those agencies more skilled in antitrust matters). But a primary point of such an overview must be the consideration of whether the efficiencies promised by a particular transaction can be achieved through less restrictive means. In the *Pacific Division Transfer Case*, the DOT simply failed to consider such questions. It refused to step outside the confines of the instant proceeding and to consider even closely related matters plainly under its own control. In so refusing the Department of Transportation failed to live up to its responsibilities. That is a cause for concern however one thinks the *Pacific Division Transfer Case* should have been decided.

Appendix: The role of non-Japanese foreign flag carriers

The concentration statistics given in the text overstate the likely importance of the secondary Asian foreign flag carriers (China Airlines, Korean Air, CAAC, Thai Airways International, Singapore Airlines and Philippine Airlines) in restraining anticompetitive behavior on the part of the major market participants. Those secondary carriers are unlikely to expand much beyond the position they now occupy.

In many instances the level of US–Japan traffic on the secondary Asian flag carriers reflects explicit agreements between those carriers and JAL on capacity and price. Those agreements serve to protect the positions of the participating carriers and help them to maintain control over lucrative traffic between their home countries.[35]

An aggressive expansion attempt by such a carrier would doubtless be resisted by the Japanese government and might even jeopardize existing pooling agreements. Moreover, even if a secondary Asian flag carrier were to obtain expanded rights in carrying passengers between Japan and the United States, it is doubtful that it could also obtain the beyond-Tokyo rights from other nations needed to establish an efficient hub at Tokyo. Certainly, such carriers could not provide service within the United States.

Notes

1. Some studies have challenged this rosy view of contestability (Graham *et al.*, 1983; Bailey *et al.*, 1985). While the conclusions of these studies may or may not be correct, the studies themselves are not free from problems. In particular, the finding that concentration affects fares depends crucially on the decision to treat concentration as exogenous. Where this is not done, the estimated effect has the wrong sign in the relevant range. Testing generally fails to reject the null hypothesis of exogeneity (although not for all tests in all years) at the 5 per cent level, and the authors take this as permitting the acceptance of exogeneity. But failure to reject the null hypothesis is not the same as accepting it. In the circumstances involved here, the fact that null hypothesis testing is weighted towards the retention of the null hypothesis, while accepting exogeneity when it is false has serious consequences, means that the test procedure is (unavoidably) the wrong way around. The results suggest that the power of the test is low, and the test statistics, while not significant at the 5 per cent level, are large enough to make acceptance of exogeneity highly questionable.
2. A full discussion of my views is given in Chapter 2.
3. Exhibit JA-RT-2, Rebuttal Testimony of Dennis W. Carlton, William M. Landes and Sam Peltzman. This testimony presented a regression study concluding that Herfindahl–Hirschman index levels do not influence fares in a cross-section of international city-pairs. While the merits of the particular regression analysis can be debated, I agree with the general conclusion that Herfindahl–Hirschman index levels are far from a sufficient statistic for assessing the likelihood of tacit collusion. United and Pan American's economic testimony was entirely restricted to this issue and to the indisputable claim (discussed below) that the post-acquisition United would be a stronger competitor in the Pacific than the pre-acquisition Pan American.
4. For a detailed discussion of economic analysis and market definition, see Chapter 3 of Fisher *et al.* (1983).
5. The conclusions are no different if Hawaii–Far East traffic is included. Hawaii–Far East service is also quite concentrated.
6. See, for example, US Travel and Tourism Administration 'Survey of International Air Travelers, In-Flight Survey', October–December (1983), pp. YOSOS4-1–YOSOS4-6. Other surveys yield consistent results. Surveys of residence are more likely to be accurate on the question of how much travel originates or terminates in a gateway city than are direct ticketing counts, since many travelers to the Far East buy separate tickets for travel between their residence and a gateway city.
7. Even a non-negligible portion of United's pre-acquisition traffic through

Seattle to Japan originated at one of the two California gateways. See Exhibit DOJ-R-1, Rebuttal Testimony of Gloria J. Hurdle, Table R-2.

8. Before the acquisition, Pan American provided non-stop service between Tokyo and Los Angeles, New York and San Francisco, while United had non-stop flights between Tokyo and Seattle. Northwest provided non-stop service between Tokyo and all five gateways, and Japan Air Lines had such flights between Tokyo and every gateway except Chicago. Other foreign flag carriers flew non-stop between Tokyo and the two California cities. There were somewhat different patterns for other Asian destinations (but, as seen in Table 3.1 and discussed below, Japan–US traffic is by far the most important piece of US–Asia air travel).

9. Similarly, the importance of the United States as a business and tourist destination for Japanese travelers means that the availability of destinations other than the United States places only a weak constraint on the pricing of Japan–US mainland travel.

10. The 'Guidelines' characterize a market as 'highly concentrated' if the Herfindahl–Hirschman index is at least 1,800. They indicate that a merger in a 'highly concentrated' market will usually be challenged if it results in an increase in the Herfindahl–Hirschman index of at least 50 points. The increase here (on either definition) is 270 points.

11. Presumably for this reason the DOT refused to permit the merger of Continental and Eastern Airlines until some provision was made for transferring landing slots to Pan American for use in providing New York–Boston and New York–Washington shuttle service. For a detailed analysis of the importance of a market in slots, see Koran and Ogur (1983). Morrison and Winston (1986, pp. 60–6) find a substantial decrease in welfare from slot constraints.

12. A referee of an earlier version finds a 'wonderful irony' in the fact that I am valuing capital here. Apparently, he or she believes that my position on accounting rates of return is that no capital can ever be valued (Chapters 4, 5 and 6). That misstates my views, especially when there is a market in the used assets involved. In the present instance, even at the prices being asked for similar equipment, the value of the aircraft involved would not exceed about $650 million. Taking account of the thinness of the markets involved and the availability of substitutes, Michael Levine, testifying for American Airlines, estimated the value of the tangible assets being transferred at no more than $365.8 million (Exhibit AA-T-1, Testimony of Michael E. Levine, pp. 19–20). United's own president commented on the obsolescent nature of the planes being acquired (*Wall Street Journal*, April 29 (1985), p. 6).

13. Operating margins, as a per cent of revenues, were low on trans-Pacific routes before the merger (for example, 1984 margins were 5.8 per cent for Northwest and 7.5 per cent for Pan American). This makes it tempting to conclude that the scarcity value of the Tokyo rights was low under competition. That conclusion, however, requires information on capital values that is not easy to obtain, and hence the temptation ought to be resisted. I am grateful to the referee mentioned in the preceding note for preserving me from error here.

14. A somewhat more extended discussion of what follows is given in Exhibit NW-T-780, 'Pacific Pricing.'

15. This use of United's computer reservation system is procompetitive. The

uses discussed later are not.

16. The fringe of third country carriers was neither disposed nor able to interfere with a reduction of competition. See the Appendix.

17. Exhibit NW-R-734.

18. For theoretical discussion of the effects of mergers on competitors' profits, see Stigler (1950), Salant *et al.* (1983) and Perry and Porter (1985). Some analysts (with somewhat inconclusive results) have attempted to use the effect of a merger announcement on the prices of competitors' shares as evidence as to whether efficiencies or anticompetitive effects are likely to predominate (Eckbo, 1983; Stillman, 1983). (I am indebted to Richard Ruback for these references.) This requires one to believe that the stock market somehow knows instantly what would take trained analysts months of study to learn.

19. For an estimate of the way the public values single-line service in the context of a domestic merger case, see Carlton *et al.* (1980).

20. For a detailed discussion of the theory and literature here, see Krattenmaker and Salop (1986).

21. An American Airlines study in December 1981 found that almost 92 per cent of all sales made on its computer reservation system (Sabre) came from the first screen and more than 53 per cent from the first line. (US Department of Justice, 'Comments and proposed rules', Civil Aeronautics Board, Docket 41686 (1983), p. 81.)

22. In one case United offered to recompense a travel agent converting to its computer reservation system (Apollo) with $500,000 cash, a 10 per cent override on all transportation sold on Apollo and five years of free use of the system including absorption by United of all telecommunications line charges. ('Statement of Northwest Airlines, Inc.', Committee on Commerce, Science and Transportation, Subcommittee on Aviation, Hearings, Computer Reservation Systems, March 19 (1985), p. 64).

23. The loss in passenger convenience incurred here is large, as anyone who looks at the schedules involved or has changed terminals at Narita will quickly realize.

24. See Exhibit NW-T-765.

25. A recent report of the Department of Justice cites numerous examples of complaints about bias (US Department of Justice, 1985, pp. 33–40) and states (p. 39): 'Whether a specific algorithm . . . violates the antibias rule can be a difficult and highly fact-bound issue. The issue would not be adequately resolved by more rules, however. It can only be addressed on a case-by-case basis.'

   Competition from unbiased computer reservation systems will not solve the problem. A principal problem here is that no such system can succeed without the active participation of United and American in providing real-time information and allowing bookings to be made directly. It was the withdrawal of United and American that effectively killed the development of a joint industry computer reservation system in the mid-1970s.

26. See Note 13.

27. See *Monfort of Colorado, Inc.* v. *Cargill, Inc.*, 591 F. Supp. 683 (D. Colo. 1983), *aff'd.*, 761 F.2d.570 (10th Cir. 1985); *Christian Schmidt Brewing Co.* v. *G. Heileman Brewing Co.*, 600 F. Supp. 1326 (ED Mich. 1985), *aff'd.* 753 F.2d. 1354 (6th Cir. 1985), *cert. dismissed*, 105 S.Ct 1155 (1985); *White Consolidated Industries, Inc.* v. *Whirlpool Corp.*, 612 F. Supp. 1009

(ND Ohio 1985); *Pennzoil Co. v. Texaco, Inc.*, 1984-1 Trade Cas. (CCH) para. 65,848 (ND Okla.), *aff'd.*, 1984-1 Trade Cas. (CCH) para. 65,896 (10th Cir.); *Cia. Petrolera Caribe, Inc. v. Arco Carribean, Inc.*, 754 F.2d 404 (1st Cir. 1985); *Chrysler Corp. v. General Motors Corp.*, 589 F. Supp. 1182 (DDC 1984).

28. The Department of Justice took a strong stand in this regard in *Monfort*.
29. Similarly, a new Japanese carrier will not be able to acquire a US feeder system.
30. It would have taken several years for Northwest to acquire such a fleet, crucial to the development of a feeder system, by non-merger means.
31. *Final Opinion and Order*, pp. 50–1. The *Tentative Opinion and Order* is equally terse on this subject (p. 35).
32. *Final Opinion and Order*, pp. 35–6.
33. *Final Opinion and Order*, p. 39.
34. *Final Opinion and Order*, p. 38.
35. See Exhibit NW-T-790.

References

Bailey, E.E., Graham, D.R. and Kaplan, D.P. *Deregulating the Airlines.* Cambridge Mass.: MIT Press, 1985.

Carlton, D.W., Landes, W.M. and Posner, R.A. 'Benefits and costs of airline mergers: a case study'. *Bell Journal of Economics*, Vol. 11 (1980), pp. 65–83.

Eckbo, B.E. 'Horizontal mergers, collusion and stockholder wealth'. *Journal of Financial Economics*, Vol. 11 (1983), pp. 241–73.

Fisher, F.M., McGowan, J.J. and Greenwood, J.E. *Folded, Spindled and Mutilated: Economic Analysis and US v. IBM.* Cambridge Mass.: MIT Press, 1983.

Graham, D.R., Kaplan, D.P. and Sibley, D.S. 'Efficiency and competition in the airline industry'. *Bell Journal of Economics*, Vol. 14 (1983), pp. 118–38.

Koran, D. and Ogur, J.D. *Airport Access Problems: Lessons Learned from Slot Regulation by the FAA.* Washington, DC: Federal Trade Commission, Bureau of Economics, May 1983.

Krattenmaker, T.G. and Salop, S. 'Anticompetitive exclusion: raising rivals' costs to achieve power over price'. *Yale Law Journal*, Vol. 96 (1986), pp. 209–93.

Morrison, S. and Winston, C. *The Economic Effects of Airline Deregulation.* Washington, DC: Brookings Institution, 1986.

Perry, M.K. and Porter, R.H. 'Oligopoly and the incentive for horizontal merger'. *American Economic Review*, Vol. 75 (1985), pp. 219–27.

Salant, S.W., Switzer, S. and Reynolds, R.J. 'Losses from horizontal merger: the effects of an exogenous change in industry structure on Cournot–Nash equilibrium'. *Quarterly Journal of Economics*, Vol. 98 (1983), pp. 185–99.

Sibley, D.S., Jollie, S.B. 'Antitrust Policy in the Aviation Industry'. Washington, DC: Civil Aeronautics Board, 1982.

Stigler, G.J. 'Monopoly and oligopoly by merger'. *American Economic Review, Proceedings*, Vol. 40 (1950), pp. 23–34.

Stillman, R. 'Examining antitrust policy towards horizontal mergers'. *Journal of Financial Economics*, Vol. 11 (1983), pp. 225–40.

US Department of Justice 'Merger Guidelines'. *Federal Register*, Vol. 49 (1984), 26284.

US Department of Justice *1985 Report of the Department of Justice to Congress on the Airline Computer Reservation System Industry*. Washington, DC: US Government Printing Office, 1985.

4

On the misuse of accounting rates of return to infer monopoly profits (1983)

Accounting rates of return are frequently used as indices of monopoly power and market performance by economists and lawyers.[1] Such a procedure is valid only to the extent that profits are indeed monopoly profits, accounting profits are in fact economic profits and the accounting rate of return equals the economic rate of return.

The large volume of research investigating the profits–concentration relationship uniformly relies on accounting rates of return, such as the ratio of reported profits to total assets or to stockholders' equity as the measure of profitability to be related to concentration.[2] Many users of accounting rates of return seem well aware that profits as reported by accountants may not be consistent from firm to firm or industry to industry and may not correspond to economists' definitions of profits. Likewise, they recognize that accountants' statements of assets, hence also stockholders' equity, may fail to correspond to economically acceptable definitions, because accounting practices do not provide for the capitalization of certain activities such as research and development and do not incorporate allowances for inflation. This is to say, they are well aware of certain measurement problems which arise in using available accounting information to measure profitability. They seem, however, totally unaware of a much deeper conceptual problem,

Written jointly with John J. McGowan. McGowan was Vice-President, Charles River Associates. He died on April 7, 1982. This chapter is based on work done for Fisher's testimony as a witness for IBM in *United States* v. *IBM* (69 Civ. 200, US District Court, Southern District of New York). We are indebted to Larry Brownstein, Steven Hendrick, and especially Karen Larson and Leah Hutten for computational and programing assistance. Any errors are our responsibility.

namely, that accounting rates of return, even if properly and consistently measured, provide almost no information about economic rates of return.[3]

The economic rate of return on an investment is, of course, that discount rate that equates the present value of its expected net revenue stream to its initial outlay. Putting aside the measurement problems referred to above, it is clear that it is the economic rate of return that is equalized within an industry in long-run industry competitive equilibrium and (after adjustment for risk) equalized everywhere in a competitive economy in long-run equilibrium. It is an economic rate of return (after risk adjustment) above the cost of capital that promotes expansion under competition and is produced by output restriction under monopoly. Thus, the economic rate of return is the only correct measure of the profit rate for purposes of economic analysis.[4] Accounting rates of return are useful only insofar as they yield information as to economic rates of return.[5]

Now, it should be obvious that only by the merest happenstance will the accounting rate of return on a given investment, taken as the ratio of net revenue to book value in a particular year,[6] be equal to the economic rate of return that makes the present value of the entire net revenue stream equal to the initial capital cost. Indeed, as we shall see below, accounting rates of return on individual investments generally vary all over the lot. Hence, only if such fluctuations are somehow averaged out by a firm's investment behavior over time will its accounting rate of return even be roughly constant – let alone approximate the economic rate of return.[7]

It is easy to show that such averaging requires that the firm grow exponentially, investing in the same mix of investment types each year – an investment type being defined by a time shape of net revenues. Even in such an unrealistically favorable case, the accounting rate of return will generally depend on the rate of growth, equalling the economic rate of return only by accident. Furthermore, the relationship between the accounting and economic rates of return depends on the time shape of net revenues.

Hence, only by accident will accounting rates of return be in one-to-one correspondence with economic rates of return. We show by example below that the effects involved cannot be assumed to be small – indeed, they can be large enough to account for the entire interfirm variation in accounting rates of return among the largest firms in the United States.

The plan of the chapter is as follows. The first section summarizes the theoretical results which are proved and elucidated in the Appendix. These results establish the relationships among the various rates of return, time shapes and rates of growth, and demonstrate in principle that accounting rates of return are not informative. The balance of the chapter analyzes a series of relatively simple examples to show that the theoretical effects are not so small that they can be neglected in practice. Indeed, they are very large. A ranking of firms by accounting rates of return can easily invert a ranking by economic rates of return.

Before proceeding, we note that some of the theoretical results given below are not new. Ezra Solomon (1970) wrote a number of articles culminating in one dealing with the case of exponential growth. Thomas Stauffer (1971) published various theorems a year later and also attempted to make adjustments to accounting rates of return to correct for alternative cash flow profiles in testimony for the FTC in the ready-to-eat-cereal litigation.[8] J. Leslie Livingstone and Gerald Salamon (1971) have also studied and attempted to determine a relationship between the accounting and internal rates of return. Yet, perhaps because Solomon's focus was on the correct concepts of rate of return and cost of capital for rate regulation, or perhaps because none of the studies cited makes clear just how large the effects involved can be, the importance of these matters for more general industrial organization research appears to have gone largely unnoticed. It is our hope that the self-contained discussion of this chapter and, especially, the magnitudes of the effects exhibited in the examples below will remedy this.

Summary of theoretical results

The main theoretical results, which are proved and elucidated in the Appendix, are as follows:

1. Unless depreciation schedules are chosen in a particular way, so that the value of the investment is calculated as the present value at the economic rate of return of the stream of benefits remaining in it[9] – a choice which is exceptionally unlikely to be made – the accounting rate of return on a particular investment will differ from year to year, and will not in general equal the economic rate of return on that investment in any year.
2. The accounting rate of return for the firm as a whole will be an average of the accounting rates of return for individual investments made in the past. The weights in that average will consist of the book value of those different investments which in turn depend on the depreciation schedule adopted, and, particularly, on the amount and timing of such investments.

3. Unless the proportion of investments with a given time shape remains fixed every year, and unless the firm simply grows exponentially, increasing investments in each and every type of asset[10] by the same proportion for every year, the accounting rate of return for the firm as a whole cannot even be expected to be constant, let alone be equal to the economic rate of return.

4. Even where the firm does operate in such an unrealistic manner – the case most favorable to the accounting rate of return – the accounting rate of return will vary with the rate of growth of the firm, and will not generally equal the economic rate of return.

5. The only reliable inferences concerning the economic rate of return that can be drawn (and only in such an unrealistically favorable case) from examination of the accounting rate of return stem from the fact that the accounting rate of return and the economic rate of return will be on the same side of the firm's exponential growth rate. If the accounting rate of return is higher than the growth rate, then the economic rate of return is also higher than the growth rate. If the accounting rate of return is lower than the growth rate, then the economic rate of return is lower than the growth rate. If the accounting rate of return equals the growth rate, and in this case *alone*, the economic rate of return is guaranteed to be equal to the accounting rate of return.[11]

6. Even in the unrealistically favorable exponential growth case, the accounting rate of return depends *crucially* on the time shape of benefits, and the effect of growth on the accounting rate of return also depends on that time shape. In particular, it is not true that rapidly growing firms tend to understate their profits and slowly growing firms tend to overstate them. The effect can go the other way.[12]

7. All these results apply both to before- and after-tax rates of return.

The likely size of the effects

We now show by example that differences between the accounting and economic rates of return can be quite large indeed. For the sake of economy we examine only differences in after-tax rates of return. We assume a corporate tax rate of 45 per cent, and (for most examples) fix the after-tax economic rate of return at 15 per cent while varying growth rates and depreciation methods and the time shape of benefits.[13] Enormous variations in the accounting rates of return are readily generated.

The 'Q-profile'

We start with an investment whose benefits begin immediately and last for six years, and follow the time shape exhibited in column 2 of Table 4.1. For convenience we refer to this shape as the Q-profile.[14] The figures in column 2 are scaled to produce an after-tax economic rate of return of 15 per cent on an initial investment of $100 when sum-of-the-years' digits depreciation over a six-year life is used. The remainder of the table shows the calculation of the corresponding accounting rate of return each year.

Plainly, the after-tax accounting rates of return vary substantially. They never equal the after-tax economic rate of return (15 per cent), and exceed it in every year with positive net profits. Real-life firms do not generally exhibit such variation in their accounting rates of return because the averaging effects of growth, as it were, attribute profits from past investment to the book value of investments whose profit results are yet to come, rather than to the declining book value of such past investment.

While such an averaging effect tends to stabilize the accounting rate of return, it becomes a hodgepodge devoid of information about the economic rate of return. This point is illustrated by Table 4.2, which presents asymptotic accounting rates of return assuming constant exponential growth for three different versions of the Q-profile, each with the same tax rate (45 per cent) and after-tax economic rate of return (15 per cent).[15] The first version (the case of Table 4.1) has no delay between investment and the beginning of the benefit stream, and depreciation is taken over the resulting six-year life. The second version has a seven-year life including a one-year delay between investment and initial return. The third has an eight-year life including a two-year delay between investment and initial return. Except for the lag at the beginning and differences in scale, the gross benefit stream is the same in each case. The first panel of Table 4.2 gives accounting rates of return on beginning-of-year assets; the second panel gives those on end-of-year assets.

Several things are apparent from Table 4.2. First, the accounting rates of return only equal the economic rate of return of 15 per cent when the growth rate is also 15 per cent and when the accounting rate of return is measured on beginning-of-year assets. Otherwise, the accounting rates vary from seven points below to almost eleven points above the economic rate of return.

Second, it is not true (as is sometimes stated) that more rapid depreciation, other things equal, tends to understate accounting rates of return. In this example, when the rate of growth is below 15 per cent,

Table 4.1 After-tax accounting rates of return* (per cent) for the Q-profile; six-year life; no delay.

Year	Gross profits (Cash-flow before-tax)	Depreciation	After-tax profits	Beginning-of-year assets		End-of-year assets	
				Net	Accounting rate of return	Net	Accounting rate of return
1	23.3	28.6	(2.9)	100.0	(2.9)	71.4	(4.1)
2	44.1	23.8	11.2	71.4	15.7	47.6	23.5
3	51.9	19.0	18.1	47.6	38.0	28.6	63.3
4	40.5	14.3	14.4	28.6	50.3	14.3	100.7
5	20.2	9.5	5.9	14.3	41.3	4.8	122.9
6	7.8	4.8	1.7	4.8	35.4	0	Infinite

* Tax rate: 45 per cent; After-tax economic rate of return: 15 per cent; Sum-of-the-years' digits depreciation. It is assumed that the initial loss of $5.30 can be deducted from the firm's other profits.

Table 4.2 Asymptotic accounting rates of return (per cent) on three versions of the Q-profile.*

Growth rate	Six-year life (no delay)			Seven-year life (one-year delay)			Eight-year life (two-year delay)		
	Straight line	Declining balance	Sum-of-years' digits	Straight line	Declining balance	Sum-of-years' digits	Straight line	Declining balance	Sum-of-years' digits
Beginning-of-year assets									
0	15.2	17.8	18.1	18.1	21.3	22.0	21.0	24.7	25.9
5	15.2	16.9	17.0	17.0	19.1	19.4	18.9	21.1	21.7
10	15.1	15.9	15.9	16.0	17.0	17.1	16.9	17.9	18.1
15	15.0	15.0	15.0	15.0	15.0	15.0	15.0	15.0	15.0
20	14.8	14.1	14.1	14.0	13.2	13.1	13.3	12.4	12.3
25	14.7	13.3	13.3	13.1	11.5	11.4	11.7	10.1	9.9
30	14.5	12.5	12.6	12.2	10.0	9.9	10.3	8.0	7.8
End-of-year assets									
0	15.2	17.8	18.1	18.1	21.3	22.0	21.0	24.7	25.9
5	14.5	16.1	16.2	16.2	18.1	18.5	18.0	20.1	20.7
10	13.7	14.5	14.5	14.6	15.4	15.5	15.3	16.3	16.5
15	13.0	13.0	13.0	13.0	13.0	13.0	13.0	13.0	13.0
20	12.4	11.8	11.8	11.7	11.0	10.9	11.1	10.3	10.2
25	11.7	10.6	10.7	10.5	9.2	9.2	9.4	8.1	7.9
30	11.1	9.6	9.7	9.4	7.7	7.6	7.9	6.2	6.0

* See Table 4.1

declining balance and sum-of-the-years' digits depreciation produces a higher accounting rate of return than straight-line depreciation for given growth rates, time profiles and economic rates of return. The effect is reversed when the growth rate exceeds the economic rate of return of 15 per cent. This illustrates a general proposition: more rapid depreciation *increases* the accounting rate of return (measured on beginning-of-year assets) when the growth is less than the economic rate of return, and *decreases* the accounting rate of return when the growth rate exceeds the economic rate of return.[16] Since this is the only point about depreciation which we wish to demonstrate, we provide only results for sum-of-the-years' digits depreciation in the rest of this chapter.[17]

In all the examples in Table 4.2, firms growing at rates greater than the economic rate of return of 15 per cent have accounting rates of return on beginning-of-year assets less than the economic rate of return, while those growing at rates less than the economic rate of return all have accounting rates of return on beginning-of-year assets greater than the economic rate of return.[18] Contrary to what might be expected, this qualitative relationship provides no practical basis for adjusting accounting rates of return so that they will accurately reflect economic rates of return.

Table 4.2, for example, shows that firms which use sum-of-the-years' digits depreciation and grow at 5 per cent have accounting rates of return on beginning-of-year assets which range from 17.0 to 21.7 per cent. Thus, even for firms with the same growth rate and depreciation method, the required adjustment varies from 2 to 6.7 percentage points depending upon the time profile. Clearly, the time profile, depreciation method and growth rate must all be known before accounting rates of return can be adjusted to reflect economic rates of return.

In the foregoing examples, for a given time shape, faster-growing firms have lower accounting rates of return than slower-growing ones with the same economic rate of return. We have seen that even if this were a universal phenomenon, it would not provide a way to adjust accounting rates of return to reflect economic rates of return, since different firms will generally have different time shapes and therefore require different adjustments. The difficulties are even worse in practice, because the accounting rate of return can actually *rise* with the growth rate, causing *slower*-growing firms to have their economic rates of return *under*stated. Thus, even the strong assumption that firms have the same time profile is insufficient to permit adjustment of accounting rates of return; the specific profile must also be known in order to make inferences about the ranking of economic rates of return.

We demonstrate this phenomenon by taking the original Q-profile (six-year life and no delay) and spreading the last year's gross profits out evenly over five years (Years 6–10) instead of having them all in Year 6. Table 4.3 shows that this small change in the profile produces an increasing relationship between the growth rate and the accounting rate of return. The original results for sum-of-the-years' digits depreciation are reproduced for ease of comparison.

Focusing on the first column (ten-year life), we see that the accounting rate of return on beginning-of-year assets actually begins by rising with the growth rate, reaching the value of the economic rate of return (as it must) at a 15 per cent growth rate, and then going slightly above it before falling back again. (It is a special feature of this particular example that these values are all close to the economic rate of return of 15 per cent.) The behavior of the accounting rate of return on end-of-year assets is different. This magnitude falls with the growth rate (in this example), but it exhibits still another phenomenon. As opposed to the previous example, where the accounting rates of return on both beginning- and end-of-year assets were above the economic rate of return of 15 per cent for low growth rates and below it for large ones, here the accounting rate of return on end-of-year assets starts *and finishes* below the economic rate of return of 15 per cent. There is *no* rate of growth for which the accounting rate of return on end-of-year assets equals the economic rate of 15 per cent.

The impossibility of making inferences about relative profit rates should be obvious even within the confines of these examples, all of which represent only relatively slight variations on the same profile. *Every one of the firms exhibited in Table 4.3 has the same underlying after-tax economic rate of return. Yet their after-tax accounting rates of return on end-of-year assets vary from 6.0 to 25.9 per cent.*[19]

Further, it is impossible to infer anything about relative profitability by attempting to adjust for growth rates. For example, each row of Table 4.3 involves firms with the same growth rate, so that there is nothing to adjust for in comparing them; yet, except for the special row corresponding to the point where the growth rate is equal to the true after-tax economic rate of return, the after-tax accounting rates of return continue to vary. For the row corresponding to 5 per cent growth, for example, after-tax accounting rates of return vary between 13.8 and 20.7 per cent. For the row corresponding to 25 per cent, they vary between 7.9 and 12.0 per cent. Further, it is not correct to say that slow-growing firms have accounting rates of return that overstate their economic rate while fast-growing firms have accounting rates of return that understate them. Continuing to use accounting rates of return on end-of-year assets, the firm just introduced (ten-year life) has an accounting rate of return which understates its economic rate of return at all levels of growth. If one uses beginning-of-year assets, it has ac-

Table 4.3 Asymptotic accounting rates of return (per cent) on four versions of the Q-profile.*

Growth rate	Ten-year life (no delay, last year spread)	Six-year life (no delay)	Seven-year life (one-year delay)	Eight-year life (two-year delay)
Beginning-of-year assets				
0	13.9	18.1	22.0	25.9
5	14.5	17.0	19.4	21.7
10	14.8	15.9	17.1	18.1
15	15.0	15.0	15.0	15.0
20	15.1	14.1	13.1	12.3
25	15.1	13.3	11.4	9.9
30	15.0	12.6	9.9	7.8
End-of-year assets				
0	13.9	18.1	22.0	25.9
5	13.8	16.2	18.5	20.7
10	13.5	14.5	15.5	16.5
15	13.0	13.0	13.0	13.0
20	12.6	11.8	10.9	10.2
25	12.0	10.7	9.2	7.9
30	11.5	9.7	7.6	6.0

* See Table 4.1.

counting rates of return which tend to understate its economic rate of return at low rates of growth and (slightly) overstate it at higher ones.

Moreover, the phenomenon of accounting rates of return increasing with the growth rate can be considerably more marked if we use other profiles. Table 4.4 shows the before-tax benefit stream (corresponding to an initial investment of $100, an economic rate of return of 15 per cent and sum-of-the-years' digits depreciation over a six-year life) for two other profiles (X firm and Y firm). Table 4.5 shows the after-tax accounting rates of return for these firms when they grow exponentially at various rates. The after-tax accounting rates of return on beginning-of-year assets rise rather rapidly with the growth rate. The after-tax accounting rate of return on end-of-year assets also rises with the growth rate. However, as was also the case for the variation on the Q-profile examined earlier, it does not rise by enough to get to the economic rate of return of 15 per cent.

Conclusions

That the accounting rate of return – after tax as well as before tax – is a misleading measure of the economic rate of return is evident from examining cases of single projects such as in Table 4.1. The cases shown in later tables are unduly *favorable* to the accounting rate of return

Table 4.4 Before-tax benefit streams from an investment of $100.*

Year	X firm ($)	Y firm ($)
1	90.2	107.0
2	27.1	10.7
3	18.0	10.7
4	9.0	10.7
5	9.0	10.7
6	9.0	10.7

* See Table 4.1.

Table 4.5 Asymptotic accounting rates of return (per cent) for X and Y firms.*

Growth rate	Beginning-of-year assets		End-of-year assets	
	X firm	Y firm	X firm	Y firm
0	12.9	12.5	12.9	12.5
5	13.6	13.3	13.0	12.7
10	14.3	14.2	13.0	12.9
15	15.0	15.0	13.0	13.0
20	15.7	15.8	13.0	13.2
25	16.3	16.6	13.0	13.3
30	16.9	17.3	13.0	13.3

* See Table 4.1.

in that they mask its behavior by averaging. That averaging effect is achieved by the quite unrealistic assumption that investment by the firm always brings in the same time shape of returns, and that the firm grows each year by increasing its investments at the same percentage rate. Even on such favorable terms, it is impossible to infer either the magnitude or direction of differences in economic rates of return from differences in accounting rates of return. This is because such inferences require not only correction for growth rates, but *also* knowledge of the time shapes of returns.

The level and behavior of the accounting rate of return are both sensitive to the type of time shape used. Even within the Q-profile example, the rates vary depending on when the time shape begins and how the last few years are spread out. There is every reason to suppose that firms differ in the time shapes of their investments, and that a particular firm's investments will also differ among themselves. Thus, comparisons of accounting rates of return to make inferences about monopoly profits is a baseless procedure.

This conclusion can be most dramatically demonstrated by juxtaposing accounting rates of return for firms with different time shapes and *different* economic rates of return. When this is done, it is easy to see that firms with *higher* accounting rates of return can have *lower* economic rates of return. Table 4.6 gives after-tax economic rates of return and after-tax accounting rates of return on end-of-year assets for three growth rates (0, 5 and 10 per cent), and for each of the six time shapes already discussed as well as two other 'one-hoss shay' time shapes.[20] For *each* growth rate, the examples are chosen so that the eight firms represented are ranked in *ascending* order of economic rates of return and in *descending* order of accounting rates of return – a complete reversal even with growth rates constant.

Examination of Table 4.6 shows again that no inference about relative after-tax economic rates of return is possible from after-tax accounting rates of return. For example, the lowest after-tax economic rate of return in Table 4.6 is that for the *Q*-profile with an eight-year life at a zero growth rate. For that firm, the after-tax economic rate of return is 13 per cent. Yet, its after-tax accounting rate of return on end-of-year assets is 21.6 per cent, the second *highest* accounting rate of return in Table 4.6, and a value well above that of 15.8 per cent for the *Y* firm at zero growth, corresponding to a 19.2 per cent economic rate of return. The 21.6 per cent accounting rate of return so encountered is even above the 18.9 per cent figure obtained for the *Y* firm at 10 per cent growth – a figure which corresponds to an economic rate of return of 23.2 per cent, the highest in Table 4.6, and more than 10 percentage

Table 4.6 After-tax economic rates of return (*E*) and asymptotic accounting rates of return on end-of-year assets (*A*) for eight time shapes.*

	Growth rate					
	0 per cent		5 per cent		10 per cent	
Profile	*E*	*A*	*E*	*A*	*E*	*A*
Q-profile						
eight-year life (two-year delay)	13.0	21.6	16.0	22.6	17.8	21.2
seven-year life (one-year delay)	14.0	20.2	17.0	21.6	18.8	20.9
One-hoss shay						
six-year life (no-delay)	15.0	20.0	18.1	21.4	19.7	20.7
four-year life (no delay)	16.0	19.8	19.0	21.3	20.0	20.289
Q-profile						
six-year life (no delay)	16.1	19.6	19.05	21.2	20.05	20.287
ten-year life (no delay; last year spread)	18.0	16.9	20.0	18.5	22.0	19.8
X firm	19.0	16.2	21.0	17.8	23.0	19.2
Y firm	19.2	15.8	21.2	17.4	23.2	18.9

* Tax rate: 45 per cent; Sum-of-the-years' digits depreciation.

points above the economic rate of return of 13 per cent for the *Q*-profile with an eight-year life at zero growth. Similar examples of reversals occur throughout the table.

Nor can one eliminate these effects by correcting somehow for differences in rates of growth. The table as constructed exhibits a reversal of the ordering of economic and accounting rates of return with the rate of growth held constant. Rate of growth effects have thus *already* been removed from each pair of columns to an extent beyond that which one could hope to achieve in practice. Moreover, it is not true that faster-growing firms should have their accounting rates of return adjusted upwards relative to slower-growing ones. Consider the comparison between the *Q*-profile with a ten-year life at zero growth and the *Q*-profile with an eight-year life at 5 per cent growth. The faster-growing firm has an accounting rate of return (22.6 per cent) already greater than that of the slower-growing firm (16.9 per cent), but its economic rate of return (16.0 per cent) is *below* that of the slower-growing firm (18.0 per cent). Adjusting the faster-growing firm's accounting rate of return *upwards* relative to that of the slower-growing one will make things *worse*, not better.

As all of this makes clear, there is no way in which one can look at accounting rates of return and infer anything about relative economic profitability or, *a fortiori*, about the presence or absence of monopoly profits. The economic rate of return is difficult – perhaps impossible – to compute for entire firms. Doing so requires information about both the past and the future which outside observers do not have, if it exists at all.[21] Yet it is the economic rate of return which is the magnitude of interest for economic propositions. Economists (and others) who believe that analysis of accounting rates of return will tell them much (if they can only overcome the various definitional problems which separate economists and accountants) are deluding themselves. The literature which supposedly relates concentration and economic profit rates does no such thing, and examination of absolute or relative accounting rates of return to draw conclusions about monopoly profits is a totally misleading enterprise.

Appendix
A: Before-tax analysis

The accounting rate of return on individual investments

We begin our analysis of the problem by considering the before-tax accounting and economic rates of return on a single investment. Later we shall consider the firm as being made up of a series of such investments which may be (but need not always be) of the same type. The after-tax case is treated below and shown to be isomorphic, although more complex.

An investment may be thought of for heuristic purposes as a 'machine' costing one dollar. If this is invested at time 0, the firm experiences a stream of net benefits as a result. Such benefits include all changes in revenues and costs (other than the initial capital cost) which accrue to the firm as a result of making the investment. The flow of such benefits at time θ is denoted by $f(\theta)$.[22]

The economic rate of return on a machine, r, is that discount rate which makes the discounted value of the benefit stream equal to the capital costs of the investment. In other words, r satisfies

$$\int_0^\infty f(\theta) \exp(-r\theta) \, d\theta = 1 \tag{4.1}$$

We assume that the integral in Equation 4.1 is monotonically decreasing in r so that Equation 4.1 has a unique positive solution. This will be true if the negative portion of the net benefit stream (if any) precedes the positive portion. This is the usual case.[23]

Now the firm adopts a depreciation schedule for this machine. Let $V(\theta)$ denote the book value of the machine as of time θ. Then $-V'(\theta)$ is the rate of depreciation at θ, where the prime denotes differentiation. Plainly, $V(0) = 1$, and it makes sense to suppose that $V(\infty) = 0$, although this latter condition is not really needed.

Accounting profits attributable to this machine at time θ will be equal to net benefits less depreciation. We can think of the accounting rate of return for this machine as the accounting rate of return which the firm would have if this were its only asset. Denoting that rate by $b(\theta)$,

$$b(\theta) = (f(\theta) + V'(\theta))/V(\theta) \tag{4.2}$$

The first question which comes immediately to mind is that of when $b(\theta) = r$ for all θ within the life of the machine. We prove this will occur if and only if the depreciation schedule adopted by the firm always values the machine at the discounted value of the future benefit stream, discounting at the economic rate of return, r (see Hotelling, 1925).

Theorem 4.1: $b(\theta) \equiv r$ if and only if

$$V(\theta) = \int_\theta^\infty f(u) \exp(-r(u - \theta)) \, du \tag{4.3}$$

Proof: (a) Suppose Equation 4.3 holds. Differentiating with respect to θ, we obtain

$$V'(\theta) = -f(\theta) + rV(\theta) \tag{4.4}$$

which when substituted in Equation 4.2 yields $b(\theta) = r$.
 (b) Suppose $b(\theta) \equiv r$. Then, from Equation 4.2

$$V'(\theta) \equiv rV(\theta) - f(\theta) \tag{4.5}$$

This is a linear differential equation with an additive forcing function $(-f(\theta))$. Its solution is therefore in the form

$$V(\theta) = C \exp (r\theta) + z(\theta) \tag{4.6}$$

where $z(\theta)$ is any particular solution of Equation 4.5 and C is a constant to be determined by the initial conditions. However, by Part (a) of the proof, the integral on the right-hand side of Equation 4.3 is a particular solution of Equation 4.5. Hence $z(\theta)$ can be taken as that integral. Do this and note that $z(0) = 1$ by Equation 4.1, the definition of the economic rate of return. Since we have $V(0) = 1$, setting $\theta = 0$ in Equation 4.6 yields $C = 0$, and the theorem is proved.

Thus even where the firm has a single simple investment with no ambiguity about marginal against average economic rates of return, the accounting rate of return will not equal the economic rate of return except for a particular choice of a depreciation schedule – which choice we may term 'economic depreciation'.

The reason for this is not hard to find. The book value of the firm's assets reflects the investment expenditures made in the past less the depreciation already taken on them. The benefits for which such investments were made are at least partly in the future. Yet the accounting rate of return takes gross profits before depreciation as the benefit flow which happens to be currently occurring. Unless depreciation is chosen so as to reflect the change in *future* benefits in the appropriate way, there is no reason to suppose that such a calculation should equal the economic rate of return, and Theorem 4.1 shows that the two will generally not be equal.

Will firms tend to adopt an 'economic depreciation' schedule yielding book value as in Equation 4.3? This is pathologically unlikely. Except in the simple 'Santa Claus' case of $f(\theta) = k \exp (-\lambda\theta)$ which corresponds to exponential depreciation or other similarly special cases corresponding to straight-line or other standard depreciation methods, the benefit stream from investment when plugged into Equation 4.3 will not yield depreciation schedules anything like those used by real-life firms to optimize after-tax profits given Internal Revenue Service (IRS) rules or those schedules used for non-tax purposes. Real investments will almost invariably have complicated time shapes for their benefit streams. Further, even relatively simple shapes yield economic depreciation schedules which are quite far from actual ones. To see this, one need only observe that if $V(\theta)$ satisfies Equation 4.3, there is no reason that $V'(\theta)$ must always be negative. Indeed, if the time stream of benefits starts low and then has a hump a few years out, taking economic depreciation would require writing up the value of assets for the first few years. Yet there is nothing bizarre about such an example.

We must, therefore, with pathologically unlikely exceptions, expect that the accounting rate of return on a particular machine, $a(\theta)$, will generally not equal the economic rate of return r. (How far off it can be is demonstrated by examples.) This should make us suspect that the same thing will generally be true of the firm as a whole, and we now go on to explore that question.

The accounting rate of return for the firm as an average

It is fairly plain that the best hope for an accounting rate of return equal to the economic rate of return will occur if all investments made by the firm are exactly alike, since otherwise (as shown below), changes in the mix of investment types will change the accounting rate. So we begin by considering the case in which all machines are like the machine above.

It now becomes necessary to distinguish calendar time, denoted by t, from the age of a machine, denoted by θ. We let $I(t)$ be the value of investment made at t (equals the number of machines purchased). Let $K(t)$ denote the book value of the firm's assets at t and $\pi(t)$ the value of its accounting profits at t. Then,

$$
K(t) = \int_{-\infty}^{t} I(u) V(t - u) \, du
$$

$$
= \int_{0}^{\infty} I(t - \theta) V(\theta) \, d\theta
\tag{4.7}
$$

where $\theta = t - u$. Similarly,

$$
\pi(t) = \int_{-\infty}^{t} I(u) [f(t - u) + V'(t - u)] \, du
$$

$$
= \int_{0}^{\infty} I(t - \theta) \, [f(\theta) + V'(\theta)] \, d\theta
\tag{4.8}
$$

$$
= \int_{0}^{\infty} I(t - \theta) V(\theta) b(\theta) \, d\theta
$$

using Equation 4.2.

Hence, letting $a(t)$ be the firm's accounting rate of return at t:

$$a(t) \equiv \frac{\pi(t)}{K(t)}$$

$$= \frac{\int_0^\infty [I(t - \theta)V(\theta)] \, b(\theta) \, d\theta}{\int_0^\infty I(t - \theta)V(\theta) \, d\theta}$$

(4.9)

so that we have proved

Lemma 4.1: At any time, t, the accounting rate of return for the firm as a whole is a weighted average of the individual accounting rates for its individual past investments, the weights being the book values of those past investments.

It should be obvious that this result would also be true if machines were not always of one type.

We now ask whether such an average will equal the economic rate of return. First consider whether the average can even be independent of t. This can happen in two ways. First, $b(\theta)$ might be independent of θ. We know from Theorem 4.1 that this will happen for $b(\theta) \equiv r$ only for the case of economic depreciation already discussed which we rule out. It is easy to show that $b(\theta) \equiv q \neq r$ is impossible.[24]

The other way in which $a(t)$ might be independent of t would be if the relative weights in the average did not change over time.[25]

$$\frac{I(t_1 - \theta)V(\theta)}{I(t_2 - \theta)V(\theta)} = k$$

(4.10)

whence

$$\frac{I'(t_1 - \theta)}{I(t_1 - \theta)} = \frac{I'(t_2 - \theta)}{I(t_2 - \theta)}$$

(4.11)

for all (t_1, t_2). Evidently it must then be the case that

$$I(t) = M \exp(gt)$$

(4.12)

for some constant growth rate g.

The remainder of our investigation will concern the case of exponential growth with the scale factor, M, set equal to unity. This case is the most favorable to accounting rates of return approximating economic rates of return, since in its absence accounting rates of return will not even be constant, even though the economic rate of return is well defined and constant.

The effect of the growth rate in exponential growth

We are now dealing with a case in which the accounting rate of return is (at least asymptotically) constant and given as

$$a = \frac{\int_0^\infty [\exp\,(g(t-\theta))V(\theta)]\,b(\theta)\,d\theta}{\int_0^\infty \exp\,(g(t-\theta))V(\theta)\,d\theta} \tag{4.13}$$

where a denotes the (asymptotic) constant value. This is still a weighted average of the accounting rates of return on individual investments. Plainly, the growth rate g affects the weights. Since the accounting rates of return on individual investments will almost always not be constant in view of Theorem 4.1, changes in the weights will usually affect the average.

The present section studies such effects and asks, in particular, what inferences can be drawn concerning the economic rate of return, r, from knowledge of the accounting rate of return, a, and the growth rate g, without information on the time shape of benefits, $f(\cdot)$, since the latter information is plainly never available from the books of the firm – even assuming it is known in detail to the firm's forecasters.

The first thing to say in this regard is that while (as we shall show) there exist values of g for which $a = r$, these values will be the exception. One cannot expect accounting and economic rates of return to coincide even in the most favorable case of exponential growth and a single investment type except by the merest accident. What information *can* be gleaned from the accounting rate of return is analyzed in this section.

It will be convenient to set up the problem a little differently from the analyses above. Let $\pi^*(t)$ denote the gross profits of the firm before depreciation. Let $\delta(t)$ denote total depreciation taken at time t. Let $K^*(t)$ denote the *undepreciated* value of the firm's capital stock. Let $D(t)$ denote the total depreciation already taken on that stock. Finally, let $a^* = \pi^*(t)/K^*(t)$, so that a^* is the accounting rate of return which would be observed if there were no depreciation. The following relationships hold:

$$a = \frac{\pi^*(t) - \delta(t)}{K^*(t) - D(t)} \tag{4.14}$$

$$\pi^*(t) \equiv \int_{-\infty}^{t} \exp(gu)f(t - u)\,du$$

$$= \int_{0}^{\infty} \exp(g(t - \theta))f(\theta)\,d\theta \tag{4.15}$$

$$= \exp(gt) \int_{0}^{\infty} \exp(-g\theta)f(\theta)\,d\theta$$

$$= \exp(gt)\pi^*(0)$$

$$K^*(t) \equiv \int_{-\infty}^{t} \exp(gu)\,du \tag{4.16}$$

$$= \exp(gt)/g$$

$$\delta(t) = \int_{-\infty}^{t} \exp(gu)V'(t - u)\,du$$

$$= \int_{0}^{\infty} \exp(g(t - \theta))V'(\theta)\,d\theta \tag{4.17}$$

$$= \exp(gt)\delta(0)$$

$$D(t) = \int_{-\infty}^{t} \delta(u)\,du$$

$$= \int_{-\infty}^{t} \exp(gu)\delta(0)\,du \tag{4.18}$$

$$= \delta(0)\exp(gt)/g$$

Evidently, we have proved:

Lemma 4.2: $\delta(t)/D(t) = g$.

We now study the effects of g on a^*.

Lemma 4.3: (a) If $g = r$, then $a^* = r = g$.
(b) $d \log a^*/d \log g < 1$.
(c) a^* and r are always on the same side of g.
That is, $a^* < g \leftrightarrow r < g$; $a^* = g \leftrightarrow r = g$; $a^* > g \leftrightarrow r > g$.

Proof: (a) Using Equations 4.15 and 4.16,

$$a^* = g\pi^*(0)$$

$$\equiv g \int_{0}^{\infty} \exp(-g\theta)f(\theta)\,d\theta \tag{4.19}$$

If $g = r$, then $\pi^*(0) = 1$ by the definition of the economic rate of return, Equation 4.1, whence $a^* = g = r$.

(b) From Equation 4.19,

$$\log a^* = \log g + \log \pi^*(0) \tag{4.20}$$

but examination of $\pi^*(0)$ shows that it is necessarily decreasing in g since it is the discounted integral of future benefits from a single machine discounted at the rate g. Thus $d \log a^*/d \log g < 1$.

(c) These statements follow directly from (a) and (b).

Using Lemmas 4.2 and 4.3, we can now proceed to the main result of this section for the magnitude of interest, the accounting rate of return a, itself.

Theorem 4.2: a and r are always on the same side of g. That is,

$$a < g \leftrightarrow r < g; \qquad a = g \leftrightarrow r = g; \qquad a > g \leftrightarrow r > g.$$

Proof: By definition, $\pi^*(t) = a^* K^*(t)$. By Lemma 4.2, $\delta(t) = gD(t)$. Substituting in Equation 4.14

$$a = \frac{a^* K^*(t) - gD(t)}{K^*(t) - D(t)} \gtreqless g \tag{4.21}$$

according as $a^* \gtreqless g$. The desired result now follows from Lemma 4.3.

A diagram may be illuminating here. In Figure 4.1, the growth rate is measured on the horizontal axis and rates of return on the vertical axis. The 45° line indicates where growth rates and rates of return are equal. Theorem 4.2 states that the accounting rate of return must be above the 45° line to the left of the dashed line at $g = r$; it must pass through H, the point of intersection of the dashed line and the 45° line; and it must be below the 45° line to the right of the dashed line.

Can we say more than this? The answer is in the negative without information on the time shape of benefits $f(\cdot)$. In particular, it is *not* the case that the direction of change of a with respect to g is signed. Nor is it true that r must lie between a and g. These facts are exemplified in the text.

B: After-tax analysis

These same results apply to the analysis of the relationship between the after-tax economic rate of return and the after-tax accounting rate of return. This is obvious if the depreciation schedule used is not that used for tax purposes; in that case, the effect of taxes is just to change the benefit profile with the analysis the same as before, given the new benefit profile $f(\cdot)$. Moreover, the same thing is true if tax depreciation

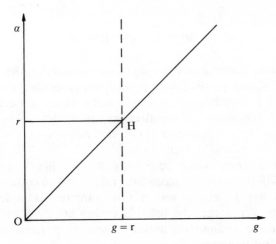

Figure 4.1   Pictorial representation of Theorem 4.2.

is used. To see this, let α be the tax rate $0 < \alpha < 1$ (assumed constant for simplicity). Let r' denote the after-tax economic rate of return. Then r' satisfies

$$\int_0^\infty [(1 - \alpha)f(\theta) + \alpha d(\theta)] \exp(-r'\theta)\, d\theta = 1 \qquad (4.22)$$

where $d(\theta)$ denotes depreciation on an asset of age θ and $f(\theta)$ denotes its *before*-tax benefits, as before.

This reflects the fact that the choice of a depreciation schedule, $d(\cdot)$, affects after-tax returns. Define

$$f^*(\theta) \equiv [(1 - \alpha)f(\theta) + \alpha d(\theta)] \qquad (4.23)$$

We now show that the analysis of the before-tax case applies directly to the after-tax case with $f^*(\cdot)$, the after-tax benefit schedule, replacing $f(\cdot)$, the before-tax benefit schedule.[26]

To see this, observe that the denominator of the accounting rate of return (whether total capitalization or stockholders' equity) will be the same before and after taxes. The numerator in the after-tax case, after-tax profits less depreciation, will be:

$$\int_{-\infty}^t (1 - \alpha)\,[f(t - \theta) - d(t - \theta)]\,I(\theta)\,d\theta$$

$$= \int_{-\infty}^t [(1 - \alpha)f(t - \theta) + \alpha d(t - \theta)]\,I(\theta)\,d\theta$$

$$\qquad (4.24)$$

$$-\int_{-\infty}^t d(t - \theta)\,I(\theta)\,d\theta$$

$$= \int_{-\infty}^{t} f^*(t - \theta)I(\theta)\, \mathrm{d}\theta - \int_{-\infty}^{t} d(\theta)I(\theta)\, \mathrm{d}\theta$$

But this is the *same* numerator as would be encountered in the before-tax analysis for a firm with the same depreciation schedule, but *before*-tax benefits $f^*(\cdot)$. For such a firm, r' would be the before-tax economic rate of return. Hence analysis of the after-tax case is identical to that of the before-tax case with an appropriate adjusted definition of the benefit schedule. All previous results apply to it.[27]

Thus, in after-tax analysis as in before-tax analysis, there is no reason to believe that differences in the accounting rate of return correspond to differences in economic rates of return. Our computer examples show the effects can be very large; the belief that they are small enough in practice to make accounting rates useful for analytic purposes rests on nothing but wishful thinking.

Notes

1. Aside from *United States* v. *IBM*, see, for example, Joseph Cooper (1976), p. 15; the various industry studies in Walter Adams (1970); and the discussion by Philip Areeda and Donald Turner (1978), Vol. II, pp. 331–41.
2. See the comprehensive reviews of this literature by Leonard Weiss (1979) and more recently by F.M. Scherer (1980), pp. 267–95. Additional accounting problems raised by attempting to measure profitability by line of business are discussed extensively in George Benston (1979).
3. A referee suggests that even the crudest accounting information tells us IBM is more profitable than American Motors (AMC), but we disagree. Surely accounting information tells us IBM generates more dollars of profits per dollar of assets than does AMC but, as the examples below demonstrate, that information alone does not tell us which firm is more profitable in the sense of having a higher economic rate of return.
4. This is literally true only if the cost of capital is first subtracted. In what follows below, we follow the usual empirical practice of measuring all rates of return before such subtraction.
5. The existence of a uniquely defined economic rate of return – which we now assume for the theoretical analysis below and which occurs in all the examples – is guaranteed only if the net revenue stream stemming from an investment has any negative terms occurring before the positive ones. If the economic rate of return fails to be unique, then, while present value calculations using the cost of capital remain the correct method for analyzing profitability, profitability cannot be summarized correctly by *any* rate of return, including accounting rates of return.
6. Throughout this chapter we work with accounting rates of return defined as ratios of profits to book values of capital. Similar (but not identical in detail) results apply to accounting rates of return on stockholders' equity. The precise relations involved can, in principle, be inferred from the results given below. (Such results do apply directly to accounting rates of

return on stockholders' equity even in detail if we consider the firms being analyzed to hold neither debt nor retained earnings.)

7. For discussion purposes – and in our examples below – we assume that the firm achieves the same economic rate of return on all its investments, and thus speak of 'the' economic rate of return for the firm without worrying about differences between average and marginal rates. This is, of course, the most favorable case for the accounting rate of return for the firm as a whole.

8. The proofs given below are different from Stauffer's proofs, and, we think, more suitable for our present purposes than his where the propositions coincide.

9. Such a 'natural' depreciation formula – which we shall term 'economic depreciation' – was first suggested by Harold Hotelling in 1925. It is somewhat misleading, however, to say that the fundamental conceptual problems discussed in this chapter are basically matters of depreciation accounting. Rather, there exists a particular form of depreciation which will correct those problems which stem from a fundamental difference between the economic and accounting rates of return. These problems arise even where machines never wear out. An example is given in Chapter 1.

10. Two assets are said to be of the same 'type' if they yield the same time shape of benefits.

11. It is worth pointing out that these results apply to accounting rates of return on total assets, not directly to accounting rates of return on stockholders' equity. Further, they apply to accounting rates of return on beginning-of-year, not end-of-year or yearly average assets. As the examples below show, the problem of making inferences from accounting rates of return on end-of-year (or average) assets is even worse – if possible – than when beginning-of-year assets are used.

12. Compare Cooper (1976), pp. 132–3.

13. The figure of 15 per cent was roughly the average *accounting* rate of return in US manufacturing corporations in 1978 (*Economic Report of the President*, US Council of Economic Advisers (1979), pp. 279–91). If accounting and economic rates of return tended to coincide, 15 per cent would be a reasonable choice for the economic rate of return. Since the rates do not generally coincide, the choice is immaterial. Choosing a lower economic rate of return would reduce the range of accounting rates of return in the results below (for the *same* examples), but would not affect the conclusions.

 With a fixed capital investment, a given time shape of gross profits before depreciation and taxes results in different after-tax economic rates of return for different depreciation methods. To fix the after-tax economic rate of return for a given time shape, therefore, we adjust the height of the gross profit–benefit stream proportionally to produce the desired after-tax economic rate of return.

14. This shape was (erroneously) suggested during *United States* v. *IBM* as being typical of IBM's experience. We use it for convenience.

15. In this context, exponential growth takes place by repeated investment in the same type of project; i.e. all investments have the same time shape of benefits. This is obviously an unrealistic assumption, but one which is more likely to produce equality between accounting and economic rates of return than more realistic assumptions.

16. By Theorem 4.1 (p. 92), the changeover point is also where the growth rate

equals the accounting rate of return on beginning-of-year assets.

17. There is one additional point about depreciation which we shall not bother to exemplify. Since the depreciation method chosen affects the time shape of the after-tax benefit stream, the relationship of after-tax accounting rates to the growth rate is particularly sensitive to the depreciation method. It can even happen that faster growth increases accounting rates of return for one choice of depreciation method and decreases them for another – all for the same pre-tax benefit time shape and the same after-tax economic rate of return. This makes adjustments for growth even harder to make than appears from the examples below.

18. So simple a relationship does not hold if the accounting rate of return is based on end-of-year assets.

19. Here and later, the results for beginning-of-year assets are similar.

20. The one-hoss shay time shapes have a constant return (no lag) for four and six years, respectively, and zero returns thereafter.

21. If one made the strong assumption that the same time shape of returns held for all investments made by a given firm throughout its life, then it might be possible to recover that time shape by regression of gross returns on a distributed lag of past investment. We are indebted to Zvi Griliches for this suggestion.

22. The time origin is arbitrary. The flow of benefits is assumed to depend on the age of the machine only. Thus an investment at time t brings in benefits of $f(\theta - t)$ at time $\theta \geq t$. Time dependence of the benefit stream can be handled by thinking of it as equivalent to investment in different kinds of machines at different times.

23. If Equation 4.1 has more than one solution, then the economic rate of return is ill-defined and there is even less point in considering whether the accounting rate of return yields information about it.

24. To see this, observe that a proof essentially the same as that of Theorem 4.1 would show that $b(\theta) \equiv q$ if and only if

$$V(\theta) = C \exp (q\theta) + z(\theta) \qquad (4.25)$$

where

$$z(\theta) = \int_{\theta}^{\infty} f(u) \exp (- q(u - \theta))\, du \qquad (4.26)$$

but $V(0) = 1$ so that $C = 1 - z(0) \neq 0$ if $q \neq r$. Then Equation 4.6 yields $V(\infty) = \pm \infty$ depending on $q \gtrless r$ and this is not possible.

25. For a *given* distribution of $b(\theta)$ there might be other possibilities, but these would be even more special than the case of economic depreciation already discussed. The statement in the text is true if $a(t)$ is to be constant despite unknown variations in $b(\theta)$ with θ.

26. A word about the treatment of inflation seems appropriate here. In the before-tax analysis it does not matter whether we work in real or nominal dollars (so long as we are consistent). In the after-tax case, however, the fact that depreciation which is deductible for tax purposes must be in nominal terms appears to raise some difficulty. That difficulty is only apparent however. Suppose that we begin by working in real terms. The nominal nature of the depreciation deduction plus the effects of inflation affect the depreciation schedule measured in real terms. We show, how-

ever, that any after-tax case with *any* depreciation schedule is isomorphic to a before-tax case. The effects being considered will, of course, influence *what* that before-tax case is, but they will not alter the existence of such a case. Hence, while the nominal nature of depreciation (like any other factor affecting the depreciation schedule) will affect what the numerical value of the real after-tax accounting rate of return is, it will not change our results.

27. It is interesting (and revealing of the full unity of the before- and after-tax analyses) to note what happens in the case of 'economic depreciation' examined above. In that case, it turns out that the (pathologically unlikely) choice of an economic depreciation schedule involves the *same* depreciation schedule whether economic depreciation is chosen before or after tax. Assets are valued at the present value of all remaining benefits either before or after tax; it makes no difference. Further, that choice of depreciation schedule makes the after-tax economic rate of return r' relate to the before-tax economic rate of return r, in the natural (but – except with this depreciation schedule – not inevitable) way: $r' = r(1 - \alpha)$. To show these things, return to the differential equation (Equation 4.5) from which we derived the formula for economic depreciation in the before-tax case.

$$V'(\theta) = rV(\theta) - f(\theta) \tag{4.27}$$

Consideration of the before-tax analysis shows that if and only if $V(\cdot)$ satisfies this and $V(0) = 1$, then

$$V(\theta) = \int_{\theta}^{\infty} f(u) \exp\left(- r(u - \theta)\right) du \tag{4.28}$$

the present value of future benefits. Now, choose $V(\cdot)$ and hence $d(\cdot)$ to satisfy Equation 4.28 and therefore Equation 4.27. Then

$$(1 - \alpha)V'(\theta) = r(1 - \alpha)V(\theta) - (1 - \alpha)f(\theta) \tag{4.29}$$

$$V'(\theta) = r(1 - \alpha)V(\theta)$$

$$- [(1 - \alpha)f(\theta) + \alpha d(\theta)] = r(1 - \alpha)V(\theta) - f^*(\theta) \tag{4.30}$$

since $d(\theta) \equiv - V'(\theta)$. But this is the same form as Equation 4.27. Hence, as in Equation 4.6:

$$V(\theta) = \int_{\theta}^{\infty} f^*(u) \exp\left(- r'(u - \theta)\right) du + C \exp\left(r'\theta\right) \tag{4.31}$$

with $r' \equiv r(1 - \alpha)$. Here, C is a constant of integration; however $C = 0$, since Equation 4.28 shows that $V(\infty)$ is finite. Since $V(0) = 1$, we have

$$1 = \int_{0}^{\infty} f^*(u) \exp\left(- r'u\right) du \tag{4.32}$$

which shows that r' is the after-tax economic rate of return. From Equations 4.28 and 4.31 with $C = 0$, $V(\theta)$ is both the before- and the after-tax present value of the remaining benefit stream at θ, whence economic depreciation is the same in both cases. See Paul Samuelson (1964).

References

Adams, Walter, *The Structure of American Industry*, New York: Macmillan, 1970.

Areeda, Philip and Turner, Donald F., *Antitrust Law: An Analysis of Antitrust Principles and Their Application*, Boston: Little, Brown and Co., 1978.

Benston, George J., 'The FTC's line of business program: a benefit–cost analysis', in Harvey Goldschmid, ed., *Business Disclosure: Government's Need to Know*, New York: McGraw-Hill, 1979, 58–118.

Cooper, Joseph D., *Proceedings of the Second Seminar on Economics of Pharmaceutical Innovation*, Washington: American University, 1976.

Hotelling, Harold, 'A general mathematical theory of depreciation', *Journal of the American Statistical Association*, September 1925, **20**, 340–53.

Livingstone, J. Leslie and Salamon, Gerald L., 'Relationship between the accounting and the internal rate of return measures: a synthesis and analysis', in J. Leslie Livingstone and Thomas J. Burns, eds., *Income Theory and Rate of Return*, Columbus: Ohio State University, 1971, 161–78.

Samuelson, Paul A., 'Tax deductibility of economic depreciation to insure investment valuations', *Journal of Political Economy*, December 1964, **72**, 604–6.

Scherer, F.M., *Industrial Market Structure and Economic Performance*, Chicago: Rand McNally, 1980.

Solomon, Ezra, 'Alternative rate of return concepts and their implications for utility regulation', *Bell Journal of Economics*, Spring 1970, **1**, 65–81.

Stauffer, Thomas R., 'The measurement of corporate rates of return: a generalized formulation', *Bell Journal of Economics*, Autumn 1971, **2**, 434–69.

Weiss, Leonard W., 'The concentration–profits relationship and antitrust', in Harvey J. Goldschmid *et al.*, *Industrial Concentration: The New Learning*, Boston: Little, Brown and Co., 1974.

US Council of Economic Advisers, *Economic Report of the President*, Washington: USGPO, 1979.

5

The misuse of accounting rates of return: Reply (1984)

After he had made his remark about the Emperor's new clothes, the boy was quite surprised at the reaction. One commentator pointed out how hard the boy had made it for established experts on imperial robes to testify about what they just *knew* to be true. His comments were at least amusing, but others tended to be more strident. Indeed, some designers and fashion critics (particularly those involved in line-of-royalty fashion reporting) accused the boy of trying to destroy not only the clothing business, but all of business generally. They pointed out that the boy's model emperor was unrepresentative of true emperors and, anyway, emperors and clothes-wearing tended to be correlated. Still others said that, while it was true that the Emperor had no clothes, he did carry a stick, and, under some assumptions, sticks could be sceptres.

While a few people did say that they agreed with the boy, they were mostly people who had already remarked on the state of imperial undress. Indeed, since a number of people had said much the same thing in the past, the boy wondered why he should have provoked such strong reactions. Perhaps, he thought, it was because he had been unduly blunt in referring to His Majesty as 'that naked jaybird' or because he had published his findings in the very prestigious *Court Journal*.

Moral: Don't interfere with fairy tales if you want to live happily ever after.

What did we say?

Judging from some of the comments I have received on Chapter 4, only some of which were published with this reply, you would think that John

I am grateful to Joen E. Greenwood, Paul Joskow and Robert Larner for comments, but retain responsibility for error.

McGowan and I had defaced a national monument. We have been accused of claiming that all accounting data are useless, of making it difficult for expert economists to testify about monopoly, and even of implying that 'most of applied economics is misguided'. To put things in perspective, let's examine what we did say.

McGowan and I pointed out that the profit rate about which economic theory speaks is the internal or economic rate of return. It is that rate, if any, which provides the signal for the entry or exit of firms and resources. Hence, studies which use profit rates as though they were the objects analyzed in the theory must use profit rates which measure the economic rate of return if those studies are to be worth anything at all. This is particularly true of studies either of individual firms or of cross-firm or cross-industry comparisons which seek to identify high rates of return with monopoly power.

Such studies use accounting rates of return, defined as current profits divided by either total capitalization or the value of stockholders' equity.[1] For convenience, we concentrated on the first alternative, although our qualitative conclusions applied to both. We ignored well-known difficulties such as the treatment of intangibles in order to concentrate on the conceptual problem involved.

That problem is as follows. The numerator of the accounting rate of return in question is current profits; those profits are the consequence of investment decisions made in the past. On the other hand, the denominator is total capitalization, but some of the firm's capital will generally have been put in place relatively recently in the expectation of a profit stream much of which is still in the future. While the economic rate of return is the magnitude that properly relates a stream of profits to the investments that produce it, the accounting rate of return does not. By relating *current* profits to *current* capitalization, the accounting rate of return fatally scrambles up the timing.

Moreover, this defect is not something that can be corrected by averaging, nor is it merely a start-up problem. It persists even in steady-state growth. Unless the firm values its assets in the particular way long ago pointed out by Harold Hotelling (1925), its accounting rate of return will not equal the economic rate of return. Further, that particular valuation method is totally impractical. For firms to use it would sometimes require taking negative depreciation; for observers to do so would require knowing the economic rate of return, so that computing the accounting rate would be pointless.

Without the use of Hotelling valuation, the accounting rate of return is not very informative, to say the least. In particular, even in the most unrealistically favorable case, that of exponential growth, the most that can be said is that the accounting and economic rates of return are always on the same side of the growth rate – a fact that is not very helpful. In a series of computer-generated examples, McGowan and I showed that the effects involved could be very large indeed, so that firms with the same economic rate of return could have widely different accounting rates of return. We also showed that ranking of firms by accounting rates could invert their ranking by economic rates of return.

One way of describing the causes that lie behind such phenomena is as follows. The accounting rate of return in exponential growth depends on the time shapes of benefits that flow from investments and on the rate of growth of the firm. It is true, given the rate of growth and the general appearance of the time shape of benefits, but not its level, that the accounting rate of return and the economic rate of return will be positively associated, but that association is not strong enough to allow one to ignore the obviously realistic possibility that growth rates and time shapes differ over firms. Particularly in the case of time shapes, so little is actually known that one assumes away differences at one's peril (and, I may add, if one knows the time shape of benefits including its level, one knows the economic rate of return without further ado).

I should have thought that, given such results, the burden of proof would be on those who wish to continue in the belief that accounting rates of return can be used as valid indices of economic profit rates. Surely, more is called for than the simple assertion that our examples are unrepresentative and that it is well known that accounting rates of return measure profits. That is particularly so because, on the contrary, it is – or ought to be – well known that this is not the case. Many of our results were not new, and, as we pointed out, many of the same points had been made by others.[2]

End-of-year versus beginning-of-year rates

I now turn to the specific comments published with this reply, concentrating on that of William F. Long and David J. Ravenscraft (1984) (L–R). As do L–R, I begin with what may at first seem a minor matter, the treatment of end-of-year versus beginning-of-year assets.

Long and Ravenscraft (1984) assert that McGowan and I incorrectly calculated accounting rates of return on end-of-year assets. They claim that this must be so because our end-of-year-assets rates of return are lower than or equal to our beginning-of-year-assets rates of return and state:

> If there is depreciation, and if the same accounting profit value is divided by the two asset values, the end-of-year accounting rate of return must be larger than the beginning-of-year accounting rate of return (p. 494).

This is flatly false. So long as the firm has positive net investment, end-of-year assets will exceed beginning-of-year assets. Non-negative net investment occurs in our computer-generated examples for every case of exponential growth, and positive net investment for positive rates of growth. It is not hard to see that, in exponential growth, the accounting rate of return on beginning-of-year assets will exceed that on end-of-year assets by a factor of one plus the growth rate, and this is true of the results given in Chapter 4. It is not true of the supposedly 'corrected' results given by L–R.

This part of L–R's treatment of the beginning- versus end-of-year assets question may be only indicative of their keen sensitivity even in trivial respects to an analysis that criticizes the accepted way of doing things in this area, but the remainder of that treatment is symptomatic of a more fundamental misunderstanding. They claim that the fact that accounting rates of return on end-of-year assets perform even less well in our examples than accounting rates of return on beginning-of-year assets is an artifact stemming from the fact that we defined the economic rate of return in beginning-of-year terms. They observe:

> The continuous time results derived in F–M's Appendix hold in discrete time for accounting profit rates defined with beginning-of-year assets as the denominator, if the growth rate and internal rate of return are defined in beginning-of-year terms. However, it [*sic*] also holds for accounting profit rates defined with end-of-year assets as the denominator, provided the growth rate and internal rate of return are defined in end-of-year terms. (pp. 494–5)

They also point out that suitable redefinitions will make our results hold for accounting rates of return defined on any given convex combination of beginning- and end-of-year assets.

This is certainly true[3] and just as certainly completely irrelevant. What L–R fail to realize is that the issue is not whether one can redefine the magnitudes of economic theory (here the economic rate of return) so that certain theorems (our results) will be true of their relations to the magnitudes used in practice (here accounting rates of return on end-of-year assets). Rather the issue is whether the magnitudes used in practice bear any useful relationship to the magnitudes of economic theory. The fact that one can invent something called the 'end-of-year internal rate of return' and show that its relations to the accounting rate of return defined on end-of-year assets are such as to obey the theorems in the Appendix to Chapter 4 is not a reason for using the accounting rate of return defined on end-of-year assets.

This is an important point and it is worth going into in more detail. The economic rate of return is the magnitude which gives the signal for entry or exit of resources. That is because firms can compare the economic rate of return offered by a particular investment opportunity with the cost of capital. At least in those cases in which rate of return calculations are appropriate at all, such comparisons will yield the correct actions for long-run profit maximization.[4]

Now consider the internal rate of return which L–R propose to define on end-of-year assets. That rate is undefined for assets such as one-year bonds whose payoff comes entirely in one year. That means that firms deciding between one-year bonds and other assets cannot use the L–R-defined rate of return to make that decision. More generally, that rate of return cannot be used to decide among different investments that have significant positive payoffs in the first year or to compare such investments with others; indeed, if one examines L–R's general formula, one finds that any two-period investment with positive cash flow in both years and the cash flow in the first year greater than the investment cost has an L–R rate of return greater than 1 and is to be preferred to any two-period investment with first-year cash flow below the investment cost *no matter what the sizes of the second year cash flows are*. Similar anomalies arise for longer cash flow profiles. In the light of this, what difference does it make whether or not such an internal rate of return relates to the accounting rate of return on end-of-year assets in the way given for continuous time rates in the Appendix to Chapter 4?

I have discussed this in some detail because it is symptomatic of the reluctance on the part of those involved in the use of accounting rates of return to take a serious look at what it is that such rates of return are supposed to be measuring. Long and Ravenscraft are so anxious to rescue accounting rates of return on end-of-year assets that they make an elementary error (inconsistently treating net investment) and have apparently forced their calculations to show the impossible. Worse, they show that they can define magnitudes (their redefined internal rates of return) which relate to the particular version of accounting rates of return they wish to defend in the same (not very useful) way that the usual internal rate of return relates to the accounting rate of return on beginning-of-year assets; but they fail to notice that the magnitudes they define no longer have the property that the usual internal rate of return does of being something in which the analysis is interested.[5]

The burden of proof and the role of examples

The same tendency to defend rather than consider runs through much of the rest of L–R's criticisms. As already remarked, given our results, one would think that the burden of proof was on those who wish to go on using accounting rates of return as measures of economic profit. Since our examples merely illustrate some general theorems, that burden cannot be sustained by arguing that our examples are unrealistic; one must show rather than presume that the problems do not arise for real firms.

In this connection, it is instructive to consider L–R's valid point that since our examples considered the accounting rate of return on total assets rather than on equity (the firms in our examples had no debt), our use of 15 per cent as the value of the economic rate of return was incorrect. If we were going to choose a rate representative of accounting rates of return, we should have used the average accounting rate of return on total assets (7.8 as opposed to 15 per cent in 1978). Quite so. But consider what they say next:

> If an economic rate of return of 7.8 percent is used instead of 15 percent, and the set of growth rates is centered on 7.8 percent, the maximum deviation from the economic rate of return on beginning-of-year assets is 3.9 vs. 10.9 percentage points in F–M's Table 2 or 50 vs. 73 percent of the economic rate of return. (Long and Ravenscraft, 1984, p. 495)

Apparently, a 50 per cent error is a small one. Moreover, while it is undoubtedly true that the spread of accounting rates of return in such an exercise would be reduced *for these particular examples*,[6] it must be remembered that the examples in Table 4.3 are all variations on a particular theme suggested by an earlier critic who thought that earlier examples generating a still wider range were chosen to be unrepresentative (see Chapter 4, p. 83, Note 14, and our book with Joen Greenwood, 1983, p. 242). Other, more widely varying examples would yield an even wider spread, so that no comfort can be taken from the prospect that accounting rates of return may be 'only' 50 per cent in error.

Similar remarks apply to L–R's contention that our examples are misleading because most of them involve accelerated depreciation. The spread of accounting rates of return for a given economic rate of return is quite large enough in the straight-line depreciation cases given in Table 4.2 to show that accounting rates of return cannot be used as measures of economic rates of return. Furthermore, that spread would be wider still for different examples.[7]

To sum up: our examples only illustrate the general theorems involved. Only those who are determined to believe without any serious theoretical basis that accounting rates of return measure economic rates of return can find L–R's arguments persuasive.

Correlation between accounting and economic rates of return

Plainly, what is needed is an affirmative showing that accounting rates of return in fact measure what they are supposed to, and L–R do indeed make some gestures in that direction. They suggest that accounting rates of return and economic rates of return are likely to be correlated; they make some 'indirect' tests of whether conclusions based on accounting rates of return are likely to be in error; and they claim that accounting rates of return meet the market test of being widely used.

It would be surprising if accounting rates of return were not correlated at all with economic rates of return. As pointed out above, given the growth rate of the firm and, especially, given the general appearance of the time shape of benefits accruing from a typical investment, then (at least in exponential growth) the accounting rate of return will be positively associated with the economic rate of return because both will be positively associated with the level of the benefit stream. It is this fact which allows management of particular companies with reasonably constant time shapes and growth rates to use accounting rates of return as 'hurdle rates' as discussed by Michael van Breda (1984) in his comment. It would be surprising to find that such positive association fails to persist when time shapes and growth rates vary over firms; one expects variables with a positive coefficient in a multiple regression to show some positive zero-order correlation with the dependent variable.

How strong is that correlation in fact? That is very hard to know, precisely because we do not know the economic rates of return of most firms (and if we did, any information provided by the positive correlation in question would be superfluous). Long and Ravenscraft cite Thomas Stauffer (1980) to the effect that the correlation is 0.79 over nine selected industries and speculate that this understates the correlation for all industries. Unfortunately, the basis for this is quite weak – and inevitably so. Stauffer's estimation of internal rates of return for the nine industries studied rested (as was inescapable) on specific assumptions about the time shapes of benefits which he thought characterized those industries. Those assumptions were plausible, but they could not be precise calculations. Since we know that the relation between the accounting and economic rate of return is very sensitive even to relatively small variations in the assumed time shape (see Table 4.3, p. 88), the correlation which L–R derive from Stauffer's results can only be taken as somewhat suggestive. No general conclusion can be drawn.

More important than the exact size of the correlation, however, is the fact that it plainly is not very close to one. Given that, the issue is not how high the correlation is but whether differences between accounting and economic rates of return are related to variables used in statistical studies. If they are, then studies which use the accounting rate of return as a proxy dependent variable for the economic rate of return are likely to give misleading or unreliable results.

This point is well made in a pair of studies by Gerald Salamon (1985)

and by Salamon and Mark Moriarty (1983). They observe that Mc-
Gowan's and my results show that the choice of a depreciation method
affects the relation between the economic rate of return and the accounting rate of return; since there is evidence that the choice of depreciation method is related to firm size, conclusions as to the relations
between firm size and profitability which stem from the use of the
accounting rate of return must be viewed with caution. Salamon estimates economic rates of return for a selection of firms (assuming a
particular parametric family of time shapes) and shows that conclusions
on the size–profitability relation are indeed affected. He and Moriarty
reach a similar result as to the conclusions of the literature on the
relations of advertising and profitability. While these results depend on
the assumptions as to time shape, it would be perilous indeed to conclude that they are not general. Only very detailed investigation can
rescue the accounting rate of return and the studies based on it.

The L–R 'indirect' evidence

Long and Ravenscraft do not offer such detailed investigation; instead
they offer indirect evidence. Some of that evidence is indirect indeed.
The fact that distortions in line-of-business profits coming from common
cost allocations or non-market transfer prices may leave line-of-business
profits correlated with profits measured differently has no bearing whatever on the problems at issue here. More important, evidence relating
to studies using profit rates on *sales* is similarly irrelevant.

I cannot understand how even the most casual reader of Chapter 4
could think that McGowan and I were discussing any accounting rate of
return other than that on assets or on stockholders' equity. In particular,
our results plainly have nothing to do with the usefulness or lack thereof
of the accounting rate of return on sales. Yet L–R treat this as though it
affected the relevance of our results, and Stephen Martin (1984) in his
comment uses Chapter 4 as an occasion to write about the relations
between the accounting rate of return on sales and the Lerner measure
of monopoly power as though such relations bore on what we did discuss. I shall comment on this matter below; for the present, however, I
wish to stay with the question of the relevance of the L–R discussion of
results involving the rate of return on sales to the applicability of our
results.

Long and Ravenscraft calculate regression statistics for a structure–
profits regression using profits/sales and gross profits/gross assets as
alternative dependent variables. They find similar results in both regres-

sions.[8] They then reestimate using profits before depreciation in the numerators of the dependent variables and attempt to interpret the results as to the likely effect of the distortions introduced by different depreciation methods on the relations between the accounting rate of return and the economic rate of return. They find in the case of profits/sales as the dependent variable that five out of twenty-three coefficients are affected (including the coefficient of minimum efficient scale as Salamon's results would suggest). Changes in the case of the gross profits/gross asset regression were even less significant. Long and Ravenscraft appear to draw some comfort from these results.

It is unnecessary to consider whether five out of twenty-three is large or small. These results are meaningless. Consider first the results using profits/sales as the dependent variable. Adding depreciation back into the numerator of the dependent variable produces a variable with no content in terms of economic analysis. Depreciation, however difficult its computation, represents a real economic cost. Profits before depreciation no more relate to the Lerner measure than do profits before subtraction of labor costs. To the extent, therefore, that the L–R results do not change when gross profits are used, one must question the meaning of their results when net profits are used in the dependent variable. As it is, all that can be concluded from these results is that depreciation/sales in the L–R sample is related in particular ways to at least five of the variables they use.

The case as regards the regressions using gross profits divided by assets is similar. Such a 'depreciation-adjusted' accounting rate of return is no more likely to be closely related to the economic rate of return than is the unadjusted accounting rate. Indeed, since depreciation represents real costs, such an adjusted rate of return makes even less analytical sense than do the usual measures.[9] To find that such an adjustment leaves results unaffected is to cast grave doubt on the results if it says anything at all.

The results reported by L–R using accounting rates of return on end-of-year or middle-of-year instead of beginning-of-year assets are likewise irrelevant. Since none of these measures correctly reflects the economic rate of return, the most that can be concluded from the fact that results using each are similar is that the differences among them are less important than the differences between the economic rate of return on the one hand and such measures as a group on the other. Since accounting rates of return on beginning-of-year and on end-of-year assets are likely to be highly correlated,[10] any other result would be surprising, whatever the facts as to the economic rates of return of the firms involved.

The 'market test'

I now turn to the question of the market test of acceptance of accounting rates of return. Here again, L–R are quite confused. McGowan and I attacked the use of accounting *rates of return* – L–R behave as though we had attacked the use of data on accounting *profits*, and that is simply beside the point. Accounting profit data have their problems as measures of economic profits, but those problems are relatively well understood and were certainly not the subject of Chapter 4. It is unnecessary further to comment on L–R's discussion leading up to their somewhat hysterical comment that 'the implication of F–M's work, if correct, is that most of applied economics is misguided' (Long and Ravenscraft, 1984, p. 495).

The only market test that is of any relevance, then, concerns the direct use of accounting rates of return themselves. That use is explained along the lines given above as to the reasons for positive correlation between accounting and economic rates. In the absence of better information, firms (and investment houses) may use accounting rates of return as rules of thumb – 'hurdle rates' as van Breda puts it. Careful comparisons for a given firm over time or among firms in the same industry may yield some rough information because growth rates and benefit profiles may be roughly the same (although even this is open to question). But, if accounting rates of return really measured economic rates of return, there would be no need for potential investors or financial analysts to use anything else, and they plainly do, examining, among other things, rates of growth and, especially, prospective cash flows. In any event, such use of accounting rates of return by the lay public cannot substitute for analysis of their properties by the economist.

The Lerner measure and the rate of return on sales

I now leave the discussion of Long and Ravenscraft and comment briefly on issues which arise in the rather more sensible comments of the other authors involved in the discussion. The first such subject, as has already been indicated, is that of the use of profits divided by sales as a measure of monopoly profits. This is the subject – indeed the only subject – of Stephen Martin's (1984) comment.

I have already indicated that this topic seems to me irrelevant as a criticism of McGowan and me. Chapter 4 was plainly about the use of profits divided by assets or by equity. To reply that profits divided by sales may be a useful measure is not to reply at all. This is therefore not the appropriate place to discuss the failings of the return-on-sales-as-a-measure-of-monopoly-power literature. (See Chapter 6.) Since the topic has been brought up, however, I shall add a few remarks.

1. Nobody supposes that profits divided by sales are an interesting profit rate measure because they tell one something about the desirability of moving resources in or out of a given area. If profits divided by sales are interesting, it is because, under constant returns to scale, the rate of return on sales is related to the Lerner measure of monopoly power, not because that rate of return is truly a profit rate in the sense that economic theory uses that term. I stand by our statement that 'the economic rate of return is the only correct measure of the profit rate for purposes of economic analysis' (p. 80).

2. The use of profits divided by sales as reflective of the Lerner measure is something which needs to be approached with considerable caution. It seems to me quite dangerous to assume constant returns when dealing with analyses involving firm size and concentration.

3. Even the Lerner measure itself seems to me to be of limited usefulness. There is a clear sense in which, for a given firm and (possibly) for a given industry, the higher the Lerner measure the greater the monopoly power, but it is not so clear in what sense this is true when different firms or industries are to be compared as in statistical studies. There is no natural metric here and it is not clear how high is high, or even whether higher is necessarily more powerful.

4. This can be related to the first point made above by observing that the Lerner measure is not directly related to the economic rate of return. An industry with a high Lerner measure and a low economic rate of return does not strike me as ripe for antitrust action; an industry with a high economic rate of return which is unaccounted for by any reason other than the possible presence of monopoly[11] does so strike me, even if it has a low Lerner measure. In this sense I would include even the rate of return on sales (which we certainly did not have in mind) in the statement by McGowan and me that 'Accounting rates of return are useful only insofar as they yield information as to economic rates of return' (p. 80). Whether the Lerner measure has that property is an open question.

Concluding remarks

I can, I think, do no better than to conclude with a brief comment on Ira Horowitz (1984). His paper is at least amusing, and there is no point in being overly solemn about it. Nevertheless, to the extent that it is to be taken seriously, one searches in vain for any argument that McGowan and I were mistaken. Rather, the underlying assumption again appears to be that everyone knows that high accounting rates of return are indicative of monopoly power and that therefore this must be true.

I thus read Horowitz as saying that McGowan and I have made it harder for economists to give loose but pontificating testimony for which there is no solid analytic foundation. Particularly considering the origins of Chapter 4 in *United States* v. *IBM*,[12] I am not going to lose any sleep over that. Certainly, John McGowan would have considered it the highest possible praise.

Notes

1. We did not discuss the use of profits divided by sales. I take this up below.
2. I wish to take this occasion to rectify an inexcusable scholarly oversight on our part. While we cited a number of predecessor writings, we failed to cite that of G.C. Harcourt (1965); this was particularly unfortunate because of all the literature, Harcourt's valuable article is perhaps the one most closely related to our own work. In this connection, it is perhaps useful to point out that J.A. Kay's criticism (1976) of Harcourt is quite misleading. For example, Kay states (result (*i*), p. 449) that if the accounting rate of return on a particular project is constant over the life of that project, then that accounting rate of return equals the internal rate of return. He fails to note that such constancy can only occur if Hotelling valuation ('economic depreciation') is used (see Theorem 4.1, p. 92 and also p. 95, Note 24). More important, Kay's calculation of the economic rate of return for the firm as a whole from a time-series of accounting rates and a terminal valuation either requires that the firm be wound up, in which case, all that is involved is a direct knowledge of the time shape of benefits or else requires that the terminal valuation used be Hotelling valuation which requires knowledge of the economic rate of return. See also F.K. Wright (1978).
3. L–R's definition of the appropriate internal rate of return to use on end-of-year assets is given in their footnote 2 and elaborated in their working paper (Long and Ravenscraft, 1983).
4. As is well known, there are occasions on which rules based on rate of return comparisons are not equivalent to present value maximization which always yields the correct rule, but in such circumstances the literature which uses accounting rates of return to make inferences about profits cannot possibly be correct. Contrary to what some of my correspondents appear to believe, McGowan and I were not recommending internal rate of return calculations as a substitute for present value maximization.
5. There are, of course, problems involved in discrete time models as to the handling of cash flows that come in and investments that are made in the course of a year, but they are not the ones being discussed here.
6. Whether the particular figures given by L–R can be trusted in light of their results on end-of-year accounting rates is a different matter.
7. And, I may add, large firms – including those that may be suspected of having monopoly power – tend to take accelerated depreciation.
8. It is typical of L–R's underlying attitude toward the issues that arise when the dependent variable used may not measure what it is supposed to meas-

ure that they should state: 'the strongest statistical results arose in the profits/sales regression, which lends support to the choice of profits/sales over profits/assets as the dependent variable in such regressions' (Long and Ravenscraft, 1984, p. 495).

9. Long and Ravenscraft have at least avoided the pitfall of adding depreciation back to the numerator of the accounting rate of return while leaving depreciated assets in the denominator. Such an adjustment is not unknown to those attempting to make inferences from accounting rates of return; it was made by Alan McAdams in his testimony for the government in the *IBM* case. Since IBM took relatively faster depreciation than did most of the computer firms with which it was being compared, the results were predictable as an arithmetic artifact. See Fisher *et al.* (1983), pp. 236, 257.

10. Indeed, as pointed out above, in exponential growth the two rates of return will be proportional for firms with the same growth rate.

11. This is by no means an easy thing to discover. There are many other roles for and sources of profits besides monopoly. See Fisher *et al.* (1983), Chapter 7.

12. See Fisher *et al.* (1983), Chapter 7.

References

Fisher, Franklin M., McGowan, John J. and Greenwood, Joen E., *Folded, Spindled and Mutilated: Economic Analysis and US v. IBM*, Cambridge Mass.: MIT Press, 1983.

Harcourt G.C., 'The accountant in a golden age', *Oxford Economic Papers*, March 1965, **17**, 66–80.

Horowitz, Ira, 'The misuse of accounting rates of return: comment', *American Economic Review*, June 1984, **74**, 492–3.

Hotelling, Harold, 'A general mathematical theory of depreciation', *Journal of the American Statistical Association*, September 1925, **20**, 340–53.

Kay, J.A., 'Accountants, too, could be happy in a golden age: the accountant's rate of profit and the internal rate of return', *Oxford Economic Papers*, November 1976, **28**, 447–60.

Long, William F. and Ravenscraft, David J., 'The usefulness of accounting profit data: a comment on Fisher and McGowan', Working Paper No. 94, Federal Trade Commission, June 1983.

Long, William F. and Ravenscraft, David J., 'The misuse of accounting rates of return: comment', *American Economic Review*, June 1984, **74**, 494–500.

Martin, Stephen, 'The misuse of accounting rates of return: comment', *American Economic Review*, June 1984, **74**, 501–6.

Salamon, Gerald L., 'Accounting rate of return' *American Economic Review*, June 1985, **75**, 495–504.

Salamon, Gerald L. and Moriarty, Mark M., 'Alternative profitability measures and tests of economic hypotheses: an application to the advertising–profitability issue', mimeograph, May 1983.

Stauffer, Thomas R., *The Measurement of Corporate Rates of Return and the Marginal Efficiency of Capital*, New York: Garland, 1980.

van Breda , Michael F., 'The misuse of accounting rates of return: comment', *American Economic Review*, June 1984, **74**, 507–8.

Wright, F.K., 'Accounting rate of profit and internal rate of return', *Oxford Economic Papers*, November 1978, **30**, 464–8.

6

On the misuse of the profits–sales ratio to infer monopoly power (1987)

Introduction

It is popularly supposed that under constant returns the Lerner measure of monopoly power – (price minus marginal cost)/price – is equal to the ratio of profits to sales. This chapter shows that proposition to be generally false, although it can be true in certain special cases. Moreover, the resulting errors can be quite large and are likely to be systematically related to the variables used in regression studies purporting to test the structure–conduct–performance paradigm.[1]

The reason is not hard to find. Constant returns means constant returns to all factors including capital, so that unless proper account is taken of the user cost of capital (e.g. Hall and Jorgenson, 1967), the profits–sales ratio will misstate the Lerner measure.[2] It will often be the case, however, that the user cost cannot easily be estimated from the firm's own accounts. Capital is a factor that necessarily enters the production of output at different points in time. Its costs are joint because its use involves economies of scope. Unless there is an active market in used capital goods that forces the firm to make marginal decisions about the acquisition or disposition of old capital, the way the firm allocates those joint costs to different years – the way it takes depreciation – need not reflect true user costs.

There is, of course, a depreciation schedule that will reflect such costs. This is 'economic depreciation' (Hotelling, 1925). That depreciation schedule implies a valuation of capital ('Hotelling valuation') at

I am indebted to Paul L. Joskow for helpful discussions and to the Editorial Board and referees of the *RAND Journal of Economics* for constructive criticism, but retain responsibility for any error.

the present value of the associated remaining net revenue stream using the firm's risk-adjusted discount rate. But such valuation is revenue-oriented; it does not reflect cost, and, without an active market in used capital goods, there is nothing to force a firm to use it. While Hotelling valuation will serve as a useful benchmark in the analysis below, that is all it is. Real firms do not (and often cannot) generally employ it.

The existence of capital-measurement problems with the profits–sales ratio has been noticed in the literature. Liebowitz (1987), in particular, attacks the use of that ratio, and Martin (1983, pp. 28–32) discusses some of the issues. But the full analytics of the problem appear not to have been spelled out, nor has its importance been realized.

That importance is substantial. There is a very large literature using the profits–sales ratio as the dependent variable in regressions purporting to test various propositions of the structure–conduct–performance paradigm (e.g. Weiss, 1974; Martin, 1983; Ravenscraft, 1983; Domowitz *et al.*, 1986). Whatever view one takes as to how associations between profits and structural variables should be interpreted (Demsetz, 1973), it matters whether those associations are really there. Yet the dependent variable in such regressions may be subject to substantial error from the capital-valuation problems studied here. Moreover, contrary to the assertion that one can assume that such errors are distributed independently of the right-hand-side variables used in such studies (e.g. Martin, 1983, p. 32), I show below that such independence generally does not hold.

Moreover, the use of the profits–sales measure to infer monopoly power is not restricted to regressions. The staff of the Federal Trade Commission's Line-of-Business Program proposed to use the data generated by that program to identify targets of antitrust prosecution on the basis of profits–sales ratios (Long *et al.*, 1982). Further, Scherer, who briefly testified for the Antitrust Division in the *IBM* case, asserts (1984, p. 620, emphasis added):

> IBM's normal strategy was to set prices exceeding manufacturing costs by at least a factor of four. *If this does not reflect monopoly power, what does?*

Thus, the problem considered here is of some importance for antitrust policy.

Formal model: Hotelling valuation

To begin, consider the simplest possible case in which the firm produces output, x, from capital and labor inputs, K and L, respectively. Capital is bought at time 0 and used thereafter. Production at time t takes place according to a standard, differentiable neoclassical production function: $x = F(K, L, t)$. Time is included in the production function to incorporate the effects of physical depreciation of the capital stock. (L and x are functions of t, but this has been omitted from the notation – as will also be true for all other variables.)

Denote the wage of labor by w, the price of the product by p and the marginal revenue of the firm by $R'(x)$. The discount rate used by the firm is denoted by r, and we normalize so that the price of a unit of new capital is always unity.[3] As of time $\theta \geq 0$, given the amount of capital in place, the present value of the firm is

$$M(K, \theta) = \int_\theta^\infty [pF(K, L) - wL]e^{-r(t-\theta)}dt \qquad (6.1)$$

where we assume that the firm plans to choose L optimally. Denoting differentiation by subscripts, we can write the marginal internal benefit of having additional capital at time θ as

$$V^*(\theta) \equiv M_K(K, \theta) = \int_\theta^\infty R'(x)F_K e^{-r(t-\theta)}dt \qquad (6.2)$$

This is Hotelling valuation – the valuation whose derivative with respect to θ,

$$V^{*\prime}(\theta) = R'(x)F_K + rV^*(\theta) \qquad (6.3)$$

corresponds to economic depreciation.

Now assume that new capital can be bought and sold freely at time 0, but that there is no market for used capital, so that capital once put in place must be used forever. It is obvious that, if capital is purchased to maximize present value, $V^*(0) = 1$. Further, it is natural to assume that $V^*(\infty) = 0$. Without a market in used capital at intermediate dates, however, there is nothing to tie $V^*(\theta)$ to outside phenomena, and nothing that leads to the firm's use of it on its books.

In fact, real firms are unlikely to use Hotelling valuation. One important reason for this is as follows. Since $V^*(\theta)$ depends not on costs but on revenues, it will generally depend on future wages and the future state of demand. Hence $V^*(\theta)$ will, in fact, depend on calendar time as well as on the age of the capital stock. This means that the use of Hotelling valuation would require that capital of a given age have different valuations in two successive years simply because labor market or output market conditions change, even though such changes were perfectly foreseen.

The reason that this matters is that (for a single project), the use of the profits–sales ratio to estimate the Lerner measure implies that Hotelling valuation is being used. To see this, observe that Equation 6.3

implies that the user cost of capital – depreciation plus imputed interest – is equal to the marginal revenue product of capital. This, plus constant returns, and the first-order condition for present-value maximization with respect to labor $(R'(x)F_L = w)$, make the profits–sales ratio equal the negative reciprocal of the elasticity of demand.

This result, however, holds only when the firm uses a depreciation schedule corresponding to $V^*(\theta)$ – 'economic depreciation' defined in Equation 6.3. If *any other* depreciation schedule is used, then the desired equality does not follow, at least in the case of a single project.

I must add one more word before proceeding. The user cost of capital includes imputed interest. Hence, profits must be adjusted for this if the profits–sales ratio is to equal the Lerner measure. In practice, this is seldom, if ever, done directly. Because r – the risk-adjusted cost of capital – is not known, most studies that make any adjustment for the opportunity cost of capital do so by omitting it from the computation of profits and putting the value of capital divided by sales on the right-hand sides of regressions. If Hotelling valuation were used and if the capital–output ratio had no other effect on the Lerner measure, then the coefficient of that variable would be r.[4]

Suppose that imputed interest is omitted from costs and the value of the capital–sales ratio is included as an independent variable in a regression in which profits/sales is the dependent variable. Let b denote the resulting regression coefficient of the capital/sales variable. One gets equivalent results by subtracting r times that variable from the dependent variable and obtaining a regression coefficient on the right-hand side of $(b - r)$. Such a subtraction, however, amounts to adjusting accounting profits by subtracting imputed interest at the correct interest rate, r, but with the firm's own (non-Hotelling) valuation of capital. In what follows, I assume this to have been done and consider the consequences for estimating the Lerner measure as though it were done explicitly.

A stationary environment: the most favorable case

Despite the fact that real firms do not use Hotelling valuation, there does exist a case in which, for a growing (as opposed to a single-project) firm, the profits–sales ratio will equal the Lerner measure under constant returns. That case requires us to ignore the important issue of time dependence discussed above and to go to the most favorable case of an essentially stationary environment.[5] In this case we can simplify notation by defining $f(\theta)$ as the instantaneous marginal revenue product at θ of capital of age θ $(R'(x)F_K$ in the previous notation). Then, from Equation 6.3, we have

$$f(\theta) = -V^{*\prime}(\theta) + rV^*(\theta) \tag{6.4}$$

Now denote the amount of investment that the firm makes at time u by $I(u)$.[6] Let $V'(\theta)$ denote the depreciation actually taken by the firm on a unit of capital of age θ. This implies a book-value schedule for such capital, $V(\theta)$, given the natural assumption that $V(0) = 1$.[7] Then the sum of total depreciation and total imputed interest at time t as taken on (or implied by) the firm's books is:

$$A \equiv \int_{-\infty}^{t} I(u)[-V'(t - u) + rV(t - u)]du \tag{6.5}$$

By contrast, the depreciation and imputed interest that correspond to economic depreciation and Hotelling valuation are given by

$$B \equiv \int_{-\infty}^{t} I(u)[-V^{*\prime}(t - u) + rV^*(t - u)]du$$

$$= \int_{-\infty}^{t} I(u)f(t - u)du \tag{6.6}$$

using Equation 6.4.

Let L^* be the true value of the Lerner measure. Then $L^* \equiv (p - R'(x))/p$, where p is price. Equivalently,

$$px = xR'(x)/(1 - L^*) \tag{6.7}$$

Let L be the profits–sales ratio. Then

$$L - L^* = \frac{B - A}{px} = \frac{(B - A)(1 - L^*)}{xR'(x)}$$

$$= \left(\frac{B - A}{B}\right)\left(\frac{B}{xR'(x)}\right)(1 - L^*) \tag{6.8}$$

This expression separates the error in the use of profits/sales into three parts. The first is the relative error in the cost of capital; the second is the ratio of true capital cost to output valued in terms of marginal revenue rather than price; and the third is one minus the Lerner measure itself.

The appearance of the third factor $(1 - L^*)$ strongly suggests that the error in the use of profits/sales as an estimate of the Lerner measure is very unlikely to be uncorrelated with variables that affect the Lerner measure and thus appear in regression studies. That will indeed be the case unless the effects of $(1 - L^*)$ are somehow cancelled by the other effects in Equation 6.8, in particular, by the appearance of $xR'(x)$.

We can see that such cancellation cannot be a general phenomenon by examining a leading (if simple) example with a special production technology. That examination is required in any case to generate a usable expression for evaluating the possible size of the error.

To construct this example I alter the description of the technology slightly and assume that one unit of capital of age θ is equivalent to a fixed number of units, $a(\theta)$, of new capital. Then it is natural to measure capital in efficiency units, each of which has the same marginal product. Consideration of Equations 6.3 and 6.4 above, however, shows that the marginal revenue product of capital of age θ must be $f(\theta)$, so $a(\theta)$ is proportional to $f(\theta)$ so that we can renormalize by choosing the units of output to make $a(\theta) = f(\theta)$. From Equation 6.6 B is then the capital stock in the new efficiency units.

More precisely, suppose that, at time t, the labor assigned to capital of vintage u is $L(t, u)$ and that the output produced thereby is

$$x(t, u) = F(f(t - u)I(u), L(t, u)) \tag{6.9}$$

This states that the effects of capital age can be captured as capital-augmenting technical change. Since we are assuming constant returns and that all labor has the same wage, it follows from a well-known theorem on capital aggregation (e.g. Fisher, 1969, pp. 559–60) that total output is given by the production function:

$$x = F(B, L) \tag{6.10}$$

where L is the total amount of labor employed by the firm. Note that Equations 6.3 and 6.4 imply that we have measured capital so that the marginal *revenue* product of B is unity.

Now consider changes over time with w and $R'(x)$ held constant. Since $F(\cdot, \cdot)$ is homogeneous of degree one and L will be chosen to have marginal physical product equal $w/R'(x)$, the ratio of L to B will be constant. It follows that x/B will also be constant and that $xR'(x) = mB$ for some constant m. Substituting in Equation 6.8 yields

$$L - L^* = (1 - L^*) \frac{B - A}{mB} \tag{6.11}$$

The constant, m, depends on w and on $R'(x)$, but is otherwise technologically determined. It is illuminating to evaluate it in an even more special case. Suppose that the technology is Cobb–Douglas, so that

$$F(B, L) = B^a L^{1-a} \tag{6.12}$$

Then the fact that the marginal revenue product of B is unity implies that $xR'(x) = B/a$, so that $m = 1/a$, and Equation 6.11 becomes

$$L - L^* = a(1 - L^*) \frac{B - A}{B} \tag{6.13}$$

The appearance of the Cobb–Douglas parameter in this way is no accident. Returning to the more general case of any constant-returns production function given in Equation 6.11, we see that Euler's theorem and the fact that the marginal revenue product of B is unity imply that $xR'(x) = B + wL$. Hence, $1/m \equiv B/xR'(x) = 1 - wL/xR'(x)$. Thus, $1/m$ turns out to be one minus labor's share of the value of output when that value is in terms of marginal revenue rather than of price. As in the Cobb–Douglas case, this will depend on the parameters of the production function, but it should come as no surprise that the errors that come from the mismeasurement of capital bulk larger when (true) capital costs are a large share of total costs than they do when that share is small. This must clearly be a general phenomenon, as is the fact that the term in $(1 - L^*)$ does not cancel out of the error formula.

I shall return to a discussion of the error formula below, and also to the use of the Cobb–Douglas, capital-augmenting example. For the present, however, I want to return to the relatively more general (but still very special) case of a stationary environment with an arbitrary production function to examine the question of whether *without* Hotelling valuation, it is possible that $B = A$ and that profits/sales equals the Lerner measure.

The simplest case: exponential growth

I shall consider only the simplest and most favorable case, that of exponential growth in which $I(u) = e^{gu}$. While not very realistic, this is at least a case in which one can imagine the stationarity assumption to hold with demand and all variables growing at the same rate, g.

Define $C(g) \equiv e^{-gt}(B - A)$, so that $C(g) = 0$ is equivalent to profits/sales equalling the Lerner measure. Letting $\theta = t - u$, we see that in the exponential growth case

$$C(g) = \int_0^\infty [rV^*(\theta) - V^{*'}(\theta) - rV(\theta) + V'(\theta)]e^{-g\theta}d\theta$$

$$= \int_0^\infty [f(\theta) - \hat{f}(\theta)]e^{-g\theta}d\theta \tag{6.14}$$

Here, $\hat{f}(\theta) \equiv -V'(\theta) + rV(\theta)$ and has the interpretation of the stream of benefits which, if it occurred, would make $V'(\cdot)$ (the depreciation schedule actually used by the firm) economic depreciation and $V(\cdot)$ Hotelling valuation.

Integration by parts of the terms in Equation 6.14 involving $V'(\theta)$ and $V^{*'}(\theta)$ gives[8]

$$C(g) = (r - g) \int_0^\infty [V^*(\theta) - V(\theta)]e^{-g\theta}d\theta \qquad (6.15)$$

This immediately yields the following theorem.

Theorem 6.1: In the exponential case profits/sales equals the Lerner measure if $g = r$.

This result parallels that for the relation between the accounting rate of return and the economic rate of return in the exponential growth case (Chapter 4). In both cases when the growth rate is equal to the discount rate, the accounting and economic measures are the same.

In the case of the accounting and economic rates of return, it was possible to proceed further than this to show that the two rates of return must always lie on the same side of the growth rate. Unfortunately, there is no parallel result in the present case, and, indeed, without further assumptions, the behavior of $C(g)$ does not appear to obey any interesting restrictions beyond that of Theorem 6.1.

To see this, observe that Equation 6.14 shows $C(g)$ to be the present value of the difference between two benefit streams, $f(\cdot)$ and $\hat{f}(\cdot)$, discounted at interest rate g. Since that difference can change sign an arbitrary number of times, $C(g)$ can easily have several (indeed an infinite number of) roots, of which r must be one. Further, $C(g)$ will generally not be monotonic in g. So long as $f(\cdot)$ and $\hat{f}(\cdot)$ are unrestricted except by $V(0) = 1 = V^*(0)$ and $V(\infty) = 0 = V^*(\infty)$, this appears to be all that can be said. (These propositions are exemplified below.)

In practice, however, it may be possible to proceed further than this by imposing additional assumptions. Suppose that firms accelerate depreciation *relative to Hotelling depreciation* so as to make the value of their capital stock never greater and sometimes less than would be the case under Hotelling valuation.[9] In such a case a definite result does emerge.

Theorem 6.2: Suppose that $V(\theta) \leq V^*(\theta)$ for all $\theta \geq 0$, with the strong inequality holding for some set of values of θ of non-zero measure.[10] Then $C(g)$ has the sign of $(r - g)$, so that profits/sales overstates the Lerner measure if $g < r$ and understates it if $g > r$.

Proof: Under the stated condition, the integral in Equation 6.15 is positive.

Of course, a similar result holds with reversed signs if it is $V^*(\cdot)$ that is accelerated relative to $V(\cdot)$ in the above sense. Further, essentially the same proof leads to the following theorem.

Theorem 6.3: Suppose that Firms 1 and 2 are identical except that Firm 1 uses a depreciation schedule that results in a capital valuation always less than or equal to that of Firm 2 (and less for non-trivial time periods). Then, for identical growth rates, g, the difference between the profits/sales ratio of Firm 1 and that of Firm 2 will have the sign of $(r - g)$.

Note that at low rates of growth (generally the ones of interest) accelerating depreciation does *not* decrease the profits/sales ratio. Of course, this is a result of the steady-state nature of what is going on. Accelerated depreciation means lower depreciation and imputed interest on assets acquired in the past, even though it means higher depreciation on newly acquired assets. A similar result holds for the accounting rate of return (Chapter 4).

The size and behavior of the error: examples

We can also use the exponential case in combination with the Cobb–Douglas, capital-augmenting example to get some rough idea of the size and behavior of the errors that may be involved in the use of the profits–sales ratio. In so doing we must keep in mind that stationarity and exponential growth are unrealistically favorable assumptions for that use.

Consideration of the error formula Equation 6.13 (or Equation 6.11) shows that the crucial thing to do is to tabulate $(B - A)/B$ – which I shall denote as Z – for a series of examples. Each example requires a choice of $f(\cdot)$ subject to the restriction $V^*(0) = 1$ (and $V^*(\infty) = 0$). I do this in various ways described below. Each example is computed for three different types of depreciation schedule: straight-line, the continuous-time equivalent of sum-of-the-years' digits and exponential decay starting at twice the straight-line rate and switching to straight-line when the latter method becomes faster.

The tabulation is done for three values of r : 0.10, 0.15 and 0.20. In choosing such rates, it is important to realize that one must work in terms of nominal rather than real interest rates,[11] and that the rate must include a risk premium so, in practice, different values of r apply to different firms.[12] For each value of r the values of Z are calculated for *nominal* growth rates, g, from 0 to 0.25 in steps of 0.05. The lower values of g are the ones of most interest.

As we should expect from Theorem 6.1, at given low nominal growth rates, Z tends to be lower in absolute value when the nominal discount rate is low than when it is high. This suggests that the problems with profits/sales as an estimate of the Lerner measure are likely to be relatively less severe when real interest rates are low than when they are high. It is not clear that this is a general property, however. In any case, those problems do not generally become absolutely small.

To evaluate the size of the errors, rearrange Equation 6.13 to express the error in terms of the observable L rather than the unobservable L^*. The result is:

$$L - L^* = a(1 - L)\left(\frac{Z}{1 - aZ}\right) \qquad (6.16)$$

Ravenscraft (1983, pp. 30–1) gives a mean value for L from the line-of-business data for 1975 of 0.0648 with a maximum value of 0.5371 and a negative minimum – all values with no subtraction of imputed interest. By comparison, figures based on both line-of-business and *Census of Manufactures* data for 1972 show a mean of 0.2188 with a maximum of 0.4232 and a minimum of 0.0096 – again with no subtraction of imputed interest.[13]

The calculation of an appropriate value for a is a bit trickier, since the traditional Cobb–Douglas estimate of approximately 0.25 for the entire United States is based on value-added rather than total sales data and includes all kinds of capital.[14] If one is willing to assume that the problems discussed in this chapter are small on the average and hence that both depreciation and the value of depreciable capital for all business are roughly right, then one can get an order-of-magnitude estimate by calculating the share of depreciable assets in total sales.

For all non-financial corporate business in 1974, 1975 and 1976, the *Economic Report of the President, 1984* (p. 235) gives 0.112, 0.137 and 0.141, respectively, as the value of 'capital consumption allowances with capital consumption adjustment' per unit of gross domestic output. We can compute the ratio of gross domestic output to sales in manufacturing for the same three years by using figures from the same source (pp. 232, 276) as 0.306, 0.279 and 0.267, respectively. As for imputed interest, the 1977 *Census of Manufactures* (Vol. 1, pp. 1–2, 5–3) shows the ratio of gross book value of beginning-of-year depreciable assets to the value of shipments to be approximately 0.30 during the same period. This suggests a value for a of approximately $(0.036 + 0.3r)$. For $r = 0.10$, this gives $a = 0.066$; for $r = 0.15$, $a = 0.081$; for $r = 0.20$, $a = 0.096$. In what follows I shall take $a = 0.08$.

We can now calculate the factor by which to multiply Z in considering the results below. At $a = 0.08$ and for most of the values of Z in the results, the term $(1 - aZ)$ is sufficiently close to unity that we can ignore it.[15] Doing so, we can apply just the multiplier $a(1 - L)$ to the tabulated results. As this depends on L (a crucial point, as already remarked), no

Table 6.1 Multipliers for Z in error formula.

L	$a(1 - L)$	$a(1 - L)/L$
0	0.080	∞
0.05	0.076	1.52
0.07	0.074	1.06
0.1	0.072	0.72
0.2	0.064	0.32
0.3	0.056	0.18
0.4	0.048	0.12
0.5	0.040	0.08

single value is really appropriate. Table 6.1 gives the values of this expression for the range of values of L reported by Ravenscraft (1983) both in absolute terms and relative to the value of L itself. Because the reported values of L do not include a subtraction of imputed interest, the multipliers given are excessively low. This is especially true when the multiplier is expressed as a fraction of the observed L and L lies near the mean of its distribution.

Given the range of values for Z tabulated below, these multipliers are large enough to make the potential errors in the calculation of the Lerner index very large. This is less likely to be so at the upper end of the distribution of observed values of L than it is for smaller values. At the mean of that distribution according to line-of-business data, the multiplier in ratio terms is about unity and makes the potential errors large enough to be a matter of concern.

Table 6.2 gives the values of Z for a one-hoss-shay case in which $f(\theta)$ is constant for ten years and zero thereafter. Not suprisingly, in view of Theorem 6.2, the values of Z exhibit a simple pattern here; they are positive for low growth rates and negative for high ones and pass through zero, as they must, at $g = r$. As we should also expect, for $g < r$, the use of sum-of-the-years' digits depreciation yields the absolutely highest value of Z, with straight-line depreciation yielding the absolutely lowest values and exponential depreciation values somewhere in between the two.

Unfortunately, the suggestion in these results that straight-line depreciation, which is used by most firms but far less so by large firms (Salamon, 1985, p. 497), leads to relatively small errors is not borne out when we turn to other examples. Table 6.2 happens to be one of the more favorable cases for the use of profits/sales and for straight-line depreciation.

Table 6.3 shows that even what appears to be a relatively minor change in the benefit profile, $f(\cdot)$, can make an enormous difference. That table, like Table 6.2, presents the results for a ten-year one-hoss-

Table 6.2 Values of $Z = (B - A)/B$; ten-year, one-hoss shay.

g	$r = 0.10$			$r = 0.15$			$r = 0.20$		
	Straight-line	Exponential	Sum-of-the-years' digits	Straight-line	Exponential	Sum-of-the-years' digits	Straight-line	Exponential	Sum-of-the-years' digits
0	0.0518	0.1100	0.1572	0.0937	0.1651	0.2231	0.1353	0.2149	0.2794
0.05	0.0256	0.0556	0.0780	0.0614	0.1106	0.1474	0.0995	0.1610	0.2071
0.10				0.0300	0.0551	0.0724	0.0645	0.1064	0.1353
0.15	−0.0244	−0.0555	−0.0752				0.0311	0.0524	0.0658
0.20	−0.0471	−0.1097	−0.1461	−0.0279	−0.0536	−0.0685			
0.25	−0.0679	−0.1615	−0.2116	−0.0535	−0.1046	−0.1320	−0.0285	−0.0498	−0.0498

Table 6.3 Values of $Z = (B - A)/B$; two-year delay followed by ten-year, one-hoss shay.

g	r = 0.10			r = 0.15			r = 0.20		
	Straight-line	Exponential	Sum-of-the-years' digits	Straight-line	Exponential	Sum-of-the-years' digits	Straight-line	Exponential	Sum-of-the-years' digits
0	0.1719	0.2291	0.2754	0.2710	0.3345	0.3861	0.3624	0.4264	0.4784
0.05	0.0929	0.1242	0.1472	0.1939	0.2403	0.2744	0.2902	0.3428	0.3814
0.10				0.1038	0.1291	0.1460	0.2062	0.2444	0.2699
0.15	-0.1078	-0.1448	-0.1672				0.1097	0.1304	0.1429
0.20	-0.2312	-0.3114	-0.3551	-0.1184	-0.1481	-0.1643			
0.25	-0.3712	-0.5008	-0.5647	-0.2520	-0.3161	-0.3476	-0.1235	-0.1477	-0.1596

shay case but with the benefits from the capital good beginning only two years after the expenditure for that good is made. At a growth rate of 5 per cent, this results in roughly tripling the values of Z generated by straight-line depreciation and roughly doubling those generated by exponential and sum-of-the-years'-digits depreciation. The resulting errors can easily be on the order of 30 per cent at the point of means of the observed distribution of L.

The results in Table 6.4 are a bit different. They also correspond to (absolutely) large percentage errors, but they illustrate a different phenomenon. In that table $f(\theta)$ has been chosen to decline exponentially for ten years at a unit rate of decay, in other words, $f(\theta) = Ce^{-\theta}$ for $0 \leqslant 10$, after which $f(\theta)$ becomes zero. The new feature in this table is that the values of Z are negative at low growth rates and positive at high ones – the reverse case of Theorem 6.2.

As one should expect from Theorem 6.3 in these circumstances, it is now the least rapid depreciation method, straight-line, that yields the (absolutely) largest errors at low rates of growth. It is therefore no surprise that shifting the function, $f(\cdot)$, which corresponds to Table 6.4, by delaying its start by two years, reduces rather than increases the absolute values of the errors for low rates of growth. Such a shift moves economic depreciation closer to the three depreciation schedules examined. For some growth rates, this makes the errors for some methods positive and those for other negative. While some of the errors naturally become absolutely small, not all of them do, and one cannot predict the size of the errors (or their sign) without knowing the benefit profile, $f(\cdot)$. These results are given in Table 6.5.

Table 6.5 illustrates still another phenomenon. The results for exponential and sum-of-the-years'-digits depreciation are not monotonic in the growth rate and sometimes change sign at rates of growth other than r. This is so since we have now reached cases in which $[f(\theta) - \hat{f}(\theta)]$ can change sign more than once (cf. Equation 6.14).

Of course, the values of Z given in Table 6.4 are excessively large (absolutely) because the example used to generate them is extreme and involves a very rapid exponential decline in benefits. Suppose, then, that one decreases the exponential decay rate from one to zero, eventually reaching the one-hoss-shay case of Table 6.2. As this happens, the errors at low growth rates will go from being absolutely large and negative to being absolutely large and positive. They will not all pass through zero at the same decay rate, however, and there is no reason at all to assume that the 'realistic' cases are the ones that happen to have small errors.

Indeed, in the present state of our knowledge, we cannot assume that the realistic shapes for $f(\cdot)$ are so simple as those used in the tables.

Table 6.4 Values of $Z = (B - A)/B$; ten-year exponential decline (Ce^{-tl}).

g	r = 0.10			r = 0.15			r = 0.20		
	Straight-line	Exponential	Sum-of-the-years' digits	Straight-line	Exponential	Sum-of-the-years' digits	Straight-line	Exponential	Sum-of-the-years' digits
0	-0.3637	-0.2801	-0.2122	-0.5218	-0.4018	-0.3044	-0.6667	-0.5134	-0.3889
0.05	-0.1579	-0.1223	-0.0956	-0.3021	-0.2339	-0.1829	-0.4343	-0.3363	-0.2629
0.10				-0.1325	-0.1031	-0.0829	-0.2539	-0.1976	-0.1589
0.15	0.1226	0.0959	0.0790				-0.1123	-0.0879	-0.0724
0.20	0.2187	0.1721	0.1449	0.1046	0.0823	0.0693			
0.25	0.2951	0.2334	0.2003	0.1882	0.1488	0.1277	0.0902	0.0713	0.0612

Table 6.5 Values of $Z = (B - A)/B$; two-year delay followed by ten-year exponential decline (Ce^{-tl}).

g	r = 0.10			r = 0.15			r = 0.20		
	Straight-line	Exponential	Sum-of-the-years' digits	Straight-line	Exponential	Sum-of-the-years' digits	Straight-line	Exponential	Sum-of-the-years' digits
0	-0.1909	-0.1088	-0.0421	-0.2240	-0.1174	-0.0307	-0.2290	-0.1057	-0.0055
0.05	-0.0779	-0.0407	-0.0134	-0.1184	-0.0540	-0.0066	-0.1306	-0.0468	-0.0148
0.10				-0.0462	-0.0167	0.0030	-0.0640	-0.0127	0.0214
0.15	0.0511	0.0194	0.0002				-0.0221	0.0017	C.0160
0.20	0.0814	0.0215	-0.0111	0.0259	-0.0000	-0.0141			
0.25	0.0949	0.0094	-0.0328	0.0352	-0.0141	-0.0385	0.0061	0.0153	-0.0259

More complex shapes will generate more complex behavior of the errors, *and there is plainly no way without knowledge of such shapes that one can correct the use of the profits–sales ratio.* Higher growth rates can mean either higher or lower errors, and accelerated depreciation can move L closer to or farther from L^*. Moreover, all of this takes place in the unrealistically favorable case of a stationary environment. Simple use of the profits–sales ratio to make statements about the monopoly power of individual firms is a risky business.

Regression studies and 'random' errors

This does not end the matter, however, for profits/sales is used as a measure of monopoly power in regression studies in which it is the dependent variable. In such studies errors in the dependent variable become part of the error term. This has led some practitioners (e.g. Martin 1983, p. 32) to assume that such errors create no problem because one might just as well assume them uncorrelated with the variables used in the regression.

Such an 'independence assumption' is risky when the errors can be large, and we cannot make it in the present case. Indeed, the error involved in the use of the profits–sales ratio to measure the Lerner index is systematically related to the variables used in regression studies. The first reason for this is that, as shown above, the error formula Equation 6.13 (or Equation 6.11) contains a term in $(1 - L^*)$, so that errors will be absolutely larger for firms with low values of the Lerner measure than for firms with high ones.

There is an obvious way around this problem, however. It is to use $\log(1 - L)$ rather than L itself as the dependent variable. So far as I have been able to discover, this particular form of the dependent variable has never been employed, and, if there were no other problems, it would be worth redoing existing studies in this form.

Unfortunately, there are other problems with the independence assumption that such a choice of dependent variable cannot cure. This is so since the remainder of the error is correlated with the variables used in regression studies. I comment briefly on some of the effects involved.

Capital intensity

As already observed, investigators frequently attempt to account for imputed interest by using the capital–output ratio as a regressor. We saw above, however, that relatively capital-intensive firms will have relatively high (absolute) errors. While we cannot say what sign those errors are likely to have, there is no reason whatever to suppose that they can safely be assumed to be zero.

In fact, there may be some weak evidence here as to the sign of such errors. Liebowitz (1987) points out that the coefficient of the capital/sales variable is often found to be significantly and embarrassingly negative. While there can be other reasons for this, one possibility is that this results from negative values of $(B - A)/B$, as in Table 6.4.[16]

Depreciation methods

It is obvious that the choice of depreciation method influences the errors.[17] Salamon (1985, p. 497) points out that a number of studies have found that large firms tend to use accelerated depreciation methods. This will lead to a bias in the coefficient of a firm size variable and, generally, to biased coefficients of all variables in profits/sales regressions including firm size. On the other hand, Salamon (1985, p. 503) states that 'there is mixed evidence about whether firms in industries of different sales concentration have systematically different accounting methods . . . and there is no evidence to suggest that' the choice of accounting method is systematically related to advertising intensity.

Growth rate

The size of the error is influenced by the growth rate of the firm. Studies that do not include the growth rate as an explanatory variable will have errors correlated with any independent variable correlated with growth rate. Firm size and market share appear candidates here, since they will be influenced by past growth.

Even the inclusion of the growth rate requires the assumption that the environment is stationary in the sense described above. Further, the influence of the growth rate depends on the shape of the benefit profile, so that controlling for differences in growth rates is unlikely to work when dealing with firms in widely different industries.

Risk

The value of r used makes a sizable difference in the errors. Yet r differs among firms because it includes a risk premium. Some variables, such as research and development expenditures, may be related to participation in risky activities; others, such as the Hirschman–Herfindahl index may relate to the risky nature of the industry involved.

Conclusion

The profits–sales ratio is an unreliable estimate of the Lerner index. Simulated examples show that the errors involved in using it may be large in practice, even in the favorable case of a stationary environment and exponential growth. Further, even the direction of error cannot be easily determined, nor is there a simple way to recast profits/sales so as to recover the Lerner index from accounting data.

I believe that the detection of monopoly power requires detailed investigation of the facts of particular industries. This means a careful industry study that considers and analyzes the firms and markets in question by examining such issues as barriers to entry and the ability of competitors to expand. Such analyses are not easy, and because of their generally qualitative nature, they appear less certain than do quantitative studies. That apparent lower certainty is not real, however. The use of simple indexes to measure monopoly power suppresses large amounts of information. It can only be justified if those indexes really measure what they are supposed to do. So far as the use of the profits–sales ratio is concerned, that is not the case.[18]

Notes

1. The same difficulties occur in the use of the accounting rate of return on capital value or on equity to infer monopoly profits, and hence the relations of the profits–sales ratio to the Lerner measure bear considerable resemblance to the relations of the accounting rate of return on capital to the economic rate of return studied in Chapter 4. Those who hope that the use of the profits–sales ratio instead of the accounting rate of return will avoid such problems will be disappointed. See Long and Ravenscraft (1984), Martin (1983, 1984), and, most recently, Domowitz *et al.* (1986, especially p. 3, footnote 6).
2. The problem is not limited to constant returns and the profits–sales ratio. Any attempt to calculate the Lerner measure must involve at least an implicit measurement of marginal cost. Such a measure, if direct, must take capital costs properly into account to produce a valid result (Liebowitz, 1987). For simplicity, I assume constant returns throughout this chapter, as does most of the empirical literature, although that seems a questionable assumption when studying the effect of variables such as market share or concentration that are related to firm size.
3. For simplicity, I assume that the price of a new unit of capital does not change over time, so that there are no gains or losses stemming from

capital price changes.

4. In practice, as Liebowitz (1987) points out, that coefficient is often found to be significantly negative. I shall comment later on one possible reason for such a finding.

5. To make this consistent with net investment by the firm, one must suppose that demand shifts in a very special way and that the firm invests to secure the same marginal revenue in all periods.

6. For simplicity, I assume that the firm uses only one type of capital; generalization is easy.

7. I also assume that $V(\infty) = 0$.

8. I am indebted to Richard Arnott for suggesting this way of proceeding, which simplifies and slightly strengthens an earlier version.

9. Note that this is not equivalent to 'accelerated depreciation' in the ordinary sense. In particular, it need not rule out straight-line depreciation.

10. This proviso essentially rules out the case in which valuations are discontinuous and the valuation used by the firm is below Hotelling valuation only at isolated points.

11. While the profits–sales ratio appears to be free of the effects of inflation, this is not the case. The book value of capital is in terms of original cost, as are depreciation and imputed interest. This means that changes in the price level do matter.

   Working in nominal terms is not in conflict with the assumption made in Note 3 that the price of capital is always unity. In the case of a stationary environment, that assumption is equivalent to the assumption that the marginal revenue product of a dollar's worth of capital is always the same. If output and capital prices rise at the same rate, that will be true. Note, however, that this means that growth rates must also be interpreted in nominal terms, so that a real rate of growth of zero means growth at the inflation rate. This should be borne in mind in considering the tables below.

12. For simplicity, the entire analysis and the examples have been worked out in before-tax terms. It is not hard to show that the same analysis applies if after-tax magnitudes are used, with $f(\cdot)$ interpreted as the *after*-tax benefit stream (Chapter 4).

13. Since 1975 was a year of recession, the values of L for that year may be low in some sense. It is not entirely clear, however, in what sense this is so. Monopoly power does not disappear in recessions. Further, the fact that real firms do not live in stationary environments makes the error in the use of L vary with market conditions and makes *every* year special.

   In any event, Ravenscraft reports the average value of the smaller of unity and the ratio of line-of-business sales in 1975 to sales in 1974 as 0.9166. This suggests at most a 10 per cent upward adjustment in the 1975 figures for L. Similarly, the overall profits and sales figures given in the *Economic Report of the President, 1984* (p. 318) show that the overall profits–sales ratio for 1975 was only about 13 per cent below that for 1974 or 1976. The implied adjustments to the 1975 figures are too small to make any substantial difference to the ensuing discussion.

14. I am indebted to F.M. Scherer for calling this to my attention and to Zvi Griliches for discussion of the issues involved.

15. At an absolute value of Z of 0.5, taking account of that term would increase the multiplier being calculated by about 8 per cent if Z is positive and would decrease it by about the same amount if Z is negative.

16. It could also result from a negative correlation between Z and capital intensity that stemmed from a systematic relation between capital intensity and the shape of $f(\cdot)$.

17. Because the influence of the depreciation method used depends in a complex way on the shape of the benefit profile, $f(\cdot)$, using right-hand-side variables to represent the choice of depreciation method selected will not solve this problem.

18. Several recent articles have used Tobin's q as the dependent variable in regressions intended to test hypotheses about monopoly power (Lindenberg and Ross, 1981; Salinger, 1984; Smirlock *et al.*, 1984). Such a use has much to recommend it, but it is not generally free of the problems discussed in this chapter. For firms that do not face a complete set of perfect second-hand capital markets and therefore do not use Hotelling valuation, the denominator of q must be estimated rather than observed. Even where all capital is tangible – and intangible capital presents a serious problem here – such estimation typically uses new capital goods prices and a depreciation schedule that differs from economic depreciation.

References

Demsetz, H. 'Industry structure, market rivalry and public policy'. *Journal of Law and Economics*, Vol. 16 (1973), pp. 1–10.

Domowitz, I., Hubbard, R.G. and Petersen, B.C. 'Business cycles and the relationship between concentration and price–cost margins'. *RAND Journal of Economics*, Vol. 17 (1986), pp. 1–17.

Fisher, F.M. 'The existence of aggregate production functions'. *Econometrica*, Vol. 37 (1969), pp. 553–77.

Hall, R.E. and Jorgenson, D.W. 'Tax policy and investment behavior'. *American Economic Review*, Vol. 57 (1967), pp. 391–414.

Hotelling, H. 'A general mathematical theory of depreciation'. *Journal of the American Statistical Association*. Vol. 20 (1925), pp. 340–53.

Liebowitz, S.J. 'The measurement and mismeasurement of monopoly power'. *International Review of Law and Economics*. Vol. 7 (1987), pp. 89–99.

Lindenberg, E. and Ross, S. 'Tobin's q-ratio and industrial organization'. *Journal of Business*, Vol. 54 (1981), pp. 1–32.

Long, W.F. and Ravenscraft, D.J. 'The misuse of accounting rates of return: comment'. *American Economic Review*, Vol. 74 (1984), pp. 494–500.

Long, W.F., Lean, D.F., Ravenscraft, D.J. and Wagner, C.L., III. *Benefits and Costs of the Federal Trade Commission's Line-of-Business Program, Vol. 1: Staff Analysis.* Washington, DC: Federal Trade Commission, Bureau of Economics, September 1982.

Martin, S. *Market, Firm and Economic Performance.* New York: Salomon Brothers Center for the Study of Financial Institutions, Graduate School of Business Administration, New York University, 1983.

Martin, S., 'The misuse of accounting rates of return: comment'. *American Economic Review*, Vol. 74 (1984), pp. 501–6.

Ravenscraft, D.J. 'Structure–profit relationships at the line-of-business and industry level'. *Review of Economics and Statistics*, Vol. 65 (1983), pp. 22–31.

Salamon, G.L. 'Accounting rates of return'. *American Economic Review*, Vol. 75 (1985), pp. 495–504.

Salinger, M.A. 'Tobin's q, unionization and the concentration–profits relationship'. *RAND Journal of Economics*, Vol. 15 (1984), pp. 159–70.

Scherer, F.M. 'Review of F.M. Fisher, J.J. McGowan and J.E. Greenwood, *Folded, Spindled and Mutilated: Economic Analysis and US v. IBM.*' *Journal of Economic Literature*. Vol. 22 (1984), pp. 620–1.

Smirlock, M., Gilligan, T. and Marshall, W. 'Tobin's q and the structure-performance relationship'. *American Economic Review*. Vol. 74 (1984), pp. 1051–60.

Weiss, L.W. 'The concentration-profits relationship and antitrust' in H.J. Goldschmid *et al.*, eds., *Industrial Concentration: The New Learning*, Boston: Little, Brown, 1974.

7

On predation and victimless crime (1987)

The question of how one should test for predation has long been a lively subject for debate among antitrust lawyers and economists. That debate was given greatly renewed life by the publication of Areeda and Turner's seminal article in 1975[1] and has continued vigorously ever since.[2] It has largely concerned questions of what cost tests should be used to detect deliberate below-cost pricing. While such discussions are important, they are not the whole story, however. By concentrating on what predation is all about, one can sometimes avoid the necessity of making close decisions or elaborate analyses of data.

On any sensible definition, predation involves the sacrifice of short-run profit for long-run monopoly gain. This leads naturally to a two-pronged test.

First, a predatory act is one that departs from what one expects to see under competition. It necessarily involves doing something that is not profit-maximizing if one does not take into account the supracompetitive profits to be earned because of the elimination or reduction of competition. An act that stands on its own bottom as profit-maximizing without such supracompetitive profits is an act that one expects to see competing firms engage in.

How does the Areeda–Turner approach fit in with this prong of the test? Areeda and Turner consider the simplest possible (although still quite complex) case of a single-product firm. Ideally, they would prohibit selling below marginal cost. Such sales are plainly not profit-maximizing on their own; they cost more than they take in. Areeda and Turner,

This chapter is based on remarks given at the antitrust meeting organized by the MIT Conference Board, March 6, 1986.

correctly realizing that direct estimation of marginal cost is usually impractical, suggest using average variable cost as a substitute measure. Some debate has centered around whether the measure should be average variable cost – which makes sense if the original standard was short-run marginal cost – or average total cost – which may correspond more closely to a standard of long-run marginal cost.[3] But however such issues are decided, the ultimate question for this prong of the test should not be in doubt. Is the action involved profit-maximizing on its own or does it require the profits consequent on its destruction of competition to make it worthwhile?

There is, however, a second prong to the test for predation. In order to be predatory, a suspect action must plausibly be supposed to have an anticompetitive result. There has to be a victim if the act is to be considered a smoking gun. Simply finding, with the benefit of hindsight, that a firm took an action that was not profit-maximizing may mean that one has not understood all aspects of profit maximization or it may simply mean that the firm made a mistake. A predatory act is one that is not profit-maximizing *without* the supracompetitive profits to be made after competition is damaged; it is one that is profit-maximizing *with* those profits. It is not an antitrust offense to lose money.

I emphasize the two-pronged nature of the test because it is all too easy to forget what we are testing for in considering the first prong – departure from profit maximization. While courts have often remembered that apparent predation cannot be real unless there are barriers to entry, most of the attention has focused on how one tells whether an action is below cost. Here, as in other areas of antitrust, the search for a 'bright line' standard has sometimes tended to obscure the purpose for which the standard is sought. What is more, consideration of the second prong of the test – and hence the purpose for which the test is to be used – can illuminate the controversies surrounding the first prong.

The best-known allegation of predation in the *IBM* case[4] involved IBM's production and pricing of the 360/90 series in the early 1960s.[5] The 360/90 was in its day a supercomputer and intended by IBM as its entry in a part of the market then being entered and swept by Control Data Corporation (CDC) with its 6600 machine. Even after the dismissal of the government case as 'without merit', the 360/90 story continues to be viewed with suspicion. It was the one incident that Assistant Attorney General William Baxter thought 'a reasonably credible predatory pricing episode', calling it 'the best plausible episode by a very considerable margin'.[6] Russell W. Pittman of the Antitrust Division staff has published a detailed analysis concerning it.[7]

For present purposes, the principal allegation of predation can be summarized as follows.[8] At different times before the announcement of the 360/90 there were different forecasts within IBM as to how many machines would be placed. A few months before announcement, one forecast estimated the number of placements at 15; just before announcement another forecast estimated it at 24. (In the event, only 17 machines were placed, and only 13 were placed outside of IBM.) The Antitrust Division claimed that the placement of 15 machines would have made the program unprofitable, and that the later, larger forecast was not a real one, being cooked up to avoid antitrust liability.

For the present, assume that claim to be true. Then the release of the 360/90 was certainly below cost. Was it therefore predatory? It helps to look at the second prong of the test.

At the very least, there is something odd going on here. We have a situation in which the predatory product would be profitable at a small but relatively high volume of production and unprofitable at a still smaller and relatively low one. On the logic of the Division's position, it would have been even more predatory had IBM not truly expected to place *any* 360/90s *and thus swept CDC before it.* This is not the way in which predatory pricing works. Such pricing involves losing *more* money the more is sold so that the extra sales will drive out competition. Here it is contended that greater sales would *not* have been predatory even though greater sales by IBM would presumably have been worse for CDC – the supposed victim. One need look no further to conclude that the 360/90 was not predatorily priced.

This is not the end of the matter, however. Let us examine the allegation again in Areeda–Turner-like terms. Since greater output would have been more profitable than less, it must be the case that the 360/90 was priced above marginal cost. But we are assuming, *arguendo*, that an output of 15 was expected and would have been unprofitable. Then the price must have been below average *total* cost at that output. Whether the price was below average *variable* cost, we cannot tell directly; the principal purpose of the average variable cost test, however, is to allow average variable cost to serve as a surrogate for the usually hard-to-measure marginal cost. In this case, either the surrogate is a poor one or the price was above average variable cost.

The difference between average variable cost and average total cost has to do with the difference between the short and long runs, since in the long run all costs are variable. Hence we might suppose that a price between average variable and average total cost must be below long-run marginal cost even though it can be above short-run marginal cost. This is not always the case, however. Indeed, in the present instance, it cannot be true if the cost estimates are relevant to the analysis of predation.

There are two possibilities. Either the estimate that a placement of 15 would be unprofitable included costs already expended and sunk by the time the estimate was made or it did not. If the estimate of unprofitability did include sunk costs, then it was totally irrelevant to the announcement decision and contains no information as to whether that decision was predatory.

Suppose, on the contrary, that such sunk costs were not included. From the point of view of the announcement decision, the costs involved were surely long-run. No output had yet been produced and what was being costed was the entire program. Since we know the price to have been above marginal cost and below average total cost, the two cannot have coincided.

This is not a surprise. The difference between total and variable costs consists of fixed costs. If these are large, then average total costs will fall substantially as output increases, implying marginal costs below average total costs. Where, as here, there are sizable costs still to come associated with research and development, no vague appeal to constant returns to scale can sweep this under the rug.

But this brings us to the really sensible question. Plainly it would not have been predatory to produce a greater number of 360/90s. Was it predatory to announce and produce the 360/90 *at all*? The revenues involved in going from an output of 15 to one of 24 may have exceeded the costs, but this does not mean that it was profitable to go from an output of zero to one of 15. While the 360/90 cannot have been predatorily priced, the facts so far do not prevent the inference that it was predatorily produced.

Here again it pays to look at the second prong of the test – the effect on competition – rather than simply stopping with the supposed showing that the program was unprofitable. Within IBM it was forecast that the potential placement of all machines of such size in the United States was about 70. Since that forecast is not suspect, it is simply not possible that IBM – especially if it really believed it would place only 15 machines – expected the 360/90 to drive CDC, the principal producer of large computers, from the marketplace.

Further, such expectations would have been wildly incorrect. CDC placed 94 of their Model 6600/6700 (as opposed to IBM's placement of 17 Model 360/90s). They achieved their goals for the 6600 in both gross revenues and profits. By CDC management's own account, the 6600 was 'particularly' successful, and CDC was able to 'dominate' the field in large computers from 1964 to 1969 (by which time, of course, the litigation had begun and public statements became more circumspect).

If this is so, however, why did IBM deliberately introduce an unprofitable machine? The simple answer is that they didn't – even continuing to make the very dubious assumption that the pre-announcement forecast of 24 was spurious and ignoring the possibility that the cost estimates may have included costs already sunk by the time of the announcement decision. The accounting system that forecast the program to be unprofitable with 15 placements quite naturally took no account of two things. First, IBM reasonably expected to and did in fact receive unquantifiable benefits from undertaking the program in the form of technological fallout useful across the product line as well as public relations benefits from being at the leading edge of the field. Second, some of the costs of the program would have been incurred anyway as IBM went on to develop later computers. They were therefore not fully attributable to the 360/90 program, as was realized by IBM management at the time. Careful and very detailed analysis of cost attribution shows that the program was expected to be profitable even without regard for the unquantifiable benefits it was correctly expected to bring.

Such careful analysis is (and was) laborious and time-consuming, however. The argument over the 360/90 in the *IBM* case stands as a classic example of the reasons for Areeda and Turner's view that a rule based on long-run analyses – particularly analyses of investment decisions – would generally be unworkable and would prompt potential abuse in the form of 'the threat of baseless but costly litigation'.[9] That is true so long as one restricts attention only to the first prong of the test – the job of deciding whether long-run decisions were deliberately unprofitable. As the 360/90 story illustrates, that job need not have been done. Had the Antitrust Division not been so obsessed with the attempt to satisfy a supposedly objective standard and considered sensibly the ultimate purpose of the analysis, there would have been no need to go further.[10]

That lesson, of course, is not restricted to the *IBM* case. Wherever predatory actions are alleged, it pays to analyze how the type of predation alleged could have been successful. If one looks first to see how the actions involved could plausibly have had a victim and led to monopoly profits, one can inform or even eliminate the lengthy and detailed analysis of costs and prices that will otherwise be involved.

Notes

1. P. Areeda and D. Turner, 'Predatory pricing and related practices under Section 2 of the Sherman Act', **88** *Harvard Law Review* 697 (1975).
2. For an excellent review of the literature and cases, see J.D. Hurwitz and W.E. Kovacic, 'Judicial analysis of predation: The emerging trends', **35** *Vanderbilt Law Review* 63 (1982).
3. See P. Areeda and D. Turner (1975) at 75–82.
4. *United States* v. *International Business Machines Corp.*, Docket No. 69

Civ. (DNE) (SDNY dismissed 1982). I served as IBM's principal economist witness.

5. The series included the produced machines, the 360/91 and the 360/95 (which superseded the planned 360/92 before production). For simplicity, I refer to all of these computers as the '360/90', the differences among them being immaterial to the present discussion.

6. Department of Justice Press Conference, January 8, 1982, Transcript at 19–20.

7. R.W. Pittman, 'Predatory Investment: *US* v. *IBM*', 2 *International Journal of Industrial Organization*, 341 (1984).

8. For detailed discussion, see Pittman (1984), or F.M. Fisher, J.J. McGowan and J.E. Greenwood, *Folded, Spindled and Mutilated: Economic Analysis and US v. IBM* 277–82 (Cambridge Mass.: MIT Press, 1983). Detailed references to the trial transcript are given therein and will be omitted here.

9. Areeda and Turner (1975), at 719–20.

10. This seems an appropriate place to dispel one of the persistent myths about the *IBM* case, the supposed fact that IBM paid CDC $100 million as part of the settlement of CDC's private antitrust case. In fact, the settlement included the transfer to CDC of IBM's Service Bureau Corporation. The supposed $100 million payment was the transfer of the vested pension fund assets of the Service Bureau Corporation, a transfer accompanied by an equal transfer of liabilities. Had we known that we would be taken to task for neglecting to mention this supposed payment as evidence that there must have been something in the 360/90 story, my coauthors and I would have discussed it in our book on the case. See especially H.S. Houthakker, 'Review of Fisher, McGowan and Greenwood', **93** *Journal of Political Economy* 618, 620 n.5 (1985). See also R.J. Dennis, 'Review of Fisher, McGowan and Greenwood', **70** *Cornell Law Review* 580, 591 (1985).

8

Matsushita: Myth v. analysis in the economics of predation (1988)

Matsushita

The following chapter was part of a discussion of the *Matsushita* case (*Matsushita Elec. Indus. Co. v. Zenith Radio Corp.*, 475 US 574 (1986)). That case involved a suit by US manufacturers of television sets against a large number of Japanese firms. The plaintiffs claimed that the Japanese firms had engaged in a twenty-five-year-long conspiracy to charge predatorily low prices so as to capture the US market. Among the practices complained of were an apparent agreement by the Japanese firms not to go below certain minimum prices and to limit US customers to no more than five companies per Japanese firm. The Supreme Court eventually affirmed the District Court's grant of summary judgment for the defendants creating an important precedent when they did so. They observed, in effect, that summary judgment can be appropriate where the plaintiff's theory makes no sense. The court focused on the length of time involved in the supposed predation period and the fact that US firms still had some 50 per cent of television set sales at the end of so long a period. Kenneth Elzinga wrote a very sensible article discussing these aspects. The following was my shorter comment and companion piece.

Introduction

Antitrust can be a dry subject. The structural analysis that is usually required may be of great importance, but the general public and even the legal profession fail to find it as stirring as economists think they should. The thrill of calculating a Herfindahl–Hirschman index or even of correctly measuring barriers to entry is not known to those with ordinary tastes.

By contrast, the analysis of conduct, of the dirty tricks played by would-be monopolists or conspirators, has a fascination that appeals even to the palate uneducated by exposure to serious economics. Moreover a focus on conduct leads to a search for 'smoking gun' documents – a search that lawyers revel in and that can produce results that juries can understand (or think they do) far better than arguments over market definition and similar subjects. In addition, such a focus fits nicely with the Populist strain of the antitrust tradition, with its mistrust of large and powerful firms as in some way deliberately evil.

Behind all this there is the natural human appreciation for a good story, preferably with heroes and villains. The best such stories are the simplest – morality plays with the forces of good and evil locked in combat (and the jury invited to root for the good guys or, in the context of this discussion, the home team). But perhaps the most apt metaphor of all is that of the fairy tale, with the monopolist as the giant, for example, menacing the tiny competitors. Antitrust stories are surrounded by such myths and legends, popularly believed, but often without much sound basis in fact or economic analysis.

One of the most persistent of antitrust fairy tales is that of predation, with the predator in the role of the wicked witch. Predation can and sometimes does occur, but far less often than is alleged. Further, the economic analysis of predation is considerably more sophisticated than the simple legends.

The *Matsushita* case, in which I had some involvement,[1] was a particularly good example of the fairy tale of predation. The principal myths that usually surround the kernel of possible truth were all present (together with a few more especially designed for the particular case). Further, this tale had the added excitement of potentially allowing a jury to rescue the US victims from a scheming set of foreign villains. Fortunately, the District Court and, later, the majority of the Supreme Court recognized the fairy tale for what it was and refused to allow it to be told to a jury.

As all this suggests, Professor Elzinga and I are in substantial agreement on the analysis of *Matsushita*.[2] My presentation will therefore not differ so much in substance as in detail and occasionally in emphasis. I shall concentrate on listing the myths about predation illustrated by plaintiffs' case.

The myths of predation

Myth Number One: All That Is Required to Prove Predation Is to Show Pricing Below Cost.

This is the most widespread and important myth of all. Predation involves an act that is not profit-maximizing without counting the supranormal profits that follow the destruction of competition. But it is also an act that *is* profitable when those profits are counted. Since (as we all know and as is illustrated below) the question of whether prices are below cost is not a simple one, any test for predation must be in two parts. It is not enough to argue that the act or price involved was not profitable by itself. One must also show that the act or price was reasonably expected to bring the supranormal profits that would make it profitable. If not, then someone – possibly the defendant in its business decisions, but more likely the plaintiff's attorneys and experts in their analysis – has made a mistake.

The latter part of this test alone can often be dispositive. In the first place, predation is not a victimless crime. By its nature, predation must drive out or suppress competition. Where this is not a reasonable outcome, predation cannot be at work.[3] In the *Matsushita* case, the large market shares of the US firms still remaining after decades of supposed predation imply that the Japanese alleged predators must either have had more than the usual dogged determination or been unusually stupid.

Second, one can reasonably ask whether the supranormal profits to be made once predation has destroyed competitors can possibly justify the loss taken during the predation period. In *Matsushita*, the Supreme Court saw very clearly that this justification was most unlikely, and Professor Elzinga has provided a clear and convincing analysis showing that the game could not reasonably have been worth the candle.

One can go somewhat farther in this case, however, because Elzinga's conclusion that the Japanese firms' investment in predation was a definite loser holds for a monopoly predator as well as for the supposed cartel. The fact that the predation alleged in *Matsushita* was supposedly accomplished through a conspiracy further illustrates why it made no sense.

On plaintiffs' theory, each of the Japanese companies absorbed losses for a long period of time. For those losses to have been worthwhile, each company must have firmly believed that it would later be compensated by significant gains. To put it mildly, such assurance of payoffs would not have been easy to arrange even with explicit and constant communication among the companies.

Consider, first, expectations as to the post-predation period when the ill-gotten gains are to be shared. For a company to be convinced that its predatory sacrifices will be duly and proportionally rewarded, it must believe that the cartelized market will be rigorously divided. This is not impossible, but cartels have a way of falling apart, and a cartel would have to be very long-lived to reap the rewards justifying a long predatory period.

Second, each company in a predatory conspiracy has an incentive not to cooperate. If the US firms are to be driven out by taking losses, then it pays to let others take the losses, instead of taking them oneself.

There is, of course, an exception to all this. If taking the losses oneself also brings on the gains, then one will have an incentive to play one's assigned role. This would certainly be the case if brand loyalty persisted beyond the predation period and played an important part in customer decisions. In such a case, a firm that acquired a high market share during the predatory period would be assured of a high share when prices later rose.

Of course, in a situation of persistent brand loyalty, it is even less clear than usual how one is to interpret pricing 'below cost'. If customers who purchase now develop a preference for a particular company's product, then it may very well be profit-maximizing to offer low prices now in order to make profits later; this needs no anticompetitive intent or effect. For example, if quality and dependability are important to customers, then they may pay more for a brand with which they have had good experience or which has developed a wide reputation for quality than for one that is as yet untried. In this situation, the return from the sale of a product is not merely its price, but also the profits that can later be made when the product's reputation has been established. Taking the latter profits into account can make it profit-maximizing to compete by initially selling at a price that is below cost.

Put aside such problems, however, and suppose that below-cost selling is undertaken for predatory reasons and effect, and that brand loyalty ensures that a high market share gained during the predatory era will persist into the recoupment period. Such a story needs no conspiratorial embellishments. If such persistent brand loyalty existed, each separate firm would have an incentive towards predation, and there would be no need to conspire to get others to do so.

If, on the other hand, brand loyalty is of minor importance (as appears to be the case with television sets), then it is hard to see how the conspirators could be kept from cheating and assured of a fair division of the spoils. Moreover, it is also hard to see how supranormal profits could be expected at all in such a case. Without really persistent (and irrational) brand loyalty, there appear to be no barriers to entry into the production and marketing of television sets in the United States, and predatory destruction of domestic competition would not last into the period of supranormal pricing.

There is a bit more to it than this, however. If one shuts one's eyes very tightly and sprinkles a little fairy dust, one can manage to interpret part of plaintiffs' case as plausibly directed at these issues. I refer to the agreement on minimum prices ('check' prices) and to the 'Five Company Rule'.

Nobody likes to lose money unnecessarily, and predators are no exception to this rule. One can imagine a situation in which a particular Japanese company competes for a contract by offering low prices. The customer (a Sears, perhaps) bargains by claiming that it has a lower offer from a different supplier (presumably another Japanese company), but does not reveal that supplier's identity. Since the object of the predatory exercise is to drive out the US firms and not to fight each other, an agreement on minimum prices, set below the costs of the US firms, might permit the Japanese companies to avoid pricing their product lower than necessary.

Similarly, one might imagine that a rule restricting each company to five US customers would have the effect of focusing the predation by making each predator compete for a different set of customers and would ensure that each predator took its share of losses. The problem here is that the 'Five Company Rule' did not work this way in practice. Not only could and did each Japanese company make one of its customers a US subsidiary which could then sell to anyone, but the Rule restricted rather than mandated selling. As Elzinga remarks:

> From an economic perspective, the Five Company Rule runs contrary to the hypothesis of a low price export conspiracy. An organizer of a predatory cartel might have to say, 'you must sell to these five' but not 'you are *limited* to these five' (Elzinga, 1988, at 961; see Note 2).

Putting aside such doubts, there is the obvious question of how minimum prices and restricted customer allocations could have damaged the plaintiffs. Here, I think, the plaintiffs deserve a little more credit than they are usually given. To the extent that such devices were necessary for the operation of the predatory conspiracy, they contributed to the losses suffered by plaintiffs. This, I think, was the soundest of plaintiffs' arguments, or would have been had they articulated it well and consistently. (It did not, of course, sit well with the argument that plaintiffs were also damaged by a conspiracy to *violate* the minimum price agreement.)

In any case, even to reach this part of the plaintiffs' argument requires one to believe several impossible things before breakfast (as the White Queen says to Alice). In particular, one must believe that the predatory conduct complained of would make sense for a single, unified predator, and, as already discussed, it certainly did not. Further, one must suppose a very complex and sophisticated use of the minimum price agreement and the Five Company Rule in an environment with low entry barriers. In fact, the obvious explanation of the minimum-price agreement and the Five Company Rule lies in the desire of the Japanese to avoid unnecessary friction in trade relations with the United States.

Myth Number Two: Deep Pockets, Warchests and the Subsidization of Predation.

This myth is less important than the first, but, in different forms, probably just as widespread. In one form (the 'warchest'), it is the myth that supranormal profits in one market are used to subsidize predatory actions in another, and that this observation itself adds something to the analysis of predation. In *Matsushita*, the subsidizing profits involved were said to have been earned by an alleged high-price conspiracy in Japan. In its more general form (the 'deep pocket'), the myth asserts that the possession of a large source of cash is an important aspect of the predatory enterprise.

Of the two versions, the 'warchest' story is the more colorful and the easier to dispose of. If cash resources are to be devoted to the financing of a predatory campaign, what difference can it make where those resources come from? (I come later to questions of price discrimination and below-cost pricing.) The decision to invest funds in predation would be the same whether the funds had been earned in legitimate activities, laundered by the Mafia or supplied as unrestricted donations by philanthropists.

The 'deep pocket' version, however, has a bit more to it. Predatory campaigns do involve losses, and hence the investment of funds. This requires that the funds be available. If capital markets are imperfect, firms that have internal sources of funds (deep pockets) may be better able to make such investments – or any investments – than firms without such sources.

Note, incidentally, that this argument implies that plaintiffs did have an interest in proving a conspiracy in the Japanese home market. If the only source of funds for investment in predation came from that conspiracy, then predation abroad required conspiracy at home. This might have made plaintiffs' evidence on the home-market conspiracy more than a prejudicial irrelevance.

The problem, of course, is that it is hard to believe that such funds could not have been found elsewhere. If investment in predation was really profitable, surely large companies would find the funds for it from other sources. While it is indeed implausible that lenders would have provided funds for so risky a venture as the alleged predatory conspiracy in *Matsushita*, this is not because of any imperfections in the capital market. Rather, it is because the investment required was plainly going to be unprofitable.

To put it another way, not only is it hard to see why outside lenders would put up the money for such an adventure, it is hard to see why anyone would. As Elzinga states:

> If enormous profits were, in fact, being made in the Japanese home market, this might have afforded the Japanese sellers the ability to finance a costly predatory campaign in the United States. It does not provide the motive (Elzinga, 1988, at 963–4; see Note 2).

Myth Number Three: Charging Different Prices in Different Markets Implies Below-Cost Pricing in the Low-Price Market.

This myth is closely related to the charge of dumping which was also an issue in the *Matsushita* case.

In *Matsushita*, the analytic core of the plaintiffs' claim on this point was as follows. The Japanese companies were alleged to charge higher prices in Japan than in the United States. Because a television set sold in the United States could have been sold in Japan for a higher price, selling it in the United States was thus a below-cost sale, taking opportunity costs into account.

I put aside the factual question of whether prices for comparable items were in fact higher in Japan than in the United States (defendants claimed they were not), and consider the analytic issues involved. Here, one must consider different assumptions about market structures, and I shall begin by taking the extreme form of the plaintiffs' claims about the Japanese home market.

Suppose then, for the moment, that a single firm had monopolized the Japanese home market and was shipping products into the United States at a lower price than the monopoly price in Japan. Does a proper treatment of opportunity costs imply that the United States price is below cost because a television set sold in the United States could have been sold at a higher price in Japan?

The answer to this question is in the negative. The return that such a monopolist gives up if it sells a television set in the United States rather than in Japan is not the price in Japan but the marginal revenue there. A profit-maximizing monopolist producing for two markets from a common set of plants will operate so as to equalize marginal revenue in the two markets. If one market is competitive and the other monopolized, it will operate so as to make price in the competitive market equal to marginal revenue in the monopolized one. Since marginal revenue is below price in the monopolized market, a lower price in the

United States than in Japan is perfectly consistent with profit-maximization, and thus does not imply below-cost pricing in the United States.

A similar analysis applies when an oligopoly rather than a monopoly is involved. If, as plaintiffs alleged, the Japanese market was cartelized and supranormal profits were earned, then those profits were earned through a restriction of output. As with the monopolist, the opportunity cost incurred by selling output in the United States rather than in Japan was not the price in Japan but the full effects of expanding output in Japan on the cartel's supranormal profits there. These effects made the marginal return from the sale of more output in Japan less than the Japanese sales price.[4]

Finally, suppose that the Japanese market were competitive. Here the story is a bit more complex, but not more favorable to plaintiffs (whose case as presented, of course, involved a heavy claim that the Japanese market was cartelized). In the first place, if the two markets were really separate, then there would be no reason to expect the two competitive prices to be the same.

This does not end the matter, however, because the two markets were not separate; the same facilities were used to produce television sets for both. In this circumstance, the competitive equilibrium of price equal to marginal cost should have produced the same price in each market, since marginal costs were (*arguendo*) the same.

The problem here is that one cannot conclude from this argument and the (alleged) fact of lower prices in the United States than in Japan that below-cost selling was taking place in the US market. All that one can say is that it cannot be true that both markets were in competitive equilibrium. Since the appealing hypothesis (and the one urged by the plaintiffs) is the usual inference that the high-price market (Japan) was not competitive, it is hard to make much of this argument in a US antitrust action about predatory prices.

Moral

Below-cost pricing is an oft-repeated fear. Especially when foreign competition is involved, competitors are likely to complain when market prices are below their own costs, or even if prices are below what they would like them to be. While the story of predation is analytically sound, in the sense that it provides a consistent theory in which below-cost pricing takes place, the special nature of the story makes its applicability narrower than legend would suggest. Many economists find the predatory story hard (although not impossible) to believe. Fortunately, in *Matsushita*, where the story was truly incredible, the Supreme Court also refused to believe it.

Notes

1. *Matsushita Elec. Indus. Co.* v. *Zenith Radio Corp.*, 475 US 574 (1986). The original case was *Zenith Radio Corp.* v. *Matsushita Electric Industrial Co.*, 513 F. Supp. 1100 (ED Pa. 1981) in which the District Court decided for the defendants on a motion for summary judgment. That decision was reversed by the Court of Appeals for the Third Circuit in *Re Japanese Electronic Products Antitrust Litigation*, 723 F.2d 238 (3d Cir. 1983), and the Third Circuit was in turn reversed by the Supreme Court. After the decision by the Third Circuit, I was retained by counsel for defendants as a consultant and a potential expert witness should the case be retried.
2. Elzinga 'The new international economics applied: Japanese televisions and US consumers', **64** *Chi.-Kent L. Rev.* 941 (1988).
3. On this point, see Chapter 7.
4. Plaintiffs suggested that the restriction of output required for the high-price conspiracy in Japan left the Japanese companies with excess capacity, which in turn enabled them to sell at a low price in the United States. Assuming this was true, it is hard to see what it has to do with predation. Such an argument simply suggests that the marginal costs of producing goods for the US market were sufficiently low as to make low prices profitable. While it may be true that the US prices in such a case would be below the average variable cost of all output (domestic and export) taken together, they would not be below the average variable cost of the output at issue – the output produced for export. To make such an argument is to misunderstand the point of the Areeda-Turner average variable cost criterion. (Areeda and Turner 'Predatory pricing and related practices under Section 2 of the Sherman Act', **88** *Harvard L. Rev.* 697 (1975)).

9
Can exclusive franchises be bad? (1985)

The problem

Suppose the manufacturer of a certain product contracts with a dealer to distribute that product; the dealer is given an exclusive franchise making him the only distributor in a given area. Does this constitute a restraint of trade, and if so, is it a harmful one?

The answer depends in the first instance on the competitive position of the manufacturer. Where there is substantial competition for the manufacturer's product ('interbrand competition'), the manufacturer, even if fully integrated, has no market power and can confer none on the dealer. In this type of situation an exclusive franchise may be granted for efficiency or marketing-incentive reasons (for example, to avoid the free-rider problem), but it can have no anticompetitive implications.[1]

The situation in which interbrand competition is either weak or absent is more complex. In that case, an antitrust interest in limiting exclusive distribution arrangements may appear warranted on the basis of the following argument: An exclusive franchise eliminates rivalry among distributors in the sale of the manufacturer's product (intrabrand competition). As with all reductions in competition, this is contrary to the public interest. Although it may be true that the manufacturer could legally achieve the same reduction in competition by

I am indebted to R.L. Bishop, P.A. Diamond, J. Farrell, G. Hay, E. Rasmusen, L. Solomon and L. White for helpful comments but retain responsibility for error.

integrating forward and also acting as an exclusive distributor, there is no reason for making it easy to reduce competition in distribution by allowing market power to be passed on to an independent distributor. Indeed, such an arrangement risks permitting the franchisees to exercise some market power of their own. It may permit restriction on the sales of the manufacturer's goods in attempts to reap monopoly profits in reselling the goods; such a restriction is both inefficient and harmful to consumers.

This argument is inadequate, however, for the matter is deeper than it might appear. Where a monopoly franchisee restricts output, the ultimate customers will not be the only ones affected, for the profits of the manufacturer will also be reduced. Because the manufacturer will realize this before granting the franchise, an exclusive franchise will be given only if such an output restriction by the franchisee is in the manufacturer's interest or if the negative effect on profits is overcome by such efficiencies as may be involved in such a setup. If there is reason to believe that the manufacturer has the same interests as does society in avoiding output restriction by the franchisee, there will be no occasion for antitrust action as the fact that the manufacturer chooses to set up an exclusive franchisee shows that reasons of efficiency must outweigh any anticompetitive effects resulting from the arrangement.

Is there, then, a reason for believing that the interests of the monopoly manufacturer in avoiding output restriction by franchisees coincides with those of society? The growing literature on the subject claims that there is and thus that it should be presumed that any such arrangement is in the interests of society if it is freely entered into by the manufacturer.[2] The reason given is that output restriction by the dealer shifts the manufacturer's derived demand curve inward; thus, at any given price charged the dealers, the manufacturer's output will be greater if the dealers compete to resell the product than if a monopoly dealer deliberately restricts output. Because this situation cannot be in the manufacturer's interest, efficiency rather than avoidance of competition must account for the granting of such a franchise.

Although this reasoning is undoubtedly correct as far as it goes, it does not go far enough, for it fails to take into account the possibility that the manufacturer's profits may not consist only of the profits to be made by selling to dealers. If the manufacturer sets up a monopoly dealer who then earns monopoly profits, the manufacturer may be able to extract some or all of those monopoly profits from the dealer as a franchise fee. This raises the possibility that the manufacturer may be better off with a monopoly, output-restricting franchisee than with competitive dealers, even though society is worse off. The remainder of this chapter is devoted to an examination of this possibility.[3]

In that examination it is important to bear in mind that we are always operating under the assumption that the manufacturer is a monopolist. This means that the first-best case of full competition at all levels is not attainable, so that we are comparing second- and third-best situations.

Costs and supply curves

In order to study the issue in its purest form, I consider a situation in which the costs of distribution do not depend on the way the manufacturer organizes the distribution function; thus, efficiency considerations do not arise. I assume, therefore, that the costs of selling and distributing any given output are the same whether selling and distributing are done by a single monopoly dealer, by a group of competitive dealers, or by the manufacturer integrating forward. Particularly because it turns out that the question of the existence and nature of decreasing returns in distribution plays a crucial role, this assumption requires discussion.

In the long run, a competitive industry exhibits some attributes of constant returns to scale. This can occur if each enterprise, in fact, operates under conditions of constant returns; more generally, though, it occurs because, in long-run equilibrium, each firm operates at the minimum point on its average-cost curve. Provided the minimum cost output is small enough, the latter situation resembles constant returns if the cost curves are all the same, and this is ensured by definition: differences among firms are defined as rents rather than costs.

Despite the appearance of constant returns at the industry level, however, and despite the fact that competitive supply curves coincide with marginal-cost curves, the long-run supply curves of competitive industries generally are not flat. This is so for more than one reason.

First, the definition that treats interfirm differences as rents rather than costs is merely a definition. However such differences are treated, they may be real ones. In that case, at low prices, only the most efficient or most favorably situated firms will enter the industry. Unless there are constant returns at the firm level, only a limited output will be produced by such firms. As price rises, additional firms (the less efficient or less favorably situated ones) will be attracted; thus higher prices are required to call forth greater output.

Second, even though firms are all the same, the costs of different units of output may differ. In distribution, for example, it may be easy to find or attract some customers but progressively more difficult to find or attract others. This may be related to the first phenomenon – for example, if stores in population centers naturally have lower selling costs than stores in outlying areas – but it need not be.

Third, negative externalities may be involved. In the case of distribution, for example, sending out many salespeople may create a situation in which the salespeople interfere with each other. The necessity of providing enough taxis to keep rider waiting time to some minimum may mean that the waiting time of taxis between customers rises when there are more customers to be served. Such cases lead to rising industry costs.

The final case also involves an externality, although here the phenomenon involved is an externality only to the industry involved, not to the production system as a whole. As price rises and output expands – either through expansion of existing firms or through new entry – the demand for the inputs necessary to produce the expanded output will tend to bid up the prices of those inputs. The firms in the industry will experience this as an upward shift in costs; it is an important part of the process that leads average costs in competition to equal price. From the viewpoint of the economy as a whole, however, such factor-price increases simply produce a rising supply curve for the product in question.

In each of these four somewhat related cases, then, it is possible to have costs the same for a monopolist as for a competitive industry. If this occurs with rising marginal costs, increasing output creates inframarginal rents; that is, it costs less to produce earlier units of output. In the first three cases listed above, such rents under competition will accrue to the competitive firms; in the last case (that of rising factor prices), they will accrue to the factors of production.

By setting up an exclusive franchise rather than competitive dealers, the monopoly manufacturer creates a situation in which such rents can be captured by the exclusive franchisee in the first three cases and siphoned off by the manufacturer through a franchise fee. If this siphoning cannot occur with competitive dealers, the acquisition of such rents may provide a reason for divergence between the interests of the manufacturer and those of society.

In the first case listed above (real differences among firms), the manufacturer may be able to extract the rents in question from competitive dealers by discriminating in the price charged different dealers for the product or, more simply, by charging different dealers different franchise fees. To do this, of course, the manufacturer must know how much rent will be earned by each dealer, but that involves precisely the same knowledge that would be needed to arrive at the optimal franchise fee to charge a monopoly dealer: rents earned by each dealing enterprise whether or not they are separately owned and operated.

Further, the manufacturer may be able to set the fees optimally by auctioning off the franchises. Thus, unless there is some reason why different franchise fees cannot be charged to differently situated dealers, this case is not one in which the manufacturer's interests differ from those of society and will not be discussed further.

I shall also not consider at length the fourth case listed above, rising input prices. In that case, rents accrue initially to the factors of production; they can be captured by the manufacturer only if the exclusive franchisee can exercise monopsony power over one or more *input* markets. An exclusive franchise that gives rise to the creation of such monopsony power might well be contrary to antitrust policy; but, whereas it is important to note the possibility, it is not directly related to the problem under discussion, which involves monopoly in the *output* market. This possibility does, however, provide an example in addition to that below of a case in which the manufacturer's interests in deciding on franchising arrangements do not coincide with those of society.

The two remaining cases (different costs for different units of output, and negative externalities in distribution) are the ones of substantial interest for the remainder of this chapter. In those cases, the rents accrue initially to the dealers rather than the factors of production. Moreover, although the manufacturer may be able to siphon off rents earned by a monopoly dealer, generally this will not be accomplished if there are competitive dealers. This is because, in these two cases when there are competitive dealers, while everyone may realize that rents are there to be earned, it will not be known in advance which dealers will earn them (and this may remain true even in later years). Thus, to siphon off the rents, the manufacturer must generally integrate forward or set up a single dealer to act as an identifiable conduit (in the externality case, the externality involved must be internalized).

I now analyze these two cases in detail, although there is no further need to distinguish them. I thus assume that the costs of distribution are the same under any form of market organization and that, whereas the manufacturer can acquire any inframarginal rents in distribution if there is a monopoly dealer, this cannot be so if there are competitive dealers. I shall also assume that there are no fixed costs to distribution; this is sensible, since we are dealing with a long-run decision and, in any case, the assumption makes relatively little difference in what follows. The marginal costs of distribution are assumed to be either constant (constant returns to scale) or rising (decreasing returns to scale). Under competition, the marginal cost curve becomes the supply curve.

The following analysis is largely a mathematical one; the nontechnical reader, however, will find heuristic discussion interspersed with the mathematics.

Model and notation

Let x denote the output sold by the manufacturer to the dealer or dealers and then to the ultimate customers; let p denote the price paid by the customer. Price and quantity are related by the inverse demand curve, $p = D(x)$, which I assume to be three times continuously differentiable. In accordance with the fact that the manufacturer is a monopolist and that there is no interbrand competition, $D'(x) < 0$. Total revenue at retail is denoted by $R(x) \equiv px$.

In the case where there is a monopoly dealer (or the manufacturer is fully integrated forward), the costs of dealing are given by the function $C_2(x)$. Because there are no fixed costs in dealing, $C_2(0) = 0$. It is assumed that $C_2(x)$ is three times continuously differentiable, with $C_2'(x) > 0$ and $C_2''(x) \geq 0$, so the technology of distribution exhibits either constant or decreasing returns to scale. (For convenience, I assume that whichever kind of returns to scale is involved holds everywhere in the relevant range; this makes no essential difference.) Because costs are assumed to be independent of market organization, the marginal cost curve for distribution, $C_2'(x)$, is the industry supply curve when there are competitive dealers.

The manufacturer's own costs of distribution are given by $C_1(x)$, assumed to be twice continuously differentiable. The behavior of its marginal costs is unrestricted, except by Equations 9.2 to 9.4 below.

In addition to the assumptions already made, I assume the following:

$$R''(x) < 0 \qquad (9.1)$$

so that marginal revenue is decreasing in output.

$$R''(x) - C_1''(x) - C_2''(x) < 0 \qquad (9.2)$$

so that, although there can be increasing returns in manufacturing, they are limited so as to ensure strict concavity of overall profits. Further,

$$R''(x) - C_1''(x) - 2C_2''(x) - xC_2'''(x) < 0 \qquad (9.3)$$

which, as we shall see, ensures strict concavity of manufacturing profits when there are competitive dealers. All three assumptions – Equations 9.1 to 9.3 – can be weakened to hold only in the relevant regions, but there seems little point in doing this, as they are not very special.

I also assume that at the point at which the first-order conditions for profit maximization by a manufacturer facing a monopoly dealer are satisfied:

$$2R''(x) - C_1''(x) - 2C_2''(x) + xR'''(x) - xC_2'''(x) < 0 \qquad (9.4)$$

This is the appropriate second-order condition; it need not be assumed to hold elsewhere.

Full integration versus competitive dealers

It will be convenient to compare three situations. In addition to considering the case in which the manufacturer sets up an exclusive franchise and that in which competition is encouraged among dealers, I consider the possibility that the manufacturer integrates forward and takes over the distribution function. In such a fully integrated case, the manufacturer obviously can capture all the profits that exist in the system; that will be the preferred case if there are no other reasons not to integrate. It is helpful to begin by comparing this case to the case in which the manufacturer sells to competitive dealers at a fixed price.

In the fully integrated case, the manufacturer's profits are given by:

$$\pi^1(x) \equiv R(x) - C_1(x) - C_2(x) \qquad (9.5)$$

Denoting the profit-maximizing output by x^*, that output must satisfy:

$$R'(x^*) = C_1'(x^*) + C_2'(x^*) \qquad (9.6)$$

The second-order condition is given by Equation 9.2.

Now suppose instead that there are competitive dealers. Let the price at which the manufacturer sells to the dealers be denoted by p_m. Because the dealers receive $(p - p_m)$ before their own costs, and because their competitive supply curve is given by $C_2'(x)$, the price the manufacturer must offer to get the dealers to sell any given output x must satisfy:

$$p_m = D(x) - C_2'(x) \qquad (9.7)$$

which thus gives the manufacturer's own derived inverse-demand curve.

In this case, the manufacturer's profits are given by:

$$\pi_m^2(x) \equiv p_m x - C_1(x) = R(x) - C_1(x) - xC_2'(x) \qquad (9.8)$$

Let x_c be the profit-maximizing output; the first-order condition for a maximum is:

$$R'(x_c) = C_1'(x_c) + C_2'(x_c) + x_c C_2''(x_c) \qquad (9.9)$$

The second-order condition is given by Equation 9.3.

We can now prove Theorem 9.1.

Theorem 9.1:   (A) If there are constant returns to scale in distribution $[C_2''(x) \equiv 0]$, then the competitive case and the fully integrated case yield the same outputs, the same retail prices and the same profits to the manufacturer.

(B) If, on the other hand, there are decreasing returns to scale in distribution $[C_2''(x) > 0]$, then the competitive case yields *lower* profits to the manufacturer and results in a *lower* output and a *higher* retail price than does the fully integrated case.

Proof: (A) If $C_2''(x) \equiv 0$, then, from Equation 9.9, x_c satisfies Equation 9.6. Since, by Equation 9.2, x^* is unique, $x_c = x^*$, and $D(x_c) = D(x^*)$. Finally, since $C_2(0) = 0$ and $C_2''(x) \equiv 0$, $C_2(x)$ is a ray through the origin, and $x C_2'(x) = C_2(x)$. Comparison of Equations 9.5 and 9.8 now shows $\pi^1(x^*) = \pi_m^2(x_c)$.

(B) In this case, $C_2''(x) > 0$, so that Equation 9.9 implies:

$$R'(x_c) > C_1'(x_c) + C_2'(x_c) \tag{9.10}$$

The concavity of overall profits, Equation 9.2, then shows that $x_c < x^*$, so that $D(x_c) > D(x^*)$. Since $C_2(0) = 0$ and $C_2''(x) > 0$, marginal costs exceed average costs, so that $x_c C_2'(x_c) > C_2(x_c)$. It follows from the fact that x^* is the unique overall profit-maximizing output that:

$$
\begin{aligned}
\pi^1(x^*) > \pi^1(x_c) &= R(x_c) - C_1(x_c) - C_2(x_c) \\
&> R(x_c) - C_1(x_c) - x_c C_2'(x_c) \\
&= \pi_m^2(x_c)
\end{aligned} \tag{9.11}
$$

and the theorem is proved.

Thus, in choosing between the fully integrated and competitive cases, the interests of the monopoly manufacturer coincide with those of society.

It is easy enough to give a heuristic explanation of what is going on.[4] Consider the case in which there are decreasing returns. With competitive dealers, there are inframarginal rents that cannot be captured by the monopoly manufacturer. By fully integrating forward, the manufacturer can own these rents. Thus it is not surprising that profits are greater in the latter case.

To put it another way: with competitive dealers, the manufacturer must allow the dealers a retail margin sufficient to pay them the marginal cost of the last unit of output. This must be done in order to induce the dealers to put forth the necessary effort and resources to distribute that output. Further, that same marginal cost must be paid on each unit of output. Because marginal costs are increasing, a profit (rent) on the inframarginal units is created, since the manufacturer will be paying more than is needed to call forth the necessary effort and resources to get those inframarginal units distributed. By integrating forward, the manufacturer can internalize these profits, in effect, exercising price-discrimination in what is paid for the resources involved in distribution, paying only what is necessary for each unit.

This is closely related to the more surprising result that retail price will be less and output greater under full integration than with competitive dealers. Under full integration the monopolist considering expanding output by one unit must recognize that marginal revenue falls short of price because price on all previous units must be lowered in order to sell the next one. With competitive dealers, the manufacturer must not only take that same phenomenon into account but must also realize that selling the next unit of output will involve raising the amount dealers are paid per unit.[5] In effect, at any output, the marginal revenue corresponding to the manufacturer's derived demand curve falls short of the marginal revenue corresponding to the retail demand curve because of the increasing marginal costs that must be paid to dealers. This naturally leads to a lower output and a higher retail price than result when those increasing marginal costs are internalized.

To put it another way, the monopoly manufacturer with competitive dealers can be thought of as a monopsonist in the purchase of dealer services. This provides a reason for restricting output in addition to that provided by the downward-sloping retail demand curve taken into account in either case. In the fully integrated case, the monopoly manufacturer can be viewed as a perfectly discriminating monopsonist so that there is no further output restriction.

When there are constant returns in distribution, however, all these phenomena disappear. There are no inframarginal rents to be extracted and no increasing marginal costs to be paid. The manufacturer, whether integrated or with competitive dealers, must pay the same constant marginal distribution cost per unit on all units. The manufacturer receives all the profits in either case and has no incentive to prefer one to the other, setting the same output and thus the same retail price in both.

Competitive dealers versus a monopoly dealer

These results, though interesting, do not bear directly on the main question: the manufacturer's choice between competitive dealers and an exclusive franchise monopoly dealer. Because profits are greatest in the fully integrated case, this choice assumes that full integration is not possible for efficiency or other reasons. (For example, the particular product may customarily be carried by supermarkets or mass marketers, and it may not make sense for the manufacturer to engage in such activities directly.)

To begin our examination of this choice, suppose there is a single, monopoly dealer. As in the competitive case, the manufacturer sets a price, p_m, for selling to the dealer. The dealer takes this price as given and maximizes profits:

$$\pi_d^3(x) \equiv R(x) - C_2(x) - xp_m \tag{9.12}$$

In doing so, the dealer will, of course, set the retail price, p, but this is equivalent to choosing an output, x, so we may as well consider that x as chosen directly. This means the dealer chooses x to satisfy:

$$p_m = R'(x) - C_2'(x) \tag{9.13}$$

which is thus the manufacturer's derived inverse-demand curve for this case.

Given Equation 9.13, the manufacturer's profits are given by:

$$\pi_m^3(x) = p_m x - C_1(x) = x[R'(x) - C_2'(x)] - C_1(x) \tag{9.14}$$

The manufacturer chooses p_m to maximize this; that choice is equivalent to a choice of x. Let $\hat{x}$ be the profit-maximizing output. The first-order conditions for a maximum are:

$$R'(\hat{x}) = C_1'(\hat{x}) + C_2'(\hat{x}) + \hat{x}C_2''(\hat{x}) - \hat{x}R''(\hat{x}) \tag{9.15}$$

The second-order conditions are given by Equation 9.4.

The total profits available to the manufacturer in this case, however, are not merely $\pi_m^3(\hat{x})$. By charging the dealer a franchise fee for the privilege of having the monopoly at retail, the manufacturer can extract $\pi_d^3(\hat{x})$ and achieve *total* profits:

$$\pi_T^3(\hat{x}) \equiv \pi_m^3(\hat{x}) + \pi_d^3(\hat{x}) \tag{9.16}$$

We must investigate whether the manufacturer would prefer this to having competitive dealers and achieving $\pi_m^2(x_c)$.[6]

Postponing discussion until after the results, we prove Theorem 9.2.

Theorem 9.2: The competitive case always results in a *greater* output and a *lower* retail price than does the case of a monopoly dealer. However, while profits *at the manufacturing level* are always greater in the competitive than in the monopoly case, *total* profits, including the franchise fee in the monopoly case, can be either greater or less, so that the manufacturer's interests need not coincide with those of society in choosing between the two cases.

Proof: by Equations 9.1 and 9.15, we find:

$$R'(\hat{x}) > C_1'(\hat{x}) + C_2'(\hat{x}) + \hat{x}C_2''(\hat{x}) \tag{9.17}$$

The concavity of profits in the competitive dealer case, (Equation 9.3), now shows that $\hat{x} < x_c$, so that $D(\hat{x}) > D(x_c)$. Since $R'(x) < p = D(x)$, comparison of Equation 9.7 with 9.13 shows that, for any given output, p_m is lower in the monopoly dealer case than in the competitive dealer case. Thus:

$$\pi_m^2(x_c) > \pi_m^2(\hat{x}) > \pi_m^3(\hat{x}) \tag{9.18}$$

where the first inequality follows from the fact that x_c is the unique output at which $\pi_m^2(x)$ is maximized.

It remains to show that $\pi_T^3(\hat{x})$ can be either greater or less than $\pi_m^2(x_c)$. Here, it suffices to provide examples.

(A) To see that $\pi_T^3(\hat{x}) < \pi_m^2(x_c)$ is possible, suppose that there are constant returns in distribution ($C_2''(x) \equiv 0$). By Theorem 9.1, $\pi_m^2(x_c) = \pi^1(x^*)$. But

$$\pi_T^3(\hat{x}) \equiv \pi_m^3(\hat{x}) + \pi_d^3(\hat{x})$$
$$= [R(\hat{x}) - C_2(\hat{x}) - \hat{x}p_m] + [\hat{x}p_m - C_1(\hat{x})] \tag{9.19}$$
$$= R(\hat{x}) - C_1(\hat{x}) - C_2(\hat{x}) \equiv \pi^1(\hat{x})$$

Since $x_c = x^*$ is the unique output which maximizes $\pi^1(x)$, and $\hat{x} \neq x_c$, it follows that $\pi_m^2(x_c) > \pi_T^3(\hat{x})$. Evidently, this will also be true under decreasing returns, provided returns do not decrease too sharply.

(B) To see that $\pi_T^3(\hat{x}) > \pi_m^2(x_c)$ is also possible, suppose that the inverse (retail) demand curve, $D(x)$, is:

$$p = 1 - x \tag{9.20}$$

and that the manufacturer has zero marginal costs and a fixed cost, $F \geq 0$, so that

$$C_1(x) = F \tag{9.21}$$

(By continuity, the results will also hold if marginal costs are positive but low enough.) Finally, suppose that the cost of distribution, $C_2(x)$, is given by:

$$C_2(x) = x^2 \tag{9.22}$$

In the competitive case, the manufacturer chooses x_c to satisfy Equation 9.9, which now becomes

$$1 - 2x_c = 2x_c + 2x_c \tag{9.23}$$

so that $x_c = 1/6$ and $p = 5/6$. From Equation 9.7, $p_m = 1/2$. Profits, $\pi_m^2(x_c)$, are given by Equation 9.8 evaluated at $x = 1/6$, and they are readily seen to be $1/12 - F$. The competitive dealers receive infra-marginal rents amounting to $R(1/6) - C_2(1/6) - (1/6)p_m = 1/36$.

In the monopoly case, on the other hand, the manufacturer chooses $\hat{x}$ to satisfy Equation 9.15, which now becomes:

$$1 - 2\hat{x} = 2\hat{x} + 2\hat{x} - (-2)\hat{x} \tag{9.24}$$

so that $\hat{x} = 1/8$ and $p = 7/8$. From Equation 9.13, $p_m = 1/2$, as before (this is not a general property). Profits at the manufacturing level, $\pi^3_m(\hat{x})$, are given by Equation 9.14 evaluated at $x = 1/8$ and are readily seen to be $1/16 - F$, so that $\pi^3_m(\hat{x}) < \pi^2_m(x_c)$, as must be the case. However, total profits, $\pi^3_T(\hat{x})$, are given by:

$$\begin{aligned}\pi^3_T(\hat{x}) &= R(1/8) - C_1(1/8) - C_2(1/8) \\ &= 3/32 - F > 1/12 - F = \pi^2_m(x_c)\end{aligned} \tag{9.25}$$

Thus the dealer monopoly profits extracted by the manufacturer through a franchise fee are 1/32, enough to make the manufacturer's total profits (including the franchise fee) greater than the profits that would be earned in manufacturing if there were competitive dealers. The theorem is proved.

For the sake of completeness, in the example used in Part (B) of the proof, x^*, the profit-maximizing output in the fully integrated case, satisfies Equation 9.6, which now becomes:

$$1 - 2x^* = 2x^* \tag{9.26}$$

so that $x^* = 1/4$ and $p = 3/4$. Total profits are then given by Equation 9.5 evaluated at $x = 1/4$, and they are readily seen to be $\pi^1(x^*) = 1/8 - F$. The example is summarized in Table 9.1.

Once again it is possible to give a heuristic explanation of the results. The fact that in the competitive case output is greater and retail price lower than in the case of a monopoly dealer reflects the monopoly dealer's motivation to restrict output. Even though the manufacturer takes this motivation into account in setting the price for selling to the dealer, the effect cannot be overcome completely. As compared with the competitive case, the manufacturer who contemplates expanding

Table 9.1 Comparison of profits for full integration against monopoly and competitive dealers.

	Full integration	Competitive dealers	Monopoly dealers
Output (x)	$\frac{1}{4}$	$\frac{1}{6}$	$\frac{1}{8}$
Retail price (p)	$\frac{3}{4}$	$\frac{5}{6}$	$\frac{7}{8}$
Wholesale price (p_m)	—	$\frac{1}{2}$	$\frac{1}{2}$
Manufacturing profits	—	$\frac{1}{12} - F$	$\frac{1}{16} - F$
Dealer profits or rents	—	$\frac{1}{36}$ (rents)	$\frac{1}{32}$
Total profits or rents	$\frac{1}{8} - F$	$\frac{1}{9} - F$ (manufacturing profits plus dealer rents)	$\frac{3}{32} - F$

output must not only take into account the rising (or constant) marginal cost of the dealer, but also the fact that the dealer will regard the payment received for selling the next unit of output as less than the retail margin on that unit by the reduction in revenue that will be incurred on the inframarginal units. This gives the manufacturer an added incentive to reduce output, for marginal revenue from the derived demand curve is lower than in the competitive case.

The reason that manufacturing profits must be lower in the case of a monopoly dealer than in that of competitive dealers is straightforward. Manufacturing profits will be lower because the manufacturer's derived demand curve will be lower at any price set when there is a monopoly dealer than when dealers compete to sell that output. That is the reason the literature gives for believing that the manufacturer will prefer competitive dealers if there are no counterbalancing considerations of efficiency.[7]

The catch, of course, is the behavior of the franchise fee; when this fee is taken into account, the manufacturer may prefer either arrangement. When, for example, there are constant returns to scale in distribution, there are no inframarginal rents to be captured and no dealer will pay a franchise fee. In this circumstance, the fact that manufacturing profits are lower in the case of the monopoly dealer will be controlling (particularly since, by Theorem 9.1, the manufacturer can achieve maximum profits by using competitive dealers). By continuity, the same will be true if returns to scale in distribution do not decrease too sharply, so marginal costs do not rise too quickly. When returns are decreasing and marginal costs are rising fast enough, however, the rents that can be captured through a franchise fee in the monopoly dealer case can be large enough to offset the lower manufacturing profits to be made, compared with the case of competitive dealers.

A monopoly dealer versus full integration: implicit contracts

Before proceeding to the implications of these results for antitrust policy, one other matter must be considered. In the analysis of the monopoly dealer case, I assumed that the manufacturer proceeds as follows. Knowing that dealers will act so as to maximize their own monopoly profits, the manufacturer sets the price at the manufacturing level (p_m) to maximize profits at the manufacturing level, extracting the dealer's profits through the franchise fee. The question arises whether the manufacturer can do better than that – indeed, whether the maximum profits of full integration can be achieved – by setting the manufacturing price, p_m, taking into account its effects not only on manufacturing profits but also on the size of the franchise fee the dealer will be willing to pay, thus maximizing total rather than simply manufacturing profits. If so, then, under decreasing returns in distribution, a monopoly dealer will always be preferred to competitive dealers by the manufacturer. Further, such a preference will be in society's interest, since achievement of the same profits that accrue under vertical integration necessarily requires the same output and retail price; as we have seen, these are better for consumers than the output and retail price that occur in the case of competitive dealers.

Ignoring for a moment the question of whether such actions are feasible, the simplest way for the manufacturer to set manufacturing price and franchise fee to obtain the maximum total profits would be to set the manufacturing price competitively, that is, at the marginal cost of manufacturing. This would enable the monopoly dealer to earn all possible monopoly profits, and the manufacturer could then extract the profits as a franchise fee.

Formally, suppose the manufacturer sets $p_m = C_1'(x^*)$. The monopoly dealer then chooses x according to Equation 9.13, so that x satisfies:

$$R'(x) - C_2'(x) = C_1'(x^*) \tag{9.27}$$

Obviously, by Equation 9.6, this is satisfied at $x = x^*$; further, it is satisfied nowhere else, in view of Equation 9.1 and the assumption that $C_2''(x) \geq 0$. Thus the resulting output and retail price are the same as in the fully integrated case; the dealer earns all the profits that can be earned, and the manufacturer can extract those profits as a franchise fee.

Whether this is possible depends on the formal and implicit relations connecting the manufacturer and the monopoly dealer. Suppose, for example, we are considering an arrangement that will last only one year and will never be repeated. In this case, no dealer would agree to pay such a franchise fee without an enforceable contract specifying the level of p_m. Any dealer would know that once the franchise fee is agreed on it will be in the manufacturer's interest to set p_m so as to maximize profits at the manufacturing level – that is, to set p_m to satisfy Equation 9.15, which would leave the dealer with profits lower than the agreed-on franchise fee. Thus, unless the manufacturer can be bound to charge only marginal cost $[C_1'(x^*)]$, the policy under discussion will not be feasible. Because a similar statement holds for any franchise fee higher than $\pi_d^3(\hat{x})$, the best the manufacturer can do is to follow the policy described in the preceding section.

Obviously this problem does not arise merely in short-lived relationships. No matter how long an arrangement is to last, if the franchise fee is fixed at the outset, any dealer will require a binding commitment as to manufacturing-level price before agreeing to any fee higher than $\pi_d^3(\hat{x})$, the maximum profits that can be earned in distribution when the manufacturer sets p_m to maximize manufacturing profits. What matters is not the length of the arrangement but whether it is to be repeated.

If the arrangement is not a one-time affair, however, then it is at least possible that the policy under discussion could work without an explicit binding commitment on the part of the manufacturer as to the level of p_m. This is so because knowingly imposing losses on the dealer by extracting a very high franchise fee and then departing from an implicit commitment to charge marginal cost will lead the dealer to terminate the relationship and will warn other dealers not to take it over. Knowing this, the dealer may be willing to rely on the manufacturer's long-run self-interest to enforce marginal cost-pricing, thus enabling the manufacturer to earn the maximum possible profits in the way described. The more frequent the setting of the franchise fee, the more likely this is to occur.

Just how likely it is to occur at all may depend on circumstances, however. In complex situations where there is uncertainty as to demand and costs, where change is expected to occur, and where the dealer cannot monitor the manufacturer's costs, the dealer and any potential replacements may be unable to tell whether the losses come from the manufacturer's departure from an implicit agreement or from some other source. Knowing this, the manufacturer may be tempted occasionally to cheat on such an agreement. In such circumstances, potential monopoly dealers may not be willing to agree to franchise fees much above their estimate of what they can earn if the manufacturer does cheat. Even though the manufacturer may still be able to earn higher profits with a monopoly dealer than would be the case in the non-cooperative case analyzed in the preceding section, it may not be possible to come close to the profits, output and retail price that would occur under full integration. Thus it will still be true that cases exist in which society, but not the manufacturer, would be better off with competitive dealers.

The case we have been discussing is one in which the manufacturer seeks to set a very high franchise fee and is bound to the price at the manufacturing level. It is also possible that the manufacturer will seek to bind the dealer to a minimum output and a maximum price at the retail level in exchange for a low franchise fee and the award of the franchise (or the threat of its termination). This would enable the manufacturer to move all profits to the manufacturing level (as opposed to the previous case, where they are moved to the retail level) and thus attain the equivalent of the fully integrated case.

Again what matters is the observability of behavior – in this case, the behavior of the dealer. If the selling and promotion of the product is not simple but requires a multidimensional effort on the part of the dealer, then the manufacturer may not be able to tell whether the dealer is living up to an implicit agreement, and an explicit agreement may be difficult or impossible to write or monitor. In such cases, the manufacturer may still prefer an unrestricted or imperfectly restricted monopoly dealer to having competitive dealers even though doing so runs counter to society's preferences.

Conclusions

I now summarize the results and consider their relevance for the antitrust treatment of exclusive franchising.

Where full integration is possible and easy, or where there are constant returns or near-constant returns to scale in distribution, the interests of the manufacturer coincide with those of society. In such cases it is to be presumed that setting up a monopoly dealer occurs for reasons of efficiency.

When, however, full integration is not possible and returns to scale in distribution appear to be decreasing, the conclusion reached may be different. In such cases, the question arises whether the manufacturer is achieving results equivalent to those of full integration in some way other than actually integrating. In the simplest case, for example, because the problem faced by a manufacturer with a monopoly dealer is one of output restriction, is the manufacturer imposing a minimum output or a maximum price restriction on the dealer? If so, the manufacturer may simply be achieving the fully integrated result in a different way; both the manufacturer and society will prefer that result to one achieved with competitive dealers even if no efficiency considerations are involved.

Note the implication here. Although it is true that an important and sometimes controlling question is whether the manufacturer could have done the exclusive distributing, in cases in which that is not possible, certain kinds of *more* restrictive arrangements are to be preferred to less restrictive ones. This is particularly important when one leaves the simplest case of a single homogeneous good with all costs known and considers the possibility that selling a complex product line may involve the dealer exerting efforts in several dimensions, some of which may be observable to the manufacturer only imperfectly. In such a case, the advantages of full integration may not be achievable at all. If they are achievable, achievement may require placing quite detailed restrictions on the dealer. The analysis in this chapter suggests that, so long as manufacturer-imposed restrictions require the dealer to put forth greater rather than less effort, they are positively desirable.

Especially in complex cases, however, restrictions on the dealer may not allow the manufacturer to come close to achieving the equivalent of full integration. Where they do allow this to be achieved, and thus guarantee that society's interests are protected (in this second-best situation), franchise fees cannot be substantial, for the agreements will themselves siphon off dealer rents.

Where franchise fees are substantial, the principal result discussed in this chapter comes into play. A high franchise fee is a mechanism through which a manufacturer can extract rents from a monopoly dealer. Where rents arise from decreasing returns in distribution due to externalities or different costs for different units of output, such an arrangement may be preferred by the manufacturer to a system of competitive dealers, even though no efficiency or marketing-incentive reasons are involved. Whereas it *may* be true that such preferences coincide with those of society, that result certainly is not inevitable. Such arrangements, therefore, should not be considered presumptively lawful; rather, the presence of a high franchise fee should signal the need for further investigation.

Notes

1. The possible relevance of the 'free-rider' problem goes back to Telser's discussion of fair trade. See L. Telser, 'Why should manufacturers want fair trade?' *Journal of Law and Economics* **3** (October 1960), pp. 86–105. The discussion in the text ignores the possibility that the manufacturer enters into an exclusive dealing arrangement because the dealer has monopsony power either over the manufacturer's product or over other inputs needed to sell or service that product. In such a case, such monopsony power might itself raise antitrust questions, but those questions would not arise solely (or even primarily) because of the exclusive franchise itself.
2. See R. Bork, 'The rule of reason and the *per se* concept: Price-fixing and market division (II)', *Yale Law Journal* **75**, pp. 397–405, especially pp. 402–3; R. Posner, 'Antitrust policy and the Supreme Court: an analysis of restricted distribution, horizontal merger and potential competition decisions', *Columbia Law Review* **75** (1975), pp. 283–8; 'Case Comment', *Harvard Law Review* **88** (1975), p. 641; R. Bork, *The Antitrust Paradox* (New York: Basic Books, 1978), pp. 288–91; P. Areeda and D. Turner, *Antitrust Law* (Boston: Little, Brown, 1978), vol. 3, paras. 734a, 734d.
3. See G.F. Mathewson and R.A. Winter, 'An economic theory of vertical restraints', *RAND Journal of Economics* **15** (1984), pp. 27–8 for an analysis of the various instruments available to the manufacturer.
4. There is a strong family resemblance here to the variable proportions literature on vertical integration. See Richard Schmalensee, 'A note on the theory of vertical integration', *Journal of Political Economy* **81** (1973), pp.

442–9; and Frederick R. Warren-Boulton, 'Vertical control with variable proportions', *Journal of Political Economy* **82** (1974), pp. 783–802. The constant-returns case can be thought of as one in which distributor input is required in fixed proportion to manufacturer output while the decreasing returns case corresponds to variable proportions.

5. All these 'payments' of marginal costs, in fact, come from allowing the dealers a larger retail margin. The manufacturer sets that margin by setting the price to dealers and calculating what the resulting competitive-dealer retail price will be. In practice, the manufacturer may be able to offer dealers special incentives for special effort, thus, in effect, price discriminating in the margin offered for the distribution of different units of output. Such price discrimination is unlikely to be perfect, however. I ignore such phenomena.

6. Note that the strategy which leads to Equation 9.16 appears to yield the maximum profits the manufacturer can obtain with a monopoly dealer. The question of whether this is so and of whether the manufacturer can do better and even attain the results of vertical integration with such an arrangement is discussed in the next section.

7. See Note 2 above.

10

Returns to scale in research and development: What does the Schumpeterian hypothesis imply? (1973)

The problem and the literature

Joseph Schumpeter (1942) argued strongly in *Capitalism, Socialism and Democracy* that 'the large-scale establishment or unit of control' was to be preferred to the small, competitive firm. He did not deny the static theory of competition; he argued that inefficiency at any given moment of time was more than offset by the increase in the rate of productivity growth promoted by the large-scale monopoly firm. The attractiveness of this idea is obvious, and it has been discussed widely in the half century since Schumpeter's book appeared. It has also been subjected to empirical tests, the most popular of which is to ask if the proportion of workers or expenditures in firms used in research and development (R & D) activities increases with firm size. As usual with such tests, the richness of Schumpeter's hypothesis has been sacrificed on the altar of precision. The role of market power, being hard to measure, is typically forgotten, and only Schumpeter's reference to the size of firm is retained. Even on these narrow grounds, however, the proposition tested is not the same as Schumpeter's, and a theoretical argument is needed to get from one to the other.

We have attempted to provide such an argument and have discovered the surprising result that the test is in fact *not* a test either of Schumpeter's ideas on the size of firms or of the soundness of the policy prescriptions derived from them.

In addition, Schumpeter's own clearly implied conclusions that rates

---

Written jointly with Peter Temin.

of productivity growth will be higher or that more innovations will be forthcoming if small firms are combined into big ones also do not follow from a reasonable formulation of his assumptions concerning returns-to-scale in R & D.

These conclusions have been obscured by the informal nature of the discussion, which has taken its cue from Schumpeter's own discussion. Schumpeter differentiated market power and firm size in his discussion, but he made no effort to disentangle their separate effects on the assumption that monopolists tend also to be big. He made two points. First, the 'monopoly firm' will have greater *demand* for innovations because its market power will increase its ability to profit from the innovation. Second, the 'monopoly firm' will generate a larger *supply* of innovations because 'there are advantages which, though not strictly unattainable on the competitive level of enterprise, are as a matter of fact secured only on the monopoly level' (Schumpeter 1942, p. 101).

The argument about the demand for innovations has been formalized and rejected by Arrow (1962), who showed that the existence of market power *before* the innovation reduced the profits to be expected from a given change in costs. The argument about the supply of innovations has never been formalized. Schumpeter's (1942) synthesis of size and market power has been criticized, but the argument has continued to be carried on variously with reference to one or the other.

Most of the discussion of the supply side, however, has concentrated on size, despite Schumpeter's (1942, p. 101) explicit disclaimer that 'mere size is neither necessary nor sufficient' for the superiority of the monopoly firm. Two arguments have been given. The first argument relating scale to the supply of innovations asserts that there are economies of scale in R & D expenditures. This has two parts. First, a larger R & D staff can operate more efficiently than a small one. Second, an R & D staff of a given size operates more efficiently in a larger firm.

A large R & D staff is presumed to be more efficient because it allows room for more specialized personnel. With a large staff, engineers can concentrate on particular areas of a firm's activities and develop expertise in them. There will be more engineers who have been with the firm a long time and whose accumulated experience is at the service of the firm. And there will be room for pure scientists, supervisors, technical writers or other communications personnel. A large R & D staff also helps a firm hire research firms to work for it, because the in-house R & D personnel can formulate the research project to be done and communicate the firm's needs to the outside research organization.

A given R & D staff will operate more efficiently in a larger firm, according to this argument, because of the risks underlying any research. Since it is impossible to predict the nature of new knowledge, a given R & D expenditure may or may not produce knowledge useful to a particular line of activity. If a firm is engaged in only one activity, it takes the risk of producing knowledge it cannot use. The more activities undertaken by the firm, the smaller this risk is. A large firm tends to have more diversified activities than a small one, and it therefore stands to gain more from a given R & D expenditure.

This argument assumes that there is no market for new knowledge *per se*. If there were, a firm that discovered something of no use to itself could sell it to another firm, and there would be no risk to the firm deriving from the unknown applicability of the knowledge. Pure knowledge, however, is not a widely traded commodity; it is linked to personnel, or machines, or organizations. Consequently, the diversified firm stands to gain more from a given volume of R & D than a smaller, less diversified firm.

The second argument relating firm scale to innovation asserts that there are economies of scale in the financial market. Large firms have access to more financial markets than small firms. Their credit standing is more widely known. They can borrow more cheaply than small firms, and they can borrow more money before they reach the point where each dollar borrowed costs more than the last one.

As a result, large firms can support larger R & D staffs relative to their size than can small firms; that is, a firm that is twice as large as another can have an R & D staff that is more than twice as large. This will increase the flow of innovations per worker in large firms if the R & D staffs are not less efficient. In addition, larger firms will be more willing to take risks because the greater ability to borrow reduces the risk that any specific loss or failure will result in bankruptcy. A large firm, therefore, can afford to make more mistakes or to lose more gambles than a small firm can before it succeeds in a risky endeavor.[1]

Neither of these arguments is directly testable; economies of scale are very hard to measure, particularly in R & D. Investigators, therefore, have tried to test these arguments by examining a supposed consequence of them, namely, that the inputs into R & D activities, measured by the size of the R & D staff or by R & D expenditures, increase more than proportionately with firm size. Villard (1958), Schmookler (1959), Worley (1961), Hamberg (1964), Mansfield (1964), Scherer (1965a and b) and Comanor (1967) have all investigated this question – with varying results. Markham (1965) has summarized and criticized such studies, while Grabowski and Mueller (1970) asserted that the data are not good enough to run a serious test.

These articles are critical of each other and of the results reached, but none of them suggests that the test itself is inappropriate.[2] Yet it is clear that it is only an indirect test of the existence of economies of scale and that its relevance to the existence of such economies has to be demonstrated. It should also be clear that this test also is not a direct test of the policy prescription usually derived from Schumpeter's arguments.[3] That policy is one of favoring the growth of large firms, presumably because a large firm will innovate more than a collection of small firms of the same aggregate size. This rationale is identical neither with the assertion of economies of scale nor with an assertion about the allocation of resources in large firms.

There are, then, three separate sets of propositions at issue: Schumpeter's, those about the effect of firm size on the allocation of the firm's resources, and those about the effect of firm size on the volume of innovations. These different propositions can be formalized as follows. (For ease of exposition, we use the allocation of the labor force as an index of the firm's resources, but the results do not depend on this interpretation.) Let R equal the number of R & D workers in a firm and S equal the total number of workers in the firm, which we will take as our index of firm size. Let $N = S - R$. Let $F(R, N)$ be the dollar value of the *per worker* output of the R & D staff, or the average labor productivity of research and development. It is made a function of the size of the R & D staff and of the operating staff of the firm. In other words, $RF(R, N)$ is the difference in the profits (exclusive of direct R & D costs) obtained by a firm of operating staff size N which engages in R & D to the extent measured by R and those which would be obtained by the same firm if it did no R & D. We return to this below.

We implicitly assume throughout later sections that inputs other than labor are combined efficiently with the labor inputs and that there is complete certainty about the output of R & D. These assumptions enable us to come to grips with how little can be proved in the area of interest even with the most stringent of models. (To link this discussion directly with the empirical discussion of expenditures as well as with the discussion of the labor force, S, R and N can be interpreted directly as expenditures, making the wage rates introduced below into costs of capital.)

The most obvious way to formalize Schumpeter's arguments, and the way which seems most in agreement with the literature,[4] is in terms of inequalities on the partial derivatives of $F(R, N)$. Thus, if a larger R & D staff is supposed to be more efficient than a smaller one (for given operating firm size), we would expect average R & D productivity to rise with R:

$$F_1 > 0 \qquad\qquad (10.1a)$$

(where subscripts denote differentiation in the obvious way). Similarly, if a given R & D staff is more efficient in a larger firm, average R & D product should increase with N:

$$F_2 > 0 \tag{10.1b}$$

We shall refer to Inequalities 10.1a and 10.1b as Schumpeter's hypotheses. The test of these hypotheses used in the literature is to attempt to see whether R rises more rapidly than S when S changes over firms, that is, to see whether:

$$\eta \equiv \frac{S}{R}\frac{dR}{dS} > 1 \tag{10.2}$$

On the other hand, the rationale for combining small firms into large ones is the Schumpeterian conclusion that the total R & D output of the firm, RF, rises more than proportionately with S, or that:

$$\varepsilon \equiv \frac{S}{RF}\frac{d(RF)}{dS} = \eta + \frac{S}{F}\frac{dF}{dS} > 1 \tag{10.3}$$

Schumpeter's own argument would appear to be that Inequalities 10.1a and 10.1b imply Inequality 10.3. The empirical literature seems to have asserted that Inequalities 10.1a and 10.1b imply Inequality 10.2, which then in turn implies Inequality 10.3.

We shall show that most of this is incorrect. Indeed, we shall show that, without additional special assumptions, about the only interesting true implication that can be drawn here is that Inequalities 10.1a, 10.1b and 10.2 plus a marginal version of Schumpeter's hypothesis *together* imply Inequality 10.3. Since it turns out, however, that Inequality 10.2 is neither necessary nor sufficient for Inequalities 10.1a and 10.1b and also neither necessary nor sufficient for Inequality 10.3, empirical analysis of Inequality 10.2 is of very little interest. Moreover, the Schumpeterian conclusion (Equation 10.3) follows neither from the empirically testable Equation 10.2 nor from the Schumpeterian hypotheses, Equations 10.1a and 10.1b, taken separately.

It is important to emphasize that our model can hardly be considered an adequate formalization of Schumpeter or, indeed, of the innovative process. For one thing, no treatment can be adequate in this regard which leaves out uncertainty. The effects of uncertainty, however, seem to involve the reasons behind Inequalities 10.1a and 10.1b, not the relation between those inequalities and Inequalities 10.2 and 10.3. Our model contains the features which seem to lie behind the intuition that the effects of the two types of increasing returns in R & D are to make research inputs and research outputs go up more than proportionally with firm size. We show that such intuition is in fact incorrect and that there is thus no *prima facie* reason for believing that such conclusions follow. This is not to deny that they might indeed follow in a better or more elaborate model of the innovative process as envisaged by Schumpeter, but that possibility must now be considered mere speculation in the absence of proof.

To put our conclusions another way, we shall show that, in general, empirical estimates of η are of no value in confirming or disproving the hypothesis that $F_1 > 0$ and $F_2 > 0$. Moreover, unless one is willing to *assume* both $F_1 > 0$ and $F_2 > 0$ as well as a marginal version of Schumpeter's hypothesis, an empirical finding that $\eta > 1$ does not imply $\varepsilon > 1$.

The only exception to this occurs if one is willing to assume that $F(R, N)$ is homogeneous of some degree – an assumption for which there is not the slightest justification, since $F(R, N)$ is not a production function with two factors of the ordinary sort. In this case, a finding that $\eta > 1$ does imply that at least one of F_1 and F_2 is positive. Further, in this case, it is not necessary to assume that $F_2 > 0$ to infer $\varepsilon > 1$ from the fact that $\eta > 1$, although one must still assume $F_1 > 0$ and a marginal version of Schumpeter's hypothesis. However, if one also (that is, in addition to homogeneity, etc.) assumes that $F_2 > 0$, then the fact that $\eta > 1$ can be deduced from the assumptions, and empirical investigation is a waste of time.

In short, few propositions in the literature follow from the others. Empirical verification of $\eta > 1$, in particular, is useful only in a very restricted class of cases in which one is already willing to assume so much about the relationships involved that it is hard to see why one is not willing to go farther. And the balance is delicate. Typically, to assume even a little more in such cases is to make empirical verification that $\eta > 1$ unnecessary.

Formal analysis

Every firm hires R & D workers at a wage, w, and operating workers at a wage, v, which may or may not be the same.[5] Its revenues may be thought of as divided into two parts: first, the revenues which it would earn were it not to engage in R & D but have operating staff of N; second, the additional revenues (or cost savings) which it obtains because it does engage in R & D. The latter revenues are represented by $RF(R, N)$ and the former are denoted by $G(N, \alpha)$, where α is a shift parameter whose use will be explained in a moment.[6] For convenience, we shall denote the *net* revenues which would be obtained by the firm with no R & D by $H(N, \alpha) \equiv q(N, \alpha) - vN$. The firm chooses R and N to maximize profits, Π, given by:

$$\Pi = RF(R, N) - wR + H(N, \alpha) \tag{10.4}$$

Before proceeding, some comments are in order. First, as already remarked, we assume, for simplicity, that the dollar return to R & D is known with certainty (this may be taken as the present value of a future stream of returns). However, the additive form of Equation 10.4 is perfectly general, as already explained.

Second, it is important to bear in mind that $H(N, \alpha)$ is not merely a production relationship but also includes the effects of demand conditions and wages. In particular, increasing or decreasing returns to scale in production affect $H(N, \alpha)$ but are not equivalent to statements about H_1.

Finally, we come to the role of the shift parameter, α. If there were no shift parameter in the model, all firms would be identical and there would be nothing to compare between large and small firms. Hence we must allow firms to differ in some respects. There are really only two general ways to allow for such differences. One of these is to allow the dependence of H on N to be different for different firms; this is what we have done. The shift parameter, α, may be thought of as indexing a difference in production functions or in demand conditions (or, for that matter, in the wage of production workers, v). Except for notational convenience, there is no reason why α cannot be a vector.

The other way to allow for differences between firms would be to have a shift parameter appearing in $F(R, N)$ (or affecting w). This would be pointless for the present analysis, however, since it is clear that all results of interest would turn on exactly how such a shift parameter entered. To put it differently, the non-appearance of a shift parameter in $F(R, N)$ means that the net gain to any firm engaging in R & D over what it would have earned without such activities is dependent only on size and not on special opportunities open to special firms. If this area of analysis means anything at all, it must be on the presumption that small and large firms differ only as to size in their R & D opportunities and that were they the same size (in both R and N) those opportunities would be the same. Otherwise no proposition in this area could possibly be generally valid.

We have thus placed our shift parameter only in $H(N, \alpha)$. Our technique of analysis is as follows. Since the firm chooses R and N to maximize Equation 10.4, R and N, and therefore S, are implicitly determined as functions of α. By obtaining $dR/d\alpha$, $dN/d\alpha$ and $dS/d\alpha$, we will be able to examine dR/dS, dN/dS and the remaining derivatives of interest, where the derivatives are all taken parametrically on α, the only exogenous variable which shifts. It will turn out that the precise way in which α enters matters not at all.

We begin then by maximizing Π with respect to R and N. The first-order conditions are:

$$F + RF_1 - w = 0 \tag{10.5a}$$

and

$$RF_2 + H_1 = 0 \tag{10.5b}$$

The second-order conditions are:

$$2F_1 + RF_{11} < 0 \tag{10.6a}$$

$$(2F_1 + RF_{11})(RF_{22} + H_{11}) > (F_2 + RF_{12})^2 \tag{10.6b}$$

Differentiating Equation 10.5a totally with respect to α, yields:

$$(2F_1 + RF_{11})\frac{dR}{d\alpha} + (F_2 + RF_{12})\frac{dN}{d\alpha} = 0 \tag{10.7}$$

or

$$\frac{(dR/d\alpha)}{(dN/d\alpha)} = -\frac{F_2 + RF_{12}}{2F_1 + RF_{11}} \tag{10.8}$$

We now wish to evaluate dR/dS, where the derivative is taken along a curve, movements along which are determined by changes in α. Recalling that $S = R + N$, and using Equation 10.8, we obtain:

$$\frac{dR}{dS} = \frac{dR/d\alpha}{dS/d\alpha} = \frac{dR/d\alpha}{dR/d\alpha + dN/d\alpha} = \frac{(dR/d\alpha)/(dN/d\alpha)}{(dR/d\alpha)/(dN/d\alpha) + 1}$$

$$= \frac{F_2 + RF_{12}}{F_2 + RF_{12} - (2F_1 + RF_{11})} \tag{10.9}$$

Note that neither α nor H enters this expression directly.

Recalling that $\eta = (dR/dS)(S/R)$, the first thing we can immediately say about the relations between Schumpeter's hypotheses (Equations 10.1a and 10.1b) and their supposed implication (Equation 10.2) is expressed in Theorem 10.1.

Theorem 10.1: The inequalities, $F_1 > 0$ and $F_2 > 0$, do not even suffice to determine the sign of η, let alone imply that $\eta > 1$.

Proof: It is obvious that the sign of $(F_2 + RF_{12})$ is entirely unrestricted by the first- and second-order conditions and the two Schumpeterian inequalities.

In other words, even though the average product of research and development may rise both with the size of the R & D staff *and* with the size of the operating division, larger firms may find it profitable to have not merely relatively smaller but *absolutely* smaller R & D staffs than smaller ones. The reason for this is not hard to find;[7] $\eta < 0$ only if $(F_2 + RF_{12}) < 0$, in view of Equation 10.6a. The latter expression, however, gives the effect of an increase in the size of the operating division on the *marginal* product of the R & D staff. If this is negative, then a firm with a larger operating division will find that it has to cut back on its R & D staff in order to make the latter's marginal product equal to the wage.

It is perhaps natural to assume that this does not happen, and we shall do so in a moment. It is considerably less natural to argue that such an assumption is really what is meant by the Schumpeterian argument that increasing the size of the operating division increases the returns to R & D. That argument seems to us to be embodied in the statement about *average* product, $F_2 > 0$, and it seems stretching to claim that it means that the *marginal* product of the R & D staff rises with the size of the operating division. Indeed, our view is reinforced by the fact that it is hard to see how one could argue that this half of the Schumpeterian argument refers to increasing marginal products without also arguing that the other half does also. The latter view, however, would lead to the observation that the Schumpeterian hypothesis is in direct contradiction to the second-order condition (Equation 10.6a). For firms in equilibrium, it cannot be the case that the marginal product of R & D staff is increasing with the size of the staff itself (although it can be the case at uneconomically low staff sizes), since otherwise there would be nothing to limit the size of the staff.[8] Thus, it seems difficult to argue that Schumpeter's hypothesis as to the effect of the size of the operating division should be interpreted as a statement about marginal product without also being led into a view that another part of his hypothesis cannot be true for observed firm sizes.

We shall ignore Theorem 10.1 in what follows, however, and assume that it is indeed true that dR/dS is positive. In other words, we henceforth assume:

$$F_2 + RF_{12} > 0 \tag{10.10}$$

With this assumption, it is possible to obtain some (not very strong) positive results. We begin by showing:

Theorem 10.2: If $F_2 + RF_{12} > 0$, then $0 < dR/dS < 1$ and $0 < dN/dS < 1$.

Proof: The first statement follows directly from Equations 10.9, 10.10 and the second-order condition, Equation 10.6a. The second statement follows from the first and the fact that $S = R + N$.

In other words, larger firms will have both absolutely larger R & D staffs and absolutely larger operating staffs than smaller ones. Note that only the marginal-product hypothesis (Equation 10.10) is involved in this; the average-product hypotheses (Equations 10.1a and 10.1b) play no role.

Those hypotheses do play a role, however, in:

Theorem 10.3: If $F_1 > 0$, $F_2 > 0$ and $F_2 + RF_{12} > 0$, then $\varepsilon > \eta$.

Proof: From the definitions:

$$\varepsilon = \eta + \frac{S}{F}\frac{dF}{dS} = \eta + \frac{S}{F}\left(F_1\frac{dR}{dS} + F_2\frac{dN}{dS}\right) \tag{10.11}$$

The theorem now follows from Theorem 10.2.

Corollary: $F_1 > 0$, $F_2 > 0$, $F_2 + RF_{12} > 0$ and $\eta > 1$ imply $\varepsilon > 1$.

Thus, our expanded version of Schumpeter's hypotheses *together with* their supposed consequence as to the relative size of R & D staffs in large and small firms suffice to imply the Schumpeterian conclusion about the relative output of R & D from large and small firms. Unfortunately, as we shall see below, $\eta > 1$ is required for that conclusion and does not itself follow from Schumpeter's hypotheses even with the addition of the marginal product hypothesis (Equation 10.10).[9]

Indeed, without further assumptions, no further positive results seem available. One such further assumption would be to restrict F to be homogeneous of some degree. If one is willing to do so, very strong results can be obtained, as follows.

Theorem 10.4: If F is homogeneous of degree m, then

$$\eta \gtreqless 1 \qquad \text{according as} \qquad m \gtreqless 0.$$

Proof: By Equation 10.10, the denominator of the right-hand expression in Equation 10.9 is positive, so

$$\eta \gtreqless 1$$

according as

$$(S - R)(F_2 + RF_{12}) + R(2F_1 + RF_{11}) \gtreqless 0 \tag{10.12}$$

However,

$$(S - R)(F_2 + RF_{12}) + R(2F_1 + RF_{11})$$

$$= R(RF_{11} + NF_{12}) + 2RF_1 + NF_2$$
$$= (m - 1) RF_1 + 2RF_1 + NF_2 \tag{10.13}$$
$$= m(RF_1 + F) = mw$$

where we have used, successively, Euler's theorem applied to F_1, Euler's theorem applied to F, and the first-order condition (Equation 10.5a). The theorem now follows immediately, since the wage is positive.

Corollary 1: If F is homogeneous of some degree, then $F_1 > 0$, $F_2 > 0$, and $F_2 + RF_{12} > 0$ imply both $\eta > 1$ and $\varepsilon > 1$.

Proof: By Euler's theorem, $F_1 > 0$ and $F_2 > 0$ imply that F is homogeneous of positive degree. The corollary now follows from Theorem 10.4 and the corollary of Theorem 10.3. Note that Equation 10.10 must still be assumed for this result.[10]

Corollary 2: If F is homogeneous of some degree, then $F_1 > 0$, $\eta > 1$ and $F_2 + RF_{12} > 0$ imply $\varepsilon > 1$.

Proof: If $F_2 > 0$, then the result follows from Corollary 1, so we may as well assume $F_2 \leq 0$. Using Equation 10.11 and the fact that $S \equiv R + N$,

$$\varepsilon = \eta + \frac{S}{F}\left[F_1 \frac{dR}{dS} + F_2\left(1 - \frac{dR}{dS}\right)\right]$$
$$= \eta + \eta\,(F_1 - F_2)\,\frac{R}{F} + \frac{S}{F} F_2$$
$$= \eta + \eta\left(\frac{RF_1 + NF_2}{F}\right) + (1 - \eta)\,\frac{S}{F} F_2 \tag{10.14}$$
$$= \eta\,(1 + m) + (1 - \eta)\,\frac{S}{F} F_2$$

where m is the degree of homogeneity of F, and the last equality follows from Euler's theorem. Since $\eta > 1$, the term multiplying F_2 is negative and, since $F_2 \leq 0$, $\varepsilon \geq \eta(1 + m)$. By Theorem 10.4, however, $\eta > 1$ implies $m > 0$, proving the corollary.

Thus, if we could assume F homogeneous of any degree, Corollary 1 assures us that all the results which are supposed to flow from Schumpeter's hypotheses (plus Equation 10.10) would indeed do so. Moreover, Corollary 2 states that, with that assumption, observing that $\eta > 1$ would make the Schumpeterian hypotheses that $F_2 > 0$ irrelevant in concluding that $\varepsilon > 1$, provided we are still willing to assume $F_1 > 0$ *and* Equation 10.10. Even here, however, $\eta > 1$ does not imply $F_1 > 0$ and $F_2 > 0$ (although it certainly does imply that at least one of these is true by Theorem 10.4). Moreover, it does not imply Equation 10.10 or that $\varepsilon > 1$.[11]

Even so, it would clearly be very helpful – particularly in view of Corollary 1 – to be able to assume homogeneity. Unfortunately, however familiar to economists, there does not seem to be any reason to suppose that F has such a property.[12] Without it, the desired results simply do not follow, as we now show.

Theorem 10.5: $F_1 > 0$, $F_2 > 0$ and $F_2 + RF_{12} > 0$ imply neither $\eta > 1$ nor $\varepsilon > 1$.

Proof: It is obvious that even Equation 10.10 is not enough to bound η away from zero, since $F_2 + RF_{12}$ can be made as small as desired. This clearly makes it very unlikely that $F_1 > 0$, $F_2 > 0$ and Equation 10.10 imply $\varepsilon > 1$, but there seems no way to prove this save by providing a counter-example (which, by the corollary to Theorem 10.3, will also exhibit $\eta < 1$). We do so by choosing a form for F which has all the appropriate properties in a region surrounding the equilibrium point; far away from equilibrium, the function would have to be altered, but this presents no difficulty.

Accordingly, in the relevant region, we choose:

$$F(R, N) = 40(2^{20})\, R^{0.1}\, N^{0.1} - R^3\, N^2 \tag{10.15}$$

For appropriate choice of $H(N, \alpha)$ and w, we shall show that $R = 1$, $N = 2^{10} = 1024$ is an equilibrium. Since $H_1(2^{10}, \alpha)$ and $H_{11}(2^{10}, \alpha)$ are essentially at our disposal, this amounts to verifying a number of inequalities.

$$F(1, 2^{10}) = 79(2^{20}) > 0 \tag{10.16}$$

$$F_1(1, 2^{10}) = 5(2^{20}) > 0 \tag{10.17}$$

$$F_2(1, 2^{10}) = 6(2^{10}) > 0 \tag{10.18}$$

Hence both F and its two first partials are positive. It follows that Equation 10.5a will be satisfied at the point in question for an appropriately chosen positive wage [$w = 84(2^{20})$].[13] Further, Equation 10.5b will be satisfied for $H_1 (2^{10}, \alpha) = -6 (2^{10})$. Thus $R = 1$ and $N = 2^{10}$ can satisfy the first-order conditions for positive w and appropriate H.

Turning to the second-order conditions:

$$2F_1(1, 2^{10}) + F_{11}(1, 2^{10}) = -3.2(2^{20}) < 0 \tag{10.19}$$

satisfying Equation 10.6a. Since H_{11} can be taken as negative as desired, Equation 10.6b can also be satisfied.

Checking Equation 10.10 we have:

$$F_2(1, 2^{10}) + F_{12}(1, 2^{10}) = 0.8(2^{10}) > 0 \qquad \text{(10.20)}$$

Hence, the function and equilibrium point chosen satisfy all the assumptions. We now compute η and ε at the point in question. Using Equations 10.9, 10.19 and 10.20:

$$\eta = \frac{S}{R}\frac{dR}{dS} = (2^{10} + 1) \left(\frac{0.8(2^{10})}{0.8(2^{10}) + 3.2(2^{20})} \right) = 0.25 \qquad \text{(10.21)}$$

approximately. Using this, Equation 10.14 and our other numerical results:

$$\varepsilon = \eta + \eta(F_1 - F_2)\frac{R}{F} + \frac{S}{F}F_2 \qquad \text{(10.22)}$$

$$= 0.25 + \frac{0.25[5(2^{20}) - 6(2^{10})] + 1025(6)(2^{10})}{79(2^{20})} = 0.34$$

approximately. This completes the proof.

There remain two questions of interest. First, were empirical work to show that $\eta > 1$, would one then be entitled to conclude that at least one of F_1 and F_2 was positive, or entitled to conclude that $\varepsilon > 1$? Second, even though $F_1 > 0$ and $F_2 > 0$ do not imply either $\eta > 1$ or $\varepsilon > 1$, do $F_1 < 0$ and $F_2 < 0$ imply either $\eta < 1$ or $\varepsilon < 1$? In the latter case the Schumpeterian hypothesis would at least be necessary for the Schumpeterian conclusion, even though we know that it is not sufficient.[14] We dispose of these possibilities with another counter-example.

Theorem 10.6: (a) $\eta > 1$ does not imply $F_1 > 0$ or $F_2 > 0$; (b) $\eta > 1$ does not imply $\varepsilon > 0$, let alone $\varepsilon > 1$; (c) $F_1 < 0$ and $F_2 < 0$ do not imply $\eta < 1$ or $\eta < 1$.

Proof: Choose

$$F(R, N) = (2 - \lambda)(10^{-2})RN^4 - R^2N^2 - 60N + k \qquad \text{(10.23)}$$

where $\lambda > 0$ and $k > 0$ are parameters which we will specify later. We will show that $R = 1$, $N = 10$ can be an equilibrium point.

In the first place, by choosing k sufficiently large, $F(1, 10) > 0$. Evaluating F_1 and F_2:

$$F_1(1, 10) = -100\lambda < 0 \qquad F_2(1, 10) = -40\lambda < 0 \qquad \text{(10.24)}$$

For large enough k, $F(1, 10) + F_1(1, 10)$ will be positive, so that Equation 10.5a can be satisfied at a positive wage. Further, since H is at our disposal, Equation 10.5b can also be satisfied.

Turning to the second-order conditions:

$$2F_1(1, 10) + F_{11}(1, 10) = -200(1 + \lambda) < 0 \qquad (10.25)$$

so that Equation 10.6a is satisfied, while Equation 10.6b will be satisfied for appropriate choice of H_{11}.
Checking Equation 10.10:

$$F_2(1, 10) + F_{12}(1, 10) = 40 - 80\lambda \qquad (10.26)$$

which will be positive for $0 < \lambda < 0.5$.
We now evaluate η at the equilibrium point.

$$\eta = \frac{S}{R}\frac{dR}{dS} = 11\left[\frac{40 - 80\lambda}{40 - 80\lambda + 200(1 + \lambda)}\right] \qquad (10.27)$$

$$= 11\left(\frac{1 - 2\lambda}{6 + 3\lambda}\right)$$

This will be greater than unity for λ sufficiently small, proving (a) and the first part of (c).
Turning to the evaluation of ε at the equilibrium point, we have:

$$\varepsilon = \eta + \eta(F_1 - F_2)\frac{R}{F} + \frac{S}{F}F_2$$

$$= 11\left(\frac{1 - 2\lambda}{6 + 3\lambda}\right) - 11\left(\frac{1 - 2\lambda}{6 + 3\lambda}\right)(60\lambda)(1/F) \qquad (10.28)$$

$$- 11(40\lambda)(1/F)$$

By choosing k sufficiently large and λ sufficiently small, the last two terms can be made as small as desired and ε made to approach $\eta > 1$. This proves the second part of (c). On the other hand, by making k small enough, F can be made close to zero, and, if λ is also taken small enough, this can be done so as to keep Equation 10.5a satisfied at positive wage. Indeed, it is clear that the operative restriction is the latter one, so that, using Equation 10.24, k must be chosen so that $F(1, 10) > 100\lambda$. By choosing k close to this bound, however, we leave everything else unaffected and ε can be made to approach:

$$\varepsilon^* = 4.4\left(\frac{1 - 2\lambda}{6 + 3\lambda} - 1\right) \qquad (10.29)$$

and for λ sufficiently small this approaches -3.67, approximately. Hence ε can also be made to approach -3.67, and (b) is proved.

This completes our analysis. We have shown the rather disappointing result that the Schumpeterian hypotheses and conclusions have relatively little to do with each other without further assumptions. Moreover, the empirical test which has been attempted in the literature has relatively little to do with either. One cannot do comparative statics without second derivatives.

Notes

1. On average, of course, the big firm will have to do as well as the small one to remain profitable. This argument refers not to the average but to the variation around the average.
2. But Griliches (1962, p. 353) casts a skeptical eye on the theoretical discussion as well as the empirical evidence and suggests that the whole matter is of second-order importance as a determinant of the rate of growth of inventive activity.
3. Comanor (1965) attempts such a direct test and then interprets the results in terms of economies of scale. The results of this chapter show that such an interpretation is not necessarily appropriate. We are indebted to John M. Vernon for this reference.
4. Schumpeter did not say and the subsequent literature also has not specified whether he was talking about the effects of size on average or marginal products. It is more natural when thinking of increasing returns to interpret Schumpeter and the literature as we have done here in terms of average products than in terms of marginal products. In addition, there are logical difficulties with the marginal interpretation (which we note below) that preclude its easy acceptance. But we consider that version later, in any case.
5. As remarked above, we have chosen to simplify matters by working with a single explicit factor input. If other factors are implicitly included, their costs per worker are included in w and v, which may then not be constants. To allow for such non-constancy would merely complicate the analysis without changing its conclusions.
6. This division of revenues may also correspond to a real division in which the output of R & D is sold outside the firm, but such an interpretation is unnecessarily special.
7. We are indebted to Robert Hall for discussion of this point.
8. Bela Balassa has pointed out to us that this need not always be the case. If capital markets are imperfect and interest rates rise with the amount borrowed, then the marginal cost of R & D might rise with R (and possibly decline with N). In such a case, the marginal productivity of research workers might be increasing in equilibrium since their marginal cost would be also. This case is readily handled in our analysis. Replace w in Equation 10.4 by $w + g(R, N)$, where $g(R, N)$ reflects the increasing marginal-cost effect being considered. If we define $F^*(R, N) \equiv F(R, N) - g(R, N)$, the analysis can then proceed essentially as before with $F^*(R, N)$ replacing $F(R, N)$. Since our principal finding is that assumptions about the derivatives of $F(R, N)$ are essentially unrelated to propositions about η or ε, the fact that the derivatives of $F^*(R, N)$ will differ from those of $F(R, N)$ matters not at all, although the statement of theorems such as Theorem 10.3 would have to distinguish carefully between $F(R, N)$ and $F^*(R, N)$.
9. Remark: it might be thought that Equation 10.10 need not be separately assumed in order to obtain the corollary, since $\eta > 1$ already implies that

$dR/dS > 0$. This is not true, since without Equation 10.10 it would be possible to have $dN/dS < 0$ if η were sufficiently great; Equation 10.10 is a sufficient condition for $dR/dS > 0$, not a necessary one.

10. Remark: if F is homogeneous of degree greater than or equal to unity (which does not follow from $F_1 > 0$ and $F_2 > 0$), then Equation 10.10 need not be separately assumed. In that case, $F_1 > 0$ implies $F_{11} < 0$, from the second-order condition (Equation 10.6a). Euler's theorem appled to F_1 then shows $F_{12} > 0$, which, together with $F_2 > 0$, yields Equation 10.10.

11. Even assuming Equation 10.10, $\varepsilon > 1$ cannot be deduced from homogeneity and $\eta > 1$ without assuming $F_1 > 0$. Examining Equations 10.9, 10.14 and the calculation in the proof of Theorem 10.4, it can be shown that there are cases in which η is close to unity and m close to zero, and the sign of $\varepsilon - 1$ is determined by appropriate choice of the term in $(-SF_2/F)$. Consideration of the examples in the proofs of Theorems 10.5 and 10.6 below reveals that the latter term is essentially unrestricted in magnitude.

12. F is not a production function in two factors in any reasonable sense. The two variables represent the effects of one direct input and a kind of externality, and the usual arguments for homogeneity do not apply.

13. The units are irrelevant, of course. We could count our workers, for example, in groups of 100, so the firm analyzed would have a total work force of about 100,000 and an R & D staff of 100.

14. Obviously, the proof of Theorem 10.3 shows that $F_1 < 0$, $F_2 < 0$ and $\eta < 1$ imply $\varepsilon < 1$. This is not of much interest, since we know that $\eta < 1$ does not imply $F_1 < 0$ and $F_2 < 0$. The only other possibility that might be of some interest is that $\eta < 1$ implies $\varepsilon < 1$, which is clearly false, as consideration of Theorem 10.3 reveals.

References

Arrow, K.J. 'Economic welfare and the allocation of resources for invention' in *The Rate and Direction of Inventive Activity*. Princeton, NJ: Princeton Univ. Press (for Nat. Bur. Econ. Res.), 1962.

Comanor, W.S. 'Research and technical change in the pharmaceutical industry'. *Rev. Econ. and Statis.* 47 (May 1965): 182–90.

Comanor, W.S. 'Market structure, product differentiation and industrial research'. *QJE* **81** (November 1967): 639–57.

Grabowski, H. and Mueller, D. 'Industrial organization: the role and contribution of econometrics'. *AER* **70** (suppl.; May 1970): 100–4.

Griliches, Z. 'Comment' in *The Rate and Direction of Inventive Activity*. Princeton, NJ: Princeton Univ. Press (for Nat. Bur. Econ. Res.), 1962.

Hamberg, D. 'Size of firm, oligopoly and research: the evidence'. *Canadian J. Econ. and Polit. Sci.* **30** (Feburary 1964): 62–75.

Mansfield, E. 'Industrial research and development expenditures: determinants, prospects and relation of size of firm and inventive output'. *JPE* **72** (August 1964): 319–40.

Markham, J. 'Market structure, business conduct and innovation'. *AER* **55** (suppl.; May 1965): 323–32.

Scherer, F.M. (a) 'Size of firm, oligopoly and research, A comment'. *Canadian J. Econ. and Polit. Sci.* **31** (May 1965): 256–66.

Scherer, F.M. (b) 'Firm size, market structure, opportunity and the output of patented inventions'. *AER* **55** (December 1965): 1097–125.
Schmookler, J. 'Bigness, fewness and research'. *JPE* **67** (December 1959): 628–35.
Schumpeter, J.A. *Capitalism, Socialism and Democracy*. New York: Harper & Bros., 1942.
Villard, H. 'Competition, oligopoly and research'. *JPE* **66** (December 1958): 483–97.
Worley, J.S. 'Industrial research and the new competition'. *JPE* **69** (April 1961): 183–6.

11

The Schumpeterian hypothesis: Reply (1979)

Professor Rodriguez (1979) caught us in an elementary error. Basically, we failed to notice that if one assumes that the average product per worker is increasing, then the marginal product must be above the average product. It certainly follows that if all workers are paid the marginal product there will not be enough to go around, and the firm would be better off shutting down its research establishment.

Rodriguez is not correct, however, when he concludes that this means that all our results are invalid. As a matter of fact, our principal results become stronger when this error is corrected.

It is instructive to see why this is so. We wanted to show that the Schumpeterian hypothesis had less empirical content than had been assumed widely in the literature and that previous tests of it were invalid. To do this, we had to define the Schumpeterian hypothesis more precisely than had been done previously. We were trying to show that Schumpeter's hypothesis had very few empirical implications, so we bent over backward to define his hypothesis strictly, since more restrictive assumptions enable more theorems to be proven. We bent so far backward, as Rodriguez has pointed out, that we lost our balance. We defined the hypothesis so strictly that we contradicted ourselves. But when we straighten up – when we adopt a looser, internally consistent definition of the Schumpeterian hypothesis – we inevitably find that even fewer positive theorems can be proven. It follows that all of our negative conclusions about the limitations of the Schumpeterian hypothesis are reaffirmed. Only the discussion of our special cases is changed.

Written jointly with Peter Temin

We showed, more specifically, that testing to see whether expenditures on R & D go up more than proportionally with firm size provided no information about returns to scale even if F_1, the derivative of the average return per research worker, was positive. As Rodriguez points out, that derivative cannot be positive in equilibrium. Firms cannot be in equilibrium in a region in which average returns per research worker are increasing. This means (assuming that firms are in fact in equilibrium) that, where we observe firms, average returns per worker must be decreasing (or zero if zero profits are earned in the research activity). But that is consistent with very large increasing returns to scale (in the sense of increasing average returns) over a range starting at zero and going up to a large research-establishment size smaller than that actually observed; it is also consistent with no increasing average returns per research worker anywhere. It should not come as a surprise then that observing the equilibrium behavior of firms and comparing it from firm to firm yields essentially no information about the existence or size of the unobservable range in which average returns per research worker do increase.

To consider this in detail, suppose we consider what increasing returns to scale in R & D can be taken to mean in light of the error which Rodriguez points out. (We assume the reader is familiar with Chapter 10, whose notation we adopt here). We originally assumed that both $F_1 > 0$, so that average returns per research worker were increasing with the size of the research staff, and $F_2 > 0$, so that average returns per research worker were increasing with the size of the production staff. As Rodriguez points out, $F_1 > 0$ cannot be maintained. One way to proceed would be simply to take F_1 as unrestricted. But it might be argued that increasing returns to scale in R & D ought to mean at least that F_1, while negative, is small in absolute value compared with F_2. A sensible way to describe this is to assume that if both R and N increase in the same proportion, so that both the research and production divisions of the firm grow at the same rate, then average returns per research worker go up. It is easy to see that this amounts to assuming

$$RF_1 + NF_2 > 0 \qquad\qquad (11.1)$$

This statement that returns to scale are increasing as we move along a ray in $R-N$ space is consistent with profit maximization at positive levels of research. Note that it is weaker than the assumption that both $F_1 > 0$ and $F_2 > 0$. It therefore should not be surprising that if one substitutes Equation 11.1 for $F_1 > 0$ one can prove even less than before. Moreover, since given that $F_1 \leq 0$, Equation 11.1 implies $F_2 > 0$, assuming Equation 11.1 will enable us also to examine what cannot be proved from the weaker assumption that $F_2 > 0$.

All of the original theorems remain valid (with appropriate changes in the assumptions) with the sole exception of Theorem 10.3. For example, our original statement of Theorem 10.1 said that the two inequalities, $F_1 > 0$ and $F_2 > 0$, do not even suffice to determine the size of η (the elasticity of research output with respect to firm size), let alone imply that $\eta > 1$. *A fortiori,* this remains true when the two weaker inequalities, $F_2 > 0$ and Equation 11.1, are substituted for the original two.

Theorem 10.3 indicated a positive result. It noted conditions under which $\varepsilon > \eta$ (where ε is the elasticity of research output with respect to firm size). Rodriguez has shown that the assumed conditions would never be observed.

Theorem 10.4 remains valid, but its corollaries need to be restated rather more than the theorems. The restated corollaries are as follows:

Corollary 1′:   If F is homogeneous of some degree, then $\eta > 1$ if and only if Equation 11.1 is true.

Corollary 2′:   If F is homogeneous of some degree, then $\eta > 1$ implies $F_2 > 0$, but $\eta < 1$ does not imply $F_2 \leqslant 0$.

Corollary 3′:   In the homogeneous case: (a) $\eta = 1$ implies $\varepsilon = 1$; (b) if $F_2 \leqslant 0$, then $\eta < 1$ and $\varepsilon < \eta < 1$; (c) if $F_2 > 0$ *and* $F_{12} > 0$, then $\eta > 1$ implies $\varepsilon > \eta > 1$ and $\eta < 1$ implies $\varepsilon < \eta < 1$.

It remains true in the homogeneous case that one can get some positive results. In particular, testing to see whether or not the elasticity of research input with respect to size is greater than 1 is indeed a test of Inequality 11.1, the increase of average returns per research worker as both divisions grow proportionately. Further, if it turned out that that elasticity was just equal to unity, then the elasticity of research output with respect to firm size would also be equal to unity.

One does not get much further than this in a very useful way, however. If one found that $\eta < 1$, *and* one were willing to assume that the Schumpeterian hypothesis that $F_2 > 0$ did not hold, then one could conclude that $\varepsilon < 1$. But it is not true that the finding that $\eta < 1$ implies $F_2 \leqslant 0$, even in the homogeneous case. If $F_2 > 0$, then conclusions about ε from findings about η – which are equivalent to findings about Inequality 11.1 – appear to require the *very* strong assumption that $F_{12} > 0$. This does not seem very helpful.[1]

In sum, then, our conclusion that there are no strong connections between the propositions involved in this area is strengthened by correction of the error found by Rodriguez. Except for the homogeneous case, all the positive results disappear. Such additional positive results as occur in our treatment of the homogeneous case above occur simply because of the focus on Inequality 11.1 instead of on $F_1 > 0$ and $F_2 > 0$, rather than (in general) because of the correction. It is possible to say even less than before except in the homogeneous case, and we remind the reader that there is no special plausibility to the homogeneous case in this context.[2]

Notes

1. It is not true that the extra conditions in Corollary 3' are redundant. Homogeneity alone does not imply that η and ε are on the same side of unity (or that $\varepsilon > \eta$). This is so for essentially the reason stated in Note 11 of Chapter 10. In particular, the function $F(R, N) = R^a N^\beta + bN$ with $-1 < a < 0$, $a + \beta = 1$, $b > 0$ has the property that $\varepsilon < \eta$ and further, for large enough R, $\varepsilon < 1 < \eta$. The calculations involved are tedious, however, and we leave them to the reader who can manage to cling to the homogeneous case.
2. In this connection, perhaps we may comment briefly on F.M. Scherer's privately circulated comment on our article (Scherer, 1973). Scherer argues that the case in which returns to R & D are homogeneous of some degree in R is really the interesting one and different from ours. He suggests indeed that all Schumpeterian tests would be appropriate if such returns are homogeneous of degree one in R. But Scherer's homogeneous case is the *same* as ours since if such returns are homogeneous of degree $m + 1$, then average returns are homogeneous of degree m and conversely. In particular, in Scherer's case of homogeneity of degree one, $F(R, N)$ must be homogeneous of degree zero (and may be constant). If one is willing to assume that, then $\eta = \varepsilon = 1$ and there is no point to testing anything.

References

Rodriguez, Carlos A., 'A comment on Fisher and Temin on the Schumpeterian hypothesis', *JPE* **87** (1979) 383–5.
Scherer, F.M., 'Research and development returns to scale and the Schumpeterian hypothesis: comment', Mimeographed. Berlin: Internat. Inst. Management (1973).

12

Games economists play: A non-cooperative view (1989)

Introduction

For some thirty years following World War II, most bright young economists did not go into industrial organization. It was not hard to see why this was so. The quick, big payoffs in economics tend to go to theorists, and industrial organization was a subject in which theory was not only unsatisfactory, but moribund. The promise of the Chamberlin–Robinson revolution of the early 1930s had not been fulfilled, and, while institutional and verbal-theoretic writings on the subject were sometimes illuminating, there was no hard analytic theory formalizing the structure–conduct–performance paradigm. Oligopoly, in particular, showed no signs of analytic tractability.

Today, the atmosphere is altogether different. The profession is full of young theorists whose principal occupation is industrial organization. Indeed, industrial organization has become *the* hot topic for microtheorists. Journals, meetings and seminars abound in research on oligopoly, and, judging by the market, this is a booming industry.

Of course, the principal reason for the change is the rise of game theory and its applications in these areas. Von Neumann and Morgen-

An earlier version of this chapter was presented as an invited lecture at the Australasian meetings of the Econometric Society, Christchurch, New Zealand, August 1987. I am grateful to the organizers of those meetings for the opportunity and to Drew Fudenberg, John Riley, Jean Tirole and Michael Whinston for comments and criticism but absolve them of responsibility for errors or for the views expressed. In view of what I have to say about 'new developments on the oligopoly front' in the last thirty years, I wish to dedicate this chapter to my friend and colleague, Franco Modigliani, on the occasion of his becoming Institute Professor Emeritus.

stern's great work was published in 1944 and hailed immediately by theorists (von Neumann and Morgenstern, 1944). Jacob Marschak, indeed, stated in reviewing it (Marschak, 1946, p. 115): 'Ten more such books and the progress of economics is assured.' Nevertheless, it was not until the last decade that game theory came to the ascendant as the premier fashionable tool of microtheorists.

That ascendancy appears fairly complete. Bright young theorists today tend to think of every problem in game-theoretic terms, including problems that are easier to deal with in other forms. Every department feels it needs at least one game theorist or at least one theorist who thinks in game-theoretic terms. Oligopoly theory in particular is totally dominated by the game-theoretic approach. The field appears to be in an exciting stage of ferment.

To understand why I believe that such excitement is not warranted, it is necessary to step back, briefly review the history of oligopoly theory before the game-theory revolution, and consider what it is that one wants theory to deliver.

Oligopoly theory before game theory[1]

As we all know, oligopoly theory began with Cournot (1838) and his two bottlers of mineral spring water. Cournot assumed that each seller takes the other's output as constant and derived an equilibrium as the point at which each seller's output is optimal, given the other.

There are two well-known apparent problems with the Cournot solution in its original form. One is that there appears to be no reason to limit the activities of the sellers to setting outputs. This led Bertrand (1883) and Edgeworth (1897) to consider similar assumptions as to price-setting, and, indeed, capacities, research and development expenditures, advertising and other variables can also be objects of strategic choice. The solution is quite dependent on just what it is that one takes the oligopolists to be setting.

The second apparent problem with the Cournot assumption is that the participants in the model are very stupid. Each of them takes the other's output as given, but the very process of adjustment shows them not only that this is mistaken, but that, in fact, the rival's output reacts to that of the given seller. This led von Stackelberg (1934) to inquire as to what would happen if one of the sellers woke up and then to generalize (or try to) as to what might happen if they both did. This line of development led to a messy collection of cases, which can best be summarized by saying that the results depend very heavily on just what each oligopolist is assumed to be conjecturing about its rivals.

What *should* such conjectures be? It is fair to say that, at this stage of the theory, there was *and probably could not be* be a good answer to this question if one considers the agents involved to be perfectly sensible. This is so since *any* conjecture as to rival's behavior appears to lead to a change in that behavior if the rival realizes that one is making it. So long as one remains within a static, one-shot context, there is no really satisfactory way of treating this. (One of the positive things one can say about game-theoretic developments is that they clarified what is involved here. See Tirole, 1988, Chapters 6 and 8.)

In any event, the major change in the way the profession thought about such subjects was brought about by Edward Chamberlin, in work incorporated in his *Theory of Monopolistic Competition* (1933).[2] Chamberlin pointed out that the oligopolists being studied could figure out their problem quite as well as economists could. He suggested that they would reach the cooperative solution – called the 'joint-maximization' solution – at which total profits are maximized. While that solution is not what we would now call a 'Nash equilibrium', and any of the rivals can improve itself by deviating, Chamberlin argued that such deviations will not happen because they are foreseen to be ultimately self-defeating.

Of course, as was quickly recognized, the joint-maximization solution is not a fully compelling answer. For one thing, the temptation to cheat is very strong. Put in modern terms, the oligopolists are in a prisoners' dilemma, and it will not be easy to be sure that the cooperative solution holds up unless explicit communication is permitted. Indeed, in a changing world oligopolists may not be sure where the joint-maximization solution is and may misinterpret moves toward a changed joint-maximization position as attempts to cheat on the tacit agreement.

Second, save in the convenient but unrealistic case of pure symmetry, if side payments are not allowed, some oligopolists may not like the joint-maximization solution very much. (For example, that solution may require high-cost firms to shut down.) If they like it less than they would a non-cooperative outcome, Chamberlin's reasoning will break down.

Despite these defects (or perhaps because of them), it is fair to say that Chamberlin's suggestion changed the way in which we think about oligopoly in practice. The study of any real oligopoly has largely become the study of how the joint-maximization solution is or is not achieved and of the reasons why. One need search no further for an example than the story of OPEC.

One also need not search very far to conclude that there is not much hard theory in all this. As early as William Fellner's classic *Competition among the Few* (1949), one finds a complete description of the issues involved in deviation from joint maximization. That description would hardly be different today, but while the issues are well described in Fellner, they are not formalized in any very adequate way.

To sum up, as of the early 1950s, the state of oligopoly theory could reasonably be described as follows: a great many outcomes were known to be possible. The context in which the theory was set was important, with outcomes depending on what variables the oligopolists used and how they formed conjectures about each other. A leading class of cases concerned the joint-maximization solution and when it would or would not be achieved. The answer to the latter question was also known to be very dependent on the context and experience of the oligopolists. Plainly, the theory was in a messy and unsatisfactory state.

The application of game theory to oligopoly

I want now to consider what it is that we know about oligopoly after some years of intensive application of game theory. I begin by going back to Cournot's duopolists bottling water from a mineral spring. Here we know the following: if the two duopolists each choose only output, and if the game they are playing is played only once, then the Cournot solution is the (usually unique) Nash equilibrium of the game. In other words, the Cournot solution gives the only pair of outputs at which each duopolist is playing its best response, given the output of the other one.

This hardly seems much of an advance. Cournot knew that his solution had this property, even if he did not phrase it in such terms. Yet the fact that the Cournot solution is a Nash equilibrium has caused a rash of revitalized interest in it. Indeed, so fascinated are some economists by this fact that I know of two cases of quite distinguished academics who either proposed to testify or did testify in antitrust cases that one should analyze real markets by using the Cournot solution. One, indeed, proposed to testify that in deciding whether to allow a merger in the petroleum industry, one should predict the effects on output and prices in terms of the change in the Cournot solution.

That, I think, is theory run riot. The petroleum industry does not consist of firms playing the one-shot Cournot output-choosing game. Neither does any other real-life industry. That makes the one-shot game totally uninteresting. Further, even on its own terms, the fact that the Cournot solution is a Nash equilibrium is only a complex way of translating what Cournot already knew. It has the merit of avoiding the rather silly Cournot dynamic story of adjustment in which the Cournot conjecture is repeatedly proved false. So far as I can see, however, that is its only merit.[3]

Indeed, once one has more than two oligopolists, even the fact that the Cournot solution is a Nash equilibrium loses its appeal. This is so since the Nash equilibrium concept itself is not the only appealing one. As B. Douglas Bernheim (1984) and David Pearce (1984) have independently pointed out, the arguments that make Nash a sensible concept also apply to what they call 'rationalizable equilibrium'. A Nash equilibrium is appealing because so long as you play your Nash strategy, it pays me to play mine, and *vice versa*. But suppose I think that you think that I will not play Nash. Then it may pay me not to play Nash, and that may validate your conjecture. Rationalizable equilibria (of which Nash equilibria are a subset) are points at which the strategies played are justified by a consistent (if possibly incorrect) system of conjectures as to what A thinks B thinks A thinks B thinks A will play, and so forth. Bernheim has shown that, with three or more oligopolists, there is a whole continuum of rationalizable equilibria in the one-shot Cournot output-choosing game.

Put this aside for the moment, however, and concentrate on the popular Nash equilibrium concept. Much of the game-theoretic study of oligopoly consists of analyzing one-shot games in contexts richer than that of quantity-setting. When one does so, one gets richer results. A great many interesting stories have been told in this way. In terms of general propositions, however, about all that one can say is that the results depend heavily on the context – on the particular setting in which the oligopoly game is supposed to be played.

As already remarked, however, real industries are not involved in one-shot games. The whole literature at least from Chamberlin's insight on through the limitations of joint maximization revolves around the fact that repeated experience matters. To put it another way, Chamberlin's view that symmetric oligopolists will certainly not be stupid enough to fight rests on the notion that they must go on living with each other. It is perfectly true that if the game is played only once, the joint-maximization solution cannot be the outcome of the prisoners' dilemma. Tacit collusion is only made possible by the fact that the game, or games like it, will be played again or that the prisoners will have to deal with each other in later contexts.

What, then, does game theory have to say about repeated games? Alas, nothing remarkably helpful to the general analysis of oligopoly. The best known result here is the so-called 'folk theorem', which states that, in an infinitely repeated game with low enough discount rates, any outcome that is individually rational can turn out to be a Nash equilibrium (Fudenberg and Maskin, 1986). Crudely put: anything that one might imagine as sensible can turn out to be the answer. While the folk theorem itself requires a number of assumptions, the existence of an embarrassingly large number of equilibria appears to be a fairly general phenomenon. This is a case in which theory is poverty-stricken by an embarrassment of riches.

Faced with this problem, there are two ways in which one might go. The first of these is to try to solve it by refining the notion of equilibrium used. This is a sensible thing to do, and there have been some advances here. (See Fudenberg and Tirole, 1989, for an excellent summary.) Unfortunately, those advances do not cure the problem of the existence of a vast multiplicity of equilibria.

Nor can one much improve matters by tacking on considerations of Pareto optimality. This is often done by authors simply asserting (rather uncomfortably) that the players will naturally not choose Nash equilibria that are Pareto-dominated. The problem here is that this tacks on to the pure concept of Nash equilibrium the view that certain equilibria stand out from others. That may very well be true, and, if it is, it may be an important insight, but in that case the question of *why* certain equilibria stand out becomes the central question. Further, Pareto efficiency often does not reduce the equilibrium set to a happily small size.

To return to the oligopoly context, at least with low enough discount rates and an infinite horizon, one of the Nash equilibria in any repeated game will be the old joint-maximization solution, and this is likely also to be the case with less extreme assumptions.[4] By definition that solution is Pareto efficient (for the oligopolists). To observe that Pareto-efficient solutions may have special properties is, in part, to repeat Chamberlin's insight that oligopolists are likely to choose the joint-maximization solution. The question of when this will or will not happen then becomes one of paramount importance. But we have been here before.

I shall have some more favorable things than this to say about the game-theoretic approach to oligopoly, but the following summarizes my general view of where things stand: a great many outcomes are known to be possible. The context in which the theory is set is important, with outcomes depending on what variables the oligopolists use and how they form conjectures about each other. A leading class of cases concerns the joint-maximization solution and when it will or will not be achieved. The answer to the latter question is also known to be very dependent on the context and experience of the oligopolists.

Of course, these are the very words I used in describing the pre-game theory state of oligopoly theory. I must add, however, that, in a way, I have been overly generous to the results of game theory here. I stated that 'a leading class of cases concerns the joint-maximization solution and when it will or will not be achieved'. In fact, while I strongly believe that this ought to be a central question of oligopoly theory, game theory, with its concentration on equilibria, has partially succeeded in obscuring its importance.[5]

Generalizing theory and exemplifying theory

To say in such sweeping terms that game theory has still left oligopoly theory with a large variety of outcomes and with the same problems as before is not necessarily to say that game theory has failed or has produced no useful results. To go deeper into the matter requires a consideration of what it is that one should ask a theory to do.

In fairly broad terms, there are two styles of theory in economics. I shall refer to these as 'generalizing theory' and 'exemplifying theory', respectively. They both have very important uses.

Generalizing theory proceeds from wide assumptions to inevitable consequences. It speaks in terms of what must happen, given the background circumstances. Good examples here involve general equilibrium. In that area, existence theory or, perhaps even better, the two welfare theorems give broadly (but, of course, not universally) applicable results. One need not look on so grand a stage for examples of generalizing theory, however. At the level of the individual consumer, Slutsky's equation and the other properties of the substitution terms are propositions that apply under very wide circumstances. They provide general propositions describing what must happen, given fairly general assumptions.

Of course, there is no reason that generalizing (or any other) theory must be purely qualitative. I most certainly do not mean to exclude from generalizing theory the kind of proposition that states that certain effects depend on the values of various variables, with the parameters left to be estimated by econometric means. In the world of empirical economics, such propositions are central, with the role of theory being to specify the important variables and, if we are lucky, to tell us something about admissible functional forms. Generalizing theory can be, and usually is, parameter-dependent.

Whether qualitative or quantitative, however, the grand propositions of generalizing theory are not always available. Further, in finding them it may be useful to work inductively, building up general propositions from simpler cases. This leads to the use of exemplifying theory – also sometimes termed 'MIT-style theory' – which is very widespread in the profession.

Exemplifying theory does not tell us what *must* happen. Rather it tells us what *can* happen. In a good exemplifying-theory paper, the model is stripped bare, with specializing assumptions made so that one can concentrate on the phenomena at issue. (For example, rather than trying to deal with a hard problem in full generality, it may be useful and illuminating to assume that all consumers have the same constant relative risk-aversion utility function.) When well handled, exemplifying theory can be very illuminating indeed, suggestively revealing the possibility of certain phenomena. What such theory lacks, of course, is generality. The very stripping-down of the model that makes it easy (or even possible) to see what is going on also prevents us from knowing how the results will stand up in more general settings.

Returning to my main subject, it should be plain that (with or without game theory) the status of the theory of oligopoly is that of exemplifying theory. We know that a lot of different things *can* happen. We do not have a full, coherent, formal theory of what *must* happen or a theory that tells us how what happens depends on well-defined, measurable variables.[6]

It is true, of course (as a reader of this chapter has pointed out), that the folk theorem is itself an example of generalizing theory, although a negative one. It tells us that we cannot hope for a general oligopoly theory based only on cost and demand functions and free of the context in which oligopolists operate. But that result (which is not exactly a great surprise) is precisely the point. We need a generalizing theory as to how that context influences the outcome.

Such a theory is presently lacking. At present, oligopoly theory consists of a large number of stories, each one an anecdote describing what might happen in some particular situation. Such stories can be very interesting indeed. Elie Wiesel (1966, preceding numbered pages) has said that 'God made man because He loves stories', and economists (not merely game theorists) are plainly made in the divine image in this respect.

The following is a case of exemplifying theory at its best.[7] In the *IBM* antitrust case, one of the claims was that IBM had engaged in something called 'premature announcement'.[8] While it is not clear exactly what the US government had in mind, 'premature announcement' must mean that in some sense IBM announced products sooner than it should have. Now, in the computer industry, it was (and to some extent still is) common practice to announce products before they are ready to be shipped. Such an announcement was a rather formal matter, marking the beginning of the taking of orders. Since computers tended to be built to order rather than to stock and since customers needed time to prepare for the installation of a new computer, there were good reasons for announcing in advance of shipment, and every manufacturer did so. The question then arises of what 'premature' announcement can mean. In my testimony and my book on the *IBM* case (Fisher *et al.*, 1983), I argued that unless an announcement was made in bad faith (in which case, with rational customers, it was unlikely to represent a practice that could be successfully repeated), it could not be 'premature' in the sense of being anticompetitive. While I still believe that to be usually true (and certainly to have been true given the facts of the *IBM* case), Joseph Farrell and Garth Saloner (1986) have produced a counter-example, showing that there are circumstances in which early truthful announcements can be anticompetitive. This occurs because of network externalities not taken into account by customers opting for a given technology.

On the other hand, there is a danger to such stories. Economists are so fond of theoretically consistent tales that they sometimes overlook the fact that exemplifying theory does not provide an inevitable description. The case of the economists who proposed to apply Cournot to the petroleum industry is one example. Another is occasionally provided by articles having to do with network externalities. In that area the authors, having constructed an interesting and plausible story as to how a firm might unfairly limit the ability of competitors to hook-up their machines, tend to assume without close examination that the story must fit the facts of the *IBM* or other antitrust cases.

Such lapses may be considered the understandable excesses of youthful zeal, and they do not limit the usefulness of exemplifying theory, properly understood. That usefulness, however, is naturally limited. Exemplifying theory must always remain a collection of stories unless those stories point the way to some unifying principle – to a generalizing theory.

Towards a general theory of oligopoly

In the case of oligopoly, what would such a generalizing theory be? What questions would it answer? This is fairly easy to say, although very hard to accomplish.

As we have seen, oligopoly theory is a collection of stories. We have a large and increasing number of formal anecdotes in which the outcome appears to depend heavily on the context. The role of a true generalizing theory of oligopoly is to tell us the nature of that dependence, in older terms, to tell us how conduct and performance depend upon structure.

I can put this rather pointedly in terms of an example. Everything we know about oligopoly, both with and without game theory, tells us that the characteristics of particular oligopoly environments can substantially influence the outcome. As a teacher of mine (probably Carl Kaysen) once remarked some thirty years ago, it may very well be the case that one cannot understand the history of the US rubber tire industry without knowing that Harvey Firestone was an aggressive guy who believed in cutting prices. Maybe so. But then, as someone else (probably Mordecai Kurz or Kenneth Arrow) remarked to me a few years ago, the job of theory is to discover what characteristics of the rubber tire industry made such aggressive behavior a likely successful strategy. Absolutely right. That question would be answered if we had a generalizing theory of oligopoly. As it stands, we are a long way from an answer.

To see what I have in mind in a more general context, consider the question of policy towards horizontal mergers. In the United States such a policy forms an important, and sometimes controversial, part of our antitrust policy. As part of that policy, the Department of Justice has issued 'Merger Guidelines' that state when a merger is or is not likely to be opposed. While the standards set forth in the 'Guidelines' do not have the force of law, they play a very powerful role in influencing what mergers do or do not take place, and there is a lamentable tendency for the authorities to take them as carved in stone instead of as tests to see whether further investigation is warranted.[9]

A principal feature of the 'Guidelines' is the stress they put on the Herfindahl–Hirschman index of concentration (HHI). That index is defined as the sum of squares of the shares of the firms in the market multiplied by 10,000, for ease of scaling. To get an idea of the orders of magnitude involved, observe that a market with n equally-sized firms will have an HHI of $10,000/n$, so that five equal firms mean an HHI of 2,000, while 10 equal firms mean an HHI of 1,000. The HHI has a number of fairly natural arithmetic properties.

The problem is that we have little idea as to whether the HHI has any *economic* properties. Thus, when the 'Guidelines' speak of opposing a merger which increases an HHI already over 1,800 by at least 100 points, it is impossible to say with any precision whether a sensible policy is being described.

This difficulty arises for more than one reason. First, while it seems sensible that the practice of tacit collusion – the tendency towards the cooperative, joint-maximization solution – is more likely, the more concentrated the industry, other things equal, oligopoly theory is remarkably silent on the question of what concentration levels are dangerous. Indeed, there is little theory showing that the esthetically appealing HHI is the correct measure. Second, while it seems likely that increased concentration matters, other things equal, we are very far from having a decent specification of just what those other things are and how to measure them. A policy that uses concentration levels in different industries should be based on a theory that takes account of the many other phenomena that make industries differ in terms of the likelihood of tacit collusion. We have no such theory. We do not even know what the crucial phenomena are, save in a very general way. Most of what we know, we knew forty years ago.

There have, of course, been repeated attempts to solve this problem by empirical studies using cross-sectional regressions across industries. These attempts have not been successful. Not surprisingly, what repeatedly shows up in such studies is the lack of a generalizing theory to inform the empirical efforts. We do not even know what dependent variable to use, and the studies in question commonly use dependent variables, such as the accounting rate of return or the profits–sales ratio, that exemplifying theory shows to be fatally flawed (see Chapters 4, 5 and 6.) The specification of the right-hand side of the regressions or of the direction of causation is not in much better shape (Demsetz, 1973).[10]

The authors of such studies may not always be good theorists, but good theorists are not helping them much. A primary aim of oligopoly theory should be the synthesizing of the individual stories of exemplifying theory to the point where such empirical studies can be done sensibly. We are not near such a point, and, worse, theorists working in the area do not seem to have that end in view.

Has game theory helped?

Despite the fact that we do not seem close to a generalizing theory of oligopoly or, more generally, of the structure–conduct–performance relationship, it may not be fair to say that little progress has been made. After all, to a very large extent, the problem lies in the underlying phenomena themselves rather than in the methods used to investigate them. It appears plain that oligopoly is a very rich subject with many different kinds of outcomes possible. Hence, before a generalizing theory becomes available, it is crucial to develop a rich set of cases from which to generalize. The development of such a set is the job of exemplifying theory.

In this regard it may be argued that the game-theory revolution has been particularly important. By systematizing the way we think about particular examples, game theory may be paving the way for the generalizing theory that we need. On this view, even if game theory merely retells informal anecdotes in a formal manner, it is performing an important service by systematizing our thought and helping us to understand what the crucial features of those anecdotes are.

As my discussion of the example of 'premature announcement'

shows, I certainly agree that formal argument and exemplifying theory are important. Nevertheless, I do not believe that game theory is in fact preparing the way for generalizing theory.[11] This is so for two reasons. First, game theory in normal form is an inconvenient language with which to prepare the way for the generalizing theory of oligopoly. Second, while game theory in its extensive form may very well be a highly useful language in this regard, most of the existing literature has concentrated on one-shot games, and these are not the interesting ones. I now consider these two points in greater detail.

Game theory can be utilized by considering games in either their normal or their extensive forms. In normal form a game is reduced to a vector-valued function that maps the strategies chosen by the different players into the payoffs. (In the case of discrete, two-person games, this is simply a matrix.) This form is convenient for proving theorems.

Unfortunately, the normal form is not a convenient one for the study of oligopoly or, more generally, of the effects of market structure on conduct and performance. Those effects appear to depend very much on the context. In particular, the ease with which tacit collusion (joint maximization) does or does not take place has much to do with the particulars of the situation in which the oligopolists find themselves. How uniform is the product? How is cheating detected? How are prices quoted, and do most transactions take place at list prices? And so forth. These are all questions of context, and they are suppressed when one represents that context only in terms of strategies describing the actions that will be taken under every conceivable contingency.

I want to be very clear about this. I am not saying that rich contexts cannot be modeled in normal-form game theory. Of course they can. What I am saying is that normal-form game theory is not a convenient way to do it – not a convenient language, as it were. Because it suppresses rich contextual detail, normal-form theorizing about oligopoly makes it awkward at best to come to grips with the central generalizing problem: how do the different aspects of the context interact to produce conduct and performance? Looking at Nash equilibria in normal-form games is not likely to lead to a high payoff here.

The same objection, however, certainly does not apply to game theory in its extensive form, an area that has recently been more and more developed. Here I quote my colleagues, Drew Fudenberg and Jean Tirole (1987, p. 176). I do so at some length, because this passage seems to me to be an excellent statement of the uses of game theory in industrial organization by two thoughtful, first-class practitioners. It is a statement with which I agree, despite my generally skeptical tone.

> Game theory has had a deep impact on the theory of industrial organization.
> . . . The reason it has been embraced by a majority of researchers in the field

is that it imposes some discipline on theoretical thinking. It forces economists to clearly specify the strategic variables, their timing and the information structure faced by firms. As is often the case in economics, the researcher learns as much from constructing the model (the 'extensive form') as from solving it because in constructing the model one is led to examine its realism. (Is the timing of entry plausible? Which variables are costly to change in the short run? Can firms observe their rivals' prices, capacities or technologies in the industry under consideration? etc.)

A drawback of [*sic*] the use of game theory is the freedom left to the modeller when choosing the extensive form. Therefore, economists have long been tempted to use so-called reduced forms, which try to summarize the more complicated real world game, as for example, in the literature on conjectural variations, including the kinked demand curve story. This approach is attractive, but has several problems. The obvious one is that the modeller can only be sure that the reduced form yields the solution of a full-fledged model if he has explicitly solved the model. Also, reduced forms are most natural for the description of steady states, and are thus ill-suited to describe battles for market shares (like price wars, predation, entry and exit), or to study the adjustment paths to outside shocks or government inter-vention. (Reduced forms are not robust to structural changes.) While the reduced-form approach is simpler, and so more amenable to applications, we believe that the focus on 'primitives' implied by the extensive-form approach allows a clearer assessment of the model. Furthermore, the diversity of 'reasonable' extensive forms may to some extent reflect the wealth of strategic situations in industries.

This seems to me to recognize quite correctly the importance of context, and hence the importance of doing exemplifying theory by using extensive forms. Unfortunately, generalizing theory is more easily done in normal form, but I strongly believe that extensive-form game theory is the way to systematize our thinking about examples.

Alas, the examples that we are accumulating in this fashion are not the important ones for generalizing theory because of the one-shot/repeated-game distinction discussed earlier. Most of extensive-form oligopoly game theory is an accumulation of examples showing what can happen in one-shot games in different contexts. But the crucial question for oligopoly theory is not that of the outcome of one-shot games. Rather it concerns the factors and circumstances leading to cooperative, joint-maximizing outcomes in repeated games. There, as already mentioned, little is known, and the folk theorem strongly suggests that simply analyzing Nash equilibria (still less more general concepts of equilibrium) cannot tell us what we want to know.

Let me give an example here. Douglas Bernheim and Michael Whinston (1987) have circulated an excellent discussion paper on the effect of multimarket contact on collusive behavior. In it they attempt to formalize the notion that firms that face each other in many markets are more likely to collude than firms facing each other in only one. They show that in fairly general circumstances multimarket contact raises the incentive for collusion – changing the relative costs and benefits of cooperating versus cheating to make cooperation relatively more attractive. This is an example of the game-theoretic analysis of oligopoly at its best. It comes fairly close to doing what I am asking for – formally explaining how changes in the context can influence the likelihood of collusion.

Nevertheless, the paper falls short of that goal. It only shows (indeed, it only *can* show) that multimarket contact makes collusion more attractive. But collusion is always attractive if it can be sustained and will often be a Nash equilibrium in the repeated game. The question that Bernheim and Whinston do not (and probably cannot) fully address is that of how (or whether) multimarket contact assists oligopolists in achieving the collusive equilibrium; they only show that increasing such contact increases the oligopolists' *desire* to achieve collusion.

The point is that one suspects that – unlike Shakespeare's dictum on drink and lechery (*Macbeth*, Act ii, Scene iii) – multimarket contact does both provoke the desire *and* assist the performance. In this case the 'performance' has to do with the mechanism of coordination, with the way in which the oligopolists grope their way to the collusive outcome instead of to some other equilibrium. Here, multimarket contact is likely to assist because it provides the oligopolists with increased experience in dealing with and signaling to each other. It is true that the 'desire' will also assist by changing priors so that a given ambiguous move is less likely to be interpreted as cheating than were collusion relatively less attractive. But the full, rich, contextual story of how multimarket contact affects the ability to get to joint maximization cannot be told by concentrating on Nash equilibria.

In short, I think game-theoretic oligopoly theorists are studying the wrong thing. They are accumulating a wealth of anecdotal material about one-shot oligopoly games when what one wants to know concerns the factors that lead the collusive equilibrium to be chosen in repeated games. So far as I can see, modern oligopoly theory has made little progress on that centrally important question.

I close by briefly commenting on another example, this time a very well-known one that in a general (although not a specific) sense exemplifies my problems with this literature. I refer to the famous articles on Selten's (1978) chain-store paradox (Kreps and Wilson, 1982; Milgrom and Roberts, 1982). These authors consider the following question. Suppose that there is a monopolist faced with a succession of possible entrants (either a chain store with possible entrants in a variety of local markets or, more conveniently for my purposes, a firm with potential entrants arising over time). As each potential entrant appears, the incumbent firm can either fight or allow entry. It is assumed that fighting can keep a particular entrant out but that the relative costs and benefits are such that, were there only one entrant, it would be preferable for the incumbent to allow entry and accept a reduction from monopoly to duopoly profits than to fight successfully. Further, assume that this is common knowledge.

In this situation the incumbent firm will certainly not fight a single entrant. One might suppose, however, that with multiple entrants the incumbent will fight early entrants to establish a reputation for toughness. Not so. Since the incumbent will certainly not fight the last entrant and the last entrant will know this, there is no point in fighting the next-to-last entrant. Since everyone can figure this out, the incumbent cannot gain by fighting the second-to-last entrant or, by extension, by fighting anybody. Hence, there is no reputation for toughness to be gained.

Of course, this result seems somehow wrong when there are enough potential entrants, and the articles under discussion do a quite interesting job of altering things slightly to come up with a different answer. The authors show that so long as entrants believe that there is a slight probability that the incumbent is irrational, it may pay the incumbent to fight.

This is a first-rate piece of analysis and an early example of the utility of employing the extensive form. It has also led to further work on reputation effects (see, for example, Kreps *et al.*, 1982; Fudenberg and Levine, 1989). Nevertheless, in my view the point of the original analysis is open to question.

The reason the 'paradox' arises in the first place is that it is assumed that there is a last potential entrant. Without that, the story does not unravel, and it is easy to see that engaging in predatory behavior for the sake of reputation will make sense.[12] But real-life incumbents do not face a well-defined finite set of potential entrants. Corporations in most contexts are assumed to have an infinite time horizon and surely cannot believe that any particular fight will be the last. One need go no farther to find a possible reason for predation in such contexts.

This being so, why go to such admittedly elegant lengths to study the question with finite entry? The reply given me some years ago by one of the authors is that the answer of infinite entry is uninteresting.

In one sense that reply is absolutely right. The infinite-entry answer does not compare in elegance and sophistication with the one given by the four authors. But in another sense, the reply exemplifies what is wrong with modern game theory as applied to industrial organization and especially to oligopoly. There is a strong tendency for even the best practitioners to concentrate on the analytically interesting questions rather than on the ones that really matter for the study of real-life industries. The result is often a perfectly fascinating piece of analysis.

But so long as that tendency continues, those analyses will remain merely games economists play.

Notes

1. For a summary of the early literature and full references, see Fellner (1949).
2. It is interesting to note that Joan Robinson, in her *The Economics of Imperfect Competition* (1933) which is often paired with Chamberlin's book, simply failed to understand the oligopoly problem altogether. She assumed (p. 21) that the behavior of each oligopolist can be modeled by creating a demand curve *taking the optimal reactions of rivals into account* and then having the oligopolist set marginal revenue equal to marginal cost. This totally begs the question of what those optimal reactions are – and the fact that one cannot know the answer to that before creating the theory is the central core of the oligopoly problem. Chamberlin put in considerable effort during his lifetime to differentiate his product from that of Joan Robinson. In the oligopoly dimension, at least, he was right.
3. The fact that the static Cournot outcome can be an equilibrium in a dynamic game is more interesting, however. (See Maskin and Tirole, 1987.)
4. If it were true that joint maximization is an equilibrium only under well-defined special circumstances, we would have a very useful, strong result. I do not believe this to be the case, however.
5. This is not to say that it is uninteresting to know when joint maximization is or is not an equilibrium and what the properties of collusive equilibria are. (See Fudenberg *et al.* (1989) and Green and Porter (1984).)
6. A reader of this chapter objects, stating that we surely know that detection lags or secrecy hurt collusion. That is quite true, but we have known it for a long time. Formal theory has not added much to our knowledge here nor provided us with a way of assessing the importance of such effects against others.
7. Carl Shapiro's article (Shapiro, 1989) largely consists of a survey of the accomplishments of game-theoretic analysis in producing exemplifying theory in industrial organization. I do not quarrel with the proposition that such accomplishments exist; indeed, every article I discuss here is one that I regard favorably. That only reinforces my pessimistic view as to the nature of the progress being made towards generalizing theory.
8. *United States* v. *International Business Machines Corporation*, Docket Number 69, Civ. (DNE) Southern District of New York (Dismissed 1982). For a detailed discussion of the 'premature announcement' issues, see Fisher *et al.* (1983, pp. 289–99).
9. For a fuller discussion of merger policy and the 'Guidelines', see Chapter 2.
10. In his article (Shapiro, 1989), Carl Shapiro points to the empirical literature as generally supporting a smooth relationship between market structure and performance in the form of price–cost margins. For the reasons given, I regard that evidence as a very weak reed on which to lean.
11. The proposition that game theory systematizes thought and thus leads to

generalizing theory is reminiscent of the argument that used to be given for the teaching of Latin. It was said that Latin might or might not be interesting for its own sake but that studying it helps to systematize the way one thinks about language. Speaking as one who studied Latin for four years, I believe that argument to have been correct. I do not believe the parallel proposition about game theory.

12. Indeed, with an unbounded set of entrants, the entire problem reduces to Pascal's wager: the rational person prays when faced with the infinite! See Milgrom and Roberts (1982, pp. 305–6) for a formal demonstration.

References

Bernheim, B.D. 'Rationalizable strategic behavior'. *Econometrica*, Vol. 52 (1984), pp. 1007–28.

Bernheim, B.D. and Whinston, M. 'Multimarket contact and collusion'. Harvard Institute of Economic Research Discussion Paper No. 1317 (1987).

Bertrand, J., Review of Cournot's *Recherches*, *Journal des Savants* (1883), p. 503.

Chamberlin, E. *The Theory of Monopolistic Competition*. Cambridge Mass.: Harvard University Press, 1933.

Cournot, A. *Recherches sur les Principes Mathématiques de la Théorie des Richesses*, Paris (1838).

Demsetz, H. 'Industry structure, market rivalry and public policy'. *Journal of Law and Economics*, Vol. 16 (1973), pp. 1–10.

Edgeworth, F.Y. 'La Teoria Para del Monopolio', *Giornale degli Economisti*, Vol. 15 (1897), p. 13.

Farrell, J. and Saloner, G. 'Installed base and compatibility: innovation, product preannouncements and predation'. *American Economic Review*, Vol. 76 (1986), pp. 940–55.

Fellner, W. *Competition among the Few*. New York: Alfred A. Knopf, 1949.

Fisher, F.M., McGowan, J.J. and Greenwood, J.E. *Folded, Spindled and Mutilated: Economic Analysis and US v. IBM*. Cambridge Mass.: MIT Press, 1983.

Fudenberg, D. and Levine, D.K. 'Reputation and equilibrium selection in games with a patient player'. *Econometrica* Vol. 57 (1989), pp.759–78.

Fudenberg, D. and Maskin, E. 'The folk theorem in repeated games with discounting and with incomplete information'. *Econometrica*, Vol. 54 (1986), pp. 533–54.

Fudenberg, D. and Tirole, J. 'Understanding rent dissipation: on the use of game theory in industrial organization'. *American Economic Review: Proceedings*, Vol. 77 (1987), pp. 176–83.

Fudenberg, D. and Tirole, J. 'Noncooperative game theory for industrial organization: an introduction and overview' in R. Schmalensee and R. Willig, eds., *Handbook of Industrial Organization*, Amsterdam: North Holland, 1989.

Fudenberg, D., Levine, D. and Maskin, E. 'The folk theorem in repeated games with imperfect public information'. Mimeograph, 1989.

Green, E.J. and Porter, R.H. 'Noncooperative collusion under imperfect price information'. *Econometrica*, Vol. 52 (1984), pp. 87–100.

Kreps, D.M. and Wilson, R. 'Reputation and imperfect information'. *Journal of Economic Theory*, Vol. 27 (1982), pp. 253–79.

Kreps, D.M., Milgrom, P., Roberts, D.J. and Wilson, R. 'Rational cooperation in the finitely repeated prisoner's dilemma'. *Journal of Economic Theory*, Vol. 27 (1982), pp. 245–52.

Marschak, J. 'Neumann and Morgenstern's new approach to static economics'. *Journal of Political Economy*, Vol. 54 (1946), pp. 97–115.

Maskin, E. and Tirole, J. 'A theory of dynamic oligopoly, III'. *European Economic Review*, Vol. 31 (1987), pp. 947–68.

Milgrom, P. and Roberts, D.J. 'Predation, reputation and entry deterrence'. *Journal of Economic Theory*, Vol. 27 (1982), pp. 280–312.

Pearce, D.G. 'Rationalizable strategic behavior and the problem of perfection'. *Econometrica*, Vol. 52 (1984), pp. 1029–50.

Robinson, J. *The Economics of Imperfect Competition*. London: Macmillan, 1933.

Selten, R. 'The chain-store paradox'. *Theory and Decision*, Vol. 9 (1978), pp. 127–59.

Shapiro, C. 'The theory of business strategy'. *RAND Journal of Economics*, Vol. 20 (1989), pp. 125–37.

Tirole, J. *The Theory of Industrial Organization*. Cambridge Mass.: MIT Press, 1988.

US Department of Justice 'Merger Guidelines', Federal Register Vol. 49 (1984), 26284.

von Neumann, J. and Morgenstern, O. *Theory of Games and Economic Behavior*. Princeton: Princeton University Press, 1944.

von Stackelberg, H., *Marktform und Gleihgewicht*, Vienna and Berlin (1934).

Wiesel, E. *The Gates of the Forest*. New York: Holt, Rinehart & Winston of Canada, 1966.

13

New developments on the oligopoly front: Cournot and the Bain–Sylos analysis (1959)

The recent review article by Franco Modigliani on books by Sylos Labini and Bain[1] reports on new and interesting work on the empirical and theoretical consequences for the study of oligopoly of considerations of entry and potential competition. The theoretical model he presents, however, may at first glance cause a feeling of *déjà vu*, since the behavior assumed in it seems at least reminiscent of Cournot. I discuss this question here primarily with reference to the way in which the *results* of the Bain-Sylos model as presented by Modigliani compare with the *results* of a Cournot model enlarged to take account of entry. I do not discuss the question whether the behavior assumed in one model can be considered more realistic than that assumed in the other or, indeed, the question whether either behavioral assumption can be considered plausible.

For convenience, I restrict my attention to what may be termed the 'pure' case of the Bain–Sylos model. Here the product is homogenous and, for each firm (potential entrants included), long-run average cost is assumed to be perfectly constant for output greater than, or equal to, a certain minimum optimal size, $\bar{x}$, and prohibitive for output below that size. The level of long-run average (equals long-run marginal) cost for outputs greater than or equal to $\bar{x}$ is k. In perfect competition,[2] equilibrium price would be k and total industry output X_c, that output for which the demand and marginal-cost curves intersect. Modigliani defines the size of the market, S, as the ratio of competitive output to minimum optimal size: $S = X_c/\bar{x}$.

In the model presented by Modigliani, a 'Sylos' postulate' is made:

I am indebted to Franco Modigliani for discussion of the basic content of this chapter. All errors are mine, however.

that potential entrants behave as though they expected existing firms to adopt the policy most unfavorable to them, namely, the policy of maintaining output while reducing the price (or accepting reductions) to the extent required to enforce such an output policy (p. 217).

On this assumption, it follows immediately that the smallest entry-blocking industry output, X_0, is

$$X_0 = X_c - \bar{x} = X_c \left(1 - \frac{\bar{x}}{X_c}\right) = X_c \left(1 - \frac{1}{S}\right) \tag{13.1}$$

since, if industry output is equal to or larger than this, the entry of one more firm, even at minimum size, will reduce (or be thought by potential entrants to reduce) the price to the no-profit point or below. Presumably, under these circumstances, the firms already in the industry will agree, tacitly or explicitly, to produce a total output of X_0 (unless, of course, entry is 'blockaded' and the output which maximizes joint profits is greater than X_0; I shall assume that this is not the case). Note that this result is, by and large, independent of the *shape* of the demand curve. It depends only on the intersection of the demand and average (marginal)-cost curves and on the cost structure assumed.

Now, the 'Sylos' postulate' looks somewhat familiar. Potential entrants assume that the output of other industry members is independent of their own. The classical Cournot model of oligopoly, however, makes a very similar, but much stronger, assumption, namely, that *every* member of the industry assumes that the output of all other sellers is independent of its own. Cournot, however, did not consider entry. Let us consider an enlarged Cournot model in which, with the same cost structure already discussed, every producer, whether in or out of the market, behaves as though the output of all other producers was independent of its own action.[3] Note that it follows that producers already in the market will ignore potential entrants in making their decisions.

Throughout the following analysis of this model, I assume for simplicity that potential entrants make their decisions in response to equilibrium, long-run prices only so that the process of adjustment among the sellers already in the market does not itself induce entry by temporarily raising price above the entry-inducing level. I also assume that entrants enter one at a time. Neither of these assumptions is necessary.

Let $n + 1$ be the smallest integer that is equal to or greater than S, that is, $S = n + 1 - \rho$, where $1 > \rho \geqslant 0$. It follows that $X_c = (n + 1 - \rho) \bar{x}$, and that $X_0 = (n - \rho) \bar{x}$.

Let us call a given industry output, X, *feasible for m sellers* if and only if X can be produced by m sellers each producing at least at minimum optimal size. In other words, X is feasible for m sellers if and only if $X \geq m\bar{x}$. There are four cases to consider.

Case 1: The demand curve facing the industry is linear. Let $X_1(m)$ be the equilibrium industry output in this case for m sellers in the ordinary Cournot model, disregarding feasibility considerations and ignoring entry. Consider the enlarged Cournot model. It is well known[4] that

$$X_1(m) = \frac{m}{m+1}X_c = \frac{m}{m+1}(n+1-\rho)\bar{x} \qquad (13.2)$$

For $m < n$, we have

$$X_1(m) \geq \frac{m}{m+1}(m+2-\rho)\bar{x} > \frac{m}{m+1}(m+1)\bar{x} \qquad (13.3)$$

$$= m\bar{x}$$

so that $X_1(m)$ is feasible for m sellers. However, it is also true that

$$X_1(m) \leq \frac{n-1}{n}(n+1-\rho)\bar{x}$$

$$= \left[n-1+\frac{n-1}{n}(1-\rho)\right]\bar{x}$$

$$< (n-1+1-\rho)\bar{x} \qquad (13.4)$$

$$= (n-\rho)\bar{x} = X_0$$

Therefore, if there are fewer than n sellers, they will produce the output given by the classical Cournot model; however, this will be less than the minimum entry-blocking output, and another seller will enter the market, upsetting the equilibrium. This will continue until there are n sellers in the market.

Now let us consider $X_1(n)$. We have

$$X_1(n) = \frac{n}{n+1}(n+1-\rho)\bar{x} = \left(n - \frac{n\rho}{n+1}\right)\bar{x} \qquad (13.5)$$

If S is an integer, so that $\rho = 0$, we have

$$X_1(n) = n\bar{x} = X_0 \qquad (13.6)$$

so that $X_1(n)$ is feasible for n sellers and coincides with the Bain–Sylos solution. Entry is thus blocked and equilibrium attained.

If, however, S is not an integer, $\rho > 0$, and Equation 13.5 yields

$$n\bar{x} > X_1(n) > (n-\rho)\bar{x} = X_0 \qquad (13.7)$$

so that $X_1(n)$ is neither feasible for n sellers nor efficiently entry-blocking. In this case, a corner solution will hold, namely, each of the n sellers will produce at minimum output. Industry output will then be $n\bar{x} > X_0$, so that final equilibrium will be reached at an industry output greater than that of the Bain–Sylos model.[5]

In the following cases, we let $X_s(m)$ be the equilibrium industry output for m sellers in the ordinary Cournot model, disregarding feasibility considerations. We assume, for simplicity, that $X_s(m)$ is unique, but the discussion could be extended to eliminate this assumption. Let $x_{si}(m)$ be the corresponding equilibrium output for the ith seller and let P be price. Then[6]

$$x_{si}(m) \frac{\mathrm{d}P}{\mathrm{d}X} + P = k \tag{13.8}$$

and, by addition,

$$X_s(m) \frac{\mathrm{d}P}{\mathrm{d}X} + mP = mk \tag{13.9}$$

For reasonably well-behaved demand curves, $X_s(m)$ will be a monotonically increasing function of m. I shall assume that this is the case.

Let us distinguish the cases where $X_s(n) = X_1(n)$, $X_s(n) < X_1(n)$, and $X_s(n) > X_1(n)$. If $X_s(n)$ is fairly close to $X_1(n)$, so that a linear approximation well represents the portion of the demand curve between the two points,[7] these cases can be illustrated graphically in the following manner.

In Figure 13.1, DD' is the demand curve, and the horizontal line the marginal (average)-cost curve. The line EF is drawn tangent to DD' at B, the point corresponding to $X_1(n)$. It cuts the marginal-cost curve at A, with corresponding industry output X_A. Since, if EF were actually the demand curve instead of only an approximation to it, $X_s(n)$ would be $(n/n + 1)X_A$, while $X_1(n)$ is actually $(n/n + 1)X_c$, we may conclude that (roughly) $X_s(n) \gtreqless X_1(n)$ according as $X_A \gtreqless X_c$. This is easily seen to be equivalent to the statement that (roughly) $X_s(n) \gtreqless X_1(n)$ according as the absolute value of the elasticity of demand at B is greater than, equal to or less than the absolute value of the elasticity of demand at B when the demand curve is a straight line through B and C.

Case 2: $X_s(n) = X_1(n)$. This is similar to Case 1, save that $X_s(m)$ may not be feasible for m sellers for some or all $m < n$. In any case, whether $X_s(m)$ is produced or whether a corner solution $X = m\bar{x}$ obtains for m sellers, entry will not be blocked for $m < n$. The analysis of the case of n sellers is exactly the same as in Case 1. Industry output will always be $n\bar{x}$, but this will always be greater than X_0 except in the case where S is an integer, so that ρ is zero.

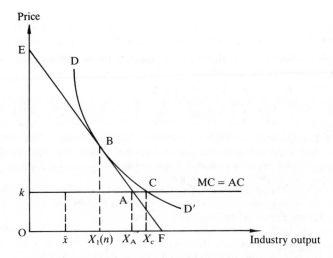

Figure 13.1 The pictorial representation of Case 1.

Case 3: $X_s(n) < X_1(n)$. As before, the solution for m sellers when $m < n$, whether $X = X_s(m)$ or $X = m\bar{x}$, will not be entry-blocking. The solution for n sellers, however, will always be the corner solution $X = n\bar{x}$,[8] and, as before, this will always be greater than X_0 save in the case of integral size of market.

Case 4: $X_s(n) > X_1(n)$. Here it is possible that $X_s(m) \geq X_0$ for some $m < n$. In this case, equilibrium will be reached with fewer than n sellers. The case of $X_s(m) = X_0$, of course, can be expected to happen only by accident. If $X_s(m) < X_0$ for all $m < n$, equilibrium will be reached with n sellers[9] at $X = n\bar{x} > X_0$ if $\rho > 0$ and $X_1(n) < X_s(n) < n\bar{x}$ both hold and at $X_s(n) > X_1(n) \geq X_0$ otherwise.

To summarize, we have found that equilibrium is reached in the enlarged Cournot model with industry output at X_0 only exceptionally in Case 4 and only for S an integer in Cases 1–3. Since this latter circumstance could likewise occur only by accident, we may conclude that, in general, equilibrium industry output will be larger and price lower in the enlarged Cournot model than in the Bain–Sylos model as presented by Modigliani. Finally, since the enlarged Cournot model predicts not only the equilibrium industry output and price but also the equilibrium number of sellers and the way in which the equilibrium industry output is divided among them, while the Bain–Sylos model makes no such prediction, it is clear that, so far as their respective results are concerned, these two models are indeed different. Thus, so far as these results are concerned, the Bain–Sylos model is truly a 'new development on the oligopoly front'.[10]

Notes

1. 'New developments on the oligopoly front', *Journal of Political Economy*, **LXVI** (June 1958), 215–32.

2. That is, in a perfectly competitive market with a different cost structure for the individual firm but the same aggregate-cost function. If desired, the statement in the text may be taken simply as defining the no-profit industry output and price.

3. In other words, given the cost structure, this is a classical Cournot model with Sylos' postulate holding for all potential entrants. The model discussed above, similarly, was a Chamberlinian joint maximization model with the same postulate holding.

4. For discussion of the ordinary Cournot model see E.H. Chamberlin, *The Theory of Monopolistic Competition* (7th ed.; Cambridge Mass.: Harvard University Press, 1956), Appendix A, pp. 221 ff.

5. Here and later, as in the Bain–Sylos model, we ignore the possibility that if $\rho = 0$ and we somehow started with $n + 1$ sellers, profits would be zero but not negative, so that there might be no incentive to exit.

6. See Chamberlin (1956) of Note 4.

7. The following construction, of course, is equivalent to expanding the demand function in Taylor's series around $X_1(n)$ and ignoring terms of higher than first degree.

8. By the way, it is obvious that Equation 13.8 cannot hold for any seller with $x_{si}(m) > \bar{x}$ if $\bar{x}(\mathrm{d}P/\mathrm{d}X) + P < k$ and the demand curve is downward-sloping. Hence, if a corner solution obtains for any seller, it obtains for all.

9. Note that $X_s(m) \geq X_c$ is impossible, by Equation 13.9, if the demand curve is downward-sloping.

10. The true analogy, of course, is with a Cournot 'leadership' model with all firms already in the industry playing the collective leader to the potential entrant's follower. This is another story, however.

14

The stability of the Cournot oligopoly solution: The effects of speeds of adjustment and increasing marginal costs (1961)

In an interesting recent paper,[1] R.D. Theocharis argues that the Cournot solution to the oligopoly problem is dynamically stable if and only if there are less than three sellers; for precisely three sellers, perpetual but bounded oscillations are obtained; and for more than three sellers, there is always instability.

This chapter argues that Theocharis' results are in large part due to the type of adjustment to disequilibrium which he assumes the sellers to make and due also to his assumption of constant marginal costs. We show that, if one considers a somewhat wider class of adjustment processes[2] (of which the Theocharis process is, in a sense, a limiting case), the Cournot solution is not necessarily unstable no matter what the number of sellers (although the tendency to instability does rise with the number of sellers for most of the processes considered). Indeed, we show that, for a process which is, in a sense, at the opposite limit of the class considered from the Theocharis process, the Cournot solution is invariably stable, no matter what the number of sellers. For processes other than this limiting one, we establish necessary, sufficient and sometimes necessary and sufficient conditions for stability in the large.

We further show that within the class of adjustment processes considered (which, remember, includes the Theocharis process), increasing marginal costs are always a stabilizing factor. Finally, we show that as the number of sellers goes to infinity, if each seller continues to behave *à la Cournot* but neglects its own influence on price, and if the

I am indebted to Robert L. Bishop and Robert M. Solow for discussion of parts of this chapter. They are not responsible for its errors.

Theocharis process is employed, our results lead to the well-known stability conditions for the cobweb model. However (and not surprisingly), the Cournot model is always more likely to be stable whatever the number of sellers if each seller takes its own effect on price into account than if it does not.

Aside from any interest which this paper may hold for the history of doctrine, it may also be of some moderate interest for the current discussion of the stability of competitive equilibrium, since it affords an example of a model whose stability properties depend closely on the type of adjustment process assumed to hold for the individual participants. In particular, it turns out that the stability properties of the system depend crucially on the speeds of adjustment involved and on other market parameters if a difference equation system is used, whereas, in the corresponding differential equation system, there is almost no such dependence. This perhaps mildly suggests that it may be important to worry in more general discussions about the adjustment process at the individual level, rather than simply assuming that some market variable (aggregate or average) adjusts in some specified (but sometimes mysterious) way.

We begin by summarizing Theocharis' model.[3] Let there be n sellers, with respective non-negative outputs $x_1, x_2, \ldots, x_n$. Let p be the *ex post* market price and t be time. It is assumed that the market demand curve is:

$$p_t = a - b \sum_{i=1}^{n} x_{it} \qquad (14.1)$$

where $a, b > 0$ and (since p_t is non-negative)

$$a/b \geq \sum_{i=1}^{n} x_{it} \geq 0 \qquad (14.2)$$

Each seller is assumed to have total cost C_i ($i = 1, \ldots, n$) with *constant* marginal cost c_i ($i = 1, \ldots, n$).

Each seller expects that the output of every other seller will not change from $t - 1$ to t. On this assumption, it expects p_t to be a function of its output alone. In other words, letting p_t^i stand for the price expected by the ith seller:

$$p_t^i = a - bx_{it} - b \sum_{j \neq i} x_{jt-1} \qquad (i = 1, \ldots, n) \qquad (14.3)$$

Given Equation 14.3, the profit anticipated by the ith seller is $p_t^i x_{it} - C_i$, and this will be maximized for:

$$\frac{\partial}{\partial x_{it}}(p_t^i x_{it} - C_i) = a - 2bx_{it} - b \sum_{j \neq i} x_{jt-1} - c_i = 0$$

$$(i = 1, \ldots, n) \tag{14.4}$$

Let x_{it}^* be the (unique) value of x_{it} satisfying Equation 14.4. Clearly,

$$x_{it}^* = \frac{a - c_i}{2b} - (1/2) \sum_{j \neq i} x_{jt-1} \qquad (i = 1, \ldots, n) \tag{14.5}$$

or, letting x_t and x_t^* be the n-component column vectors whose elements are the x_{it} and x_{it}^*, respectively:

$$x_t^* = T_n x_{t-1} + w \tag{14.6}$$

where w is an n-component column vector, whose elements are the $(a - c_i)/2b$ and T_n is an $n \times n$ matrix:

$$T_n = \begin{bmatrix} 0 & -1/2 & -1/2 & . & . & . & -1/2 \\ -1/2 & 0 & -1/2 & . & . & . & -1/2 \\ . & & & . & & & . \\ . & & & . & & & \\ . & & & . & & & -1/2 \\ -1/2 & . & & . & . & . & -1/2 & 0 \end{bmatrix} \tag{14.7}$$

Theocharis now assumes (implicitly) that each seller adjusts its output completely and instantaneously, that is, that:

$$x_t = x_t^* \tag{14.8}$$

This gives rise to the system of difference equations:

$$x_t = T_n x_{t-1} + w \tag{14.9}$$

Since w is a constant vector and T_n is non-singular, the stability of the system (Equation 14.9) depends only on the latent roots of T_n. The system will converge to equilibrium if and only if all such roots are less than one in modulus.

As it happens, the latent roots of T_n are all real and can be determined at sight. There is one root equal to 1/2 which occurs with multiplicity $n - 1$, and the remaining root is $\left[-\frac{(n - 1)}{2} \right]$. Since the absolute value of this last root is less than, equal to or greater than unity according as $n \lessgtr 3$, the system is stable only for two sellers (or, trivially, for one). For three sellers, there are perpetual but finite oscillations, and for more than three, the system explodes.[4]

Now, a great deal of the weight of this result falls on the assumption as to the adjustment mechanism – Equation 14.8. It is not surprising to discover that a model in which each seller makes complete and instantaneous adjustments, simultaneously assuming each other seller's output to remain unchanged, is unstable. On the contrary, it is some-what surprising to find convergence for $n = 2$. It therefore seems of interest to investigate the stability properties of the system under more usual assumptions about the adjustment mechanism.[5]

We consider two related types of adjustment. Let K be an $n \times n$ diagonal matrix with diagonal elements $K_1, \ldots, K_n$ all positive.[6]

The first class of adjustment mechanisms which we shall consider is:

$$x_t - x_{t-1} = K(x_t^* - x_{t-1}) \tag{14.10}$$

Here, the K_i are speeds of adjustment. They are the fractions of the distance from actual to desired output which are covered in one time period. (When discussing Equation 14.10, we should thus expect $K_i \leqslant 1$, for all $i = 1, \ldots, n$, but this will not be of later importance.) Clearly Equation 14.8 is a limiting case of Equation 14.10, with $K = 1$.

Now, the magnitudes of the K_i depend (other things being equal) on the length of the time unit involved in Equation 14.10. That unit is the smallest interval at the end of which the situation is reviewed by at least one seller – the smallest interval over which x_t^* remains the same. Given the fraction of the desired distance which would be covered in a year, say, the K_i will be smaller, the shorter is that interval. In the limit, where at least one seller continuously reviews decisions, we have (dropping the time subscript):

$$\dot{x} = K(x^* - x) \tag{14.11}$$

where $\dot{x}$ is the n component column vector of the time derivatives of the elements of x. We shall refer to Equations 14.11 and 14.10 as the 'continuous' and the 'discrete' adjustment processes, respectively. (In general, we should expect the K_i in Equation 14.11 to be small relative to the K_i in Equation 14.10, other things being equal, but there is no need to restrict their magnitude other than to assume that they are non-negative.)

It may be objected, however, that adjustment processes like Equation 14.10 (for $K \neq 1$) and especially Equation 14.11 are inconsist-ent with the Cournot assumption that each seller expects all the others to maintain output. This is not the case. All discussions of the Cournot model allow the sellers to receive new information as to the outputs of their rivals. No seller is ever assumed to look once and for all at other outputs and then never to look again. Rather, the seller is assumed to look, then adjust, then look again, and so forth. (This may not seem like very sensible behavior – but that is a criticism of the Cournot assumption itself.) Cournot oligopolists may be stupid, but they are not stubborn. Were this not so, practically any point could be an equi-librium. This being the case, there seems nothing inconsistent in assuming that sellers can receive information while making adjustments as well as afterwards, and this is all that is required for $K_i < 1$ in Equation 14.10. Indeed, the behavior of the sellers is more reasonable for the K_i all small, for if adjustments are made very slowly relative to the time interval at which decisions are reviewed and rivals' outputs surveyed, the assumption that rivals maintain constant output will turn out to be a considerably better approximation than in the case of Equation 14.8 where adjustments are made very rapidly relative to the frequency of decision reviews. (This is another way of observing that instability, given Equation 14.8, is not surprising). We may therefore be quite comfortable about examining the consequences of Equations 14.10 and 14.11 within the context of the Cournot model.

As already indicated, however, it is desirable to generalize the model in another way before proceeding – to include the possibility of increasing (or decreasing) marginal costs. This is so for at least two reasons. First, there is a sense in which we already expect constant or decreasing marginal costs to be a destabilizing factor, for sharply rising marginal costs clearly inhibit variations in output and thus make the constant rivals' output assumption a better one. It is of interest to see if this is the case and to see in just what way such an effect occurs. Second, we shall use linear marginal cost curves; however, even this simple extension allows us to broaden our results beyond those immediately obtained. Specifically, by allowing non-constant marginal costs, we make it possible to apply our results (under certain assumptions) to the case of stability in the small for non-linear demand and cost curves, since such curves may be approximated by linear (but not constant) ones in the neighbourhood of equilibrium.

We thus alter Theocharis' assumption as to costs and assume instead that the ith seller's total cost curve, C_i, is of the form:

$$C_i = g_i + c_i x_i + 1/2 d x_i^2 \qquad (i = 1, \ldots, n) \qquad (14.12)$$

(where $g_i \geq 0$ and we shall further restrict c_i and d below), so that marginal costs are of the form $c_i + dx_i$. Marginal costs will thus be increasing, decreasing or constant according as $d \gtreqless 0$ (note that we may thus always specialize our results to study the Theocharis case). Observe that while the intercepts of the marginal costs curves are allowed to differ among sellers, the slopes are not.[7]

Under this assumption, Equation 14.4 becomes:

$$a - 2bx_{it} - b \sum_{j \neq i} x_{jt-1} - c_i - dx_{it} \doteq 0 \qquad (14.13)$$

$$(i = 1, \ldots, n)$$

and thus:

$$x_t^* = F_n x_{t-1} + v \tag{14.14}$$

where F_n is an $n \times n$ matrix with 0 everywhere on the principal diagonal and $\left[-\dfrac{b}{(2b + d)} \right]$ everywhere else; and v is an n-component column vector whose typical element is $\dfrac{(a - c_i)}{(2b + d)}$. (Note that this reduces to Equation 14.6 when $d = 0$.)

Now, we cannot allow the parameters of the cost curve (Equation 14.12) to be completely unrestricted. Aside from the restriction of the g_i to be non-negative (fixed costs not less than zero), there are a few other reasonable restrictions which we shall impose.

In the first place, for x_{it}^* to truly maximize profits, we must have the second order condition:

$$2b + d > 0 \tag{14.15}$$

Second, it seems fatuous to regard a seller as 'in' the market in any sense, unless there is some admissible situation in which a non-negative profit can be made by producing a positive output. Clearly, however, the profit of the ith seller is a decreasing function of all other outputs, other things being equal; we need therefore only look at the case when all other outputs are zero – if non-negative profits are not anticipated here, they will never be anticipated. For the ith seller's output also to be zero, moreover, the expected profits cannot be positive (in the long run they will be zero). Since, in view of the second order condition (Equation 14.15) marginal profits are a decreasing linear function of own output, non-negative profits can never be expected unless marginal profits at zero output are non-negative. (Even if they are zero, loss of money will be expected by producing more than an infinitesimal amount.) Hence it is reasonable to require at least:

$$a \geqslant c_i \qquad (i = 1, \ldots, n) \tag{14.16}$$

Third, while we are prepared to admit $d < 0$, so that marginal costs may decline, we are not prepared to allow marginal costs to decline so far as to become non-positive so that a greater output can be produced at the same cost as or more cheaply than a smaller one. On the other hand, since we have assumed linear marginal cost curves, it would be self-defeating to require that marginal costs be strictly positive for *all* positive outputs, since this would require $d \geqslant 0$ and would rule out *any* decreasing marginal cost curve. Fortunately, we may reasonably compromise by requiring positive marginal costs for all outputs admissible under Equation 14.2 (we can always pretend that linearity ceases after that and that marginal costs eventually cease to fall). In view of the assumed linearity of the marginal cost curves, however, it suffices to require positive marginal cost at both ends of the admissible range, thus:

$$c_i > 0, \qquad d(a/b) > -c_i \qquad (i = 1, \ldots, n) \qquad (14.17)$$

However, Equations 14.16 and 14.17 together imply a further restriction on d. Suppose that $d \leq -b$. Then, multiplying both sides of that inequality by (a/b) (a positive number), we obtain $-a \geq d(a/b)$, and, from the second part of Equation 14.17, $-a > -c_i$ $(i = 1, \ldots, n)$. Multiplying these last inequalities by -1, however, we obtain $a < c_i$ $(i = 1, \ldots, n)$, which directly contradicts Equation 14.16. It must therefore be the case that:

$$d > -b \qquad (14.18)$$

so that marginal costs cannot decline as fast as price.

It is interesting to observe that, while all these restrictions have apparently little or nothing to do with stability, it is in fact the case that Equation 14.18 is a necessary condition for the stability of every system considered in this chapter.[8]

It will be convenient to begin with the continuous adjustment process, Equation 14.11. Substituting from Equation 14.14 and suppressing the time subscript:

$$\dot{x} = K(F_n x + v - x) = K(F_n - I_n) x + Kv$$
$$= KA_n x + Kv \qquad (14.19)$$

where $A_n = F_n - I_n$, so that A_n is an $n \times n$ matrix with -1 everywhere on its principal diagonal and $-\dfrac{b}{(2b + d)}$ everywhere else.

Since KA_n is non-singular and Kv is constant, the stability properties of Equation 14.19 depend only on the characteristic roots of KA_n. We may immediately state the fundamental properties of those characteristic roots on which all later results depend. (The proof is somewhat cumbersome and is deferred to the Appendix.)

Theorem 14.1: The characteristic roots of KA_n are all real and negative. Specifically, let λ_i denote a root of KA_n $(i = 1, \ldots, n)$; then, if the K_i and the λ_i are numbered in ascending order of absolute magnitude:

$$\left(-\frac{b + d}{2b + d}\right) K_i \geq \lambda_i \geq \left(-\frac{b + d}{2b + d}\right) K_{i+1}$$
$$(i = 1, \ldots, n - 1) \qquad \text{(a)}$$

the equalities holding if and only if $K_i = K_{i+1}$.

$$\left[-\frac{(n + 1) b + d}{2b + d} \right] K_1 \geqslant -K_1 - \left(\frac{b}{2b + d} \right) \sum_{i=2}^{n} K_i \geqslant \lambda_n$$

$$\geqslant -K_n - \left(\frac{b}{2b + d} \right) \sum_{i=1}^{n-1} K_i \geqslant \left[-\frac{(n + 1) b + d}{2b + d} \right] K_n$$

(b)

the equalities holding if and only if all the K_i are equal.

It follows immediately that:

Theorem 14.2: The system (Equation 14.19) is always stable.
Note that this result in no way depends upon the number of sellers.
Note further as a special case, that even for $d = 0$, as in Theocharis, the system is invariably stable.

The case of the discrete adjustment process (Equation 14.10) is a little more complicated. Substituting from Equation 14.14:

$$\begin{aligned} x_t &= K(F_n x_{t-1} + v - x_{t-1}) + x_{t-1} \\ &= (KA_n + I_n) x_{t-1} + Kv = B_n x_{t-1} + Kv \end{aligned}$$

(14.20)

where $B_n = KA_n + I_n$.

Now, the difference equation system (Equation 14.20) will be stable if and only if the characteristic roots of B_n are less than one in absolute value. However, it is evident that each such root is equal to $1 + \lambda_i$ for λ_i a root of KA_n. Since, by Theorem 14.1, all the λ_i are real, a necessary and sufficient condition for stability is that $0 > \lambda_i > -2$ $(i = 1, \ldots, n)$. Further, since the former inequality will always hold, we need only concern ourselves with the latter one. Finally, this being so, we need only concern ourselves with λ_n. Theorem 14.1 thus yields immediately:

Theorem 14.3: (a) A sufficient condition for the stability of Equation 14.20 is that

$$K_n < 2 - \left(\frac{b}{2b + d} \right) \sum_{i=1}^{n-1} K_i$$

Hence, it is also sufficient that

$$K_n < 2 \left[\frac{2b + d}{(n + 1)b + d} \right]$$

(b) A necessary condition for the stability of Equation 14.20 is that

$$K_1 < 2 - \left(\frac{b}{2b + d} \right) \sum_{i=2}^{n} K_i$$

Hence, it is also necessary that

$$K_1 < 2 \left[\frac{2b + d}{(n + 1)b + d} \right]$$

(c) If all the K_i are the same, a necessary *and* sufficient condition for the stability of Equation 14.20 is that

$$K_i < 2 \left[\frac{2b + d}{(n + 1)b + d} \right]$$

Observe that the Theocharis results follow directly from the last statement if $K_i = 1$ and $d = 0$.

These results are rather interesting. It turns out that it is sufficient for stability that the largest speed of adjustment be less than some critical magnitude and necessary that the smallest speed of adjustment be less than the same or a similar magnitude. That magnitude declines with the number of sellers and rises with the slope of the marginal cost curve, so that more sellers tend toward instability and increasing marginal costs toward stability. However, given the number of sellers, it is always possible to find speeds of adjustment such that the system is stable, regardless of what that number is (this follows from the fact that the limiting continuous case is always stable). Further, for any number of sellers, it is always possible to find marginal cost increasing so fast that the system is stable for all speeds of adjustment less than 2 (that is, provided that the sellers do not more than overshoot their target each period by as far again as the distance to the target).

Of course, the fact that the speeds of adjustment can always be low enough to produce stability is hardly surprising. We have already remarked that the assumption of constant rivals' outputs will seem a better approximation when decisions are reviewed frequently and adjustments made relatively slowly than when decisions are reviewed infrequently and adjustments made relatively quickly. It is thus quite sensible that equilibrium should be approached by a group of sellers all making that assumption, provided that adjustments are made sufficiently slowly relative to the frequency of decision review.

Similarly, since increasing marginal costs tend to inhibit large output variations and thus to make the constant rivals' output assumption a better one, it is reasonable to find increasing marginal costs a stabilizing factor.

We may add a few points of minor interest. First, in the case where all speeds are unity, Theorem 14.3 (c) shows that Equation 14.20 is stable if and only if:

$$(n - 3) < d/b \tag{14.21}$$

For $d = 0$, we get the Theocharis case, and it is interesting to observe that $n = 3$ is just on the borderline of instability.

Finally, we may inquire as to what happens to stability when each seller continues to assume all rivals' outputs constant but neglects its own effect on price (this can happen for n very large or marginal costs so sharply rising that such effect is negligible for all contemplated outputs) so that price is assumed constant. It would be tedious to go through the whole business again on this assumption, but it is evident from Equation 14.13 that the effect is to change the term in various denominators from $2b + d$ to d. Since $b > 0$ by assumption, the effect of this must always be destabilizing. The second-order condition for a maximum now requires $d > 0$, and the critical magnitudes of Theorem 14.3 are clearly reduced. Restricting ourselves to (c) of that theorem for simplicity, we obtain the result that now a necessary and sufficient condition for stability in the discrete adjustment case is:

$$K_i < 2 \qquad \left[\frac{(n+1)b}{2 - K_i} \right] K_i < d \qquad \text{(14.22)}$$

Since in this case we may aggregate the marginal cost curves to secure the market supply curve, we may restate this result in terms of the slope of that curve. Letting that slope be denoted by e and observing that $d = en$, we have as necessary and sufficient conditions for stability in this case:

$$K_i < 2 \qquad \left(\frac{n+1}{n} \right)\left(\frac{K_i}{2 - K_i} \right) b < e \qquad \text{(14.23)}$$

In particular, for all $K_i = 1$, as n goes to infinity, this approaches:

$$b < e \qquad \text{(14.24)}$$

that is, the market demand curve must be sloped less steeply than the market supply curve, the well-known stability condition of the cobweb model.

Appendix

In proving Theorem 14.1, it will be convenient to drop, until later reinstated, the convention that the K_i are numbered in ascending order of size.

Lemma 14.1: $\text{Det } (A_i) = (-1)^i \left(\frac{b+d}{2b+d} \right)^i \left(1 + \frac{ib}{b+d} \right)$
$(i = 1, \ldots, n)$

Proof: It is apparent by inspection that A_i has a characteristic root of multiplicity $i - 1$ equal to $\left[\dfrac{b}{(2b + d)} - 1\right]$ and a characteristic root equal to $\left[-\dfrac{(i - 1)b}{(2b + d)} - 1\right]$. However, the determinant of any matrix equals the product of the characteristic roots thereof, so

$$\text{Det }(A_i) = \left(\frac{b}{2b + d} - 1\right)^{i-1}\left(-\frac{(i - 1)b}{2b + d} - 1\right) \tag{14.25}$$

$$(i = 1, \ldots, n)$$

which yields the lemma on some rewriting.

Now, for $1 \leqslant m \leqslant n$, let $K(m)$ be an $m \times m$ diagonal matrix with $K_1, \ldots, K_m$ on the principal diagonal ($K(n) = K$). For a variable λ, let $P_m(\lambda)$ be the characteristic polynomial of $K(m)A_m$, that is:

$$P_m(\lambda) = \text{Det }(I_m\lambda - K(m)A_m) \tag{14.26}$$

For brevity, let $f = \left[\dfrac{(b + d)}{(2b + d)}\right]$. Consider $P_m(-fK_1)$. We prove:

Lemma 14.2: $P_m(-fK_1) = f(K_m - K_1)P_{m-1}(-fK_1)$ $(1 < m \leqslant n)$

Proof: As is well known,

$$P_m(\lambda) = \sum_{i=0}^{m}(-1)^iV_i(m)\lambda^{m-i} \tag{14.27}$$

where $V_0(m) = 1$ and $V_i(m)$ is the sum of all ith order principal minors of $K(m)A_m$ for $i = 1, \ldots, m$. However, it is apparent from inspection of $K(m)A_m$ that:

$$V_i(m) = W_i(m) \text{ Det }(A_i) \qquad (i = 0, \ldots, m) \tag{14.28}$$

where Det (A_0) is defined as unity as is $W_0(m)$, and $W_i(m)$ is the sum of all ith order principal minors of $K(m)$ for $i = 1, \ldots, m$. Since $K(m)$ is diagonal, this means that (for $i = 1, \ldots, m$) $W_i(m)$ is the sum of the products of all sets of i of the first m of the K_j, regardless of order.[9]

Now, let $U_i(m)$ be defined as the similar sum of the products of any i of the first m of the K_j, *excluding* K_1, for $i = 1, \ldots, m - 1$. Define $U_0(m) = 1$ and $U_{-1}(m) = 0 = U_m(m)$. Then:

$$W_i(m) = U_i(m) + K_1U_{i-1}(m) \qquad (i = 0, \ldots, m) \tag{14.29}$$

Substituting Equation 14.29 into Equation 14.28 and the result into Equation 14.27:

$$P_m(\lambda) = \sum_{i=0}^{m} (-1)^i [\mathrm{Det}\ (A_i)]\ [U_i(m) + K_1 U_{i-1}(m)]\lambda^{m-i}$$

$$\hspace{2cm} (14.30)$$

$$= \sum_{i=0}^{m} f^i\left(1 + \frac{ib}{b+d}\right) [U_i(m) + K_1 U_{i-1}(m)]\lambda^{m-i}$$

where the second equality follows from Lemma 14.1 and the fact that $2i$ is necessarily even.

Now, evaluating Equation 14.30 at $\lambda = -fK_1$ yields:

$$P_m(-fK_1) = \sum_{i=0}^{m} (-1)^{m-i} f^{m-i} f^i\left(1 + \frac{ib}{b+d}\right)[U_i(m) + K_1 U_{i-1}(m)]K_1^{m-i}$$

$$= f^m\left\{\sum_{i=0}^{m}(-1)^{m-i}K_1^{m-i}\left(1 + \frac{ib}{b+d}\right)U_i(m)\right. \hspace{1cm} (14.31)$$

$$\left. - \sum_{j=-1}^{m-1}(-1)^{m-j}K_1^{m-j}\left[1 + \frac{(j+1)b}{b+d}\right]U_j(m)\right\}$$

so that, remembering that $U_{-1}(m) = 0 = U_m(m)$:

$$P_m(-fK_1) = f^m\left(\frac{-b}{b+d}\right)\sum_{i=0}^{m-1}(-1)^{m-i}K_1^{m-i}U_i(m) \hspace{1cm} (14.32)$$

Now, observe that (defining $U_m(m-1) = 0$):

$$U_i(m) = U_i(m-1) + K_m U_{i-1}(m-1)$$
$$(i = 0, \ldots, m) \hspace{1cm} (14.33)$$

Substituting this into Equation 14.32, we have:

$$P_m(-fK_1) = f^m\left(\frac{-b}{b+d}\right)\sum_{i=0}^{m-1}(-1)^{m-i}K_1^{m-i}[U_i(m-1) + K_m U_{i-1}(m-1)]$$

$$\hspace{2cm} (14.34)$$

$$[U_i(m-1) + K_m U_{i-1}(m-1)]$$

and, since $K_m = (K_m - K_1) + K_1$, this becomes:

$$P_m(-fK_1) = f^m\left(\frac{-b}{b+d}\right)(K_m - K_1)\sum_{i=0}^{m-1}(-1)^{m-i}K_1^{m-i}U_{i-1}(m-1)$$

$$+ f^m\left(\frac{-b}{b+d}\right)\sum_{i=0}^{m-1}(-1)^{m-i}K_1^{m-i}U_i(m-1) \hspace{1cm} (14.35)$$

$$- f^m\left(\frac{-b}{b+d}\right)\sum_{j=-1}^{m-2}(-1)^{m-j}K_1^{m-j}U_j(m-1)$$

However, since $U_{-1}(m - 1) = 0 = U_{m-1}(m - 1)$, the last two sums cancel and we may rewrite the first as:

$$P_m(-fK_1) = (K_m - K_1)f^m\left(\frac{-b}{b + d}\right)^{m-2}\sum_{i=0}^{m-2}(-1)^{m-1-i}K_1^{m-1-i}U_{i-1}(m - 1)$$

$$(14.36)$$

which, on comparison with Equation 14.32, at last yields the lemma.

Lemma 14.3. $P_n(-fK_h) = f^{n-1}\left(\dfrac{b}{2b + d}\right)K_h\prod_{i\neq h}(K_i - K_h)$

$$(h = 1, \ldots, n)$$

Proof: Since we have dropped any convention about the numbering of the K_i, we may, without loss of generality, take $h = 1$. Repeated application of Lemma 14.2 now yields:

$$P_n(-fK_1) = f^{n-1}P_1(-fK_1)\prod_{i=2}^{n}(K_i - K_1) \qquad (14.37)$$

and the lemma follows immediately from direct evaluation of $P_1(-fK_1)$.

We are finally in position to prove Theorem 14.1. We now resume the convention that the K_i are numbered in order of increasing size. (Note that in view of Equation 14.18, $-f < 0$.) It is evident from Lemma 14.3, that $-fK_h$ is a root of KA_n if and only if K_h and either K_{h-1} or K_{h+1} or both are equal. There are two cases that remain to be examined:

Case 1: $K_{h-1} \neq K_h \neq K_{h+1} \neq K_{h+2}$. Here, P_n cannot be zero at either $-fK_h$ or $-fK_{h+1}$. However, from Lemma 14.3, $P_n(-fK_h)$ has precisely $h - 1$ negative factors while $P_n(-fK_{h+1})$ has precisely h negative factors. It follows that $P_n(\lambda)$ changes sign between $-fK_h$ and $-fK_{h+1}$ and thus that KA_n has a real root between those two points.

Case 2: $K_h \neq K_{h+1}$ but either $K_{h+1} = K_{h+2} = \ldots = K_{h+r}$ or $K_h = K_{h-1} = \ldots = K_{h-s}$ or both, for at least one of $r > 1$, $s > 0$ holding. It will suffice to take $r > 1$, $s = 0$ as the proof is similar for all other subcases. It is evident from inspection of KA_n that if $r > 1$, KA_n has a characteristic root equal to $-fK_{h+1}$ of multiplicity $r - 1$. However, by the factor theorem of algebra, $P_n(\lambda)$ can be written as:

$$P_n(\lambda) = (\lambda + fK_{h+2})(\lambda + fK_{h+3})\ldots(\lambda + fK_{h+r})Q_{n-r+1}(\lambda)$$

$$(14.38)$$

where $Q_{n-r+1}(\lambda)$ is a polynomial in λ of order $n - r + 1$ and is not zero at $\lambda = -fK_{h+1}$. From Lemma 14.3, however:

$$Q_{n-r+1}(-fK_h) = f^{n-r}\left(\frac{b}{2b + d}\right)K_h \prod_{i \neq h,h+2,\dots,h+r} (K_i - K_h)$$

(14.39)

while $Q_{n-r+1}(-fK_{h+1})$ is a similar expression with $h + 1$ substituted for h. Hence, as before, $Q_{n-r+1}(\lambda)$ must change sign between $\lambda = -fK_h$ and $\lambda = -fK_{h+1}$. This completes the proof of part (a) of the theorem.

Part (b) of the theorem is considerably easier. First, observe that the first and last inequalities (and the statement about when they hold) follow from the convention as to the ordering of the K_i. As to the middle two inequalities, since KA_n is negative and indecomposable, the desired result follows immediately from extension of a well-known theorem of Solow.[10]

Notes

1. 'On the stability of the Cournot solution on the oligopoly problem', *Review of Economic Studies*, Vol. XXVII (2), 1959–60, 133–4.
2. We argue below that the processes considered are by no means inconsistent with the traditional Cournot behavioral assumption.
3. For later convenience, we alter his notation somewhat, and consider the general n seller case explicitly rather than generalizing (as he does) from the case of $n = 3$.
4. Incidentally, Theocharis gives the solution to Equation 14.9 incorrectly for $n > 2$, although the error does not affect the result as regards stability. Since, as just observed, $1/2$ is a root of multiplicity $n - 1$, the solution contains terms in $t^{i-1}(1/2)^t$ for $i = 1, \dots, n - 1$. Only the first of these appears in Theocharis' Equations 8, 10 and 11 (Theocharis, 1960–1, 134; see Note 1).
5. The adjustment assumptions about to be introduced are common in the stability literature when applied to market prices; it is not so common to make them hold for the adjustment of individual outputs. However, as already remarked, the results here obtained mildly suggest that such a procedure might have interesting consequences for the discussion of stability of more general models than the present one.
6. It is not hard to generalize to the case where some or all of the K_i are zero, but such generalization is tedious and of little interest when carried out in detail. Briefly, if $K_1, \dots, K_s$ are zero, then the first s sellers maintain constant output. Since the remaining sellers take those outputs as given, the dynamic system becomes a system explaining movements in the last $n - s$ outputs which is identical to the system that would be obtained for $n - s$ sellers, save for the equilibrium position. This being so, all results obtained below carry over, provided that n is interpreted to be the number of sellers with non-zero K_i and stability understood to mean stability of the

second kind (since where the system converges to an equilibrium, there is no guarantee that such an equilibrium will be the Cournot one; rather it depends on the initial outputs of the sellers with zero K_i).

7. While it would be mildly interesting to generalize by removing this restriction, it is unlikely that such a generalization would qualitatively alter our results, and there does not seem to be any easy way to accomplish it. The reader will be better able to appreciate this after reading the Appendix and reflecting on the additional complexity caused by allowing the K_i (which enter in a relatively simply way) to differ.

8. Given Equation 14.15, $d > -b$ is a necessary (as well as a sufficient) condition for the crucial quantity $[-(b + d)/(2b + d)]$ of Theorem 14.1 below to be negative. For $d < -b$, that quantity is positive and Equation a of Theorem 14.1 holds with the inequalities reversed (the proof being unchanged as is Equation b). The matrix KA_n then has $n - 1$ positive real roots and all systems studied are obviously unstable. For $d = -b$, KA_n has a zero root of multiplicity $n - 1$. For $n = 2$, this yields – at best – stability of the second kind, while for $n > 2$ it yields instability since all solutions will include a polynomial time trend of order $n - 2$.

9. That is, for example, K_1K_2 only appears once in the sum, not once as K_1K_2 and once as K_2K_1.

10. R.M. Solow, 'On the structure of linear models', *Econometrica*, Vol. 20, No. 1 (January 1952), 36–8.

PART 2
Regulation of television

15

Community antenna television systems and the regulation of television broadcasting (1966)

Under existing institutional arrangements in the United States, the broadcast signal of a television station has many of the aspects of a pure public good. If a signal is broadcast over the air to a certain community, all members of that community can receive and enjoy it, provided they possess receiving sets. Further, television sets are sold under supply conditions that presumably involve the costs of their construction, but surely have nothing to do with the cost of production of the signals they receive. In general, no attempt is made to charge the latter cost directly to television (TV) viewers.

This is not to say that such costs could not be so charged in principle. Experiments with pay-TV have been made with varying degrees of success; however, there is no reason to believe that, in the absence of free television competition, a system of exclusively pay-TV would not be viable. (And, if it would not, ought the service to be provided at all?) It is technically feasible to charge viewers according to use of the service. Alternatively, a less economically efficient arrangement might be used whereby any owner of a receiving set is taxed a flat amount every year and the proceeds used to finance television broadcasting. Such a system is used in most other countries. It has the merit of financing the service by charging the users, but the defect of not discriminating between heavy and light users. Further, it imposes a single flat charge

My knowledge of the matters discussed was largely first acquired during my preparation of testimony on behalf of the National Association of Broadcasters before the Federal Communications Commission. That testimony concerned the impact of cable television (then called 'community antenna television systems') on local broadcast station's audience and revenue. The research is reported in detail in Chapter 16. I am indebted to V.E. Ferrall, Jr, and A.Y. Naftalin for discussion of many of the issues here considered. The responsibility for the views here expressed is solely mine, however.

covering all programs broadcast during the year rather than different charges for different programs which are, in fact, different products. In such a system, programming decisions are made without regard to the state of demand for individual programs when individually priced. Rather they are made on the basis of the state of demand when all individual programs are priced at zero once the fixed charge has been paid, or on the basis of what the producing authority for other reasons thinks ought to be broadcast.[1]

The system used in the United States has all the defects of such an arrangement without the merit of charging television viewers as such for the cost of providing the programs. Television viewing is mainly financed through advertising, so that viewers are subsidized by the consumers of advertised products. In these circumstances, the choice among alternative programs is only a very indirect market choice and one which certainly fails to reflect the state of demand which would obtain if programs were priced at cost rather than at zero. In this system, the long-run costs of placing and keeping a television station on the air are not defrayed by those who use its services in their capacity as television viewers.

Even given the inefficiency of such an arrangement for reflecting consumers' tastes and production costs, it has not been the case that one could safely rely on the competition of stations for advertisers to optimize resource allocation subject to the limitations of that arrangement. Nor does that competition obviously produce those programs which might in some sense be said to be in the best public interest. This is the case in part because of the limitations on entry into local television markets which have until fairly recently been inherent in the technology and history of the industry.

The very high frequency broadcast band (VHF) happens to be that in which television broadcasting first became feasible. Unfortunately, that band contains only twelve channels (2–13). Even after ultra high frequency (UHF) broadcasting opened the technical possibility of an additional seventy channels (14–83), in most communities the fact that most existing receivers were able to receive only VHF limited entry to the twelve channels of the VHF band. While this situation is slowly changing due to the All-Channel Law (which went into effect in 1964) requiring all new sets to be capable of UHF reception, VHF broadcasting has been and still is the most profitable if not the only economically viable means of television broadcasting in most major television markets.

In addition, television signals cannot be received off the air without special relaying apparatus, unless the receiver and the transmitting tower are in a direct line of sight. In particular, signals cannot be directly received beyond the horizon or through mountainous terrain.

This circumstance means that while programs may be nationally produced, the sources of broadcast signals in each local area have to be local sources. This has led (at least in principle) to the possibility of a system of local control over programming and of diversity from market to market, a possibility greatly fostered by the deliberate policy of the Federal Communications Commission (FCC). The wish to promote such diversity as a matter of public policy, the considerations of equity between neighboring communities, and the fact that communities are sufficiently close that the 'natural television reception area' of each generally overlaps that of others, has led the FCC naturally to restrict licensing of television stations in a given locality not merely to the twelve VHF channels but to those channels not assigned to neighboring communities. The result has been that only the largest cities have as many as seven VHF channels available (and one of these is generally reserved for educational television) while most communities have three at most.

In this situation, it is not reasonable to rely on atomistic competition to produce optimal results even given the limitations of the arrangements for recouping costs already discussed. Indeed, we do not rely on such competition. The FCC has generally strongly encouraged local television stations to show programs of a public service nature and has been particularly interested in the promotion of locally originating live programs.

This is a reasonable interest. The effect of the line-of-sight limitation in promoting a diversity of broadcast sources and local control over local program choice may be largely lost if local stations find it most profitable to rely on network or other national sources for programs. While it is possible that such profitability may reflect an overall similarity in tastes among television viewers everywhere, the non-existence of a mechanism for charging the viewers the long-run marginal production costs of the programs they watch makes it impossible to know this. It is at least not obvious that, if all programs were properly priced, local programs would be less profitable than national ones for local stations. In insisting that local broadcast stations originate local programming (which frequently operates at a loss under present arrangements), the FCC may be partly redressing the inefficiencies of the current institutional arrangements for financing television production. Moreover, such a policy may act to inform and change the tastes of the viewing public and (as the FCC doubtless believes) may well be justified on grounds other than that of economic efficiency. Indeed, the policy of diversity of control over mass communication media is obviously founded in public purposes outside of economics.

In any case, the effect of such a policy is the subsidization of local programming by the profits from network affiliation and broadcasting.

Those profits are available for this purpose in part because of the technologically imposed limitations on entry into local television markets.
Thus, any innovation which partly removes such limitations is likely
also to have an upsetting effect on the FCC's policy of favoring local
autonomy.

Such innovations have, in fact, been made, and their growth has
been rapid. One might expect this given the existence of entry-inducing
profits in local television markets, particularly if such innovations permit relatively low-cost extension of existing services into markets which
could not fully support an additional broadcast station. There are now
two principal means of overcoming the line-of-sight limitation on the
reception of the signal of a given station. These are boosters and satellite stations, on the one hand, and community antenna television systems (CATVs), on the other.[2]

A booster is a device to pick up a given television signal and instantaneously rebroadcast it with increased power. It is particularly useful in
mountainous terrain where it enables a television station to reach communities and areas which are separated from it by mountains.

For our purposes, a satellite station may be considered a large booster.
It is a television station which originates no (or almost no) programming but rebroadcasts the programs of its parent station. In so doing it
gives the parent station coverage of a much wider area than that station
could reach by itself. Typically, advertising time on parent and satellite
stations is sold as a single unit.

There are three features of the booster or satellite station arrangement which are important for our purposes. First, such arrangements
typically involve only the signal of a single station; second, the rebroadcast signal can be received (as can any ordinary television signal) by
any receiver within range. This leads to the third point. Boosters and
satellites are generally not financed directly by viewers as such in the
communities to which they bring the given signal. All these points distinguish boosters and satellite stations from CATVs and all of them help
to explain why CATVs have had a far higher rate of growth and are
believed to present a much more pressing regulatory problem than
boosters and satellite stations.

The influence of the first feature is evident. Since boosters or satellite
stations typically involve but a single signal, they are not so attractive to
viewers in a local television market as is a device which brings in many
signals at once. Next, since off-the-air signals can be received by all
viewers, a television station (or other entrepreneur) contemplating the
installation of a booster to serve a given community cannot hope to
profit from the investment by charges on the viewers served (unless, in
true public-goods-analysis fashion, the community can be persuaded to

use its taxing power and build the facility itself).[3] As is the case (under present institutional arrangements) with the construction and operation of a television station itself, the profits from the construction of a booster or a satellite station must therefore come from the additional demand for advertising time on the parent station generated by the existence of the additional audience which the new facility will allow advertisers to reach when their commercials appear on the parent station. While such a return has frequently been (and still is) present in sufficient measure to justify the construction and operation of a booster, particularly in communities with little or no pre-existing television service, it clearly depends *ex ante* on forecasts of the size of the extra audience which will actually view the station's rebroadcast signal.[4] It is further dependent on the desire of advertisers to reach the entered market via the given station rather than in some other way (which may already be in use).[5]

Thus, especially as a means of entry into markets with some existing television service, boosters and satellite stations may not always seem so attractive a proposition as some device which can gain revenues directly from the users without non-user benefits and which is attractive to users because it brings in several different television signals rather than one. Such a device is the CATV.

The original CATVs were simply giant television antennas. Such an antenna set up on a mountain can receive signals that are blocked by the terrain from reception in the valley below. The signals are then fed by cable to the television sets of subscribers to the system rather than being rebroadcast and picked up off the air as is the case with signals passed through boosters. While most CATVs still (1965) operate in this way, a growing number of large systems use microwave relay to beam the desired signals from a point near their origin to the CATV master antenna in the community served. In this way, CATVs are able to bring in the signals of television stations over very considerable distances. From their original purpose of providing television service to communities with little or no television service they have grown very rapidly and are now extensively used even in communities with two or more signals available off the air. They serve to bring in (sometimes with better reception than is available off the air) a full line of network programs as well as the signals of commercial and educational independents.[6]

CATVs charge their users directly (although not in proportion to the use made). They also carry several signals. Thus, as indicated above, they are a less risky and more profitable means of entry into local television markets than are boosters and satellite stations, which presumably accounts in large measure for their relative growth. Originating in 1952,

CATVs now service about 1,785,500 television homes and their subscriber growth during 1964 was more than 30 per cent.[7]

While CATVs have grown and prospered, their growth has naturally had its effects on existing television stations with signals receivable off the air in the communities served by CATVs. Such effects have become a matter of concern to the FCC. To a brief description of those effects and a discussion of whether that concern is properly placed we now turn.

A CATV locating in the market area of an existing television station affects that station's revenues by reducing its viewing audience. This it does primarily through offering viewers a substantial range of alternative signals, so that its effect (so far as subscribers are concerned) is rather like that of the entry of several new broadcast stations into the given area. There are, however, three reasons which (where applicable) make a CATV's impact on the audience and revenues of an existing local station more pronounced than is suggested by the view that it simply involves the provision of alternative signals to a given number of viewers.

In the first place, a CATV subscriber generally does not retain the ability to view programs off the air after the set is connected to the CATV cable. Even in the minority of cases in which this is not so, a special switching device must be activated to change from CATV to off-the-air reception. This means that a CATV which does not carry the signal of a given station and whose subscribers could otherwise receive that signal off the air pre-empts part of that station's audience or at least places that station at a substantial disadvantage in competing for the subscribers' viewing time.

Second, CATVs in relatively small markets typically bring in all the signals from a large city's stations. Further, most stations are affiliated with one or more of the three major networks and thus show principally network programs in prime evening time. Thus, a CATV which locates in the market area of an existing station and which carries that station's signal is quite likely also to carry the prime time programs of that station from another source, either simultaneously or on a somewhat different schedule depending on the scheduling of network programs by different stations. Such a CATV does not merely provide its subscribers with programs competing with those shown by the local station; it provides the identical product except for the dial position or, possibly, the time the programs are scheduled.

Finally, there is evidence that the average CATV subscriber in one- and two-station markets watches television considerably more than the average off-the-air viewer able to receive a similar set of signals.[8] In part this may be due to the better average signal quality which may be afforded the average CATV viewer as opposed to the signal quality of off-the-air reception available to the average viewer in a small market able to receive a similarly large numbers of signals from overlapping distant sources. In part at least it is probably due to the self-selection of subscribers. It is the avid television fan who is most likely to pay for the services of a CATV system. To the extent that this is the case, a CATV does not merely affect a station in whose area it locates by affecting the viewing habits of a part of that station's market chosen, as it were, at random; it affects the habits of a part of that station's market which accounts for a disproportionately large share of that station's audience measured in terms of actual viewing.

All these things mean that CATVs, while aiding the stations whose signals they bring to viewers otherwise unable to receive them, have a substantial long-run impact on the revenues and profits of stations in whose market areas they locate.[9] The FCC has viewed this as a matter of public concern and has adopted for CATVs using microwave relays, and proposed to adopt for all CATVs,[10] rules essentially requiring CATVs to carry the signals of local stations and not to duplicate the programs of those stations from fifteen days preceding to fifteen days following the time they are shown (news and special events programs excepted).[11]

The rule that a CATV shall not simply pre-empt part of a local station's market by not carrying its signals to viewers who could otherwise receive it is patently in the public interest since it prevents the foreclosure of part of the market. The non-duplication rule is less clearly so, especially when simultaneous duplication is not involved. The FCC clearly wishes to protect local stations, but the protection of competition does not generally mean the protection of particular competitors. We must therefore consider whether the FCC's favoring of local stations is a well-grounded policy. We shall do this by considering the general arguments as to whether CATV entry into local markets should be unimpeded by regulatory action rather than by discussing the wisdom of the non-duplication rule in particular.

The argument in favor of unregulated CATV expansion is simple and apparently strong. CATVs provide a service the cost of which the users are apparently willing to pay for. To argue that regulation is desirable in such a situation, one must argue that the general presumption that such a service is worth providing is invalid in the instant case for reasons special to the CATV broadcasting industry.

There are indeed such reasons. We saw above that FCC policy, the line-of-sight limitation and barriers to entry into local television markets have led to a situation in which local programming is subsidized by the profits earned by broadcast stations on other types of programs. We argued that for reasons of public interest such local programming may be desirable or that it may be that viewers, if charged directly, would support such programming. Yet CATV competition drawn by those very profits tends to lessen or eliminate them. If follows that such competition may very well lead to a substantial alteration in local programming, reducing or even ending such local programming – to an end to such local diversity as the FCC has been able to foster under the line-of-sight limitation.

Yet this is not a result which can reasonably be said to be presented to the individual CATV subscriber upon subscription. If local programs are valued then the amount which the subscriber is willing to pay for CATV services is greater than would be the case if it were known that local programs would be changed by the act of subscribing. Even if this were explained in detail, it would make no difference, since the public good character of television financing makes it not in the interest of any individual subscriber to take into account the effect of CATV on local stations even if it would be in the collective interest of all such individuals to do so. In the absence of a system in which viewers bear directly the full costs of the programs they watch, there can at the least be no presumption that because CATVs are profitable the particular marginal costs of providing CATV services are worth incurring.

Moreover, even if CATV subscribers would in any case subscribe at profitable rates knowing with certainty that they were buying a package which included the resulting effects on local programming, it would still not necessarily be the case that CATV expansion should be unregulated. By their nature, CATVs are largely restricted to towns and cities where a relatively short cable can serve many viewers. The local stations whose programming may be affected, however, do not merely serve the CATV subscribers. Rather, they broadcast over a considerably greater area. If local programming is changed as a result of CATV competition, therefore, there is an external effect on the television services available to non-subscribers. The resulting possible disutility to such viewers is obviously not included in the CATV costs paid by subscribers.[12]

Finally, aside from these arguments, the technological situation is changing in a way that may mean that CATVs if temporarily inhibited would not be profitable in a few years in many of the markets which they have entered and are entering. The effect of the All-Channel Law is clearly to remove one of the limitations to local-market entry by new broadcast stations as the existing stock of television sets depreciates. A market which currently has not a full network lineup of VHF stations because it has not been assigned three VHF channels (for reasons of signal overlap) may very well support additional UHF stations, both network-affiliated and independent, when most sets can receive them. Were such stations in existence, CATV services would be far less attractive to subscribers. With unregulated CATVs in the principal towns of a given area, however, entry of such UHF stations is likely to be substantially inhibited. Moreover, such UHF entry will serve the surrounding area and local diversity of programming is obviously less likely to be inhibited by local competition than by competition from large-city stations brought in on CATVs.

In short, given the economically highly inefficient institutional arrangements in local television broadcasting and given the changing technological situation, the FCC's policy of mild regulation of CATVs may be a reasonable one. Indeed, it may clearly be the case that non-carriage and duplication protection of local stations does not go far enough. Yet it is well to be cautious. The effects of the All-Channel Law are as yet in the uncertain future and the diversity of programming provided by big city independent stations which are carried on CATVs may be more important than the local diversity provided by profit-subsidized local programming. In not inhibiting CATV growth beyond the mild restrictions involved in the carriage and non-duplication rules – restrictions which reduce only mildly the alternatives open to CATV subscribers – the FCC may be giving proper weight to these considerations and to the fact that CATV subscribers are willing to pay for the services they are getting, even if the full costs of those services are not recovered thereby. Whether such a restrained policy is in fact sufficient to allow the growth of UHF stations and to offset the effects of CATVs on the local programming available to subscribers and also to non-subscribers is difficult to say at the present time.

One further point. It is clear that the encouragement of local diversity in television is a legitimate aim of public policy. This is particularly evident if we recall the non-economic benefits of such a policy in a free society. Regulation of CATV may be necessary to preserve that diversity in the presence of the economically inefficient methods now used to sustain it. Yet one cannot but feel that such regulation is but another patch on a set of arrangements not particularly well suited to public ends. If local programming and local control are to be encouraged, it might be more efficient to subsidize local stations directly than to restrict their competitors.

Addendum (1990)

The twenty-five years since this chapter was written saw repeated efforts by the FCC to grapple with the cable issue. Those efforts first imposed then relaxed regulation, and were largely ended by judicial decisions to the effect that much federal regulation of cable was unconstitutional. In the meantime, cable grew to become a major competitive force in television.

Notes

1. It should be noted that the argument of this chapter does not turn on the question of whether consumer tastes would be 'uplifted' if programs were differently priced. Nor does it depend on knowing how to price programs in an industry in which the marginal cost of an additional viewer is zero. It merely involves the obvious fact that the present institutional arrangements for TV financing are not those of a Pareto optimum so far as recovering costs from users is concerned.
2. The use of communications satellites of course provides another means of transmitting television signals beyond the horizon. By 1990, this technology was used principally to distribute signals to cable systems, with direct satellite-to-home broadcasting of relatively small importance.
3. Incidentally, even this may leave rural viewers subsidized. Many boosters are indeed financed by local cooperatives or local television set retailers and repairmen rather than by broadcast stations.
4. It is at least possible that such forecasts may be misleading if based on surveys of the potential audience. The public-good nature of a booster signal makes it in the interest of anyone who would like to have such a signal available to overstate the amount of viewing which will be done, as they will not pay for the signal in their capacity as viewer.
5. In the long run, the addition of one television home to the average audience estimated as actually viewing a station's programs in prime evening time (and the associated addition to non-prime time viewing) is worth about \$26–29 in yearly revenue to the station (in 1963 dollars). See Chapter 16 for the estimation of this figure.
6. Large CATV systems have even been proposed for New York City – a return to their original purpose as a means of providing better signal quality, with tall buildings replacing mountains as the signal barrier.
7. Based on April 1964 estimates of the National Community Television Association (the CATV trade association) and November 1964 estimates of the American Research Bureau. An alternative estimate puts subscribers at the end of 1964 at 1.4 million and growth at about 15 per cent per year. See D. M. Blank, 'The quest for quantity and diversity in television programming', *American Economic Review, Papers and Proceedings*, LVI (May 1966), 448–56.
8. This is discussed in Chapter 16.
9. The size of that impact is estimated in Chapter 16.
10. The difference stems from the question of the Commission's jurisdiction over non-microwave CATVs.
11. While the original version of this chapter was in press, the FCC issued revised rules. Those rules reduced the duplication protection to the same day on which a program is shown and essentially prohibited CATVs locating close to stations in the 100 largest markets from bringing in signals not already receivable off the air. This change does not affect the analysis

of the chapter, which does not run in terms of particular rules in any case.

12. It should be noted that the argument does not depend for the most part on local programs being the ones which are sacrificed when revenues fall (or fail to rise). Any change in the programming of the local station induced by the effects of CATV competition is an externality in the context of the present institutional arrangements.

16

Community antenna television systems and local television station audience (1966)*

The nature and significance of the problem

The regulation of community antenna television systems in their competition with local television stations is a matter of continuing concern for Federal Communications Commission policy. This chapter reports what was the first systematic study to estimate the effects of that competition on local station audience and revenue and analyze the determinants of local television station audience. It is written from the standpoint of 1964, using data available as of that time.

A community antenna television system (CATV) is a master antenna, usually located on a mountain-top or other favorable reception point, which receives television signals and then transmits them over a network of coaxial cable to subscribers. Subscribers' television sets are connected directly to the cable system. The CATV antenna receives

* At that time cable television systems were called 'community antenna television systems'.

Written jointly with Victor E. Ferrall Jr in association with David Belsley and Bridger M. Mitchell. The research here reported was done for the National Association of Broadcasters and submitted to the Federal Communications Commission. Details omitted below for reasons of space and underlying data are available in the public records of the FCC, Dockets Nos. 14895 and 15233, FCC Reports, Vol. 38 (1965).

We are indebted to many people for discussion and suggestions. Space forbids thanking all of these, but we are especially indebted to Alan Y. Naftalin. Valuable assistance was provided at various stages by members of the staffs of the FCC, Vitro Laboratories and the American Research Bureau (ARB).

Most computations were performed at the Sloan School of Management Computer Facility at MIT. Data handling and programming was in the main directly done by Mitchell and Belsley, but assistance was also rendered by John Hand, William Oakland and others. The departure of introducing econometric analysis into an FCC proceeding could not have been undertaken without Bernard Koteen.

signals either directly off-the-air, as does a home antenna, or by microwave. Once a television home becomes a CATV subscriber and is connected to the CATV cable, it does not receive programs off-the-air.[1]

The average CATV system today carries four or five channels. Most newly constructed CATVs are equipped to carry twelve signals. All presently existing CATVs provide only very high frequency (VHF) service (Channels 2–13), i.e. no ultra high frequency (UHF) service (Channels 14–83). The signals of UHF stations, when carried by a CATV, are converted to VHF.

Most CATVs are presently located in communities served by, at most, two reliable off-the-air services. High signal-distribution costs have to date limited CATV development to urban areas with relatively dense populations. At present, there is no foreseeable prospect of CATVs bringing service to rural areas. In general, therefore, CATVs are relegated by costs to urban centers and by demand to cities and towns sufficiently small or remote not to enjoy all three network signals off-the-air.

CATVs affect the audience of the local television stations with which they compete by:

(a) excluding their subscribers from the potential audience of those local stations[2] whose signals are not carried by the CATV;
(b) carrying a local station but also carrying the same programs by one or more additional channels; and
(c) bringing in different programming from distant stations which would otherwise be unavailable in the market.

With few exceptions, CATVs do no programming. All of the programs they provide are originated by broadcast stations. To date, there has been no substantial providing of 'pay-TV' programming by CATVs. CATV and pay-TV are technologically compatible, however, since both are wire transmission systems. Industry statements suggest that a combination of the two types of service in the future is anticipated and likely.

The rate of growth of CATV systems is impressive and increasing. The first CATV was built in 1952. Today, CATVs service about 1,785,500 television homes. No evidence of slackening in the rate of growth exists, subscriber growth during 1964 having been more than 30 per cent.[3]

Recent applications for municipal franchises to operate a CATV suggest future growth may include large cities with three or more local stations. Franchise applications have been filed in cities such as New York, Philadelphia and Cleveland. In New York, CATV will provide no signals not available off-the-air. Rather, it will offer better quality reception of local stations. Reception in some urban areas is particularly poor because of shielding caused by tall buildings.

Thus, CATVs are capable of providing two services: programming not available off-the-air because of distance factors; and programming not available off-the-air because of topographical or other reception impediments.

We are concerned in this chapter with measuring the extent of economic impact on local stations of not being carried or of being duplicated by a CATV.

At the time this study was done, proposed rules had been prepared by the Federal Communications Commission requiring microwave-fed CATVs located within the Grade A contour[4] of a television station to carry the signal of that station and to refrain from duplicating its programming by carrying the same program broadcast by another station. Non-duplication protection was extended to prohibit carrying such a program within fifteen days of the time (both before and after) it was carried on the protected local station.[5] The proposed rules were limited to microwave-fed CATVs, which include less than one-quarter of all CATVs, because the Commission's jurisdiction over the microwave common carriers serving them was unequivocal. One the other hand, its jurisdiction over CATVs which received signals directly off-the-air seemed less certain.

The economic impact of CATV on local stations is, however, totally unrelated to the technological method by which a CATV obtains the signals it transmits. For this reason, our study did not distinguish between microwave and non-microwave CATVs. In addition, we focused on a service area roughly approximating the B contour for each station, an area similarly defined but much larger than the A contour.[6] For most stations, the B contour is the economically significant potential audience area. In fact, a significant portion of the audience of many smaller stations, particularly in remote areas, is drawn from areas beyond the B contour.

On April 23, 1965, final rules were adopted by the Commission with respect to microwave CATVs.[7] The new rules provide both 'must carry' and fifteen days before and after non-duplication protection. Both are extended to the B contour, as our study suggested, rather than to the A contour as originally proposed.

At the same time as the new rules were adopted, a new rule-making procedure was begun looking toward:

(a) application of the new microwave CATV rules to all CATVs and
(b) consideration of additional CATV questions such as:
     'leap-frogging;'[8]

the impact of CATVs on existing and potential non-network UHF stations; and

the relationship of CATV to pay-TV.[9]

The question of the economic impact of CATVs on local stations is therefore one of importance for current policy decisions.[10]

The audience–revenue relation

CATVs affect local station revenues by affecting the local station audience. When the audience changes, so, in the long run, does the attractiveness of a station to advertisers and the rates which the station can charge. This section reports estimates of the audience–revenue relationship, providing dollar values for assessing the impact of CATVs on the audience analyzed below.

Because time series data on some of the key variables used below are unavailable, and because the confidentiality of individual revenue data would force a rather aggregate time series analysis, we studied a cross-section of television stations. For the audience–revenue relation, the cross-section included every television station for which audience and revenue data were available. For the regression to explain audience size, we used every station for which data were available and which is located in a one- or two-station market.[11] There were 127 such stations, which will be termed 'study stations', below. The audience–revenue relationship was also estimated separately for the study station group.[12]

Audience was measured as the average number of television homes viewing each station during prime time.[13] For our purposes the accuracy of audience estimates[14] is not so important as might be supposed. Whether or not the estimates are accurate, they are relied on by advertisers.[15]

Revenue data were for total broadcast revenue net of selling commissions as reported to the FCC for the year 1963.[16]

Letting M denote revenue in dollars and A denote average prime time audience in television homes, the regression of M on A for all 487 stations[17] for which data were available yields:

$$M = 103,300^a + 26.63^d A \qquad R^2 = 0.897^d$$
$$(45,270) \qquad (0.39) \tag{16.1}^{18}$$

This should be interpreted as stating that an addition of one home to average prime time viewing (i.e. one home viewing three and one-half hours nightly) is worth on the average $26.63 in yearly revenue.

To check this result for possible non-linearities over the full range of audience size, similar regressions were performed for the same data divided into quartiles by audience size and for one- and two-station market stations only. Regression slopes were not substantially different from that just presented. The slope was $29.03 for the one- and two-station market stations.

Audience was, therefore, valued at about $27 of yearly revenue per average prime time home, a somewhat conservative estimate for one- and two-station markets.

The determinants of station audience: the form of the model

If we had separate data on the viewing of a given station by CATV subscribers and by television homes receiving the station's signal off-the-air, we could consider separately the viewing habits of the two groups. Unfortunately, such data do not exist.

We can expect, however, that actual viewing (measured by A) is related both to potential audience (i.e. market) size and to factors affecting viewing habits of television-homes in the potential audience.

These two elements apply both to CATV and off-the-air viewing. Thus, let N_1 be the number of television homes in the potential off-the-air audience of a study station and N_2 the potential CATV audience, i.e. subscribers to CATVs carrying the study station's signal.[19] In broad outline, our model is:

$$A = N_1 F^1 + N_2 F^2 + u \tag{16.2}$$

where u is a random disturbance, F^1 is a function to be specified which determines the viewing of the average member of the study station's off-the-air potential audience, and F^2 is a function (not necessarily the same as F^1) also to be specified which determines the viewing of the average member of the study station's CATV potential audience.[20]

The heart of the model lies in the specification of the variables entering F^1 and F^2 and in the definition of the two potential audiences measured in N_1 and N_2.

We shall discuss measurement of N_1 below. Since our sample is a cross-section at a moment in time, it would be pointless to include in potential CATV audience (N_2) CATV subscribers who cannot in fact receive the study station. Such subscribers contribute nothing to A.[21] We have, therefore, included in each study station's potential CATV audience only those CATVs which carry its signal.

The variables in F^1 and F^2 refer to the competition given a study station by some defined group of stations. For F^2 these are the stations carried on the CATV; for F^1 the stations received off-the-air. We compute the variables entering F^2 for each relevant CATV and average over all such CATVs in a station's audience area,[22] weighting the components of the average by the number of subscribers to the various CATVs involved. In the off-the-air case, a similar weighted average is computed for F^1, but off-the-air weights are rather more complicated. They are discussed below, along with the definition and measurement of N_1. For the present, we ignore such averaging and consider viewers faced with a defined group of stations including the study one.

The variables

Off-the-air viewing of a local station is primarily influenced by the number and quality of substitutes for its programming.[23] The number of alternative *signals* is not, however, a good measure of the extent of substitute availability since two or more competing stations may carry the same programs. Thus, the primary variable in our analysis is the number of 'program alternatives' to the study station's programming, available to its potential audience. This variable is denoted by Q and was measured as follows.

Five categories of program alternatives were defined. If a non-study station devoted forty or more of the forty-nine half-hours of prime time per week to the programs of one of the three networks, the station was classified as an affiliate of that network.[24] Stations which showed practically no prime time network programming were classified as independents.[25] Finally, stations which were not independent but which did not show as much as forty half-hours of prime time of any single network's programs were counted in a separate category and referred to as 'multiple affiliates', whether or not they carried more than one network.

The value of Q for a group of stations confronting a study station was the number of non-empty categories. The natural logarithm of $(1 + Q)$ was taken as the relevant variable in our regression, since it yields a reasonable approximation to the competitive effect of an *additional* alternative spread over pre-existing ones, i.e. an effect roughly proportional to $1/(1 + Q)$.

Not all program alternatives, however, are equally attractive. Also, the five classifications used in measuring Q were somewhat arbitrary. Additional variables were therefore needed.

The measurement of Q implicitly assumed that an independent alternative offers the same competition to a study station as does a network alternative.[26] This is not the case. Network programs, on the average, are far more popular than non-network programs.[27]

Accordingly, we entered separately a variable which equaled unity if the group of stations concerned included an independent and zero otherwise. This variable was denoted by I.[28] Since independents are included in Q, a positive coefficient for I indicates that independents provide relatively slight competition to study stations.

Next, multiple affiliates are counted in Q as providing a single program alternative. But two multiple affiliates may carry different programs. To account for this possibility, we entered as variables the number of stations in the multiple category and a measure of the duplication among them.[29] These two variables did not affect the results, doubtless because intramultiple duplication is relatively infrequent and generally does not occur in the areas where most of the potential audience of a study station is located and because the effect of such intramultiple duplication on study station audience is quite indirect.

A more important problem concerning multiple affiliates, however, is not that they may provide more than a full alternative, but that they may provide less because they duplicate programs shown on competing pure network affiliates. To take account of this, we introduced a variable, C, which, given the value of Q, represents competition among a study station's competitors, i.e. a partial cancellation of the competitive effect on the study station measured by Q.

The multiple affiliate-network duplication variable, C, was computed as follows. Let X_A^A, X_C^C and X_N^N represent the average fractions of weekly prime time devoted to network programming stations classified as ABC, CBS and NBC affiliates, respectively.[30] Let X_A^M, X_C^M and X_N^M similarly represent the fraction of weekly prime time devoted by the composite of multiple affiliates (calculated as described below) to ABC, CBS and NBC programs, respectively. Then:

$$C = X_A^A X_A^M + X_C^C X_C^M + X_N^N X_N^M \tag{16.3}$$

This may be thought of as the expected fraction of weekly prime time during which programs shown by the multiple affiliate are the same as those shown (possibly not simultaneously) by one of the pure network affiliates, assuming each network's programs are selected independently by both pure and multiple affiliates.

Of course, such an independence assumption is not valid. Popular programs are more likely to be carried than are others. In the present context, however, this is not important since X_A^A, X_C^C and X_N^N are all close to one. Thus, if a multiple affiliate showing ABC programs competes with a pure ABC affiliate for which X_A^A is one, the multiple affiliate's programming is surely duplicated. The first term of C represents this, adjusting for the possibility that X_A^A is a bit less than one.

Where only one multiple affiliate competes with the local station, X_A^M, X_C^M and X_N^M are the actual fractions of weekly prime time devoted to the respective networks. Where more than one multiple affiliate was involved, X_A^M, for example, was computed as the probability that a half-hour of weekly prime time contained an ABC program on at least one station in the multiple category.[31] The sums X_A^M, X_C^M and X_N^M calculated in this way for a composite multiple alternative may exceed unity since two or more multiple affiliate stations may show a total of more than forty-nine prime time half-hours of network programming.[32]

Intracompetition duplication must be accounted for so that the true program competition faced by our study stations can be gauged. But the focus of our model is measuring the impact of CATV duplication of study stations' programming on their audience. Clearly, a station's audience will be reduced if its potential audience can view its programming on other stations. Given the definition of Q, however, the impact of duplication of study station programming, measured by a separate variable, D, may register as either positive or negative. Since a station which duplicates the local station is included in Q, the coefficient of the duplication variable (D) will be positive if a duplicating signal reduces local station audience less than does a completely different program alternative; negative if it reduces audience more.

In fact, off-the-air duplication is generally found at the fringes of a station's market area, away from areas of densest potential audience. Where such duplication does occur in a station's prime market area, the distant duplicating signal tends to be inferior to the local station signal. Duplication on CATV is different (and far more significant), since on CATV all signals tend to be of acceptable quality.

D is computed in the same way as was C. It measures the fraction of prime time network programs carried on a study station which are also carried on at least one other competing station assuming independence of program choice.[33] Where duplication between pure and multiple network affiliates exists, the assumption of independence of program choice was again used to avoid double counting.[34]

That assumption necessarily will give an approximately right result where at least one of a pair of stations whose duplication is being measured devotes nearly all its prime time programs to a single network. Nearly all such programs shown by the other station will be duplicated. In a minority of cases, however, both the study station and a duplicating station were multiple affiliates. In such a case, D is likely to underestimate the duplication involved. For example, suppose that the study station and another station each show seven half-hours (1/7 of weekly prime time) of CBS programs in prime time weekly. In the computation of D, we would estimate that only one such half-hour is duplicated $((1/7)(1/7)(49) = 1)$. In fact, however, nearly all such programs are likely to be duplicated, since both stations will tend to carry the seven most popular CBS half hours. The precise magnitude of the resulting error is uncertain, but its direction is clear.

Define:

$$Z = \begin{cases} 0, \text{ if the study station is } not \text{ a multiple affiliate} \\ X_A^S X_A^M + X_C^S X_C^M + X_N^S X_N^M \text{ otherwise} \end{cases} \quad (16.4)$$

X^S denotes study station fraction of prime time devoted to a given network's programming; X^M is the same measure for the composite multiple affiliate; and the subscripts identify the networks.

Note that $Z = 0$ if the study station is not a multiple affiliate, if it does not face a multiple affiliate, or if it has no network in common with the multiple affiliate faced. In all these cases, the effect under consideration cannot arise.

Now, let q equal the total fraction of weekly prime time devoted to network programs by the study station, i.e.

$$q = X_A^S + X_C^S + X_N^S \quad (16.5)$$

The variable used in our regression is denoted by G:

$$G = \begin{cases} 0 & \text{if } Z = 0 \\ q - D & \text{if } Z > 0 \end{cases} \quad (16.6)$$

G measures the maximum understatement of duplication afforded by D in the cases under discussion. Where duplication of a particular network's programming carried by a local station results solely from a multiple affiliate, D's understatement of duplication cannot exceed $q - D$, since q is the total fraction of prime time during which duplication can take place. In general, G proved to be small, its mean for CATV-carried competition being about 0.06. Its inclusion in the regression, however, did have a significant effect on the results.

Off-the-air potential audience and the measurement of overlap

Relevant potential audience delineation is no problem with respect to CATVs. It is all subscribers to CATV carrying a local station. The other signals carried on those CATVs are the relevant competitors.

Off-the-air television reception in the United States, however, does not fall into isolated areas, but rather forms a series of overlapping markets. Identifying the potential off-the-air audience and the intersection of potential audience of two or more stations is a problem of some magnitude.

Potential off-the-air audience, N_1,[35] can be measured either as the number of television-homes in a station's audience area able to receive that station's signal (ATR) or the number of television-homes in a station's audience area which watch that station at least once a week – the station's 'net weekly circulation' (NWC).[36]

ATR data theoretically do not depend on the nature of the competing signals. In fact, they do. Replies to ATR questionnaires depend in part on the orientation of rooftop aerials. That orientation depends, in turn, on the same competitive factors as does NWC. In addition, unless people do in fact watch a signal, their judgment as to reception is qualitative and subjective.

NWC is affected by the same or similar competitive forces as is actual viewing audience, notably the number and quality of program alternatives available to that household.[37] To measure potential audience by NWC data, therefore, would clearly understate the effects of off-the-air competition.

On the other hand, since the focus of our study is the impact of CATV competition – *vis-à-vis* off-the-air competition – on total local station audience, optimally we would consider only the portion of that total audience obtained from CATV potential audience (subscribers). But separate data on off-the-air and CATV audiences are unavailable. Use of NWC data as our measure of potential off-the-air audience, however, allows us to exclude those television-homes technically able to receive a local station, but which do so infrequently at most.[38] In other words, to the extent that such television-homes are excluded, the dependent variable (audience) is purified of off-the-air effects.[39] The relative significance of CATV competition in our model – which treats the total local station audience as a function of the potential off-the-air audience as affected by off-the-air competition plus the potential CATV audience as affected by competition on CATVs – is, therefore, increased and the estimate of CATV effects made more efficient.[40]

We thus took NWC data as our primary potential audience measure but performed the analysis using ATR data as well. The ensuing discussion is in terms of ATR data for ease of exposition.

The most recent ATR data for each county and station were collected in 1960.[41] In order to be able to subtract CATV subscribers from the total potential audience to get the total off-the-air potential audience, it was necessary to adjust ATR data to the 1963–64 base as follows.

The total number of television-homes able to receive a given station in each county was computed directly from the survey data. For each county, the number of subscribers to CATVs carrying that station and located in that county in 1960 was subtracted to give 1960 off-the-air ATR data. This was divided by the number of television-homes in that county in 1960 less the total number of subscribers to CATVs in that county in 1960 to give the relative frequency of ATR homes among all non-CATV television-homes in that county for 1960. ATR data for 1963 were then calculated by multiplying that relative frequency by the number of that county's 1963 television-homes similarly adjusted to remove CATV subscribers.[42]

The described relative frequencies were then used to determine competitive overlap, i.e. to estimate the number of homes in each county able to receive a specified group of stations. Independence was again assumed, i.e. the probability that a household picked at random from a given county could receive Station A was assumed to be independent of whether it could receive Station B. The probability that it could receive both was thus computed as the product of the separate probabilities of receiving each, and so forth.

The smaller the geographical unit surveyed, the less likely independence is to be violated, e.g. Station A to be received in only one corner of a county and Station B only in another corner. Departures from independence are only potentially serious if neither station is received in nearly all *or nearly none* of the homes in the county. Counties are the smallest areas for which data are available. Moreover, large departures from independence tend to occur at the margin of a study station's market, where its signal is less strong and the population less dense, since densely populated counties are nearly completely covered by at least one station. Since the variables as used in our regression are weighted by the potential audience of the study station in each county, the potential impact of non-independence is further reduced.[43]

Study stations for which 1960 county data were unavailable[44] were deleted, as was any study station sharing a large part of its audience with such stations.[45] County ATR and NWC frequencies for non-study stations which competed with study stations and for which 1960 data were unavailable were judged by inspection of the A and B contours of the relevant stations and the audience areas of stations similarly situated. Such estimates were few, required only for counties of overlap with a study station and used only in overlap computations to compute weights in averages.

Finally, nine study stations known to have non-duplication agreements with particular CATVs in their audience area were deleted as the evaluation of the effects of the various agreements presented special problems.

The remaining sample size was 127.

The results and their interpretation

The basic regression result using NWC data was:

$$A = 1926^{b} + N_1 (0.5322^{d} - 0.3466^{d} \log (1 + Q_1)$$
$$ (791) (0.0292) (0.0375)$$
$$+ \ 0.1535^{d} C_1 + \ 0.4943^{d} I_1 + \ 0.0707^{a} D_1)$$
$$(0.0381) (0.0644) (0.0333)$$
$$+ \ N_2 (0.7574^{c} - \ 0.6898^{a} D_2 - \ 1.2285^{a} G_2)$$
$$(0.2707) (0.3397) (0.5586)$$

$$(16.8)^{46}$$

$$R^2 = 0.9468^{d}$$

We discuss below the effects of adding $\log (1 + Q_2)$, C_2 and I_2.

Since A is measured in average number of television-homes viewing the study station in prime evening time, we may take the coefficients as referring to the behavior of an average television-home.

The implication of the off-the-air constant term (which is reliably estimated in view of the great range of the off-the-air variables) (0.5322) is that homes unable to watch any alternative save the study station watch that station about 53 per cent of prime time on the average – about 1.86 hours per evening. If C_1, I_1 and D_1 all equal zero, and Q_1 equals 1, average viewing of the study station is estimated as about 29.4 per cent. If television-homes divide their viewing equally among alternatives, this yields 58.8 as the per cent of prime time as average total viewing with one alternative. If we introduce a second alternative ($Q_1 = 2$) and triple the result, estimated average total viewing is 46.8 per cent. The decline when two alternatives are introduced is natural, since in one- and two-station markets the assumption that C_1, I_1 and D_1 are all zero is likely to be violated with two or more alternatives. A positive value for any one of these three variables would raise estimated average viewing.[47]

The positive coefficient of C_1 indicates that when the multiple alternative included in Q_1 does duplicate the pure network alternatives, competition with the study station is less severe than otherwise, given the value of Q_1.

The positive coefficient of I_1 indicates that, given the number of alternatives as measured by Q_1, independent stations are less attractive than network stations. The unreasonably high coefficient of I_1 (0.4943) appears to be a distortion resulting from the use of NWC data. This is so since many homes watch independent stations sometimes that do not watch them as much as once a week, particularly because few independent station programs – relative to network programs – are weekly series. Thus, NWC data underestimate I_1 relative to the other variables by underestimating the intersection of the potential audiences of study and independent stations. This results in an overestimation of the coefficient of I_1. When ATR data are used, the coefficient of I_1 is much lower (see Note 46). Since ATR data do not underestimate I_1, this supports the argument.

The coefficient of D_1 is positive (but small) indicating that off-the-air duplication (which is likely to be from a distant station with a relatively poor quality of signal) generally provides less competition to a study station than does a non-duplicating alternative.[48]

Turning to CATV effects, CATV viewer data are much less reliable and the importance of the behavior studied to total audience behavior much less than in the case of off-the-air viewers. In addition, the range of some CATV variables is less in our sample than that of off-the-air variables. CATV coefficients while still significant, at least at the 5 per cent level, thus have relatively much bigger standard errors than do off-the-air coefficients and several effects fail to show up at all.

There is almost no variation in the value of $\log(1 + Q_2)$ over CATVs. Thus, though the number of program alternatives available to subscribers is obviously important, its effect cannot be measured in our sample. Nearly every CATV studied carries a full network line-up in addition to the study station. The average value of Q_2 is about 3.14 and the variance is very small.[49] We must therefore be content with the omission of the term in Q_2, *realizing, however, that since nearly all CATVs have the same number of alternatives, the effect of Q_2 is included in the constant term in the CATV parenthesis.*

If C_2 is included, the other point estimates are not much changed and the coefficient of C_2 is of the same order of magnitude as that of C_1 (about $- 0.19$). That coefficient, however, has a very large standard error and the standard errors of other coefficients rise somewhat. This is not surprising, since the effect of C_2 is an indirect effect on substantially less than 10 per cent of the potential audience of the stations. C_2 is, therefore, not included. Its inclusion, however, would not materially change the remainder of the discussion.

I_2 is also not included. If used, it receives a small *negative* coefficient with a huge standard error and the other coefficients are not particularly affected. In view of the sizable and significantly positive effect found for I_1, the failure of I_2 to have a like effect suggests that for CATV viewers, as opposed to off-the-air viewers, independent stations do not provide significantly less competition to study station viewing than do affiliated stations.[50] This may reflect a better quality signal on CATV than off-the-air or imply that CATV viewers on the average watch television more than do similarly situated off-the-air viewers.

The effect of CATV duplication on study station audience

The coefficient of D_2, the primary estimate of the fraction of study station prime time duplicated, in Equation 16.8 indicates that a duplication increase of 10 per cent reduces study station prime time viewing by an average subscriber household by about 6.8 per cent. This works out to about twenty-one minutes of viewing per additional half-hour duplicated at the margin.[51] The variability of D_2 about its mean, however, is sufficiently small as to make us regard with caution any attempt to measure the full effect of duplication by multiplying D_2 times its coefficient.

Indeed, there are several reasons for regarding the expression in the CATV parenthesis of Equation 16.8 as probably a linear approximation to a highly non-linear relationship – an approximation not valid outside the narrow range of variability of D_2 afforded by the sample.[52]

The constant term in the CATV parenthesis in Equation 16.8 (0.7574) does *not* imply that the average CATV subscriber would watch the study station about 76 per cent of the time if there were no competition. Rather, as seen above, it includes in itself the effect of the average number of alternatives available (3.14).[53] This makes it unlikely that the audience–duplication effect is linear, since, if so, *total* estimated viewing by CATV subscribers is well over 100 per cent of prime time (a bit much, even for addicted fans).

The constant term in question makes sense, however, if non-linearity is present. In this case, 0.7574 is the intercept not of the audience–duplication relationship itself, but of the tangent to it at the average level of duplication in the sample, that tangent being the linear approximation which we estimate. Thus, if a curve such as AB in Figure 16.1 is the true relationship, the crucial property being strict concavity toward the origin in the relevant range, and $A'TB'$ is the tangent drawn

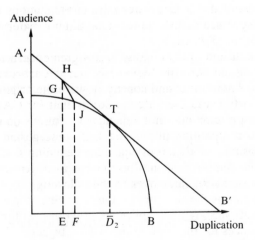

Figure 16.1 Effect of non-linearity in audience–duplication relationship.

at the point of mean D_2, $\bar{D}_2$, then clearly, the estimated intercept, A', will lie above the true intercept, A.

That such concavity occurs in our analysis is supported by the experiment with D_2^2 reported in Note 52 and by the size of the measured intercept.[54] It is also strongly indicated by the coefficient of G_2, the variable representing the maximum understatement in duplication measured by D_2 in a certain class of cases.[55] That understatement is generally small, averaging about 0.06 in our sample.

Assume to begin with that the average value of D_2 where G_2 is positive lies to the left of $\bar{D}_2$, at a point such as E in Figure 16.1. If D_2 truly measured duplication for these cases, then the audience as estimated from the linear approximation would be EH. Because of the hypothesized non-linearity, however, the true audience would be less, namely, EG. If there were nothing to distinguish these positive G_2 cases from the others in the sample, that overstatement would stand. In such cases, however, entering G_2 as positive has the effect of moving measured duplication to the right of E, say to $F = E + G_2$ and reduces the true audience to FJ.[56] This means, however, that the drop in the estimated audience from EH (which would be estimated if G_2 were not included) to FJ (the true average audience where G_2 is positive) will all be attributed in the regression to G_2. The coefficient of G_2 will thus be essentially the slope of the line HJ. Sliding F (which always lies to the right of E) to all possible positions, it is clear that the resulting slopes are always (absolutely) greater than that of $A'TB'$ save when F and $\bar{D}_2$ coincide. Indeed, if EF is very small, that slope approaches minus infinity.

Now move E to $\bar{D}_2$ or to the right of $\bar{D}_2$ and repeat the argument. Again we obtain the slope of $A'TB'$ as a lower (absolute) bound on the slope of HJ, and it is easy to see that the latter slope is not (absolutely) bounded from above.

That the observed coefficient of G_2 is considerably greater than that of D_2, therefore, is consistent with the hypothesis that the audience–duplication relationship is non-linear and concave toward the origin.

Why does such concavity exist? That answer lies in the fact that the audience for a particular program does not depend solely on the nature of that program and its competition during the same time period. It depends also on the position of that program in the evening line-up of programs on the same station. Specifically, there is a tendency for audiences for a given program to carry over to the following program and to tune in early, thus raising the audience for the preceding program.

Now, if the study station shows unduplicated programs around a duplicated one, its audiences for those programs will be bigger and the carry-over effect for the duplicated program larger than if the surrounding programs are also duplicated. Indeed, the total audience for the duplicated program (both for the study station and the duplicating one) will be larger if that program is surrounded by unduplicated programs than if it is surrounded by duplicated ones. It follows that duplication is reinforcing; the duplication of a given half-hour by a single station will approximately cut the study station's audience for the duplicated program to half the total audience for that program, but extensive duplication will also cut the total audience for the given program. This will make the audience–duplication relationship concave to the origin.[57]

In sum, empirical evidence and theoretical arguments suggesting concavity are considerable.

Conclusions: the economic impact of CATV

When a CATV obtains new subscribers they may be viewed as an increase in N_2 and an offsetting decrease in N_1. This, however, assumes that the off-the-air viewing habits of new CATV subscribers were the same before subscribing as those of average off-the-air viewers similarly placed. Our results, however, imply that CATV subscribers watch television considerably more than non-subscribers with the same number of program alternatives, as is plausible if those who pay for television are those who like it most.[58]

At the point of means for our sample, $D_2 = 0.72$ and $G_2 = 0.06$. Since the sum of the two variables provides an upper limit on duplication, average prime time duplication lies between 72 and 78 per cent. At the same point of average duplication, CATV viewers are estimated to view the study station about 18 per cent of prime time. Assuming average duplication to be 75 per cent (the result is insensitive to minor variation) and assuming that only one station at a time duplicates the study station, then, on CATV, the study station receives the full audience of an alternative for 25 per cent of the time and approximately half that audience for 75 per cent of the time.[59] As the sum of these is 18 per cent of prime time, an unduplicated alternative on CATV is viewed about 29 per cent of prime time. The average number of alternatives carried, the effect of which is already reflected in the 18 per cent figure, is 3.14. To these, the study station adds 25 per cent of a distinct alternative (the fraction of prime time in which it is not duplicated). Multiplying 29 per cent by 3.39, we obtain about 98 per cent as the fraction of prime time in which *some* alternative is being viewed by the average CATV household. While this figure can only be taken as a crude approximation, it is so far above the comparable figure of about 53–58 per cent for the *average* off-the-air household as to suggest strongly that

CATV subscribers are more avid television watchers.[60] This conclusion is supported by industry experience.[61]

Of course, such greater viewing on CATV than off-the-air may be the result of other factors as well. For example, average clarity of the CATV signal may be better than that of average off-the-air reception.[62] Even so, it seems clear that treating new CATV subscribers before subscription as equivalent to average off-the-air viewers (as we shall generally do) underestimates the impact of CATV.

Estimating withdrawals from off-the-air potential audience simply as subtractions from N_1, we can use Equation 16.8 to evaluate the loss to a study station of the addition of 1000 subscribers in its audience area to a CATV which does not carry its signal. If those subscribers were not previously in the study station's potential audience, e.g. if they move into the station's audience area and immediately subscribe to CATV, then there is no loss. If they previously had no alternative other than the study station, that station's audience drops by 530 television-homes in the average prime time half-hour. If the subscribers had one other program alternative, the comparable figure is 294 television-homes.[63] The corresponding dollar figures of annual revenue are $14,310 and $7,938. The figures fall if there were previously more alternatives, but most CATV subscribers come from viewers with limited alternatives available off-the-air.

For CATVs which carry the local station with average duplication, the effects are as above with an offsetting gain of about 180 television-homes or $4,860.[64]

As for the effects of duplication itself, the *marginal* effect of duplication is about 21 minutes per half-hour or about $380 per thousand subscribers per year for an extra half-hour of duplication. The full effect is harder to estimate in view of the non-linearity already discussed. Some indication is given by our estimate that the audience of an unduplicated alternative on CATV is about 29 per cent of potential audience. Subtracting the actual audience at average duplication, the effect of average duplication is about 11 per cent of potential audience which is 110 television-homes per 1000 subscribers or $2,870 in annual revenue.

The magnitude of these numbers should be assessed in the light of the present rapid rate of increase of CATV subscriptions and of the fact that the average study station had 6,300 CATV subscribers in its audience area and an off-the-air NWC of 105,000 in 1964. For the fourth quartile (in terms of viewing audience) of such stations, the corresponding figures are 5,500 and 27,900. Average profit for study stations was $165,000 net of depreciation and proprietary payments and $258,000 gross of such payments. For the fourth quartile, the corresponding figures are a loss of about $200 and gross profits of $37,500.

It is thus evident that CATVs locating in the audience area of study stations, especially in the audience area of smaller stations, have a great potential impact on profits.[65] That impact is greater to the extent that CATVs locate close to the stations and thus pick up most of their subscribers from viewers previously in the study station's potential off-the-air audience. It is lower to the extent that CATVs locate relatively far from study stations and extend potential audience by adding subscribers not previously a part of it. If the present tendency for CATVs to be constructed so as to bring in more signals rather than to reach outlying communities with no other television coverage continues, the extension effect can be expected to become relatively less important than it has been in the past.

In our judgment the essential summary facts of our study are these:

1. CATV's economic impact on station revenues is substantial.
2. A significant percentage of existing stations, particularly in small markets, cannot withstand a relatively small increase in CATV penetration in their audience area without concomitant cost reduction.
3. A substantial percentage of potential new station entrants, particularly UHF[66], are likely to be discouraged from entry by a relatively small increase in CATV penetration in their potential audience areas.

In sum, therefore, the impetus of CATV is toward the reduction of local television service and the expansion of national television service through the broader distribution of existing major market stations of cities such as New York and Los Angeles or ultimately through the creation of new cable networks – either pay-TV or free-TV – or both. There is no necessary evil in such change. It is, however, opposed to long-existing Congressional and Commission policy which favors as much local service as possible, provided by as many separately-owned stations as possible.

Before closing, a word of caution is in order. The impacts measured in our study must be regarded as *ceteris paribus* and long-run estimates. This is generally true of cross-section results and is no less so in the present case. In particular, a loss of audience is likely to be accompanied not by an immediate loss of advertising revenue (though this may occur in the long run) but by the failure of the station involved to share in general rate increases and to attract new business. CATVs are thus more likely to injure broadcast stations by preventing future than by nullifying past profits.

Notes

1. It is technologically feasible to provide switching devices to permit CATV subscribers to obtain satisfactory reception with their own antennas. Such

devices, however, were rarely furnished in the 1960s.

2. Hereafter a station which competes with a CATV, i.e. which provides off-the-air service in the town served by the CATV, will be simply identified as a 'local station'.

3. Based on April 1964 estimates of the National Community Television Association (the CATV trade association) and November 1964 ARB estimates. An alternative estimate puts subscribers at the end of 1964 at 1.4 million and growth at about 15 per cent per year. See D. M. Blank, 'The quest for quantity and diversity in television programming', *American Economic Review, Papers and Proceedings*, LVI (May 1966).

4. The 'Grade A contour' is a technically determined geographic area defined, in the Commission's Rules, by the intensity of signal broadcast by a station. Even between stations broadcasting on the same frequency with the same power and antenna height, it can vary substantially because of terrain differences. Typically, however, it includes the city in which the station is located and extends out 25 or more miles in all directions from the transmitter.

5. Such 'non-simultaneous' non-duplication protection is particularly important to stations located in markets with less than three stations. In such markets, stations frequently carry the programs of more than one network and, as a result, often carry some programs on a delayed basis, i.e. not at the same time they are carried on the network. In such situations, a distant major market station brought into the local station's market by a CATV is likely to carry the same programs as the local station, but at different times.

6. See Note 4. Frequently, the B contour has a radius of from 60 to 70 miles from the transmitter.

7. FCC, *First Report and Order*, Dockets Nos. 14895 and 15233, FCC Reports, Vol. 38 (1965), p. 683.

8. Distribution by a CATV of distant signals in preference to signals closer to it.

9. *Notice of Inquiry and Notice of Proposed Rule Making*, Docket No. 15971, FCC Reports, 2d Series, Vol. 1 (1965), p. 543.

10. For a discussion of the policy issues see Chapter 15.

11. As defined by the FCC. This group was selected as that on which the impact of CATV in its present stage of development was likely to be of sufficient relative importance to permit measurement. It is also the group most likely to be presently aided by the FCC's proposed regulations. The selection of some subgroup of stations was necessary to reduce an already overwhelming data collection and handling job.

12. Including 45 similar stations for which audience and revenue data were available but for which all data used below were not.

13. This time was 7.30–11.00 p.m. in the Eastern time zone and comparable hours elsewhere. Data were for March 1964. Average prime time audience was used for reasons of convenience. Non-prime time audience is highly correlated with prime time audience across stations.

14. Made by ARB on the basis of diaries placed in television homes.

15. While a similar argument does not apply to the other ARB-measured variables used below, for those variables it suffices that the true variables be highly correlated with the measurements across stations.

16. 1963 was the last year preceding the March 1964 ARB survey for which financial data were available. While it would have been possible to use

ARB audience data for March or October 1963, this would have led to some problems with other variables. The difference between 1963 and March 1964 is negligible when considering a cross-section of stations. Wherever possible, we used March 1964 data.

17. Or parent and satellite stations combined, when separate data were unavailable.

18. The following notation will be used throughout for significance levels:

[a] Significant at 5 per cent level or better.
[b] Significant at 2 per cent level or better.
[c] Significant at 1 per cent level or better.
[d] significant at 0.1 per cent level or better.

19. As explained above, these two groups are almost always separate, i.e. viewers typically cannot receive signals both on cable and off-the-air.

20. While Equation 16.2 does not admit a constant term, the actual regressions run were not forced through the origin. In the absence of precise knowledge as to the functional forms for F^1 and F^2, a constant term may permit a better approximation than would be yielded by such forcing. Further, in the presence of a large number of observations, the efficiency gained by such forcing would be slight even if specification of the forms of F^1 and F^2 were precise.

Second, the possibility of heteroskedasticity in Equation 16.2 is obvious. As a correction, we also ran the same regressions deflated by number of television homes in the audience area of each study station, i.e. the geographical area over which data on A are collected. It is not obvious that such a correction is optimal, but it is probably crudely correct. The results do not differ greatly from those reported below, although the noise level for some of the estimated coefficients of the CATV variables rises.

21. Such subscribers are in the potential audience of the study station only in the sense that should that station be carried on the CATV to which they subscribe, they would then enter its potential viewing audience. This is true of every CATV with respect to any station.

22. That is, in those counties accounting for at least 98 per cent of the station's net weekly circulation (the number of homes viewing at least once a week).

23. Non-television substitutes were not considered. They probably do not differ greatly in their effects over the stations in our study group.

24. Forty half-hours is an arbitrary point chosen for convenience. The results would not be much affected by using forty-one or thirty-nine, or even a bit more.

25. Educational stations were counted separately from the measurement of Q for CATV viewers and not at all for off-the-air viewers, since the appropriate data on them do not exist. Entering a variable representing their presence or absence for CATV viewers changed nothing in the results. Canadian stations were counted as independents. (In general, only one of them, at most, is present in any relevant group.) Mexican and other foreign language stations were ignored as not serving the same viewers as study stations.

26. None of our study stations was independent.

27. Variables intended to reflect the intrinsic popularity of programming were computed using both the fraction of prime time devoted to network programs and the average *national* ratings of the network programs shown (there are no comparable ratings for non-network programs) in various

combinations. These variables had little effect because average ratings for a full line-up of network programming vary relatively little over study stations.

28. In view of the form in which it was decided to use Q, it might have been slightly preferable to enter $[\log (1 + Q - 1) - \log (1 + Q)]$ instead of I. Since, however, I is almost never unity unless Q is three, such a variable would be very highly correlated with I. Incidentally, there is almost never more than one independent in any relevant group of stations in our study, so the possibility of two independents carrying the same programming does not arise.

29. Duplication was computed in similar fashion to the duplication measures described below. We also allowed for the possibility that the multiple affiliate category as a whole shows more than forty-nine half-hours of prime time – that is, shows more than one network simultaneously – in dealing with duplication of the study station and duplication of the network categories, as about to be described.

30. Averages were used for pure network affiliates instead of the more complicated aggregation procedure used for multiple affiliates and described below because:

    (a) the difference in the figures computed would have been negligible since all fractions are close to unity;
    (b) possible error in cases with more than one station in a given network category is minimal;
    (c) the additions to an overwhelming computational burden which would have been required were too expensive to justify the small gain.

    The maximum fraction of prime time so devoted might be more plausible than either the average or the result of such computation, but the average and the maximum are close here.

31. Again, our computation assumed program choice independence which, although a more questionable assumption in this case, affects computation of C (and of D, below) in, at most, a minor manner, considering the possible deviations from it.

32. Instead of counting the presence of any number of multiples as a unit addition to Q, we might have counted the addition as equal to the number of distinct half-hours divided by forty-nine. In effect, we did about the same thing by using the number of multiple stations and their duplication of each other as separate variables.

33. Non-network programs are assumed throughout not to be duplicated. This assumption is a computational necessity and, during prime time, generally valid.

34. Note that most double counting is automatically avoided by grouping stations into program alternatives. This approach ignores the possible greater impact of more than one duplicating signal since only duplicating program alternatives are counted. Accordingly, we constructed a variable measuring the average number of signals duplicating a study station's programming. It proved to be highly correlated with D (since the importance and frequency of groups of stations in which more than two show the same program is small) and added nothing to the results.

35. The subscript 1 is used throughout to denote off-the-air variables. CATV variables are identified by the subscript 2.

36. Statistics on both measures are available by county from a survey conducted by ARB in 1960. The survey did not distinguish between homes receiving the signal off-the-air and homes on CATV. We deal with this problem below.
37. This is borne out in the data. If N_1 denotes NWC potential audience and N_1' denotes ATR potential audience (the other symbols have already been defined), then, measuring the variables as described below in the text:

$$N_1 = -1870 + N_1'(1.508^d - 0.7029^d \log (1 + Q_1) + 0.4045^d C_1$$
$$(1902) \quad (0.066) \quad (0.0785) \quad (0.0551)$$
$$+ 0.4890^d I_1 + 0.0976 D_1) \qquad R^2 = 0.9753^d \qquad \textbf{(16.7)}$$
$$(0.0627) \quad (0.0704)$$

This should be regarded as a linear approximation to the relationship under discussion. All coefficients have the proper sign as in the audience regressions below. Sample size is 136.
38. That is less than once a week.
39. A non-simultaneous explanation of the causes of non-viewing by the television-homes excluded by using NWC data is given in Equation 16.7 above.
40. Note, however, that the estimated expected effect of a CATV gaining a subscriber chosen at random from the television-homes in a given county will be the same in both cases, since,

$$\frac{\text{viewing}}{\text{NWC}} \times \frac{\text{NWC}}{\text{TV-homes}} = \frac{\text{viewing}}{\text{ATR}} \times \frac{\text{ATR}}{\text{TV-homes}}$$

41. This was also the date of the most recent NWC data.
42. 1963 county on television homes data were the most recent available. The above description ignores minor data inconsistency problems which occasionally arose. For example, the reported number of 1960 subscribers to CATVs carrying the given station in a few counties slightly exceeded total county NWC data for that station. The obvious adjustments were made in such cases to keep relative frequencies between zero and one, the frequencies being set at the appropriate end of the zero–one interval.
43. The independence assumption cannot be strictly correct, since if no station covers 100 per cent of a county's television homes, that assumption implies the existence of television-homes able to receive no station. In part this reflects data inaccuracies (not every county is surveyed for all stations received in it: less than 100 per cent coverage in some counties with only one station listed as received). In any case, inspection showed this to be a thoroughly minor phenomenon, as one might expect, since it can be important only where a small number of stations are received in a county and none of them is received in nearly all homes. This situation occurs only in rather thinly populated areas which receive small weight in any case. By definition, it cannot happen in the counties close to a local station which are most important in its audience area. Note further that the uncovered homes which matter are not all uncovered homes but only those which in fact are in the local station's potential audience.
44. In most cases, because after 1960 the station came on the air, substantially changed its facilities or built a satellite. In a few cases, 1963 data were available from ARB on stations with facilities changes since 1960, and

such data were employed.

45. As judged by location and A and B contours.
46. Using ATR data, the result was:

$$A = 2051 + N_1 (0.5849^d - 0.4139^d \log (1 + Q_1) + 0.1850^d C_1$$
$$(1051) \quad (0.0340) \quad (0.0402) \quad (0.0286)$$
$$+ 0.2907^d I_1 + 0.0790^d D_1) \quad \text{(16.9)}$$
$$(0.0325) \quad (0.0373)$$
$$+ N_2 (0.6991^a - 0.6281 D_2 - 1.3436 G_2) \quad R^2 = 0.9071^d$$
$$(0.3585) \quad (0.4460) \quad (0.7389)$$

The effect of off-the-air competition is higher than in Equation 16.8 while the point estimates for the CATV variables are essentially unchanged. The noise level is higher than in that equation. Finally, the overly large coefficient of I_1 compared with that of $\log (1 + Q_1)$ has disappeared, as discussed below.

47. In addition, it is possible that, in one- and two-station markets, the average quality of signals available to viewers able to view more than two stations tends to be lower and less reliable than that of signals available to viewers able to view fewer stations, as the former viewers are likely to be located in fringe areas.

48. After performing the analysis, a program error was discovered which led to minor underestimation of D_1 in some cases. The values of D_1 as computed are clearly very highly correlated with the true values. The errors are all in the direction of underestimation. This means that the estimated coefficient of D_1 (0.0707) is biased upwards and the true effect is even smaller than that indicated by Equation 16.8. Since that indication is already one of a very small effect and since the error cannot appreciably affect our other results, we did not invest in the approximately 15 hours of computer time required to correct this error. Note that such an error does not extend to the computation of D_2, the important duplication variable in this study.

49. Indeed, the correlation between N_2 and $N_2 \log (1 + Q_2)$ (the relevant variables as the regression is computed) is over 0.99.

50. In view of the nature of a large part of the programming of independents, this is consistent with the results of pay-TV experiments indicating that subscribers to pay-TV systems are more interested in motion pictures and sports than in anything else. See D. M. Blank, cited in Note 3.

51. Average CATV duplication of study stations is about 0.72 of prime time as measured by D_2.

52. We experimented with the introduction of D_2^2 in the regression. D_2 and its square, however, are, too collinear over the sample range for this to provide much help in assessing the extent of non-linearity. If only the square is used, the constant term in the parenthesis does fall substantially without much else being changed. This reinforces the belief that the audience-duplication relation has the non-linear shape hypothesized below.

53. The comparable term in the off-the-air parenthesis (0.5322) does not include this effect, which is separated out by including Q_1.

54. The concavity hypothesis was formulated, however, before experimentation with D_2^2 and, as it happens, before the effects of introducing G_2 were examined.

55. See above, pp. 253–4.
56. This discussion ignores, for simplicity, the fact that G_2 merely provides an upper bound on the underestimation of duplication. The essential point is not affected by this.
57. Note that if the duplication is always from the same station and there is no reason to expect that station to be preferred to the study one (because it shows more popular unduplicated programs, for example), then duplication can be expected to halve the study station's audience for a program unless it also affects total audience for that program. An effect on the total is thus required for concavity.
58. This is consistent with the evidence as to the viewing of independent stations by CATV subscribers, as opposed to off-the-air viewers, discussed above.
59. The assumption implicit is that viewers are indifferent between the local and duplicating station and, therefore, the two stations tend to split the audience evenly during periods of duplication. If a CATV provides comparable quality signals for both stations, the assumption is reasonable.
60. Interestingly, ARB reports .CATV subscribers are more reliable about maintaining and returning survey diaries, indicating that they are more devout as well as more avid.
61. As evidenced in private conversations with industry personnel.
62. We are indebted to David M. Blank for this suggestion.
63. The standard errors of these figures are 29.1 and 9.2, respectively. Using Equation 16.9 in place of Equation 16.8 gives similar results.
64. The standard errors rise by approximately 44.9 and 57.1 television-homes in the two respective cases.
65. As shown above, there is a very high correlation between station audience size and revenues. CATVs do not, of course, affect station costs.
66. Because, compared to VHF, UHF is more expensive to operate, the coverage area is often smaller and all persons with VHF-only television sets are excluded from a UHF station's potential audience.

17

The audience–revenue relationship for local television stations (1980)

Introduction

Cable television systems increase the geographic distribution and reception quality of television station signals and can provide alternative
forms of programming. Cable, therefore, increases competition for
viewers among television stations in a given geographic area and increases the potential audience for those stations whose signals are carried on cable systems. In these ways, cable systems may alter both the
size and the geographical distribution of audiences for local stations.

Local television stations derive almost all of their revenue from the
sale of time for commercial announcements to advertisers. As described
below, the time sold is essentially fixed so that the demand for advertising time determines the price and revenue received by stations. The
prices advertisers are willing to pay depend upon the size of the audience which their commercial announcements are likely to reach and on
certain demographic characteristics of the audience, such as income,
age, sex and in some cases, its location. This chapter estimates the demand curve for television advertising in terms of certain characteristics
of the 'product' – viewer attention – sold by stations. It reports estimates of the relationship between television station revenue and audience size derived from data on 601 local television stations for 1976.[1]

Written jointly with John J. McGowan and David S. Evans.

This chapter reports on research sponsored by the National Association of
Broadcasters. We should like to express our appreciation to the staff of the Federal
Communications Commission for their time, courtesy, patience and assistance in
arranging for our use of confidential data and of the FCC computer facilities.

Interest in this relationship stems from the Federal Communication Commission's (FCC) attempts to regulate cable television systems.[2]

Since cable systems may change the size and other characteristics of the audiences of local television stations, they may also change the revenues of such stations. The possible adverse effects of cable systems on the financial condition of local television stations through audience diversion and revenue loss have led the FCC to constrain the number, type and location of broadcast television signals which cable systems can carry. These signal carriage rules are the object of continuing controversy among broadcasters, cable operators, television program producers, sports teams and leagues, and public interest groups. The research reported here was undertaken in connection with the FCC's latest evaluation of its signal carriage rules in its *Inquiry into the Relationship between Television Broadcasting and Cable Television*, Docket No. 21284 US Federal Communications Commission (1979b). Its intent is to provide systematic estimates of the demand for advertising to aid in assessing the financial effects of audience diversion to cable.

Determinants of local station revenue

All commercial television stations derive revenue from the sale of commercial 'spots' directly to local, national and regional advertisers. Commercial spots are broadcast both within and between programs. Those broadcast between programs are referred to as 'adjacencies'. The time available for spots within programs is limited by the National Association of Broadcasters Code to which the overwhelming majority of stations subscribe. Consequently, the time available for the direct sale of commercial spots to advertisers is essentially determined by the total hours broadcast by a station, except for one complication, namely, network affiliation.

Most local television stations are affiliated with either the American Broadcasting Company (ABC), the Columbia Broadcasting System (CBS) or the National Broadcasting Company (NBC). Stations affiliated with one of these networks have first call on programs offered by the network for broadcast in the station's locality. When a local station chooses to broadcast a program offered by a network, it agrees to carry the commercial spots which the network inserts in the program and sells to national advertisers. The station thus foregoes the sale of spots within programs provided by a network company. However, it still derives revenue from the sale of adjacencies directly to avertisers. Furthermore, it receives payment at a negotiated rate, known as network compensation, from the network which provides the program.[3]

Hence, there is likely to be different relationships between total revenue and audience for affiliated stations and for non-affiliated or independent stations, as they are known. In addition, the relationship between audience and revenue from sales directly to advertisers for affiliated stations is likely to differ both from that relationship for independent stations and from the relationship between audience and network compensation for affiliated stations. The audience–revenue estimates reported below allow for these differences in three ways. First, we provide separate estimates of the audience–revenue relationship for total revenue and for revenue from direct sales to local and national advertisers for the entire sample of stations allowing for different intercepts for affiliated and independent stations. Second, for affiliated stations, we provide separate estimates of the audience–revenue relationship for total revenue, for revenue from direct sales of spots to advertisers, and for network compensation. Third, for the sample of independent stations, we provide separate estimates of the audience–revenue relationship for total revenue.

For direct sales of spots to advertisers, we expect price and revenue to be positively related to audience size, since advertisers are strongly interested in the total circulation of their advertising messages. Advertisers may also be concerned with the location of stations' viewers. Certainly, an advertiser whose sole or primary place of business is in the same locality as a television station would value viewers located close to the station more highly than viewers located at substantial distances from the station and from the advertiser's place of business. National advertisers may also value viewers located close to a station more highly than distant viewers, since the close viewers are less likely to be reachable by messages which are broadcast by stations in other localities.

In the estimates presented below we were able to allow for the existence of differences in the value of audience, depending upon its location in relation to the station, by decomposing audiences into four groups. Total audience for a station, as reported by *Arbitron*, is determined by sample surveys of viewing behavior by households in the station's total survey area (TSA). Generally, audience estimates are also provided for two smaller areas contained within the station's TSA. These are the metro region (MRA) and the area of dominant influence (ADI), which includes the MRA. Thus, total viewing can be separated into three 'rings': viewing within the MRA, viewing outside the MRA but within the ADI, and viewing within the TSA but outside the ADI. Finally, viewing outside the ADI of a station can be segregated into that which is due to homes located in adjacent ADIs and that which is in non-adjacent ADIs. We would expect the estimated value of audience to local and national advertisers to be highest for audience in the MRA, lower for audience located outside the MRA but within the ADI, and still lower for audience outside the ADI.

The value of audience is likely also to differ according to time of the day or week. This is perhaps most clearly seen for affiliated stations' revenue from direct sales to advertisers. The proportion of time devoted to broadcasting network programs varies by time of day and day of the week for affiliated stations. The proportion of network programs is highest during the prime evening hours (8–11 p.m. Eastern, Mountain and Pacific time; 7–10 p.m. Central time) and is lower by varying amounts during day time, early evening and late evening. Consequently, the amount of time available for direct sale to advertisers during each hour of programming differs among these day-parts and so the value of audience is also likely to vary. The age and sex distribution of audiences also varies among day-parts, and this provides another reason to expect the value of audience for both affiliated and independent stations to vary by day-part. We have allowed for these differences by providing estimates of the various audience–revenue relationships in which total audience is segregated into prime-time viewing, day-time viewing, early fringe viewing and late fringe viewing.

The question of whether segregation of audiences by geographic and temporal location matters to the revenue relationship is an important one. If it does, then regulatory judgment as to the effects of audience diversion to cable must be concerned with when and where the diverted audience is and cannot rely on overall estimates. Thus, for example, a study sponsored by the FCC found that cable systems locating near existing stations are likely to divert audiences in the fringe periods surrounding prime time (Park, 1979, pp. 20–21, Table 2). Our estimates below show that such diversion would often be the most serious in terms of revenue. In considering relaxation of its rules, therefore, the FCC ought not to content itself with general estimates of audience diversion but must take such locational factors into account.

Results when audience is subdivided by location

Results for all stations and all revenue

In addition to the location of audience in space or time, we have allowed for other effects in the audience–revenue relationship. Table 17.1 gives the definitions of the variables used. These will be discussed as we proceed.

The dependent variable used in each case was revenue divided by the total number of television households in the station's TSA. Some

Table 17.1 Definition of variables.

TR	= Annual total revenue
NC	= Annual total revenue from network compensation
LNR	= Annual total revenue from sales of local and national advertising
PS	= Dummy variable which equals unity for observations on the combined operations of a parent station and its satellite(s) and zero otherwise
UA	= Dummy variable which is unity for UHF affiliates and zero otherwise
VI	= Dummy variable which is unity for independent VHF stations and zero otherwise
UI	= Dummy variable which is unity for independent UHF stations and zero otherwise
HY	= Median annual income per household
TSAH	= Total households in a station's total survey area
MVH	= Average quarter-hourly number of households within a station's metropolitan region viewing the station
ADIVH	= Average quarter-hourly number of households within a station's area of dominant influence viewing the station
TSAVH	= Average quarter-hourly number of households within a station's total survey area viewing the station
AADIVH	= Average quarter-hourly number of households in adjacent areas of dominant influence viewing the station
TSAVHDT	= Average quarter-hourly number of households within the station's total survey area viewing the station during daytime hours.* Daytime includes the hours of 6.00 a.m. to 4.30 p.m. and 1.00 a.m. to 2.00 a.m. Monday through Friday plus 6.00 a.m. to 7.30 p.m. and 11.00 p.m. to 2.00 a.m. on Saturday and Sunday.
TSAVHEF	= Average quarter-hourly number of households within the station's total survey area viewing the station during early fringe time*. Early fringe time includes the hours 4.30 p.m. to 7.30 p.m. Monday through Friday.
TSAVHPT	= Average quarter-hourly number of households within the station's total survey area viewing the station during prime time*. Prime time includes the hours 7.30 p.m. to 11.00 p.m. Sunday through Saturday.
TSAVHLF	= Average quarter-hourly number of households within the station's total survey area viewing the station during late fringe time*. Late fringe time includes the hours 11.00 p.m. to 1.00 a.m. Monday through Friday.

* Adjusted to make units comparable. See text. Definitions of day-parts are for Eastern time.

of the other variables are similarly divided. It is thus important to distinguish between 'audience' or 'viewers' and 'households'. 'Audience' is a measure of the number of households actually viewing the station. 'Households', on the other hand, is a crude measure of relative market size. It is the total number of TV homes in the station's TSA. We shall often interpret the results in terms of the revenue gained by acquiring an additional viewing household. This will be measured in revenue per *viewing* household. It is to be distinguished from measures of revenue per TSA household. Changes in the number of households reflect changes in scale; changes in the number of viewers reflect actual changes in the viewing of the station.[4]

We begin with the results for all television stations and all revenue given in Table 17.2. Consider first the effects of audiences on revenue when audiences are divided into the three 'rings' defined earlier. The coefficient of audience in the MRA is $156 per year for an additional household quarter-hour of viewing. The estimate is significant at the 0.1 per cent level. The coefficient of audience in the middle ring, ADI (but not in the MRA), is approximately $113 and highly significant. The coefficient of audience in the outer ring, TSA (but not in the ADI), is $97 and again highly significant.

We thus see a consistent pattern of results in terms of the effects of audience on revenue, as measured by the coefficients so far discussed. Audience is plainly important for revenue, but that importance tends to decrease as the location of the audience moves outward from the station. This makes sense in terms of the hypotheses about advertiser behavior advanced above.

In a further attempt to differentiate audiences by location, we introduced a variable, $AADIVH$, which measures the size of a station's audience that is located in adjacent $ADIs$, i.e. in nearby markets. Audience which is not located in nearby markets and is not within the station's ADI is likely to be cable audience in distant cities. Since the audience measured by $AADIVH$ is included in the audience measured by $TSAVH - ADIVH$ (the outer ring), the coefficient on $AADIVH$ measures the difference between the value of outer-ring audience in nearby markets and the value of outer-ring audience in distant markets. We find uniformly that this coefficient is not merely insignificant but essentially zero (in the present instance, it is $0.38). This indicates that distant audiences are valued similarly independently of whether they are in nearby markets and suggests that being carried on distant cable systems is *not* worth more than being received off-the-air in the outer ring, a fact of obvious regulatory relevance.[5]

Such locational effects are not due to chance. An *F*-test of the proposition that all three coefficients are the same (and that the adjacent audience coefficient is zero) gives a probability to that hypothesis so low as to be not readily computable from tables.[6]

Further, the result that audience located far away from the station is not worth so much as audience located near it is supported by an additional result in the regression. For some stations in our sample (very few), there is a parent–satellite relationship where the satellite station merely retransmits the programs of the parent. In such cases, data are for both parent and satellite combined. Since it is obviously possible that audience spread out over both parent and satellite is not worth the same as a more tightly located audience of the same size, we introduced a dummy variable into the regression which is one when a

Table 17.2 Estimates of the audience–revenue relationship with audience divided according to location (figures in parentheses are standard errors).

| Sample | Dependent variable | Independent variables* | | | | | | | | | | | R^2/s.e.e.† |
		Constant	PS	VI	UA	UI	HY	$\dfrac{MVH}{TSAH}$	$\dfrac{(ADIVH\cdot MVH)}{TSAH}$	$\dfrac{(TSAVH\cdot ADIVH)}{TSAH}$	$\dfrac{AADIVH}{TSAH}$	$\left(\dfrac{TSAVH}{TSAH}\right)^2$	
All	$\dfrac{TR}{TSAH}$	−4.309	−1.838 (0.592)	0.827 (0.423)	−0.571 (0.221)	−1.088 (0.326)	0.558 (0.060)	156.38 (10.09)	113.48 (11.80)	96.8 (18.54)	0.38 (2.56)	345.90 (94.08)	0.839 29.5
Affiliates	$\dfrac{TR}{TSAH}$	−4.637	−1.840 (0.609)	—	−0.632 (0.229)	—	0.611 (0.060)	149.25 (10.80)	108.86 (12.38)	91.08 (19.36)	0.78 (2.70)	398.59 (100.35)	0.833 28.3
Independents	$\dfrac{TR}{TSAH}$	−0.192	—	—	—	−1.309 (0.414)	0.152 (0.120)	144.50 (41.45)	180.38 (72.76)	202.34 (85.97)	−7.48 (7.63)	997.25 (928.26)	0.888 30.4
All	$\dfrac{LNR}{TSAH}$	−4.269	−1.863 (0.564)	1.272 (0.403)	−0.462 (0.211)	−0.826 (0.310)	0.535 (0.050)	153.58 (9.62)	97.37 (11.25)	90.67 (17.67)	0.62 (2.45)	228.30 (90.94)	0.823 31.4
Affiliates	$\dfrac{LNR}{TSAH}$	−4.573	−1.865 (0.578)	—	−0.531 (0.217)	—	0.588 (0.060)	145.79 (10.25)	91.92 (11.75)	84.04 (18.38)	1.00 (2.56)	287.88 (94.08)	0.818 30.8
Affiliates	$\dfrac{NC}{TSAH}$	−0.064	0.025 (0.130)	—	−0.101 (0.049)	—	0.023 (0.010)	3.62 (2.31)	16.94 (2.64)	7.04 (4.13)	0.23 (0.58)	111.01 (21.95)	0.601 54.9

* see Table 17.1 for definitions of variables.
† Standard error of estimate as a per cent of mean revenues per household.

parent and satellite are involved and zero otherwise. The coefficient of this variable is −1.84, significant at the 1 per cent level. Hence, with everything else equal, including the size of the audience, a station in which the audience figures are for both parent and satellite will have approximately $1.84 per TSA household less in yearly revenue than a station for which the same audience figures are for a single station only. This supports the earlier finding about audience location. One would expect local advertisers, in particular, to be less interested in audience on a satellite station located at some distance from the parent than in audience of the parent itself.

Note that if this hypothesis is correct, then we ought to see a difference below in considering results for network compensation versus local and national advertiser revenue. The effect of the parent–satellite dummy ought to be present and negative for local and national advertising revenue, but there is no reason to expect it to be present for network compensation. Presumably, networks do not care where the audience they are reaching on a particular station is located as long as that station is the primary means of reaching that audience. This turns out to be the case.

The results indicate that audience characteristics have two other effects on revenue. The simpler effect is that of household income. We find that, other things equal, an increase of $1,000 in the median income of households in the TSA increases station revenue by $0.56 (with standard error of $0.06) per such household. Richer populations are worth more to advertisers and hence to stations.

The more complex effect is that given by the coefficient of the square of audience-per-household.[7] Multiplying through by TSA households, we see that in terms of total revenue this variable is equal to total TSA audience multiplied by TSA audience per TSA household. We shall refer to the latter factor (audience per household) as a measure of 'penetration'. It is like a rating variable, although it is not in fact a rating which is ordinarily computed. The coefficient of the non-linear term – the square of audience per household – is 346 (with standard error of 94). For the average value of penetration in our sample, the non-linear term adds approximately $26 to the other audience effects.

A positive non-linear effect implies that advertisers do not, for example, view two spots on a station reaching a given audience as equivalent to a single spot on a station reaching an audience twice as large. Advertisers may value the single spot on the large-audience station more than the two spots on the small-audience one, even though the total audience appears to be the same in the two cases, because the audiences for the two spots on the station with the smaller audience may have some viewers in common, while the audience for the single spot on the station with the larger audience provides a greater number of *different* viewers. If advertisers value a message to a marginal viewer more highly than a marginal message to an inframarginal viewer, then there will be a positive non-linear effect of audience on revenue.

Both the non-linear term and the non-audience effects cause the marginal value of audience to differ from the average value of audience and thus to give rise to a variable elasticity of revenue with respect to audience. Our estimates indicate that for a VHF affiliate with average audience size and characteristics, the elasticity of revenue with respect to audience is approximately one, whereas without the non-linear effect the elasticity would be less than one. In general, the elasticity is greater than unity for stations with above-average penetration and somewhat less than unity for stations with low penetration. For given characteristics, the elasticity tends to be bigger for UHF affiliates and particularly for UHF independents because of the UHF handicap term which we discuss below.

The other effects estimated in the equation being considered are simple. We introduced three dummy variables to attempt to measure the difference, if any, between the audience–revenue relationship for network-affiliated and independent stations on the one hand and UHF (Channels 14–80) versus VHF stations (Channels 2–13) on the other. In each case the coefficient to be discussed measures the difference in dollars per TSA household between the revenue received by the type of station under consideration and that received by a VHF affiliate similarly situated.

It is important to realize that these are effects, given audience size, so that, in particular, the UHF effect found here reflects a UHF handicap that is not simply due to smaller audiences for UHF stations. Apparently, advertisers are less willing to pay for audience on UHF stations than on VHF stations, possibly because they believe that a given set of homes can be more efficiently reached on other stations.[8] Note that this is consistent with our findings from the non-linear effect, that advertisers prefer stations with greater penetration even given audience size.

The largest effect is that for UHF independents. We find that they tend to receive $1.09 less per TSA household than do VHF affiliates, with the effect significant at the 1 per cent level. The magnitude of this effect is best understood by expressing it in units comparable to those of the coefficients of the audience variables discussed above. If a UHF independent were lucky enough to achieve the average audience per TSA household of all stations in our sample, it would receive about $27 per viewer less than a VHF affiliate with the same audience size. Since UHF stations typically have below average audiences, the effect is even greater. A UHF independent with half the average audience per TSA household would receive about $55 less per viewer than a VHF network affiliate. These should be compared with the $97–$156 range for the marginal effects of audience on revenue (ignoring the non-linear term). This means that, for small UHF independents, the effect of audience on revenue is rather greater than one of strict proportionality.

UHF affiliates do somewhat better than this. We find that they get about $0.57 per TSA household less than VHF affiliates (significant at the 1 per cent level). The measures of the UHF handicap in revenue per viewing household comparable to the $27 and $55 figures for UHF independents are $14 and $28, respectively.

In short, there is a definite UHF handicap, not merely in the ability of UHF stations to attract audiences, but also in the revenue they receive, given such audiences. This can be seen again when we look at the variable which describes whether the station is a VHF independent. As opposed to UHF independents, which we found did definitely worse than anybody else, we find that VHF independents actually tend to do better than anybody else. Our point estimate is that, other things equal, VHF independent stations tend to get approximately $0.83 per household more than VHF affiliates (barely short of significance at the 5 per cent level). In terms of revenue per viewing household, the effect is an advantage of about $21 for a VHF independent with the average audience per TSA household of all stations, and rather more for VHF independents with smaller audiences.

Why should this be? VHF independents obviously receive much less network compensation than VHF affiliates, but they may do considerably better in terms of revenue from local and national advertisers. When we examine the latter type of revenue in the results below, we find that this is indeed the case and that the effect is statistically significant.

This completes our discussion of the results for the first principal equation estimated, that for all stations and all types of revenue when audiences are divided by geographical location but not by time of day.[9] We now turn to the results when revenues are subdivided.

Non-network revenue and network compensation

In this section we discuss the results obtained when total revenue is divided into two component parts, namely, network compensation and all other broadcast revenue, the latter being local and national advertising revenue.[10]

The equation for local and national advertising revenue for all stations appears in the fourth row of Table 17.2. In general, the coefficients are quite similar to those for total revenue already discussed. There are only two differences worth mentioning: the non-linear effect is smaller (but still significant), and there is an increase in the coefficient of the dummy variable for VHF independents.

The latter difference is an interesting one. Previously, we estimated that VHF independents have an advantage relative to VHF affiliates of about $0.83 per household, or almost $21 per viewing household at the point of means for the sample. However, the effect was not quite significant at the 5 per cent level. The effect here is larger, being $1.27 per household (about $32 per viewing household at the point of means); it is significant at the 1 per cent level. The VHF independent effect in the total revenue equation is reduced because of the inclusion of network compensation, which is largely irrelevant to independent stations.

Thus, given the size of their audiences, VHF independents receive much less network revenue than network affiliates, since the former carry far fewer network programs. The independents have correspondingly more spots to sell to local and national advertisers than do network affiliates, and therefore receive more of that type of revenue. Overall, they are at an advantage so far as the effects measured by the coefficients under discussion are concerned, because those effects only measure differences in revenue for stations with audiences held constant. Network affiliates receive some of their compensation, as it were, in the form of network programs, which attract larger audiences. These comparisons do not, of course, say anything about the comparative profits of independents and affiliates.

Whereas the local and national revenue regression is quite similar to the total revenue regression, the network compensation regression differs in a number of important respects. That regression is presented (for affiliates only) in the last row of Table 17.2. Let us discuss the simpler effects first.

Once again UHF affiliates are at a disadvantage *vis-à-vis* VHF affiliates (significant at the 5 per cent level). The parent–satellite dummy variable has a zero effect. This makes perfect sense. Whereas local advertisers, in particular, plausibly care much less about audience reached on a satellite station and located far from the advertiser, such considerations can hardly matter to networks or their advertisers.

Not quite so obvious, however, is the reason for finding that network compensation appears to be substantially unaffected by household income, with the full effect of household income on total revenue occurring for local and national advertising revenue. One explanation of this is as follows. Networks, in selling to national advertisers, do not sell time over their individual affiliates. Rather, with rare exceptions, trans-actions between networks and advertisers are based on the presumption that all or almost all affiliates will carry the programs in which the ad-vertisers' messages are placed. Thus, the prices paid by advertisers re-flect the size and characteristics of the entire network audience. Some differences in audience characteristics from station to station, such as income, may not be important to advertisers in purchasing advertising from networks, and thus may not influence network compensation.[11]

The somewhat more surprising results, however, concern the direct effects of audience on network revenue. If one looks at the effect of audience in the three rings, one sees a dramatic difference from the results already discussed. The effects are not only much smaller, but the middle ring is worth more than the others, and the outer ring may be worth more than the inner one (although only the coefficient for the middle ring is significant).[12]

Recall that the dependent variable in these regressions is always revenue per household, not total revenue. This means that *even with all other effects held constant, revenue varies with market size*, because it varies with the total number of TV homes in the survey area. Hence, the audience effects in the network compensation equation are con-sistent with the following approach to the determination of that com-pensation. Cities are classified by total size. In general, the signals of network affiliates cover the MRA, and the network expects to reach the audience in the MRA proportional to that size. Hence, little extra credit is given for reaching MRA audience, that already being taken into account in the consideration of market size. Some credit, however, is given for reaching audience outside the MRA, particularly audiences in outlying suburbs, since this is less likely to be fairly uniform over different markets and will depend on the efforts and characteristics of the individual station. That this may indeed be the case is also suggested by the fact that R^2 for this regression, while still quite acceptably large, is substantially lower than for the other regressions. With the depend-ent variable being revenue *per household*, this would be the case if considerably more of the variation in the dollar value of revenue were accounted for by variation in total households in this regression than in the others.

The remaining effect in the network compensation regression is the non-linear effect. It is obviously different from zero, but it is substan-tially smaller than in either the total revenue or the local and national advertising regression. Once again, nevertheless, stations with high penetration get more for audience than stations with low penetration. This is consonant with the effects which we have just discussed: a sta-tion with unusually high penetration can claim that merely looking at market size does not take account of how well it is doing for the network.

This completes our detailed discussion on the results obtained when audiences are divided by location, but not by day part. The other rows of Table 17.2 contain similar results of separate regression studies of network affiliates and independent stations, respectively. In general, they are consistent with the effects already discussed, although, of course, since there are many fewer independent stations than network-affiliated stations, the standard errors are rather higher for the independent station regression than for the network-affiliated regression.[13] In comparing those regressions, recall that the difference between them is the result of allowing all effects to be different for the two groups of stations rather than, as in the regressions discussed in detail above, assuming that all effects are the same except for differences which are constant per household.

Results when audience is subdivided by day-part

The results reported thus far have divided audience by space, but not by time. Differing values at different locations mean that the effects of audience diversion to cable depend on *where* they occur. Now we consider subdividing audience in time, according to what part of the broadcast day is involved. Different values here will mean that the extent of audience diversion to cable must be also subdivided as to time – the effects will depend on *when* they occur.

Unfortunately, multicollinearity prevents us from being able to examine location and time effects at once. This is not surprising: the fraction of the audience occurring in a particular day-part tends not to vary much as we go from inner ring to outer ring for a particular station. Accordingly, this section drops the locational division and concentrates on division in time. Since the other results (dummy variables, non-linear effects, etc.) are similar to those discussed above, we shall not repeat that discussion.[14]

The day-parts we study are: daytime, early fringe, prime time, and late fringe, defined as in Table 17.1. It is important to understand the units in which the audience variables are measured. Audience has so far been measured as number of viewing households per average quarter-hour. When the audience is divided into day-parts, however, this is not a convenient set of units, because there are different numbers of quarter-hours in different day-parts. This means that, measured in such units, the audience variables for different day-parts would not sum to total audience. More important, if what matters for revenue is total audience hours, then the same average audience per quarter-hour in two day-parts of different lengths will result in different revenues. This would mean that the regression coefficients, indicating revenues, would have to be corrected for the length of the period before testing the question of whether two revenues were equal. It is convenient, therefore, to adjust the units in which the audience variable is measured so as to make equal revenue effects in different day-parts correspond to equal regression coefficients and so as to have the audience in different day-parts sum to total audience.

This was done as follows. Audience per quarter-hour in a given day-part was multiplied by the number of quarter-hours per week in that day-part.[15] This produced total audience viewing hours in the day-part per week. It would have sufficed to use the variables in that form, but this would have led to units not comparable to those used in the regressions already discussed. Accordingly, we then divided by the number of quarter-hours in the broadcast week. Hence, our audience variables are weighted averages. The audience in prime time, for example, is the average audience per quarter-hour of prime time multiplied by the fraction of the broadcast week represented by prime time. With this choice of units, equal value of an audience hour in two different day-parts will be represented by two equal regression coefficients in the results.

The results are given in Table 17.3. For all stations, line 1 refers to revenue from all sources and line 4 to revenue from local and national advertisers. The results for the audience coefficients are quite similar for the two regressions, so we discuss in detail only the results for total revenue.

Division into day-parts appears to matter to a substantial degree. Indeed, an additional household in early fringe is worth more than 50 per cent more than an additional household in prime time ($340 versus $195). An additional household in late fringe is worth about 2½ times a household in prime time ($506 versus $195). The three regression coefficients for these time periods are all significant at well beyond the 1 per cent level. An additional household during daytime appears to be worth nothing. (The estimated effect is slightly negative but not significantly different from zero, and is quite consistent with a small positive effect.) The F-test of the null hypothesis that the coefficients are equal rejects it at far beyond the 1 per cent level.[16]

That conclusion holds up when we divide stations into independents and network affiliates. The results for network affiliates are presented in rows 2, 5 and 6 of Table 17.3. Looking at the results again for total revenue and for local and national revenue, we see the same pattern as before (not surprisingly, since network affiliates are most of the stations). Again, it appears to be true that early fringe is worth more than prime time, and late fringe worth more than early fringe, with daytime worth very little. Again, the possibility that such differences are due to chance is vanishingly small.

Early and late fringe audiences are more valuable than prime time to network affiliates, because there are more commercial minutes per hour in these periods and because a higher proportion of them is sold directly by the local station, since the stations carry less network programming in the fringe periods than they do in prime time. Fringe audiences are probably more valuable than daytime audiences because the demographic characteristics of the fringe audiences are more desirable to advertisers and also because a higher proportion of commercials is sold directly to advertisers.

The results for network compensation are somewhat different (as they were in the regressions where audience was divided by geographical location). Here, the differences between the various day-parts are far less marked. It appears to be true that neither prime time nor daytime audiences are worth much at all, the coefficients being insignificantly different from zero. Late fringe and early fringe appear to be worth somewhat more. The coefficients of those variables are significant at the 5 per cent level. The null hypothesis of no difference is rejected at the 5 per cent level, but not at the 1 per cent level.

The conclusion that audiences in different day-parts are worth different amounts holds for independent stations as well, although here the relative values of the day-parts appear to be somewhat different. The results are reported in row 3 of Table 17.3. Here, daytime audiences are definitely worth something, the coefficient being significant at the 1 per cent level. Prime time audience appears to be worth very little and late fringe audience also very little. (The latter has a large negative coefficient, but one which is not significantly different from zero.) What is worth the most is early fringe, which appears to be far more valuable than prime time and more than twice as valuable as daytime. (The early fringe coefficient is significant at well beyond the 1 per cent level.) The null hypothesis of no difference in the audience coefficients is rejected at the 1 per cent level.

Early fringe and daytime audiences are probably more valuable to independents than to network affiliates, because all commercial minutes are sold directly to advertisers by independents, while the demographic characteristics of their audiences are similar to those of affiliates. The low value of prime time and late fringe audiences to independent stations relative to network affiliates probably reflects less desirable demographic characteristics of independent station audiences in those time periods. Late fringe audiences for affiliates largely consist of audiences for network programs into which the affiliates can slip

Table 17.3 Estimates of the audience–revenue relationship with audience divided according to day-part (figures in parentheses are standard errors).

Sample	Dependent variable	Constant	Independent variables*										R^2/s.e.e.†
			PS	UA	VI	UI	HY	$\frac{TSAVHD}{TSAH}$	$\frac{TSAVHEF}{TSAH}$	$\frac{TSAVHPT}{TSAH}$	$\frac{TSAVHLF}{TSAH}$	$\left(\frac{TSAVH}{TSAH}\right)^2$	
All	$\frac{TR}{TSAH}$	−4.633	−2.427 (0.593)	−0.488 (0.221)	0.981 (0.459)	−0.897 (0.341)	0.589 (0.060)	−21.62 (28.55)	340.08 (57.83)	194.71 (26.89)	506.18 (75.78)	383.85 (94.08)	0.839 29.5
Affiliates	$\frac{TR}{TSAH}$	−4.799	−2.466 (0.608)	−0.566 (0.228)	—	—	0.625 (0.060)	−27.87 (30.41)	287.70 (63.38)	198.06 (28.24)	517.40 (79.14)	445.63 (100.35)	0.834 28.7
Independents	$\frac{TR}{TSAH}$	−0.356	—	—	—	−1.488 (0.415)	0.176 (0.110)	153.88 (72.78)	401.51 (115.47)	27.46 (98.39)	−174.76 (251.37)	930.76 (812.22)	0.900 28.5
All	$\frac{LNR}{TSAH}$	−4.948	−2.550 (0.579)	−0.371 (0.216)	1.516 (0.448)	−0.604 (0.333)	0.599 (0.050)	−26.73 (27.87)	315.35 (56.45)	195.82 (26.25)	465.43 (73.99)	264.99 (90.94)	0.814 32.2
Affiliates	$\frac{LNR}{TSAH}$	−5.099	−2.593 (0.590)	−0.467 (0.222)	—	—	0.640 (0.060)	−33.91 (29.54)	253.81 (61.55)	204.00 (27.42)	473.17 (76.87)	339.32 (97.22)	0.811 31.4
Affiliates	$\frac{NC}{TSAH}$	−0.300	0.128 (0.136)	−0.099 (0.051)	—	—	0.015 (0.010)	6.03 (6.79)	33.89 (14.14)	−5.94 (6.30)	44.23 (17.66)	106.62 (21.95)	0.567 57.2

* See Table 17.1 for definitions of variables.
† Standard error of estimate as a per cent of mean revenues per household.

their own spot advertising. Apparently, even given the size of the audience, such spots are more valuable to advertisers than are spots in the programs carried by the independents during late fringe. Although audiences appear generally more valuable to network affiliates than to independents, the effect is particularly marked for late fringe and reversed for daytime audiences.

To sum up, audiences in different day-parts are worth different amounts to stations. In particular, early fringe is worth much more than prime time, and for network affiliates late fringe is worth even more. Policy decisions which concern audience diversion must take this into account by examining the temporal as well as the spatial aspects of such diversion.

Conclusions

In attempting to evaluate the impact of cable penetration on local television broadcast station revenue, the FCC staff has assumed that the likely effect can be measured merely by looking at the effect of cable on audience (US Federal Communications Commission, 1979b). Such a procedure implicitly assumes unitary elasticity between total audience and total revenue. The economics of station revenue determination and the results presented here indicate that such an assumption is likely to lead to inaccurate estimates of the effect of audience diversion on local station revenue. Our results indicate that the effect of a given percentage diversion of audience on a station's revenue will differ significantly, depending upon the station type (independent, affiliate, UHF or VHF), the size of the station's audience, the location of the audience which is diverted and the day-part in which the diversion occurs.

Notes

1. The data used cover 533 network affiliates and 68 independent stations for 1976. Data for all non-revenue variables were taken from publicly available sources, such as *Arbitron* and *Television Fact Book*. Revenue data by station, however, are maintained confidentially by the FCC and were made available for internal use in runs on the FCC computer.
2. Earlier estimates of such a relationship were reported in Chapter 16.
3. For an extensive discussion of network compensation arrangements see US Federal Communications Commission (1979a). Stations also enter into arrangements similar to the network-affiliate relationship with companies other than ABC, CBS and NBC, including more limited network organizations, such as Operation Prime Time. National advertisers may

also supply programs to local stations under barter agreements where, in exchange for carrying the program, the station provides a number of spots to the advertiser free of charge and retains some time for direct sale of spots to other advertisers.

4. The use of the total survey area as the primary measure of scale is open to question. The relation between TSA households and the 'true' potential audience of a station varies widely. This may be particularly true when comparing UHF and VHF stations and we shall have to take account of this below. An obvious alternative would be to use total households in the station's ADI as the scale deflator, but this has similar problems. Because the scale deflator is used to divide not only revenue, but also the various audience measures, this choice does not materially affect our ability to interpret the results in terms of revenue per viewing household. Some deflation is necessary for heteroskedasticity and for the linear form of the equation to make sense.

5. There is a problem in the data here (discovered late in the study) which must be mentioned. For about 5 per cent of the sample, *Arbitron* reports audience in adjacent ADIs as zero for all-day viewing but positive for individual day-parts. The results in the text (here and later) are obtained by adding together the day-part audiences (in appropriate units) to obtain a total for the entire day. We also ran regressions dropping such observations and regressions treating the adjacent audience variable as really zero in such cases. For both alternative sets of regressions, the results were the same. With two exceptions, the regression coefficients and standard errors changed almost not at all from those given in the text. The two exceptions were those which we would expect – the coefficients of the adjacent audience variable itself and of the outer ring audience. The latter coefficient increased substantially, but its standard error increased by a greater factor (*t*-statistics going from 5 to 3). That increase was offset by a large but insignificant negative coefficient of the adjacent audience variable. If such alternate results are believed, there is at least a suggestion that audience reached by distant cable is worth considerably more than the rest of the audience in the outer ring. However, the greater standard errors of such results and the persistent estimation at zero of the adjacent audience effect, if one uses the obviously sensible correction applied in the results in the text, lead us to reject such alternatives.

6. $F(3,590) = 14.7$. The 1 per cent point is around 3.8.

7. The audience involved here is the total TSA audience. The households, as always, are total TSA households. It would be possible, in principle, to determine whether there are similar effects to those about to be described when the squared term is disaggregated for location of audience, but collinearity would be a problem, and the number of runs we were allowed on the FCC computer limited experimentation.

8. The data are for both intermixed markets (i.e. markets containing both VHF and UHF stations) and deintermixed ones, but the introduction of a dummy variable reflecting intermixture did not indicate a significant difference.

There is a possibility that some of the effect may be a statistical artifact due to differences between UHF and VHF stations in the length of the broadcast day. The estimated effect seems much too large to be accounted for by this, however.

9. Some experimentation was done with variables reflecting audience demographics and special station and market characteristics (i.e. a dummy

10. We did not attempt to estimate separate relationships for these two types of revenue because we were advised that the data were unreliable.

11. Network advertisers can display their preferences for audience characteristics, such as income, by their choice of programs in which they buy time for their commercial messages.

12. The hypothesis that all three coefficients are the same is still rejected at far beyond the 1 per cent level.

13. The ring effect appears reversed for independent stations, but the standard errors are much larger. The F-test of the hypothesis that audiences are worth the same independent of location fails to reject it even at the 50 per cent level.

14. The multicollinearity problem means that the F-tests for division by time and those for division by space are not fully independent. Indeed, the estimated coefficients for either division might be thought to involve both effects. This is unlikely to be a major problem, however, since the multicollinearity occurs precisely because the temporal division of audience for a given station is largely independent of its spatial division. It is not unreasonable to assume that this is also true of variations among stations. Although it is not possible to estimate an equation with a joint breakdown by ring by day-part (i.e. 12 ring–day-part variables) it would be possible to estimate a simultaneous breakdown of audience by ring and by day-part (i.e. 3 rings and 4 day-parts). However, this would require another computer run not available to us.

15. Per week, rather than per day, because there are differences between weekends and week days in the definitions of the day-parts as given in the data.

16. F is approximately 14. The 1 per cent point is approximately 3.8.

References

Park, R.E. 'Audience diversions due to cable television: response to industry comments'. *Rand Note* N-1334-FCC, November 1979.

US Federal Communications Commission. 'An analysis of the network-affiliate relationship in television'. Preliminary report of the Network Inquiry Special Staff. Washington, DC: October 1979a.

US Federal Communications Commission. 'Report in Docket 21284,' FCC 79-241, 71 FCC 2d 632 (Economic Inquiry Report). Washington, DC: 1979b.

18

The Financial Interest and Syndication Rules in network television: Regulatory fantasy and reality (1985)

In principle, a basic tenet of US economic policy involves reliance on the forces of the free market. More than any other country, the United States claims to act on the fundamental proposition of economic analysis that unfettered competition produces economic efficiency. We claim to resort to government regulation only when there is good reason to believe that the assumptions which underlie this fundamental proposition are violated or that some other social end overrides efficiency considerations. Indeed, one major way in which we use government action is in antitrust policy, which is supposed to ensure that market functioning remains free of private (as opposed to governmental) interference.

Such a policy is not easy to pursue in practice, partly because there is always continual pressure to deviate from it for the benefit of one group or another and partly because correct application of a free-market policy requires a sophisticated understanding of the economic analysis of the ways in which markets and competition do or do not operate. As a result, it can be both tempting and easy for regulatory authorities to overregulate, sincerely believing they are accomplishing a socially

This chapter first appeared in a book dedicated to the memory of John J. McGowan, who worked with me for many years on the matters discussed. As explained below, it is taken from my statements submitted to the Federal Communications Commission on behalf of CBS, Inc. in BC Docket No. 82-345 ('In the Matter of Amendment of 47CFR §73.658(j)(l)(i) and (ii), the Syndication and Financial Interest Rules'). Over our many years of involvement with these subjects, John McGowan and I spoke with and received comments from a large number of people, and it is not possible to thank them all here. Particular thanks, however, go to John Appel, William Baumol, David Blank, David Boies, Robert Bolick, Steven Edwards, Paul Joskow, Stephen Kalos, George Vradenburg III, Robert Larner, Donald Prutzman, Paul Saunders and especially Robert S. Rifkind. As usual, errors are mine, not theirs.

beneficial end, whereas, in fact, they are aiding one interest group or another. Similarly, it is tempting (and easy) for regulatory authorities to mistake the complaints of particular competitors for a symptom of injury to competition itself. In this regard, the history of the Financial Interest and Syndication Rules for network television provides a cautionary tale.

The program-development process

I begin this chapter by telling that tale in broad outline, giving the history and summarizing the relevant economic analysis. That analysis itself is given later.

In oversimplified outline, the process of developing and producing entertainment series for network television operates as follows. Someone with an idea convinces one of the three major networks (ABC, CBS or NBC) that the idea is worth trying. The network commissions the writing of a script. If the script looks promising, the network then pays a fee for production of a pilot episode. If the pilot appears sufficiently attractive, the show proceeds to production for network exhibition, with the network paying for the right to exhibit it. Then, if successful when shown, the network can decide to renew, showing the series in later seasons. Eventually, if the show has a long, successful run on the network, it may (usually at the end of the network run) go into 'syndication', with old episodes being exhibited by individual stations across the country.

The terms on which the development and network exhibition of series take place are generally agreed on in advance. That is, at the beginning of the project, the network and the packager producing the show agree on the fee the network will pay for the script, the pilot and each episode in each year of network exhibition. In practice, however, fees for successful shows are often renegotiated upward in the second or later years of their network runs.

Both parties to such agreements are investing in a risky proposition. Most projects never get to pilot, and most pilots never get to series. Further, most series do not last beyond their first year, and fewer still even make it into syndication. (All of this, of course, is due largely to competition among the networks and between the networks, other sources of television programs, and other media for viewers and advertisers. A monopoly network, free of the rigors of competition, could show what it wished.) The networks invest large sums in these projects every year, recovering only from successful shows. Packagers receive payments from the networks, but they also bear some of the risk, sometimes profiting only if the show makes it to syndication.

Before approximately 1970, the networks bore a greater share of such risks than they do at present. Before 1970, networks often acquired certain rights and interests beyond the right of network exhibition in return for their investment. Often a network would purchase a financial interest in the profits, if any, to be made from the series; often it would acquire the right to distribute the series in syndication, if things ever got that far (although syndication rights were almost never acquired from the major studios that had their own syndication arms). Such rights or interests typically were acquired at the outset of the project, when they were highly speculative. By selling them to the network, packagers laid off risk, acquiring money immediately in exchange for lottery tickets, so to speak, that were unlikely ever to pay off.

Not surprisingly, packagers who produced successful shows came to regret having sold winning lottery tickets to the networks. When, during or after a show's first network season, it became likely that it would be profitable or go into syndication, the packager saw that more money would have resulted from that success had the risky rights been retained in the first place. To successful packagers it seemed as though the networks were reaping the rewards of success, whereas the packagers themselves were not. Further, since the price paid for the risky rights and interests was not stated separatedly but was included in the various fees of the original agreement, it was easy to overlook the fact that the networks were also paying such prices for rights and interests in unsuccessful shows. In part, the successful packagers' view resulted in renegotiation of the fees for later network seasons; in large part, though, that view found expression in complaints to the regulatory authorities that the networks were extorting financial interests and syndication rights from the packagers. Unfortunately, both the Federal Communications Commission (FCC) and the Department of Justice listened.

The rules and the antitrust cases

In 1970, the FCC forbade the networks to acquire financial rights and interests in series or to distribute series in syndication. The Commission appears to have believed that by 'protecting' packagers from the power of the networks in this way, packagers' profits would be high enough to permit packagers to engage in the production of first-run syndicated programs (programs produced directly for exhibition by television stations without having first been seen on a network). It is hard to understand the reasoning behind this. First-run syndication was not made more profitable by the rules, so there was no reason to expect packagers to invest more in projects for first-run syndication after the rules than they had done before; indeed, they did not do so.[1] The Commission appears to have been motivated at least partly by a desire to protect the packagers from the networks – and here it was joined by the Antitrust Division of the Justice Department.

Despite the fact that the FCC had already forbidden acquisition of the things in question, in 1972 the Justice Department sued each network, seeking to have such acquisitions forbidden again as contrary to the antitrust laws. The lawsuits involved can only be termed bizarre. The Antitrust Division did not allege that the networks acted in any way in concert. Rather, ignoring the intense rivalry of the networks for viewers and advertisers, and therefore for programs, the Antitrust Division sued each network separately, accusing each network of having a monopoly *of the programs it showed*. The acquisition of the rights and interests already forbidden by the FCC's rules was attacked as monopolistic extortion from the packagers, and the Division sought to have such acquisitions forbidden a second time.

It was at this point that John McGowan and I became involved. Charles River Associates (of which John was a vice-president) and I were retained by counsel for CBS as economic consultants in *United States* v. *CBS* and related matters (I was a potential expert witness). We served in that capacity until the case was settled by consent decree in 1980. Afterward, in the fall of 1981 and the winter of 1981–82, we acted as consultants to NBC on related matters. (This was one of the last projects John worked on before his death.) Finally, in 1982–83, Charles River Associates and I worked again for counsel for CBS in connection with the FCC's proposed repeal of the Financial Interest and Syndication Rules. This chapter is based on the statements submitted to the FCC in that matter and heavily draws on the work John and I did earlier.

There were several reasons why neither the FCC's rules nor the Justice Department's antitrust claims made sense. First, the networks in fact competed with each other; no one network could possibly have a monopoly. Second, even if networks had monopoly power over packagers, forbidding acquisition of financial interests and syndication rights would leave that power unaffected. The networks, acquiring fewer rights and interests when investing in programs, would simply pay less, and any monopolistic exploitation of packagers would show up in lower initial prices. Moreover, exactly the same thing would be true if the networks *did not* have monopoly power; the price paid for a smaller bundle of rights would decline. Whatever the market structure, the direct effect of forbidding such acquisitions would simply be to force packagers to bear more of the risk of series development than they would have otherwise.

This was particularly unfortunate because, as I show in detail below, the networks are the natural and efficient bearers of risk in this situation. As opposed to (at least) small packagers, they can spread their risks by investing in many projects rather than in one. Further, they can invest so as to take advantage of the audience-flow effects that result from planning an entire network schedule rather than having random placement of programs (and, of course, a given network has a better idea than anyone else what sort of programs its own future lineups will require). Finally, networks are in the best position to exploit programs over time in terms of promotion, taking into account the effects on later syndication during the years of the network run. While it is true that other risk-bearers can do one thing networks cannot – spread their risks over projects developed for *different* networks – the fact that networks regularly acquired the rights and interests in question shows that this effect was less important than the risk-bearing efficiencies of the networks. Again, acquisition of those rights and interests had nothing to do with any supposed network monopoly power. The networks would have acquired those rights and interests whether or not they had monopoly power, provided it was profitable and efficient for them to do so.

The regulations embodied in the FCC's Financial Interest and Syndication Rules – and then again in the consent decrees that settled the Antitrust Division's suits against the networks (when the networks decided the expense of further litigation was not worth avoiding being forbidden twice to do something they were already forbidden to do once) – thus could not accomplish their stated ends. Like much poorly thought out regulation, however, the rules were not without effect. By keeping the most efficient risk-bearers from acquiring the risky rights and interests involved, the rules forced others to bear the risks. Some packagers (the major studios and the already successful independents) were relatively well able to do so. Others – particularly those attempting to break into the business (or to break away from employment with the major studios) – were not. The inevitable effect of the rules, therefore, was to force risk-averse packagers into the arms of their competitors. Ironically, the rules, themselves incapable of improving the income of packagers by weakening any monopoly power the networks may have had, could improve certain packagers' income by lessening competition among the packagers themselves. Certain competitors (the successful packagers) were protected, but only at the expense of competition itself.

The proposed repeal of the rules

These facts did not go unremarked. The networks asserted them, and so did independent analysts.[2] Eventually, when the FCC (with the usual suspicion of network power) set up a special staff to study networks, that staff reported in 1980 that the Financial Interest and Syndication Rules served no legitimate purpose, were likely to have the effects outlined above, and should be repealed.[3] In 1982, the FCC asked for comments on such repeal and, after what may have been the most heavily lobbied proceeding in history, in August 1983 tentatively decided to rescind the Financial Interest Rule totally while substantially altering the Syndication Rule.[4] In doing so (over the anguished protests of those protected from competition by the rules), the FCC essentially adopted the position of the Reagan Administration's Antitrust Division. It seemed a reasonable forecast that similar alterations in the misguided consent decrees might be forthcoming.

'Warehousing'

Alas, the story does not end completely happily – if indeed it ends at all.

First, whereas both the FCC and the Justice Department abandoned the positions that led to the imposition of the rules (and the lawsuits) in the first place, and although they apparently agreed that the Financial Interest Rule served only negative purposes, they nevertheless found a wholly new rationalization for limiting the networks' ability to acquire and use syndication rights. That rationalization, suggested by the Justice Department and agreed to by the FCC, was as follows.

Suppose there were a single network – a monopoly as far as network exhibition is concerned. If such a network acquired syndication rights to all the programs it exhibited, it might turn out to be to the network's advantage to 'warehouse' the programs, delaying their release into syndication. Such a monopoly network, by keeping the best off-network shows away from independent stations, would hamper the ability of those stations to compete with network affiliates exhibiting newer shows. (Another possible strategy would be to offer the shows to independents on differentially unfavorable terms.) Although such a policy would require sacrifice of the revenues to be earned from syndication, it might nevertheless pay if independent competition were damaged sufficiently.

The trouble with this scenario, of course, is not that it *could not* be true but that it bears no relation to the facts of the real world, either now or in the foreseeable future. There is not a single monopoly network but three vigorously competing networks. For those networks to engage in such a 'warehousing' policy would require them either to collude explicity, violating the antitrust laws, or to act in parallel without collusion. Such parallel action would be extremely difficult, since it would involve a whole series of decisions as to what programs to release to syndication and in which localities. The temptation to cheat on any implicit (or explicit) understanding would be very high, for holding back a worthwhile program would represent a sacrifice of syndication revenues to the 'warehousing' network, whereas any benefit accruing from injuring independent stations would be reaped by all networks equally. Further, such benefits would be reaped directly not by the networks themselves but by their affiliated stations, most of which are independently owned. Finally, even disregarding all this, the networks could not pursue such a policy without controlling the bulk of syndication rights. Even before the Syndication Rule, the three networks jointly acquired only a small fraction of such rights; in 1968 only 18.5 per cent of syndicated program sales by hours were made by networks.[5] There seems little prospect that the networks would or could acquire a very much larger share after repeal with numerous other syndicators bidding for the rights and with vigorous competition for programs among networks (and from other, newer competitors such as cable). Even if they did, they could not do so quickly; so there would be plenty of time for regulatory action.

The FCC agreed that a 'warehousing' scenario was highly unlikely. Nevertheless, in its tentative decision, it took that scenario as a basis for restricting the networks (at least until 1990) – forcing them to sell off any syndication rights within six months of cancellation of a show's network run or after five years of network exhibition, whichever comes first. The effect of such a provision (suggested by the Antitrust Division) would indeed be to remove much of the interference with efficient risk-taking embodied in the old rules. That provision would still interfere with the efficient promotion and use of programs over time, however, for it would force an arbitrary time of release to syndication. Further, the provision would remove three strong competitors – the networks – from the ultimate syndication market, imposing an undoubted decrease in competition for fear of an admittedly far-fetched possibility of such a decrease in the future.

The inefficiencies and diminished competition that would be brought about by the continued syndication prohibitions in the FCC's Tentative Decision were ameliorated, however, by a proposed termination of the rules in 1990. With a seven-year 'transition period' to full competition in the syndication business, even the theoretical fear of network collusion/

withholding in off-network series syndication would be put where it should be – to rest. The burden of justifying continuation past 1990 of regulatory-induced inefficiencies and barriers to network entry in off-network series syndication would also be put where it should be on proponents of continued regulation.

The proposed end of restrictions in 1990, however, would still have come years later than it should, for restrictions on the syndication activities of the networks should not have been imposed in the first place and should not be retained even in the milder form proposed. Between 1970 and 1983, the FCC and the Antitrust Division moved from basing policy on considerations that could not possibly have been true under any circumstances to basing it on considerations that, while they could be true with some conceivable set of facts, bear no resemblance to reality. That is, frankly, a major gain, but it is not enough.

Postscript

The question whether the justification for the proposed milder restriction makes any sense did not matter, however. The packagers, led by the major motion picture producers, did not cease their lobbying activities when the FCC issued its tentative decision in August 1983, nor did they limit those activities to the FCC. In late October, while the FCC was considering its ultimate decision, Congress was considering bills postponing repeal for five years, and the Senate Appropriations Committee attached an amendment to a fiscal 1984 supplemental appropriations bill prohibiting the FCC from spending funds to implement repeal until May 31, 1984.[6] In early November, President Reagan intervened, ordering the Departments of Commerce and Justice (which, of course, still had the consent decrees in force) to alter their positions in support of repeal.[7]

In this context, economic analysis may not be the determining factor in policy-making. Nevertheless, I now set forth the analysis of the rules in detail.

Economics of network television

The commercial television business requires assembly of a package consisting of programming, station time and advertising. This assembly involves transactions with several different groups – local stations, which offer time for sale; advertisers, who offer to buy time directly or indirectly to broadcast their commercial messages; and program suppliers, who offer programs to attract viewers for advertisers' messages.

The three major television networks are in the business of assembling packages consisting of programming, station time and advertising messages. To a minor extent they obtain programs by producing them themselves; primarily, however, the networks get programs by purchasing broadcast rights from independent program producers and owners. They acquire station time from their affiliates and other local stations in exchange for direct compensation and the opportunity to sell some of the available commercial time. They sell time to national advertisers whose commercial messages are placed in the programs offered for broadcast by the networks to local stations.

All told, the three major networks are the leading assemblers of these packages of programming, station time and advertising messages, but they are not alone in the business. Local stations, both network affiliates and independents, assemble such packages. They may do this by producing programs or by acquiring broadcasting rights from others and then broadcasting the programs over their own stations and selling time for commercial messages to local, regional and national advertisers. Others assemble such packages as well, including:

(a) advertisers who produce programs or purchase broadcast rights from others, insert their own commercial messages in the programs, and offer them to stations which can then sell additional commercial time within and adjacent to the programs;

(b) program producers, who sell time for commercials within their programs to national advertisers and offer the programs to local stations, which can sell additional commercial time within and adjacent to the programs; and

(c) advertiser-supported cable television networks.

Thus many non-network entities are essentially in the same business as the networks. Networks account for large shares of total TV advertising sales, however, and network programs attract a large share of viewing households both in prime time (7.30–11.00 p.m. in the Eastern time zone and comparable times elsewhere) and at other times in the day. Network purchases of television broadcast rights doubtless account for a highly significant portion of all such purchases. The existence of television networks and their important role in television broadcasting are attributable to three factors: scale economies in program viewing; economies of integrating the functions of program development, time acquisition and advertising sales; and advantages in financing the risks of program development.

Scale economies in program viewing

Networks benefit from scale economies in program viewing. Advertisers buy viewer attention. The larger the number of viewers who watch a program, the more it is worth to advertisers and the more they are willing to pay for spots within and adjacent to it. Further, the size of the audience for a program tends to depend on the effort devoted to producing it. Consequently, a program's audience share in a given market tends to be an increasing function of the resources, measured in dollars, expended in producing it. In short, relatively expensive programs tend to draw relatively larger shares because their production requires relatively more time and resources and because the more talented and popular actors, writers, directors and other personnel command relatively higher salaries and fees.

Because relatively expensive programs tend to draw relatively larger audience shares, there is a clear advantage to exposing programs to as large a potential audience as possible. In addition, a television program broadcast in one locality can be broadcast in other localities at almost no additional cost. Thus economies of scale can be achieved by broadcasting a program in more and more communities. Because attractive programs are expensive, economies of scale can be substantial. Broadcasting in almost all communities, as opposed to communities accounting for only half as many TV households, may make the difference between a profitable and an unprofitable program. By exploiting these economies of scale, networks can sell commercial spots at prices that cover program and other costs and provide a reward for their efforts, yet at prices that make television a cost-effective medium for advertisers. The existence of networks and their role in bringing together programs, stations and advertisers thus are a natural consequence of economies of scale in program viewing.[8]

Economies of integration

Economies of scale explain why networks can be expected to perform the function of bringing programs, program producers, stations and advertisers together as a broker might. Because economies of integration are intertwined with the economies of scale, however, networks are more than brokers; they invest in program development and acquisition, determine the dates and hours at which their programs are offered for broadcast, contractually obligate themselves to offer programs and pay compensation to affiliates, and solicit agreements to provide commercial spots to national advertisers.

The limited number of hours available for television viewing combines with the relatively small number of broadcast stations in each community to make the selection of programs to develop or acquire, offer and broadcast critical for achieving large audiences, providing an effective advertising medium, and yielding adequate profits. Program development and acquisition is a risky undertaking that involves large financial commitments well before the programs are broadcast, when audiences are unknown and revenues sufficient to cover program costs cannot be guaranteed. These risks can be reduced, however, if those who invest in program development and acquisition have reasonable assurance that their programs will be broadcast to nationwide audiences, thereby increasing the chance that revenues sufficient to cover costs will be generated. Affiliation agreements between networks and local stations help assure networks that the programs offered will be broadcast to nationwide audiences, so long as these programs are at least as attractive to audiences and stations as are other programs available. With that assurance networks are more willing to invest in program development and acquisition than they would be if they had to depend wholly on the individual decisions of loose and changing groupings of local stations. That investment results in programs more attractive to large numbers of viewers and affiliates than would otherwise have been produced, making affiliation advantageous to stations. Thus it is economically efficient for a single institution (a network) to integrate the function of offering programming to a large number of stations with that of development and acquisition of programs.[9]

It is also efficient for the same entity that develops programs to determine the date and time at which programs are offered for broadcast. Scheduling is important because the audience for a given program depends not only on its own inherent attractiveness to viewers but also on the attractiveness of other programs broadcast at the same time and on the attractiveness of the programs that precede and follow it. The inability or failure of developers of programs, assemblers of station time, or sellers of time for national advertising to take into account these counterprogramming and audience-flow effects decreases the effectiveness of such agents in performing their respective functions. Only by performing all three of them in conjunction with scheduling can a network maximize its audiences, its efficiency as an advertising medium, and its profits.

The benefits of the economies of integration noted above accrue to program producers, advertisers, stations and television viewers. Program producers benefit because integration increases networks' willingness to invest in programs. Advertisers benefit because more costly and attractive programs will be offered by networks and because they can reach nationwide audiences by dealing with a few networks rather than myriad local stations. Local stations affiliated with networks benefit because they can expect the network to offer them more attractive programming than they could otherwise obtain. Finally, viewers benefit from the greater attractiveness of the programs made possible through the network arrangement. Indeed, were this not the case, networks would cease to exist, for their economic efficiency lies ultimately in their ability to attract viewers.

Benefits from economies of scale and integration accrue to networks in the form of profits they might not otherwise earn. These profits are the returns that attract and reward networks for successfully performing the roles of scheduling and bringing advertisers, programs and stations together – and, most especially, for assuming the risks inherent in program development and acquisition. Those risks and their management underlie the effects of the rules on program supply.

Financing the risks of program development and acquisition

As I have observed, developing and acquiring television programs is a risky undertaking. Large financial commitments, often involving several million dollars, must be made well in advance of broadcasting and network receipt of revenues, at a time when the size of audience and revenues is speculative. Few program projects – even among those that are exhibited – survive long enough to earn a positive return on the investment made in developing them. Several economic factors explain why networks do most of the financing and why they bear most of the risk.

The most important factor explaining network participation in program development is that the risk can thereby be pooled; it is less risky to develop several programs at one time than to develop a single program, even if all programs have the same chance of success. A particular development project may be a smashing success, a miserable failure or something in between. Among a group of development projects some may be highly successful, some highly unsuccessful and some moderately successful. As a result, returns from projects which are average and above average tend to counterbalance losses on failures. Moreover, as the number of projects increases, the return on investment for the group of projects tends to become more predictable, thus reducing the risk of investing in program development. Ability to reduce risk by investing in numerous development projects explains why those who finance program development usually invest in many projects at a time and why – given the limited number of programs that can be shown on networks, and thus the limited opportunity for risk-pooling –

there are relatively few organizations financing program development in this way. These effects are particularly important for prime-time program development where investments for programming tend to be higher than for programs exhibited at other times.

The efficiencies of risk-pooling may also be achieved to some extent by non-network organizations which are large enough to finance numerous development projects simultaneously. Because a network must finance enough projects to fill its entire schedule, however, no other organization financing fewer projects can achieve greater benefits from risk-pooling. Moreover, networks have an additional advantage in being able to realize the economies of integration discussed above. These economies are not available to other organizations – for example, major motion picture studios – even where those organizations are large enough to achieve risk-pooling benefits equal to those of a network.

To amplify this point: networks are more efficient financers of program development than other large organizations that can realize the benefits of risk-pooling because networks are in a superior position to appraise the risks of development. Their superiority stems from their familiarity with all relevant phases of the television business and their corporate commitment to it. As a result, the risks of program development are somewhat less for networks than for potential financers of program development appraising the risks from outside the industry. Further, the interdependence of the success or failure of individual programs through audience-flow effects means that networks, which schedule the programs, will know better than others which projects are likely to result in programs most complementary to their schedule. They can thus reduce the risks of program development by investing in a suitable combination of programs. Other financers of program development must bear the risk that the collection of programs in which they invest will not meet the needs of a single network able to schedule the programs to maximize their joint value but rather will be split among different networks. Thus, for example, such financers might find that their programs are scheduled against each other, a risk no network bears.[10]

It is important to note here that the ability of a network to achieve the economies of scheduling does not depend on its owning syndication rights or financial interests. Indeed, a network's schedule is unlikely to be much influenced by such ownership, since consideration of audience and advertising revenue during the network run will be far more important. The fact that the networks are the entities that perform such scheduling, however, enables them to be more efficient investors, bearing less risk when investing in a given number of programs than would other program financers.

Even in the unlikely situation where a network, in putting together its schedule for the coming season, has to decide between two programs that are alike in ratings, cost and in all other respects save that the network holds a syndication interest in one program and not the other, it is not clear that it would be undesirable for the network to favor the program in which it held a syndication interest. Such behavior may have social benefits; networks are in the best position to invest efficiently in the development and promotion of a program over time. When networks share in the returns from post-network exhibition, the promotion and scheduling of a program during its network run can be done with an eye on the total benefits to be earned over the life of the program. Acquisition by the networks of interests in post-network runs thus promotes efficient investment in program development and promotion.

Finally, but most important, development tends to be financed by the networks because they have the most direct and substantial interest in ensuring a supply of attractive programs to offer to their affiliates. Indeed, the networks have a compelling interest in an assured supply of attractive programs. The entire relationship between a network and its affiliates and the network's ability to achieve economies of scale in programming rests on the network's ability to assure its affiliates of a continuing supply of attractive programs. Were that supply to deteriorate substantially, affiliates might well find it to their advantage to refuse network programs and ultimately to withdraw from affiliation.

This analysis shows that the role played by networks in financing television production is dictated by the fundamental economic circumstances of this industry. That role is unrelated to the presence or absence of monopoly or monopsony power. The nature of the market for television programming makes it efficient to shift risk from producers to the networks through the contracting process.

Arrangements for efficient risk-sharing

Because networks have special advantages in bearing risks, they are willing to pay more for rights that carry risky payoffs than suppliers require to compensate them for giving up those rights. Hence, in a competitive market one expects to see mechanisms developed for making such transfers while reducing risks as much as possible. Here, such mechanisms take the form of a sequential development process, together with contractual provisions transferring some combination of options and ownership interests of uncertain value to networks in exchange for their providing funds to suppliers for program development.

Sequential investment in program development, often called a 'step deal', means that program development does not proceed by committing all at once the resources needed to develop a program and its many episodes. Rather, development proceeds in several stages requiring increasing financial commitments and providing additional information useful in deciding whether and how to proceed. In the early stages expenditures are relatively modest as ideas are developed, initial scripts are drafted and potential talent is identified. Many projects are terminated at this stage, with only the more promising being developed further. The most promising projects are developed into pilots – essentially sample episodes of prospective series which, however, are often longer and more expensive to produce than are typical series episodes. Pilots selected as candidates for series production may be further developed. If a series is scheduled for broadcast, the network typically places an order for six to thirteen episodes. Additional episodes are ordered only for programs sufficiently attractive to viewers to lead the network to expect that the series will cover the costs of the additional episodes and contribute to a positive return on the network's development investments.

The strategy of reducing risks by pooling development projects derives from the ability to offset losses on failed projects with gains from successful ones. Obviously, this strategy would not work if program producers could sell to other broadcasters the rights to successful programs whose development was financed by one network, or if they could raise license fees for successful programs so high that the developing network would not earn enough to provide a satisfactory return on its total development investment.

One way to preserve the advantages of risk-pooling is for networks to develop programs themselves and thus own the broadcast rights outright. Indeed, networks have always done some program production, but it has not been their major mode of operation. Most programs, especially prime-time entertainment series, have been developed and produced by independent program producers under contract for individual programs to the television networks.[11] Most network-produced programs have been news, public affairs or daytime programs. Risks on prime-time entertainment series have been absorbed by the networks through contractual provisions.

Contracts under which programs are developed and series episodes are supplied typically are negotiated early in the development process. The contracts may be quite informal and are often renegotiated. They provide for network payments of specified amounts at each stage, contingent upon the network's desire to proceed further, and include a schedule of license fees the network will pay for any episodes it orders. In addition, the network obtains exclusive rights to offer each episode for broadcast in the United States a limited number of times (typically twice). Although the network usually has a continuing option to proceed or to order new episodes, the option term is limited, and the contract specifies dates by which each network option must be exercised.[12] If the network chooses not to exercise an option, the contract lapses, and rights revert to the program producer. Although all contractual provisions vary from contract to contract and from network to network and additional terms may be included, the essential structure of these agreements provides to networks a geographically and temporally limited exclusive option to offer programs whose development they have financed. Without such options, networks would earn little or no return by financing program development and eventually would withdraw from that function.

Before the imposition of the Financial Interest and Syndication Rules, networks absorbed risk through additional contractual provisions granting them financial interests in certain non-network uses of programs in exchange for development financing. Those provisions absorbed risk because the rights sold to networks by suppliers represented investments that were profitable only if the program was successful. Attractive television programs produced for networks often earn revenues from a number of sources other than network exhibition; those revenues, however, are important only if the network run is successful and long enough.

The first source of this type of revenue is foreign syndication – revenues paid by broadcasters in foreign countries for rights to broadcast programs developed and produced by independent suppliers in the United States. Because US networks acquire rights only for the United States, foreign syndication of a program can and does proceed simultaneously with broadcast of the program by stations in the United States. Another source of revenue is domestic off-network syndication, that is, the licensing for broadcast by local television stations, independent and affiliated, of programs previously offered by networks to local stations. Off-network syndication often occurs after new episodes of a series are no longer being offered by any of the three major television networks, but syndication can occur at any time the network does not have the exclusive right to offer the program. Still another source of revenue is merchandising – the sale of toys, clothes and other goods associated with a program or its characters.

Before the rules were established, networks frequently participated in these non-network uses of programs, sometimes by obtaining the right to act as distributor or licensor of one or more rights to foreign syndication, domestic syndication or merchandising and, more often, by sharing in profits from some of the non-network uses of program.

The possibility of sharing revenues from non-network uses through these financial interests and syndication rights provided a mechanism for allocating risks between networks and program producers. To the extent that networks purchased financial interest or syndication rights, they assumed risks because potential syndication fees and non-network earnings were, if anything, even more speculative than the potential earnings of programs on the networks. Networks were willing (and better able than independent producers) to bear these risks because of their pooling ability and the economies of integration they enjoyed. Concomitantly, to the extent suppliers sold rights and financial interests to networks, they shed risk since they exchanged items of uncertain value for the value given in return by the network, that is greater fees and advances than would have been given had the rights not been sold. Further, to the extent that networks could anticipate participating in non-network earnings, both the prospective return to financing program development and network financing increased.

To absorb risk efficiently, networks or other financing entities must be able to reach agreements with program suppliers that reflect mutual desires. This means contracts for programs must be capable of transferring risk from suppliers with an interest in one or a few programs to networks with an interest in many. Otherwise networks could not pool risks, and suppliers could not reduce risks by transferring them to networks.

A logical way to transfer risk is for networks to make one or more early cash payments in partial return for the acquisition of rights whose value is uncertain and greater than zero only if the program succeeds. One way in which risk was transferred to a network before the Financial Interest and Syndication Rules was to sell it some combination of distribution rights, merchandising rights and profit shares as part of the original deal under which the network agreed to pay for program development.

It must be emphasized that such exchange of distribution rights and profit shares for initial cash payments was in the interests of both networks and suppliers involved in a particular project. Networks, with the advantages of risk-pooling and economies of integration, could afford to pay more for rights or profit shares than suppliers needed to compensate them for their valuation of the rights and interests given up and more than suppliers could get by selling those rights and interest to others who lacked the advantages of risk-pooling and integration. Suppliers doubtless would have preferred to receive the same amount of financing *without* selling rights or profit shares, but competition among them prevented their doing so. Similarly, networks would have preferred to acquire rights or profit shares while paying less for program development than they actually did, but competition among networks for the network rights and among networks and others for distribution rights and profit shares prevented their doing so. The agreements reached reflected the networks' superior ability and willingness to assume risks and suppliers' desire to reduce them, as well as reflecting competition among networks and other distributors for rights, on the one hand, and competition among suppliers to sell broadcast and distribution rights, on the other.

The issue of monopsony

Despite the mutual benefits to be derived from selling profit-sharing and syndication rights to networks, some suppliers complained that they were forced to grant those rights and that they would have been willing to accept the greater risks involved in retaining the rights. Complaining suppliers, however, did not say they would be willing to accept both *more* risk *and* smaller network payments for program development; they said only that they preferred more to less, not that they would have been willing to accept less from networks in exchange for keeping the rights and options.[13]

The suppliers' real complaint may have been that they felt the total fees they received for the bundle of rights sold to networks were less than they would have received in a competitive market, rather than a specific complaint about the terms on which networks paid for program development. At least implicitly they seemed to believe that networks are too few and competition among them insufficiently vigorous.[14] Similarly, an important factor motivating the FCC's adoption of the Financial Interest and Syndication Rules was its perception that the three networks possessed monopsony power, that is, that the networks enjoyed market power as buyers in the program-supply market. If there is competition on the buyers' side of the program supply market, as well as on the sellers' side, surely the rules are unnecessary.

In fact, singly, the networks lack monopsony power; they compete vigorously among themselves for programming. Ultimately, networks compete among themselves for advertising revenues and with other suppliers of national advertising media, such as local television stations, radio stations, magazines, periodicals and other media. Because successful competition for advertising depends on attracting large audiences, networks compete for the attention of viewers. The networks' need to attract viewers causes them to compete vigorously for the programming with which to do it. In addition, because networks cannot reach national audiences with the relatively few stations they own and operate, they must compete with other sources of programs to attract affiliates and induce them to broadcast the network-offered programs. This competition for programs and television exhibition rights has increased and will continue to increase as a result of new distribution technologies, for example, cable and pay television, multipoint distribution systems and direct-broadcast satellites.

Moreover, careful analysis demonstrates that even if the networks had monopsony power, the Financial Interest and Syndication Rules would have left that power unaffected. The contract between a network and a program supplier is a complex bundle of interrelated rights and terms. For example, price, option length and exclusivity are important contractual terms in addition to whatever rights or financial interests the network might seek to acquire, at least prior to the rules. These terms can and do vary widely and from contract to contract. Because the rules created no more buyers and because they did not (and could not) regulate *every* contract term, they could not take away monopsony power even if it existed; the most they could do was to prevent its effects from being exercised in specific ways. If networks have significant monopsony power and can force program suppliers to accept lower than competitive prices, the rules do not change this characteristic of the market. Preventing a network from acquiring financial interests or syndication rights merely reduces the amount paid to a supplier, for the supposedly monopsonistic network will take into account the supplier's additional sources of income from selling to others rights the network can no longer acquire. In both a monopsonized and a competitive market, the rules lower the fees paid to packagers for network exhibition by an amount equivalent to the value of the rights that can no longer be transferred. (See the Appendix to this chapter.)

Thus, whatever the state of competition for programs, ability to transfer some risks from program suppliers to financers of program development increases economic efficiency and is in the interest of financers and suppliers as a group, particularly new and potential entrants (although, as we shall see, they may not be in the interest of large, established suppliers). The Financial Interest and Syndication Rules impaired the ability of program suppliers to transfer risks to networks and thereby detracted from economic efficiency. They could not have limited monopsony power even had such power existed.

Effects of the rules in the marketplace of syndicated television programming: 'warehousing'

By the time the repeal of the Financial Interest and Syndication Rules was under consideration in 1982–83, their inability to curb network power in the acquisition of program packages had been recognized. The regulatory authorities, however, raised a new issue: possible network power in the sale of off-network syndicated programs. In particular, the FCC and the Department of Justice were concerned that in the future networks might withhold some or all series from domestic syndication, delay entry of series into domestic syndication, or engage in other behavior calculated to make independent television stations less effective competitors of the network affiliates.

As we shall see, this concern was misplaced; indeed, the rules cause undesirable effects in the marketplace for syndicated television programming by eliminating the networks as competitors in that business. The rules do not permit ABC, CBS and NBC to engage in the business of syndication, including syndication of motion pictures, in the United States. Depriving the buyers of syndicated programming of access to three additional sellers can only tend to keep prices higher than they otherwise would be. Keeping efficient, viable competitors out of a market cannot be an appropriate purpose of government regulation.

Those buyers of programming hurt by the rules are principally network-affiliated and independent television stations. Other firms buy syndicated programming as well, however. They include cable systems, 'superstations' such as WTBS-TV in Atlanta, and emerging firms exploiting new technologies, such as direct-broadcast satellite.

The concern that elimination of the rules would damage rather than enhance competition is unfounded, for two reasons:

(a) the networks lack the market power to make such behavior (referred to generally as 'warehousing') effective strategy; and

(b) even if they possessed such power, the networks lack the incentive to exercise it.

First, in view of the vigorous competition among the networks and the competitive structure of the syndication business (which would be made even more competitive by the addition of three networks as sellers), warehousing would not be an effective method of hurting independent stations. For any advantage to be gained by withholding or delaying product or offering it to independent stations on discriminatory terms, the networks would, among themselves, have to control syndication of virtually all off-network programming of significant audience-attracting power, and all three networks would have to engage in collusion. These conditions were not satisfied before promulgation of the rules, and there is no evidence that warehousing occurred. Nor is there reason to believe that such conditions would exist or that warehousing would occur if the rules were repealed.

Before passage of the rules, the networks, either individually or collectively, were not dominant in syndication. In 1968 the three networks together had only 18.5 per cent of syndicated program sales by hours.[15] There is no reason to suppose that networks would have a larger share if the rules were repealed. Such a share, even if held by a single network, patently would be insufficient to permit that network to damage independent stations through warehousing. Other programming would always be available from other sources to ensure that independent stations remained competitive with network affiliates. Thus, even if they colluded, networks could only injure themselves by foregoing syndication fees and engaging in warehousing; they could not effectively injure independent stations.

Moreover, collusion among networks is also required to make warehousing work. In the absence of collusion, a warehousing network would forgo syndication fees without being able to prevent independent stations from access to the programs syndicated by its network rivals. There would be no benefit from this behavior unless the other networks were sure to engage in it as well. Yet the chances of collusion are too remote to justify the rules. Whatever else may have been said about the networks, it has never seriously been said that they collude; their competitive behavior is obvious and vigorous. Further, any collusive arrangement among the networks, short of a complete refusal to deal, would be almost impossible to police. The temptation to cheat would be strong, since significant additional revenue could be earned without losing the benefits of the conspiracy. Also, cheating would be difficult to detect, since the terms of the sales contracts are not public and the product is necessarily differentiated. How, for example, could one network be sure that another did not arrange the release of a particular program in a particular market earlier or on more favorable terms than collusion would dictate? Release can occur well before a program is actually shown, and contracts can involve rights to exhibition over several years. Further, the decision as to whether a particular program has been warehoused long enough is not one that lends itself to implicit or vague agreement.

The second reason that fears of network warehousing are unfounded is that it is difficult to imagine a situation in which a network would have an economic incentive to engage in program warehousing. It must be recognized that the beneficiaries of any injury to independent stations through warehousing would be the affiliates, which would gain some of the viewers the independents lose, and the other syndicators, including the other networks, who would sell their syndicated programs in substitution for warehoused product. The warehousing network would derive little direct benefit. To achieve an indirect benefit, the network would have to find a way to garner for itself some of the affiliates' increased profits. Whether and to what degree it could do that is speculative. Moreover, to the extent that independent stations were driven out, the bargaining power of the affiliates *vis-à-vis* the network would be increased, because the network would then lack alternative stations with which to affiliate. This would tend to shift profits to affiliates, not to the networks.[16] Therefore, it is practically inconceivable that a network would (even if it were able to collude with respect to syndicated programming) forgo profits from syndication in hopes that it could somehow siphon off some of the affiliates' increased profits or earn greater advertising revenues by virtue of its affiliates' increased audiences.

An additional check on potential network warehousing behavior is the interest of non-network participants in the profits of syndicated programs. Although the holder of syndication rights decides when and where to sell and collects a fee for the sales, others typically are entitled to share the profits from syndication. The syndicator is thus under a fiduciary obligation to such participants to maximize the profits obtainable from exploitation. Warehousing would lead to disputes and lawsuits that warehousers would be likely to lose. It would also destroy the reputation of the network as a syndicator and make it difficult for the network to get programs to syndicate in the future or to get others to invest in programs it would syndicate.

Accordingly, concern over network warehousing in the syndication marketplace to the detriment of independent stations is unjustified. The possibility of its occurring surely is too speculative and remote to justify the loss of competition that the rules impose. Moreover, if the networks, which now have essentially no syndication rights, were ever to acquire a share of such rights so large as to make warehousing less speculative, there would be plenty of time for action.

Effects on industry groups and the public of disrupting efficient risk-sharing

Whereas the possibility of an undesirable warehousing effect of repeal of the Financial Interest and Syndication Rules is speculative, the undesirable effects of retention are clear. The rules affect virtually all participants in the television industry and, of course, the viewing public. Among the firms affected are the networks, network competitors, major studios, independent program suppliers, potential new program suppliers, performing artists and other talent, affiliated television stations, independent television stations and advertisers. The effect of the rules on each of these groups and on the viewing public is analyzed below. In reading that analysis it must be kept in mind that imposition of the rules in 1970 was only one factor affecting a changing industry. The analysis thus sets forth what the effects of the rules must have been relative to what would otherwise have happened, not relative to pre-rule history.

The reductions in the efficiency of risk-bearing induced by the rules must be reflected in the amounts the networks are willing to pay for program development. The rules limit the value to the networks of the right to offer a program for network broadcast in the United States. Because entertainment programs are less valuable to networks, other factors being the same, than they were prior to the rules, the networks spend less on developing and acquiring such programs than would have been the case without the rules. The networks thus reduce payments for program development, license fees and program promotion expenses below what they otherwise would be. The payments networks offer to independent suppliers of entertainment programs with a given level of attractiveness fall, and the network resources devoted to program development decline, other factors being the same.

Suppliers of programs, selling fewer rights to networks than before, thus receive lower payments because of the rules. They face the possibility of increased 'deficit financing' where the 'deficit' consists of production costs less *only* the network exhibition fee. The profits needed to induce suppliers to remain in the business must come from the returns they earn on the rights they now cannot sell to networks.[17] But those rights promise only a risky return. Because suppliers are less efficient risk-bearers than are networks, those rights are worth less to them than they are to the networks (otherwise they would not have been sold), and suppliers are less willing to invest in making them pay off than networks would have been. Hence, overall investment in program development falls because of the rules, and programming attractiveness suffers, to the detriment of the viewing public (see the Appendix to this chapter).

Because the networks after the rules can share in the returns from risky ventures to a lesser extent than before the rules, they also have an incentive to alter their programming mix. They can be expected to acquire broadcast rights to fewer risky programs and to more less risky programs. For example, the networks can be expected to offer fewer entertainment series and to invest fewer resources in the entertainment series they do offer while offering more theatrical films and devoting more resources to movies made for television. In a competitive market, investment choices of this sort would be dictated by viewer preferences, free of interference from regulatory rules. The influence of the rules on programming choice thus skews the programming mix away from that which would have been dictated by viewers in the absence of the rules.

Further, because the rules apply only to the three existing commercial television networks and do not limit the rights other potential financers of program development and acquirers of entertainment programs may obtain, they place the networks at a distinct disadvantage in responding to increasing competition from alternative video distribution technologies, such as cable networks. Although the full effect of such competition lies in the future as such exhibitors increasingly move into financing their own first-run projects, it is plain that broadcast television networks have been hobbled in the competitive race by the rules; their competitors have not.

The rules have had differential effects on program suppliers. The rules relatively benefit the major studios, since, by virtue of their size, they are better able to absorb the risks of program development than are some of the independent producers with whom they compete. As a result, other factors being the same, one would expect an increase in the share of the major studios in the program-supply market and a decrease in the market share of smaller, independent producers.

In addition, after the rules, the major studios are the least expensive available source of risk capital for program development. Producers who want to shift some of the risk of program development, and who before the rules would have considered selling rights or interests to a network, are now largely limited to the major studios or perhaps other large distributors. Thus producers can expect to receive lower payments for the sale of profit-sharing and syndication rights. Because no other type of purchaser of the rights can bear risk as efficiently as the networks, the rights will be worth less to major studios or other large distributors than to the networks, and such purchasers will offer less for the rights. Thus the rules are likely to have particularly adverse effects on entrants and potential entrants into program supply. Because these firms tend to be small and to lack a track record, they are at a disadvantage relative to established program suppliers in obtaining funding for developing new programs. They develop few programs at once, so they are at a disadvantage as risk-bearers relative to established firms, especially the major studios. As a result, entry into program supply becomes more difficult, established firms are less likely to be displaced, and concentration among program suppliers increases relative to what would have happened without the rules.

More specifically, without the option of obtaining development funding from the networks, program suppliers can either turn to other sources of funding, finance program development themselves or use both methods of financing. Whatever their choice, they end up with higher costs or less revenue than in the absence of the rules. Since non-network firms are less efficient than the networks in absorbing the risks of program development and acquisition, any specified rights to syndication distribution and profit sharing are worth less to them than to the networks, and they will offer the supplier less compensation for the rights than the networks would have offered.

On the other hand, to the extent that the suppliers finance program development themselves, their costs rise because they, too, are less efficient at risk-bearing than are the networks. Whether the supplier funds program development from retained earnings, the sale of new equity or borrowing, stockholders or creditors will demand a premium that reflects the greater risks borne by the supplier. Thus the costs of every supplier following this financing strategy rise, but the costs of new, smaller suppliers rise disproportionately more than the costs of the larger, established suppliers, leading to a reduced rate of entry and an increase in concentration among program suppliers.

It is important to note in this regard that existing program suppliers (especially the major ones) may feel that the rules benefit them. Even though decreasing the available options for development funding can directly benefit no supplier, it will hurt small suppliers or potential entrants more than larger, established suppliers. Therefore, even though any particular established supplier would prefer to shift *its* risk to the networks, established suppliers as a group may be better off if *no* supplier can do so and potential entrants are hampered. By adopting the Financial Interest and Syndication Rules, the FCC may have facilitated a cartel arrangement which suppliers could not have brought about themselves and which prevents or hampers new suppliers from joining (and competing with) the club.

It is not at all clear, however, that the gains to the larger established program suppliers from the rules will persist. If the program-supply industry was competitive before the rules, and the rules do not fundamentally alter its competitive structure, any profits above the competitive level created by the rules will attract new firms to the industry, and entry will continue until profits fall to a competitive level. On the other hand, if the program-supply industry was not competitive before the rules, or if the rules, by increasing concentration or impeding entry, fundamentally change the structure of the industry, higher profits may continue even in the long run. If the rules increase long-run profits, it will be because the commission, through its regulations, has created market power or facilitated its exercise.

The effects of the rules on performing artists, writers and other talent are closely tied to their effects on the viewing public. Thus the effects on the two parties can be discussed together. The rules induce a change in the programming mix of the networks. Because the networks cannot earn as much from their programming investments as before, they invest less in programming and move resources away from more innovative (hence, riskier) programming to less risky, tried-and-true types of programming. The networks offer fewer entertainment series and more sports events and movies, both theatrical films and movies made for television. They do so, even though a successful entertainment series will attract larger audiences than successful movies, because the risks associated with entertainment series are greater. The new mix of programs, however, is not simply a market response dictated by viewers but is induced by a change in the allocation of risk caused by regulatory intervention in the marketplace.

These changes in risk and program mix have implications as well for performing artists, writers and other talent. Demand for their services declines as the networks invest less in programming. In addition, as part of their risk-reducing strategy, the networks will tend to favor programs with performing artists and writers who have a proven track record. Rewards to 'stars' thus increase relative to rewards to less well known talent. Just as in the case of the effects of the rules on program suppliers, in the long run fewer actors and writers will have the opportunity to develop a professional reputation. The result contributes to less diversity in programming than otherwise would be dictated by viewers.

Viewers, therefore, see less diverse and less innovative programming on network television than would occur in the absence of the rules. Indeed, that effect may carry over into non-network television, especially cable, by making it unnecessary to compete with networks in innovative programming. If such new sources of programming as cable press their advantage over the restricted networks by acquiring relatively innovative first-run programs, viewers desiring such programs will find that they are available only at the price of a subscription fee rather than on free network television.

The Financial Interest and Syndication Rules have effects on television stations, both affiliated and independent. Because affiliated stations receive less attractive programs from the networks, their entertainment series tend to fall in popularity relative to the programs viewers can watch on independent stations, cable systems or other media. A decline in the audience size of prime-time entertainment series lowers potential advertising revenues and the value of network affiliation. The corresponding improvement in the relative position of independent stations is only a short-run phenomenon, however. Over time, the stock of programs broadcast by independent stations turns over, and the less attractive programs produced after the advent of the rules make up a larger portion of their broadcasts. In the long run, both affiliated and independent stations tend to lose market share to other media and earn a lower level of revenue and profits.[18]

Finally, the rules have an effect on advertisers. As network programming attracts smaller audiences as a result of the rules, advertisers will find that network television is a relatively less cost-effective means of reaching potential customers and will reallocate their expenditures to other media. Moreover, even if the rates for network advertising fall to reflect smaller audience size, advertisers cannot be fully recompensed because, with smaller audiences, they lose some of the benefits from utilizing the otherwise most effective medium.

Thus the rules disrupt efficient market operation and risk-sharing. They cannot limit network power, and they are, if anything, anticompetitive through their elimination of the networks as sources of financing to packagers (especially new packagers) and sources of syndicated programs to stations. The retention even of the limited form of the rules proposed by the FCC in 1983 can be justified only from the point of view of private rather than public interest.

Appendix

This appendix demonstrates three propositions concerning the Financial Interest and Syndication Rules. The first is that the rules, by restricting the rights that can be sold to networks, have the effect of lowering the total equilibrium price paid by the networks for television programming, *ceteris paribus*. The second proposition is that the rules also lower the attractiveness to viewing audiences of television programming produced and sold to the networks. The third proposition is that the rules skew the choice of program types in favor of less risky or less innovative programs. The analysis assumes that networks compete for programs.

In analyzing the effects of the Financial Interest and Syndication Rules on the price and attractiveness of television programming, it is important to bear in mind that the transaction between a network and a program supplier involves a package comprising a bundle of rights in the program, including a set of property rights related to its network exhibition and, prior to the rules, sometimes to its syndication or other secondary uses. Because the rules essentially restrict the set of property rights the networks may acquire to those involving network exhibition, a package of programming available to the networks after adoption of the rules is inferior to one available before the rules, even if the program components of the two packages are of the same quality or audience attractiveness.

Hence, when I say that the rules necessarily lower the price paid by networks for programming, I mean the *total* price. In fact, the amount of money paid for the bundle of rights which the rules still permit networks to acquire goes up, making programming more costly. However, that money price does not go up sufficiently to offset the fact that certain rights are no longer being sold. The total money actually paid by networks goes down – but only because networks get less for what they pay. The price paid by networks for the rights they still get goes up.

I shall analyze the effects of the rules on three variables. The first variable is the price the networks pay for the packages of programming they acquire. Second is the level of attractiveness to audiences of the programs the networks acquire. Third is the cost to the networks of acquiring a program with a given level of attractiveness to viewing audiences.

It is important to realize that 'attractiveness' as used here is defined as the attractiveness of a program to viewing audiences. Related to this, in the demonstration below, the 'quantity' of programming is to be thought of not as measured in numbers of programs but as measured in total audience – in short, 'attractiveness'.

To evaluate the effects of the rules on the prices networks pay to suppliers and on the level of program attractiveness to audiences, consider D_0D_0 and S_0S_0, the demand and supply curves for program attractiveness prior to adoption of the Financial Interest and Syndication Rules (see Figure 18.1). It is simplest to think of these curves as relating to a single program. The supply curve slopes upward because generally it takes more inputs to make a program more attractive. Essentially, the demand curve is the networks' demand for viewer attention – 'attractiveness'. The equilibrium price and attractiveness, P_0 and Q_0, respectively, are determined by the intersection of D_0D_0 and S_0S_0.

Before the rules, independent producers were free to sell various financial or distribution rights related to syndication to the networks, along with the network exhibition rights. The rules essentially forbid the sale of such non-network financial or distribution rights to a network. This prohibition tends to shift both demand and supply curves. The demand curve shifts down by the amount of the value of the syndication-related rights to the networks, V_d. That is, because the networks now receive a smaller bundle of rights when they acquire television programming, they are willing to pay less. The post-rule demand curve is labeled D_1D_1.

The supply curve also shifts down – here, by the amount V_s – the value of the financial interests to the independent producers who now retain those rights. In other words, the producers now retain more of the rights and as a result are willing to accept a lower price from the networks. The new supply curve is labeled S_1S_1.

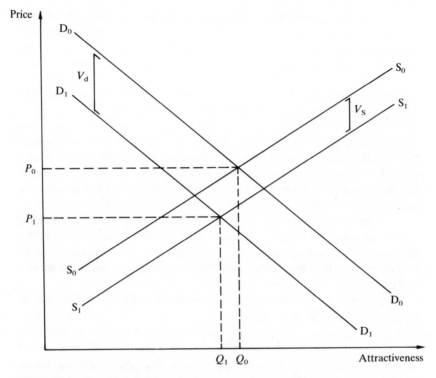

Figure 18.1 Supply and demand of programming attractiveness.

Because both supply and demand curves have shifted downward, it is clear that the new (post-rule) equilibrium price, P_1, must lie below the old (pre-rule) equilibrium, P_0. What happens to the equilibrium attractiveness depends on the relative shifts in demand and supply curves. Downward shifts in the demand curve tend to reduce attractiveness, *ceteris paribus*, whereas downward shifts in supply increase attractiveness, *ceteris paribus*. Figure 18.1 shows a decrease in equilibrium attractiveness from Q_0 to Q_1. This decrease occurs because the figure is drawn so that the downward shift in the supply curve, V_s, is smaller than the downward shift in the demand curve, V_d. This result is not an accident. The assumption that the demand curve shifts by more than the supply curve (i.e. $V_d > V_s$) reflects the fact that the networks can absorb the risk associated with the non-network financial interests more efficiently than program suppliers. That is, rights to off-network syndication and profit-sharing are more valuable to the networks than to the suppliers.

To prove that the equilibrium price and attractiveness of television programming will fall under the Financial Interest and Syndication Rules, under the assumption that financial interests are more valuable to the network than to the independent producers, consider the following. Let

$$q^d = D(P + a) \tag{18.1a}$$

$$q^s = S(P + b) \tag{18.1b}$$

where q^d and q^s are, respectively, the program attractiveness demanded and supplied, $D(\cdot)$ and $S(\cdot)$ are the demand and supply functions, P is program price and a and b are shift terms. The shift term a is equal to 0 before the rules and equal to V_d when the rules are in effect, since the price which calls forth a given level of quality demanded must fall by V_d after adoption of the rules. The shift term b is equal to 0 before the rules and equal to V_s once the rules are in effect. Define $K = V_s/V_d$. Because the networks are better equipped than the program suppliers to handle the risk associated with financial interests and syndication rights, $0 < K < 1$.

In equilibrium, the attractiveness demanded will equal the attractiveness supplied. That is:

$$D(P + a) = S(P + b) = S(P + Ka) \tag{18.2}$$

both before and after the rules. Differentiating this expression totally with respect to a yields:

$$D'\left(\frac{dP}{da} + 1\right) = S'\left(\frac{dP}{da} + K\right) \tag{18.3}$$

Rearranging terms gives:

$$\frac{dP}{da}(S' - D') = -KS' + D' \tag{18.4a}$$

$$\frac{dP}{da} = \frac{-KS' + D'}{S' - D'} < 0 \tag{18.4b}$$

The derivative of P with respect to a is negative, since K is positive, S' is positive and D' is negative, making the numerator of this expression negative and the denominator positive. This implies that price will fall as fewer financial interests can be transacted.

As noted above, the equilibrium attractiveness, q, is determined by the intersection of the supply and demand curves. That is,

$$q = D(P + a) = S(P + Ka) \tag{18.5}$$

both before and after the rules. Differentiating totally with respect to a yields:

$$\frac{dq}{da} = D' \left(\frac{dP}{da} + 1 \right) = S' \left(\frac{dP}{da} + K \right) \tag{18.6}$$

Substituting the expression for dP/da and rearranging terms gives:

$$\frac{dq}{da} = D' + \frac{D' - KS'}{S' - D'} D' = \frac{S'D' (1 - K)}{S' - D'} < 0 \tag{18.7}$$

Thus, in equilibrium, the attractiveness to audiences of television programming declines as the fraction of syndication-related rights that cannot be transacted increases.

There is another way to think about this. The analysis so far indicates that, with the Financial Interest and Syndication Rules, networks offer smaller total payments to program suppliers because the programs offered to the networks are now worth less to them. That is, the networks spend less to obtain a set of property rights that are more restricted than they were previously able to negotiate. Although the networks are paying less and receiving programming of lesser attractiveness to audiences, it is important to realize that the cost of the rights actually conveyed for programming of a *given* level of audience attractiveness has *increased*.

To the extent suppliers are not as efficient as the networks in bearing risk, syndication rights and financial interests are worth less to program suppliers than they would be to the networks in the absence of the rules. Hence, program suppliers must choose between receiving lower total payments for the full set of property rights in their programs from the network and a distributor together and retaining the syndication rights themselves but at an increased exposure to risk. Smaller payments for syndication-related rights must be offset by higher payments for network exhibition rights if the program suppliers are to recover their full costs, including a competitive return on their investment. If the program suppliers instead choose to retain syndication-related rights, they will demand a risk premium for their greater exposure to risk. With either outcome, the networks must pay a higher price for the level of programming quality they obtain.

In diagrammatic terms, think in terms of the supply curve not for the production of programming in attractiveness units, as in Figure 18.1, but for the supply of that programming for the network run *only*. That supply curve represents what the suppliers will accept for conveying the rights to the network run and can be thought of as the total they will accept for producing the programs less the value to them of non-network uses. Because the rules prohibit sales of non-network rights to the customers who value them most, their effect is to reduce the value of such rights and, hence, shift upward the supply curve for the network run. This produces an increase in the price networks must pay for the rights they can still get for programs of given attractiveness; naturally, it causes a decline in the amount of attractiveness they are willing to buy.

The full set of price effects can be illustrated by an analogy. Suppose a customer of a clothing store is accustomed to buying suits with two pairs of pants, although the store also sells suits with one pair of pants. One day the store sells only suits with one pair of pants. The customer pays less for the suits but obtains only one pair of pants. Suppose the suits with one pair of pants now cost more than they did previously, although not as much as did suits with two pairs of pants. It is true that the customer is paying less for the suits, but only because there is now only one pair of pants instead of two. The cost of such a suit is now more than it would have been earlier for a suit with one pair of pants.

So far, the analysis relates to the supply of and demand for attractiveness for a given program. That means the demand curves are drawn with the prices of other programs constant. The analysis applies to all programs, however; hence, the other prices will change. Clearly, the prices that will be most affected are those for programs in which financial interests and syndication rights are most important. These are the risker, more innovative programs. Thus the prices of those programs (for the rights actually acquired under the rules) will go up relative to the prices of less risky programs. The prices of theatrical movies, for example, will not be directly affected. The result of this change in relative prices will be to shift network demands away from risky or innovative programs toward less risky, less innovative programs, even though, on average, viewers would prefer the mix of programs that would occur without the rules.

Notes

1. Production for first-run syndication did increase, but this was largely due to the concurrent adoption of the Prime Time Access Rule, which effectively limited networks and off-network syndication by network affiliates to the last three hours of prime time. The gap was largely filled with game shows rather than shows of 'network quality', such programs as the popular 'Muppet Show' being rare exceptions.
2. See, for example, Stanley Besen and Ronald Soligo, 'The regulation of television program production and distribution: some preliminary thoughts', mimeographed (copy placed in Network Inquiry Docket, 21049); Robert Crandall, 'FCC regulation, monopsony and network television program costs', *Bell Journal of Economics and Management Science* **3** (Autumn 1972), pp. 483–508; also 'The economic effect of

television-network program "Ownership"', *Journal of Law and Economics* **14** (October 1971), pp. 385–412; Bruce Owen, Jack Beebe and Willard Manning, *Television Economics* (Lexington, Mass.: Lexington Books, 1974).
3. Network Inquiry Special Staff of the Federal Communications Commission, *Final Report on New Television Networks: Entry, Jurisdiction, Ownership and Regulation* (1980), vols. I and II (cited below as 'Staff Report'); *Recommendations of the Network Inquiry Special Staff to the Federal Communications Commission* (December 1980).
4. FCC BC Docket No. 82-345, 'Tentative Decision and Request for Further Comments', August 4, 1983.
5. Staff Report, vol. II, p. 578.
6. See 'Reagan upstages the networks in syndication', *Business Week* (November 7, 1983), pp. 51–2.
7. 'The President's priorities', *New York Times* (November 7, 1983), p. A22.
8. Direct economies achievable by spreading high program costs over large potential audiences probably do not explain why each of the three television networks has roughly 200 affiliates rather than some much smaller number. The 200 largest TV markets contain more than 99 per cent of the TV homes, and the top 100 contain approximately 85 per cent. The additional saving in cost per viewer obtainable by expansion into the 50 or 100 least populous markets is probably small and may not compensate for the costs of interconnection, together with payments to the affiliates at the level made to affiliates in larger markets. Stations in smaller markets, however, desire to affiliate with a network because of the benefits of affiliation to them rather than because of the economies they provide to the network. A network reaps most of the economies of scale from spreading expensive programs by having affiliates in the largest 100 to 150 markets. At that point there is considerable advantage to stations in the smallest 50 to 100 markets from affiliating with a network and gaining the right to broadcast highly attractive programs. These smaller stations may even be willing to affiliate on terms that require them to absorb some or all the costs of interconnection and accept lower rates of network compensation. See Staff Report, vol. II, p. 115.
9. Note, however, that these efficiencies result in programs with mass appeal. Such programs, which may display depressing similarities, generally are not uplifting and educational. In this chapter, program 'quality' and 'attractiveness' are judged by audience size. This is not, of course, the only possible criterion.
10. The fact that non-network entities can spread risks over different networks, thus insuring themselves against the collapse of a given network's entire schedule, does not appear important.
11. Network production of entertainment programs for prime-time broadcast is now severely restricted by the terms of consent decrees signed in or before 1980 by the networks as a result of the antitrust cases brought by the Department of Justice.
12. These option terms are also limited by the consent decrees.
13. Cf. Staff Report, vol. I, p. 508. In addition, as discussed below, major suppliers (and, perhaps, even all established suppliers) might prefer that *no one*, especially not their competition, be able to transfer such rights. Established suppliers have this preference not because it is in the interest

of any one supplier to be barred from transferring rights but because existing suppliers, better able to bear risk than are new ones, gain an advantage over new and potential suppliers if no one can shift risk. That advantage, by reducing the competition they face, can outweigh the disadvantage to existing suppliers of being prevented themselves from shifting risk.

14. In other contexts, suppliers have complained that competition among the networks is too vigorous, as manifested by a tendency for networks to cancel series that do not demonstrate success after the broadcast of the first few episodes.

15. Staff Report, vol. II, p. 578.

16. One potential benefit would be larger network advertising revenues if warehousing were to increase the audiences of the networks' affiliates at the expense of independent stations during times when network programs are broadcast. It should be kept in mind, however, that the network affiliates would not attract the entire potential audience of the independent. Only some fraction of that audience would turn to the network's affiliate in the absence of the warehoused program. Others would watch programs on other stations, and still others would not turn on their television sets. In addition, as a practical matter, independent stations tend to use off-network series most heavily at times when network service is not offered.

    A warehousing network might also derive direct benefit in the five markets in which it owns and operates stations. Such local markets, however, are among those in which independent stations are most numerous and strongest and off-network syndicated programs are most valuable. Thus, the syndication profits that would have to be foregone to gain any additional profits for the station owned and operated by the network would be large. In addition, most of the benefits from keeping programs from independent stations would accrue to the other two network stations, which, with a few exceptions, are also owned and operated by their networks in the pertinent markets. Thus, most of any possible benefit from warehousing in owned and operated station markets would accrue not to the warehousing network, but to its rivals.

17. Suppliers may attempt to get around this by shifting risk to the networks in other ways, for example, by longer option terms. Options, however, were limited in 1980 by the consent decrees; in any event, if longer options were an efficient way of transferring risk, they would have been sold before the rules.

18. The rules may have worked to make entry into television broadcasting more difficult. To the extent that new independent stations rely on off-network syndicated products for their programming fare, in the long run they will find fewer off-network syndicated programs available as the networks reduce the number of entertainment series they offer for broadcast.

PART 3

Quantitative methods and the law

19

The mathematical analysis of Supreme Court decisions: The use and abuse of quantitative methods (1958)

> *Glendower:* I can call spirits from the vasty deep.
> *Hotspur:* Why, so can I, or so can any man;
> But will they come when you do call for them?
> (Shakespeare, *Henry IV, Part I*, Act III, Scene 1)

In the 1950s, more and more political scientists speculated on the possible applications of mathematical analysis to political phenomena.[1] It is the position of this chapter that such discussion, when in the abstract, serves little purpose, for the question of whether or not quantitative techniques can fruitfully be so applied is essentially an empirical one and can only be resolved by experiment. Yet even a specifically experimental approach becomes challengeable if it can be shown to misunderstand and hence misemploy otherwise sound techniques. The claim to have solved problems whose mathematical features have not, in fact, been comprehended seems especially harmful in a field where the application of mathematics is as yet in its infancy, and this not only because minor impurities at the base of a growing framework may assume major proportions at its apex, but because exposure of error may breed unjustified disenchantment or give solace to those who prefer a casual, imprecise impressionism in the social sciences. In this chapter, we propose to explore the mathematical nature of a particular problem – that of predicting Supreme Court decisions from a knowledge of the 'facts' of the case – and to examine what can and cannot be asserted

I am grateful to George Kateb of Amherst, John R. Meyer of the Harvard Economics Department and especially Henry Kariel of Harvard, for discussion of some or all of the points here made. Ellen Jo Paradise of Radcliffe College (now Ellen Paradise Fisher) read all the cases involved and participated greatly in this study from its inception. All errors are mine, however.

about it from a mathematical point of view. We also intend to examine the validity of one solution to this problem which has been proposed.

Ever since Pritchett's book on the Roosevelt Court,[2] a good deal of the interest of the proponents of the use of mathematical analysis in political science has centered around the possibility of using quantitative techniques to classify the justices, to predict their decisions or otherwise to analyze their actions.[3] Fred Kort's recent article, 'Predicting Supreme Court decisions mathematically: a quantitative analysis of the "right to counsel" cases',[4] attacks the prediction problem with apparent success. Kort seems to have succeeded in reducing the Supreme Court's actions in the state 'right to counsel' cases to a mathematical formula which perfectly predicts the Court's decisions. In fact, not only does Kort successfully predict twelve out of fourteen decisions considered – the other two lie in a zone of uncertainty – he is also successful in predicting the decision in the most recent case of this type to come before the Court, a case which arose after the publication of his article.[5] If it is true that the only test of an empirical science is its ability to predict, then Kort's achievement is indeed impressive. An examination of what can and cannot be legitimately inferred from the attainment of what can predicting formula, both as regards the behavior of the Court and as regards the worth of the particular formula used, might well serve as the starting point in our exploration of the mathematical properties of the prediction problem in this area.

The problem, as set forth by Kort is as follows: take certain 'objective' variables or 'pivotal factors' – essentially the 'facts' of the case as stated in the Supreme Court opinion[6] – which appear in the cases to be analyzed, and assign to them numerical weights, in such a manner that when these weights are added for all the factors present in a particular case, the resulting sum is higher in all cases decided in favor of the original defendant than in any case decided against the original defendant. (We shall refer to these two groups of cases as 'pros' and 'cons' respectively.) Moreover, since the pivotal factors are defined so as to favor the original defendant if they are present, the weights assigned must all be non-negative (that is, positive or zero) since a negative weight would imply that the presence of the factor in question was detrimental to the original defendant. We set forth the condition which it is necessary and sufficient to impose on the behavior of the Supreme Court to ensure that the problem can be solved and solved perfectly – that is, we establish the behavioral assumption which is equivalent to the existence of a perfect prediction formula of the type described.

To find that condition, it is convenient to restate the problem in slightly more formal terms. Let us number the pivotal factors consecutively from 1 to n, where n is the number of factors. Corresponding to the *i*th pivotal factor (*i.e.* to the general factor) we can define the variable X_i which is to equal one for a particular case if that factor is present and is otherwise to equal zero.[7] The prediction problem posed now becomes the one of finding *n* non-negative numbers, one for each factor, which we shall call $A_1, A_2, \ldots, A_n$ such that the expression:

$$A_1X_1 + A_2X_2 + A_3X_3 + \ldots + A_nX_n \tag{19.1}$$

has a higher value for all pro cases than for any con. However, if this is to be the case, then, clearly, there must[8] exist a positive number, *K*, such that the value of the above expression is greater than *K* for any pro case and less than *K* for any con. Letting the superscripts, *p* and *c*, indicate any pro case and any con case, respectively, we may write this as:

$$A_1X_1^p + A_2X_2^p + \ldots + A_nX_n^p > K$$
$$> A_1X_1^c + A_2X_2^c + \ldots + A_nX_n^c \tag{19.2}$$

However, it is clear that nothing in the above would be changed if we doubled all the *A*s and doubled *K*, or halved them, or tripled them. It will be convenient, therefore, to divide inequalities (Inequalities 19.2) by the value of *K* and thus fix the scale of the *A*s.[9] If we let $a_1 = A_1/K$, $a_2 = A_2/K$, and so forth, we have:

$$a_1X_1^p + a_2X_2^p + \ldots + a_nX_n^p > 1$$
$$> a_1X_1^c + a_2X_2^c + \ldots + a_nX_n^c \tag{19.3}$$

Now, let us suppose – to take a simple example – that only two pivotal factors are possible, represented by X_1 and X_2. Then the prediction problem can be represented graphically, as in Figure 19.1, as the problem of finding a line that slopes downward such that all points representing pros lie above it and to the right and all points representing cons lie below it and to the left. The equation of the line in this case would be:

$$a_1X_1 + a_2X_2 = 1 \tag{19.4}$$

and the requirement that it slope downhill is the requirement that a_1 and a_2 be non-negative.[10]

Similarly, if we had three pivotal factors, the problem would be that of finding a plane which cut off a corner of a box (the dimensions of the box being represented by X_1, X_2 and X_3) in such a way as to catch all points representing cons and no points representing pros between it and the box corner. The equation of the plane would be given by:

$$a_1X_1 + a_2X_2 + a_3X_3 = 1 \tag{19.5}$$

In general, the problem is that of finding a 'hyperplane' (the generalization of the line or plane to more than three dimensions) such that all

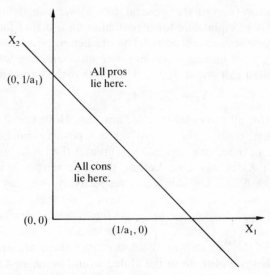

Figure 19.1 Graphical representation of prediction problem in the analysis of Supreme Court decisions.

pros lie above it and all cons below it, the hyperplane being represented by:

$$a_1X_1 + a_2X_2 + \ldots + a_nX_n = 1 \tag{19.6}$$

This is what is expressed by Inequalities 19.3.

Now, it happens that the condition under which such a hyperplane or such a set of numbers $a_1, \ldots, a_n$ will exist (indeed, under which an infinity of such hyperplanes or sets of numbers will exist, as shown below) is a rather plausible assumption to make about the behavior of the Court. That condition is now set out formally and its meaning explained.

Condition 1: Suppose that we observe a pro case with a certain number, say F, of the factors present. Then we must never observe a con case with the *same* F factors present. (Whether or not other factors are present in the second case is irrelevant.)

What this means in terms of the Court's behavior is quite simple. Condition 1 says that if the Court decides a case in favor of the original defendant, then there must be no other case in which the original defendant has in his or her favor *at least* exactly the same things as in the first case and receives an adverse decision. A transparently clear precedent must not be violated.

Equivalent statements to Condition 1 are:[11]

Condition 1′: If we observe a con case with a certain number, say G, of the factors present, we must never observe a pro case where no factors are present that are not included in the original G factors.

Condition 1″: If we observe a con case with a certain number, say H, of the factors *absent*, then we must never observe a pro case where those *same* H factors are absent. (Whether or not other factors are absent in the second case is irrelevant.)

These conditions are the obverse of Condition 1. What each of them says is that if the Court decides a case *against* the original defendant, then there must exist no case in which the Court decides *for* the original defendant in spite of the fact that in his or her favor there are *at most* exactly the same things as for the original defendant in the first case. Again, transparently clear precedents are not violated.[12]

Since Conditions 1′ and 1″ are equivalent to Condition 1, we do not need to assume them. *Condition 1 alone is a necessary and sufficient condition for the existence of an infinite number of solutions to the prediction problem posed and the fact that a perfect predictor has been found implies no more than Condition 1.* In particular, without further justification it implies very little about the validity of the particular set of weights used. We shall return to this below. We shall refer to this statement as **Theorem 19.1**.

We omit the proof of Theorem 19.1 for the general case of n factors as beyond the scope of the present not overly technical article. Reflection on the two dimensional case about to be presented graphically should convince the reader, however.[13]

In the case of only two factors, already partially discussed, we have the following situation. First, the only possible points are those marked by dots in Figure 19.2, the points $(0, 0)$, $(1, 0)$, $(1, 1)$ and $(0, 1)$. The interpretation of Condition 1 in this case is simply that if any of these points is a pro, so are all points which can be reached from that point by following the arrows as drawn. Conversely, if any of these points is a con, so are all points which can be reached from it by following the arrows backwards.[14] This being so, there are only six possible configurations, shown in Figures 19.3a–f (pros being marked P and cons C), and for each of these an infinite number of lines like that of Figure 19.1 can be drawn which slope downhill, have non-negative intercepts (note Figure 19.3b),[15] and have all pros (if any) above and all cons (if any) below them. One such line is drawn in each figure. The reader should be

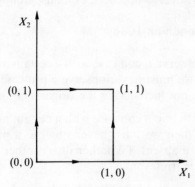

Figure 19.2 Interpretation of Condition 1.

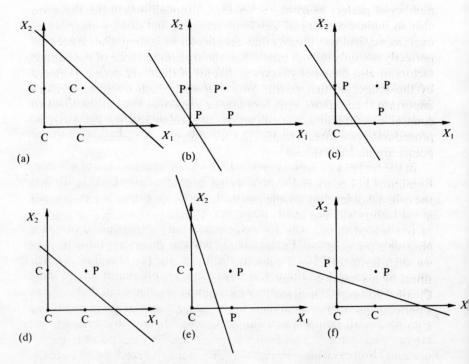

Figure 19.3 Possible configurations of pros and cons of Figure 19.2.

satisfied that the line drawn is by no means unique. Finally, Condition 1 is indeed necessary as well as sufficient, for no such line can be drawn given any configuration of pros and cons other than those depicted. As already remarked, a similar situation obtains in the general case of more than two factors.

Theorem 19.1 is a basic theorem in this problem. It ensures that prediction really is possible (and perfect!) given a relatively mild assumption about the Court's behavior. However, it also ensures that such prediction is a trivial affair. We shall return to this point in the last section. Here we explore the implications of Theorem 19.1 for the gaining of knowledge of the Court's behavior through the construction of perfectly predicting linear weighting schemes.

Now, if we turn Theorem 19.1 around it tells us that the mere fact that a given set of weights predicts perfectly implies relatively little about the way in which the Court actually behaves, about the 'true' weights, if any; for Condition 1 implies the existence of an infinite number of perfect weighting schemes. (Although, of course, there are also an infinite number of weighting schemes that don't work.) Moreover, as we shall see, the fact that a particular weighting scheme predicts perfectly not only tells us little about the true importance of the various factors, it also does not guarantee that all of them are even considered by the judges or that factors with extremely high weights are more important than factors with very low or zero ones (*i.e.* in the 'right to counsel' cases it tells us nothing about the relative importance of various procedural guarantees under the Fourteenth Amendment). These points are now developed.

In the first place, suppose that we have a set of n factors which satisfy Condition 1. Let us add to this set an additional factor, namely, that the original defendant's name has the letter 'd' in it. The resulting set of $n + 1$ factors will also satisfy Condition 1 since the presence or absence of our added factor will not (one trusts) affect any decision. If we observe a pro case with this factor and certain other ones present, then we shall never observe a con case with all the same factors present, since, by assumption, Condition 1 is satisfied for the original n factors. Clearly, however, Theorem 19.1 would then permit the construction of a perfectly predicting weighting scheme which assigned our added factor a positive (although relatively small) weight. Formally, we have:

Theorem 19.2: If Condition 1 is satisfied for any subset of a set of factors, it is also satisfied for the full set.

Corollary 1: The fact that a given weighting system perfectly predicts does not guarantee that all factors given positive weights are actually considered by the Court.

Table 19.1 Correlation of Kort's ranking and 'backwards' ranking.

Factor	Kort's rank*	'Backwards' rank
Coercion or intimidation to plead guilty	1	25[‡]
No assistance of counsel between arraignment and trial	2	11[†]
No explicit waiver of the 'right to counsel'	3	11[†]
Detention and trial in a hostile environment	4	20.5[†]
Crime subject to capital punishment	5.5[†]	4
Arraignment without the assistance of counsel	5.5[†]	11[†]
Request of additional time, etc., denied	7	7.5[†]
No previous experience in court	8	17
No advice of the 'right to counsel'	9.5[†]	5
Request of assigned counsel denied	9.5[†]	15
No assistance of counsel at the trial	11	11[†]
No assistance of counsel at the time of sentencing	12	11[†]
Youth	13	18
Detention incommunicado	14	22
Deception of the defendant	15.5[†]	19
No explicit presentation of charges	15.5[†]	23
Opportunity of consultation with own counsel denied	17	7.5[†]
Illiteracy	18	2
Crime subject to life imprisonment	19	6
Accelerated trial	20	3
Crime subject to twenty or thirty years' imprisonment	21	16
Crime subject to five or ten years' imprisonment	22	1[‡]
Consequences of the plea of guilty not explained	23	20.5[†]
Procedural or substantive error	24	14
No assistance of counsel at any other phase of the proceeding	25	24
Jurisdictional issue	¶	¶

* Derived from Kort, *American Political Science Review*, Vol. 51 (March, 1957), Table III, p. 9.
[†] In cases of ties, the tying factors have been awarded the average place.
[‡] Sic!
¶ This factor does not appear in the second group of cases and hence cannot be given a 'backwards' rank. It ranks just above 'Consequences of the plea of guilty not explained' in Kort's original weighting system.

In point of fact, to return to Kort's analysis as a case in point, it is indeed the case that some of his factors are irrelevant in the sense that they add nothing to the ability to predict, speaking on the basis of the sample he considers. First, I am completely unable to see why Kort's twenty-sixth factor – 'presence of a jurisdictional issue' (see Table 19.1 above) – is at all legitimate. Even if the Court actually treats a jurisdictional issue as though it affects the merits of a case, this is surely something which should be the *result* of the analysis, not something to be assumed. Besides, why on earth should we assume that the presence of a jurisdictional issue automatically favors the defendant? It seems to me that here we have a very real application of the principle just given, that predictive success does not imply relevance of all factors used.

Second – and more important – it is logically impossible to do as Kort claims to have done, namely, to assign weights to twenty-six factors on the basis of fourteen observations.[16] This may be seen from an examination of Figures 19.3a–f. Only in the trivial cases, Figures 19.3a and b, does it suffice to observe only one point in order to be able to draw the dividing line. In Figures 19.3e and f it takes two different points and in Figures 19.3c and d three different points to fix the position of the line. Moreover, in these cases it will not suffice to observe just *any* set of points. In Figure 19.3f, for example, one must observe the two points (0, 1) and (1, 0), for the position of the line cannot be inferred from any other two points (*e.g.* observing only the points (0, 0) and (1, 1) would not enable one to tell which of the four cases of Figures 19.3c–f obtained and this would be true no matter in how many cases we observed them). More generally, with the utmost in luck, it would take twenty-six observations to determine twenty-six weights solely from the decisions as rendered. This would occur in the case analogous to Figures 19.3e or f where one observed twenty-six cases each with a different factor present and found that all but one of them sufficed to make the case a pro. In general, we must observe enough different points to be able to infer the entire configuration of pros and cons. This is obviously not the actual situation. (Note that if it were, the prediction problem could be solved by common sense. We shall revert to this below.) This is elementary even to the casual student of statistics, at least in similar situations. Finally, given the particular twenty-eight cases which Kort observes, even all the observations he has, his 'test group' as well as his 'source group', are not enough to allow him to infer weights for his twenty-six factors. The sample of cases used simply does not contain so much information; and if it did, prediction would be trivial.

We may conclude, therefore, that some of Kort's factors should really have zero weight. However, this does not mean that they are unimportant in the Court's decisions. It merely means that they do not aid prediction, that no inference concerning their 'true' weights is possible. The fact that the prediction is perfect provides no test of the importance of these factors. In fact, it is likely that the most important factors are of the least aid in prediction, in a sample of cases of this sort, and therefore can properly (*i.e.* without outside information such as judicial pronouncements about their importance) be given only very low or zero weights.

A simplified example will make this clear. Suppose that there were only three possible factors, which we may call *A*, *B* and *C*. Suppose, further, that in reality *A* is by far the most important of these, so important, in fact, that no case in which *A* does not appear can ever be a pro. However, while *A* is thus necessary for a pro, let us suppose that it is not sufficient, that is, we suppose that either B or C is required in addition to A for a case to be strong enough to be a pro. On the other hand, B and C together do not suffice for a pro, as already assumed. It is then clear that a weighting scheme which tells us something about the relative importance of A, B and C in the eyes of the Court must give A the highest weight. But now consider: if A is really as important as we have made it, if it is really necessary for a pro, the Supreme Court will refuse to consider cases that do not have A present. Certainly, at best it will consider only a very few such cases, and we may suppose that it does not consider any. But in that case, A is useless for prediction purposes, *so long as we look only at cases actually considered by the Court.* If all cases, cons as well as pros, have factor A present, then, again solely on the basis of the 'objective' evidence, we cannot distinguish it from a factor which is not considered at all (the case discussed above) and must logically assign it zero weight, even though, in fact, it is the most important factor.[17] Another way of saying this is that the cases that actually come before the Supreme Court do not form a random sample of all cases of their type. Generally, such cases, as students of US constitutional law never tire of pointing out, are not the easier ones. Conceivably, as suggested in the next section, a *proper* analysis of a random sample of all cases considered *or refused* by the Court would yield information about the true relative importance of all the various factors,[18] but analysis of a sample such as the present one is unlikely to yield valid information concerning the more important factors.

In this section, we have tried to show that mathematical analysis is indeed possible in this area, in the sense that it is possible to find an infinite number of perfectly predicting formulas, given a rather plausible assumption about the Court's behavior. We have also argued, however, that little meaning can be attached to the fact that a particular weighting scheme successfully predicts all cases. In particular, weights can properly be given to as many factors, at most, as there are cases; not all factors with positive weights may be considered relevant by the Court; and there is no guarantee, if only cases actually decided by the Court are considered in the analysis, that factors with zero weights are less important than those with positive weights in the minds of the judges. In short, any inference about the worth of a particular weighting scheme must come from the way in which it is derived and the assumptions on which it rests and not from predictive success. Such success is indeed a necessary condition for the acceptance of a particular weighting scheme as indicative of the true relative importance of the various factors. What we have shown is that it is emphatically not a sufficient one.

It follows, then, that the worth of a prediction formula must be judged by standards other than that of predictive success. Accordingly, we now briefly examine the relative merits of two perfectly predicting methods of solution, the method used by Kort and the so-called method of 'discriminant analysis', which is already well known in the quantitative literature of the other social sciences. That is, we discuss what assumptions each method requires for its validity and what could be inferred from its results as to the true relative importance of the various factors if the method were applied to a random sample of all cases decided or refused by the Court.

If predictive success does not imply that a given method of solution of the prediction problem is at all useful, what should we require of a solution? We have already indicated part of the answer in Theorem 19.2 and Corollary 1. The method of solution must at least have the property that it assigns positive weights *only* to the minimal set of factors for which Condition 1 is satisfied, and it must assign *at most* as many weights as there are cases. That is, the solution must not infer more than is strictly present in the data. If the situation is such that, so far as the sample of cases studied is concerned, no inference is logically possible as to the effect of a given factor (because it is never observed to determine a decision, for any observed combination of the other factors, *i.e.* because the number and variety of cases observed is not sufficient to fix the position of the desired hyperplane), then a proper solution must not mislead us by appearing to make such an inference.

We may say a good deal more than this, however. A proper method of solution should have the property of being generalizable – of being inherently capable of application in other areas besides the present one, the 'right to counsel' cases. In general, this will only be the case if the assumptions on which the method is based are comprehensible and communicable. This is the most important point of all. It is of no use to know that a method works in a particular area. As we have seen, so will many other methods. What we must know is the circumstances under which the method will work in other areas. We must understand the way in which it works and the assumptions that are required for it. Put this another way. The test of a theory is indeed its ability to predict, but to say that a theory has been thus tested, we must not only have prediction, we must also have a genuine, sufficiently inclusive theory. Mathematics is not a mystic device. It is a powerful and understandable tool for manipulating certain concepts. But the assumptions which lead to certain manipulations rather than to others must always correspond to assumptions about the real-world problem to which the mathematical tool is being applied – in the present case, to assumptions about the behavior of the Supreme Court. If such assumptions cannot be communicated to others – including non-mathematicians – then mathematics has been used illegitimately. The theory involved, if any, is not a theory about the real world, and the results can have no meaning save as a curiosity.

We now briefly consider the Kort solution. As indicated earlier, Kort takes twenty-eight cases and divides them (chronologically) into two groups of fourteen each. He then derives his weighting scheme on the basis of the first of these, the 'source' group, and tests it on the second, the 'test' group. We saw above that this is impossible without assuming more than is in the data since the number of factors far exceeds fourteen, the number of cases in the source group. If Kort's method is valid, then, it must be because of the inherent plausibility of its assumptions and not because it provides a direct inference to the position of the dividing hyperplane (Equation 19.6). That is, the Kort solution cannot simply be considered a legitimate method of locating the required hyperplane by looking at the characteristics and results of the various cases. No legitimate method can assign twenty-six non-zero weights on the basis of this sample. If we are to accept it, it must be because we believe that it really does provide an insight into the 'true' weighting scheme of the Court, and not because it predicts well. Unfortunately, the methods used by Kort do not seem to provide such insight.

Kort begins by assigning to each factor a 'preliminary value' (p.v.). This is done by looking at the pro case in the source group in which the factor in question appears with the least number of other factors.[19] The p.v. is the number of votes for the original defendant in that case, divided by the total number of factors present. Kort states that this represents

> making temporarily the initial minimum assumption (contrary to fact and subject to later correction) that, as the votes of all justices are equal, so the weights of all factors are equal in the minds of the justices favoring the petitioner in the case where the given factor is most influential.[20]

Accepting this takes a little effort – I fail to see, for example, why the fact that the votes of the justices are equal should imply anything at all about the relative weights of the factors in their minds – but, given that Kort realizes the assumption to be unrealistic, I could manage to swallow it were it not for what follows.[21]

And what follows really fills one with awe. For each case in the source group in which the factor in question appears, Kort computes an 'intermediate value' (i.v.) for that factor. (The final weight assigned to each factor is the average of the intermediate values over the cases in which it appears.) This is done according to the following imaginative formula (where s is the number of votes for the original defendant in the case in question):

$$\text{i.v.} = s[10\sqrt{(\text{p.v. of factor in question} + 5)}$$
$$- (1/10)(\text{sum of p.v.s of other factors in case})^2] \quad \textbf{(19.7)}$$

Kort says of this formula that it involves the 'necessary technical modifications of the preliminary values, to avoid minus quantities'. It is, of course, true that the formula accomplishes this end, but it is certainly not a necessary consequence of the need for non-negative weights. One could, instead, for example, multiply the p.v. of the factor in question by 23.99π, add 482, and subtract the sum of the other p.v.s. More simply, one could take the p.v. of the factor in question, subtract the sum of the other p.v.s and add the smallest constant which would keep everything non-negative. Either of these would mean just as much as Kort's formula and the second would be a good deal less complicated.[22] Surely, Kort's formula is completely uninterpretable in terms of the behavior of the Supreme Court.

Moreover, while it is true, as we have seen, that any acceptable weighting scheme must involve only non-negative weights, surely such a property should be the *result* of a weight-setting method and not be built into it as an assumption. Put another way, if we set out to find perfectly predicting weights, or to estimate the 'true' weighting system, and find negative weights, this tells us immediately either that there is something wrong with our estimation methods or that Condition 1 is being violated, that the Court has been inconsistent. It is convenient to have this as a check on our assumptions – it happens that the method outlined below permits this – and we should emphatically not build our whole weight-setting scheme on the assumption that the true weights are non-negative.

Finally, before leaving our discussion of Kort's analysis, we may mention two empirical matters.[23] We have already discussed the bias which results from considering only cases actually decided by the Court. A further danger results from the way in which Kort identifies his factors, namely, from a perusal of the Court's opinion.[24] Examination of *Canizio* v. *New York*, 327 US 82, will make this clear. In this case, Canizio's counsel first appeared for him at the time of his sentencing, he having meantime pleaded guilty to a charge of robbery. The Supreme Court, however, through Mr Justice Black, held that the fact that the counsel could have withdrawn the plea of guilty, under New York law, meant that Canizio had had, in effect, benefit of counsel throughout. Prediction of the result of this case, on the basis of Kort's article, would have been difficult indeed, since one would first have had to predict this interpretation of the facts. In point of fact, if one treats the *Canizio* case as one in which the defendant had no assistance of counsel at any time before sentencing, Kort's methods misclassify it as a pro. In short, prediction of Supreme Court decisions on the basis of the 'facts' of the case as listed at the beginning of the majority opinion may well be possible. It is not likely to be terribly interesting. A more worthwhile endeavor would be to take as factors the facts as given in the lower court opinion, since the Supreme Court claims not to decide questions of fact, save where the opinion of the lower court is clearly erroneous.

Second, it is possible to make an easy empirical test of the merits of Kort's weighting scheme. If, in fact, the justices are applying a consistent weighting scheme in the twenty-eight cases he considers, then it should make no difference whether we proceed as he does from the first fourteen cases to the last fourteen or *vice versa*; either way, the order of factors in importance should be approximately the same, if the estimation method used is at all valid. This is far from being the case, however. The order of factors as given by Kort and their order from this 'backwards' test are given in Table 19.1. It is evident that the two are very different indeed. The Spearman coefficient of rank order correlation[25] for the twenty-five factors that appear in both lists is only 0.307. (A value of plus one indicates perfect correspondence between the two rankings. A value of zero indicates no relationship between them.) Since this could occur by chance about fifteen times out of one hundred if there were really no relationship, we conclude that the two rankings are not significantly related and hence that the Kort formula does not lead to a consistent weighting scheme. Of course, this also implies that the formula would not work in areas other than that of the 'right to counsel' cases.[26]

If the Kort solution is not a proper one, then, what is? We have already mentioned a solution well known in the quantitative literature of the other social sciences, the method of 'discriminant analysis'.[27] This general method is precisely designed to solve the sort of problem with which we have to deal – the assignment of weights to the various attributes of certain items in such a way that the resulting linear function best discriminates between two specified classes into which the items fall. In terms of our problem, it provides an easy method for finding the hyperplane which 'best' divides the pros from the cons.

The question of what is meant by 'best' may be asked, however, since we have shown that an infinite number of hyperplanes perfectly discriminate in the instant case. The following are the desirable properties of discriminant analysis in the present problem:

1. Discriminant analysis provides an efficient and infallible method for making the maximum permissible inference as to the factor weights implied by the data. If two factors contain only the same information regarding the decision, they will be assigned equal weights.

2. If the data only contain information about a subset of factors (see Theorem 19.2 and Corollary 1), discriminant analysis will assign positive weights only to the factors in that subset. All other factors will receive approximately zero weight.

3. A related point is, if, in fact, there are not enough different cases observed to allow the specification of as many weights as there are factors, discriminant analysis will assign zero weight to those factors concerning which the sample provides no information.[28]

4. Since the assumption of non-negative weights is not built into discriminant analysis, an easy test is provided for the consistency of the Court.[29]

Finally, and most importantly, the assumption required for the application of discriminant analysis is eminently plausible and communicable. As a matter of fact, we are already quite familiar here with that assumption. It is nothing more nor less than our own Condition 1, the condition that the Court not violate clear precedents. (If Condition 1 is violated, there are several appropriate statistical techniques available for prediction, of which discriminant analysis is one. The use of such techniques might then add something, moreover, to our ability to predict, unlike the present instance. See below.) It is thus clear that discriminant analysis, unlike the methods used by Kort, is perfectly generalizable. If the problem can be perfectly solved, discriminant analysis will solve it. If not, then it will show us that the Court has not been consistent and will offer one of several good and legitimate predictors. The assumption required for the application of discriminant analysis is thus quite clear; it is the condition that a solution to the problem exists. As already stated, the application of this method to a better sample of 'right to counsel' cases considered or rejected by the Court would yield an unbiased estimate of the relative importance of all of Kort's factors in the minds of the justices.[30]

One might even go farther than this. Individual justices, as well as the Court as a whole, may be expected to obey Condition 1. Discriminant analysis would then furnish information about the way in which the individual justices rank the various factors, and, conceivably, comparison of such rankings could yield useful information for the classification of the justices into groups – or it might imply that they cannot be classified. In either case, such analysis might be worth performing.

When all this is said and done, however, some words of caution must be added for those who esteem a viable social science and an open-ended society. Discriminant analysis will indeed solve the prediction problem which we have been discussing; however, we have chosen rather to emphasize the estimation of the factor weights implied in the line of cases analyzed. The reason for this emphasis is simple. Theorem 19.1 ensures that, if Condition 1 is satisfied, a solution exists, but it also ensures that, if Condition 1 is satisfied, a solution is trivial so far as perfect prediction is concerned. *The circumstances which permit the legitimate construction of a perfectly predicting scheme are precisely those under which all cases that arise present no new features and are covered by clear precedents such as those described in Conditions 1 and 1".*

Other cases cannot be predicted with any assurance, since we can never be sure that a factor, concerning whose weight we have no information, will not be important enough to alter the decision. It was not discriminant analysis that enabled us to draw the dividing lines in Figures 19.3a–f. It was simple inspection combined with Condition 1. To repeat, if – as is not the case in the sample of 'right to counsel' cases examined by Kort – the number and variety of cases observed are sufficient to allow the construction of a perfectly predicting hyperplane by discriminant analysis or any other legitimate technique (*i.e.* to allow the assignment of weights to *all* relevant factors), then they are also such as to provide a clear precedent for every future case, given Condition 1. Discriminant analysis is a potentially useful tool for analyzing the behavior of the Court in complicated situations. It is not of much use as a perfect predictor in those same situations, however; it only does efficiently what common sense can do as well and no other method can do better. Mathematics can perfectly predict on the basis of the presence or absence of factors in a case only in those areas where the law has attained a settled state and where public policy and opinion are such as to require that it remain settled. These are the frozen areas of easy prediction, however, so that mathematics can add only to the power to analyze, not to the power to predict. In other, more complicated, more interesting and more inherently important areas where the law is still developing or where public policy requires that it should continue to develop, mathematical analysis provides no substitute for the opinions of the Court. Law, even mathematical law, is made by men.[31]

Notes

1. For examples see especially the work of Herbert A. Simon. See also Anthony Downs, *An Economic Theory of Democracy* (New York: Harper, 1957); L.S. Shapley and Martin Shubik, 'A method for evaluating the distribution of power in a committee system', *American Political Science Review*, Vol. 48 (Sept. 1954), pp. 787–92; and Kenneth J. Arrow, 'Mathematical models in the social sciences', in Daniel Lerner and Harold D. Lasswell, eds., *The Policy Sciences* (Stanford: Stanford University Press, 1951), pp. 129–54.
2. C.H. Pritchett, *The Roosevelt Court* (New York: Macmillan, 1948).

3. Perhaps the ultimate expression of this has been provided in Harold D. Lasswell, 'Current studies in the decision process: automation versus creativity', *Western Political Quarterly*, Vol. 8 (Sept. 1955), pp. 381–99. Lasswell suggests (p. 398) that the time is approaching when machines will be sufficiently well developed to make it practicable for trial runs to be carried out in which human decision-makers and robots are pitted against one another. When machines are more perfect a bench of judicial robots, for example, can be constructed.

   We shall see here, however, that the time 'when machines are more perfect' is likely to come only when the law in a particular area has become so settled that the construction of 'a bench of judicial robots' is both trivial and unnecessary.

4. *American Political Science Review*, Vol. 51 (March, 1957), pp. 1–12.

5. *Moore* v. *Michigan*, 355 US 155 (December, 1957).

6. Examples are: youth of the defendant; no assistance of counsel at various times in the proceedings; coercion to plead guilty; crime involved subject to capital punishment; and so forth. A complete list of the factors used by Kort is given in Table 19.1 below. We discuss the problem of their identification in the next section.

7. In the case of factors which can appear more than once in a case we can choose either of two procedures. Either we can let the variable corresponding to such a factor take on a value for a particular case equal to the number of appearances of the factor in the case, or we can define a separate one–zero variable for each appearance – that is, treat each new appearance as a separate factor. Which treatment is chosen makes little difference. The second is most convenient for expository and the first for computational purposes.

8. Unless a case with no factors present is a pro, in which case K will be zero. This is trivial, however. See Note 15 below.

9. This procedure is called 'normalization'. It amounts to changing the scales on a graph by multiplying or dividing them by the same number. As in changing the scales on a graph, it is purely a convenience and doesn't change anything.

10. Strictly speaking, since a_1 or a_2 can be zero, the line might be vertical or horizontal. The important point is that it can't slope uphill. That this construction is indeed the geometrical equivalent of Inequalities 19.3 in two dimensions may be seen as follows. For any point above the line (Equation 19.4), say (X_1^0, X_2^0), there must exist a point on the line, say (X_1^1, X_2^1) such that $X_1^0 \geqslant X_1^1$ and $X_2^0 \geqslant X_2^1$ with at least one inequality holding. If a_1 and a_2 are both positive, the left-hand side of Equation 19.4 will be greater for (X_1^0, X_2^0) than for (X_1^1, X_2^1), that is, greater than unity. (If one of the *a*s, say a_1, is zero, the expression may equal unity, but then the first factor doesn't count anyway and two cases with equal X_2 are really identical.) Similar remarks hold, *mutatis mutandis*, for points below the line, and a similar situation obtains in the more general case of n factors.

11. The reader should be satisfied that the following two statements are really equivalent to Condition 1 and hence to each other, in the sense that any one of the three conditions implies the other two.

12. Note, however, that we do not require the existence of cases in which they are actually followed. Cases presenting such clear features are, of course, not likely to come before the Court. What we require is merely the weak

condition that if such a case does arise it is decided in the obvious way. Our conditions would be satisfied if no such cases ever arose in fact.

13. (Added in 1990) In fact, the theorem is incorrect insofar as it asserts the existence of a *linear* perfect predictor (cf. Note 18 below). With a high enough number of factors, this need not be the case, although it will be so if cases tend to differ in enough distinct ways (as was true of the case analyzed by Kort).

The proof that Condition 1 implies the existence of a (not necessarily linear) perfectly predicting surface is as follows.

Let S^P be the set of all points, Z, such that Z represents a pro case. Let H^P be the convex hull of S^P. Suppose that there is a point, Y, representing a con case, such that Y lies on or above H^P. Let $\overline{X}$ be the point of H^P such that $Y_j \geqslant \overline{X}_j, j = 1, \ldots, n$. There exist points representing pro cases, say $X^1, \ldots, X^r$, and scalars $k_1, \ldots, k_r$, with $k_i \geqslant 0$ all i and $\Sigma\, k_i = 1$, such that $\overline{X} = \Sigma\, k_i X^i$.

Let X^* be one of the X^i, such that the corresponding scalar is positive. Since all components of the vectors involved are either one or zero, it must be the case that $\overline{X}$ has a positive component everywhere X^* has a one. But then Y must have a one everywhere X^* does. So every factor present in the pro case represented by X^* is also present in the con case represented by Y, and this violates Condition 1.

It follows that the boundary of H^P is a perfectly predicting surface. A similar proof using Condition 1' shows that the boundary of H^c, the convex hull of the points representing con cases is also such a surface. If the two convex hulls do not intersect, then the two sets will be separated by (infinitely many) hyperplanes each of which will be perfectly predicting linear surfaces.

14. The reader should be satisfied that these statements really are the interpretation of Condition 1 and its equivalents.

15. Figure 19.3b is the trivial situation mentioned in Note 8 above where a case with no factors present is a pro. Here Inequalities 19.3 do not apply, since division by zero is impossible. However, any set of positive weights will perfectly predict. The line drawn in the figure illustrates one such set.

16. That is, it is impossible to draw the requisite hyperplane using only the results of fourteen cases. *At best* only fourteen weights could be determined. Kort is guessing *at least* twelve of the weights. We shall return to this below.

17. Although, of course, *any* weight we assigned would do as well in Inequalities 19.2. The point is that there is no information in the cases considered as to what the 'true' weight should be.

18. I have, throughout this chapter, ignored the fairly obvious point that the effects of the various factors in the minds of the justices are almost certainly not additive as Kort assumes. The fact that a defendant is young and illiterate does not simply add something to his or her chances; it also increases the weight given to the various procedural guarantees in question and similarly for factors involving the seriousness of the punishment. However, since Theorem 19.1 ensures the existence of perfect linear (*i.e.* additive) predictors, this does not seem practically important. If a linear predictor always works as well as a non-linear one, it is difficult to find much meaning in the statement that the latter is correct. Besides, information about the relative importance of youth, illiteracy, previous experience in court and the like in influencing the weight given to

the various procedural guarantees can be inferred from the linear analysis, which is also much simpler to perform.

19. If the factor does not appear in a pro at all, the con in which it appears with the greatest number of votes for the original defendant is taken.

20. Kort, p. 6.

21. It is indeed quite possible that Kort's procedure here provides a roughly correct way of telling which factors are most important. This surmise is not supported by the test given below, however.

22. Only Kort knows the truth here, but one suspects that he arrived at his formula after first trying other simpler ones (such as the second one given in the text) on the data. If the data used in such a procedure included the cases in the 'test group' then that group in reality formed part of the 'source'.

23. I regret that I could not be as generous to Dr Kort in this chapter as he has been to me in promptly and graciously providing me with a list of the appearances of the various factors in each case, as noted by him.

24. I here pass over a number of minor disagreements. I do not understand, for example, why Kort observes the factor 'jurisdictional issue' only in *Rice* v. *Olson*, 324 US 786, when *White* v. *Ragen*, 324 US 760, was actually dismissed for want of jurisdiction.

25. See F.C. Mills, *Statistical Methods* (New York: Henry Hott & Co., 1955) 3d ed., pp. 311 ff.

26. The 'backwards' weighting scheme, by the way, would misclassify at least two of the cases – not counting *Canizio*. Since a scheme that gives each of the factors equal weight does equally as well, this is not impressive. Again, if the Kort solution is correct, it ought to work equally well both ways.

27. A technical and detailed description of this method, which was first applied in taxonomy and has since found major uses in psychology and sociology, may be found in G. Tintner, *Econometrics* (New York: John Wiley & Sons Inc., 1952), pp. 96–102. The mechanics of the method are too complex to be dealt with here.

28. As we have seen, in samples such as that used by Kort, these will generally be the factors of most interest and importance. We have hence not bothered to perform the analysis on Kort's sample.

29. Note, however, that such violation of Condition 1 could always be found by simple inspection so that such a test provides merely an efficient check. The actual test is as follows. Perform the analysis with the full set of factors, discard all factors with negative weights (such weights should be approximately zero) and recompute. Repeat this until only non-negative weights are obtained. (This should happen immediately.) If the weights thus found do not perfectly discriminate, then the Court has been inconsistent. Observe that some of the discussion requires linearity. See Note 13 above.

30. We add a technical point. If the sample is such that the appearances of two or more factors are not independent (*e.g.* if two factors always appear together), no inference as to the weights of all such factors will be possible because there will be more unknowns to find than independent equations to solve. In particular, to take Kort's factors as an example, the four 'seriousness of punishment' factors are not all independent since one and only one of them must appear in any given case; the value of the variable corresponding to any one of them will equal one minus the sum of the values of the variables corresponding to the others. It is thus impossible to

observe or infer the effects of any one of them, 'other things being equal'. In cases like this, discriminant analysis is impossible without removing one of the factors (*i.e.* assigning it zero weight or combining it with some other factor). In the present example, the factor 'crime subject to five or ten years' imprisonment' should be given a zero weight and removed since *every* case has at least this much punishment (assuming that the more serious the punishment the higher the weight of the factor). See Daniel Suits, 'The use of dummy variables in regression equations', *Journal of American Statistical Association*, Vol. 52 (Dec. 1957), pp. 548–51. I am indebted to John R. Meyer for this reference.

31.   Indeed, this statement proved prophetic. Within five years of the original publication of this chapter, the Supreme Court violated Condition 1, overturned the principal 'right-to-counsel' case (*Betts* v. *Brady*, 316 US 455 (1942)) and held that criminal defendants have a general right to counsel. (*Gideon* v. *Wainwright*, 372 US 335 (1963)). A highly readable and informative history is given in Anthony Lewis, *Gideon's Trumpet* (New York: Random House, 1964).

On the feasibility of identifying the crime function in a simultaneous model of crime rates and sanction levels (1978)

Introduction

In recent years, considerable social science research activity has been directed toward empirically estimating the deterrent impact of criminal sanctions. With few exceptions, the analyses have found a negative and often statistically significant association between crime rates and sanction measures such as clearance rates,[1] interpretable as a measure of probability of apprehension given crime; the ratio of imprisonments to crimes, interpretable as a measure of probability of imprisonment given crime; and time served in prison, a measure of severity of punishment given imprisonment (e.g. Gibbs 1968; Ehrlich 1973; Sjoquist 1973).

While these negative associations are consistent with the hypothesis that deterrence exists at a measurable level, several reviews (Greenberg 1977; Gibbs 1975; Nagin 1978) have questioned these results on several grounds. The key issues raised by Nagin are as follows.

1. The processes underlying the generation of data on crimes and sanctions offer alternative explanations for the observed inverse association between crime and sanctions. Variations, either across jurisdictions or over time, in police practices in the recording of offenses reported to them by the public or in the subsequent unfounding[2] of recorded offenses may in themselves generate an inverse association between published crime rates and any sanction variable using published

Written jointly with Daniel Nagin, whose contributions were partially supported by PHS research grant no. 1 ROI MH 28437-01 from the National Institute of Mental Health, Center for Studies of Crime and Delinquency.

counts of crime in its denominator (e.g. clearance rate, prison commitments per crime). Jurisdictions that record fewer reported crimes and/or unfound more recorded crimes will tend to have lower crime rates and higher measures of such sanction rates. Overt manipulation of clearance and crime reports will serve to generate an even larger negative association between crime rates and the clearance rate. High clearance rates and low crime rates are used as indicators of an effective police department. Police departments may use their discretion not to record or to unfound a reported offense to manipulate reductions in published crime rates. Concurrently, by offering suspects leniency if they admit to previously unsolved crimes, the police can also inflate clearance rates. The negative association between clearance rates and crime rates may simply reflect the varying intensity across jurisdictions with which such practices occur.

Similarly, the observed inverse association between prison commitments per crime and the crime rate may also be a reflection of the plea bargaining process. Plea bargaining will have the effect of understating in published statistics the actual number of prison commitments for more serious offenses because the commitments will be recorded for a less serious offense (e.g. assault charges may be disposed of as disorderly conduct). If plea bargaining is more prevalent in judicial systems that are overcrowded by increased crime, an inverse association between commitments per reported crime (a measure of probability of imprisonment) and crime rates will be induced that is not a reflection of deterrence.

2. The inverse association between crime and sanctions also reflects, at least in part, incapacitation effects rather than deterrent effects. In places where the probability of imprisonment is larger and/or time served is longer, a greater proportion of the criminal population will be incarcerated, *ceteris paribus*. The crime rate will thereby be reduced by physically restraining a greater proportion of the criminal element from committing crimes.

3. Motivated by a belief that crimes and sanctions mutually affect one another, many recent analyses have postulated simultaneous systems in which crime is presumed to affect sanctions and sanctions are presumed to affect crime. To separate empirically the mutual effects, *a priori* restrictions must be imposed on the behavior of the system. These restrictions have taken the form of selectively excluding significant exogenous variables from one equation in the system while including them in one or more of the other equations in the system. The restrictions are made on the assumption that a variable has a direct causal effect on the dependent variable in the equation in which it is included but has no direct effect on the dependent variable in the equation from

which it is excluded. If these exclusions are seriously in error, then the estimated coefficients are as unsuitable for inferring the effect of sanctions on crime as those estimated by non-simultaneous estimation procedures. The restrictions used to identify the crime-generating function are often implausible, consequently raising serious doubts as to the interpretability of the estimated parameters.

The purpose of this chapter is to pursue the identification problem raised in Point 3 by addressing the question of whether it is possible to identify and estimate the deterrent effects of sanctions under a maintained hypothesis that crimes and sanctions mutually affect one another.

When two factors, x and y, are simultaneously related, regressions of y on x and x on y cannot tell us the magnitude of the respective effects of x on y and y on x, since their mutual effects on each other will be confounded in both of the respective regression coefficients. For example, one cannot estimate the causal effect of price, P, on quantity demanded, q_D, by simply regressing q_D on P because P also affects the quantity supplied, q_S, which in equilibrium equals q_D. Statistical procedures exist that provide methods for identifying and estimating the mutual effects of simultaneously related variables provided certain conditions are satisfied. It can be shown, however, that if those conditions are not satisfied, then there is no way the effects can be estimated. Before discussing these methods, we shall first discuss the reasons for believing that crime affects sanctions as well as that sanctions affect crime.

Economists have argued that for a given level of resources devoted to the criminal justice system (CJS), increased crime rates saturate the resources of the CJS. The effect of the overutilization of CJS resources is a reduction in the level of sanctions delivered per crime, S. Specifically, if we define a relationship $S = h(C, E)$ that defines S as a function of crime rate, C, and CJS resources, E, then the resource saturation hypothesis would predict that $\partial h/\partial C < 0$ and $\partial h/\partial E > 0$.

A specific example of the resource saturation hypothesis is a predicted negative effect of crime rate on the clearance rate, holding E constant. Although the police will clear more crimes in absolute terms when crime rates increase, the percentage cleared (i.e. the clearance rate) will decrease (Figure 20.1).

The resource saturation hypothesis is explored in analyses done by Avio and Clark (1974), Carr-Hill and Stern (1973) and Ehrlich (1973). In each of these analyses the structural equation for sanction level showed a negative and significant association of crime rate with the dependent variable, sanction level. However, because of problems related to identification of the sanction functions (in addition to those related to the identification of the crime function), their results indicat-

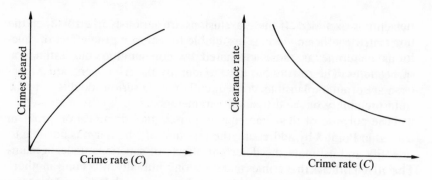

Figure 20.1   Relationship between number of crimes cleared and clearance rate per crime for a fixed level of resources under the assumption of decreasing marginal productivity for police resources.

ing a negative effect of crime on sanctions must be regarded as tentative.

Blumstein and Cohen (1973) and Blumstein *et al.* (1976) have offered still another reason for believing that crime rates will negatively affect sanctions. They have hypothesized that society is willing to deliver only a limited amount of punishment. As crime rates increase, a relatively constant level of punishment is maintained by adjusting the standards defining criminal behavior, reducing the probability of sanctions being imposed or the severity of sanctions imposed or all of these. This might involve a general reduction in sanctions in response to an overall increase in crime or a more selective response that is limited to specific crimes. While Blumstein, Cohen and Nagin have provided empirical support for the 'limits on punishment' hypothesis, their results are also tentative and require further investigation.

Both the 'resource saturation' and 'limits on punishment' hypotheses predict a negative effect of crime on sanctions. Some have argued the plausibility of increased crime rates causing a toughening of sanctions. This hypothesis is raised, for example, by Forst[3] and Avio and Clark (1974). Empirical evidence supporting this position is scant.[4] Avio and Clark (1974) observed a positive association between crime rate and sentence length. The enactment of the New York Repeat Offender Law and the Massachusetts Gun Law also support the 'toughening' position.[5]

The possibility of simultaneity between crime and sanctions, no matter what its cause, raises serious obstacles to empirical analysis and requires that simultaneous estimation be used to estimate the deterrent impact of sanctions in the simultaneous association of crime and sanctions. The separation of the two effects cannot be achieved unless *a priori* assumptions about the specific nature of the simultaneous relationship are invoked. These assumptions, which are called 'identification restrictions', are the keystone of simultaneous equation estimation, for data alone are not sufficient for estimating the structural parameters of a simultaneous system 'no matter how extensive and complete those observations may be' (Fisher 1966, p. 2).

In the next section, the identification problem will be discussed and its basic role in simultaneous equation estimation illustrated.

The identification problem

Simultaneous estimation procedures were developed because classical regression techniques are inadequate for estimating the structural equations in a simultaneous system. In particular, when two variables, x_t and y_t, are simultaneously determined as indicated by the system of Equations 20.1 shown below (such variables are referred to as endogenous), then a simple regression of y_t on x_t will generate a biased and inconsistent[6] estimate of b, the parameter defining the direct effect of x_t on y_t, and likewise a regression of x_t on y_t will generate a biased and inconsistent estimate of d, the parameter defining the direct effect of y_t on x_t.

$$y_t = a + bx_t + \epsilon_t \tag{20.1a}$$

$$x_t = c + dy_t + u_t \tag{20.1b}$$

The respective regression coefficients are not consistent estimates of the structural parameters, b and d, because the mutual interaction of x_t and y_t makes it impossible to assume that either is independent of the stochastic disturbances, ϵ_t and u_t. Since ϵ_t influences y_t and since y_t influences x_t, it cannot be the case that x_t and ϵ_t are uncorrelated. Hence a regression of y_t on x_t will confound the effect of x_t on y_t with that of ϵ_t on y_t and will not produce a consistent estimate of b.[7]

Indeed, in the present case, not only will ordinary regression techniques produce inconsistent parameter estimates, but no consistent estimator of those parameters exists. *There is no consistent way to estimate them from the data.* The problem can be seen in Figure 20.2 which presents the non-stochastic components of Equations 20.1a and 20.1b. Because x_t and y_t mutually affect one another, we will observe only a single equilibrium point (x_0, y_0). (If the stochastic terms were introduced, then the equilibrium points would be scattered about (x_0, y_0).) This single equilibrium point does not provide sufficient information for estimating either of the two equations, Equations 20.1a and 20.1b, that produced it. For example, the equilibrium (x_0, y_0) could just as well have been generated by the system shown in Figure 20.3.

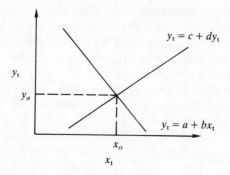

Figure 20.2   A simplified model of a simultaneous relationship between two variables.

Indeed, there are an infinite number of such systems that could have generated (x_0, y_0). There is no way to use the data to distinguish the true system from the others. Algebraically, this amounts to observing that any linear combination of Equations 20.1a and 20.1b will produce an identical equilibrium (x_0, y_0). There is no way of distinguishing the true Equation 20.1a or Equation 20.1b from any such linear combination.

Nevertheless, estimating structural equations involving simultaneously related variables is often possible.[8] Under certain conditions, discussed below, simultaneous estimation procedures do provide methods for consistently estimating the true structural equations that generated the observed associations among the simultaneously related variables. However, the true system must satisfy these conditions if the identification problem just exemplified is to be avoided and consistent estimation is to be possible.

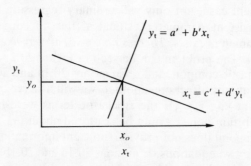

Figure 20.3   Example of an alternative system that generates the same equilibrium point as shown in Figure 20.2.

The necessary conditions for estimating the true structural equations involve the imposition of *a priori* assumptions about the behavior of the system. Most commonly, these take the form of assuming that variables whose values are determined outside the system ('exogenous variables') or values of endogenous variables determined in prior periods ('predetermined variables') directly affect one or more of the endogenous variables but not all of them. Such restrictions aid in the identification of the structural equation from which the exogenous or predetermined variable is excluded. The exclusion of a variable from one or more equations, however, does not aid in the identification of the structural equations that do include that variable.

To illustrate how such exclusions can identify a structural equation, consider again the system of Equations 20.1. As the system is specified, neither equation is identified and neither can be estimated consistently by any method. As indicated earlier, the impossibility of estimating the system is a reflection of there being an infinite set of equation systems that could generate (x_0, y_0).

Suppose, however, that an exogenous variable, T_t, is suspected to have an effect on y_t, but is *known* to have no effect on x_t. Equation 20.1a could then be respecified as:

$$y_t = a + bx_t + fT_t + \epsilon_t \qquad \textbf{(20.1a')}$$

Additionally, assume for concreteness that $f < 0$.[9]

In Figure 20.4, the non-stochastic component of (20.1a') is presented as a function of x_t for three different values of T_t. Consistent with the assumption that $f < 0$, Figure 20.4 shows that for any given value of x_t, y_t is smaller for larger values of T_t.

In Figure 20.5, Equation 20.1b is superimposed on Equation 20.1a' for the different values of T_t. The three points where Equations 20.1a'

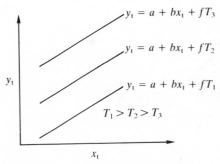

Figure 20.4 y_t as a function of x_t and an exogenous variable, T_t.

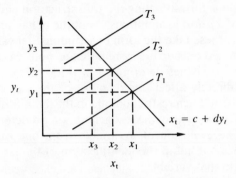

Figure 20.5 The identifying role of an exogenous variable, T_t, in a simplified model of a simultaneous relationship between two variables.

and 20.1b intersect indicate the equilibrium values of x_t and y_t for the three different values of T_t.

If these three equilibrium points were observed and connected, then the structural Equation 20.1b for x_t would be *uniquely* determined. Note, however, that Equation 20.1a′, the structural equation for y_t, is still not identified; no variables included in Equation 20.1b are excluded from Equation 20.1a′.

The fact that Equation 20.1a′ is not identified can be seen in Figure 20.6, where an alternative set of equations for y_t would generate identical equilibrium values of x_t and y_t. Again, there are an infinite number of versions of Equation 20.1a′ that would generate the observed equilibria; however, there is only a single version of Equation 20.1b, the true one, that could do so.

It is important to stress, however, that the identification of Equation 20.1b is predicated on f, the coefficient of T_t, being different from zero.

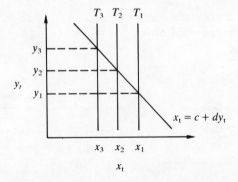

Figure 20.6 An alternative set of y_t functions that generates the same equilibrium points as shown in Figure 20.5.

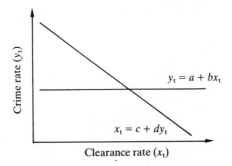

Figure 20.7 A simplified model of the relationship between crimes and sanctions in which sanctions do not affect crimes but crimes do affect sanctions.

If f were equal to zero, the situation would revert to that in Figure 20.2; a single equilibrium point (x_0, y_0) would be observed; and Equation 20.1b would no longer be identified.[10]

When more than two variables simultaneously affect one another, the conditions for identification become somewhat more complicated (see Fisher 1966). Before outlining these conditions, a simplified model of the simultaneous relationship between crime and clearance rates will be examined to illustrate the importance of proper identification for making correct causal inferences.

Suppose, in Equations 20.1, x_t is the clearance rate in period t, and y_t is the crime rate in period t. Also, suppose that unbeknownst to us, clearance rates do not in fact affect crime rate (i.e. $b = 0$), but increased crime rates do decrease clearance rates (i.e. $d < 0$). Under the assumption of $b = 0$, a graphical characterization of the unobserved (and as was shown unidentifiable) system is given in Figure 20.7.

Suppose, however, that the average sentence in period t, T_t, *does* affect crime rates, with longer sentences reducing the crime rate. Thus, the augmented specification of the crime rate equation would be as in Equation 20.1a', which is repeated below:

$$y_t = a + bx_t + fT_t + \epsilon_t \qquad (20.1a')$$

The presumed effect of T_t on y_t is illustrated in Figure 20.8.

In Figure 20.9, the clearance rate function is superimposed on the crime functions in Figure 20.8. As was shown previously, the *clearance rate function* is now identified. By connecting the observed intersections in Figure 20.9, the exact specification for the clearance rate function can be determined. The *crime function*, however, remains unidentified and it will remain unknown and unknowable to us that, indeed, higher clearance rates do not deter crime.

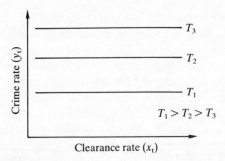

Figure 20.8 The crime rate as a function of the clearance rate and the average sentence (T_t).

Suppose, however, it were arbitrarily assumed that sentence, T_t, affected clearance rates and not crime rates. Then the mechanics of simultaneous estimation would have allowed an equation for the crime rate to be estimated. That equation, however, would be identical to the one obtained by drawing a line through the equilibrium values of x_t and y_t. Thus, the estimated relation would actually be the relationship describing the effect of crime rate on clearance rate and not clearance rate on crime rate, and so would be completely wrong. In this case, we would conclude that clearance rates have a deterrent effect on crime when in fact they have none.

The very real possibility of making erroneous causal inferences when a model is identified through erroneous assumptions underscores the point that identification is not a minor technical point of estimation. If an equation is not identified, one cannot estimate it. If one tries to do so using false restrictions to identify the equation, one will draw completely erroneous conclusions from the estimated relationship.

It is thus essential that when exclusion restrictions are used for identification, the restrictions must be carefully justified on the *a priori*

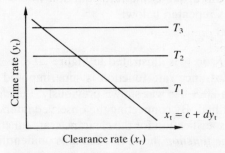

Figure 20.9 The identifying role of average sentence (T_t) in a simplified model of the relationship between crime and sanctions.

grounds that the excluded variables do not directly affect the value of the endogenous variable on the left side of the equation from which they are excluded. If a variable is excluded from an equation merely to facilitate estimation, then the coefficient estimates will remain inconsistent and thus unsuitable for inference about the behavior of the system. Moreover, identifying restrictions must be assumed *a priori* and the nature of the problem is such that restrictions needed to identify can never be tested using data generated by the model under investigation.[11]

In analyzing the mutual association of crime and sanctions, the possibility of making erroneous causal inferences about the causal effect of sanctions on crime is particularly high. Since there are good reasons for believing that crime has a negative causal effect on sanctions, we would expect to observe a negative association in the data between crime and sanctions even if sanctions do not deter crime. Such negative associations are well documented in the deterrence literature (e.g. Ehrlich 1973; Sjoquist 1973; Tittle 1969). Having observed the negative association, we are left with the delicate problem of determining the extent to which it is produced by the negative deterrent effect of sanctions on crime as opposed to the negative effect of crime on sanctions (if the latter effect is indeed negative).[12]

In view of the importance of the identification problem, we shall review some of the restrictions that have been used by some authors to identify the crime functions so that the validity of their findings on the deterrent effect of sanctions can be put into perspective. When evaluating the validity of such restrictions, one should keep in mind that crime-function restrictions presume that the variables involved affect either sanctions, police expenditures per capita (a variable commonly hypothesized to be simultaneously related to crime), or other endogenous variables included in the model, but do not directly affect the crime rate itself.

Ehrlich (1973) identified his crime function by excluding from it (but including elsewhere in his model) the following variables:

1. The crime rate lagged one period
2. Police expenditures per capita lagged one period
3. Unemployment rate of civilian males aged 35–39
4. Per cent of males aged 14–24
5. Per cent of population living in Standard Metropolitan Statistical Areas (SMSAs)
6. Males per female
7. A southern regional variable
8. Mean years of schooling of population over age 25
9. Total population.[13]

In Carr-Hill and Stern (1973), the crime function is identified by excluding:

1. Total population
2. Proportion of reported crimes that are violent
3. A measure of the proportion of the population that is middle class.

Avio and Clarke (1974) estimate a model in which crime rates, clearance rates, and police expenditures per capita are simultaneously determined. The crime function is identified by excluding:

1. Population density
2. The total population
3. Police expenditures lagged one period
4. Motor vehicle registrations per capita lagged one period
5. Crimes against persons lagged one period.

In all these papers, identification of the crime function relies on the exclusion of socioeconomic variables (SES) and lagged endogenous variables from the crime function. It is difficult to imagine any plausible arguments for the exclusion of the SES variables. Intercorrelation among these SES and demographic correlates of crime makes it difficult to determine which among them do have a causal association with crime, but it is simply not plausible to assume that such SES variables do not have a direct effect on crime, while also assuming that each does directly affect either sanctions or police expenditures per capita.[14]

Further, two of the analyses also use the exclusion of lagged endogenous variables to identify the crime function. For the estimation procedures employed, the use of such restrictions to identify rests crucially upon an assumption of no serial correlation in the stochastic disturbance terms in the equations, because these estimation procedures treat lagged endogenous variables as uncorrelated with current disturbances. If current and lagged disturbances are correlated, this assumption cannot be true. (This point will be discussed in greater detail below.) While methods exist to handle serial correlation, the analyses discussed do not use such methods. There are cogent reasons, which will also be discussed, for believing:

(a) the assumption of no serial correlation to be incorrect and
(b) there is positive serial correlation in the disturbances for the type of data used in these analyses.

Assuming that crime and sanctions are simultaneously related, our conclusion is that it is most unlikely that the authors mentioned have successfully identified and consistently estimated the deterrent effect of sanctions. Consequently, one can have little confidence that the estimated sanctions coefficients are consistent. Moreover, the magnitude of the inconsistency seems likely to be substantial since the restrictions used to identify seem unlikely to be even approximately correct (see Fisher 1961). Consequently, the resulting parameter estimates cannot be used for causal interpretation.

A crucial question is then: Can the crime function ever plausibly be identified, i.e. can we ever hope to find variables that influence sanctions but have no direct effect on crimes? This question, which is the central topic of this chapter, is the focus of the next section. The question of the feasibility of identifying the crime function requires an appreciation of some more generalized identification concepts. Thus, before we turn to the topic of feasibility, we shall develop these concepts.

Some more generalized identification concepts

The prior discussion has focused on the requirements for identifying the structural equations in a system where only two variables are simultaneously related. We shall now generalize to a situation where M variables simultaneously affect one another.

Suppose we specify the interrelationship of the M variables by:

$$y_1 = a_{12}y_2 + a_{13}y_3 + \ldots + a_{1M}y_M \\ + b_{11}x_1 + b_{12}x_2 + \ldots + b_{1N}x_N + \epsilon_1$$

$$y_2 = a_{21}y_1 + a_{23}y_3 + \ldots + a_{2M}y_M \\ + b_{21}x_1 + b_{22}x_2 + \ldots + b_{2N}x_N + \epsilon_2 \qquad \textbf{(20.2)}$$

$$\vdots$$

$$y_M = a_{M1}y_1 + a_{M2}y_2 + \ldots + a_{MM-1}y_{M-1} \\ + b_{M1}x_1 + b_{M2}x_2 + \ldots + b_{MN}x_N + \epsilon_M$$

where

y_i = the ith endogenous variable ($i = 1, \ldots, M$)
a_{ik} = the coefficient defining the magnitude of the direct ('causal') effect of y_k on y_i
x_j = the jth non-endogenous variable ($j = 1, \ldots, N$)
b_{ij} = the coefficient defining the magnitude of the jth non-endogenous variable's direct effect on y_i
ϵ_i = the stochastic component of the ith structural equation.

As was shown previously, when variables are simultaneously related, the empirical observations of the system's behavior, no matter how well measured or extensive they may be, are not sufficient for consistently estimating the structural relationships. Consider the first structural equation in the system of Equations 20.2. Estimation of the relationship would require generating $M - 1 + N$ parameter estimates. However, the limits of empirical information are such that only N independent pieces of information can be obtained from the data to estimate the $N + M - 1$ parameters of this equation. This corresponds to the fact that only the N non-endogenous variables, the x_j, can be varied independently. The M endogenous variables, the y_i, are determined (except for stochastic effects) once the x_j are set. If there were no stochastic effects, we could think of performing experiments (or having nature perform them for us) by setting the values of the x_j and observing the effect on the y_i. There would be, however, only N independent ways of setting the N non-endogenous x_j, and further experiments would be redundant.

In the stochastic case, the corresponding fact is that we are entitled to assume (at most) that each of the N non-endogenous x_j is uncorrelated with the disturbances, ϵ_i, and in particular with the disturbance from the first equation, ϵ_1. The y_i cannot be so uncorrelated.

If $M = 1$ so that there were no simultaneity, then these N zero correlations would suffice to allow the consistent estimation of the first (and only) equation by ordinary regression. In that case, only exogenous variables would appear on the right side of that equation and the N zero correlations would satisfy the necessary conditions for ordinary regression to generate a consistent estimator – namely, that the regressors be uncorrelated with the disturbance. Where $M > 1$ and there is simultaneity, these N zero correlations are not enough to recover the $M - 1 + N$ parameters of the first equation.

Another way of putting it is to say that analysis of the data can at most only tell us about the full effects (direct and indirect) of the x_j on the y_i (from the 'reduced form' in which the equations are solved for the y_i only in terms of the x_j and ϵ_i). The direct effects of the x_j on the y_i (the b_{ij}) and the direct effects of the y_i on each other (the a_{ik}) cannot be recovered from the data without at least $M - 1$ additional independent pieces of information for each equation.[15] Such additional information must come from outside, *a priori* considerations.[16]

The situation is completely isomorphic to the logical impossibility of finding a unique solution to a system of linear equations in $M + N - 1$ unknowns, when only N independent equations are available. A unique solution can only be obtained if $M - 1$ additional independent equations, comparable to our restrictions, are imposed. The identification restrictions in simultaneous equation estimation provide the $M - 1$ additional restrictions that sufficiently augment the empirical information to allow the estimation of the structural equation.

The $M - 1$ additional equations in the system of linear equations in $M + N - 1$ unknowns are as important in specifying a unique solution as the N original equations. Similarly, the identification restrictions are as important in the determination of the coefficients as the observational information.

The additional $M - 1$ restrictions can be (but need not be) generated by assuming that $M - 1$ of the parameters in the equation are zero. The $M - 1$ restrictions could be generated if we assumed $a_{1i} = 0$ $(i = 2, \ldots, M)$, which is to assume that y_1 is *not* simultaneously related to any of the other y_is. Since the x_is are assumed to be uncorrelated with ϵ_I, the coefficients of the first equation could then be consistently estimated by ordinary least squares.

Suppose, however, that we conclude that *a priori* considerations allow us only to assume that $(M - 1) - k$, where $0 \leqslant k < M - 1$, of the a_{1i}s are zero. We must still estimate $k + N$ parameters, which can still not be done using only the N pieces of empirical information available.[17] The additional k pieces of information can be generated if *a priori* considerations would allow us to assume plausibly that k of the N non-endogenous x_j do not enter the first equation but do enter one or more of the other equations (i.e. k of the $b_{1j} = 0$ but $b_{ij} \neq 0$ for some $i \neq 1$). By assuming that k of the b_{1j} are zero, it becomes unnecessary to estimate them. Thus the N pieces of empirical information can be used to estimate the remaining N parameters consistently. It must be emphasized, however, that the remaining N parameters will only be consistently estimated if the *a priori* considerations that led to the assumptions that $M - 1 - k$ of the a_{1i}s and k of the b_{1j}s were zero are correct.[18] Thus, any empirical conclusion hinges critically on the validity of those *a priori* premises.

When only $M - 1$ restrictions can be imposed and the equation in question is identified, it is said to be 'just identified'. This terminology derives from the fact that if we can generate only $M - 2$ restrictions, then the equation will not be identified (i.e. unidentified). Being short only a single restriction means that there exists more than one, and in general an infinite number of equations that are consistent with the data. All such equations are observationally equivalent to the true one. Thus, it must be remembered that from the perspective of the existence of a consistent estimator, one is no better off having $M - 2$ restrictions than zero restrictions. In either case, no consistent estimator will exist and no causal inference can be made about the equation for y_1. In some of the models to be examined in the next section, this point will return to haunt us.

Sometimes it is also possible to generate more than $M - 1$ restrictions and to identify the equation in more than one way. In such instances, the equation is said to be 'over-identified' and, since we have more than N pieces of information to estimate less than N parameters, estimation, of course, remains possible.

Before turning to the next section on the feasibility of identifying the crime function, several important points must be made. In order of importance, they are as follows. First, if an equation is just identified, then the restrictions used to identify it cannot be tested with the data being analyzed. The untestability of the restrictions follows from the fact that a model cannot even be estimated unless we assume they are true. (For example, the clearance rate's specification (Equation 20.1b) cannot be estimated unless we assume that T_t does not enter Equation 20.1b. Since we cannot estimate Equation 20.1b if T_t does enter it, then we cannot test whether it should enter Equation 20.1b.)

A related point follows when a model is over-identified, that is, when there are alternative ways to just-identify it. One can estimate the model under a variety of subsets of just-identifying restrictions, with each of the resulting model estimates being contingent upon the validity of the just-identifying subset used. If one has little or no faith in the validity of any one of the subsets, then even if one gets the same results under each subset (for example, sanctions do not deter crime), then one cannot conclude that those results are valid.

Second, any additional restrictions beyond a set of $M - 1$ just-identifying ones can be tested. Those tests are, however, contingent upon the validity of the $M - 1$ just-identifying restrictions. If one has faith in the validity of these $M - 1$ restrictions, then one can have faith in the validity of the empirical tests of the additional over-identifying restrictions. But, if one has little faith in the validity of the just-identifying restrictions, one can have only little faith in the validity of the test of the remaining restrictions. One implication of this point is that if one generates a set of over-identifying restrictions – but in this set there does not exist a subset of just-identifying restrictions whose validity is unquestionable (or nearly so) – one cannot gain a valid test of the set of restrictions by exhaustively testing each restriction under the assumption that the remaining ones are correct.[19]

On the feasibility of identifying the crime function

In this section, we shall examine the central issue of this chapter: can the crime function be plausibly identified? We shall proceed by first examining the simplest model in which a single crime type and sanction type are simultaneously related. Several categories of just-identifying restrictions, none of which are mutually exclusive, will be analyzed for their strengths and weaknesses. The single-crime-type, single-sanction-type model overly simplifies the real phenomenon of multiple crime types and multiple sanction types. However, to date no analyses have attempted to estimate models in which more than one crime and sanction type are simultaneously related. More important for our purposes, such simple models will serve to highlight the strengths and weaknesses of some different categories of just-identifying restrictions. These points will remain valid in analyzing more complex models.

We shall then consider the more complex but more realistic models in which

(a)   a single-crime type is simultaneously related to multiple-sanction types and
(b)   multiple-crime types and a single-sanction type are simultaneously related.

We shall not consider under a separate heading the most complex model in which multiple crime and sanction types are simultaneously related, because the problematic feasibility of identifying such a model will become clear from the discussion of the preceding two model types. The principal focus of our discussion will be the identification of simultaneous models. The mutual association of crime and sanctions may, however, occur with time lags rather than simultaneously. In the Technical Note we shall point out the difficulties with results based upon path models, which are a specific class of lagged models, and then discuss the difficulties likely to be encountered in estimating more general classes of lagged models.

None of the models that will be discussed will explicitly include SES variables. While SES variables should indeed be included in a specification of the crime function, we do not envisage the exclusion of SES variables being plausibly used for identification restrictions. Such exclusions would have to be predicated upon *a priori* considerations that allow one to assume that the excluded SES factor directly affects some other endogenous variable in the system but not crime. Currently we simply do not have a sufficiently well-developed and validated theory of the socioeconomic factors affecting crime and sanctions plausibly to assume that some SES factor can be excluded from the crime-generating model but included elsewhere in the system. Some new insight in this regard would, of course, be very useful.

The absence of explicit consideration of SES effects should not be interpreted as indicating that we believe these effects to be inconsequential; their effects are undoubtedly substantial, but the mechanism of their operation is simply not understood well enough plausibly to employ SES variables for identification purposes. Thus, our discussion omits SES variables only for expositional convenience. Most models would include such variables, at least in the crime function. However, it is the exclusion of such variables from the crime function (but not from other equations) that would aid identification.[20]

Single-crime-type, single-sanction models

Models using expenditures as an identifying omitted variable

Suppose we specify the following model:

$$C_t = f(S_t) + \epsilon_t^1 \tag{20.3a}$$

$$S_t = h(C_t, E_t) + \epsilon_t^2 \tag{20.3b}$$

where

$f(S_t)$ and $h(C_t, E_t)$ are linear functions[21]
C_t = crime rate in t
S_t = sanctions per crime in t
E_t = criminal justice system (CJS) expenditures in t
ϵ_t^i = stochastic error ($i = 1, 2$) whose properties are to be discussed.

In this model, which is also characterized by the flow chart in Figure 20.10, C_t is determined by S_t, and S_t is determined jointly by C_t and E_t. The CJS expenditures variable, E_t, enters the equation for S_t under the

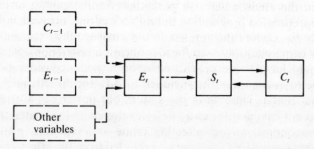

Figure 20.10 Diagram of model using expenditures as an identifying variable. The possibility that C_{t-1}, E_{t-1} and other variables affect expenditures at t but are omitted from the crime equation does not aid in the identification of the latter. This is because these variables do not appear anywhere in the sanctions–crime loop and have no effect captured beyond taking expenditures as exogenous to that loop. Another way of putting it is that the omission of such variables from the crime equation does not help to distinguish it from the sanctions equation since the variables do not appear in that equation either.

theory that increased resources devoted to the CJS, as measured by E_t, will decrease the resource saturation effect of any given level of crime, C_t (i.e. $\partial h/\partial E_t > 0$). As noted earlier, the resource saturation theory is one of the primary theories underlying simultaneous models of crimes and sanctions.

In this system, there are two endogenous variables, C_t and S_t. The crime equation includes one right-side endogenous variable, S_t. Estimation of Equation 20.3a will thus require that one identification restriction be imposed. (Within the context of the identification rules laid out in the previous section, $M = 2$ and therefore we need $M - 1 = 1$ restriction to identify Equation 20.3a.)

In this system, E_t is not included in the crime function. This exclusion, which can be used to provide the necessary single identifying restriction to estimate Equation 20.3a, is predicated upon the theory that E_t affects crime only insofar as it affects the capability of the CJS to deliver sanctions. For sanctions delivered by the courts (e.g. conviction, imprisonment) or regulated by corrections (e.g. time served in prison), such an assumption seems reasonable. However, if E_t is police expenditures and S_t is defined as the clearance rate, then the assumption that E_t has no direct effect on C_t is suspect.

The level of police expenditures is likely to influence the visibility of police, since in two identical communities, the one with greater expenditures is likely to have a larger police force. Police visibility may have an independent deterrent effect beyond S_t, where S_t is measured by clearance rate, because the potential criminal's perception of apprehension probability (which is the 'true' measure of S_t we are seeking when S_t refers to police-delivered sanctions) undoubtedly derives from multiple cues from the environment. A potential criminal cannot observe the actual apprehension probability, but rather can only measure it roughly. One such measure is the frequency with which he or she and fellow criminals with which he or she has contact are apprehended. Perhaps this frequency can be approximated by the clearance rate. The criminal's perception of apprehension probability, however, does not have to be based solely upon these undoubtedly inaccurate frequency estimates. It is likely that the estimate of apprehension probability is a reaction to additional cues from the environment – such as the intensity of the police presence.

To the extent that police visibility provides an independent cue to apprehension probability and thus acts as an independent direct deterrent distinct from the indirect effect of an increased police presence on clearance rates and hence on crime, then E_t should appear directly in the equation for C_t. Such an appearance, however, would leave the crime function unidentified.

Putting such considerations aside and presuming the exclusion of E_t

from the crime equation to be valid, that exclusion will identify the crime equation if either of the following statements is true.

1. Expenditures are fully exogenous. To assume that E_t is exogenous is to assume that neither C_t nor S_t in the current period or in prior periods affects E_t. An assumption of exogeneity seems untenable because it is likely that the level of crime affects the level of expenditures, at least across jurisdictions and probably over time. The observed positive association between police expenditures per capita and crime rate provides some evidence for the likelihood of such an effect (see, for example, McPheters and Stronge 1974).

2. Expenditures are influenced only by lagged crime rates and are therefore predetermined, although not fully exogeneous. This seems more reasonable than does full exogeneity. Due to the governmental budgeting cycle, the level of E_t is specified before the beginning of period t. That level, although probably influenced by the crime rate, is influenced by rates in prior periods, for example, C_{t-1}. Thus, E_t is a predetermined variable.[22]

Granting that E_t is predetermined, a further crucial assumption must be made about the behavior of the stochastic components, ϵ_t^i. We must specify the behavior of these stochastic terms over time. We could assume that the errors are independent over time, or we could make a less restrictive assumption that they are serially correlated. For example, we might assume that they follow a first-order autoregressive process, characterized by:

$$\epsilon_t^i = \rho_i \epsilon_{t-1}^i + \delta_t^i \tag{20.4}$$

where

ρ_i = a parameter
δ_t^i = a non-serially correlated disturbance term.

Such assumptions about the serial relationships among the ϵ_t^i are critical for identification. In our previous discussion on the limits of the empirical information in a simultaneous system, we stated that the maximum number of independent pieces of empirical information available for consistently estimating each structural equation was N, where N equals the number of non-endogenous variables in the system. This was because of the assumption that there are N non-endogenous variables that are uncorrelated with the stochastic disturbances and thus that can be varied independently. If that assumption fails for J_1 of the non-endogenous variables, then the number of pieces of empirical information for consistently estimating each structural equation is reduced to $N - J_1$. In effect, an additional J_1 of the variables become endogenous.

When using predetermined variables for identification, the possibility that the disturbances are serially correlated must be given special consideration. If the ϵ_t^i are serially correlated (for example, a first-order autoregressive process as in Equation 20.4), then the predetermined variables will necessarily be correlated with at least some of the stochastic components. In particular, E_t will be correlated with ϵ_t^1 because ϵ_t^1 is correlated with ϵ_{t-1}^1 and E_t is a function of C_{t-1}, which is in turn a function of ϵ_{t-1}^1.

When serial correlation among the disturbances is thought to be present, estimation still remains possible if one correctly specifies the specific structure of the presumed serial correlation. If one is not certain of the specific structure of the serial correlation, and one rarely is, then the less restrictive the assumption the better. For example, the first-order autoregressive assumption is less restrictive than assuming no serial correlation because the latter will occur for the special case of all the ρ_i zero. However, if the model is estimated under an assumption of no serial correlation, then the possibility of serial correlation of some specific type cannot be tested. Even less restrictive assumptions about the nature of the serial correlation (higher-order processes, for example) can be made, but some specific assumptions must be made.

Excepting a capital punishment analysis by Ehrlich (1975), all simultaneous analyses have employed estimation methods that generate consistent estimates only when there is no serial correlation of any kind among the disturbances. If the exclusion of a predetermined variable is used as an identification restriction, as with E_t in the model under consideration, the validity of using that restriction when using these methods turns on the assumption of no serial correlation. If the assumption is incorrect, then the parameter estimates will be inconsistent.

The assumption of no serial correlation among the disturbances is not only fundamental in cases like this; it reflects implicit assumptions about real effects stemming from factors influencing crime or sanctions that are captured in the disturbances because they are not explicitly included in the model. Deciding whether the assumption of no serial correlation can plausibly be maintained thus requires consideration of such factors.

In the crime function shown in Equation 20.3a, the variables not explicitly included. Nevertheless, some part of the stochastic disturbance, ϵ_t^1, would still consist of SES effects. It is impossible to include all adopted for expositional purposes. As already remarked, in practice, if Equation 20.3a were to be estimated, some SES variables would be explicitly included. Nevertheless, some part of the stochastic disturbance, ϵ_t^1, would still consist of SES effects. It is impossible to include all the SES variables influencing crime both because we do not know all of them or cannot measure them and because there are likely to be many of them, each with a small effect. In addition, if included SES variables affect crime in ways only approximated by our choice of functional form in Equation 20.3a, then departures from that approximation influence the disturbance term.

From this perspective on the factors generating ϵ_t^1, is it reasonable to assume no serial correlation in ϵ_t^1? The answer, we believe, is no. Many of the SES variables influencing ϵ_t^1 change only gradually over time. Thus, if the realized values of these variables in period t are such that the disturbance is positive in period t, it is likely that their realized values in period $t + 1$ will lead to a positive disturbance as well. Hence we should expect positive serial correlation in ϵ_t^1. One possible characterization might be the first-order autoregressive process shown in Equation 20.4, with $\rho_1 > 0$.

When using data with a cross-sectional component, the most common type of data utilized in deterrence analyses, the likelihood of serial correlation is particularly high because there is likely to be particularly wide variation in the values of excluded variables across the sampling units (usually states). Put simply, locations whose actual crime rate is higher than predicted by the systematic part of the equation in one year are likely to remain so in the next year.

The implausibility of an assumption of no serial correlation requires that estimation be done under a less restrictive assumption about the serial correlation of the stochastic terms if inconsistency is to be avoided. We shall not address the question of what sort of assumption on the nature of the serial dependence is plausible. The question deserves further attention, but it can be said that the less restrictive the assumption, the better. One possibility, given enough data, would be to allow for an autoregressive relationship of order γ, where:

$$\epsilon_t^i = \sum_{j=1}^{\gamma} \rho_{ij}\epsilon_{t-j} + \delta_t^i \tag{20.5}$$

Estimation under any assumption of serial dependence, however, requires the use of data with a time-series component. For example, the γth order autoregressive assumption would require that the time-series component in the data be at least $\gamma + 1$ periods. Pure cross-sectional data cannot be used.

To summarize, we conclude that the exclusion of the expenditures variable cannot be used plausibly to identify the crime function, at least with cross-sectional data. To do so at best requires the very implausible assumption of serial independence in the stochastic components. To estimate a model under any assumption of serial dependence requires time-series data and thereby precludes the possibility of using only cross-sectional data.

Moreover, as we have seen, the use of the expenditures restriction, no matter what one assumes about the nature of the serial dependence, hinges upon the assumption that E_t does not directly affect crime. If S_t and E_t are defined in terms of court-related activities only, this seems plausible. If E_t and S_t pertain to the police, however, then the assumption that E_t does not directly influence C_t is questionable. Expenditures on police will be closely linked to the visibility of police in the community, and police visibility may indeed be a very important factor in deterring crime. Further, if expenditures on courts and expenditures on police vary together, then one may simply be fooling oneself about identification in specifying and estimating a model in which E_t relates only to courts.

Models using prison cell utilization

In the system shown below, C_t is again a function of S_t and S_t is a function of C_t. Additonally, S_t is specified to be a function of prison-cell utilization, U_t, defined to be the ratio of the prison population in t, P_t, to total prison cells in t, K_t.

$$C_t = f(S_t) + \epsilon_t^1 \qquad \text{(20.6a)}$$

$$S_t = h(C_t, U_t) + \epsilon_t^2 \qquad \text{(20.6b)}$$

where:

P_t = the prison population in period t
K_t = prison cell capacity in period t
$U_t = P_t/K_t$

As before, SES variables are omitted for expositional convenience. To our knowledge, no deterrence investigation has included U_t in the equation for sanctions. The rationale for its inclusion again involves a resource utilization argument and, indeed, this model can be taken as a simple example in which the resource saturation hypothesis is made explicit. As prisons become increasingly crowded, pressure will be exerted to reduce utilization, U_t. In the short term (*e.g.* a year) this reduction can only be accomplished through a reduction in prison population, P_t, since expansion of existing cell capacity, K_t, would require considerably more time.[23]

One example of this effect of resource saturation at work is Federal Judge Frank Johnson's order to the Alabama Corrections Department to release a sufficient number of prisoners to alleviate prison overcrowding (see *Criminal Justice Bulletin* 1976). Judge Johnson's order resulted in the reduction of both the probability of imprisonment given conviction and time served given imprisonment.

In this single-sanction and single-crime-type model with only two endogenous variables, identification of the crime function requires that one restriction be imposed; the absence of U_t, prison-cell utilization in t, from Equation 20.6a provides the necessary restriction. To see this, consider a log–linear specification of Equations 20.6a, b:

$$\ln C_t = B_o + B_1 \ln S_t + \epsilon_t^1 \tag{20.6a'}$$

$$\ln S_t = \gamma_o + \gamma_1 \ln C_t + \gamma_2 \ln \left(\frac{P_t}{K_t}\right) + \epsilon_t^2$$

$$= \gamma_o + \gamma_1 \ln C_t + \gamma_2 \ln P_t - \gamma_2 \ln K_t + \epsilon_t^2 \tag{20.6b'}$$

In addition, if we specifically define S_t to be the probability of imprisonment given a crime and assume that an imprisoned individual is incarcerated for a single period,[24] P_t will be:

$$P_t = C_t S_t N_t \tag{20.6c}$$

$$\ln P_t = \ln C_t + \ln S_t + \ln N_t \tag{20.6c'}$$

where N_t = total population in t.[25] Substituting Equation 20.6c' in Equation 20.6b' and rearranging terms:

$$\ln S_t = \frac{\gamma_o}{1 - \gamma_2} + \frac{\gamma_1 + \gamma_2}{1 - \gamma_2} \ln C_t + \frac{\gamma_2}{1 - \gamma_2} \ln (N_t/K_t)$$

$$+ \frac{\epsilon_t^2}{1 - \gamma_2} \tag{20.6b''}$$

The exclusion of $\ln (N_t/K_t)$ from Equation 20.6a' provides the necessary restriction for identification.[26]

The validity of this identification procedure hinges upon the assumption that U_t does not directly affect crime. This assumption will fail if potential criminals have information on crowding in prisons and view the level of U_t as a partial measure of the severity of punishment. If, indeed, U_t has such an effect, then it should be included in the crime equation and the exclusion of N_t/K_t cannot be used validly to identify the crime function.

Inertia model: lagged sanctions

In the system shown below, the equation for S_t includes S_{t-1}. Its inclusion could be argued on the grounds that sanctioning practice, being bound by tradition, will adjust slowly to changes in the crime rate or indeed to any other factors influencing sanctions. As a result, S_t will be influenced by sanctions in prior periods, assumed for illustration to be represented sufficiently by S_{t-1}. Since S_{t-1} does not appear in the crime equation, the crime function is identified with some assumption on the nature of the serial dependence of the ϵ_t^i.

$$C_t = f(S_t) + \epsilon_t^1 \tag{20.7a}$$

$$S_t = h(C_t, S_{t-1}) + \epsilon_t^2 \tag{20.7b}$$

While this rationale for including S_{t-1} in the specification of S_t is highly plausible, it is not plausible at the same time to exclude S_{t-1} from the crime equation. To do so assumes that potential criminals are not influenced by sanctions in prior periods. Such an assumption has little plausibility as a crucial identifying restriction, since it implies that historical sanction levels have no influence on perceptions of current sanctions even though they do influence current sanctions themselves.

For example, suppose a rational criminal has information indicating that a certain offense is not being prosecuted as vigorously as it had been previously. Should information on sanction levels in prior periods be disregarded and decisions be based solely upon the new information on sanctions? There are several reasons that a rational criminal might still continue to consider prior information on sanctions.

First, unlike stock market prices, daily quotations of sanction levels are not available and the information that is available derives from very uncertain sources, including the criminal's own experience, the experience of criminal peers, news reports or even the published statistics utilized by deterrence researchers. When current information is poor, considering information from the past, even if it is also uncertain, is very sensible in making estimates of the current status.

Second, even if current information on a variable is good, information on prior levels provides important information on the stability or trend of the sanction over time. If, for example, potential criminals are not risk neutral, then they will want information on the distribution of potential sanctions. Prior periods may provide such useful information. Moreover, past information on sanctions may provide useful information on trends in sanctions that may also be of value to a rational criminal.

In view of the implausibility of assuming that S_{t-1} affects S_t but not C_t, we do not believe that identification can be validly achieved in this way.

A single-crime-type, multiple-sanction model

Our focus has been on simple models in which only a single sanction and single-crime type are simultaneously related. We now turn to a model in

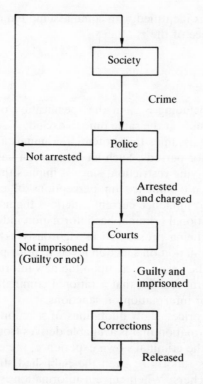

Figure 20.11 A simplified flow model of the criminal justice system.

which a single-crime type is simultaneously related to several sanction types.

In this model we attempt to capture some of the interrelationships between crime and the CJS subsystems – police, courts and corrections. These interrelationships derive from a model of the CJS put forward by Blumstein and Larson (1969) that characterizes the CJS as a flow process. A very simplified version of their conceptualization is shown in Figure 20.11.

Society generates crime, which is an input into the first of the pictured subsystems – the police. The police arrest suspects, some of whom are charged, while others are subsequently released without charge. The charged individuals are inputs to the courts subsystem. The courts in turn adjudicate the charges and some of those charged are found guilty and imprisoned, and turned over to the corrections subsystem. Others are not imprisoned, either because the charges do not lead to indictment or, if indicted, the indictment is dismissed or the defendant is acquitted – or, possibly, the defendant is convicted but not imprisoned. Finally, those individuals who are imprisoned are subsequently released to society either on parole or after having served their sentence.

The actions of each of the subsystems have implications for the possible penalties confronting a potential criminal; similarly, the amount of crime in the society has implications for the magnitudes of the flows through the subsystems.

In the models to be discussed, we attempt to capture these interrelationships between crimes and sanctions. Let us introduce the following notation:

C_t = total crimes in t
P_t^A = probability of apprehension and charge given a crime in t
$P_t^{G/A}$ = probability of conviction given charge in t
$P_t^{I/G}$ = probability of imprisonment given conviction in t
T_t = time served in period t
E_t^{Po} = police expenditures in t
E_t^J = judicial expenditures in t
E_t^{Pr} = prison expenditures in t
A_t = number of charges in t
G_t = number of convictions in t
I_t = number of imprisonments in t
U_t = prison utilization in period t
$\mu_t, \epsilon_t^i, v_t^i$ = random disturbances

$$C_t = f(P_t^A, P_t^{G/A}, P_t^{I/G}, T_t) + \mu_t \qquad \text{(20.8a)}$$

$$P_t^A = g_1(E_t^{Po}, C_t) + \epsilon_t^1 \qquad \text{(20.8b)}$$

$$P_t^{I/G} = g_3(E_t^{Pr}, G_t, U_t) + \epsilon_t^3 \qquad \text{(20.8d)}$$

since $A_t = P_t^A C_t$ (ignoring sampling variation)

$$P_t^{G/A} = g_2(E_t^J, P_t^A C_t) + \epsilon_t^2 \qquad \text{(20.8c')}$$

$$P_t^{I/G} = g_3(E_t^{Pr}, G_t, U_t) + \epsilon_t^3 \qquad \text{(20.8d)}$$

since $G_t = P_t^{G/A} P_t^A C_t$

$$P_t^{I/G} = g_3(E_t^{Pr}, P_t^{G/A} P_t^A C_t, U_t) + \epsilon_t^3 \qquad \text{(20.8d')}$$

$$T_t = g_4(E_t^{Pr}, U_t) + \epsilon_t^4 \qquad \text{(20.8e)}$$

$$E_t^{Po} = h_1(C_{t-1}, E_{t-1}^{Po}) + v_t^1 \qquad \text{(20.8f)}$$

$$E_t^J = h_2(A_{t-1}, E_{t-1}^J) + v_t^2 \qquad \text{(20.8g)}$$

$$E_t^{Pr} = h_3(U_{t-1}, E_{t-1}^{Pr}) + v_t^3 \qquad \text{(20.8h)}$$

A crucial feature of this model is the distinction among the different types of sanctions. By differentiating among such sanctions as the probability of apprehension and charge, the probability of conviction given charge, the probability of imprisonment given conviction, and time served given imprisonment, the effect of each type of sanction can, at least theoretically, be measured. Different categories of sanctions are possible and greater refinement in the number of sanction types could be made. The crucial point, however, is that, *a priori*, there are good reasons for believing that the magnitude of the deterrent effect associated with each sanction type may be different. For example, the disutility of a conviction given charge is likely to be greater than the disutility associated with charge, since the stigma of conviction is greater than that associated with only being charged.

The likelihood of differential deterrent effects associated with different sanctions has both important technical implications for estimation and significant policy implications. For the purpose of estimation, if two types of sanctions, for example P^A and $P^{G/A}$, have different effects, then it is inappropriate to estimate a single parameter for the conglomerate effect of $P^G = P^A P^{G/A}$. Further, from a policy perspective, we would not want to aggregate the two, since it may be useful to know the relative magnitudes of the separate effects. By comparing effects with costs, we can determine where resources should be allocated. If, for example, identical increases in expenditures on police and courts would achieve the same per cent increase in P_t^A and $P_t^{G/A}$, respectively, then crime reduction would be pursued more efficiently by allocating the additional expenditures to the sanction with the larger deterrent effect.

The second crucial feature of the system, which has significant implications for estimation, is the simultaneous relationship of C_t with each of the sanction variables, due perhaps to resource saturation considerations. Thus, given police resources, E_t^{Po} (which are themselves affected by the number of past crimes), the probability of arrest, P_t^A, depends on the current number of crimes, C_t, facing the police.[27] Further, although C_t only affects P_t^A directly, the levels of C_t also affect the workload of the courts and corrections subsystems 'downstream' from the police. The probability of conviction given charge, $P_t^{G/A}$, is likely to be affected by the workload of the courts, A_t, but A_t will be determined by the product of C_t and P_t^A. Since C_t is also hypothesized to be affected by $P_t^{G/A}$, $P_t^{G/A}$ and C_t will be simultaneously related.

Similarly, the probability of imprisonment given conviction, $P_t^{I/G}$, is affected by G_t, the number of convictions in t. Since G_t is the product of C_t, P_t^A, and $P_t^{G/A}$, $P_t^{I/G}$ is simultaneously related to C_t. Time served, T_t, and $P_t^{I/G}$ are also hypothesized to be affected by the utilization of prison capacity, U_t, because we expect utilization to have its predominant effect on judges and parole boards who most directly control the size of the prison population. Since U_t is affected by the size of the prison population, which is just the number of currently imprisoned criminals (and thus depends on C_t, P_t^A, $P_t^{G/A}$ and $P_t^{I/G}$), T_t will also be simultaneously related to C_t.

As the model is specified, none of the sanctions is in a direct simultaneous relationship with any other (e.g. P_t^A directly affects $P_t^{G/A}$, but $P_t^{G/A}$ does not directly affect P_t^A). In terms of the problem of identifying the crime function, the validity of this assumption about the interrelationship among the sanctions is not relevant; the model could be generalized to allow such direct simultaneous relationships without altering our conclusion about the identifiability of the crime function (Equation 20.8a).

The crime rate, C_t, is determined by four sanction variables, all of which are presumed to be simultaneously related to C_t. Therefore, at least four independent restrictions are necessary to identify the crime function. Four such restrictions are provided by the exclusion of E_t^{Po}. E_t^J, E_t^{Pr} and U_t (prison cell utilization).

The requirements for plausibly using these restrictions to identify the crime function have already been discussed. The key issues are worth restating. Since the expenditures variables are predetermined rather than exogenous (Equations 20.8f, g), it is dangerous to assume no serial correlation in the ϵ_t^i. Some more general assumptions about the nature of that serial dependence are necessary; whatever the explicit assumption, data with a time-series component will be needed. The restrictions involving the exclusion of the police expenditure variable, E_t^{Po} and U_t are particularly vulnerable to criticism, since being a measure of the intensity of the police presence in the community and the severity of punishment, respectively, it can be argued convincingly that each should also be included in the crime function. However, since the four restrictions are just-identifying and thereby necessary for estimation, we cannot test the validity of the restrictions involving E_t^{Po} and U_t, even assuming away the serial correlation problem just discussed.

In this multiple-sanction model, identification of the crime function requires the joint use of both the expenditures and cell-capacity identification restrictions, whereas in the one-sanction models, either one was sufficient to just-identify. The necessity of using both categories of restrictions to identify the crime function points to still another problem. As the number of endogenous sanctions increases, the difficulties in identifying the crime functions increase also. In the context of a multiple-crime-type model, which will be discussed next, this difficulty can become fatal to identification.

A multiple-crime-type, single-sanction model

Our discussion thus far has been limited to the consideration of single-crime-type models. We now consider the problem of identifying each of the crime equations in a multiple-crime-type model. A multiple-crime-type formulation is of interest, among other reasons, because different crime-types can have different impacts on CJS resources. An examination of their joint effect has important implications for identification.

A two-crime-type, single-sanction characterization of such a phenomenon is given below, along with the model's equivalent flow diagram, Figure 20.12.

$$C_t^1 = f_1(S_t^1) + \epsilon_t^1 \tag{20.9a}$$

$$C_t^2 = f_2(S_t^2) + \epsilon_t^2 \tag{20.9b}$$

$$S_t^1 = g^1(E_t, C_t^1, C_t^2, S_t^2) + \epsilon_t^3 \tag{20.9c}$$

$$S_t^2 = g^2(E_t, C_t^1, C_t^2, S_t^1) + \epsilon_t^4 \tag{20.9d}$$

$$E_t = h(E_{t-1}, C_{t-1}^1, C_{t-1}^2) + \epsilon_t^5 \tag{20.9e}$$

where:

C_t^i = crimes of type i per capita in t
S_t^i = sanctions per crime of type i and t
E_t = CJS expenditures in t.

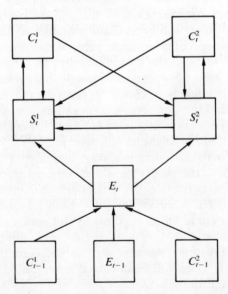

Figure 20.12 Flow diagram of multiple-crime-type, single-sanction model.

As indicated by Equations 20.9c, d, S_t^i is a function of total resources available to the CJS (E_t), the demands placed on these resources by each of the crime inputs $(C_t^i, i = 1, 2)$, and the level of the sanction imposed for the other crime type. The resource saturation theory would predict that increases in E_t would act to increase S_t^i $(\partial g^i/\partial E_t > 0)$, increases in the prevalence of either crime type would act to reduce S_t^i $(\partial g^i/\partial C_t^j < 0, j = 1, 2)$ and increases in S_t^j would decrease $S_t^i, i \neq j$ $(\partial g^i/\partial S_t^j < 0)$ because the additional resources required to increase S_t^j would be drawn from those used to maintain S_t^i.

Alternative theories of the effects of crime on sanctions might make different predictions, but the crucial point is that sanctions for each crime type are influenced by the level of both types of crime, because each crime type affects the common set of CJS resources.

Considering Equations 20.9a–d as the simultaneous system and treating E_t as predetermined by Equation 20.9c, the number of endogenous variables, M, is 4. Hence, at least three restrictions are necessary for the identification of each crime function. One such restriction is provided by the exclusion of E_t from Equations 20.9a and b under assumptions outlined previously. A second is provided by the assumption that crime of one type has no direct effect on crime of the other type. The final restriction necessary for identification of each crime function, however, rests additionally upon the assumption that sanctions for one crime type do not influence the level of crime for the other crime type (e.g. S_t^1 does not affect C_t^2). In the context of property crimes, (e.g. larceny and burglary), the possibility of such a cross-effect is quite conceivable and is indeed consistent with the basic principle that underlies the deterrence hypothesis – namely, that behavior is influenced by incentives.

If such cross-effects exist, then the two crime functions become:

$$C_t^1 = f^1(S_t^1, S_t^2) + \epsilon_t^1 \tag{20.9a$'$}$$

$$C_t^2 = f^2(S_t^1, S_t^2) + \epsilon_t^2 \tag{20.9b$'$}$$

These more general versions of the two crime functions are no longer identified; there are now only two, not three restrictions on them. Since estimation requires the imposition of three identification restrictions on each crime equation, identification would require that an additional restriction be imposed. For this simple two-crime-type, single-sanction model, the prison-cell utilization identification restriction might also be imposed.

This, however, is really only an illusory solution to the identification problem in a multi-crime-type setting. The addition of still another crime type (e.g. robbery) with S_t^3 affecting C_t^1, C_t^2 and C_t^3, and C_t^3 being affected by S_t^1, S_t^2 and S_t^3 would increase the number of endogenous variables (M) by two $(C_t^3$ and $S_t^3)$ but would increase the number of restrictions on each crime equation by only one (because C_t^3 does not directly affect C_t^1 or C_t^2). Hence we would have moved from a just-identified case of $M = 4$ with three restrictions to one of $M = 6$ with only four restrictions, and identification would fail. In general, identification of the crime functions in a multi-crime, single-sanction model seems even more difficult than in the single-crime-type case.

The difficulties in finding sufficient restrictions become even more acute when multiple sanctions are introduced into the model. If, for example, S_t^i were divided into the four sanction types discussed in the single-crime-type, multiple-sanctions model and the sanctions for each of the three crime types all had cross-effects on the other crime types, the number of endogenous variables would be 15. Thus, 12 identification restrictions would be required to estimate each of the crime functions, in addition to the automatic restrictions that only one type of crime appears in each such function.

In general, a model with n-crime types and m-sanction types would require $n \times m$ non-automatic restrictions to identify the crime functions. Hybrid versions of the model would require fewer additional restrictions. For example, one might plausibly assume that cross-effects only exist among subsets of crime types (perhaps distinguishing between property and violent crimes). From a practical perspective, however, such an approach offers little help since, for example, even a two-sanction model for the four index property crimes (i.e. robbery, burglary, larceny and auto theft) would require eight non-automatic restrictions to identify each of the separate crime functions.

In view of the difficulty in generating plausible restrictions, the estimation of the generalized multi-crime-type, multi-sanction model including cross-effects of the sanctions does not appear feasible. To the extent that the generalized model is viewed as the only plausible characterization of the simultaneous association between crime and sanctions, an argument as to the impossibility of valid identification is even more compelling than in the case of the simplified models discussed earlier.

The apparent infeasibility of identifying the generalized model hinges upon the assumption that the sanctions for C_t^i directly affect C_t^j. It may be that such cross-effects are, at most, very weak. The difficulty is that, using aggregate, non-experimental data, we cannot test for this. Moreover, a model estimated simply assuming no cross-effects would always remain suspect for having assumed that cross-effects are not operating.

Conclusion

Identication is the *sine qua non* of all estimation and especially of simultaneous equation estimation. It establishes the feasibility of determining the structure of a system from the data generated by that system. Without identification, estimation is logically impossible.

Researchers who have employed simultaneous estimation techniques to study the deterrent effect of sanctions on crime have failed to recognize fully the importance of this issue. The restrictions that they (implicitly or explicitly) use to gain apparent identification have little theoretical or empirical basis.

In this chapter we have examined a variety of plausible approaches to the identification of the crime functions in a system in which crime rates and sanction levels are simultaneously related. Our conclusions with regard to the feasibility of identification, while not wholly negative, are certainly soberly cautious. In particular, it appears very doubtful that work using only aggregate cross-sectional data can ever succeed in identifying and consistently estimating the deterrent effect of punishment on crime. If we are to know that effect and, particularly, if we are to rely on that knowledge for policy purposes, that knowledge must come from analyses of a different sort. In particular, analyses using aggregate non-experimental data must have a time-series component in the data (i.e. pure time-series or a time-series, cross-section), and the estimation procedures must account for the possibility of serial correlation in the stochastic components of the specification.

Technical note: lagged models of the mutual association of crime and sanctions

The principal focus of this chapter is the estimability of simultaneous models of crime and sanctions. In a simultaneous formulation, the mutual interaction is assumed to occur contemporaneously during the period of observation. For an observation period of a given length, a necessary requirement for a phenomenon to be simultaneous is that the impact of the actions taken by the system's actors (e.g. criminals and the CJS) be transmitted sufficiently fast so that each actor can react to the actions of the other actors within the observation period. Thus, a critical parameter is the length of the observation period. If the period is sufficiently short, then any mutual association can be modeled as non-simultaneous, whereas, if the period is sufficiently long, all such associations can be made simultaneous. In the context of the mutual association of crimes and sanctions, in which observations are generally made annually, the association is simultaneous if within a 1-year period potential criminals receive cues on the current level of sanctions being delivered by the CJS and if the level of crime in the current period also works to influence the sanctions delivered by the CJS.

If information does not flow this quickly, an alternative characterization of the mutual association involves lags. In the single-crime-type, single-sanction model, such a characterization could take the form

$$C_t = a + bS_{t-1} + \epsilon_t \qquad\qquad (20.10a)$$

$$S_t = c + dC_{t-1} + \mu_t \qquad\qquad (20.10b)$$

If the parameters of this model are to be estimated consistently by regression, the disturbances, ϵ_t and μ_t, must not be serially correlated.[28]

In our prior discussion, we elaborated upon the reasons for believing that there is, in fact, serial correlation. Hence, we would have very little confidence in any causal inferences drawn from parameter estimates that are generated by ordinary least squares.

Our pessimism about using regression is reinforced by the fact that in the simplest case, where there is only serial correlation in ϵ_t, the serial correlation will result in an overestimate of the deterrent effect of sanctions. Suppose that ϵ_t follows a first-order autoregressive process with parameter ρ. Let σ^2 denote the variance of ϵ_t. Additionally, assume that $d < 0$ (i.e. increases in C_{t-1} decrease S_t). Under these plausible conditions, if $\epsilon_{t-2} > 0$, then C_{t-2} will be larger than predicted by the structural component of Equation 20.10a. This larger-than-predicted value of C_{t-2} will drive down the value of S_{t-1}, since $d < 0$. In addition, since $\epsilon_{t-2} > 0$, ϵ_t will tend to be positive because $\mathrm{cov}(\epsilon_t, \epsilon_{t-2}) = \rho^2\sigma^2 > 0$. With $\epsilon_t > 0$, C_t would be larger than that predicted by the structural component of Equation 20.10a. We would then observe large values of C_t being associated with small values of S_{t-1}, even if $b = 0$. This negative association, however, would drive the estimate of b to a negative value.

Attempts to analyze models of the type given by Equations 20.10a and b have been limited to the sociological literature on deterrence (Logan 1975; Tittle and Rowe 1974). In these analyses, S_t is defined as arrests per crime. Tittle and Rowe found a negative and often significant path coefficient between S_{t-1} and C_t, a result that is consistent with the deterrence hypothesis, while Logan found no such association.

The path coefficient estimate of the association between S_{t-1}, and C_t is estimated in a way that is analytically equivalent to regression estimation of b in the model shown in Equation 20.10a. Therefore, these path coefficients suffer from all the ambiguities that we have discussed.

Models in which the mutual association between crime and sanctions occurs with a lag, however, are attractive because they offer an intuitively attractive characterization of this mutual association. Information on the sanctioning behavior of the CJS is probably transmitted very slowly through the kinds of cues that have been discussed. An assumption that information lag on sanctions is greater than a year may, therefore, be plausible in most instances.[29] Under such an assumption that C_t is a function of sanctions in prior periods, we could maintain the assumption that C_t affects S_t (e.g. C_{t-1} is replaced by C_t in Equation 20.10b), and the model would remain non-simultaneous – but there would still be a catch. For such a model to be consistently estimated by ordinary regression, there not only must be no serial correlation, but also ϵ_t and μ_t must be uncorrelated.

Thus, whatever the specific nature of the model employing a lagged structure, estimation must use methods that allow for the possibility of serial correlation and non-zero covariance in the stochastic terms if the estimated coefficients are to be plausibly regarded as an estimate of the causal effect of sanctions on crime.

Notes

1. The clearance rate is the proportion of reported crimes that are eventually 'solved'. In general, crimes are solved by the arrest of a suspect.
2. An offense is said to be 'unfounded' when

    (a) circumstances following the report show than no crime actually occurred (e.g. a reported theft is in fact a case of misplaced property) or

    (b) there is good reason to believe that no crime occurred (e.g. it is suspected that an offense is reported merely to implicate another individual in wrongdoing).

3. Private communication.
4. However, to the extent that identification problems arise, empirical evidence either way must be viewed with caution.
5. While this evidence is consistent with the 'toughening' hypothesis, in each case the sanction pertains either to sentences or to statutory definition. It is not clear that these official declarations materially alter the level of sanctions actually delivered (e.g. actual time served). If criminals react primarily to cues on actual sanctions, then the 'toughening' hypothesis would require evidence of a positive effect of crime on actual sanctions.
6. An estimator is said to be consistent if its probability limit exists and is the true parameter value. Intuitively, this is similar to saying that with a sufficiently large sample the parameter can be estimated with high probability with any desired precision. An estimator that is inconsistent will also, generally, be biased. The converse is often not the case.
7. The respective covariances of x_t with ϵ_t and y_t with u_t can be shown to be:

$$\sigma_{x\epsilon} = \frac{1}{1 - bd} [d\sigma_\epsilon^2 + \sigma_{u\epsilon}]$$

$$\sigma_{yu} = \frac{1}{1 - bd} [b\sigma_u^2 + \sigma_{u\epsilon}]$$

where

$\sigma_{x\epsilon}$ = covariance of x_t and ϵ_t
σ_{yu} = covariance of y_t and u_t
σ_ϵ^2 = variance of ϵ_t
σ_u^2 = variance of u_t
$\sigma_{u\epsilon}$ = covariance of u_t and ϵ_t

Since $\sigma_{x\epsilon} = 0$ and $\sigma_{yu} = 0$ are, respectively, necessary conditions for regression to produce consistent estimates of b and d, regression is an inappropriate estimation technique.

8. Ordinary least squares regression, however, remains inconsistent even though consistent estimators exist.

9. An assumption of $f > 0$ would do just as well; an assumption, however, of $f = 0$ would leave both equations unidentified as before.

10. If f is nearly equal to zero, then Equation 20.1b is still identified but there will be very little movement in the equilibrium over variations in T_t. Thus, it may be very difficult in practice to estimate Equation 20.1b.

11. However, other data generated in other ways (by experiment, for example) can be so used.

12. Indeed, in a complex model, such an observed negative association could occur even if neither direct effect is negative because of relations among the disturbance terms.

13. In his PhD dissertation, Ehrlich (1970) estimated a crime function that included the above unemployment, age and education variables and found a negative and generally significant association between crime rate and sanctions. This crime function was identified in part by the exclusion of the remaining variables listed above, a different but still apparently arbitrary set of identification restrictions.

14. Indeed, Ehrlich's own theoretical model specifies that unemployment in particular does have such an effect.

15. This is a necessary but not sufficient condition for identification. For a full discussion see Fisher (1966).

16. See Fisher (1966) for a complete discussion.

17. In the earlier discussion, $M = 2$ and $k = 0$; thus, we needed only one identification restriction.

18. Fisher (1961) shows that the magnitude of the inconsistency in parameter estimates is directly related to the degree of 'correctness' of the identification restrictions.

19. There do exist methods for testing an entire set of over-identifying restrictions symmetrically; however, such tests are not very strong as indications of which restrictions are incorrect. See Fisher (1966, Chapter 6).

20. Naturally, no model is likely to include all relevant SES variables. Omitted SES effects become part of the disturbance terms. We shall later discuss at length the behavior of omitted SES factors on these stochastic components of the model, since appropriate specification of such behavior is crucial to making consistent estimates of the parameters.

21. In this analysis, we assume for simplicity that all functions are linear. Non-linearities in the sanctions function can aid in identification, but only if one is sure of the functional form of the non-linearity and sure that similar non-linearities are not present in the crime equation. Such precise information on functional forms is seldom available and is certainly not so in this case. (See Fisher, 1966, Chapter 5, for extended discussion.) Later, we use expressions such as $f(\cdot)$ or $f(\cdot, \cdot)$ to denote functions not necessarily those of Equations 20.3.

22. It should be noted that if C_t does influence E_t directly, perhaps because the budget is adjusted in t in reaction to C_t, then E_t becomes determined simultaneously with C_t and S_t, and the crime function is no longer identified even if E_t does not appear in it. Some additional restrictions involving a non-endogenous variable are necessary.

23. To the degree that crime does influence K_t by leading to more prison-cell construction, that effect is longer-term, perhaps 5 to 10 years.

24. This model is clearly an oversimplification. In general, prison terms are often considerably longer than a year, so that the prison population is not solely a function of the current values of C_t, S_t and N_t but also depends on past incarcerations. This makes no essential difference to the points under discussion, however, save that past incarcerations could be used as an omitted predetermined variable in identifying the crime function under the assumption of no serial correlation.

25. The variable N_t is entered because C_t is expressed as crime per capita, while P_t is the total number of prisoners.

26. It might appear that we might separate $\ln (N_t/K_t)$ into two variables by writing $\ln (N_t/K_t) = \ln N_t - \ln K_t$ and then use the exclusion of both $\ln K_t$ and $\ln N_t$ from the crime equation to achieve not merely identification but over-identification. This apparent achieving of something for nothing does not succeed, however. Perhaps the easiest way to see this is to observe that the restrictions stating that both $\ln K_t$ and $\ln N_t$ do not appear in the crime equation can be written equivalently as the restriction that the coefficient of $\ln K_t$ in that equation is zero plus the restriction that the coefficient in that equation of $(-\ln N_t)$ is equal to that of $\ln K_t$. This latter restriction, however, is also satisfied in the sanctions equation and hence does not help at all in telling the two apart; if we used only that restriction we would not have identification. (This is an example of the fact referred to in a previous note that counting restrictions provides only a necessary, not a sufficient condition for identification.) To put it another way, $\ln K_t$ and $\ln N_t$ do not independently affect $\ln C_t$ and $\ln S_t$. There is only one piece of useful information to be gained from using them, not two.

27. In earlier sections, C_t was crimes per capita. Defining C_t as total crime instead of the crime rate would not affect our conclusion for this model; all state variables to be discussed, A_t, G_t, E_t^{Po}, E_t^{J} and E_t^{Pr} could be normalized by total population and thereby be redefined as rates.

28. The parameters of one of the equations could be consistently estimated if there is not serial correlation in that equation's disturbance. In general, however, if ϵ_t and μ_t are correlated either with their own past values or with each other's past values, consistency will not be present. In such general cases, the covariances of S_{t-1} and C_{t-1} with ϵ_t and μ_t will be complex expressions involving both the serial correlation behavior of ϵ_t and μ_t and their covariance.

29. In specific instances where official statements are published announcing changes in sanctioning practice (e.g. the case in which the District Attorney of San Francisco announced that prostitution would no longer be prosecuted), the assumption of a 1-year lag would be untenable.

References

Avio, K. and Clarke, S. (1974) 'Property Crime in Canada: An Econometric Study'. Prepared for the Ontario Economic Council.

Blumstein, A. and Cohen, J. (1973) A theory of the stability of punishment. *Journal of Criminal Law and Criminology* **64**(2):198–207.

Blumstein, A. and Larson, R. (1969) Models of a total criminal justice system. *Operations Research* **17**(2):199–232.

Blumstein, A., Cohen, J. and Nagin, D. (1976) The dynamics of a homeostatic punishment process. *Journal of Criminal Law and Criminology* **67**(3): 317–34.

Carr-Hill, R.A. and Stern, H.H. (1973) An econometric model of the supply and control of recorded offenses in England and Wales. *Journal of Public Economics* **2**(4):289–318.

Criminal Justice Bulletin (1976) Alabama Prison. Newsletter published by Anderson Editorial Services, Cincinnati.

Ehrlich, I. (1970) Participation in Illegitimate Activities: An Economic Analysis. Doctoral dissertation, Columbia University.

Ehrlich, I. (1973) Participation in illegitimate activities: a theoretical and empirical investigation. *Journal of Political Economy* **81**(3):521–67.

Ehrlich, I. (1975) The deterrent effect of capital punishment: a question of life and death. *American Economic Review* **65**(3):397–417.

Fisher, F.M. (1961) On the cost of approximate specification in simultaneous equation estimation. *Econometrica* **29**(2):139–70.

Fisher, F.M. (1966) *The Identification Problem in Econometrics*. New York: McGraw-Hill Book Company.

Gibbs, J.B. (1968) Crime, punishment and deterrence. *Southwestern Social Science Quarterly* **48**(4):515–30.

Gibbs, J.B. (1975) *Crime, Punishment and Deterrence*. New York: American Elsevier.

Greenberg, D. (1977) Crime, deterrence research and social policy. In Stuart Nagel, ed., *Modeling the Criminal Justice System*. Los Angeles: Sage Publications.

Logan, C. (1975) Arrest rates and deterrence. *Social Science Quarterly* **56**(3): 376–89.

McPheters, L., and Stronge, W.B. (1974) Law enforcement expenditures and urban crime. *National Tax Journal* **27**(4):633–44.

Sjoquist, D. (1973) Property crime and economic behavior: some empirical results. *American Economic Review* **83**(3):439–46.

Tittle, C. (1969) Crime rates and legal sanctions. *Social Problems* **16**(Spring): 408–28.

Tittle, C., and Rowe, A. (1974) Certainty of arrest and crime rates: a further test of the deterrence hypothesis. *Social Forces* **52**(4):455–62.

21

Empirically-based sentencing guidelines and ethical considerations (1983)

Introduction

The US Parole Board initiated the study of empirically-based guidelines to describe the decision rules it had been using implicitly. The board's purpose was to inform itself about the pattern of its own decisions. As a purely descriptive device, such a study has no ethical implications. Later the research emphasis shifted from parole to sentencing and to a more normative focus on what decisions should be. Nonetheless, the technology involved in developing empirically-based guidelines still bears a strong resemblance to the analysis of parole decisions. Ethical considerations in particular are avoided in these analyses.

This chapter examines the philosophy of empirically-based sentencing guidelines. The strong basic philosophy we pursue is to follow an empirically-based mode as far as we can, not because we are particularly attracted to the conservatism inherent in this line (whatever was done in the past must have been just, even if we cannot explain it), but because we find that surprisingly quickly our thoughts lead us to require new ethical judgments. Thus, in particular, we find that even when empirically-based guidelines are expected to do no more than reduce sentence disparity, some ethical judgment is required. If past decisions may have involved ethically irrelevant factors such as race, the purging of those factors, while possible, requires more than the judgment that they should be purged. Further ethical judgments are necessarily involved.

Written jointly with Joseph B. Kadane

The simplest case: no ethically irrelevant variables

Consider first the simplest case, in which sentences have in the past depended on a set of independent variables, all of which are believed to be ethically appropriate. Thus, for example, variables such as those describing seriousness of offense are appropriate in sentencing; variables such as race are not. We can represent this situation by the following equation:

$$S = \delta + R\alpha + \varepsilon \qquad (21.1)$$

where S is sentence length; R is a set of ethically relevant variables, α is a set of unknown slope parameters; δ is an unknown constant term; and ε is a random disturbance. (For ease of exposition, we deal for the present with the linear case only and restrict attention to sentence length as the variable to be determined.[1])

In this situation, if we suppose that the decisions of the past were ethically acceptable on the average, the justification for guidelines becomes the presence of the random disturbance, ε. That disturbance may involve factors affecting particular judges on particular days, or it may involve the factors peculiar to individual cases that lead judges to sentence differently.

There is an apparent tension here as to whether it is desirable that Equation 21.1 fit the data well or badly. If the equation fits badly, then apparently it will provide only an uncertain guide as to what past practice actually was. If the equation fits well, then the influence of the random term, ε, will be small and there will be little disparity to reduce.

In fact this apparent tension is not real, because there is a difference between how well the model fits and how closely the parameters δ and α are estimated. With large enough sample sizes or enough variation in the underlying data, it is quite possible to estimate α and δ with considerable precision while still having a large unexplained variance. In that case we could estimate average past behavior quite accurately but there would be considerable disparity in the sense of scatter around such average behavior. Note that this makes it particularly important not to use overall measures of goodness-of-fit such as R^2 as the sole or principal measures with which to assess the model. What really matters are the standard errors of the estimated parameters.[2]

If the parameters and thus past average behavior can be reliably estimated but there is considerable variation around that behavior, it may appear desirable to reduce that variation. This is the basic rationale for empirically-derived guidelines. It rests on the view that judges were correct in the past on the average but that judges themselves or society would wish to reduce the extent of individual variation around those averages. If the model has been correctly specified so that all the important variables affecting the sentencing decision have been included, and if all these variables are ethically relevant ones, this may be an appealing view, provided disparity is high. While some room for individual factors and individual judgment will always be necessary, it may seem reasonable to require judges explicitly to justify any large departures from the systematic collective wisdom.

In the context of this model, this is easy to do in principle. The process of estimating Equation 21.1 will also estimate σ^2, the variance of ε. We denote that estimate by σ^{*2}. Now choose a constant, k. Judges will be required to write an explicit justification of their actions whenever their sentence does not lie within $k\sigma^*$ of the estimated average sentence for the particular value of R present in the case decided. The predicted sentence is

$$S^* = \delta^* + R\alpha^* \qquad\qquad (21.2)$$

where asterisks denote estimates.

How should k be chosen? Given the distribution of ε (which can be approximated from the data), a choice of k is equivalent in the above procedure to requiring that judges write explicit justifications for cases that fall farther away from the average sentence than some stated fraction (e.g. 90 per cent) of cases would have done in the past. What fraction should be chosen depends on the extent to which one wishes to reduce disparity in this way. While such a choice depends in part on what one sees as the source of past disparity, it is also an ethical choice.

This is perhaps seen most easily by considering the following. There is no intrinsic reason why upward departures from avarage sentencing behavior (harsh sentences) and downward departures (lenient sentences) should be treated identically. One might, depending on one's ethical views, choose different values of k, say k_1 and k_2, for the two different types of departures, using a smaller value when departures are considered worse. Plainly, the choice of such values depends on ethical considerations; those considerations cannot be avoided by restricting the choice to $k_1 = k_2$ and treating both kinds of departures symmetrically.

Before moving into more complicated cases, one point is worth making. Using models in this way requires that the model be either correct or a close approximation. (It also requires that it be estimated using the best available practice.) If, in particular, variables are wrongly omitted from Equation 21.1 that are correlated with those included, the estimated effects will be wrong and the guidelines misleading. This will be particularly important if the omitted variables are ethically irrelevant.

To take a leading example, suppose that the true model is not Equation 21.1 but rather

$$S = \delta + R\alpha + I\beta + \varepsilon \tag{21.3}$$

where I is a single ethically irrelevant variable that, for purposes of focusing discussion, we will take to be a dichotomous variable indicating race (with $I = 0$ for Blacks and $I = 1$ for Whites). Suppose also that among the variables in R are one or more that are correlated with race. To fix ideas, suppose the variable in question is a measure of prior record. Then mistaken estimation of Equation 21.1 instead of Equation 21.3 when race has actually mattered directly in the past will lead to erroneous estimation of α. Furthermore, the derived guidelines will build in the ethically irrelevant effect of race by giving (in the simplest case) an inappropriate coefficient to prior record (among other things). In other words, such misspecification will lead to those with longer prior records being given long sentences not simply because of the effect of prior records tend to be black. Past racism will be incorporated in the guidelines and the resulting coefficients will be biased in more than one sense.

Other misspecifications will lead to a number of less dramatic results. In the limiting case in which the omitted variables are not correlated with any of the included ones, such omission will not lead to biased estimates of the parameters that describe average behavior. It will, however, lead to inefficient estimates of those parameters. In addition, the effects of such omitted variables will be attributed to disparity, whereas they may represent not random occurrences but precisely those explicable case-by-case variations that one would not wish to reduce.

Plainly, correct specification is very important. Whether we know enough to achieve it is a separate question. .

The presence of a single ethically irrelevant variable: the linear case

We now face directly the question of what to do in the situation of Equation 21.3, in which an ethically irrelevant variable such as race has influenced past decisions. (For ease of exposition we begin with the case of only one such variable, treating the more complex case below.) We have already seen how *not* to treat such a case – one must not delete the ethically irrelevant variable from the equation being estimated. A positive prescription is now required.

The problem can be posed as follows. The justification for empirically-based guidelines lies in the view that the collective decisions of the past represent, on average, an ethically desirable standard. In the present case, however, that is manifestly untrue; such decisions, by assumption, were contaminated by the use of an ethically irrelevant criterion, race, to affect sentence length. Is it possible to purge past decisions of that contaminating effect and to use the purged estimates to inform future decisions through the construction of guidelines?

The answer is 'yes' but the accomplishment of this task necessarily involves another ethical choice. Begin by estimating Equation 21.3 (in the simplest case by multiple regression). This yields estimates of δ, α, and β which we denote by asterisks. Note that α^*, in particular, is an estimate of the effects of the ethically relevant variables, R, *with the effect of race held constant*. In terms of the example used above, this procedure estimates the effect of longer prior record given race – an effect uncontaminated by the fact that Blacks tend to have longer records than do Whites. This is useful information, for it tells us (in this linear model) what the average difference in sentence was between offenders with good and those with bad records independent of race.[3] If we can decide on the base level of sentence in the guidelines for one case, then we can use the estimates to derive levels for others.

This can be described in an equivalent but perhaps more revealing way. Suppose that we estimate Equation 21.3 as described. We can then go on to use the estimated equation as determining the average sentence to be used in the guidelines and purge it of the racial effects by choosing a value for I, say I', to be used for future cases of whatever race. The average sentence used in the guidelines for cases with characteristics represented by R will then be

$$S^* = \delta^* + R\alpha^* + I'\beta^* \tag{21.4}$$

The effect of changes in R will then be measured by α^* so that the choice of I' is equivalent to the choice of a base level as above.

How should that choice be made? This is an inescapable ethical decision. To see this, consider what different choices of I' imply. To choose any value of I' is to treat all offenders in a racially neutral way but the particular choice determines how they should be treated. Thus, to choose $I' = 0$ for guideline construction is to treat later offenders on average as Blacks were treated previously. To choose $I' = 1$ is to treat them as Whites were treated previously. To choose $I' = \frac{1}{2}$ is to treat them as getting exactly the average of previous Black and White treatment. This is an essentially ethical choice that cannot be made simply by referring to the average of past experience.[4]

However I' is chosen, note that the choice of k as in the simplest case will make judges explicitly justify departures that cannot be accounted for by random variation in more than a corresponding fraction of the cases. This will force any judges who still use race in an important way to make explicit justification.

Non-linearities and more than one ethically irrelevant variable

This same analysis readily extends to the case in which the relationship to be estimated is non-linear. Suppose that Equation 21.3 is replaced by

$$S = F(R, I, \varepsilon) \tag{21.5}$$

where $F(\cdot, \cdot, \cdot)$ is some function, and we continue with a single dichotomous ethically irrelevant variable, I, for the moment (and continue the race example to fix ideas).

Noting that I still takes on the values of either zero or one, we can represent this equivalency in a different way. Define

$$\begin{aligned} F^0(R, \varepsilon) &\equiv F(R, 0, \varepsilon) \\ F^1(R, \varepsilon) &\equiv F(R, 1, \varepsilon) \end{aligned} \tag{21.6}$$

Then for either of the two possible values of I,

$$F(R, I, \varepsilon) = (1 - I)F^0(R, \varepsilon) + IF^1(R, \varepsilon) \tag{21.7}$$

This corresponds to the general case in which the sentencing behavior of judges is allowed to be completely different for Blacks from that for Whites – complete interaction; the linear case considered above is a special case of this.

In this circumstance we once again estimate the full descriptive model of sentencing behavior, Equation 21.7. This is then purged of racial effects by applying the model for a given choice of I, say I', to all future cases. The form of Equation 21.7 now makes it apparent that the choice of I' is equivalent to the necessarily ethical choice of what average between former Black and former White cases is to be used. A choice of $I' = 0$ treats all offenders as if they were Black; a choice of $I' = 1$ treats them as if they were White; a choice between zero and one determines an average.[5]

Note that this interpretation depends on the dichotomous nature of I. If I were a continuous variable we would estimate Equation 21.5 directly. A choice of I' to use in the estimated version of Equation 21.5 would then still be an ethical choice but, except in special cases, it would not correspond to a simple averaging of sentences previously given for various values of I.

If more than one ethically irrelevant variable has mattered in the past, more than one ethical choice (in addition to the choice of k above) must be made. Thus consider the case of two such variables that we take to be dichotomous. Suppose that I_1 now represents race as above and I_2 represents whether there was a guilty plea (assuming this to be ethically irrelevant) with $I_2 = 0$ denoting no such plea and $I_2 = 1$ denoting such a plea. Rewrite Equation 21.5 as

$$S = F(R, I_1, I_2, \varepsilon) \qquad\qquad (21.8)$$

Define

$$F^{00}(R, \varepsilon) \equiv F(R, 0, 0, \varepsilon)$$
$$F^{01}(R, \varepsilon) \equiv F(R, 0, 1, \varepsilon)$$
$$F^{10}(R, \varepsilon) \equiv F(R, 1, 0, \varepsilon)$$
$$F^{11}(R, \varepsilon) \equiv F(R, 1, 1, \varepsilon) \qquad\qquad (21.9)$$

Then, similar to the construction in Equation 21.7, for the possible values of I_1 and I_2, we can write

$$\begin{aligned}
F(R, I_1, I_2, \varepsilon) = {}& (1 - I_1)(1 - I_2)F^{00}(R, \varepsilon) \\
& + (1 - I_1)I_2 F^{01}(R, \varepsilon) \\
& + I_1(1 - I_2)F^{10}(R, \varepsilon) \\
& + I_1 I_2 F^{11}(R, \varepsilon) \qquad\qquad (21.10)
\end{aligned}$$

That is, there are separate relationships allowed for Blacks not pleading guilty, Blacks pleading guilty, Whites not pleading guilty and Whites pleading guilty.

The construction of empirically-based guidelines now proceeds by estimating Equation 21.10 and choosing *two* values, I'_1 and I'_2, to be used in the estimated equation that results. These choices, necessarily ethical, determine the weights to be used in averaging the previous average sentences of the four groups in guidelines to be used for all future offenders.

Note, however, that there are only two choices to be made, not more than two, despite the fact that four groups are to be averaged. This corresponds to the fact that the weights used to average the guilty plea and not-guilty plea groups must be the same for Blacks as for Whites if race is to play no role in the use of the guidelines. Equivalently, the weights used to average the Black and White groups must be the same for those pleading guilty as for those not pleading guilty if the presence or absence of a guilty plea is to play no role in the use of the guidelines.

Where n ethically irrelevant variables are involved, n ethical choices must be made. If n is large, even though *only* n such choices must be made, the view that guidelines can or should be based on past behavior rather than constructed directly from ethical or societal considerations loses much of its force, although the estimated a coefficients may still help to inform decisions.

Conclusion

We are uncomfortable with the whole enterprise of empirically-based sentencing guidelines, for several reasons. First, they are by their nature unthoughtfully conservative. What is past may be prologue, but it is surely not unswervingly just. We prefer guidelines that arise from ethical principles, deducing the shape of the guidelines from those principles, as was done in Minnesota.

Second, taking empirically-based guidelines on their own terms leads us to require ethical judgments: For example, shall we treat Blacks as we used to treat Whites, or conversely, or use an average? We anticipate that ethical experts might say 'neither' and propose a different punishment schedule entirely, but this would lead back to a Minnesota-type approach.

Finally, there is the matter of implementation. These procedures assume that the model is correctly specified. Incorrect specification can lead to reintroduction of racial bias and other kinds of substantial injustice. We should add that correct specification is very difficult to achieve.

In conclusion, empirically-based sentencing guidelines strike us as a species of computer-driven conservatism. They do not avoid hard ethical questions, and they mislead those who would construct guidelines by substituting statistical sophistication, which is useful but not essential, for ethical sophistication, which is critical.

Notes

1. For convenience of notation we have not written out terms such as $R\alpha$. The reader is free to think of R as a single variable. The more general case would have

$$R\alpha = \alpha_1 R_1 + \alpha_2 R_2 + \ldots + \alpha_k R_k$$

2. For a discussion of this and similar issues see Chapter 23.
3. Although prior record is itself a composite of several variables, we ignore this for simplicity of exposition.
4. Note, in particular, that a choice of I' to generate the same average sentence length for all cases in the sample as actually occurred builds in a judgment that such an average was 'right' despite the fact that it was influenced by the racial mix of cases in the sample. To attempt to set I' empirically by estimating I' together with α and δ to give the best fit in the sample is even worse. It can be shown to be equivalent to leaving race out of the estimated equation altogether (by absorbing $I'\beta$ into δ, the constant term), the case of misspecification considered above.

   There may be other ways to correct for the effects of race. For example, in a rather extreme form of affirmative action, one might wish to take account of the fact that Blacks are discriminated against elsewhere. Such discrimination can mean that Blacks have a worse prior record or are more likely to be unemployed than Whites. One can imagine correcting variables such as prior record or unemployment by regressing them on race, then giving those variables in Equation 21.4 the values they would have on the average if the offender were White, or the values they would have if the offender were Black, or some other common value. This would involve a correction for race more extreme than simply a uniform value for I' and would be likely to lead to wholesale reliance on regression rather than to analysis of individual offender characteristics.

5. Note that choices outside the range of (0, 1) are also possible. This would mean treating all offenders better than Whites were treated in the past or all offenders worse than Blacks were treated in the past (assuming discrimination to have been against Blacks). To do so is to depart fairly sharply from the notion that past judgments are ethically acceptable, however – the view that lies behind empirically-based guidelines.

22

Janis Joplin's yearbook and the theory of damages (1990)

Introduction: Making the plaintiff whole

The trial on liability is over, and the plaintiff has won. Now the question of the amount of damages arises. There is more than one standard that can be used here. For example, one might award damages to punish the defendant or to deter other prospective offenders. A commonly used standard in civil cases, however, is that of making the plaintiff 'whole' in the sense of exact compensation – placing him, her or it in the position that would have been occupied had the violation not taken place. Even where additional damages are to be awarded (trebling in antitrust cases, for example, or punitive damages generally), the trier of fact is often called upon to calculate the amount of compensatory damages.

Some questions arise as to how this should be done – questions not only difficult in practice but interesting in principle. Most (not all) of these stem from the fact that trials take time, so the damage award will be made long after the violation that caused the damages. In particular, to what extent should the defendant be compensated for the time value of money between the injury and the award?[1] In deciding on the award,

Written jointly with R. Craig Romaine. While this chapter is largely based on work done over the last few years, the occasion for writing it came when I was invited to a conference to discuss the paper by R.F. Lanzillotti and A.K. Esquibel, 'Measuring damages in commercial litigation: present value of lost opportunities', (Lanzillotti and Esquibel 1990). The present chapter evolved in part from that discussion. I am grateful for the invitation and hope to be forgiven for producing a related article rather than a discussion as such.

should the trier of fact use the benefit of hindsight? This chapter considers these and related issues.[2]

The rate of prejudgment interest[3]

We begin with a simple case. The violation took place at a single point of time, time 0. It involved the destruction of an asset whose value at that time is clearly known as Y. Hence, had damages been assessed at time 0, an award of Y would have made the plaintiff whole. Unfortunately, however, the processes of justice take time, and the award is to be made at time $t > 0$. How (if at all) should the plaintiff be compensated for this fact?

At first glance, it may seem that the plaintiff is entitled to interest at its opportunity cost of capital, r. After all, had the plaintiff received Y at time 0, it would have invested the funds, receiving presumably its average rate of return. Hence, by time t, the plaintiff would have had Ye^{rt}, so this is the amount that would make it whole. Another version of this argument would compensate the plaintiff at the rate it reasonably expected to earn on the destroyed asset.

The fallacy here (in either version) has to do with risk. The plaintiff's opportunity cost of capital includes a return that compensates the plaintiff for the average risk it bears. But, in depriving the plaintiff of an asset worth Y at time 0, the defendant also relieved it of the risks associated with investment in that asset. The plaintiff is thus entitled to interest compensating it for the time value of money, but is not also entitled to compensation for the risks it did not bear. Hence prejudgment interest should be awarded at the risk-free interest rate, $r^* < r$.

One can see the problem with awarding interest at the plaintiff's opportunity cost of capital by considering the following example. The same defendant destroys two identical assets belonging to two different plaintiffs, Hetty and Ravenal. Hetty is extremely risk-averse and only invests in government bonds. Ravenal, on the other hand, invests in high-risk ventures. On average, Hetty earns a low rate of return, while Ravenal earns a high one. Naturally, those returns have different distributions: Hetty always earns the same rate on every investment, while Ravenal earns a very high rate on a few investments and loses money on most others.

In this situation, it cannot be right to award Ravenal a higher amount than Hetty just because of the passage of time and their different investment strategies. Had the award been made at time 0, they would each have been awarded the same amount. To give Ravenal more than Hetty at time t is to forget that his higher average rate of return compensates him for the risk associated with his investments. It is made up of even higher returns on successful ventures and negative returns on unsuccessful ones. The asset destroyed might perfectly well have been employed in an unsuccessful venture; that risk has not been borne.[4]

To vary the example, suppose that Hetty is a prudent investor, while Ravenal is a (very rich) compulsive gambler who always loses and would, by time t, have frittered away the asset. It cannot be right to award Hetty positive interest and award Ravenal nothing at all. In this case, Ravenal's negative returns are the price he pays for indulging his tastes for hopeless risk. He was surely not able to indulge those tastes with the asset in question; hence, he should not have to pay the price. The same general principle applies to less extreme examples with positive returns: the plaintiff should not be compensated (positively or negatively) for risks he or she did not bear.

The paper by Patell *et al.* (1982) agrees with this principle but reaches a different conclusion. It points out that the defendant's actions did not relieve the plaintiff of all risk. Even assuming that the outcome of the trial was certain, the plaintiff bore the risk that the defendant would go bankrupt before paying the damage award. Therefore, the authors argue, the plaintiff is entitled to interest that reflects that risk, interest at the rate paid by the defendant on its own bonds.

This position raises two problems. First, even corporations cannot borrow unlimited amounts at fixed rates.[5] If the value of the asset destroyed was beyond the ability of the defendant to borrow, it is not clear what should be done if one adopts the principle of Patell *et al.*

More fundamental than this is the second problem. The risk of the defendant's bankruptcy is not the only risk the plaintiff bears. It also bears the risk of losing the case. Moreover, the plaintiff has borne the expense of litigation. Truly to place the plaintiff in the same position as if the violation had not occurred would involve recompensing for all litigation risks and costs. In the US system, however, this is not usually done. We choose to distribute the risks and costs of litigation differently than do some foreign countries. But the risk that the defendant will go bankrupt during trial is properly associated with the risks of litigation, not with the violation itself. It is hard to see why that risk should be singled out as one for which the plaintiff is to be compensated. Accordingly, we retain the position that prejudgment interest should be awarded at the risk-free rate.

The treatment of taxes

It is important to realize, however, that the appropriate risk-free rate to use must take account of tax effects, as must the entire damage calculation. Making the plaintiff whole must mean making them whole after taxes, remembering that the damage award is taxable[6] as would have been lost profits and the interest earned thereon. (Naturally, one must account for the possibility that no taxes would in fact have been due.)

The simplest case to handle (and the only one to which we shall give explicit treatment) is that in which the effective tax rate paid by the plaintiff would not have been affected had the award been made in year 0 and will not be affected by the payment of the award in year t. (More complex cases do not present any interesting new matters of principle.)

For $0 \leq i \leq t$, let θ_i be the effective tax rate in year i, and r_i^* be the before-tax risk-free rate (the rate on treasury bills, say) in that year. Had the award of Y been made in year 0 (coinciding with the damage itself), the plaintiff would have paid taxes on it, invested the remainder at the risk-free rate, r_i^*, and paid taxes on the resulting earnings. The net after-tax interest that would have been retained would therefore have been at the after-tax risk-free rate, which we denote by $\hat{r}_i^*$ where:

$$\hat{r}_i^* \equiv r_i^*(1 - \theta_i) \tag{22.1}$$

Let

$$\hat{Y} \equiv Y(1 - \theta_0) \tag{22.2}$$

be the after-tax dollars that would have been retained by the plaintiff in year 0 had the award been made then. Evidently, the plaintiff's net after-tax position would be in year t:

$$\hat{S} = Y(1 - \theta_0) \prod_{i=0}^{t} (1 + \hat{r}_i^*) \tag{22.3}$$

The before-tax award that results in this after-tax amount is

$$S = \hat{S}/(1 - \theta_t) \tag{22.4}$$

Note that if the effective tax rate is the same at times 0 and t, then, when Equation 22.2 is substituted into Equations 22.3 and 22.4, the term in $(1 - \theta_0)$ will be cancelled by the division in Equation 22.4. Nevertheless, this does not mean that there are no tax effects. The result in that case is equivalent to allowing the before-tax loss of Y to accumulate interest at the after-tax risk-free rate, $\hat{r}_i^*$.

Discounting the stream of lost profits

So far, we have assumed that the damage-producing act consists of the destruction of an asset of known value, Y. In practice, this is not likely to be the case. Rather it is very often the case that the violation removed the opportunity to earn a stream of profits. In the recently concluded *ETSI* case[7], for example, plaintiffs claimed that the actions of the defendant railroads had prevented them from building a pipeline with which to transport coal in slurry form from Wyoming to the Southwest. Damages were claimed for the lost stream of profits that the pipeline would have earned.

As this example illustrates, there is no difference in principle between a claim for a stream of lost profits and a claim for the destruction of an asset. An asset is in fact worth the present value of the profit stream associated with it; to turn the matter around, the possession of a profit stream is the possession of an asset worth the present value of that stream. Hence our previous treatment applies to such cases.

To stop here, however, would be to overlook some subsidiary matters of vital practical importance. How is one to determine the profit stream to be discounted? Further, what discount rate should be used in doing the discounting? These questions are related, but we begin by focusing on the latter question.

If we consider the loss of a profit stream that would have started at time 0 to be the same as the loss of an asset at time 0, then we must begin by valuing the asset as of that time. The fact that the award will be made at time $t > 0$ can than be taken into account as already discussed.

Accordingly, having decided on an expected profit stream as seen from time zero (this is discussed below), we must discount that stream, not with a risk-free rate, but with a discount rate that includes a risk premium suitable to the risks involved. If the venture that was injured was similar to others undertaken by the plaintiff, then the plaintiff's correctly measured cost of capital as of the time of violation will be the appropriate rate to use here.[8] Otherwise, a different measure will be needed.

Maintaining the same tax assumptions and notation as before, let M_i denote the value of the before-tax lost profits that would have been earned in year i. Let r denote the value of the appropriate discount rate to be used in discounting after-tax cash flows. (Note that both the discount rate and the tax rate are taken as of time 0 to reflect the plaintiff's reasonable expectations as of that date. The issues involved in doing this are discussed below.)

The difference between this case and that already considered lies in the fact that the term $\hat{Y}$ in Equation 22.3 will not be given by Equation 22.2 with Y known, but rather by:

$$\hat{Y} = \sum_{i=0}^{\infty} M_i(1 - \theta_0) \left[1/(1 + r) \right]^i \tag{22.5}[9]$$

Note the major implication here. Lost profits for year i (the difference between 'but-for' and actual profits in year i) are not considered to be awarded as of year i and then allowed to accumulate interest. Rather, they are first discounted back to the date of violation, year 0, using a risk-adjusted post-tax discount rate. They then accumulate interest at the *risk-free* post-tax rate from year 0 to year t when the award is made.

Since the risk-adjusted rate will generally be considerably higher than the risk-free rate, this difference in treatment can amount to a very substantial difference in result, with the difference becoming larger the longer the damage award is delayed. In the *ETSI* case, for example, the plaintiff offered a calculation for a damage award to be made in 1988 (contingent on a finding of liability) as compensation for an injury suffered in 1984. Lost profits in each year were taken to be awarded as of that year and then allowed to accumulate interest (though not at the risk-free after-tax rate, as we have suggested). Compared to the calculation given by Equations 22.3, 22.4 and 22.5, the plaintiff's result overstated the damage award by as much as 100 per cent![10]

Continuing violations

So far, we have consistently assumed that the violation involved is a one-time affair resulting in the destruction of an asset or, equivalently, the loss of an opportunity. Very often, however, violations are more complex than this. Damages can result from on-going violations, from a stream of acts lasting over time. We must now consider how our analysis should be adapted to deal with such cases.

Fortunately, this is easily done in principle, although practice may often prove more difficult. We can consider each violation as a new act and award damages and interest according to the principles already given. More precisely, we must deal with a whole set of but-for worlds: the world with no violation; the world with violations ending at time 1; at time 2; and so forth.

Adapting our previous notation, we assume that the violations began at time 0 and ended at time $s \le t$. Let $\hat{G}(i, j)$ denote the after-tax profits that would have been earned at time i had there been no violations later than j ($\hat{G}(i, -1)$ denotes after-tax profits in the no-violation world.) Let r_i denote the risk-adjusted discount rate appropriate to after-tax cash flows from the plaintiff's projects as of time j and $\hat{r}_k^*$ denote the after-tax risk-free rate as of time k.

Each time period's violation brings with it (in principle) a continuing stream of lost profits. The undiscounted after-tax lost profits which occur in year i as a result of violations in year j are given by

$[\hat{G}(i, j - 1) - \hat{G}(i, j)]$. In accordance with the previous analysis, such profits are to be discounted back to the time of violation at j using the risk-inclusive rate and then compounded forward to t using the risk-free rate. This makes the total amount of the damage award after taxes:

$$\hat{S} = \sum_{j=0}^{s} \sum_{i=j}^{\infty} \frac{[\hat{G}(i, j - 1) - \hat{G}(i, j)]}{(1 + r_j)^{i-j}} \prod_{k=j+1}^{t} (1 + \hat{r}_k^*) \qquad (22.6)$$

The before-tax award is made by adjusting $\hat{S}$ to obtain S as in Equation 22.4 above.

Despite its complex appearance, this rule is really quite simple in principle. The change in the profit stream brought about by each violation is discounted back to the time of that violation and then compounded forward at the risk-free rate.

In practice, however, this is likely to be impractical. It is hard enough to estimate lost profits in a single but-for world. The task of doing so for s different but-for worlds differing by the date of assumed cessation of violations can easily be overwhelming.

There are several things to be said about this, however. First, the practical importance of making such estimates depends on the amount of carry-over effect that previous violations have on later profits. If cessation of violation would have returned the profit stream to that of the no-violation world in, say, m periods, then $\hat{G}(i, j - 1) = \hat{G}(i, -1)$ $= \hat{G}(i, j)$ for $j \leq i - m$. If m is small, then most of the terms in Equation 22.6 will be zero.

Note, in particular, that if cessation of violation would have instantly restored the no-violation profit stream ($m = 1$), then Equation 22.6 takes the much simpler form:

$$\hat{S} = \sum_{j=0}^{s} [\hat{G}(j, -1) - \hat{G}(j, j)] \prod_{k=j+1}^{t} (1 + \hat{r}_k^*) \qquad (22.7)$$

In this case, only one but-for world need be constructed – that in which no violations took place. Actual profits earned in year j are subtracted from the profits that would have been earned in that year in the no-violation world and the result brought forward from j to t by compounding at the risk-free rate.

It is also useful to note that the deviations from this relatively simple rule that occur in more complex cases are entirely due to discounting and compounding. If all the discount rates in Equation 22.6 were zero, then the terms corresponding to a given i would simply sum to $[\hat{G}(i, -1)$ $- \hat{G}(i, s)]$, the difference between profits in the no-violation world and actual profits.

Accordingly, we recommend that in practice the simple rule given in Equation 22.7 be followed. If there are small carry-over effects of previous violations, then some adjustment for discounting should be made. For example, if some fraction, g, of lost profits in year $j + 1$ can reasonably be associated with violations ending in year j, then lost profits up to $s + 1$ should be adjusted by discounting that same fraction, g, of them for one year by the risk-including rate and compounding them forward for one more year at the risk-free rate. While g will seldom be knowable, it may be reasonable to place an upper bound on it. If the upper bound is small, the effects of the adjustment involved can be readily limited, particularly because effectively only the difference between the two discount rates matters.

Naturally, such a recommendation would not apply to cases in which a major violation occurred early and would have had long-lasting effects even had there been no further violations.

Using hindsight: Janis Joplin's yearbook

Most of the analysis so far given has begged an important question. How should one estimate the stream of lost profits to be discounted? In particular, should one use hindsight, estimating what *would* have happened had there been no violation, or should one instead use only such information as was available when the violation took place? Where there are few carry-over effects from a particular violation, this issue does not matter. Where carry-over effects are large and long-lasting, it can matter very much. Since, as discussed in the preceding section, on-going violations are likely best to be treated without much adjustment for carry-over effects, the hindsight problem is most likely to be important in practice in the case of a single violation destroying an asset.[11] We now return to that case.

We have already implicitly indicated our answer to the question at issue. In choosing a discount rate with which to calculate the present value of the stream of returns associated with the destroyed asset, we chose the plaintiff's opportunity cost of capital (or other rate associated with the riskiness of the stream) *as of the time of violation*. Similarly, we used the tax rate prevailing as of that time. (See Equation 22.5, above.) If hindsight were to be used to estimate the stream of returns, there would be no reason not also to use actual discount rates and tax rates as they developed over time.

As this suggests, our position is that hindsight should not be used.[12] Rather, the stream of returns should be estimated using the information available as of the time of violation. Indeed, as we shall see, expectations as of that time are particularly relevant.

There is, of course, no question but that had the plaintiff been made whole as of the time of violation, time 0, the destroyed asset would have been valued as of that time and the plaintiff paid accordingly. The question at issue only arises because this did not happen, and the plaintiff is to be made whole as of time t, a later date.

But we have already discussed this issue. The fact that the plaintiff is to be made whole as of t means that it must be recompensed for the time value of money. This means interest at the risk-free rate on the time 0 award. Why should it mean any adjustment in the award principle itself? The reason that one might be tempted to make such an adjustment is as follows. Had the plaintiff actually not been deprived of the destroyed asset, it would have experienced a particular stream of returns. Hence, if we can tell what that stream would have been, the plaintiff can best be made whole by giving it that stream with an appropriate adjustment for interest.

This argument is wrong. The violation did not merely deprive the plaintiff of the stream of returns that would have accompanied the asset. It also relieved the plaintiff of the uncertainty surrounding that stream. To use hindsight is to ignore the latter effect. As already explained, the way in which both effects can be taken into account is to value the asset as of the time of violation, taking account of uncertainty, and then award the time value of money making no allowance for uncertainty.

Some simple examples will illustrate what is involved. The first – and the one to which we shall return – is a somewhat simplified version of a hypothetical question posed to me in a deposition in the *ETSI* case.[13] The case was to be tried by a jury in Beaumont, Texas, adjacent to the town of Port Arthur.

Janis Joplin, the rock star, went to high school in Port Arthur, Texas. Suppose that when she graduated she signed one copy of her high-school yearbook. Suppose further that nobody had any idea that Ms Joplin would one day be famous. Assume that signed high-school yearbooks were being bought and sold for $5.00 in Port Arthur, regardless of whose signatures they contained.

Assume that a thief stole and destroyed the copy of the yearbook with Janis Joplin's signature. The legal proceedings that followed took considerable time, and, by the time a damage award is to be made, Janis Joplin is known to have been a star, with her autograph selling for $1,000. Ignoring punitive issues (and assuming that the yearbook has no sentimental value), what damage award will make the plaintiff (the book's owner) whole?

The temptation, of course, is to use hindsight and award $1,000. The other answer – $5.00 plus interest at the risk-free rate – seems somehow very unfair. That perception is incorrect, however, and the temptation ought to be resisted.

The book's owner was not deprived of a yearbook containing the autograph of a rock star. He or she was deprived of a yearbook plainly worth $5.00 that contained one or more signatures. Associated with that yearbook was uncertainty as to whether any of the autographs it contained would ever be worth anything. The $5.00 price of the yearbook included the value of the small probability that they would. It also included the value of the rather more likely outcome that they would not. A book equally valued by the owner at the time could have been purchased for $5.00, and the owner could have, in effect, mitigated the damage by purchasing a replacement and acquiring an essentially identical asset.

To put this another way, we extend the example somewhat. Suppose that yearbooks without Janis Joplin's signature are worth nothing by the time of the award. Suppose that the thief had stolen and destroyed another yearbook at the same time, a yearbook without Janis Joplin's signature. It is surely unfair for the second plaintiff to be awarded nothing at all while the first one gets $1,000. At the time they were stolen, both yearbooks were considered interchangeable by their owners. The owner of the Janis Joplin yearbook has been deprived of a chance at $1,000, but so has the owner of the other yearbook. Moreover, the owner of the Janis Joplin yearbook has been relieved of the chance of discovering that his or her yearbook turned out to be worthless.

The point may be illuminated further by using a different example.[14] Suppose that the asset destroyed was the opportunity to enter into a long-term contract thought at the time to be valuable. Suppose, however, that, with the benefit of hindsight, we now know that the contract would have been a disaster, losing money for the plaintiff. Surely, one would not assess negative damages, having the plaintiff pay the defendant.

The two cases are symmetric, however. The reader who finds it hard to accept our argument should attempt to enunciate a principle on which the use of hindsight leads to paying a high award when the asset turns out to have been unexpectedly valuable and does *not* lead to negative damages when the asset turns out to have been a loser.[15]

In fact, there is no such principle. In both cases, the plaintiff was deprived of a valuable asset. The mere passage of time does not change that fact. Further, hindsight does not change the value that the asset had when it was destroyed. Making the plaintiff whole today means making it whole as of the date of the violation plus compensation for the pure time value of money. Giving the plaintiff the lost profits that hindsight suggests does not place it in the position it would have occupied without the violation; it replaces an uncertain world with a particular outcome.

Private information

This result, however, holds most plainly in the case in which the destroyed asset had a clear market value and could be replaced. In that case, one can say that the plaintiff could have mitigated the damage by replacing the asset. But suppose that the asset was not of the sort freely traded or, equivalently, that private information caused the plaintiff to place a different value on this particular asset than did the market.

To fix ideas, return to the example of Janis Joplin's yearbook. Suppose that the owner of the yearbook had information leading him or her – alone in Port Arthur – to believe it likely that Janis Joplin would someday be a star. In that case, the owner would have valued the Janis Joplin yearbook at the time of theft at more than $5.00, the price at which it could then have been sold. If that is so, then making the plaintiff whole as of the time of violation means an award as of that time of more than $5.00. It means an award as of that time of the amount for which the owner would have *sold* the book; in this case, that is greater than the price at which he or she could have bought it.

There are problems here that warrant discussion, however; they combine issues of principle with issues of practice.

Obviously, it will be to plaintiff's advantage to argue that it valued the destroyed asset especially highly. Here, the burden of proof that such valuation exceeded that which the market either did or reasonably would have placed on the asset belongs to the plaintiff. In the case of Janis Joplin's yearbook, for example, the plaintiff should have to show either contemporaneous private information or, at least, contemporaneous statements revealing that he or she thought Joplin had star potential.

Note that the extra valuation must rest on the peculiar properties of the destroyed asset. If the asset was replaceable in the plaintiff's eyes, then the replacement cost should be used. (As already remarked, replacement of the asset can be considered a form of mitigation.)

In this connection, it is a mistake to value the asset differently merely because of plaintiff's particular risk preferences. Suppose that the stream of returns reasonably expected to accompany the asset would have a rather low present value if discounted using an appropriate market evaluation of risk. Suppose that the plaintiff asserts that it was less risk-averse than the market, so that, in its eyes, that stream of returns was worth a higher value. By itself, this should make no differ-

ence. The plaintiff may not have been able to exercise its risk preferences with the destroyed asset, but there are many opportunities to
invest in risky assets, paying only the price that the market would pay
for risk. This is a different case from that in which private information
or belief about the *particular* asset made the plaintiff value it above
market price.

Naturally, the task of assessing the valuation actually put by the
plaintiff on a destroyed asset will often be difficult when the asset is not
identical to others. Proponents of a particular project within a firm will
typically have put forward rosy forecasts about its profitability. Plaintiff
will certainly produce those forecasts to show extra valuation. What
matters, however, is the extent to which top management took (or
would have taken) such forecasts seriously as a cause for action. The
refusal of an offer for Janis Joplin's yearbook puts a believable lower
bound on the value.

It is in assessing the reasonability of plaintiff's claimed valuations
that hindsight can play some role. Under most circumstances, what
actually happened is at least within the support of the probability distribution of expectations before the fact. A contemporaneous docu-
ment of plaintiff coming reasonably close to forecasting what actually
occurred is certainly to be taken seriously.

Notes

1. In what follows, we assume that injury begins when the violation occurs. If
    not, there is a question as to whether the plaintiff should be made whole as
    of the time of violation or as of the time of first injury. We ignore this. Our
    analysis can easily be adapted to either standard.
2. Many of the same issues are discussed in James M. Patell, Roman L. Weil,
    and Mark A. Wolfson (1982). Although we are in general agreement with
    the approach there taken, we differ in some particulars and consider some
    issues not there discussed.
3. Our views on the appropriate rate for pre-judgment interest have been
    informed by conversations with others, especially A. Lawrence Kolbe,
    who convinced us of the position here taken. We believe that position to
    have originated with Stewart Myers. Naturally, neither Myers nor Kolbe is
    responsible for our errors.
4. On this point we disagree with the conclusions reached in R. F. Lanzillotti
    and A. K. Esquibel (1990). The authors there argue that, if the destruction
    of the asset forces the plaintiff to borrow, then the plaintiff should be com-
    pensated by receiving interest at its borrowing rate. But the destruction
    of any asset forces even plaintiffs with deep pockets to borrow from them-
    selves, as it were, bearing the opportunity cost of foregone earnings. There
    is thus no reason to distinguish borrowing and non-borrowing plaintiffs in
    this regard. Further, in the example given in the text, Ravenal will have a
    higher borrowing rate than Hetty. But, since that higher rate stems from
    causes having nothing to do with the violation, there is no reason why

Ravenal should be compensated at a higher rate than Hetty is.

5. If the defendant is not a corporation but an individual, the same argument would suggest using the defendant's borrowing rate.

6. The Internal Revenue Code provides for an exclusion from personal income taxes damages received on account of 'personal injuries or sickness'. For a discussion of Tax Court decisions on the interpretation of 'personal injuries or sickness', see David G. Jaeger (1989).

7. *ETSI Pipeline Project et al.* v. *Burlington Northern Inc.*, *et al.*, Civil Action B-84-979-CA.

8. It is worthwhile to note that this is *not* typically the plaintiff's return on equity. The capital asset pricing model (CAPM) can be used to obtain the required return on equity and adjustment for debt structure can then be made. See, for example, Richard A. Brealey and Stewart C. Myers (1988).

9. The stream in Equation 22.5 is, in principle, extended to infinity to take account of the fact that the loss of profits resulting from the violation may extend for an indefinite time. Naturally, if it is believed that the cessation of the violation or other relief ends the loss of profits at some particular time, then the calculation can stop there too. To put it another way, the term M_i in Equation 22.5 represents the difference between profits in the 'but-for' world in which the violation never took place and profits (with losses suitably mitigated, if necessary) in the actual world. Those differences may in fact be zero after time t (or some earlier time), but they need not be so.

10. A particular feature of the plaintiff's case had the effect of exaggerating the difference between the two treatments. ETSI used different risk-adjusted discount rates for different years. Discounting for the years between 1988 and 1990 (during the construction period of the project) was at a relatively high rate, while a lower discount rate was applied for the years after 1990. This tended to exaggerate the effects of the error made in calculating the damage award, because ETSI's method implied that if the trial was delayed long enough the higher discount rate would never have been applied.

11. Note that in the case of an on-going violation, forgoing the use of hindsight does not mean valuing the entire stream of lost income from the standpoint of the start of the violation, rather it means valuing the effects of each year's violation from the standpoint of that year.

12. This is also the position taken by Patell *et al.* (1982).

13. *ESTI et al.* v. *Burlington Northern et al.* (1988). The examining attorney, Rufus W. Oliver III, was representing Houston Lighting and Power, whose interests would be served if hindsight was not used. Presumably, he chose this example to nail me firmly to the position taken in the text.

14. This example arguably applied to Houston Lighting and Power in the *ETSI* case.

15. While one might be content with a principle that leads to this result, such a principle must be avoided for the moral hazard it creates. That is, if a plaintiff always receives the benefit of an unexpectedly favorable turn of events but does not suffer the cost of an unexpectedly disastrous turn of events, then there is an incentive for potential plaintiffs to make violations easy, thereby reducing or eliminating their risks. Furthermore, plaintiffs would have an incentive to influence the timing of the trial in their favor. Patell *et al.* provide a discussion of this issue.

References

Brealey, Richard A. and Stewart C. Myers. 1988. *Principles of Corporate Finance*, 3rd ed., Chapter 9, (New York: McGraw-Hill).

ETSI Pipeline Project, et al. v. *Burlington Northern Inc., et al.* 1988. Civil Action B-84-979-CA. Deposition of Professor Franklin M. Fisher, Vol. III, pp. 85–90.

Jaeger, David G. 1989. 'Taxation of damage awards: the Tax Court's shifting standard', *Taxes*, January 1989, **67**(1): 71–8.

Lanzillotti, R. F. and A. K. Esquibel, 1990. 'Measuring damages in commercial litigation: present value of lost opportunities', *Journal of Accounting, Auditing and Finance*, **5**(1).

Patell, James. M., Roman L. Weil and Mark A. Wolfson, 1982. 'Accumulating damages in litigation: the roles of uncertainty and interest rates', *The Journal of Legal Studies*, **11**(2):341–64.

23

Multiple regression in legal proceedings (1980)

Multiple regression analysis is a device for making precise and quantitative estimates of the effects of different factors on some variable of interest. It is not a new tool, going back in its origins to Carl Friedrich Gauss, an extremely important mathematician born about 200 years ago. Nevertheless, the practical use of multiple regression has grown very substantially over the past twenty-five years or so. This growth is due partly to the development of modern statistical methods, partly to increasing availability of decent statistical data, and perhaps most of all to the development of the electronic computer. Some of the increasing use of multiple regression and related techniques has occurred in connection with legal proceedings of various kinds, although lawyers and judges have often tended to view such use with general (and occasionally healthy) distrust.

In light of the increasing prominence of multiple regression analysis, it is important for lawyers to understand what it is, how it works, and what it properly can be used for. Perhaps the single most important legal use of multiple regression thus far has been the analyses of the deterrent effects of the death penalty on murder, cited by the Solicitor General in his amicus brief before the Supreme Court in the death penalty cases.[1] The fact that the studies relied on by the Solicitor Gen-

This chapter was adapted from a paper delivered before the Association of the Bar of the City of New York (Special Committee on Empirical Data in Legal Decision Making) in May 1979. I am indebted to Michael O. Finkelstein for helpful criticism but retain the usual responsibility for error.

eral were, in my opinion, fatally flawed[2] only adds to the importance of understanding the methodology involved. On a less grand level, multiple regression studies have figured in a number of other legal proceedings, and while the ones with which I am most familiar have been regulatory proceedings, there is no reason why multiple regression should not be used in other litigation as well.[3]

This chapter first explains, on a basic level, the concept of multiple regression analysis, its basic properties, and the fundamental assumptions upon which its validity rests.[4] I shall also discuss methods of measuring the accuracy and reliability of estimates generated by multiple regression. The second part of the chapter explores in greater depth the proper use of multiple regression in legal proceedings by focusing on three areas in which multiple regression studies might play a role – the examination of wage discrimination, the determination of antitrust damages, and the evaluation of punishment as a deterrent to crime.

Multiple regression analysis

Uses of multiple regression

The two primary uses of multiple regression analysis are best illustrated through an examination of actual situations in which multiple regression studies were employed. Consider the following two cases.

1. For many years after the disappearance of coal-burning locomotives, there was a perennial labor dispute concerning the preservation of the jobs of railroad firemen. Whatever the merits of that dispute (ultimately resolved, I believe, through negotiation), one of the issues in it concerned the question of whether the presence of a fireman on trains contributed to railroad safety. A study of that issue, using multiple regression, was presented in testimony before a presidential emergency board in 1970.[5]

2. Cable television systems (CATVs) have been the subject of repeated rule-making proceedings by the Federal Communications Commission. Among the issues involved in such proceedings is the effect of the entry and activity of CATVs on the profits and growth of broadcast television stations. This issue involves such questions as the influence of CATVs on the viewing audience reached by particular broadcast stations and the effect of changes in a station's audience on the revenue it receives.[6] In general, as one would expect, cable operators have claimed such effects to be small and broadcast stations have insisted they are large. The problem has been studied repeatedly by multiple

regression methods, most recently in a study of the relationship between audience size and revenues, authored in part by me and submitted to the FCC in 1978–79.[7]

In the first case, the issue is whether or not a particular variable (presence or absence of firemen) has *any* effect on some other variable (railroad safety). In the second case (the audience–revenue relationship), there is not much doubt that audience size affects television revenue – viewer attention is what stations sell to advertisers, and all parties are vitally interested in audience statistics; the problem is rather one of measuring the effect. These two uses of multiple regression are what statisticians call 'testing hypotheses' on the one hand and 'parameter estimation' on the other. In the first use, one wishes to be able to state whether or not something is true. In the second, one is more interested in the precise magnitude of the effects involved. Obviously, the two questions are closely related.

There is a third, but less widespread, use to which multiple regression analysis can be put: to *forecast* the values of some variable. A multiple regression analysis shows how certain independent variables affect a dependent variable. From that analysis, and from a forecast of the values of the independent variables (obtained from some other source), one can generate a forecast of the dependent variable. This type of 'unconditional forecast' is not always useful – which is fortunate, since such unconditional forecasts tend to be relatively inaccurate. Far more often what is of interest is a 'conditional forecast' – a prediction of what will happen to the dependent variable if another variable is changed or, looking retrospectively, what would have happened to the dependent variable had the value of an independent variable been different.

Consider the two examples already described. The question in the case of the railroad firemen did not really involve predicting the number of railroad accidents. Rather, it involved trying to decide whether the number of those accidents would be significantly greater if the railroad firemen were no longer employed. Similarly, while prediction of television station revenue would be desirable for some regulatory ends, the primary issue in the audience–revenue study was systematic measurement of the effects on revenue of changes in the size and socioeconomic characteristics of a station's audience.

The firemen example best brings out the problems involved in making such predictions. By their nature, railroad accidents involve random, chance events. Even the accident *rate* (however measured) is subject to such chance fluctuations. Simply determining whether the presence or absence of firemen makes a significant difference to the railroad accident rate may be easier than predicting the rate itself with great precision. One of the distinctive characteristics of multiple regression analysis is that it is able to provide information about the effects of the variable of interest (in this case the employment of the firemen) on the dependent variable (here, railroad accidents) without necessarily being able to predict the dependent variable itself with great accuracy.

In a way, one might describe multiple regression as a method used to extract a systematic signal from the noise presented by data. There are two primary problems involved in extracting such a signal. First, it is typically the case that the factor whose influence one wishes to test or measure is not the only major factor affecting the dependent variable – for example, the amount of traffic on the railroads has something to do with accidents as well. Second, even if one can somehow account for the effects of the other important systematic factors, there typically remain chance components.

If we could make controlled experiments, it would be relatively easy to quantify the relationship being investigated. A controlled experiment in the audience–revenue case, for example, would vary station audiences and the other variables expected to influence revenue one at a time, holding everything else constant and observing the resulting revenue. Obviously, this is impossible – there is no way we can tinker with station audiences. This means that we must be content with analyzing, as it were, the experiments performed by nature, in which more than one of the variables deemed likely to affect revenue move at the same time.

Moreover, even if we could control station audiences and hold constant the variables that we believed to be important, we would not know enough about the audience–revenue relationship to be sure of holding constant all the variables that actually affect the revenues of an individual station. It may be, for example, that the personality and effectiveness of the stations' sales representatives or the advertising policies or publishing quality of competing newspapers affect revenue. These variables are hard to measure, let alone hold constant.[8]

Inability to perform well-controlled experiments is not uncommon. Indeed, it occurs even when one is making so-called controlled experiments in the natural sciences. The difference there is that one can be fairly sure that the uncontrolled effects that one does *not* know about in detail are extremely small. When dealing with observations from the economic system (or, indeed, from any system in which the experiments are performed by nature rather than by the experimenter), there is likely to be a non-trivial, residual element of unexplained effects on the variable of interest, even after one has taken account of the major systematic effects. Multiple regression is a way of dealing with these difficulties.

How multiple regression works

An overall view

In multiple regression, one first specifies the major variables that are believed to influence the dependent variable. In our examples, this means specifying the important or systematic influences that may affect station revenue or railroad safety. There inevitably remain minor influences, each one perhaps very small, but creating in combination a non-negligible effect. These minor influences are treated by placing them in what is called a random disturbance term and assuming that their joint effect is not systematically related to the effects of the major variables being investigated – in other words by treating their effects as due to chance.[9] Obviously, it is very desirable to have the random part of the relationship small, particularly relative to the systematic part. Indeed, the size of the random part provides an indication of how correctly one has judged what the systematic part is. Multiple regression thus provides a means not only for extracting the systematic effects from the data but also for assessing how well one has succeeded in doing so in the presence of the remaining random effects.

The relationship between the dependent variable and the independent variable of interest is then estimated by extracting the effects of the other major variables (the systematic part). When this has been done, one has the best available substitute for controlled experimentation. The results of multiple regressions can be read as showing the effects of each variable on the dependent variable, holding the others constant. Moreover, those results allow one to make statements about the probability that the effect described has merely been observed as a result of chance fluctuation.

Estimating multiple regressions

Suppose that the relationship to be examined is to include only two variables, the dependent variable (Y) and one independent variable (X). Suppose further (for simplicity of exposition) that it is believed that the relationship between these variables is a straight line.[10] Such a relationship could be expressed mathematically as:

$$Y = a + bX \tag{23.1}$$

or, diagrammatically, as in Figure 23.1. The problem for the investigator is to discover the values of the parameters, a and b (i.e. the intercept and slope of the line). If the relationship really were exact – if there were no random influences at all – this would be extremely easy to do.

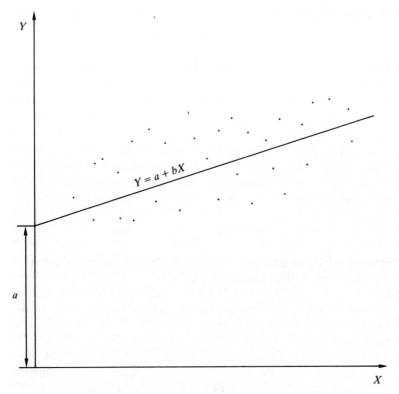

Figure 23.1 Two variables connected by a straight-line relationship with random disturbances.

One would need only to observe two points with different values of X. Since two points determine a line, it would require only routine arithmetic calculation to find the line they determine.

In real life, however, the relationships to be fitted are not exact. Rather there are random influences on the dependent variable, as described above. Hence, the correct relationship is not Equation 23.1 but rather:

$$Y = a + bX + u \qquad (23.2)$$

where u represents the random influences. Different values of u will produce different values of Y which will be either above or below the line; indeed, they will produce a scatter of points such as that shown in Figure 23.1. The task for the investigator is to cut through the noise generated by these random influences and extract the 'signal', namely, the line around which the points are scattered. This is done by picking the line that best fits the scatter of points in the sense that the sum of the squared deviations between predicted and actual Y values is minimized.[11] This is called 'least squares regression'. (The adjective 'multiple' is used when there is more than one X.)

Assumptions of least squares regression

In practice, least squares regression is not done diagrammatically but numerically (generally by computer), resulting in numerical estimates of a and b. The relation that such estimates are likely to have to the true values of a and b depends on the assumptions one is willing to make about the random disturbance term, u, and its relationship with the independent variable, X, whose effect on Y (represented by b) is to be measured.

There are essentially three major assumptions involved:

(a) that the effects of the random disturbance term are independent of the effects of the independent variable;
(b) that the values of the random term for different observations are not systematically related and that the average squared size of the random effect has no systematic tendency to change over observations; and
(c) that the sum of random effects embodied in the disturbance term is distributed normally, in the 'bell curve' generally characteristic of the distribution of the sum of independent, indentically distributed random effects.[12]

The validity of these assumptions bears on the effectiveness and reliability of least squares analysis. Various properties of multiple regression depend on the accuracy of the assumptions, different properties involving different assumptions. Moreover, the dependence is cumulative: if the early assumptions are invalid, the properties associated with the later assumptions are not likely to be present. In situations where the assumptions may fail, the use of multiple regression analysis is likely to be inappropriate.[13]

Independence of the disturbance term

The fundamental assumption of least squares regression is that the uncontrolled effects of the random disturbance (u) are in an appropriate technical sense independent of the controlled effects of the independent variable (X). (Alternatively, this can be expressed as the assumption that the disturbance term has a zero mean whatever the value of X. In repeated samples, the disturbance term for any given X is neither positive nor negative on the average.) If this were not so, then attempting to determine the effects of X on Y could not be done simply by observing different Xs and trying to average out the effects of u. In such a case, movements in X would be systematically associated with movements in u and, without a great deal of care, the estimates of b would include not merely the direct effects of X on Y, but also the associated effects of movements in the disturbance term, u.

When is such an assumption likely to fail? The simplest case to understand occurs when some large and systematic factor, other than X, has been left out of the analysis; this is called misspecification. In the revenue–audience study, for example, it turns out that average household income as well as size of audience affects television station revenue. Suppose, however, that we had not thought of this but had simply tried to estimate the effect of audience size on revenue. (Here, revenue would be Y and audience size would be X.) In effect, this would mean that we were placing household income in the disturbance term. Yet, if household income across television markets is positively associated with audience size, then part of what we would attribute to larger audience size would in fact be attributable to higher income. In other words, we would have failed to control for income levels and the lack of such control would matter.

Obviously, the assumption that one has controlled for all the important influences is basic to any attempt to measure those influences correctly. There are, however, other ways in which the assumption of independence between random disturbance and included factors can be violated. In general, this will happen when there exist relations between the dependent and independent variables in addition to the relation being estimated. I shall discuss specific examples of such cases in the section on appropriate and inappropriate use of multiple regression.

If the assumption of independence between u and X is warranted, then least squares estimates of the parameters (a and b) will have some desirable properties. First, the estimates will be *unbiased* – they will be correct on the average. This means that if one did the calculations for a sample of a particular size, and were then to repeat the procedure on numerous samples of the same size, each time obtaining different estimates for a and b, the average of the estimates so obtained would be the true values of a and b. To put it a little differently, least squares estimates have no tendency to err systematically on either the high side or the low side.

Further, if the assumption of independence is correct, least squares estimates will be *consistent*. The property of consistency means that, as the sample size increases, the probability of obtaining least squares estimates that differ from the true values by more than any given amount goes to zero. Thus, as more data become available it will become easier to extract the true values of a and b from the noise presented by the random part.

Behavior of the disturbance term

Consistency is the minimal property that one wants an estimator to have. But there are many consistent estimators and, in some situations, even many unbiased ones. Moreover, unbiasedness assures only that the estimator is right on the average; it does not indicate how far off it is likely to be in any given sample. Similarly, consistency guarantees only that one will get close to the true values of the parameters if one knows enough; it cannot determine how much one needs to know to get close. It is clearly desirable to have measures of reliability – that is, measures of how far off one can generally expect estimates to be. Moreover, within the class of unbiased or consistent estimators, it is obviously desirable to choose the one likely to be most reliable.

With an additional assumption, least squares regression turns out to be such an estimator and will itself generate estimates of its reliability. This assumption concerns the nature of the random disturbance term (u), rather than an assumption concerning its relation with X. The assumption can be divided into two parts.

First, it is assumed that if one had information about the value of u for some observations, one would not thereby gain any information about its value for other observations. For example, if the observations are on the variables over time, an unusually high and positive value for u should not be followed by a tendency for u to be high the next year; rather, successive values of u should be independent of each other. One can see why this is likely to matter. Least squares regression is a generalized form of averaging. Averaging is an excellent way to take care of random noise, provided that one is averaging over independent events. If the random disturbances from different observations are not mutually independent, however, then the averaging involved in least squares regression will not diffuse the random effects efficiently. In such a case one could do better by expressly assuming that a high disturbance term in one period indicates something about the value of the disturbance term in the following period, and then using this information to attempt to factor the disturbance out of the equation.

Second, it is assumed that there is no systematic tendency for the random disturbance (u) to be either big or small.[14] To put it differently, one assumes that the chances of a large random effect versus a small one are the same for all observations.[15] Again, one can see why this will matter. If some observations tended to have larger random effects than others, then the observations with large random effects would contain less reliable information than would the observations with small random effects. In any averaging procedure, one would want to give more weight to the latter. Since least squares regression will treat all observations equally, it will not take this into account.[16]

These assumptions will be violated if, when dealing with a series of observations over time, the disturbance term includes the effects of variables that behave systematically over time. Certainly, this is a serious possibility in econometric models. Similarly, if the observations are of individual entities, such as firms, it may very well be that the effects of particular uncontrolled events (such as political events) will be larger for large firms than for small ones. In such a case, the second part of the assumption would be violated. As with all the assumptions of least squares regression, however, one would want to be sure that the violations are really important before abandoning least squares. In the cases posited above, small departures from the assumptions would have small effects. Furthermore, the properties of least squares associated with the assumptions are so strong as to make least squares regression superior to the alternative estimators that would result from trying to cure such small departures.

Given the validity of the assumptions under discussion, least squares estimates will be *efficient*. This means that, within a wide class of un-biased and consistent estimators, least squares estimates will have the smallest variation. Thus, if one could take repeated samples, the variation of the least squares estimates around the true values of a and b would be less than the variation of other unbiased and consistent estimators; in short, the least squares estimates will be more reliable.

Normality of distribution

The last assumption of least squares imposes greater restrictions on the random disturbance, u, than the ones already discussed. The assumption is that u, for all values of X, follows the normal distribution (bell curve),[17] with a mean of zero, as already assumed. This, however, is not as restrictive as it may appear. As a general proposition of statistics, the normal distribution is characteristic of large averages of independent random effects. To the extent that the error term is made up of the sum of small random effects, that sum will tend to be distributed normally.[18]

The normality assumption, in addition to bolstering least squares' property of efficiency, implies the ability to make precise probability statements concerning how far off the least squares estimates are likely to be.[19]

Multiple independent variables

In practice, one does not usually work with relationships involving only two variables, but rather with relationships in which a dependent variable is influenced by many independent ones (railroad traffic as well as firemen employment; audience income as well as audience size). Denoting the independent variables as $X_1, X_2, \ldots, X_k$, the relationship to be estimated (assuming linearity)[20] can be expressed as:

$$Y = a + b_1X_1 + b_2X_2 + \ldots + b_kX_k + u \qquad (23.3)$$

If there is only one independent variable, this is the case already considered, the case of a straight line. When there are two independent variables, one is fitting a plane to a scatter of points in space. When there are more than two independent variables, one is fitting a hyperplane (the generalization of a plane to more than three dimensions), but the principles are still the same, although the visualization is no longer immediate. Least squares still retains all the properties listed for the simple case above.

Least squares regression takes advantage of the fact that the independent variables seldom move in perfect step together but rather move (as the name suggests) independently. By determining how the dependent variable changes when the independent variables move in a variety of different ways, the effect of each of the independent variables is extracted.

This kind of systematic extraction of the effects of each variable is important. Examination of raw data leads to facile, and sometimes erroneous, conclusions. Over time, for example, removal of firemen and increased numbers of accidents both occurred. That these events were causally connected cannot be concluded if both are also associated with increases in a third variable (railroad traffic) that plausibly affects railroad accidents. Only by systematically using the fact that railroad traffic, while associated with fireman employment in the data, is not perfectly so associated, can one find out about the independent effect of the firemen. Not controlling for railroad traffic would place it in the disturbance term of Equation 23.3 and violate the fundamental assumption of least squares that disturbance terms and independent variables are independent.

As this description suggests, it is very important that variables do in fact move somewhat independently. Suppose, for example, that in the revenue–audience study one wished to investigate the separate effects on station revenue of audiences close to a station (X_1) and audiences located farther away (X_2). Suppose, as is not the case, that whenever the nearby audience increased by 10 per cent, as one went from station to station, the far-away audience also increased by 10 per cent. Then, although one would be able to determine the influence on revenue of the *total* audience, one could not find out the separate effects on revenue of the two subdivisions of that audience. No 'experiment performed by nature' would have separated these effects in any way.

Such an extreme situation is not generally encountered in practice; rather what is encountered is something close to it. Suppose that every time the nearby audience went up by 10 per cent, the far-away audience went up by amounts that varied only slightly up or down from 10 per cent. In that case, it would be possible to estimate the separate effects generated by each subdivision of audience size, but one would be very uncertain about the estimate. Nature would not be performing experiments calculated to separate those effects with any high degree of accuracy. Such a circumstance is called *multicollinearity* – so-called because it involves an additional linear relationship among the variables on the right hand side of the equation.

Obviously, the less multicollinearity is present, the better able one will be to separate out the effects of interest. Unless multicollinearity is perfect, however, multiple regression will be able to separate the effects to some extent and, again, will do so more precisely than any other method, producing estimates with the properties discussed above as well as measures of the reliability of those estimates. The effects of multicollinearity will show up in such reliability measures (standard errors), as discussed below.[21]

Erroneous inclusion or exclusion of variables

The discussion thus far has presumed that the true systematic relationship is the one being estimated. To put it another way, we have already seen in discussing unbiasedness that multiple regression retains the desirable properties associated with it only if one has in fact included all the variables likely to have a large effect on the dependent variable and can safely assume that the remaining effects are not correlated with the independent variables included. In the audience–revenue study it was thus necessary to control for household income and not place it in the disturbance term. It is therefore important to proceed by including at some stage all the variables that one might think could possibly have a significant effect on the dependent variable. In general, one does this by first examining those variables that one thinks are actually important and then asking what happens when additional variables are included.

Note that this must be done by specifying *in advance* what variables are thought to be important. To proceed by first looking at the data and then including those factors that appear correlated with the dependent variable is a recipe for spurious results. It leads to a situation where no true test of the estimated relationship can be made. In addition, it is likely to leave out variables that truly belong in and thus lead to invalid as well as untested results. The measurement provided by least squares regression is a way of making theoretical assumptions precise or of testing them; it is not a substitute for thought.

I mention this emphatically because a number of packaged computer programs that are sometimes used involve what is known as 'step-wise regression'. Such programs build up multiple regressions in ways similar to the following. First, the program finds the independent variable in the list most correlated with the dependent variable and does a regression involving it. It then looks at the sample deviations from the regression (the differences between actual and predicted values) and asks whether those deviations are correlated with another independent variable. If so, it puts in the variable most correlated with those errors and so forth. This is not recommended. In the first place, even if none of the independent variables have anything to do with the dependent variable, proceeding in this fashion is very likely to produce the appearance of a high correlation in a particular sample. Second, variables that in fact belong in the relationship but that are correlated with the independent variables used early in the procedure tend never to get in. In general, such computer programs suffer from the same problems as attempts to look by eye at bilateral relationships that in fact involve the influence of many variables: they are likely to attribute the effects of the omitted variables to the included ones and result in biased estimates.

The opposite of building regressions up one variable at a time is to put many variables in and then see whether some of them should come out. This is a somewhat better method. Whereas there is a major effect from excluding a variable whose true coefficient is far from zero, the effect of erroneously including a variable whose true coefficient is zero is of very little consequence. Such a variable can be thought of as actually present in the relationship, with the zero coefficient simply indicating that the variable has little or no effect. The multiple regression technique then estimates that coefficient along with the other true coefficients; thus, the regression technique must extract one more parameter from the same number of observations. This is equivalent to having one less observation with which to extract the non-zero parameters.[22] If the sample size is large (there are more than 500 television stations in the United States, for example), there will be only a very small effect on the estimates of the remaining coefficients and on the prediction of the dependent variable (unless the inclusion of the extra variable adds to multicollinearity). The reliability measures and the measures of 'goodness-of-fit'[23] will take full account of the slight reduction in information involved. Where possible, therefore, it may be best to start with an overly complex model and build down.

Nevertheless, it is important to realize that such building down cannot be done without an antecedent theory; the use of computer programs that do 'backwards step-wise regression' is not recommended. Without some theory about which variables are likely to matter, throwing a great number of variables into the hopper is likely to lead to spurious results. If one tries enough combinations of variables, then, in a particular sample, one will tend to get some relationship that appears to fit well. Therefore, a properly done study begins with a decent theoretical idea of what variables are likely to be important. It then can proceed to test well-defined hypotheses about additional variables. But a study that casts about for a good-looking relationship by trying all sorts of possibilities is very likely to come up with relationships where none exist.

This leads directly to two comments relevant to lawyers. First, when having a study done by an expert, one should not be too insistent about covering every possibility at once. Rather, one should make sure that the expert proceeds by estimating a reasonable model including the major variables and then goes on to test other possibilities. If one insists that all possible variables are likely to be of equal importance, one is likely to end up with a rather doubtful result.

Second, when faced with an opposing expert who has done a regression study, one should find out how the expert decided on the variables included and how many different combinations of variables and models were tried before settling on the one that is being presented. If the basic model was tried relatively early and variations were then tried simply to see if anything else seemed to matter, the study may be sound. If, however, the basic model being presented is the end result of vast amounts of computer work, particularly mindless and mechanical computer work, then one may have a legitimate point of attack.

Measuring 'goodness-of-fit'

As I have already mentioned several times, least squares regression not only estimates the effects of the variables involved in the model but also measures the certainty or accuracy of such estimates. In addition, it provides overall measures of how well the model fits the data as a whole. There are several different measures involved and because they each measure different things, it is important to be clear on the differences among them.

Standard errors of coefficients and t-statistics

Associated with the estimated value of each regression coefficient (a and b in the above equations) is a figure known as the standard error[24] of that coefficient, which measures the coefficient's reliability. In general, the larger the standard error, the less reliable or the less accurate is the estimated value of the coefficient.

Speaking somewhat loosely, in large samples the chances are 19 out of 20 that the true coefficient lies within approximately two standard errors of the estimated coefficient. The chances are 99 out of 100 that it lies within approximately 2½ standard errors of the coefficient.[25] (In small samples the bounds tend to be wider.) Thus, for example, if the estimated coefficient is 10 with a standard error of 2, the chances are 19 out of 20 that the true coefficient lies between 6 and 14 and 99 out of 100 that it lies between 5 and 15. To say that the chances are 19 out of 20 that the true coefficient lies between 6 and 14, however, does not mean that the true coefficient is equally likely to be in any part of that range. The single most probable figure is 10. The probability of matching the correct figure decreases as one moves away from 10 and, as the slight difference between the 6-to-14 and 5-to-15 ranges indicates, that probability decreases very fast as one moves substantially away from the middle estimate.

It is conventional to use the standard error of an estimated coefficient to make a statistical test of the hypothesis that the true coefficient is actually zero – i.e. that the variable to which it corresponds really has no effect on the dependent variable. Essentially, such statements are constructed by asking how likely it is that ranges of the sort just described will include 0. This is done by taking the ratio of the estimated coefficient to its standard error. Such a ratio is called a *t*-statistic.

In large samples, a *t*-statistic of approximately 2 means that the chances are less than 1 in 20 that the true coefficient is actually 0 and that we are observing a larger coefficient just by chance. In such a case, the coefficient is said to be 'significant at the 5 per cent level'. A *t*-statistic of approximately 2½ means that the chances are only 1 in 100 that the true coefficient is 0; in that case, the coefficient is 'significant at the 1 per cent level'.[26] (In small samples, *t*-statistics must be larger for a given significance level.) In the numerical example given, the *t*-statistic would be 5 (10 divided by 2) and the probability that the true coefficient is 0 extremely small. The coefficient would be significant at much better than the 1 per cent level.

Significance levels of 5 per cent and 1 per cent are generally used by statisticians in testing hypotheses. That is, given a significance level of 5 per cent (or 1 per cent for a stricter researcher) it is safe to assume that the true coefficient is not zero and that therefore the variable being tested has some effect on the dependent variable in question. Some lawyers might question whether the use of such levels imposes too severe a standard. Why reject the hypothesis that a certain coefficient is 0 only if the probability of obtaining so large an estimate due to chance is 5 per cent or less? Where the hypothesis involved is of legal importance (for example, when a non-zero coefficient would indicate the presence of sex discrimination in wages), would it not make more sense to use a 'preponderance of the evidence' standard and require only significance at 50 per cent?

Such an approach, however, would reflect a flawed understanding of what significance levels really mean. In particular, a significance level of 50 per cent would not correspond to a 'preponderance of the evidence' standard. The significance level tells us only the probability of obtaining so large a measured coefficient *if* the true value is 0; it does *not* give the probability that the coefficient's true value *is* 0, nor does subtracting the significance level from 100 per cent give the probability that the hypothesis is not true. Because, even with a large sample, it is quite possible to obtain results differing from a coefficient's true value, it is conventionally thought that there must be a very low probability that the results have been obtained with a true coefficient of zero before it can be conclusively claimed that the variable associated with the coefficient has a definite effect on the dependent variable.

This does not mean that only results significant at the 5 per cent level should be presented or considered. Less significant results may be suggestive, even if not probative, and suggestive evidence is certainly worth something. In multiple regressions, one should never eliminate a variable that there is firm theoretical foundation for including just because its estimated coefficient happens not to be significant in a particular sample.

Nevertheless, the computation of the standard errors of the coefficients or the corresponding *t*-statistics is a matter of considerable importance. It is routinely done by professionals, with the 5 and 1 per cent significance levels generally accepted as the point at which the zero hypothesis is rejected. Failure to report such measures of reliability is a clear signal that the study is suspect.

The standard error of estimate

Another statistic often reported with the results of least squares regression is the 'standard error of estimate' or 'standard error of the regression'. This is not to be confused with the standard errors of the coefficients. The standard error of estimate is one of the summary measures reflecting the degree to which the estimated regression line or plane fits the data. In terms of the discussion given earlier, it is an estimate of how widely the points are scattered around the line.

More precisely, the standard error of estimate describes the average deviation of the actual values of the dependent variable in the sample from the values that would be predicted from the regression.[27] Thus a standard error of 0 would correspond to a perfect fit. The larger the standard error of estimate, the poorer is the fit, in the sense that the more important is the random component not being explained.

The size of the standard error of estimate will depend upon the units in which the variables are measured. For example, if we were to measure the dependent variable in pennies rather than in dollars, the standard error of estimate would also be in pennies rather than in dollars and would therefore be multiplied by 100. To judge whether the standard error of estimate is large or small, therefore, one must compare it with something else. One such comparison involves computation of the correlation coefficient, discussed below. Other comparisons involve looking at, for example, the mean value of the dependent variable and determining what percentage of that value the standard error is. In general, the standard error of estimate can be used to make probability statements about how far off forecasts from the model are likely to be. Around the mean of the sample (if the sample is of considerable size), forecasts are likely to be off by more than approximately two standard errors of estimate only once in twenty times.[28]

It is very important, however, to realize that a large standard error of estimate does not tell one anything at all about the accuracy with which the effects of the independent variables are measured. Similarly, a large standard error of estimate says nothing at all about the probability that the effects of those variables are really zero and one is observing only chance effects. (Those propositions are assessed by means of the standard errors of the coefficients and the *t*-statistics as described above.) The standard error of estimate is a way of assessing how important the random part of the model is; it does not tell one how large the effects of such randomness are on one's ability to measure the systematic part.

An example may make this clear. Suppose that a group of workers are all paid the same per-hour wage, *w*, for each hour worked. Suppose, in addition, that workers are employed for different numbers of hours. Now suppose that at the end of each week the workers take their pay and engage in a high-stakes roulette game. Then the income of each worker will be the sum of the pay from the job and the winnings or losings in the roulette game.

Now suppose that we are trying to estimate the common per-hour wage, *w*, from data on the number of hours worked and total income, but that we cannot observe take-home pay directly. We could do this by a regression in which the dependent variable was total income and the independent variable was hours worked; the coefficient of hours worked would be our estimate of the per-hour wage, *w*. The influence of the roulette game, of course, would be the random part of the model.

How would we measure the accuracy of our estimate of the per-hour wage? This would be measured in terms of the standard error *of the estimated coefficient* (*w*). If we had a large enough sample, that standard error would be very small. (This is the consistency property of least squares.) Despite this, we would still find a large standard error *of estimate* because no matter what we did, we would be unable systematically to estimate the effects of the unsystematic roulette game. In such a circumstance, we would be entitled to conclude that there were large unsystematic effects that affected our ability to predict total income. However, under no circumstances would we be entitled to conclude from that fact that we had a biased or unreliable estimate of the per-hour wage. Still less would we be entitled to conclude that changing the number of hours worked had no effect on income (i.e. that the true wage was equal to zero) or, to take the most extreme case, that workers should be indifferent about whether or not they are laid off. Statements of this sort would be signaled by very large standard errors of the estimated per-hour wage, the regression coefficient of hours worked, not large standard errors of estimate of the regression.

Thus, a large standard error of estimate of the regression tells you that you do not know *everything*. This is not the same as telling you that you do not know *anything*. This is important in practice. In the case of the firemen what is involved is the difference between being able to predict the number of accidents well and being sure that employment of firemen affected that number. While related, these are not the same thing and they are measured differently.

The correlation coefficient

The most common way of normalizing the standard error of estimate for different units is to compare it (or more properly, its square) with a measure of the total variation of the dependent variable. What such a comparison does is to split the variation of the dependent variable around its mean into a part that is explained by movements of the independent variable (the systematic part) and a part that is not so explained (the unsystematic part). The squared multiple correlation coefficient, R^2, measures the percentage of that variation that is explained by the systematic part.[29]

How should values of R^2 be interpreted? Obviously, a value of zero means that movements in the independent variables do not explain movements in the dependent variable at all. The higher is R^2, the greater is the association between movements in the dependent and independent variables. A value of unity means that the entire variation in the dependent variable is explained by the model.[30] Beyond that, this commonly used measure must be approached with a fair amount of caution, since R^2 can be affected by otherwise trivial changes in the way in which the problem is set up.[31]

The appropriate and inappropriate use of multiple regression in legal proceedings

So far, this chapter on 'multiple regression in legal proceedings' has been primarily about multiple regression. The time has come to talk about legal proceedings. I shall do this by discussing three areas where multiple regression analysis has figured: the examination of wage discrimination against women; the determination of damages in price-fixing cases; and the evaluation of punishment as a deterrent to crime. These three examples will illustrate a number of the technical points already made as well as providing some lessons concerning what multiple regression analysis can and cannot do. I believe multiple regression analysis to be an entirely appropriate tool for the examination of possible discrimination in wages, but I am very dubious about its utility in price-fixing cases and I believe it to be dangerously misleading in the examination of deterrence.

Discrimination in wages

In this example, a case is brought against a firm on behalf of a group of its women employees. They charge that the firm discriminates by paying women less than men. The object of the statistical study is to test whether this is indeed so.

Let us suppose that the facts are such that it appears to be so. The wage paid the average female employee is less than that paid the average male employee. To make things simple, let us suppose that we are considering only women and men in similar jobs.[32]. The firm defends (or is likely to defend) by claiming that the women are on the average not as qualified as the men. In particular, they are less well educated and have less job experience. They also score lower on certain aptitude tests.

This is obviously a reasonable defense, if in fact it is true. For it to be true, however, it must not only be the case that women, on the average, are less qualified according to these various measures, but also that the difference in qualifications accounts for the difference in pay. If the firm does not pay well-educated men more than less-educated men, then it can hardly claim that this is the basis for the difference between male and female wages.

Multiple regression is well suited to answer this sort of question fairly precisely. Moreover, without a multiple regression study it is difficult to see how it could be decided. The raw comparison of average wages for women and for men may make one suspicious, but it cannot tell one anything definite. Indeed, it can be misleading in either direction. For example, it would be entirely possible in a different setting that women are paid on the average just as much as men but that a multiple regression analysis would show that there is indeed discrimination because women are *more* highly qualified in the measures that account for the variation in male pay.[33]

Returning to the original problem, how can this be set up in a multiple regression framework? We begin by doing something that may seem needlessly cumbersome but will pay off later. We define a variable, S, as follows:

$$S = \begin{cases} 0 \text{ if the employee is a woman} \\ 1 \text{ if the employee is a man} \end{cases} \tag{23.4}$$

S is what is called a 'dummy' variable, used in situations where one wants to examine discrete rather than continuous variations – in particular, classification into categories. Consider the regression equation:

$$Y = a + bS + u \tag{23.5}$$

where Y denotes the income paid to a particular employee. It is not hard to see that estimating Equation 23.5 by least squares regression is simply another way of computing the difference in average pay between men and women. If $S = 0$, then, on the average, pay will be given by a; this will be the average pay of female employees. On the other hand, if $S = 1$, then, on the average, pay will be given by $(a + b)$; this will be the average pay of male employees. The difference in the averages is thus b, the coefficient of S, and testing whether that coefficient is significantly different from zero tests whether men are indeed paid more than women.

But of course, such a test is only a test of the original proposition, that men, on the average, are paid more than women and that the difference in pay is not accounted for only by random fluctuations. Such a test is better than simply looking at the difference in pay, but we have not yet tackled the problem of controlling for other variables, namely qualifications.

Such controlling is fairly easily done. For example, suppose for a moment that there were only one measure of qualifications (say, aptitude test scores), denoted by A. Consider the following modification of Equation 23.5:

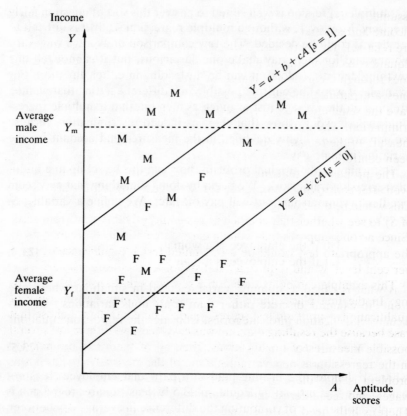

Figure 23.2   An illustrative example of the effect of sex and aptitude scores on wages.

$$Y = a + bS + cA + u \qquad\qquad (23.6)$$

Estimation of this equation by multiple regression will give an answer to the question of whether sex affects wages, with aptitude test scores constant. This may be seen diagramatically in Figure 23.2.

In Figure 23.2, employee income is plotted against aptitude test scores. Points denoting male employees are indicated by M; points denoting female employees are indicated by F. I have drawn a case in which male employees are obviously paid more than female employees on the average, but in which, again on the average, female employees score lower on aptitude tests than do male employees. Examination of the average wages without correcting for aptitude tests (equivalent to least squares regression estimation of Equation 23.5) amounts to drawing a horizontal line in the diagram (horizontal because aptitude is assumed to have no effect in Equation 23.5) at the level of average male income and another one at the level of average female income. These are relatively far apart. Correcting for aptitude test scores by estimating Equation 23.6, on the other hand, amounts to drawing two parallel lines through the male and female points respectively. The fact that the lines are parallel indicates the assumption that aptitude tests should have the same effect on wages for males and females if there is no discrimination. The difference in the intercepts is the coefficient of *S*, a measure of the remaining difference in wages after aptitude scores have been controlled for.

The proposition that males systematically earn more than females even after controlling for aptitude test scores can now be directly tested. This would be done using the *t*-statistic associated with *b* (the coefficient of *S*) to see whether that coefficient is significantly different from zero. (Since no one supposes that women earn systematically *more* than men, the appropriate test would be a one-tailed test.) 'Significance at the 5 per cent level' would require a *t*-statistic of a little more than 1.6.

This example can be extended in a few ways that are worth discussing. In the first place, there is no reason why only one measure of qualifications – aptitude test scores – should be controlled. I chose that case because the resulting diagram was easy to draw. If there are several possible measures of qualifications, then all of them can be included in the regression as new variables. One of the great advantages in this problem is that there are not many variables that plausibly explain wages, and thus interest centers simply on whether sex is one of them. There is little need to thrash about for various different combinations of variables that might be included. Rather, having found an apparent effect in the raw data, the only question is whether that effect is caused by failure to control for other plausible variables.

I have set up the problem in Equation 23.6 as though the only issue was whether a man with given aptitude was paid a fixed number of dollars more than a woman with the same aptitude. This is indicated in Figure 23.2 by the constant distance between the two sloping lines. According to the equation, women are at a constant dollar handicap whatever their aptitude, and the question is whether or not that handicap is zero. But of course, this may not be the most likely possibility. It is at least as plausible that women are at a constant *percentage* handicap, so that the difference in dollar terms is greatest for women with high aptitudes. This is easily accommodated in the analysis. I shall not attempt to draw the resulting diagram, but all that would be required would be the use of the logarithm of income instead of income itself as the dependent variable in Equation 23.6.

One might also try a somewhat subtler variation. I have set up Equation 23.6 (or its logarithmic equivalent) so that what is tested is the hypothesis that women are at a disadvantage, *given* that aptitude test scores affect wages in the same way for men and for women (the sloping lines in Figure 23.2 are drawn parallel). This is a good way to do it, but it is not the only way. One could estimate two separate regression equations – one for men and one for women – in which income would be regressed on aptitude. One could then test to see whether the regression coefficients for the two equations were the same *in all respects*. After all, it would be evidence of discrimination if the effect of aptitude tests on wages was not the same for men as for women. It is possible to construct cases in which *b* in Equation 23.6 turns out to be zero, but in which separately estimated equations would yield significantly different values of *b* for men and women. On the other hand, trying to examine several things at once (i.e. whether whole sets of coefficients are the same for men and women) will produce less powerful tests than will examining each one of them individually.

Two other features of this example deserve comment. First, I have deliberately used aptitude test scores as a measure of aptitude. It is common knowledge that such tests do not provide perfect measures of ability. However, this may not make any difference in the validity of the regression model. To the extent that true aptitude has different dimensions, the crudeness of aptitude test scores as a measure may be corrected for by the other variables to be introduced into Equation 23.6 – variables such as years of education or work experience. Second, what matters in the current problem is what the employer can observe in distinguishing aptitude. The defendant in this case will look relatively weak by claiming only that there was an unmeasurable way of evaluating aptitude and that all measurable methods are subject to error. In effect, what is important in this problem is not some underlying measure of aptitude but the measure that the employer can see and reward. An argument that aptitude tests are subject to error ought to be challenged by demand for some more reliable but objective measure. (See Chapter 25.)

Putting this aside, however, the crudeness of aptitude scores might make a substantial difference if the true variable (aptitude) were measured only by aptitude test scores with a random error. In such a case, it is possible to show that the estimates of *c*, the coefficient of aptitude test scores in Equation 23.6, would be biased toward zero. This is perhaps what one would expect, since putting in variables that contain a lot of 'noise' is likely to result in estimates suggesting that those variables do not have much systematic effect. More important, however, the bias will not be restricted to the coefficient of the variable that is subject to the error. In the present problem, the variable *S* (describing sex differences) is correlated with the variable *A* (denoting aptitude test scores), reflecting the fact that, in the sample of employees, women tend to score lower than men on aptitude tests. Such correlation means that the coefficient of *S* will also be biased and this coefficient is the one that is of interest. Unfortunately, it is not possible to say (without more assumptions) in what direction that coefficient will be biased. Under some circumstances, there are steps that can be taken to guard against the effects of measurement error, but it would take me too far afield to discuss them here. (See Chapter 25.)

The final point to be made about this example is that accurate prediction of the dependent variable, income, is not required for successful resolution of the problem. Rather what is involved here is a direct test of the significance of a particular coefficient. The precision of that test (technically its 'power') will depend on the standard error of that coefficient and not directly on how well the equation can be expected to do in predicting the dependent variable. Generally, tests like these are likely to be more successful than tests that depend directly on predictions.

What makes the wage discrimination example so suitable for multiple regression is its simplicity and the readiness with which it can be cast into the mold of a test of the significance of a particular regression coefficient. Notice in particular the following` feature: whether there is discrimination or not, one would expect the expanded version of Equation 23.6 to fit well. What is being done there is to imbed in a theory of wage determination the difference that discrimination does or does not make. At least at this level, the question of what factors other than discrimination determine wages can be considered without regard to whether or not there is in fact discrimination. Further, the presence or absence of discrimination makes a clearly definable difference in the result one would expect to find. These features stand in contrast to those of the next example.

Antitrust damages in price-fixing cases

In this example, the defendants have lost on the issue of liability in a price-fixing case, and the issue to be decided is the extent of damages. The defendants prepare a study attempting to show that the effect of fixing the price was minimal, in that the price would have been the same (or higher) without the conspiracy.[34] There are a number of ways in which this might be done, but I am very dubious about the usefulness of any of them.

One way to proceed is to take a leaf from the discrimination example just discussed. In that example, the study proceeded by controlling for several variables and, in effect, estimating what income would have been if there were no discrimination. Why not systematically estimate what prices would have been without price fixing? We might think of doing this as follows. Under competition, price is determined by the intersection of supply and demand curves. Let us assume, for simplicity, that there are no close substitutes for the product in question, so that demand depends only on the income of consumers (or the output of industrial customers) as well as on price. Supply will depend on price and on costs, which in turn depend on the prices of the factors of production. This suggests that we ought to be able to explain price by a regression equation involving consumer income and factor prices.

Although one might assume that *quantity* should be included as one of the variables that may have an impact on price, it is more appropriate to treat price and quantity independently since, in fact, the same market forces control both. This is evident from an examination of the specific equations (supply and demand curves) that determine supply and demand in the market.

Quantity, like price, is determined by the intersection of the supply and demand curves. Assuming linearity, for convenience, we can write the demand curve as:

$$Q = a + bP + cY + u \tag{23.7}$$

Here, Q denotes quantity, P denotes price and Y denotes consumer income. As before, u is a random disturbance. Similarly we can write the supply curve as:

$$Q = d + eP + fW + v \tag{23.8}$$

Here, W is a measure of factor prices and v is another random disturbance.

Equations 23.7 and 23.8 form what are called the 'structural equations' of a 'simultaneous equation system'. Such a system involves the interaction of more than one equation – equations that must be solved simultaneously. The fact that price is determined by the intersection of supply and demand is reflected by the fact that P and Q must have the same value in both equations. We can thus solve both equations together for those two variables by equating the values that each equation predicts for the 'quantity' variable. To do this, we create new coefficients (π_0, π_1, π_2, etc.) that depend on all the coefficients of the supply and demand curves. When this is done, the solution for price will look as follows:

$$P = \pi_0 + \pi_1 y + \pi_2 W + u^* \tag{23.9}$$

u^* is the random disturance, which depends on some of the coefficients in the supply and demand curves, as well as on u and v. (Precisely, it is equal to $(u - v)/(e - b)$.) The exact algebra need not detain us. There will be a similar solution for Q.

Equation 23.9 and its companion for Q are called the 'reduced form' of the model. They show price and quantity directly in terms of those variables that are determined by forces other than those being modeled (Y, W, u and v). Such reduced-form equations can be estimated by least squares regression.

It would be a mistake, however, to include Q in the equation for P. It does not appear in Equation 23.9 for the very good reason that quantity and price are jointly determined by the same forces, and it cannot be said that one of them determines the other. A regression that includes quantity on one side and price on the other might be interpreted as an attempt to estimate either Equation 23.7 or Equation 23.8 directly, but this cannot be done consistently by least squares. The easiest way to see this is as follows. A movement in the disturbance term in Equation 23.7, u, affects quantity, Q; this is essentially a random shift of the demand curve. But random shifts of the demand curve affect not only quantity but also price. Hence, shifts in u are associated with movements in P, as can be seen directly from Equation 23.9 and the fact that u^* depends on u. This means that, in estimating Equation 23.7, the fundamental assumption of least squares – that random disturbances move independently of the independent variables – is violated. Equation 23.7 can be estimated, but least squares is not the way to do it.

Thus, trying to determine what price would have been in a competitive market by regressing price on a set of variables including quantity is doomed to failure. Suppose, however, that we were more sensible and simply regressed price on income and factor price (Y and W), thus estimating Equation 23.9 directly and using that equation to predict price absent the price-fixing agreement.

This is better, but still not adequate. The problem here is that there will not be a clear distinction between the results that one would obtain if the market was affected by the price-fixing scheme and the results that one would obtain if it was not. If the market was not competitive but was seriously affected by price-fixing, price was not determined by the intersection of competitive supply and demand curves. Rather, price was determined largely by the price-fixers. But the price-fixers presumably did not set arbitrary prices but rather set prices to maximize their profits to the extent that they could.

Without going into great detail, it is not hard to see that profit maximization would have required consideration of the position and shape of the demand curve (Equation 23.7) as well as consideration of the costs of production. In the standard terms of economists, profit maximization requires the equating of marginal revenue and marginal cost. Marginal revenue will depend directly on demand and marginal cost directly on factor prices. The price and quantity that equate marginal revenue and marginal cost will, just as in Equation 23.9, depend on income and factor costs. Indeed, for price, one is quite likely to end up with an equation identical to Equation 23.9; the difference that price-fixing makes is that the coefficients in Equation 23.9 will be different under price-fixing than under competition.

This means, however, that there is no point to estimating Equation 23.9 directly and using it to forecast price. Equation 23.9 would be valid whether or not there was price-fixing and one will not be able to tell whether the predictions that it generates are competitive or non-competitive. The case was quite different in the wage discrimination example. There the issue was sharply defined as whether a certain coefficient was zero or non-zero. Here the issue might be described as involving differences in a certain set of coefficients (the πs in Equation 23.9), but we can estimate those coefficients only once and there is thus no way that we can compare the values we obtain with the unknown values that we would have obtained under either the competitive or the non-competitive hypothesis.

Does this mean there is nothing that can be done? No, but it comes close. We might proceed in a somewhat more sophisticated manner and try to estimate Equation 23.7, the demand curve, which is the same under both regimes. We might then ask what the competitive supply curve would have looked like. Theoretically this could be done, but in practice it is probably impossible. The demand curve (Equation 23.7) can be estimated. As we have seen, it cannot be estimated by least squares under the hypothesis of competition, but there are other methods of estimating it, and those methods would remain valid, in general, even under a scheme of price-fixing.[35] However, in order to find out what price would have been under competitive conditions, it will be necessary to estimate the competitive supply curve. One cannot do that directly from the observations because to do so is to assume that the observations were generated by competitive supply and demand. That, however, is what one wants to prove. Hence, one will have to look elsewhere. In general this will mean estimating the cost curve of the producers and calculating marginal cost. Even if the defendants are willing to give up the information required for this calculation, estimation is likely to prove extraordinarily difficult. Once we move away from simple one-product examples, the cost calculations (and indeed the estimation of the various demand curves as well) become quite complicated. What is involved here is a major undertaking requiring a great deal of data, most of it unlikely to be in usable form, and generating only a thin promise at the other end. Indeed, if one is going to look directly at cost information, it might be better to make a direct showing that prices approximated marginal costs. To do that, one would not need to look at demand.

There remains one possibility in this area that looks slightly more promising. Many of the problems just discussed occur because one wants to know how competition would have looked without directly assuming that competition in fact existed. If, however, there is agreement that the price-fixing conspiracy was in effect only for a limited time, then one might consider estimating the reduced form equation for price (Equation 23.9) and the companion equation for quantity, using only data from the competitive period. One could then use those equations to forecast price for the price-fixing period and study the difference in results.

This sort of program is feasible, at least in principle.[36] Unfortunately, it is unlikely to pay off in practice. One will be using the estimated equations to forecast out of the sample period. If conditions have changed (and over time they usually do) this is going to mean forecasting away from the mean of the sample. Even if the model is entirely correct, one is not going to be able to make this sort of forecast with a great deal of certainty. One is likely to find that the price at a given moment during the price-fixing period is not significantly higher than that which would be predicted by the competitive model, but that the standard error of that prediction is large. Thus, although it will be possible to test whether the difference in price is significant, it will probably be very hard to decide how much of that difference is due to random error.[37] Furthermore, variations in price in either direction can be explained away, by either plantiffs or defendants, in terms of shifts in demand or cost conditions. Hence, if what is involved is prediction over a long time, this forecasting may be worth trying, but it is not likely to be useful. As opposed to the other approaches already discussed, however, it does have the merit of providing a clear comparison of the two hypotheses involved.

Punishment as a deterrent to crime

The last topic that I shall discuss is the use of studies that purport to examine the effect of punishment as a general deterrent to crime – that is, as a deterrent to persons other than those being punished. I have already mentioned the death penalty studies referred to by the Solicitor General. In addition, there are a number of studies of other categories of crimes and types of punishment. This is not the occasion to discuss these studies in great detail; such discussions can be found elsewhere.[38]

However, a consideration of some of the reasons why these studies are unsatisfactory will illustrate points that are generally applicable to the use of multiple regression analysis.

At first glance, the problem seems to be eminently suitable for regression analysis. Nearly any examination of data in which punishment varies also shows crime varying in the opposite direction. Yearly data on murders committed in the United States (a 'time series') show the number of murders rising in years with no executions. With respect to other crimes, cross-section data show that the jurisdictions with less severe sentences tend to be the jurisdictions with higher crime rates. It plainly appears that there is a negative correlation between severity of punishment and crime rate and that the problem is merely that of assessing the magnitude of the deterrent effect.

Unfortunately, while I agree that there probably is something significant in these data, the problem of measurement turns out to be very severe. This is true for more than one reason. First, there is a problem because we do not have a very good theory of what causes crime, and thus we do not really know what other variables should be controlled for in deriving a crime equation. Second, one has to control not only for other variables in the same equation but also for the presence of additional relations between those variables and crime. Add to this the doubtful nature of much of the data and one has a serious problem.

Let me begin by considering the death penalty studies.[39] The primary study[40] used time-series data on the United States as a whole for the years 1933–1969. This is a sample of thirty-seven observations, although data on some of the variables had to be constructed. However, it turns out that the results depend almost entirely on the years after 1962. This is, perhaps, no surprise; it was primarily in those years and in the early 1970s that many jurisdictions experimented with the abolition of capital punishment. It does mean, however, that there is only a relatively limited amount of data to use in controlling for other effects, despite the seemingly large sample size. Furthermore, those same years coincided with a general upsurge in crime, not just in those crimes subject to capital punishment. Therefore, we cannot be sure that the results of the study do not simply depend on poorly understood phenomena concerning the causes of crime.

There are lessons to be learned here. First, when faced with a multiple regression study, one should try to determine whether the results crucially depend on certain of the years chosen or whether they stand up to variations in the sample. If the results do depend on certain years, one should try to decide whether there are other characteristics specially associated with these years that might have affected the results. Second, and perhaps more important, one must try to determine whether enough is known about the phenomenon being investigated (here, the causes of crime) to estimate it in terms of the model selected. If not, there will be other plausible explanations for the results achieved.

The death penalty study also turns out to depend rather crucially on the form of the equation used. There is a big difference in its results depending on whether the equation is estimated in linear or logarithmic form.[41] Of course, if one had reason to believe that the correct form of the equation was one or the other, one would simply use that form. But one does not know which form is 'correct'. Results that depend on the use of a particular version of the equation may not be valid; they depend on an unsupported assumption.[42] When one is deciding whether to execute a man, it ought to concentrate the mind wonderfully. In such matters, the studies to be relied on ought not depend on particular sample periods or choice of specifications.

Many of the problems with the capital punishment study arise because of the limited nature of the available data. An obvious alternative set of experiments would involve the use of data concerning various crimes and drawn from different jurisdictions, in order to get a large sample and a lot of variation.[43] The trouble here is as follows.

Obviously, there are reasons other than variations in punishment that crime rates vary over jurisdictions. It is therefore necessary to control for such reasons. Some possibilities for variables are unemployment rate, percentage of urban population, and so forth. Multiple regression might in fact do this.

Unfortunately, there are also reasons why punishment levels vary over jurisdictions. One of the reasons suggested in the literature has to do with crime rates. It is easy to see how this might happen. Jurisdictions with higher crime rates may adopt 'get tough' policies. Alternatively (and this is the suggestion in much of the literature), jurisdictions with high crime rates may overload their punishment facilities and thus may come to tolerate relatively common offenses somewhat more than do jurisdictions with low crime rates. In any event, there is a serious possibility that the variation in punishment levels over jurisdictions can be accounted for, at least in part, by the variation in crime rates. In this circumstance, as in part of the supply and demand example given above, the problem is not merely that one has to control for other variables, but that one has to control for the presence of another equation. To see the kind of problem that arises, consider the following vastly simplified example.

Assume, for the moment, that the *only thing* that affects crime rates is punishment. Assuming linearity, for convenience only, the crime rate equation to be estimated could then be written as:

$$C = a + bS + u \qquad (23.10)$$

Here, C is the measure of crime rate and S is a measure of punishment or sanctions levels. The coefficient *b* would represent the deterrent effect of increasing sanctions.

Suppose, however, that sanctions also depended on the crime rate and only on the crime rate. Then the equation that shows how sanction levels are determined can be written (again assuming linearity):

$$S = d + eC + v \tag{23.11}$$

In these equations *u* and *v* are random disturbances.

Given the interrelation between these two equations, one could not effectively estimate the crime equation (Equation 23.10) by least squares regression. The fundamental assumption of least squares regression is that the random disturbance term operates independently of the independent variable. All of the properties of least squares depend on this. In the present instance this would require that *u* and *S* be uncorrelated. This cannot be the case, however, because the model itself (just as in the supply and demand example given above) implies that it is not so. An upward shift in *u*, according to Equation 23.10 itself, will mean an upward shift in the crime rate, *C*. But an upward shift in the crime rate, *C*, will, according to Equation 23.11, cause a shift in the sanctions level, *S*. Hence, shifts in *u* cannot be independent of shifts of *S* and least squares regression will fail. (This may also be seen by solving Equations 23.10 and 23.11 for *C* and *S* to obtain the reduced form of the system, as was done in the supply and demand example.)

The problem is worse than this, however. To see this, ignore the random disturbances, for a moment, and suppose that Equations 23.10 and 23.11 were exact. I have graphed those equations in Figure 23.3. In such a situation, the crime rate and the sanctions level would be entirely determined by the simultaneous solution of the two non-random equations – the intersection of the two lines in Figure 23.3 at K. (The resemblance to a supply and demand graph is not accidental.) If this were really the case, the only point we would ever observe would correspond to that intersection at sanctions level denoted by S^* and crime rate denoted by C^*. But if that point were the only one observed, there would be no way of recovering Equations 23.10 and 23.11. In terms of the graph, we could not tell the true crime function (the more steeply-sloped line) apart from the sanctions function (the less steeply-sloped line) or, indeed, from any other line that went through that same point; each line could vary, in an infinite number of ways, around the point K.

Even if we put random disturbances back in, we would not get anywhere. The effect of random disturbances would be to produce a cluster of points surrounding the intersection drawn in the graph, but again, it would not be possible to recover the two underlying lines that generated this cluster or to tell the two lines apart even if we could

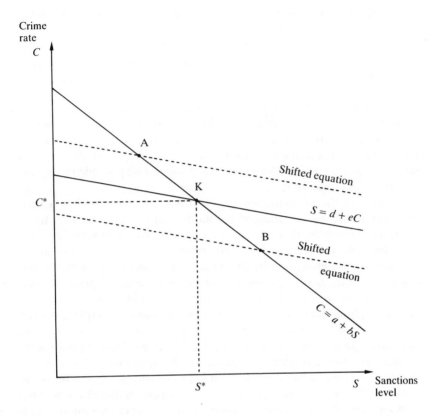

Figure 23.3 Illustration of simultaneous relations between crime rates and sanctions or punishment.

recover them. In this circumstance, the crime and sanctions equations are said to be 'not identifiable'.

This problem, one of *identification*, is a well-studied subject in econometrics.[44] I have deliberately chosen an extreme case. Unfortunately, the identification problem continues in the deterrence studies even when the extreme assumptions are relaxed.

Suppose, for example, that there was some variable that shifted sanctions levels over jurisdictions but did not affect crime rates. This would mean that there would be an additional significant variable in Equation 23.11 that was not also a variable in an expanded version of Equation 23.10. Leaving Equation 23.10 as it is, the effect would be to shift the sanctions equation in Figure 23.3 up and down. (This is illustrated by dashed lines parallel to the solid line corresponding to the sanctions equation in Figure 23.3 and marked 'shifted equation'.) If this happened, we would observe not merely one intersection of the sanctions equation and the crime equation but several intersections, points such as A and B, for example. Those points would all lie on the crime equation and, indeed, as the sanctions equation shifted back and forth because of the presence of the additional variable, the points of intersection would trace out the crime equation.

In such a situation, as the diagram suggests, there is a technique for recovering the crime equation from the data. That technique, however, is not least squares regression, because the correlation between the disturbance term and the independent variable in Equation 23.10 would generate invalid results. Moreover, it will still not be possible to recover the sanctions equation itself.

Because of the identification problem it is necessary to find a variable that shifts one equation of the model but not the equation to be identified. However, it is not only bad practice to attempt to find such variables from the data, it is literally impossible. No amount of manipulation of data generated by the model will reveal such variables; the selection of such a variable must be done as a matter of prior theory.

It is easy to see from Figure 23.3 why this should be so. If there is a variable shifting the sanctions equation but not the crime equation, then the observed points will be like the points A, B and K in the diagram. But such a pattern of intersection could also be produced by a variable shifting the crime equation but not the sanctions equation. More generally, it could be produced by shifts in both equations. Only if we *know* from theoretical, non-data-generated considerations that it is the sanctions equation that shifts can we be sure that it is the crime equation that is traced out.

In most situations, such theoretical considerations may readily be found. (For example, consumer income enters demand but not supply curves; factor costs affect supply but not demand.) This is not so in the present case, however. While there are a number of variables that may enter the sanctions equation, it is difficult, if not impossible, to think of such a variable that would not also enter the crime equation.[45] The existing studies have tried to get around this by casually assuming that variables such as unemployment influence sanctions levels but not crime. This is plainly wrong. In the present state of our knowledge, we simply do not know enough about the structure of the system generating the observations to be able validly to estimate the crime equation.

This problem has some general implications for the use of regression analysis. First, it is important to be very careful not only about controlling for additional variables, but also about the possibility that one must control for the existence of additional relationships between the dependent and independent variables. If there are such relationships, least squares will not be an appropriate estimator, and it is at least possible that no appropriate estimator will exist (although this is not common). Second, if there is another equation involved, one must find out how the expert really did the estimation. If the expert explored the data by multiple regression and then, having decided on a model re-estimated it with another estimation technique, the results are quite suspect.[46]

Finally, one should make sure that the model used is constructed on sound hypotheses based on theoretical considerations generated from outside the model itself. While multiple regression and related econometric techniques are powerful tools for analyzing data, their proper use presupposes an underlying theory of the structure generating those data. While some hypotheses concerning that structure can be tested with these tools, the theory itself cannot be discovered by computer runs and data experimentation. Thus, the expert making the study must not only understand the proper uses of the statistical tools, but must also learn something about the phenomena and hypotheses being investigated.

Conclusion

Multiple regression analysis can play a vital role in legal proceedings. Used properly, it is an accurate and reliable method of determining the relationships between two or more variables, and it can be a valuable tool for resolving factual disputes. In order for this to happen, however, multiple regression must be better understood by the legal community; in particular, there must be an understanding of both the potential uses and the limits of the technique.

It is not necessary that lawyers understand the mechanics of multiple regression in terms of what goes on inside the computer. It is necessary, however, that they understand the regression model and the assumptions being used in any given regression study, how the results of the regression bear on the hypothesis to be tested, and how the results distinguish this particular hypothesis from other hypotheses. The expert constructing the analysis should be able to explain all of this to the attorney who employs them, and an expert who cannot explain such things is likely to fall apart on cross-examination.

Lawyers will increasingly find themselves in a position where it would be profitable to use a regression analysis or where they must confront a regression study produced by an opponent. When that happens, a basic knowledge of multiple regression may be a valuable asset.

Notes

1. *Fowler* v. *North Carolina*, 428 US 904 (1976); *Woodson* v. *North Carolina*, 428 US 280 (1976); *Jurek* v. *Texas*, 428 US 262 (1976); *Proffitt* v. *Florida*, 428 US 242 (1976); *Gregg* v. *Georgia* 428 US 153 (1976). See generally *Deterrence and incapacitation: estimating the effects of criminal sanctions on crime rates* (A. Blumstein, J. Cohen and D. Nagin eds., Washington DC: National Academy of Sciences, 1978) (hereinafter cited as *Deterrence and incapacitation*), which contains, among other things, some devastating discussion of the studies involved. (In particular, see the paper by L.R. Klein, B. Forst and V. Filatov, 'The deterrent effect of capital punishment: an assessment of the estimates', in Blumstein *et al.* (1978) at p. 336.)
2. See pp. 433–8.
3. For an excellent discussion of proceedings using multiple regression studies, see M.O. Finkelstein, 'Regression models in administrative proceedings,' *Harvard Law Revue* **86** 1442 (1973).
4. I have been responsible for several multiple regression studies used in legal proceedings and, because I know them best, it is those studies on which I shall draw for examples for much of this chapter, hoping thereby to put some more interest into what otherwise might degenerate into a fairly dry and technical discussion.
5. The study is most conveniently reported in F.M. Fisher and G. Kraft, 'The effect of the removal of the firemen on railroad accidents 1962–1967', *Bell J. Econ. and Management Sci.* **2** 470 (1971).
6. These are important questions for the FCC since they bear on the extent to which regulation of cable television is needed to foster the growth of new UHF stations or to maintain the profits that subsidize the public service and other programming of local broadcast stations.
7. The study is most conveniently reported in Chapter 17. The first study of the problem was, I believe, the one that I gave as written testimony to the FCC in 1964. It is most conveniently reported in Chapter 16. Both studies were done on behalf of the National Association of Broadcasters.
8. Similarly, in the case of the firemen, even if we could experiment with firemen employment, we could not hold railroad traffic constant. Moreover, other variables affecting safety (the ones we call 'chance') are never known precisely.
9. The disturbances (the random or unsystematic part of the relationship) will then affect the dispersion of the true values of the dependent variable around the values that would be predicted from the systematic part alone.
10. I chose the straight line case as the easiest to understand, but the theory is not so restricted. There is nothing to prevent one or more of the variables in Equation 23.1 from being a square, a logarithm or the ratio of two other variables. Many (not all) mathematical relations can be cast into the form of Equation 23.1 by transforming or redefining the variables. Furthermore, most non-linear relationships can be at least approximated by straight lines.
11. Using the sum of squared deviations gives equal weight to positive and negative deviations. Further, in a multi-dimensional diagram (not drawn) it can be shown that there is a sense in which minimizing the sum of squared deviations amounts to minimizing the distance between the point which represents the actual values of the dependent variable and the point

which represents the values one would predict from the regression. Average squared values are the standard statistical measure of dispersion.

12. The word 'normal' here is a term of art referring to the shape of the distribution. The name indicates that the distribution involved is characteristic of many random variables. Most important, if a random variable is composed of the sum of other random variables acting independently and all with the same distribution, that sum tends to be distributed normally. This makes the assumption of normality the obvious one unless there is a compelling reason to depart from it.

13. As a general rule, there are methods of testing for and dealing with the failure of such assumptions, but they involve the more advanced tools of econometrics rather than least squares regression.

14. We have already assumed that the random disturbance term has no systematic tendency to be high or low – that is, that it has a mean, or expected value, of 0 for all values of X. ('Expected value' is to be thought of as the population mean. Roughly speaking it is the average value one expects to obtain if one takes a large enough sample.) That assumption involves the algebraic sign of the random disturbance term. The present assumption, on the other hand, has to do with the absolute magnitude of the disturbance term, regardless of sign. Put more precisely, the dispersion of a random variable is measured by the average or expected value of the squared deviation from its mean. This is called the 'variance'. Its square root is called the 'standard deviation'. The assumption previously made in the text was that the mean of the random disturbance term is not systematically related to X. The assumption now being made is that the variance or standard deviation of the disturbance term is not so related and is, in fact, the same for all observations.

15. Technically, this is the property that the variance of the disturbance term should be the same for all observations.

16. There are ways of taking this failure of assumption into account: not surprisingly, the technique involved is called 'weighted least squares', a variety of 'generalized least squares'.

17. See Note 12.

18. See Note 12. The 'normal' distribution is completely characterized by its mean and variance. It is hard to construct practical examples in which one would be inclined to question normality without also questioning the other assumptions about the random disturbance term. Hence, while there are tests for departure from normality, they are hardly ever used.

19. See pp. 419–21.

20. Again, I have chosen a linear form here. Least squares theory runs mostly in terms of such forms, but this is not as restrictive as it might appear, since many non-linear forms can be cast into a linear form similar to Equation 23.3 by appropriate transformations of the variables.

The basic assumption involved in linearity is that the effect of each independent variable on the dependent variable is independent of the level of the other independent variables. Thus, in the firemen example, linearity would imply that the effect of the presence of firemen on the number of railroad accidents was the same at high levels of traffic as at low levels. It would also imply that the effect was the same regardless of whether there were other crew members substituting for the firemen. Obviously, these are not assumptions on which one necessarily wants to rely.

Fortunately, it is not necessary to rely on them. If one thought, for example, that two of the variables – say X_1 and X_2 – interacted, then one could define a new variable X_3 as the product of X_1 and X_2. Least squares regression would then proceed as if X_3 were simply a different variable, but its coefficient would tell you something about the importance of such interaction.

To take a different example, it is often not very plausible to suppose (as linearity does) that the effect on the dependent variable of changing an independent variable by one unit should be the same in absolute terms for all levels of the independent variable. It is frequently more plausible to assume that a 1 per cent change in an independent variable has a constant percentage effect on the dependent variable. Such cases can be treated within the framework of linearity by entering into Equation 23.3 not the original variables themselves, but rather their logarithms. This is frequently done and has the advantage, as well, of assuming that the effect of the random error on different observations is likely to be of the same size in percentage rather than absolute terms, a matter that came up above in the discussion of one of the least squares assumptions. See pp. 414–15.

In general, the choice of the form in which to enter the variables or, more generally, the form of the relationship requires serious thinking about the way in which the relationship being estimated is likely to work. As with deciding which variable to include in the relationship in the first place, this must be done in large part by thinking about the problem rather than by hoping that the data will provide the answer. In any case, relations such as Equation 23.3 are substantially more general than might appear at first sight.

21. See pp. 419–21.

Note that the problem here occurs when two of the independent variables move together in an approximately linear fashion. If they move together non-linearly, there will not be so severe a problem. If what is involved is not another relation between two or more of the independent variables but another relation between the *dependent* variable and an independent variable, then the basic assumption of least squares will be violated and we will have a situation involving simultaneous equations as discussed below. See pp. 429–31 and 436–9.

22. This is because, for the purpose of assessing reliability of the regression estimate, what matters is the number of 'degrees of freedom' – the excess of the number of observations over the number of parameters to be estimated. The following conveys some idea of what is involved. One can always fit a line to two observations, but there are no degrees of freedom and no way of assessing the reliability of the result. If one has a third observation, then one cannot always fit a line exactly but some notion of reliability can be gained from observing how close one comes in fact. Add another variable with a coefficient to be estimated, however, and one is estimating a plane that can be fitted precisely to three observations. Thus, the addition of another coefficient to be estimated has the same effect as the removal of one observation.

23. See pp. 419–21.

24. As explained in Note 14, the two basic measures of dispersion of a random variable are its variance, the average squared deviation around its mean, and its standard deviation, the square root of the variance. The standard error of a statistic (here, the standard error of a regression coefficient) is, in a rough sense, its expected standard deviation. More precisely, it is the

square root of the average squared deviation that one would expect to obtain if one used the same estimating procedure over and over again. It is a convenient measure of the reliability of the statistic with which it is associated since the probability that the statistic differs from the true value by any given amount depends directly on the number of standard errors that the amount represents.

25. This will depend on the normality assumption, see p. 415 and Notes 12 and 18.

26. The examples of significance given in the text are for what is known as a 'two-tailed test'. For example, the significance level of 5 per cent associated with a *t*-statistic of about two is the probability of obtaining an estimated coefficient as large as that actually obtained, *either positive or negative*, if the true coefficient is actually 0. In many situations, for example, there is no issue as to whether or not a particular coefficient is positive or negative; rather, the only issue may be whether it is positive or zero. In such a circumstance, the appropriate test is a 'one-tailed test' in which 5 per cent would represent the probability of observing a *positive* coefficient as large as that actually obtained, if the true value were really zero. The *t*-statistic required for significance at a given level on a one-tailed test is less than that required for the same level on a two-tailed test. In the case of 5 per cent, for example, what is required is approximately 1.6 rather than 2.

27. It is in fact not computed as an arithmetic average. Rather, it is the square root of the average squared deviation in the sample (with an adjustment for degrees of freedom, see Note 22).

28. Related to the standard error of estimate, but not identical to it, is the standard error of forecast. This is a measure of how reliable forecasts made from the regression equation are likely to be. More precisely, it is the square root of the expected squared difference between the actual value of the dependent variable and its forecast value. The standard error of forecast and the standard error of estimate differ for the following reason. Whereas the standard error of estimate measures the extent of deviation in the sample period around the relationship as estimated, forecast errors will involve not only deviation from the estimated relationship but also the fact that the estimated relationship itself may deviate from the true relationship.

   The way in which these two standard errors differ is somewhat instructive. In general, one expects to be surest about where the true relationship is for points that fall inside the range of points already observed in the sample. One would be less sure of points less typical of the sample. The standard error of forecast does depend on how far from typical sample values the values of the independent variables for the forecast period happen to fall. It is larger the farther away from sample are such values. Given the location of the independent variables for the forecast period, however, the standard error of forecast is proportional to the standard error of estimate, which does not vary with such location.

29. The reasons for writing the correlation coefficient as a square need not detain us here.

30. How high a value of R^2 is to be expected depends on the number of degrees of freedom (see Note 22). When one has two observations with which to fit a line, for example, such a fit will always be exact and R^2 always

equal to unity. Where the line must fit many observations, then an R^2 near unity would be more impressive evidence that movements in the dependent variable are explained by movements in the independent variables.

31. Thus, for example, suppose that in the audience–revenue relationship, we had decided that the true relationship was logarithmic, with the logarithm of revenue as the dependent variable. Suppose also that one of the independent variables was the log of audience size. Suppose then that we subtracted the log of audience size from both sides, making the dependent variable the log of revenue per viewer (equal to log of revenue minus log of audience size). Obviously, the only substantive thing that this would do would be to subtract one from the coefficient of the log of the audience. But it would also change R^2, which would now measure how much of the variation in the log of revenue *per viewer* we were explaining rather than how much of the variation in the log of revenue itself. The resulting value of R^2 might thus be either higher or lower than the original value.

32. Controlling for job classification is an obvious thing to do and might be done by multiple regression. Of course this presumes that discrimination does not affect job classification.

33. See Finkelstein, 'The judicial reception of multiple regression studies in race and sex discrimination cases', *Colum. L. Rev.* **80** 737 (1980).

34. Since, under the *per se* rule, the ineffectiveness of a price-fixing conspiracy is not a defense, such a showing would be irrelevant to the issue of liability.

35. If one were willing to admit that the price-fixing agreement did have a substantial impact on price (which, presumably, one is not), least squares estimation of the demand curve might become easier, essentially because prices would have been determined in a controlled manner. On this point, see my study of aluminum demand, F.M. Fisher, *A Priori Information and Time Series Analysis* (Amsterdam: North-Holland, 1962), pp. 93–117.

36. There may be some technical problems concerning whether to estimate Equation 23.9 directly by multiple regression or to use sophisticated simultaneous equation techniques to estimate Equation 23.7 and 23.8 directly, but they need not detain us.

37. This would generally be tested by a so-called 'Chow' test. See F.M. Fisher, 'Tests of equality between sets of coefficients in two linear regressions: an expository note', *Econometrica* **38** 361–6 (1970). This would also be the test used to determine whether the entire regression of income on aptitude was the same for men and for women in the discrimination example above.

38. See, e.g. *Deterrence and incapacitation*, Note 1.

39. For a more detailed discussion and references, see Klein, Forst and Filatov, Note 1.

40. I. Ehrlich, 'The deterrent effect of capital punishment: a question of life and death', *Am. Econ. Rev.* **65** 397 (1975).

41. See Notes 10 and 20.

42. There are ways of testing whether one form is better than another. Often, however, it is hard to tell from the results.

43. Ehrlich has also performed cross-section analyses of murder, but I am less familiar with these than with his study of non-capital crimes. The latter is I. Ehrlich, 'Participation in illegitimate' activities: a theoretical and empirical investigation', *J. Pol. Econ.* **81** 521 (1973). The following comments are expanded in D. Nagin, 'General deterrence: a review of the empirical evidence', in *Deterrence and incapacitation*, Note 1, at 95, and in

Chapter 20.

44. See F.M. Fisher, *The Identification Problem in Econometrics* (New York: McGraw-Hill, 1966; Huntington: Robert E. Krieger Publishing Co., 1976).

45. On the other hand, it is not difficult to think of variables that enter the crime equation but that would not directly influence the choice of sanctions. Unemployment, for example, is far more likely to influence the crime rate than to influence sanctions. Other examples might include measures of income disparity or expenditures on security systems. If such variables really do influence crime rates, but not sanctions, then including them in the crime equation would shift that equation relative to the sanctions equation. The points of intersection traced out would all lie on the sanctions equation, which would then be identifiable and could be estimated (although still not by least squares).

46. Consider the following all too common procedure. Since multiple regression is easy to do, one experiments with multiple regression until one has a version of the estimated equation that corresponds to one's own predilections. Then one reestimates the equation by an appropriate simultaneous equation technique. If the results look very different from the least squares version one goes on exploring. This is not a way to produce consistent results.

24

Statisticians, econometricians and adversary proceedings (1986)

Introduction

This chapter concerns the problems and standards of behavior of statisticians acting as consultants and witnesses for lawyers – statisticians in the context of a system that views adversary proceedings as a way of finding the truth. Such an environment differs from that of the professional meeting or the graduate seminar, and the guidelines for successful and appropriate professional behavior (although surely not wholly distinct) are not the same in the two situations. I shall discuss a number of areas in which my own experience suggests problems and modes of behavior. Because I am an economist, the examples used are largely, but not exclusively, drawn from the use of econometrics in adversary proceedings. I believe the discussion to be of relevance for other branches of statistics, however. (For discussions of similar matters, see Royal Statistical Society 1982, including Downton 1982, Fienberg and Straf 1982, and Newell 1982; also see Finkelstein and Levenbach 1983 and Rubinfeld and Steiner 1983.)

This chapter is a revised version of a paper presented at the Economic and Social Research Council Econometric Study Group Conference in honor of J.D. Sargan, in Oxford, England, March 1984.

Having previously attempted to explain to lawyers how to deal with econometricians (see Chapter 23), I am grateful to Ellen P. Fisher for suggesting that it might be useful to approach the same subject from the opposite point of view. The work on the *Corrugated* case owes much to Stephen H. Kalos. I am also indebted to Joseph B. Kadane and two referees for helpful comments. Harry Roberts, in particular, went far beyond the usual call of duty and produced an unusually detailed and helpful report. It is in the nature of a paper such as this, however, that readers and author may disagree, and I am particularly conscious that errors and opinions are my responsibility.

My experience in this area has been reasonably extensive, lasting more than 20 years. Twenty years ago, the legal profession viewed econometrics as black magic, and the introduction of econometric evidence was a considerable innovation. Today, although econometrics may still be viewed as black magic, its use is no longer rare, for it is supposed to be capable of rather more than it is.

It is always tempting to seek certainty in quantification rather than to study all of the aspects of a truly complex problem. (The use of market share in antitrust cases is an outstanding example.) The use of statistical methods in general, and of econometric methods in particular, provides that temptation in a form often irresistible to one or the other side of a lawsuit. Such methods provide quantitative, computer-generated answers, which seem invested with a scientific accuracy. When those answers appear to favor their clients, lawyers may be very ready to believe whatever their expert is telling them, whether or not it is truly well founded. Since not all supposed experts are truly skilled, and since not all experts remain truly impartial, this can create serious difficulties. When the opposing side does not itself have expert assistance, the result may be a successful attempt to overawe judge or jury with an apparently scientific answer.

Indeed, a principal reason for capable statisticians to be interested in such activities is the lamentable fact that legal proceedings will contain statistical analyses whether or not competent persons provide them. Unless the area is to be abandoned to practitioners who are poorly trained, poorly skilled or whose professional standards are not very high, serious and competent statisticians and econometricians must enter it.

The desire to correct misuse of the tools, however, is not the only reason for statisticians – and particularly econometricians – to participate in litigation. Those who have brought statistical methods into legal proceedings, even those who have done so incompetently, have perceived correctly that the techniques of estimation, forecasting and tests of hypotheses can often be usefully brought to bear on real, practical problems of considerable private and even public interest. Whereas the use of large models or of time-series analysis to inform governmental policy is the most exciting, if not always a very successful, application of econometrics to macroeconomics, the use of econometrics in court or regulatory proceedings is, I think, the most exciting application to microeconomics. Econometricians have an opportunity to use their tools on problems that people really care about, to gain access to considerable bodies of data, and to use the expertise of those directly involved. I believe it to be important to accept that opportunity, and much of my own empirical work has come from such participation.

Explaining statistical methods

One of the most important problems faced by the statistician who participates in such activity is that of exposition. Direct testimony almost invariably includes an exposition of the statistical methods used as well as a presentation of the results. Hence if all goes well, statisticians will have to explain to a judge or a jury what it is they have done and how it should be interpreted. Even if the study is never presented in court, statistical methods will have to be explained to the clients, the lawyers with whom the statistician works. This is not an easy matter, since it is extremely rare that any of these potential audiences has had any technical training (or is even comfortable with high-school algebra). The following are some of the confusions I have encountered.

Parameter estimation

At least in general terms, the statistician will have to explain that estimates of the parameters of the model are not chosen arbitrarily. Such explanations can vary from a heuristic, diagram-using discussion of fitting a line to a scatter of points, to the assertion that estimation is done on a computer using a long-recognized method. At least the statistician's own client is likely to require the more elaborate explanation; whether a jury will do so may be a matter of tactics.

It is important to emphasize this point so that the statistician is not thought to be picking numbers out of the air and the audience will understand that statistical methods provide the best reflection of what the data say. Attorneys and others involved in the case may have their own opinions as to what the values of parameters are; they may not realize that it is not sufficient merely to object that the results do not come out as expected. Furthermore, attorneys and judges tend to view with suspicion any computational method that they do not understand in very elementary terms. That suspicion may be difficult to allay unless examples are well thought out and well presented, for as Edward Levi has remarked, 'The basic pattern of legal reasoning is reasoning by example.' (Levi 1948, p. 1)

To take a particular example, some years ago I had occasion to study the effect of cable television on local television stations in the United States (see Chapter 16). As part of that study, I estimated the value of a viewing household to a station in terms of advertising revenue. I did this by regressing station revenues on audience size using a cross-section of television stations. The regression passed very close to the origin and had a slope of about $27 per year for each additional household viewing in the average half-hour of prime evening time.

Despite the fact that the regression fitted a great many observations nearly perfectly, that estimate was attacked as obviously incorrect by some who failed to understand the units or the fact that an increase in household viewing in prime time in a cross-section of stations was highly correlated with household viewing in other parts of the day, so $27 did not merely represent advertising rates charged in the evening. Such confusions were only resolved by computations made by Martin Seiden, an economist (not an econometrician) hired by the Federal Communications Commission (FCC), the regulatory body in charge of television. (After receiving referee comments on a first draft in which this was not done and after consultation with the editor, I have decided to refer to people by name when they can in any case be readily identified from the public record.) Seiden took all television revenues in the United States and divided them by the number of television households multiplied by 60 per cent, the fraction of prime time that the average household was found in surveys to watch television. He came up with approximately $27 per household.

This was hardly a surprising finding. Consider a two-variable regression that goes through the origin, $y = xb + u$, where b is the least squares estimate of the slope so that u has sample mean zero. Denoting sample means by bars, it is immediate that $b = \bar{y}/\bar{x}$, since $\bar{u} = 0$. Hence Seiden was merely approximately recalculating the same regression coefficient that I had already given. Nevertheless, the fact that he could reach essentially the same result by elementary methods made him, and others, decide that my result was believable after all. Indeed, the number so calculated became perhaps the only quantitative result in my study that was widely accepted.

Certainly, such an experience would be less likely today. The FCC staff of those days had essentially no experience with econometrics or even with computers. (They expressed doubt that the same punchcards they used for accounting purposes could also be used for input for computations.) Nevertheless, even though potential clients are likely to be more sophisticated today, the story is still relevant. Unless care is taken to explain some of the mysteries of the science, the statistician may run into difficulties simply because some of the audience believe that their guess is just as good as the results, and perhaps better.

Ratios

The same story illustrates a different phenomenon. Most adult Americans, even those exposed to mathematics in college, are extremely uncomfortable with mathematical thinking. Even linear equations involving a single variable and a constant term, let alone equations involving several variables, are likely to be regarded with fear as 'higher mathematics'.

This requires careful attention by the statistician, especially because a layperson's idea of how to do forecasting may simply be to assume that the ratio of the dependent variable to one of the independent variables is constant. Despite the advantage of simplicity in such a 'constant ratio' approach, statisticians generally should firmly resist the temptation to use it. They should carefully explain that the constant-ratio assumption is but a special (usually a very special) case and that if the assumption is true it will be found to be so in the context of the more general and satisfactory linear model. Perhaps because of the difficulties of exposition involved in the use of more satisfactory methods, not all expert witnesses resist the temptation to use the simplistic, constant-ratio approach.

Systematic versus random elements: data mining

The tendency for laypersons to believe that they know how the study must come out is related to another problem that is frequently encountered. Statisticians are used to the idea that regression equations do not generally fit the data perfectly. They understand that although the systematic part of a regression equation involves the most important variables that theory or common sense suggests influence the dependent variable, the effects of minor or particular influences is left to the random error term. Although one naturally wants a fit as good as possible, other things equal, it is well recognized that even the best model is but an approximation. There will always be unexplained deviations from the regression plane.

Lawyers may understand this in principle, but they do not like it. Attorneys, presented with a general argument, tend to think in terms of counter-examples, and the fact that not all observations lie in the regression plane may seem to them to provide ammunition for the opponent. They tend to offer *ad hoc* explanations of at least the larger deviations from the regression plane, even in cases in which the fit is good. Furthermore, attorneys tend to be quite sensitive to the objection that not every plausible argument was taken into account. The result is a tendency to insist that the statistician explicitly model every influence that anyone can think of as possibly important.

This presents both statistician and attorney with a dilemma. On the one hand, unless the statistician explores all of the plausible alternatives, the attorney's fears may be realized: the statistician may be made to look careless on cross-examination by a failure to see if any of the suggested influences made a difference. On the other hand, the statistician cannot simply mine the data until a satisfactory model is found to fit the sample. To do so at best vitiates any claim as to the statistical properties of the model and at worst exposes the statistician to the suspicion that models have been rejected until one favoring the client is found. Since not all expert witnesses attempt to maintain full impartiality and since, as I discuss later, subjective honesty is not a simple matter even for those with the best of intentions, care must be taken to guard against such a charge.

The problem is not merely one of appearances. In scientific work, one may want to impose severe limits on exploratory data analysis in order to protect against overfitting. In legal work, on the other hand, the same stringent limits may prevent the examination of potentially relevant evidence. Yet it is dangerous either to ignore such evidence or to depart from usual scientific procedures for the sake of the type of investigation or the client.

I recommend the following mode of operation to deal with such problems. First, the attorney sponsoring the project must be made to understand the problems associated with 'data mining'. Explanation should carefully be given as to the role of the random error in picking up particular exceptions to a general rule and as to the fact that the estimated equation will describe an average tendency rather than an exact universal law.

Second, particularly in cases in which the data are insufficient to permit segregation of the sample for exploratory model building and for testing, statisticians should set down in advance the versions of the model (few in number) that they believe are most likely to be the appropriate ones. (Of course, this should be done after discussion with the attorney and with others knowledgeable about the phenomena being modeled.) If those versions prove to provide a reasonable explanation of the phenomenon under investigation (with no more than the usual reconsideration after the results are seen), the particular factors that the attorney or someone else thinks may also operate can be entered as additional variables. Often such additional factors make little difference to the results.

In this way the statistician can succeed whether or not the particular factors involved are in fact important. If they are, this will be discovered. If they are not important, as I have suggested will be the usual case, the statistician will be able to testify to that lack of importance on direct or cross-examination and will have created a record showing that the model sponsored was not arrived at after massive experimentation on the same set of data.

In some cases, of course, the matter may be easier to resolve, for the statistician may have the luxury of sufficient data with which to explore different possibilities while reserving other data for confirmatory testing. (This is perhaps more likely in discrimination cases, where the data relate to individuals, than in antitrust cases, where a model of the industry is required.) Even in such cases, the procedure just outlined is desirable. Writing the alternatives thought most plausible in advance becomes part of the necessary practice of creating a retrievable record of what decisions were taken and the reasons for them. When data are used for exploration, the reasons for changing or abandoning a model and for following up or not following up some alternative must be set forth. In any case, enough exploration must be done so that the results are shown to be relatively insensitive to plausible alternative specifications and data choices. Only in that way can statisticians protect themselves from the temptation to favor the client and from the ensuing cross-examination.

Goodness-of-fit and the nature of models

Associated with the tendency to believe that a model must fit all cases is the tendency to judge models purely on how well they fit the data, with goodness of fit being measured in the grossest sense of R^2. There is a natural view that models are supposed to do nothing other than predict, and therefore a model that superficially appears to predict well must be believed. Since it is often possible to fit the data well with models that do not reflect any structural characteristics of the phenomena being investigated, the danger here is that the laypersons involved will be impressed by poor work to the detriment of better models that do not fit or predict quite so well but are in fact informative about the phenomena being investigated.

It is easy to misunderstand what is likely to be involved here. There is a genuine scientific issue regarding the insights into structure that can be gained from structural models that fit poorly. Furthermore, there are occasions on which the structure of the phenomenon being investigated is so poorly understood that attempts to fit a structural model are not helpful. But those are precisely the occasions on which statistical methods are unlikely to provide much guidance for judge or jury. The issue in litigation is unlikely to be whether an autoregressive integrated moving average (ARIMA) model predicts better than a supposedly structural one. Rather, it is likely to be whether to believe the implications of very simple models based on trend-fitting and related techniques that have little to do with the phenomenon being studied. On other occasions with somewhat more sophisticated opponents, the question may be whether to believe a poorly constructed structural model just because it appears to fit the sample well. (See the discussion of the *Corrugated* case below.)

On the other hand, it is important to remember that, depending on the object in view, it may not be necessary to estimate a full structural model. For example, to test whether a certain firm discriminates in the wages it pays women, one need not estimate a model that attempts to mimic the decision processes of the firm. Abstracting from other difficulties, consider a structural model with two equations describing in detail the assignment of employees to jobs and the assignment of salaries for given jobs, in both cases given gender and qualifications. Such a model, if correct, can be revealing as to how discrimination operates. If the details of the job and salary assignment process are poorly understood, however, one may well do better with a single reduced-form equation that merely seeks to explain salary given qualifications and gender. In a more general context, when interest centers on a particular parameter it is useful to remember and explain that effects that bias the estimates of other parameters are not important even if they prevent a full structural explanation of the process being studied.

Significance levels and tests of hypotheses

Within the context of a structural regression model, the relevant goodness-of-fit statistics are usually the standard errors of the regression coefficients or the associated t-statistics, but these are much less easy for non-statisticians to understand than are overall measures. Furthermore, unless care is taken to explain how the precision of estimation is measured, a judge or jury can be readily confused by objections raised by the relatively untrained or the unscrupulous.

In my work in the *IBM* antitrust case, for example, I presented regressions that attempted to relate the price of computer central-processing-unit–memory combinations to characteristics such as speed and memory size. There was a very good fit. Despite the fact that t-statistics on the order of 20 were obtained for all of the regression coefficients, Alan K. McAdams, appearing as an expert for the government, testified that collinearity made it impossible reliably to separate the effects of the different independent variables and hence that little reliance could be placed on the result (see Fisher *et al.* 1983, p. 156).

Whatever else that incident illustrates, it shows that numbers, especially technical magnitudes such as t-statistics, do not speak for themselves to the lay public. In particular, familiar as they may be to the statistican, the concept of significance levels and the nature of hypothesis testing are not particularly easy for the non-statistician to grasp, and the statistician must be prepared to explain them carefully.

It is not surprising that the lay public, including the legal profession, has difficulty with hypothesis testing and the interpretation of significance levels. Such matters are not easy to explain to beginning students of statistics, and it is easy to slip into the incorrect usage of saying that significance at the 5 per cent level means that the probability that the null hypothesis is true is less than 5 per cent. It is particularly important to avoid such errors in adversary proceedings because of the importance attached to standards of proof in such proceedings.

Civil cases in the United States generally use what is called a *preponderance of the evidence* standard. This means that if it is more probable than not that a given side is correct, then that side should prevail. (See Fienberg and Kadane (1983) for a discussion of Bayesian interpretations of different standards of proof.) If the significance level is incorrectly interpreted as the probability that the null hypothesis is true, then the preponderance-of-the-evidence standard can lead to the position that the correct significance level to use in testing hypotheses is 50 per cent!

I am not making this up. A recent case involved the question of whether a particular drug has the side effect of increasing the risk of a certain condition found in the population at low levels among both drug users and non-users. A witness called as an expert in statistics by the plaintiff (who contended that the effect was present) actually took this position, at least in advising the client. Indeed, the witness went further, contending not only that the appropriate standard was a one-tailed test but also that any experiment showing a reduction of the condition among drug users compared to the population as a whole must be a mistake and should be disregarded. Needless to say, this produced a predictable antidrug conclusion.

The problem that this example presents is not that of why the analysis was wrong but of how to convince non-specialists that it is wrong. This is difficult enough when dealing with high-powered lawyers; it is an order of magnitude harder if one is trying to straighten out a jury.

The approach that I have found most useful in this area is that of using very simple examples. In the drug case just outlined, put aside the question of discarding studies showing a reduction of the condition involved. In that example, it is not hard to see that the use of the 50 per cent significance level with a one-tailed test to test the hypothesis that a particular coin is weighted toward heads leads to an absurd result. The conclusion will be that the coin is weighted if it comes up heads more often than tails no matter how small the number of tosses.

The matter is seldom so easy, however. Without the one-tail feature, it is much harder to find a description of the absurdity of using the 50 per cent significance level that is instantaneously convincing to the untrained person. The use of a two-tailed test at the 50 per cent level to test whether a coin is fair only leads to the result that fair coins will be deemed unfair 50 per cent of the time. To non-statisticians this sounds like the false proposition that rejection of the null hypothesis of fairness at the 50 per cent level means that the coin is more likely than not to be weighted.

The drug example also illustrates a deeper problem. Classical null hypothesis testing is not really suited to a situation in which retention of the null hypothesis when it is false can have very serious consequences compared to rejection of the null hypothesis when it is true. Most court cases of this type do not concern the initial decision to release the drug or even (save implicitly) the question of whether the drug should continue to be used. Suppose, however, that continued use of the drug were indeed the question at issue. If the possible undesirable side effects were enough compared to the beneficial effects of the drug, one would not want to adopt a procedure implicitly weighted in favor of retaining the drug. Yet that is what happens if one rejects the null hypothesis of no side-effects only when the observed results would be observed less than 5 per cent of the time if the null hypothesis were true. It is very tempting to suppose that one can cure this problem by using a less demanding significance level. Indeed, if the possible harm is great enough, one can understand the temptation to discard all studies showing a condition-reducing effect of the drug, even though some such results are to be expected if the drug has no side-effects.

Both of these temptations lead to suboptimal procedures, even when the decision is whether to permit continued drug use. Adjusting the significance level used directly adjusts the probability of stopping the use of a drug that does not in fact have harmful side-effects. The effect on the probability of continuing a drug that has such side-effects is only implicit, and it is neither easy to state what the optimum significance level is nor necessarily true that the optimal policy can be parameterized in this way.

Furthermore, the usual litigation context is somewhat different. That context is typically one in which the issue is whether a particular plaintiff should receive damages, not directly whether the drug should continue to be used (although the drug may be withdrawn if damages are heavy enough). The statistician must somehow meet the preponderance-of-the-evidence standard by estimating the probability that a particular plaintiff was injured. Within the framework of classical null hypothesis testing, this may be possible by setting up the null hypothesis that the increased risk caused by the drug is no more than some given amount. More satisfactory answers are likely to be even harder to explain.

Plainly, I have no very good solutions for such expository problems. The concepts involved in hypothesis testing and, perhaps even more so, in the construction of confidence intervals are hard to explain to those with no statistical training.

I can, however, offer a negative prescription. The real need to communicate with attorneys, judges and juries by speaking language they can readily understand must not be met at the cost of imprecision of speech. It is very easy to slip into locutions such as that which describes a significance level as the probability that the null hypothesis is true. Such slips only lead to trouble when the listeners are called on to make the ultimate decision.

Professional and unprofessional behavior

> In other professions in which men engage
> (Said I to myself, said I),
> The Army, the Navy, the Church, and the Stage
> (Said I to myself, said I),
> Professional license, if carried too far,
> Your chance of promotion will certainly mar,
> And I fancy the rule might apply to the Bar
> (Said I to myself, said I).
>
> (W.S. Gilbert, *Iolanthe*)

Although exposition occupies a central role, there are other problems that the statistician is likely to encounter. Some such problems concern the statistician's behavior in putting forward a study and some concern the statistician's role in criticizing the studies of others. Indeed, since statisticians (or at least supposed statistical work) may appear on both sides of a case, it is important to distinguish legitimate criticism from obfuscation and to consider how best to make clear to the judge or jury what the difference is between serious statistics and pseudo-science.

Data management: protecting oneself

The first rule in presenting one's own study ought in any context to be standard procedure but too often is not followed. It is the rule that there must be total familiarity with the data sources and total assurance that the data used are absolutely accurate. Unless one has seen it happen, one cannot imagine the skill and ferocity with which a good cross-examining attorney can make a study appear riddled with error and its author a careless fool if there are many mistakes in the underlying data. Such mistakes are easy for a judge or jury to understand, and even if the mistakes are minor, no amount of professional skill or assumption of expertise on the part of the statistician can overcome the fatal impression of carelessness that such cross-examination can produce.

Fortunately, the very participation in an adversary proceeding that makes detailed data examination likely by the opponents also makes it likely that the statistician will have the resources to make such examination fruitless – resources that unfortunately are not always available in pure research. The necessity of guarding against mistakes will generally lead the attorneys for whom the statistician works to pay for careful data management by a staff of trained assistants. (Since, as discussed later, a primary duty of that staff is to protect the statistician from being swept along by overzealous attorneys, it is best if the staff is not provided by the attorneys themselves or the ultimate client but has an outside relationship with the statistician. Possible sources are consulting firms or academic colleagues and students.)

If properly used, such a staff can provide an invaluable resource to the statistician. One staff member should be given the responsibility for data management. That person must understand that his or her responsibility is to ensure that the backup for every statement made and for all data used is accurate and available. Consistent with the use of staff to protect the statistician's subjective honesty (discussed later), it should be made clear that good performance means finding all possible problems, even if this means the discovery of apparent difficulties that prove not to be real ones.

The data-management job involves responsibility for numerical accuracy. It is advisable to have all data transcription and key punching independently done by more than one person. Such relatively mechanical matters are vitally important; however, the data-management job is not limited to them. The data-management person should also be responsible for keeping a complete record of data sources and of decisions concerning data. (A similar record of all decisions concerning model building should also be kept, as should all computer runs when possible.) Furthermore, a large part of data management can involve the evaluation of whether data really represent what they are supposed to and of whether non-statistical judgments involved can be supported. It is a mistake to leave data-management responsibility to relatively inexperienced or untrained research assistants.

I cannot stress too heavily the desirability and importance of good, systematically organized data management. It is embarrassing to have to explain why some runs were not kept or to remember imprecisely why some things were done. Even more important, there is nothing that makes it easier to withstand cross-examination about one's work than the correct belief that one knows far more about it than the attorney asking the questions. That belief rests on the invaluable assurance (which only good data management can provide) that the data are absolutely accurate and that the answer to any question about what was done can be ascertained readily.

Even a knowledgeable witness can be trapped by a skillful cross-examining attorney. Especially when tired, it is all too easy to lose one's temper, to ramble and to misspeak a sentence in a way that will be quoted forever after. This is particularly likely to happen if the cross-examiner can legitimately cast doubt on the accuracy of or the basis for the witness's conclusions. Although there is no such thing as too much preparation for cross-examination, no amount of practice can substitute for a well-founded belief in the performance of the data-management staff.

Data management: criticizing others

The problems that poor data management can produce may arise in another way. The statistician may be asked to criticize a study put forth by someone on the other side, and data errors are a legitimate focus for such criticism. A story is instructive here, however.

After the study of cable television already mentioned was submitted as testimony to the FCC, the other side (in this case the cable trade association) retained Herbert Arkin, a statistician, to criticize it. He did so in a written submission to the FCC, spending the major part of his paper on the possible (not the actual) presence of data error. After admitting that my qualifications were beyond question, he challenged the capability of the MIT graduate students who assisted me.

This, of course, meant war, but it was a war that Arkin – or at least his attorneys – fought in a strange way. He demanded that a subpoena be issued for the data so that they might be checked for error. This was strange, because the data had already been submitted with my original study, so all that such a demand could succeed in doing was to reveal that the person making it had not done his homework. In the event, the FCC staff, reporting on these issues, observed that there must be some mistake because the data had in fact been made part of the file, whereupon Arkin submitted a further letter demanding that a key to the data be subpoenaed, since data are not always in readily readable form. Needless to say, such a key had also already been provided.

In a recent unpublished letter to the editor of the *Journal of the*

American Statistical Association, Arkin stated that his attorney clients misinformed him and that he was told that neither the data nor the key was available.

There are several lessons to be drawn from this tale. The first of these is that it is not enough to suggest that errors may exist in someone else's work. Errors are always possible, but merely to point that out is not to advance at all. Instead, one must establish either that errors do exist in fact (and are of material importance) or at least that the procedures used are likely to result in error. Armchair criticism is at best less effective than actual demonstration.

Arkin was correct to ask his clients for the data and, believing that they were unavailable, to demand that they be produced so that they could be examined for error. That line of attack, however, could only be effective if followed up by actual examination. There was little point to a lengthy and general explanation of the possibility of error and little point also to general questioning of the qualifications of the MIT graduate students (who were, in fact, quite highly skilled). Without actual demonstration of the presence of error, such comments could not carry much weight. Especially when the FCC staff's observation (after several weeks) that the data had always been available was not followed by actual examination but by a demand for the also available key, the indelible impression was left that armchair criticism was all that was intended.

The second, related, lesson is more complex. Somebody obviously slipped badly in permitting Arkin to submit the demand for the key after the FCC staff had pointed out that the earlier demand had been unnecessary from the outset. Given that Arkin knew that he had been (deliberately or inadvertently) misled by his attorney clients about the availability of the data, he allowed himself to be used too easily a second time. One of the important things that a testifying expert must bear in mind is to be deeply enough involved to be certain that slips like this do not occur. Attorneys are often the easiest source of information and reliance on them is sometimes unavoidable, but the expert witness needs to act independently whenever possible. Even though the attorneys generally have a strong interest in protecting expert witnesses and their reputations, that is not their primary goal. Furthermore, when, as here, it becomes evident that the attorneys cannot be relied on, the witness must act, taking that unreliability into account.

Arkin appears to have been a victim of (at least) bungling on the part of his attorneys. As a result, much of his criticism came across as mere obfuscation – a form of attack that is tempting when dealing with an untrained audience but is unlikely to pay off against a really well-prepared opponent.

Illegitimate criticism generally

Naturally, these lessons carry over to areas of possible criticism of others beyond that of data management. Precisely because statistics and econometrics are badly understood by judges and juries, statisticians and econometricians have a special obligation not to 'hoodwink a judge who is not overwise' (in the words of Gilbert and Sullivan's Lord Chancellor) by throwing up objections that, even if valid, would not materially affect the results of the study being criticized. There is an obligation to demonstrate that the objection is not merely one that could be made to *any* econometric study and to show that the conclusions to be drawn are likely actually to be affected by the error being discussed.

For example, it is not helpful to object that error distributions may not be normal unless there is some reason to think that they are very far from normal; to do so is to play on the listeners' ignorance of the central limit theorem so as to make the assumption of normality seem very special. Similarly, as in the example from the *IBM* case referred to before, it is not a good idea to damn a study for collinearity without thinking about whether that collinearity really mattered. To do so is at best to hope that the statistician who did the study is not very good at exposition. Alas, the statistician presenting a study had better be prepared for criticisms like these.

Of course, I do not contend that serious criticism should be withheld; far from it. The statistician testifying in an adversary proceeding should expect to withstand serious cross-examination. The attorney doing that cross-examination is entitled to the best professional help from other statisticians. Only in that way can an adversary system hope to arrive at an informed judgment. What the statistician assisting in cross-examination should avoid is deliberate obfuscation that takes unfair advantage of the fact that the judicial decision-maker is untrained. Such obfuscation is unprofessional. Furthermore, if the other side is able, deliberate obfuscation will open an opportunity for a telling rebuttal.

Part of the reason that such tactics can pay off, of course, is the relatively untrained nature of the judge or the jury. This raises the possibility that the court might be aided by a special master or clerk trained in statistics. [A similar procedure was tried long ago by Judge Charles Wyszanski in the *United Shoe Machinery* case (see *United States* v. *United Shoe Machinery Corporation* 1953) when he employed Carl Kaysen, the economist, as his clerk.] In principle, this seems a good idea; in practice, courts will have a hard time identifying good statisticians (or economists) from bad ones. Furthermore, the better statisticians will be less likely than the poor ones to be willing to put in the long periods of time on relatively short notice that may be required to serve in such a capacity. Since the court is likely to rely heavily on its own expert, these are very real difficulties, although some of the problems might be alleviated if the court's expert could be cross-examined by the parties. In any event, such experiments are relatively rare.

Legitimate criticism: the Corrugated case

The statistician looking for something to criticize in adversary proceedings will probably not have to look far. This is because, as already remarked, the advent of the computer and the success of econometrics have opened the door to poor statistical and econometric testimony masquerading as serious science. I have already related some incidents suggesting that this is true; now I turn to a recent one of considerable importance. (For another discussion, see Finkelstein and Levenbach 1983).

A recent tripartite series of antitrust cases concerned allegations of price-fixing in the sale of corrugated containers (see *In Re Corrugated Container Antitrust Litigation* 1979, 1980, 1985). The first of these cases was a criminal trial in which all defendants who contested the charge were acquitted. The second, tried in 1980, was a private, civil, class-action suit that only one defendant, the Mead Corporation, contested. The third, tried in 1982 and 1983, was brought by several large corporations who had opted not to participate in the class-action trial and was defended by several manufacturers of corrugated containers.

In the class-action suit, the plaintiffs put forward an econometric model developed by John Beyer, an economist with admittedly no econometric training. That model purported to show that the alleged price-fixing conspiracy had resulted in a general overcharge to purchasers of 7 per cent. The jury found for the plaintiffs, and the result was what appears to be the largest settlement collected on behalf of a class in the history of the Sherman Antitrust Act. Beyer's model and testimony justifiably gained notoriety among members of the antitrust bar.

By the time of the 'opt-out' trial, Beyer had 'improved' his model, which now showed an overcharge of 26 per cent. This time, however, the defendants, now suitably alerted, decided that they had better retain an econometrician themselves, and they retained me. At the end of the trial, the jury found that although there was evidence of conspiracy, there was no evidence of damages to the plaintiffs – rejecting the use of Beyer's econometric model.

Beyer's model was not well grounded in economic analysis. It was generally agreed that the alleged conspiracy had ended as of sometime in the middle 1970s. (Beyer used three different months in 1975 as an ending date and opted for the one that happened to produce the largest damages.) Beyer did not build a model of the post-conspiracy period and project backwards to see what prices would have been absent the conspiracy (a procedure which, as discussed below, showed no damages). Instead, he purported to model the conspiracy period itself, project forward to the late 1970s to estimate what prices would have been had the conspiracy continued, and then assume that the ratio of conspiratorial to competitive prices would have been the same had there been competition in the earlier period.

Aside from the fact that this procedure provides at best a roundabout way of doing such a study, it suffers from the problem that it requires a model of the conspiratorial period. Models of oligopoly behavior are not notoriously successful, and the reader may wonder what Beyer did to overcome this.

He did nothing at all. Instead, he discussed matters in terms of supply and demand functions, disregarding the fact that the supply function does not exist under oligopoly. He estimated what he referred to as a 'reduced form' in which price was regressed on a number of variables that seemed likely to affect either supply or demand, including a cost index, measures of output in container-using industries and of capacity utilization and inventory adjustment in containers, and a dummy variable reflecting price controls. The model was monthly, and lagged price was also included. Finally, despite the overwhelming theoretical basis for working in deflated prices, Beyer used an index of money prices as the dependent variable, taking account of inflation by including a general price index among the regressors. This was, of course, guaranteed to produce a high R^2 over any period with high inflation.

Despite (or perhaps because of) its lack of a sound structural foundation, the model produced results that were superficially convincing. When the model was dynamically simulated, starting in the 1960s, the predicted prices tracked the actual prices quite closely until about 1975, the date that ended both the sample period and the alleged conspiracy. After that, the simulated prices, which supposedly embodied the effects of the alleged conspiracy, rose above the actual prices. This is graphically depicted in Figure 24.1. To the untrained eye, this picture seems a quite convincing demonstration that something important had happened in early 1975.

Something important had indeed happened. Whether or not the alleged conspiracy ended in January 1975, the sample certainly did. Moreover, the period of the early 1970s was marked by the imposition

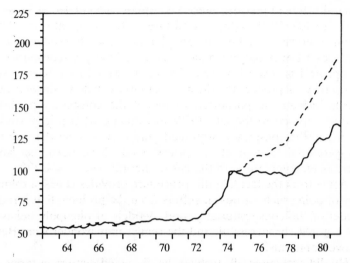

Figure 24.1 FBA corrugated container price index, actual versus simulated (December 1974 = 100): Beyer's model, estimation period from 1963:1 to 1975:1 (——, actual FBA price index; ---, simulated FBA price index).

and then the lifting of price controls, followed by the energy crisis and a recession. As a result, actual container prices rose sharply in the early 1970s and then flattened out. It seemed unlikely that these effects could be handled adequately by the use of an additive dummy variable for the price-control period. If so, then the results were likely to be driven by the events at the end of the sample period that had nothing to do with the alleged conspiracy.

This suspicion proved to be well founded. Standard Chow (F) tests firmly rejected the null hypothesis that the regression equation was the same for the early 1970s as for the 1960s. More dramatically, reestimation of the same model for different sample periods showed that all of the results crucially depended on the inclusion of the unusual years of the early 1970s in the sample. If those observations are removed and the same model estimated only on data before price controls, a very close fit is again obtained for the sample period. This time, however, the dynamic simulation no longer yields high prices for the late 1970s but produces projections of 'conspiratorial' prices *lower* than the prices actually charged after the supposed ending date of the alleged conspiracy. These results are depicted in Figure 24.2.

Indeed, the model has the characteristic that however one chooses

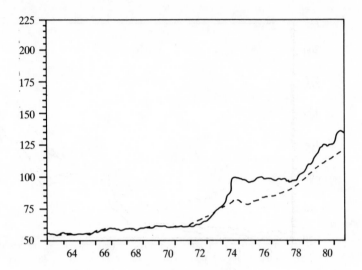

Figure 24.2   FBA corrugated container price index, actual versus
simulated (December 1974 = 100): Beyer's model, estimation period
from 1963:1 to 1971:7 (——, actual FBA price index; ---, simulated
FBA price index).

the sample period, the dynamic simulation fits the sample data quite
well and then continues along whatever trend the last few sample observations happen to be following. This is true even if one chooses a
late sample period and uses dynamic simulation to project backward,
the trend in question here being the backward trend of the first few
sample observations.

This phenomenon is illustrated in Figure 24.3, where the model is
estimated over the supposed post-conspiracy period and used to back-
cast what competitive prices would have been up to 1975. Figure 24.4
illustrates the same phenomenon when a later post-conspiracy period is
chosen. (The first few simulated observations in Figures 24.3 and 24.4
should be ignored; the simulation is given the actual value of the price
index in January 1963 as a starting point.) This is an entirely appropriate test of Beyer's model. As already observed, it is not a model with
the structural features of oligopoly and is, if anything, more suited to
the straightforward procedure of estimation on a competitive sample
period and simulation for the supposed conspiratorial period than to
the roundabout procedure for which Beyer used it.

Note that to make this criticism effective, it was not enough to point
out that the supposed 'model' was not a structural one so that it was
particularly likely that the results merely reflected the particular sample

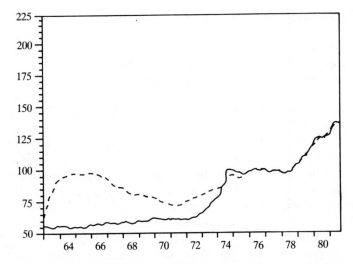

Figure 24.3 FBA corrugated container price index, actual versus simulated (December 1974 = 100): Beyer's model, estimation period from 1975:2 to 1981:8 (——, actual FBA price index; ---, simulated FBA price index).

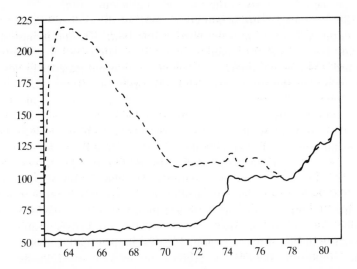

Figure 24.4 FBA corrugated container price index, actual versus simulated (December 1974 = 100): Beyer's model, estimation period from 1979:1 to 1981:8 (——, actual FBA price index; ---, simulated FBA price index).

period used; it was necessary to show that this really did matter. A similar statement holds true for a different criticism of the model, although here the materiality of the objection had to be analytically inferred rather than directly empirically demonstrated.

As already mentioned, Beyer's 'improvements' to his model between the two trials at which he testified had also 'improved' the damage estimates that his model produced, raising them from 7 per cent to 26 per cent of the revenues of the defendants. It is never wise in these matters to succumb to the temptation of presenting the result that happens to be best for one's client (a temptation that attorneys are hired to yield to but statisticians should resist); this is particularly true if one has previously testified to a different effect. In any event, the 26 per cent figure was so outrageously large that it was apparent that had prices been lower by the amount of the supposed overcharge, all of the defendants would have been bankrupt long ago.

The plaintiffs' response to the fact that the estimated damage figure was preposterously large took two related forms. First, Beyer pointed out that conspiracy shields firms from the rigors of competition; in particular, it saves them from having to be efficient. He claimed that the costs of the defendants were inflated by the lack of competition, so no inference could be drawn from the fact that prices could not have been 26 per cent lower given their actual, inefficient costs.

Second, a very important component of the costs of producing corrugated containers was the cost of linerboard (a major input). Since many corrugated container firms are integrated backwards into linerboard, the costs of linerboard reflect the internal transfer prices of that input within the integrated firms. According to Beyer, that price was artificially inflated by the alleged conspiracy with profits taken in linerboard rather than in container production.

The problem with advancing arguments such as these, which are possibilities rather than actualities, is that they have implications that can be seen by trained opponents. In the first place, as pointed out by Peter Max, another defense witness, the bankruptcy that 26 per cent lower prices would have brought about would have applied to the integrated firms, taking into account their entire operations. More pertinent for the present discussion, Beyer had used costs as an *exogenous variable* in his own regression. In so doing, he had not only accepted the supposedly fictitious linerboard prices as being real, he had also implicitly assumed that the prices produced by the alleged conspiracy did not themselves affect costs – exactly what he denied in his inefficiency argument. Although general objections as to the possibility of simultaneous equations bias can often be made, here was a case in which that bias was the more serious the more one believed the arguments given by the model builder for accepting his results.

Conclusion: professional standards and objectivity

I have lingered over the story of the *Corrugated* case, partly for its intrinsic interest and partly because it and the other stories already related exemplify a number of the problems that the statistician involved in adversary proceedings is likely to encounter and, perhaps, the principles that ought to be followed. (For another discussion of some of the matters in this section, see Fisher *et al.* 1983, pp. 350–2).

The first of these has to do with the temptation to pseudo-science. It is tempting to stun the audience with proclaimed expertise together with computer output and professionally drawn visual displays. By pandering to the belief that econometrics is in fact black magic and the statistician the shaman of the computer, it may be possible to overawe the untrained.

Such a temptation should be firmly resisted. On a practical level, such a strategy is only safe to pursue when one is sure that the other side is untrained. An unprofessional job that would not hold up in seminars is unlikely to hold up in court, and it is all to easy to underestimate the intellectual powers of the cross-examining attorney.

Moreover, it is unethical to behave in such a way. As the *Corrugated* story illustrates, the world has quite enough poor statistical and econometric testimony without serious statisticians and econometricians adding to the stock. The court, as well as the statistician's client, is entitled to the statistician's best professional efforts. Anything less is wrong. Statisticians and econometricians have a potentially large contribution to make in litigation; that contribution can only be tainted by the belief that one can get away with less than the best.

Related to this is another temptation, that of telling one's attorneys what they want to hear. The attorney is retained to make the best possible argument on behalf of the client. Wise attorneys realize that this can only be done if they also know all of the things that can be said on the other side. Expert witnesses and attorneys who become greedy and listen only to the good news may not find that the news remains good at the end of the case.

More important, statisticians have reputations to protect. For those who are prominent in the profession and are therefore among those whom I am urging to participate in such affairs, their reputation extends beyond the confines of the courtroom or the consulting practice. It is at best shortsighted to overlook this in giving testimony. Furthermore, to do so is to damage the profession itself as well as to mislead the client and the court.

It is not, however, always easy to avoid becoming a 'hired gun' (and still harder to avoid being described as one). The danger is sometimes a subtle one, stemming from a growing involvement in the case and friendship with the attorneys. For the serious professional, concerned about preserving standards, the problem is not that one is always being asked to step across a well-defined line by unscrupulous lawyers. Rather, it is that one becomes caught up in the adversary proceeding itself and acquires the desire to win. In so doing, one can lose sight of where the line is and readily acquiesce in language shaded to produce a favorable but not truly defensible result. Particularly because lawyers play by rules that go beyond those of academic fair play, it becomes insidiously easy to see only the apparent unfairness of the other side while overlooking that of one's own. Continuing to regard oneself as objective, one can slip little by little from true objectivity.

I have found it useful to do two things in this regard. First, one should insist at the outset that one must be free to make an independent investigation. If the results of that investigation are unfavorable, then one need not testify, but the results are not to be tailored to the order of the party buying (or bringing) the suit. I have had the experience of having results turn out adversely and it being clear that I could not testify; I do not believe that either the attorneys or I or our relationship suffered for it.

Second, as in data management, it is important to have an independent staff, independent of the lawyers and (to the extent possible) of oneself. Such a staff can be drawn from a consulting firm or from one's academic colleagues and students. Members of the staff (who must themselves have the appropriate technical training) should be charged with the job of protecting the expert from slipping into advocacy. In so doing, they will find it natural to make the best case for the other side; this serves the additional purpose of refining the expert's analysis and preparing the expert for cross-examination. If the staff and the expert work together on different cases (or look forward to doing so), then the staff will particularly understand that they both have a stake in the expert's continuing integrity and reputation.

As the real necessity for the use of such procedures suggests, participation in adversary procedures can be a psychologically wearing experience as well as an exciting one. The question then arises as to why serious statisticians should participate at all. I have already tried to suggest some reasons for participation, and the following story –

although only indirectly related to adversary proceedings – may serve to emphasize some of them.

Some years ago, I received a telephone call from a staff member of a prospective panel of the National Academy of Sciences inquiring whether I would be interested in serving on the panel. The panel in question was to review and consider the statistical studies on the question of whether punishment is a significant deterrent to crime (see Blumstein *et al.* 1978). The assistance of an econometrician seemed desirable, and my name had been suggested. I replied that I was very busy and had no particular interest in the subject. My caller asked whether I did not consider it my social duty to participate (a point also urged by my wife) in view of the fact that, among other things, such studies were being used in arguments before the Supreme Court in support of the restoration of capital punishment. I remained unmoved. A day or so later, the staff member called again. 'There is something I forgot to tell you,' the caller said. 'We have reason to believe that the people producing such studies do not understand the identification problem and are misusing least squares.' 'Why didn't you say so before?' I asked. '*That* is my social duty.'

References

Blumstein, A., Cohen, J. and Nagin, D. (eds.) (1978). *Deterrence and incapacitation: estimating the effects of criminal sanctions on crime rates*, Washington, DC: National Academy of Sciences.

Downton, F. (1982), 'Legal probability and statistics', *Journal of the Royal Statistical Society*, Ser. A, **145**, 395–402.

Fienberg, S.E. and Kadane, J.B. (1983), The presentation of Bayesian statistical analyses in legal proceedings', *The Statistician*, **32**, 88–98.

Fienberg, S.E. and Straf, M.L. (1982), 'Statistical assessments as evidence', *Journal of the Royal Statistical Society*, Ser. A, **145**, 410–21.

Finkelstein, M.O. and Levenbach, H. (1983), 'Regression estimates of damages in price-fixing cases', *Law and Contemporary Problems*, **46**, 145–69.

Fisher, F.M., McGowan, J. and Greenwood, J. (1983), *Folded, Spindled and Mutilated: Economic Analysis and US v. IBM*, Cambridge, MA: MIT Press.

In Re Corrugated Container Antitrust Litigation (1979), 1980–1 Trade Cas. (CCH), para. 66,163 (SD Tex. 1979); aff'd in part and remanded, 643 F.2d 195 (5th Cir. 1981); 84 FRD 40 (SD Tex.); aff'd mem., 606 F.2d 319 (5th Cir.); cert. dismissed, 449 US 915 (1980); 620 F.2d 1086 (5th Cir., 1980); 1983 2 Trade Cas. (CCH) para. 65,628 (SD Tex.).

In Re Corrugated Container Antitrust Litigation (1980), 620 F.2d 1086 (5th Cir., 1980); 1983–2 Trade Cas. (CCH) para. 65,628 (SD Tex. 1983).

In Re Corrugated Container Antitrust Litigation (1985), MDL 310; Dockets 83–2281, 83–2486 (5th Circuit, April 4).

Levi, E. (1948), *An Introduction to Legal Reasoning*, Chicago: Phoenix Books (reprinted by University of Chicago Press in 1962).

Newell, D. (1982), 'The role of the statistician as an expert witness', *Journal of the Royal Statistical Society*, Ser. A., **145**, 403–9.

Royal Statistical Society (1982), 'Discussion meeting on "The role of the statistician as an expert witness"', *Journal of the Royal Statistical Society*, Ser. A., **145**, 395–438.

Rubinfeld, D.L. and Steiner, P.O. (1983), 'Quantitative methods in antitrust litigation', *Law and Contemporary Problems*, **46**, 69–141.

United States v. *United Shoe Machinery Corporation* (1953), 110 F. Supp. 295.

25

Employment discrimination and statistical science: comment (1988)

Arthur Dempster's paper has a good deal to say about the interpretation of probability models and causal thinking, much of it uncontroversial. Rather than discuss such matters in the abstract, however, let's consider the example of employment discrimination that Dempster uses and see what it is that he is really saying.

This is not hard for me to do, because I have encountered Dempster's views on previous occasions. I was a witness for the plaintiff in two employment discrimination cases, *OFCCP* v. *Harris Trust and Savings Bank* (Department of Labor Case No. 78-OFCCP-2) and *Cynthia Baran, et al.* v. *The Register Publishing Company* (Civil N. 75–272, US District of Conn.). In both cases, I testified on matters of econometric and statistical principle rather than putting forward a study of my own, and Dempster testified for the defendant. This chapter is largely based on my experience and testimony in those cases. (I believe – but do not know for sure – that, just as my own experience in employment discrimination cases has been as an expert assisting plaintiffs' counsel, Dempster's experience, to which he refers, has been as an expert assisting counsel for defendants.)

A particular employer is accused of sex discrimination. (As does Dempster, I take this as a leading example.) In general, this means that salaries paid to female employees average less than those paid to male employees. One possible reason for this discrepancy is discrimination; another is that male employees are more productive than female ones.

This chapter was a comment on a paper by Arthur P. Dempster ('Employment discrimination and statistical science', *Statistical Science*, **3** (1988), pp. 149–61. With that information the reader should find the present chapter self-contained.

To examine the question of whether there is a gender-based wage difference holding productivity constant, a statistician estimates the model

$$Y = G\alpha + X\beta + e \qquad (25.1)$$

where (letting i denote values for a particular employee), Y_i denotes salary, G_i is 0 for female and 1 for male employees, X_i is a vector of observed employee characteristics (education, experience, age, etc.), and the e_i are assumed to be random variables (usually taken to be independent $N(0, \sigma^2)$, although this will play no role in the present chapter). α, β and σ are parameters to be estimated, and it will aid discussion to assume that the sample size is sufficiently large to enable us to take such parameters as known with certainty. A positive value of α is taken to be evidence of discrimination against females.

What is wrong with such a procedure? Dempster points out several possibilities. In the first place, he suggests interpreting the stochastic element involved by assuming that the non-discriminatory employer is computing

$$Y^* = E(Y^{**} \mid G, X^*) \qquad (25.2)$$

where X_i^* is a vector of employee characteristics known to the employer (but possibly not to the analyst), Y_i^{**} denotes 'true' employee productivity and Y_i^* denotes employee productivity as estimated by the employer in Equation 25.2. Both Y_i^{**} and Y_i^* are assumed measured in monetary units to be comparable to wages, Y_i. Discrimination is to be interpreted as paying males more than Y_i^*, i.e.

$$Y = G\alpha' + Y^*$$

with $\alpha' > 0$.

This is not the only form that discrimination can take. Depending on the state of the outside labor market, discrimination is more likely to consist of paying females *less* than the employer truly thinks they are worth than of paying them what their estimated productivity indicates and paying males more. To alter Dempster's treatment in this regard, however, would make no essential difference to either his or my discussion.

In any event, if Equation 25.2 is assumed to take a linear form, it becomes

$$Y^{**} = G\alpha'' + X^*\beta^* \qquad (25.4)$$

so that wages are determined in terms of characteristics observable to the employer by

$$Y = G\alpha^* + X^*\beta^* \tag{25.5}$$

and discrimination against females means $\alpha^* > \alpha''$. (The fact that Dempster allows α'' to be positive is an issue I discuss later. Until further notice, assume it to be zero.)[1]

Now, Equation 25.5 looks very much like Equation 25.1. It differs from it in two respects. First, Equation 25.1 contains an error term, e. Second, Equation 25.5 uses X^* rather than X, reflecting the possibility that the employer uses different information than does the statistician. The consequences of the latter difference form the main subject of this discussion. The presence of the error term in Equation 25.1 needs to be considered first, however.

Dempster's assumption that the employer is using a non-stochastic form like Equation 25.5 will not be true in real situations in any helpful way. If the employer actually uses such a procedure and does so in a demonstrable and reproducible way, then the case will go no further, and no statistician will be needed. Instead, there are two possibilities.

The first of these is that the employer actually uses Equation 25.4 (in addition to possibly discriminating) as an average guide, leaving some latitude for individual wages to be determined by individual circumstances unexplained by and orthogonal to Equation 25.4. This can be represented by the addition of a disturbance term, e. The mere fact that the employer does not actually throw dice to determine wages does not mean that there is no component that can be represented in this way. Of course wages are completely causally determined in the sense that they are what they are and that something made them turn out as they did, but the same is true of the fall of dice. The issue is whether wage (or dice) outcomes are completely determined given the information at hand.

Put this aside, however, and consider the second possibility in which the employer determines wages using a completely deterministic mechanism such as Equation 25.4. As already remarked, the problem is over if those decisions are reproducible, so we may as well suppose that the statistician and employer do not have the same information. In this case, the term in Equation 25.4 and 25.5 representing the employer's information, $X^*\beta^*$, can be thought of as the sum of two parts. The first such part is correlated with the variables used by the statistician in Equation 25.1 (G and X); the second part is orthogonal to those variables. Call the orthogonal part, e. Substitution in Equation 25.5 now yields Equation 25.1.

Of course such a substitution is not innocuous. The fact that the employer is assumed to have more information than the statistician means that the coefficients estimated by the statistician may very well not be unbiased estimates of α^* and β^*. In particular, it is possible that estimation of Equation 25.1 will lead to a positive a and therefore to a finding of discrimination even where no discrimination is present. As already indicated, that is the principal subject of this discussion.

Accordingly, I now proceed by including an error term, e, in Equation 25.5 and consider the differences between Equation 25.5 so adjusted and Equation 25.1.

We come now (not for the last time) to the question of what arguments are to be taken seriously. Every employer accused of sex discrimination will certainly argue that he (given the example it is unlikely to be 'she') can judge productivity better than the statistician can and that a regression based on the information that he, the employer, actually uses would show no discrimination.

Such an argument may, indeed, be true. But if this is all the employer says, and if he proffers no description of the inside information he possesses and offers no positive evidence as to its use, then acceptance of that argument is tantamount to finding for the employer in *all* cases. For this has nothing intrinsically to do with statistics. Against *any* evidence of sex discrimination short of a 'smoking gun' memo, the employer can always reply: 'It only looks like discrimination, but if you only had my secret (and unrevealable) information on productivity you would see that it is not.'

It is for this reason that a finding of sex discrimination based on Equation 25.1 is sometimes taken as establishing a *prima facie* case. The defendant ought to be required to put forward an affirmative showing that such a finding is wrong rather than permitted to rebut it on the basis of undisclosed productivity information.

There are two forms that such an affirmative showing can take. The strongest is a regression analysis using the employer's full information, X^*. Indeed, one might argue that if such information really plays a systematic and important role in wage decisions, then the employer can be expected to have retained or be able to reconstruct it so that it can be used. On this view, the very absence of such information makes the employer's argument suspect.

On the other hand, such a view may be too stringent. Wage decisions are not in fact made using regressions; further, data may be impressionistic and not retained. Hence, while one may be suspicious of an employer who makes the secret information argument without being able to produce the information, there may be something more to be said.

A less stringent standard is to permit the employer to argue that Equation 25.1 yields a biased estimate of a^* based on a *specific* description of the information he claims to use and the way in which the lack of that information operates if Equation 25.1 is used. This is at least an intellectually respectable argument (and one which Dempster uses).

Even so, because such arguments tend to have testable implications, I would tend to treat them skeptically if the employer produces no empirical justification. Employment discrimination cases can involve a great deal of money – enough to justify at least sampling the employees to recover the information involved.

Put this aside, however, and consider directly the argument that unincluded information can produce a positive α in Equation 25.1 when α^* is in fact zero. When will this happen?

For simplicity, suppose first that X and X^* are both single variables (suppressing any constant term in Equations 25.4 and 25.5), and that the information problem consists of the fact that X is a noisy measure of X^*. That is,

$$X = X^* + v \tag{25.6}$$

where v is uncorrelated with the 'true' variable, X^*, and also uncorrelated with G. For example, if X is the score on a particular aptitude test, X may be influenced not only by the employee's true aptitude (somehow observable to the employer through other means) but also by the state of health of the employee on the day the test was taken.

This is a classic errors-in-variables problem. We know that if X is used instead of X^* in Equation 25.5, its estimated coefficient (assumed positive) will be biased toward zero. Because the very fact that Equation 25.1 was estimated rather than relying on the raw comparison of male and female wages means that male employees are likely to have scored higher than female ones in terms of the variable used as X, G is likely to be positively correlated with X. This will produce an estimate of α^* that is biased upward. In common sense terms, the use of X rather than X^* will underestimate the true effects of X^* on wages. This, in turn, will lead to too small a correction of the male–female wage differential for productivity differences and hence to an overestimation of the effects of gender. (The matter is less simple if there is more than one variable in X or X^*, but there will be some tendency in this direction in any case.)

For my purposes, the errors in variables explanation of the source of the problem is slightly inconvenient. An equivalent way of proceeding is to substitute Equation 25.6 into the error-term-containing version of Equation 25.5, obtaining

$$Y = G\alpha^* + X\beta^* + (e - v\beta^*) \tag{25.7}$$

With $\beta^* > 0$ and $(-v\beta^*)$ part of the error term, X is negatively correlated with the error, leading to a downward bias in its estimated coefficient (and an upward bias in that of G, as before).

Harry Roberts first proposed 'reverse regression' to deal with this problem. Dempster is incorrect when he states, 'The original motivation for . . . reverse regression, as well as for the contrasting terms reverse and direct, comes from contrasting definitions of "fairness".' The use of reverse regression in that regard was a later development, apparently partly suggested by Dempster himself. (See Roberts 1979, 1980, Ferber and Green 1984, page 111 and especially, Conway and Roberts 1983, page 85). I discuss the 'fairness' concepts below.)

Reverse regression deals with the errors-in-variables problem in the following way. Suppose that Equation 25.7 is solved for X, obtaining

$$X = Y(1/\beta^*) + G(-\alpha^*/\beta^*) + [e(-1/\beta^*) + v] \qquad (25.8)$$

If this is estimated by regression, the presence of v causes no difficulty because, by assumption, it is uncorrelated with G and Y. This suggests the estimation of Equation 25.8 – reverse regression – rather than Equation 25.7 to obtain an estimate of α^*.

Of course, once it is written out in this way, one of the problems with reverse regression becomes obvious. Although the presence of v in the disturbance term in Equation 25.8 creates no difficulty, the presence of e certainly does. Assuming that the firm used Equations 25.4 and 25.5 to set wages, Y is certainly positively correlated with e and hence negatively correlated with the disturbance term in Equation 25.8. This means that estimating Equation 25.8 by regression will lead to an estimate of $(1/\beta^*)$ that is biased downward and hence to an implied estimate of β^* itself that is biased upward. Hence, reverse regression will *over*state the effects of X^* on productivity, leading (by the same reasoning as before) to an *under*estimate of α^*, the all important coefficient of G in Equation 25.5.

Note that this means that a finding that reverse regression leads to a lower estimate of α^* than does direct regression (or even a finding that reverse regression shows no sex discrimination whereas direct regression does) does not imply that the errors-in-variables problem is a serious one for direct regression.

I shall return to the serious problem for reverse regression caused by the presence of e in the disturbance term of Equation 25.8. For the present, however, put it to one side, for there are other problems to consider.

The first of these is technical. Once we drop the assumption that X and X^* are single variables, the analysis becomes more complex. For one thing, it is no longer guaranteed that the errors-in-variables problem will lead direct regression to an estimate of α^* that is biased upward (although this seems a likely outcome). More important, it is far from clear what reverse regression is to mean. The natural composite is $X^*\beta^*$, but the lack of a consistent estimate of β^* (let alone information on X^*) is what causes the problem in the first place.

There is a more fundamental problem than this, however. Whether or not X and X^* are single variables, the assumption that leads to the errors-in-variables analysis is unlikely to be satisfied. In terms of Equation 25.6, this is the assumption that v, the difference between X and X^*, is correlated with X, but not with X^*. As soon as we leave the example of aptitude test scores, that assumption stops being plausible. In practice, the employee characteristics available to the statistician are generally such things as years of education, age, experience and so forth. Although it is certainly possible that the employer observes other attributes that contribute to productivity, this is likely to mean that

$$X^* = XH + W \tag{25.9}$$

where H is a matrix of parameters and W is orthogonal to X, not to X^*. In other words, the assumption that the employer has more information than the statistician is likely to mean just that. The problem is not that such variables as education, age and experience are noisy substitutes for some 'true' productivity measure that the employer observes, but rather that such variables do not tell the whole story, so that 'true' productivity has other components as well. One need only think of examples in which the employer claims to observe on the job work effort or 'attitude' to see the point.

But if Equation 25.9 holds, then, substituting in Equation 25.5, we obtain

$$Y = G\alpha^* + X(H\beta^*) + (e + W\beta^*) \tag{25.10}$$

and this is in the same form as Equation 25.1 with the presence of $W\beta^*$ in the error term causing no difficulty, because it is uncorrelated with X. In this case (which I strongly believe to be the likely one), direct regression leads to a consistent estimate of α^*, whereas reverse regression certainly does not. Indeed (under the same conditions as before), reverse regression is likely to lead to an estimate of α^* that is biased downward, both because of the presence of e on the righthand side of Equation 25.8 as before *and* because of a similar effect from the fact that $W\beta^*$ will now also appear in the error term of that equation.

In passing, note that, as Equation 25.9 implies, further information possessed by the employer will be relevant *only* to the extent that it is orthogonal to X. For example, if the employer claims to observe on-the-job performance or 'attitude', and years of education are included in X, merely knowing that men and women score differently on the employer's measure does not invalidate the use of Equation 25.1. Because education may affect such scores, the employer's information only adds something if male–female score differentials persist when education effects are held constant. Even then, as just shown, estimation of Equation 25.1 remains consistent.

Reverse regression, then, is unlikely to be an attractive way to deal with omitted variables in the present context. Its proponents, however (including Dempster), have put forth another justification for its use. This is the possibility that the firm engages in what Conway and Roberts (1984, p. 128) call 'Hiring 2', choosing wage (and other job character- istics) first and then hiring the job applicant with the highest quali- fications. Such a procedure leads directly to reverse regression as a test for 'Fairness 2' – the carrying out of this procedure in a sex-blind way.

There are several things to be said about this argument. First, if the firm really does engage in 'Hiring 2', one of the arguments given above for the biased nature of reverse regression will certainly fail. If quali- fications are conditioned on wages and not the other way round, the appearance of e in Equation 25.8 causes no difficulty. Indeed, with 'Hiring 2', a parallel argument shows that direct regression leads to biased results.

This does not rescue reverse regression, however, for the considera- tions as to the nature of omitted variables remain the same whether or not 'Hiring 2' is involved. To see this, return to the univariate case. 'Hiring 2' means the employer chooses X^* by

$$X^* = G\lambda + Y\mu + u \tag{25.11}$$

where u is a random disturbance and λ and μ are parameters. When the statistician uses X in place of X^*, then (taking $H = 1$ in Equation 25.9 for simplicity)

$$X = G\lambda + Y\mu + (u - W) \tag{25.12}$$

But W will certainly be negatively correlated with Y, and, as before, this will lead to underestimating the extent of discrimination.

Returning to the multivariate case, this shows that reverse regression (as Dempster recognizes) will not be an adequate test for 'Fairness 2', unless $X^*\beta^*$ rather than X is used. This, however, brings us back to the question of what forms of argument should be acceptable. To justify reverse regression (and, indeed, to combat the results of direct regres- sion), the employer must be able to specify X^*. Further, for present purposes, he must specify β^*. Even if he does that, however, one ought not to accept reverse regression as the appropriate method without a credible showing by the employer that he practices 'Hiring 2' – choosing qualifications given wages – rather than 'Hiring 1' – paying wages given qualifications. If 'Hiring 2' really is used, such a showing ought not to be burdensome. Large firms tend to have written personnel policies. Even small ones can give examples of their job advertising and anecdotal testimony from personnel officers. Lacking such a showing, one ought to suspect that reverse regression – as its intellectual history suggests – is just an answer looking for a good question.

This is related to the final question I shall discuss, that of what Dempster calls 'judgmental discrimination'. Put aside all issues of statistical method, says Dempster. Suppose that 'a presumed honest attempt to assess productivity' involves a positive α'' in Equation 25.4. Then even knowledge of α^* in Equation 25.5 will not suffice as a test for sex discrimination, because a positive α^* may simply reflect a positive α''.

To accept this argument is to accept anything as a defense and always find for the defendant. A positive α'' means that the employer conditions wages on gender, *given* all the other information that he has. It means that women are seen to be less productive, not because they differ from men in education or measurable skills, or even because they want different hours or conditions of travel for child-rearing considerations. Any of those propositions could be tested because neither women nor men are all alike in such dimensions. (For example, some men are single parents and some women are not married.) Of course it is *possible* that the employer 'knows' that women and men differ for non-testable reasons, but (as in all cases of untestable private information) that ought not to be an acceptable form of argument.

Let me put this in plain English. Acceptance of 'judgmental discrimination' as a legitimate defense has nothing to do with statistics. It means allowing the employer to defend by saying: 'Of course I'm not prejudiced against women (Blacks). It's just that – *for reasons I can't explain* – they can't do a (White) man's job.' Experts ought to think hard before lending themselves to positions like this.

Acknowledgments

My original testimony on this subject benefited from conversations with Richard Gilman, Diane Heim, Bruce Levin, Debra Millenson and Mary Ellen Wynn. I retain responsibility for error.

Notes

1. (Added in present edition) In the original version a slip (pointed out by Dempster) left a term in e^{**} included in Equations 25.4 and 25.5. The present version corrects this error which basically affects only the exposition. The changes consist of the following six paragraphs plus a minor notational change below.

References

Conway, D.A. and Roberts, H.V. (1983) 'Reverse regression, fairness and employment discrimination', *J. Bus. Econ. Statist.* **1**, 75–85.

Conway, D.A. and Roberts, H.V. (1984). Rejoinder to comments on 'Reverse regression, fairness and employment discrimination'. *J. Bus. Econ. Statist.* **2**, 126–39.

Ferber, M.A. and Green, C.A. (1984). What kind of fairness is fair? A comment on Conway and Roberts, *J. Bus. Econ. Statist.* **2**, 111–13.

Roberts, H.V. (1979). Harris Trust and Savings Bank: An analysis of employee compensation. Report 7946, CMSBE, Graduate School of Business, Univ. Chicago.

Roberts, H.V. (1980). Statistical biases in the measurement of employment bias. In *Comparable Worth: Issues and Alternatives* (E.R. Livernash, ed.). Equal Employment Advisory Council, Washington.

Permissions

14. 'The stability of the Cournot oligopoly solution: The effects of speeds of adjustment and increasing marginal costs', *Review of Economic Studies*, vol. 28(2), 1961.

PART 2   Regulation of television

15. 'Community antenna television systems and the regulation of television broadcasting', *American Economic Review*, vol. 56(2) (*Proceedings*), May 1966.
16. 'Community antenna television systems and local television station audience' (written jointly with V.E. Ferrall, Jr, in association with D. Belsley and B.M. Mitchell), *Quarterly Journal of Economics*, vol. 80(2), May 1966. Copyright © 1966 Franklin M. Fisher *et al.* Reprinted by permission of John Wiley & Sons, Inc.
17. 'The audience–revenue relationship for local television stations' (written jointly with J.J. McGowan and D.S. Evans), *Bell Journal of Economics*, vol. 11(2), autumn 1980.
18. 'The financial interest and syndication rules in network television: regulatory fantasy and reality', *Antitrust and Regulation: Essays in Memory of John J. McGowan*, ed. Franklin M. Fisher. Cambridge, MA: MIT Press, 1985.

PART 3   Quantitative methods and the law

19. 'The mathematical analysis of Supreme Court Decisions: The use and abuse of quantitative methods', *American Political Science Review*, vol. 52(2), June 1958.
20. 'On the feasibility of identifying the crime function in a simultaneous model of crime rates and sanction levels' (written jointly with D. Nagin), in *Deterrence and Incapacitation: Report of the Panel on Research Deterrent and Incapacitative Effects*, eds A. Blumstein *et al.*, Washington DC: National Academy of Sciences, 1978. Reprinted with permission from the Assembly of Behavioral and Social Sciences and the National Academy of Sciences.
21. 'Empirically-based sentencing guidelines and ethical considerations' (written jointly with J.B. Kadane), in *Research on Sentencing, the Search for Reform*, eds. A. Blumstein *et al.* vol. 2, Washington DC: National Academy Press, 1983. Reprinted with permission from the National Academy Press, Washington, DC.
22. 'Janis Joplin's yearbook and the theory of damages' (written jointly with R.C. Romaine), *Journal of Accounting, Auditing and Finance*, vol 5(1), January 1990. Reprinted with permission of the University of Chicago Press.
23. 'Multiple regression in legal proceedings'. Copyright © 1980 by the Directors of the Columbia Law Review Association, Inc. All Rights Reserved. This article originally appeared in *Colum. L. Rev.* vol. 80, p. 702 (1980). Reprinted by permission.
24. 'Statisticians, econometricians and adversary proceedings', *Journal of the American Statistical Association*, vol. 81, p. 394, *Applications*, June 1986.
25. 'Employment discrimination and statistical science: Comment', *Statistical Science*, vol. 3(2), May 1988. Reprinted with permission from the Institute of Mathematical Statistics.

Index